JUSTIFIED DEADLY FORCE

AND THE MYTH OF SYSTEMIC RACISM

MIKE SIMONELLI

THE FACTS EVERYONE MUST KNOW

Charleston, SC
www.PalmettoPublishing.com

Justified Deadly Force
Copyright © 2021 by Mike Simonelli

Second Edition

Paperback: 978-1-63837-403-9
eBook: 978-1-63837-404-6
Hardcover: 978-1-68515-010-5

Author photo courtesy of Glenn Tarquinio

This book is dedicated to the memories of our fallen officers and to their loved ones that must carry on without them, we owe them all a debt of gratitude that can never be repaid. The following is a tribute to the service those brave men and woman performed to help keep us all safe. While I, the author did my best to accurately portray every incident to the best of my ability using the resources available, it is possible something was missed or misconstrued—so while they were not intentional, all mistakes are my own and I take full responsibility for them.

TABLE OF CONTENTS

I.   PROLOGUE 1

II.   INTRODUCTION 3

III. Part 1. Deadly Police Shootings: Racial Bias by the Press, Protestors, and Politicians 11

          RESEARCH STUDY INTRODUCTION 12

          LITERATURE REVIEW 14

          METHODOLOGY 22

          RESULTS 26

          RESEARCH STUDY CONCLUSIONS 52

IV.   Part 2. Justified Deadly Force of Unarmed Subjects, 2019 to 2020 57

          INCIDENTS IN 2019: 61

          INCIDENTS IN 2020: 117

          ANALYSIS 161

V.   Part 3. Felonious Line of Duty Murders of Law Enforcement Officers, 2019 to 2020 167

          INCIDENTS IN 2019: 169

          INCIDENTS IN 2020: 239

          ANALYSIS 309

VI.   CONCLUSION 317

VII. REFERENCES 329

VIII. ENDNOTES 331

PROLOGUE

I N THE AWARD-WINNING MOVIE, *THE USUAL SUSPECTS*, WHEN QUESTIONED BY THE POLICE ABOUT MYSTERI-ous criminal mastermind Keyser Söze, Kevin Spacey's character Roger Kint answers:

"Nobody ever believed he was real. Nobody ever knew him or saw anybody that ever worked directly for him, but to hear Kobayashi tell it, anybody could have worked for Söze. You never knew. That was his power. *The greatest trick the Devil ever pulled was convincing the world he didn't exist.*"[1]

A lot has changed in America since *The Usual Suspects* debuted in 1995, but one thing that has remained constant is which police incidents garner national headlines. In 1991 on the West Coast, it was the Los Angeles Police Department (LAPD) excessive use of force against Rodney King. Later in the 1990s the East Coast had its unfortunate turn with two such stories eliciting substantial press coverage and public outrage. The first was the 1997 brutal sexual attack upon Abner Louima and then the February 4, 1999, fatal police shooting of Amadou Diallo. While the Rodney King riots resulted in massive death and destruction to the Los Angeles area, it was largely contained there and ended within a week by successful employment of the California National Guard. Because the Louima attack was so heinous and out of the ordinary, Police Officer (PO) Justin Volpe was universally condemned, even among his fellow officers. Though Louima initially claimed that a racist slur was used during his beating, he later recanted that, so while his assault was completely depraved, it was not racial. The Diallo shooting and successive acquittal of the four officers involved inspired numerous songs and TV shows for the American public, but there were no riots in NYC nor national unrest.

If you notice a pattern here it is because there is one, and that same pattern is evident decades later in the 2020's. When the words "police brutality" or "police murder" are mentioned, the people that come to mind are Rodney King, Michael Brown, Eric Garner, Breonna Taylor, and George Floyd–every one of them Black. What has changed though since 1995, and for the worse, is the magnitude of rumors spread about such police incidents by mainstream news outlets, elected officials, and community leaders. The current narrative of racist policing has been pushed by the professional media with a religious-type zeal, amplified by social media influencers, and then accepted by the masses on the left as gospel. Many in the middle or the right do not subscribe to the anti-police narrative and remain silent because speaking out against America's racial grievance industry will earn them the modern-day equivalent of a scarlet letter–they will be labeled a racist. Minorities receive equally noxious labels, called Uncle Tom's, traitors to their race, sellouts, or worse. Others remain silent because they just do not have the time to research the truth and then effectively communicate it in a quick tweet, Facebook post, or letter to the editor.

This book cannot teach someone to have the courage to stand up for the truth, but it will provide the tools for those who are brave enough to educate themselves, their loved ones, and repudiate those blinded by the false god of racism. In the following pages you will see how the grievance about fatal police encounters constantly spread in the news, on political pulpits and by protestors is pure deception. This book will provide the facts behind the encounters to demonstrate how race was completely irrelevant. You will observe how the media spins stories of police shootings depending upon the race of the subjects involved. In addition, this book will also show you how little the media, activists, and even some politicians care about anyone other than Blacks killed by the police. Besides Whites, Latino's, and Asians, their indifference includes police officers feloniously killed in the line of duty. By the end, this book will prove how in this new religion of wokeness where the police are made to be the devil, the more appropriate quote for our time is:

"The greatest trick the left ever pulled was convincing America every police encounter with Blacks is based upon racism."

INTRODUCTION

"Woe to those who call evil good and good evil, who turn darkness to light and light to darkness, who replace bitter with sweet and sweet with bitter "
—*Isaiah 5:20*

I F SOMEONE SAID BEFORE 2020 THAT AMERICA HAS BECOME SO OBSESSED WITH RACIAL GRIEVANCES THAT the outrage over the police killing of one black man could easily overshadow a once-in-a-life-time global health pandemic, they would have been ridiculed and accused of being a conspiracy theorist. Sadly, thanks to the COVID-19 pandemic such a statement is neither a conjecture nor a conspiracy, but a demonstrable fact. On May 24, 2020, America, like most of the nations, was in the midst of a once-per-century global health pandemic. Its citizens throughout many of the fifty states were facing their third month of lockdowns to stop the deadly spread of the COVID-19 virus.

Also, it is to be noted that as of May 24, the police were once again seen as the good guys. Slightly reminiscent of the post-9/11 appreciation shown to the men and women in blue for the heroism they displayed along with the New York City (NYC) Fire Department (FDNY) running toward the towers, officers were acknowledged for the sacrifices they were making by continuing to serve and protect the American public. Small but much-appreciated measures of gratitude from citizens across the country could be seen on various social-media platforms, handheld signs, and written editorials. Starting in late March, businesses showed their support as well, with companies like Starbucks[2] and Wawa[3] offering free coffee to first responders and health-care workers. While the deadly plague had so many other Americans staying at home 24/7, law enforcement officers and other such essential professions were reporting for duty every day at great risk to themselves and their loved ones. The number of officers killed by COVID-19 has been astounding, and acts as a further testament to the selfless profession. As of February 10, 2021, 243 officers died of COVID since its inception, as compared to the 42 officers feloniously murdered during that same time.

The past, present, and future sacrifices of all those officers became overshadowed–as did all the concerns about masses of people being outside, social distancing, or spreading the deadly Coronavirus when an amateur video was released showing Minneapolis Police Officer Derek

Chauvin kneeling on George Floyd's neck for 8 minutes and 46 seconds on May 25, 2020. In the background of the video, upset bystanders can be heard pleading with the officers to get off Floyd and just put him into the police car. As Floyd can be seen on the ground facing the camera, crying "I can't breathe," a man angrily tells the cops, "He's not even resisting arrest" and "you're stopping his breathing"[4]. In disbelief a woman asks, "Did they just kill him?" as Floyd is observed lifeless under Officer Chauvin's knee. The video is disturbing to watch, and the obvious perception is that the officers just killed an unarmed, cooperative, handcuffed Black man. As the video went viral, outraged protestors quickly took to the streets, first in Minneapolis, then throughout America and ultimately throughout the world[5].

Within 24 hours the first protest started off with thousands of peaceful protestors gathering at the scene of Floyd's last breaths and ended later that night with violence directed at the Minneapolis Police Precinct involved. That was a pattern that played out repeatedly across the nation and throughout the summer of 2020. Unlike the relatively sporadic anti-lockdown protests, the protests over Floyd's death were widespread and destructive, and they were not bound by any COVID-19 lockdowns, social distancing, or, in many cases, restrictions of any kind. From May 26 to September 5, 2020, 12,045 protests occurred in the US, of which 633 across 47 states were lawless enough to be considered riots and another 510 involved varying levels of violence and/or looting[6]. Compounding onto the tens of millions of Americans forced onto unemployment and thousands of businesses shutdown by COVID-19, the riots left behind the most expensive amount of damage in American history[7].

The damages were projected to cost more than $2 billion[8]. Casualties of the anti-police riots included damages to at least 150 federal buildings[9]; 97 police cars burned and hundreds more vandalized[10]; and over 1,500 businesses and buildings in just Minneapolis and St. Paul were marred[11]. Human casualties of the riots were high as well, with 47 deaths[12]; at least 2,000 officers were injured[13] and dozens hospitalized. Despite the massive mayhem accompanying them, these "demonstrations" involving millions of people in at least 140 cities were actually embraced by many of the same political class that had up until May 24 been demanding that American citizens remain indoors to "stop the spread"[14].

Besides failing to address the violence conducted in her state during the riots after having been so vocally critical of the "anti-shutdown protests," Michigan Gov. Gretchen Whitmer issued a statement of "solidarity with those who are seeking equitable justice for everyone in our state"[15]. In violation of her own mandated social distancing protocols, Whitmer was photographed "shoulder-to-shoulder protesting with other officials and demonstrators"[16]. Washington D.C. Mayor Muriel Bowser too broke her mandated COVID protocols when she removed her mask for a photo op with supporters at a Black Lives Matter (BLM) mural. Contrary to his executive orders barring singing in church or celebrating the 4th of July with non-family members for fear that it would "result in increased rates of infection, hospitalization, and death, especially among more vulnerable populations"[17], California (CA) Gov. Gavin Newsom supported the millions of anti-police protestors "lifting their voices in anger—rightfully outraged at the systemic racism that persists in America"[18].

Across on the east coast, NYC Mayor Bill DeBlasio offered a similar display of contradiction as he communicated that New Yorkers were expected to continue adhering to his mandated COVID lockdown and curfew, unless they were protesting–in which case he just warned them not to be violent[19]. When the protests turned violent as they quickly did in Minneapolis, Mayor Jacob Frey, who had not told his officers to enforce social distancing among the protestors, ordered police to stand down–allowing the rioters to overrun the Third Precinct, ransack it, and set it ablaze[20]. Apparently for Frey, the political optics of a burning police precinct were better than that of officers justifiably using force to protect themselves and city property paid for by taxpaying citizens. Mayor Melvin Carter of the other twin city of Saint Paul did not concern himself with neither violence nor optics as he told protestors that he "want[s] to be very clear that we are not asking you for patience. And we're not asking you for pacifism"[21].

Just as they had joined politicians in characterizing everyday Americans as heroes for complying with statewide COVID lockdowns, after Floyd's death, the medical professionals hailed those violently rioting in the name of racial justice as patriots. Instead of condemning the mass protests as one would suspect because of their potential to spread the disease and overwhelm the hospitals, 100 health-care professionals signed a letter supporting the protests "as vital to the national public health and to the threatened health specifically of Black people in the United States"[22]. Infectious disease epidemiologist at Harvard Medical School, Julia Marcus said, "Even if COVID-19 did circulate at protests, that could be countered by the good that would come from calling attention to the danger of police violence"[23]. Another epidemiologist, Jennifer Nuzzo from Johns Hopkins agreed, tweeting, "In this moment the public health risks of not protesting to demand an end to systemic racism greatly exceed the harms of the virus"[24]. Even after COVID infected more than 1.8 million Americans by June 1, 2020, former CDC Director, Tom Frieden, supported the mass protests despite their inherent dangers for adding to those casualties.

Outrage over George Floyd's death was so powerful that it eclipsed safety protocols implemented for the recent pandemic as well as longstanding practices in America's institutional systems. Though due process ensures that justice in America typically moves at a snail's pace, it came swiftly in Minneapolis. In less than 24 hours after the incident, all four officers involved in Floyd's death were fired, and even before the autopsy report was released, Derek Chauvin was charged with third-degree murder and manslaughter on May 29. Although Governors declared it illegal for Americans to attend funerals during the Coronavirus shutdown, Floyd received three separate nationally televised and well-attended memorial services befitting a military hero. Then democratic candidate for the 2020 Presidential Race, Joe Biden, flew to Floyd's hometown to personally express his condolences to Floyd's family before the burial. In less than a month after his death the notoriously slow US House of Representatives passed a bill in his name, the "George Floyd Justice in Policing Act of 2020."

Democrats were the most vocal about Floyd's death, but Republicans chimed in as well. Texas Congressman, Will Hurd, let his feet do the talking as he marched with protestors at a rally in Houston. Utah Senator, Mitt Romney, accompanied protestors during their march near the White House, telling a reporter, "We need a voice against racism. We need many voices against racism and against brutality. We need to stand up and say that black lives matter"[25]. Senate Majority Leader, Mitch McConnell, called the protestors cause "righteous" on the Senate floor, reflecting how he believes, "most Americans are ready to consider how the memories of black Americans like George Floyd and Breonna Taylor can move us to continue combating residual racism"[26].

Between the ensuing murder, mayhem, and political grandstanding, it was impossible after Memorial Day 2020 to not see a TV news broadcast or online story segueing into how George

Floyd died after fired Minneapolis PO Derek Chauvin kept his knee on Floyd's neck for nearly 9 minutes. In just the first month after it happened, the six major cable networks of ABC, CBS, NBC, CNN, FNC, and MSNBC contributed 2,345 stories on Floyd and the aftermath of his death. Much of that aftermath was based upon the premise that Floyd's death was a symptom of a larger systemic issue of police bias against blacks. An understandable presumption, since such a death by a police officer appearing to nonchalantly crush the life out of a man would never happen to a white person. And if such a perceived murder did happen, it could not be on video because Americans would have seen it and been just as outraged as they were about Floyd's death. Wrong! A terribly similar incident occurred to a man named Tony Timpa four years earlier, but most Americans never heard of him.

On August 10, 2016, in Dallas, Tony Timpa had called 911 because he had stopped taking his medications for schizophrenia and depression, and he knew he needed help. By the time police arrived, Timpa had already been handcuffed by a store security guard and can be seen in the video lying on the grass near a busy street. Police bodycam video shows an upset Timpa on the ground as three officers respond and try to calm him. Timpa is moving around on the ground telling the police "You're gonna kill me" as they approach and then get on top of him to switch out the security guard's handcuffs with their own. Timpa may have been certifiably crazy, but his fear of not surviving the encounter proved to be legitimate. Less than fifteen minutes later Timpa would be dead.

Like the video of Floyd's death, Timpa's video shows that he stopped breathing while being held in a restrained position by the police. In his final moments Timpa, too, is seen begging for his life– more than 30 times, crying "You're gonna kill me! You're gonna kill me! You're gonna kill me!"[27] as the officer kneeled on him for 13 minutes. Also, like Floyd, the autopsy of Timpa revealed that illegal controlled substances, namely cocaine, were in his system.

Unlike Floyd's criminal behavior provoking a call to 911, it was Timpa who had called 911 crying out for help. Unlike for Floyd, Democratic and Republican leaders never even mentioned Timpa's name, protestors did not march through neighborhoods, and stores did not burn for Timpa. Unlike for Floyd's family, Timpa's family was left to mourn all alone. Unlike for the officers involved in Floyd's death, none of the officers involved in Timpa's case were fired, and after the grand jury indicted those involved– the District Attorney dismissed the charges. Unlike the amateur video of Floyd's death that was made instantly available to the public, it took a three-year court battle before police finally released the bodycam video of Timpa's death. Unlike the officers calling for a rush on rescue while surrounded by an angry crowd during Floyd's last moments, the video shows the officers mocking Timpa as he is dying. And unlike the weeks' long dawn-to-dusk media coverage of George Floyd, the six major cable networks ran a mere six stories about Tony Timpa during the three years after his death.

While both Floyd and Timpa's troubled lives held value, neither of their deaths represent an institutional problem nor a systemic racism. Timpa's case slowly worked its way through the criminal justice system, but Floyd's was immediately tried in the court of public opinion solely based upon that disturbing nine-minute video. If all the evidence presented shows that neither Floyd nor Timpa died of an overdose or "excited delirium," and the officers involved in either incident are found culpable, then they, and only they, should be held accountable for their actions. The facts involved in Floyd's death are analyzed in Part 2. As for the millions of protestors demanding black lives to matter, ask yourself: When comparing the disparities of the reactions to the deaths of George Floyd and Tony Timpa, whose life did not matter? And if you are going to generalize along racial terms, whose lives do not matter?

Blacks are led to believe that they are the victims of systemic state oppression, because the media, political class, and social justice agitators are engaged in a willful campaign of racist rhetoric anytime the victims of police incidents are Black, while ignoring similar incidents whenever the victims are White. This campaign is working, and this is why besides being mostly ignorant of what happened to Tony Timpa, those who are protesting as well as those who are supporting them claim that their outrage is not just because of what happened to George Floyd. They say this incident is just one of many in a long history of police violence against African Americans. Floyd's death has been referred to as "the tipping point"[28] after months of palpable outrage over the deaths of two other blacks, Breonna Taylor and Ahmaud Arbery. Arbery was killed by two white men who confronted him over recent neighborhood burglaries. While it was an avoidable and tragic interracial incident much like that of Trayvon Martin in 2012, the uproar over Arbery's death was just as unusual as it was with that of Martin since they were both killed during confrontation with civilians, not police. The outrage is even more unusual when contrasted against the apathy shown over other intra– and interracial incidents like the 2,574 blacks murdered by fellow blacks and 566 whites killed by blacks in a typical year such as 2019[29]. As for the deadly police shooting of Ms. Taylor, as you will read in Part 2, while analyzing the evidence, claims of racism or wrongdoing against the officers involved are complete falsehoods.

Before Arbery and Taylor, the outrage was over Michael Brown, Alton Sterling, Philando Castile, and other blacks whose deadly police shootings gained nationwide attention and riots of their own. These incidents which have been used to vilify law enforcement for years are analyzed in Part 1 and are also proven to be red herrings, distracting from the facts illustrating how rare police uses of deadly force are. More recently the anti-police propaganda extends past any individual incidents and seeks to associate today's sworn officers with slavery practices from America's early years. The association is made clear by articles such as "The racist roots of American policing: From slave patrols to traffic stops"[30] by Connie Hassett-Walker, Assistant Professor of Justice Studies and Sociology at Norwich University and stories such as "From slave patrol to storm troopers, America's police have an ugly history"[31] by Amrita Chakrabarti Myers, Associate Professor of History and Gender Studies at Indiana University.

These references to practices that were made obsolete over 150 years ago are part of a larger narrative irredeemably linking America's institutions and policing with slavery. In keeping with *The New York Times* "The 1619 Project" attempt to re-write America's founding to 400 years ago when the first African slaves were brought to Virginia, the social justice activists, academics, and politicians wed America and its police to four centuries of oppression. Days into the George Floyd-inspired riots, in an editorial published in *The Daily Beast*, actor/activist George Clooney wrote, "The anger and the frustration we see playing out once again in our streets is just a reminder of how little we've grown as a country from our original sin of slavery. This is our pandemic. It infects all of us, and in 400 years we've yet to find a vaccine"[32]. High School English Teacher and President of the Vermont-National Education Association, Don Tinney wrote in a Vermont newspaper, "We must teach the fundamental lesson of America; 400 years of systemic racism. George Floyd wasn't murdered just by the police, but by centuries of oppression"[33].

A lengthy *USA Today* article titled "Not just George Floyd: Police departments have 400-year history of racism"[34], chronicles the slave patrols and Klu Klux Klan (KKK) with the shootings of Trayvon Martin and Michael Brown. Insisting "past harms by law enforcement need to be addressed before even attempting to move forward," Michigan State University Criminal Justice, Professor Jennifer Cobbina opines, "All that is happening [right now] is steeped in 400 years of legacy of injustice"[35].

Bolstered by their massive social and legacy media platforms, such actors and academics influence the masses, and together they spur the nation's political leaders to action where it matters–in policies and legislation. In NYC, Mayor DeBlasio continued his demands for strict enforcement of the COVID-19 shutdown destroying businesses and violating constitutional rights, while simultaneously voicing his support for the anti-police protests because he sees "an entire nation, simultaneously grappling with an extraordinary crisis seated in 400 years of American racism"[36]. Washington, D.C.'s Mayor, Muriel Bowser, showed the same disparate treatment of protestors as she vowed harsh fines and jail time for anyone violating stay-at-home orders, while she defended the Floyd demonstrators, exclaiming, "We are grieving hundreds of years of institutional racism"[37]. With an eye toward future policies, CA Congresswoman Barbara Lee proposed that a "Truth, Racial Healing, and Transformation Commission" be created "to reckon with 400 years of systemic racism"[38]. President Joe Biden hinted at a focus of his administration during his inaugural address, telling the nation, "A cry for racial justice some 400 years in the making moves us. The dream of justice for all will be deferred no longer"[39].

No matter how many politicians make solemn-sounding speeches while trying to pin 400 years of injustice upon the United States of America, there was no such sovereign nation until 1776. Furthermore, as pointed out by historians, the basic premise of "The 1619 Project" by journalist (not historian) Nikole Hannah-Jones that "the American Revolution was fought to preserve slavery was a lie"[40]. Hannah-Jones and *The NY Times* have since retracted that lie but the project continues. There is no disputing that the predominantly white police in the South were used for despicable purposes in the 1800s, and like any cross-section of the population, a few bad apples exist in today's force as well. What is also beyond dispute for those not mired in previous centuries is that the profession of policing has entered a new era, a well-diversified one, which serves and protects people of all races.

For decades now, systemic racism, brutality, or anything contrary to upholding the constitutional rights for all Americans has not been permitted among the nation's law enforcement agencies. During the past 30 to 40 years, its America's dedicated law enforcement officers who have brought violent crime down across many of the nation's biggest cities, saving countless black and brown lives in the process. Far from the days of white men conducting slave patrols, the Atlanta Police Department is now a majority Black police force. And the nation's largest police department, the New York City Police Department (NYPD) with around 36,000 officers is a majority minority department. As for the continued references to Michael Brown's shooting, even former President Obama's Justice Department ruled that PO Darren Wilson was completely justified in using deadly force and did not violate any of Brown's civil rights.

Just as the "Hand's up, don't shoot" narrative of 2014 was shown to be one of the biggest lies of the year, the mantras of "blacks are killed by police at a disproportionate rate," "police are racially profiling," and "systematic killing of innocent blacks by the police," etc. … are equally deceiving.

Together they are used effectively as propaganda demonizing the police in particular and America in general. Even the studies referenced by those repeating such rhetoric are misleading because they merely manipulate and interpret the data to support their negative feelings about the police. However, this book will show you the details of the incidents behind the numbers. You can read them and make your own educated decisions about whether the officers reacted reasonably or not. When you put yourself in that officer's position, you will see that the situation was far from as simple as black and white. And perhaps, more importantly, you can judge whether there is any evidence whatsoever to make a reasonable person believe that being Black, White, or any other race had anything to do with those deadly incidents.

Throughout the coronavirus pandemic, much like the even longer climate change "emergency" preceding it, the slogan from many has been to "follow the science". This book will prove through scientific evidence that what Americans and the world are being told about fatal police incidents in America being systemically racist is systemically false. Set up in three parts, this book will walk the reader through the evidence. The first part is a scientific research study analyzing the bias exhibited by the press, politicians, and protestors toward deadly police shootings. Conducted in April 2020, this standalone study documents the racial disparities these three critical groups exhibited toward subjects of deadly police shootings from 2015 to 2018. Building off the first, the second part details the deadly police shootings of unarmed subjects from 2019 to 2020. Ninety such incidents are carefully documented, and statistics are developed from them. Then the third and final part examines the felonious line of duty murders of law enforcement officers (LEOs) during those same two years. Together, the three parts provide substantial factual evidence with which to prepare the reader to refute the lies and spread the truth about the use of justified deadly force by American LEOs. With the accompanying website, www.JDFinformation.com, readers will have a complete toolkit to call out the lying media, politicians, and social justice activists the next time they spread falsehoods through omission, half-truths, and outright lies.

PART 1.

DEADLY POLICE SHOOTINGS: RACIAL BIAS BY THE PRESS, PROTESTORS, AND POLITICIANS

M ANY IN THE MEDIA AND SOCIAL JUSTICE REALM REPEATEDLY ALLEGE THE CRIMINAL JUSTICE SYSTEM IN general and police in particular target black people, and even worse, kill them without cause. The sensationalized focus on racism hinders the American government's ability to protect its law-abiding citizens from the violent and career criminals among them. Since the killing of black males drives much of the dialogue on racism in American policing, this study examines the bias in reporting done on the basis of the race of the subject involved in deadly police shooting incidents. Bias is tested by using quantitative analyses of print and network coverage of deadly police shootings, along with two case studies that compare the difference in media coverage, activism, and political rhetoric as seen for white and black subjects of such shootings. Both quantitative analyses showed the media coverage of black subjects of deadly police shootings eclipsed that of all other races, while the case studies documented the black subjects received substantially more coverage, which framed the incident as racially biased, than their white counterparts. Rather than the police, Part 1 reveals the racial bias exhibited by the press, protestors, and politicians over deadly police shootings.

RESEARCH STUDY INTRODUCTION

I N A 2009 BLACK HISTORY MONTH SPEECH TO THE DEPARTMENT OF JUSTICE (DOJ), ATTORNEY GENERAL (AG) Eric Holder told the audience that when it comes to talking frankly about racial issues in America, "we have always been and I believe continue to be, in too many ways, essentially a nation of cowards"[41]. Since Holder's speech and after several high-profile police shootings of African Americans, a national conversation has been taking place about America's criminal justice system victimizing minorities. A 2019 Los Angeles (LA) Times headline "Getting killed by police is a leading cause of death for young Black men in America"[42] shows that a central part of that conversation is racially biased policing and excessive use of deadly force toward Black people. These accusations of racial bias and police brutality against people of color are being used to promote legislation designed to fundamentally change America's criminal justice system.

America's criminal justice system is responsible for keeping civil society from descending into mob rule, with police officers serving as front-line government representatives in daily interactions with the public. Additionally, as recent jihadist and homegrown attacks in Boston, New York City, and San Bernardino have illustrated, the police are often the first to engage with the deadly threats of terrorism occurring on American soil. As an integral component to America's national security, it is essential that the criminal justice system is seen as an impartial arbiter that enforces the law equally to all. The 2014 deadly police shooting of Michael Brown in Ferguson, Missouri, was the impetus for hundreds of anti-police protests across America, police reforms in 24 states, and the Black Lives Matter (BLM) movement gaining national notoriety[43]. Scholars have published articles alleging anger over police killing black men such as Brown contributed to the violent radicalization of African Americans who joined America's enemy–the Islamic State of Iraq and Syria (ISIS)[44]. The rhetoric of racism continues at the highest level of American politics with 2020 Democratic Presidential Candidate Vermont Senator Bernie Sanders warning how black men who do not show respect when getting stopped by the police may "get shot in the back of the head"[45].

Labels of racism are damaging enough when they target individuals or companies, but such accusations against America's criminal justice system delegitimizes the government and impairs police officers' ability to effectively serve their communities. ISIS used video of the Ferguson protests as part of racial propaganda in recruiting efforts directed at African Americans[46]. Long-time rival Russia also understood the sensitivity of race in America and used social media to stir up racial animus to disrupt America's 2016 Presidential Election[47]. Within America, there exists a constant threat of mass casualty jihadist attacks, Transnational Criminal Organizations (TCOs) bringing daily casualties to America by way of illegal drugs, and cities with homicide rates rivaling those in the third world. It is crucial to expose the facts about deadly police shootings so that America's law enforcement agencies can maintain the freedom and support to concentrate against these tangible threats of terrorism, narcotics, and crime.

STATEMENT OF THE PROBLEM

The mantra of racism in the US emboldens its enemies, divides the populace, and ultimately handicaps America's police forces. In response to the outcry from the deadly police shootings of black males in general and Stephon Clark in particular, California passed a bill effective January 1, 2020, giving its police the strictest use of deadly force guidelines in the nation[48]. It is still too early to know what effects the new law will have upon public or officer safety as the standard has been changed from what is deemed "reasonable" at the time of the shooting to what was "necessary" when examined afterward[49]. New York however is already experiencing the consequences of a major overhaul to its criminal justice system on the basis of allegations of institutional racism.

Protests over deadly police shootings of black males such as that of Akai Gurley in NYC added to the chorus, calling for changes in policing across the Empire State. When co-sponsoring the legislation that did so, NY State Senator Jamaal Baily stated, "Our criminal justice system is outdated and in its current form, it has allowed rampant injustices to happen, primarily to people of color"[50]. Just after weeks into effect, New York's new bail reform law freed violent criminals[51], drug dealers[52], and gang members[53] who could have previously been held on bail, but instead went on to commit further injustices against society. Charges of racism by social justice activists are spurring these monumental modifications to criminal justice systems by legislators, so it is important to know if such allegations are founded or if they are being exaggerated. Towards that end, this study asks the following question: How does reporting and activism compare between deadly police shootings involving minority subjects and when they involve White subjects?

There is a significant difference between police enforcing racist laws, as they were used to do in the South during segregation and being considered racist for merely enforcing race-neutral laws against minorities as it occurs now. Allegations of racism by activist groups, notable politicians, and academics amplified through a sympathetic media portray modern law enforcement efforts as racist. Since the media controls how the national conversation is framed and the killing of Black males drives much of the dialogue on racism in American policing, this paper examines the bias in reporting depending on the race of the subject involved in deadly police shooting incidents. The two-part hypothesis is (1). There will be numerically greater media coverage of deadly police shootings when the subject killed is Black than for any other race, and (2). When Blacks are the subjects of controversial deadly police shootings, media coverage will portray the incidents as examples of systemic racial bias instead of being justified, problems with police procedures, or an individual officer's bad judgment.

LITERATURE REVIEW

BLACKS KILLED AT A DISPROPORTIONATE RATE.

At the heart of the topic of deadly police shootings in America is the key finding that Black people are killed by police at a rate disproportionate to their population according to independent groups that are tracking such statistics. In reaction to concerns over government transparency, bolstered by the Justice Department's acknowledgment that its fatal police shootings database is lacking, numerous private entities track and make available such statistics for public consumption[54]. Mappingpoliceviolence.org is a website that has been tracking and displaying police violence since 2013; *Vice News*, a current-affairs web channel, has captured shooting data since 2010; and Britain's *The Guardian* newspaper offers an interactive database for all to see; but it is the database of *The Washington Post* that appears to be the preferred reference on the subject.

Apart from Roussell (2019), Jones (2017), Zuckerman (2019), Mac Donald (2016), Johnson (2019), and Fryer (2018) cited 2015 and 2016 data from *The Washington Post,* claiming that throughout America, "Blacks are shot disproportionately by police, making up 26% and 24% of victims in 2015 and 2016, respectively, despite making up only approximately 13% of the population"[55]. For some scholars, *The Washington Post* statistics are used to support their claims of racism and historical oppression as the reasons for the overrepresentation of African Americans killed by police. That White people make up the bulk of the remaining 74% and 76% of subjects in deadly police shootings for the two years, 2015 and 2016 respectively, does not raise similar concerns among researchers focused on a nexus between racism and policing. As the disparity increases to 40% of unarmed subjects killed by police being Black, making them more likely than Whites to be killed in such incidents[56] [57], calls for justice and claims of racism become even more pronounced.

ROOT CAUSES OF BLACKS BEING KILLED BY POLICE.

The deadly shootings of unarmed Black males Trayvon Martin and Michael Brown are recognized as two of the main incidents that lead to the formation of BLM and hundreds of ensuing nationwide protests[58]. Even though Martin was killed by a civilian, the incident is still included alongside Michael Brown in discussions of deadly police shootings. Both incidents are used by Jones to stress how in America "violence directed at people of color is as old as the country itself"[59]. According to him, racism is the obvious reason for this violence as well as the racial profiling and disparity of Black victims exhibited in deadly police shootings. Referring to numerous previous studies, Shjarback too contends that it "is nothing new to suggest that citizen race impacts police behavior—the police are more likely to stop, search, arrest, and use force against African Americans"[60]. Similarly, for Roussell, the disparate numbers of Blacks killed in police shootings are one of the many ways in America's dark history where the police have disproportionately targeted people of color[61]. Mills describes this more graphically as police "upholding white supremacy in American society," noting "many argue that lynching's parallel modern police shootings"[62]. Such vapid comparisons to white supremacy and lynching's fail to explain why as *The Washington Post* data shows, white people are overall more often the subjects of deadly police shootings. Additionally, the validity of Roussell's findings are questionable given the citations of Krieger (2015) and Nix (2016) as proof of racial bias in deadly police shooting decisions. A review of Krieger (2015) shows that while his paper mentions the shootings of Michael Brown and Trayvon Martin, it does not support Roussell's view. Even worse, Nix refuted Roussell's stance by citing research finding that "Black suspects seem more likely to resist arrest and/or be combative than White suspects"[63]. As a result, we should consider alternative explanations to systemic racism or biased policing.

Other researchers citing the same *The Washington Post* data, dismiss racism as the root cause and instead posit elements such as rate of criminality and pre-incident circumstances are why black people are killed at a higher rate than would be expected solely based upon their share of the population. Using 2009 crime statistics from America's 75 largest counties, Mac Donald reveals that rates of violent crimes by Blacks were significantly higher than their population would suggest, as they "were charged with 62% of all robberies, 57% of all murders, and 45% of assaults" while they were "roughly 15% of the population"[64]. Criticism that such statistics are further proof of a racist criminal justice system is refuted by numerous studies on violent crimes from 1978 through 2011 that have "found parity between the race of assailants in victim reports and in arrests"[65]. Cited as a typical example, in New York City, blacks were the perpetrators in "over 75 percent of all shootings in the city, as reported by the victims and witnesses"[66].

Higher incidences in violent crimes result in higher rates of perilous police contact, where deadly use of force is more prone than routine contact with the community. A substantive study of deadly police shootings occurring in 2015 identified a similar crime nexus with Blacks being nearly four times more likely than Whites to be killed by police in counties where violent crime by minorities was more prevalent[67]. Such elevated risk also comports with the fact that Blacks made up 40% of all cop-killers from 2005 to 2014[68]. If *The Washington Post* data proves any kind of disparity, it is how "an officer's chance of getting killed by a black assailant is 18.5 times higher than the chance of an unarmed black getting killed by a cop"[69] according to the calculations of Mac Donald.

Also taking issue with *The Washington Post* interpreting disparity in its shooting statistics to be proof of racial bias, Fryer (2018) used a formula typically used in economics to discern whether any bias existed in deadly police shootings occurring in Houston, Texas. Contrary to a racial bias against Blacks, "after controlling for suspect demographics, officer demographics, encounter characteristics, suspect weapon and year fixed effects," Fryer calculated that "blacks are 27.4 percent less likely to be shot at by police relative to non-black, non-Hispanics"[70]. A key conclusion of another comprehensive study of officer-involved shootings, this time involving the Philadelphia Police Department, is that the disparity in Blacks being the subjects of deadly police killings reflected Black male's pre-incident conduct of shooting at police, and not racial bias on behalf of the police[71].

Annual statistics of deadly police shootings are commonly cited in studies on the subject and rehashed for the public after most shootings, but an important fact often overlooked when stating "roughly 1,000 people are lethally shot by the police–about 10% of whom are unarmed"[72] is that 90% of the time the subject killed was armed. Therefore, barring any extraneous circumstances, the police officer likely acted reasonably in using deadly force against an armed subject who presented an immediate threat to the officer and/or civilians in the area at that moment. Regarding deadly police shootings of unarmed subjects, what is typically glossed over is whether those subjects were using their personal weapons (hands, feet, elbows, etc.), overpowering the officer, or trying to take the officer's gun to use against them. Instead of reporting on these and other mitigating factors of the police shooting in question, the incidents are lumped together under the banner of racial bias in policing when the subjects are Black.

HISTORY OF OPPRESSION IN AMERICA.

Another commonly included theme in literature on deadly police shootings is that the modern-day consequences are instigated by the government's past practice of using the police as its tool to oppress Blacks in the United States. Various researchers associate the history of oppression with influencing the criminal justice system to be more lenient on Black criminals and police to be more hesitant to shoot a black person as compared to a White person. Deep within America's historic South, a nationwide study of felony convictions back in 1987 "found blacks frequently received disproportionately lenient punishment"[73]. A 1994 Justice Department study of felony cases in large urban areas found Blacks "had a lower chance of prosecution" and "were less likely to be found guilty at trial"[74] than Whites. More recently, in 2016, nearly every facet of the criminal justice system was "under fire for supposedly oppressing blacks"[75] in cities and states across America.

To validate the veracity of a decades-old report that police officers shot more bullets at White suspects than they did at Black ones, James (2016) conducted a research, more relevant to this study, by using the same simulator training technology employed by police academies. Applying the scenarios commonly leading to actual deadly police shootings, James (2016) ran dozens of active-duty police officers through shoot/don't shoot situations involving White and Black subjects. Just as in their two previous studies, James documented the "officers were slower to shoot armed Black suspects than armed White suspects, and they were less likely to shoot unarmed Black suspects than unarmed White suspects"[76]. James surmised that "concerns about the social and legal consequences of shooting a member of a historically oppressed racial group"[77] was the main reason for officers to exhibit an aversion to shooting the Black subjects. As proof, James has told of an Alabama detective who blamed his fear of ending up in the media as the reason he hesitated to use lethal force and ended up getting "pistol whipped by a black suspect"[78]. In a different study analyzing disparities in actual deadly police shootings, officers' reluctance to use lethal force against Blacks was attributed to the fear of media backlash, as well as the criminal charges that might follow[79].

At the opposite end of the spectrum, other researchers suggest Blacks react violently in inter-actions with law enforcement precisely because of the historical association with police and oppression. As Jones puts it, "These historical associations may elicit trauma-related fear, depres-sion or perhaps even hyper-aggression"[80] on behalf of African Americans. Blackstone et al. (2017) repeats an earlier argument that African American's culture and past experiences have contributed to their current affinity for civil unrest. One such experience according to him was Blacks' success-ful use of violence to highlight their exclusion from the ballot box and win over popular support to gain their right to vote. A current example exhibiting that culture of civil unrest is the positive con-nection Williamson (2018) noted among Black populated areas, deadly police shootings of Black people, and recent protests against police.

PROTESTS AND GOVERNMENT LEGITIMACY.

Anti-police protests strike at the legitimacy of law enforcement which is another theme that is fun-damental to deadly police shootings. Citizens entrust the police to enforce the law equally while using the least amount of force necessary, anything less can cause the community to not cooperate or comply with the police[81]. Even worse, the public belief that the police are unfair, impartial, or unrestrained could lead to violent confrontations requiring justified and as Cruz (2015) points out, elevated use of force on behalf of the police. As Johnson (2019) stresses, the perception that police are disproportionately targeting Black people with lethal force would raise serious concerns over law enforcement's legitimacy in America–concerns that could elevate to conflict.

Several deadly police shootings of African Americans in the past ten years have fulfilled fears of impartial policing, leading to intense media coverage of violent protests in black communi-ties and putting law enforcement under a microscope. Protest is considered a "classic example of citizens challenging legitimacy of police"[82] and an act of civil unrest which Williamson (2018) analyzed was specifically related to the BLM movement. In cities with a population of 100,000 people, Williamson found that just one Black fatality at the hands of law enforcement increased the probability of a protest by over 20%[83]. The deadly police shooting of Michael Brown and the non-indictment of the officer who shot him generated two of the largest peaks of protest activity observed in Williamson's study.

Stories detailing tragic losses of life streaming across media platforms, nationwide protests and allegations of racism have combined to make deadly police shootings "one of the most divisive issues of the twenty-first century"[84]. Shjarback (2017) acknowledges that individual officers should be held accountable for any abuses of power, but the police profession must be able to effectively enforce the law. James thinks that America needs "to move beyond the post-Ferguson atmosphere where all use of force against a racial/ethnic minority person is considered biased and unreason-able until proven otherwise"[85]. Strong and sincere words from America's elected leaders could help the country move beyond this atmosphere.

POLITICAL INFLUENCE AND LEADERSHIP.

Reporting of America's elected leaders' statements on deadly police shootings impacts upon the public's divisiveness and the government's legitimacy. Most shootings do not rise to the national level so unless forced to comment on such an incident, it is unlikely that a nationally recognized elected person would insert themselves into something so controversial. Regarding the Michael Brown-related protests, Blackstone points out how politicians on both sides of the aisle appeared "hesitant to respond to the unrest, likely for fear of political repercussions of alienating either law enforcement or minorities"[86]. The overall sense from the Democrats was that they understood the Black community's frustration over the racially charged police shooting in Ferguson and supported their peaceful protests. Drawing criticism and adding to the controversy as he did so, President Obama was one Democrat who did not shy away from responding to Michael Brown's controversial death. As Lasch (2016) reiterated, besides personally addressing the shooting, which is quite rare for a President to do, President Obama sent three staff members to attend Michael Brown's funeral[87]. Showing his interest was more than just a momentary display, President Obama assigned AG Holder and dozens of Federal Bureau of Investigation (FBI) agents to investigate not only the Brown shooting but also the Ferguson Police Department.

Conversely, Blackstone et al. (2017) notes that Republicans are generally critical of criminals and supportive of law enforcement as they were for Police Officer Darren Wilson in the aftermath of the Ferguson shooting. For his part, President Trump is considered judgmental of criminals, especially those that are illegal immigrants or minorities. Eliciting harsh criticism of his own, while President Trump does not mention race, his messages on "criminal behavior" are believed by some to be "coded terms" for his racist messaging favoring white nationalism[88]. Any deadly police shooting warranting a soundbite from notable politicians is sure to be featured in one of the numerous print, TV, cable, and internet media outlets covering American current events.

MEDIA COVERAGE.

Media reporting plays an integral role in how police deadly shooting incidents are portrayed and, therefore, is an important theme in the overall discussion as well as the main focus of this study. What the media reports and how the media frames what is reported influences both how the public thinks about a particular shooting and the extent to which they see police legitimacy as an issue. In the deadly police shooting of Michael Brown, Zuckerman (2019) reports BLM and the media found an event that spoke to African Americans historic concerns of police bias and brutality. Michael Brown's shooting death by Police Officer Darren Wilson changed the way such incidents were reported, giving birth to "a news wave focused on the disproportionate impact of police violence against Black Americans"[89].

The ensuing avalanche of coverage has generated several studies analyzing media partisanship, bias, and victim blaming of the black subjects of deadly police shootings. Blackstone et al. (2017) analyzed the twitter content of legacy, cable and online news networks for the month following the Michael Brown shooting. Expecting to find "partisan bias in tweets from the three major cable news channels, Fox News (FNC), MSNBC, and CNN,"[90] Blackstone et al. (2017) surmised that the reason they did not find it was that most politicians refrained from touching the third rail that was Ferguson. What Blackstone did observe as hypothesized were tweets framing "protesters as troublemakers rather than justified demonstrators"[91]. Blackstone et al. (2017) also found that police were likewise criticized for their militarized response to the demonstrators/protestors.

Using the previously mentioned data sets from *The Washington Post, The Guardian,* and *Mapping Police Violence,* Zuckerman (2019) analyzed media reporting on the police-involved deaths of unarmed African Americans from 2013 to midway through 2016. Running a query through Media Cloud database for stories on each fatality, Zuckerman then recorded the "likes and shares received by the story on Facebook"[92]. Where stories of a typical Black victim of a police-involved fatality garnered less than ten shares on Facebook before the Michael Brown shooting, Zuckerman (2019) discovered shares averaged over 9,000 afterward. Clearly the deadly police shooting of Michael Brown tuned the public's radar and garnered sympathy to similar stories of Black subjects.

Despite the sympathetic reactions in Facebook, not all media coverage of Michael Brown, or other Black subjects killed by law enforcement, was flattering. This is to be expected as numerous researchers have documented the media's proclivity for bias by running more stories of Black criminal behavior than those involving White criminals. Adding to such research, Dukes (2017) paper on "media coverage of the deaths of six unarmed Black males (Eric Garner, Michael Brown, Akai Gurley, Tamir Rice, Tony Robinson, and Freddie Gray) by law enforcement"[93] found the coverage included racial stereotyping, references to the subjects' involvement in criminal behavior, and a focus on their physical stature. Dukes (2017) compared this "victim blaming" of the six unarmed black subjects to what rape victims commonly go through. To examine the effects of negative and positive racial stereotypes upon judgment of blame, Dukes (2017) provided details of such stereotypes to volunteers who were then questioned on culpability using scenarios resembling those of the Michael Brown and Trayvon Martin shootings. Dukes' (2017) study showed that when people were provided negative information of the subjects who were shot, they placed less blame on the shooter. These results reinforce the concern of Dukes (2017) that media framing prejudices the public to place blame on the subjects of deadly police shootings instead of on the police officers who pulled the trigger. Dukes caveats its findings with the disclaimer "we caution readers in concluding that all victims should be portrayed positively since in some cases, shooters are not at fault and victims really are to blame"[94]. According to the literature, one media outlet stood out for the very reason that they did not portray Michael Brown as the victim.

Considered biased toward conservative views while supportive of the police in comparison to its liberal-leaning CNN and MSNBC competition, FNC was singled out by researchers for victim blaming the subjects of deadly police shootings. Besides FNC host Sean Hannity claiming that Michael Brown never said, "Hands up, Don't Shoot" (Mills 2017) sees evidence of victim blaming as numerous FNC commentators described Brown's large physical size, criminal conduct of robbing the convenience store, and his violent attack upon Officer Wilson. Furthermore, Mills (2017) blames FNC for trying to pivot from the racialized "issue of police violence" to placing the blame on the Black community by claiming systemic issues of Black-on-Black crime forces the police "to enter black communities"[95] in the first place. While Lasch (2016) considered FNC's critiques of the Obama administration's reactions to the deadly shootings of Michael Brown and Trayvon Martin as part of their larger anti-Obama agenda, Mills (2017) thinks that such critiques indicate FNC's pro-White supremacy narrative.

SUMMARY.

The topic of deadly police shootings elicits strong emotional responses, as evident from the extensive social justice activism and media coverage conducted since Michael Brown was killed by a Ferguson Police Officer. These same emotional responses are manifest in the significant body of research addressing the recent deadly police shootings, with two polarized sides seeking to understand why it appears that Blacks are so often the subjects in such incidents. On one side, preferring to examine the specifics of each incident, are the authors who see factors such as criminality and pre-incident actions influencing the numbers of blacks involved in deadly police shootings. Conducting simulated shooting scenarios and examining data from both police agencies and that of *The Washington Post*, these authors find no evidence of racial bias when police officers use lethal force on African Americans.

Research authors on the other side believe instead that each incident reflects a generalized problem that America's racist past plus the fact more blacks are killed by police than their corresponding percentage of the population, can only equal one thing–racist policing today. Statistics of blacks being the victim 26% of the time when subjects are armed and 40% of the time when subjects are unarmed in deadly police shootings is the centerpiece of these literary works. A common denominator of the deadly police shootings written about by these authors are Black subjects who are cast as innocent victims. The impression given from these researchers is that the deadly police shootings of White people must either all be justified or honest mistakes, while those of Black subjects are based on racism. Missing from the research is a detailed examination on the deadly police shootings of subjects with different races to see what the facts actually are when compared to what the media said. Having acknowledged the media's influence on what and how the public knows and thinks about events, researchers have yet to question whether a media bias in reporting on deadly police shootings has carried over to how their research on that subject has been framed.

It was the power of legacy news, cable TV, and social media that took Michael Brown's death by shooting from an obscure city named Ferguson and made it a national story with racial implications within hours. The literature shows substantial increases in BLM-related protests and in the number of tweets for subsequent stories of black men killed by police after Michael Brown's death. What the literature of those advancing a racial narrative does not show is an interest in acknowledging the veracity of the claims associated with the Michael Brown shooting. In comparing police killing of civilians in Europe to America, Jones cited an author who wrote "Darren Wilson, the White police officer who killed Michael Brown in Ferguson, would not have been absolved in Europe because he 'thought' that Brown had a gun"[96]. Jones should know that Officer Wilson was found to be justified in his actions because Brown's continued attack made Wilson fear for his life, not because of any allegations Brown had a gun. In another example, Mills criticized Fox News guests for saying that "'Hand's Up, Don't Shoot' never happened" and that "Officer Wilson was the real victim that day"[97]. Given that Mills' paper was written two years after the Justice Department report exonerating Officer Wilson came out, it reinforces the importance of examining how the Michael Brown shooting has been portrayed in the media. Additionally, the positive and negative media coverage spurred by Obama's remarks on the Ferguson shooting are discussed but this topic is not explored further to see which other police shootings warranted comments by the President and those seeking that office.

Another area that is absent in a review of the literature analyzing deadly police shootings is the extent of media coverage when the subjects of those shootings are White. Apart from the deadly police shooting of Michael Brown, additional shootings mentioned in the research included those of Alton Sterling, Philando Castile, Akai Gurley, Walter Scott and Laquan McDonald–every one of them a Black male. Are there no examples of White subjects killed in similar incidents or does the research merely mirror the media's continued representation of incidents involving Black subjects and angry protestors? Are the media themselves guilty of a bias in the deadly police shootings that they choose to make front-page news?

This study seeks to answer these and other questions of media coverage which have not been addressed in the current literature on deadly police shootings. The notions of "historical oppression" and "if it bleeds, it leads" are two reasons used to explain why the deadly police shootings of Black males have received so much coverage. The veracity of these notions will be tested by comparing media coverage of other tangential incidents where "it bleeds" to see if this also applies to murdered cops and Black-on-Black homicides. Instead of looking at the media coverage of just one incident, this study will examine four years of media coverage in general and make a deep dive into four separate deadly police shootings. Since the legacy and cable news are the trusted and most available daily sources for Americans, this study will attempt to discern whether any racial preference is evident in reporting when someone is shot dead by the police. This research study will conduct two case studies comparing the media coverage generated by the deadly police shootings of two black subjects against that of two white subjects. This will perhaps be the greatest contribution of this study to the literature.

Despite studies disproving any racial bias in deadly police shootings, such shootings still provoke outrage, protests, and at times violent reactions. Since the way such shootings are portrayed in the media influences the public's reactions, it is critical to know whether the media are reporting the incidents accurately. Modern media depictions of police shootings involving minorities make it appear as though racial bias is at play on behalf of the police. Just as the perception of biased policing elicits anger and distrust from society, so too would evidence of biased media reporting. It is in this area of exploring and exposing media bias in the reporting of deadly police shootings that this study aspires to contribute to the body of knowledge.

METHODOLOGY

THEORETICAL FRAMEWORK

Since the claims of systemic racism, protests, and subsequent calls for change to the criminal justice system are made under the guise of social justice[98], this study will be framed considering social justice theory. Originally presented as a "concept of justice taking Locke, Rousseau and Kant's social contract theory to a higher level"[99], John Rawls had developed the modern social justice theory in the aftermath of the civil-rights movement of the 1960s. Reflective of the injustices that have been fought against in the preceding decades, social justice theory is based upon the belief that individuals will freely enter into a social contract whereby they will be treated fairly and equally as members of society. The first and most important principle for the theory is that everyone has "equal rights" to the same "equal liberties." with those most relevant to criminal justice being "freedom from psychological oppression and physical assault and dismemberment; and freedom from arbitrary arrest and seizure as defined by the concept of the rule of law"[100].

Adding to the importance of equality and fairness in social justice theory, another proponent, British political theorist David Miller believed that people consider "the context of a situation"[101] when judging whether or not justice is fair. The crux of the outrage over deadly police shootings is that they disproportionately "victimize" African Americans, presenting a context of unfair and unequal administration of justice which has plagued African Americans since the nation's founding. Unlike in theory, fairness and equality may be incongruous with context for modern day social justice activists outraged over deadly police shootings of black people. While reviewing reactions to deadly police shootings, this study will examine whether the social justice theory principles of fairness and context matter, or if, perhaps, the most important detail of the incident is the race of the subject killed in the incident.

HYPOTHESES.

Hypothesis 1 is that there will be numerically greater media coverage of deadly police shootings when the subject killed is black than that for any other races. This hypothesis is further broken down into four subhypotheses:

Subhypothesis 1a: Traditional newspaper coverage of deadly police shooting incidents of Black subjects will exceed that of those incidents where the subjects are not Black.

Subhypothesis 1b: Traditional newspaper coverage of deadly police shooting incidents of Black subjects will exceed coverage of Black-on-Black crime, shooting deaths of police, and positive stories of police.

Subhypothesis 1c: ABC, NBC, CBS, MSNBC, and CNN coverage of deadly police shootings with Black subjects will exceed their coverage of such shootings with White subjects and for shootings where police are the victims.

Sub-hypothesis 1d: FNC coverage of shootings where police are the victims will exceed their coverage of deadly police shootings, but their coverage of deadly police shootings will be equal among Black and White subjects.

Hypothesis 2 is that when Blacks are the subjects of controversial deadly police shootings, media coverage will portray the incidents as examples of systemic racial bias instead of being justified, problems with police procedures, or an individual officer's bad judgment. This hypothesis is further broken down into one subhypothesis:

Subhypothesis 2a: Media coverage of the Michael Brown shooting will continue framing the incident as racially biased even after the Department of Justice (DOJ) report shows that Brown was the aggressor and Police Officer Darren Wilson used justified deadly force.

RESEARCH DESIGN

To be as comprehensive as possible, the research strategy to test the hypotheses will be performed using three separate methods:

1. To test hypothesis 1, and subhypotheses 1a and 1b regarding whether reporting has been conducted equally on deadly police shootings across races, Black-on-Black crime, the killing of police officers, and positive stories of police, a quantitative analysis will be performed by examining the front page of the *USA Today* newspaper from 2015 to 2018. The number of cover stories and teasers addressing deadly police shootings will be captured for each race. In addition, stories focused on Black-on-Black crime, officers killed in the line of duty, and positive stories on policing will also be captured.

2. To test hypothesis 1, and subhypotheses 1c and 1d, this study will analyze the existence of right- or left-leaning bias toward a certain race being the subject of deadly police shooting incidents as well as bias against covering police as victims. A quantitative analysis will be conducted on the television and online coverage by ABC, CBS, NBC, FNC, CNN and MSNBC for the number of stories run mentioning the police shooting deaths of Black subjects Akai Gurley, Alton Sterling, Philando Castile, and Keith Lamont Scott; and White subjects Dillon Taylor, Daniel Shaver, Dylan Noble, and Justine Damond (Ruszczyk). Additionally, the quantity of coverage will be compared among those same media organizations for the shooting deaths of NYPD Police Officer Wenjian

Liu; Hattiesburg Police Patrolman Liquori Tate; Baton Rouge Police Corporal Montrell Jackson; and NYPD Police Officer Miosotis Familia to see if the shootings of minority police officers by criminals elicits more or less press than the subjects of deadly police shootings.

3. To test hypothesis 2 and subhypothesis 2a, a case study will be conducted using a comparative analysis on the coverage of the deadly police shootings of Michael Brown versus Justine Damond (Ruszczyk) and Alton Sterling versus Daniel Shaver. A study on deadly police shootings in the modern era would not be complete without an in-depth discussion on the Michael Brown incident. To present the fairest comparison with a white subject of an equally controversial deadly police shooting, the incident involving Justine Damond will be used because her Australian citizenship made the story one of international interest. Since Damond was shot by a black police officer it also allows for an equal comparison of whether the shooting is portrayed as racially biased. The death of Alton Sterling by police gained intense media attention and activism in part because of the sensational video of the incident which shows him being killed. A fair comparison involving a similarly emotionally charged shooting of a white subject captured on video is the incident with Daniel Shaver.

The factors leading up to each incident, the subject's actions, the police officer's culpability, and the media coverage for both sets of shootings will be compared. These factors provide a baseline to gauge how the incident is framed by the press in relation to the actual facts and ultimate innocence or guilt of the police. Since activism and political statements are significant parts of the national conversation and influence reporting on the shootings, special attention will be paid to them.

Content analysis will be conducted qualitatively to gauge whether the shooting is portrayed as racially biased. Unless it is shown to be relevant as to why the officer pulled the trigger, the races of the officer and subject involved in a deadly police shooting does not have any bearing on the incident. However, such information does have bearing when the aim is to link the officer's action explicitly or implicitly to racial bias. The media coverage will be examined with attention paid to the use of racial descriptors such as the color of the subject and officer; key words referring to America's troubled history, for example, legacy of slavery, oppression, lynching, police violence/brutality, institutional/systemic bias, discrimination in the criminal justice system, murder, victim, targeting people of color, racist/racism/racial, minority death; and including other examples of Blacks killed by police.

Besides framing a deadly police shooting as being racially biased through key words, it can also be portrayed as such through what is and is not included in the reporting. This can be accomplished by failing to report key evidence or witnesses; using emotional quotes from the subjects' family, friends, and neighbors; publishing irrelevant, uninformed statements from celebrities; minimizing or not reporting on the subject's violent/threatening actions; linking to tangential issues; and using misleading titles to make the shooting appear like murder. Similarly, a police shooting can instead be framed as a legitimate use of deadly force or bad procedures/judgment by the police. Key words for indicating blame on the police include incompetence, poor training, errors, inexperience, unprofessional, preventable, or avoidable. While such descriptions and reporting are critical of the police, they do not insinuate race as being a factor.

LIMITATIONS OF THE STUDY

The four years from 2015 through 2018 encompass the height of the anti-police protests in the nation and spans both the Obama and Trump presidential administrations. While variances in data may be attributed to the particular political party in charge, it is also possible that any drop-off in attention to deadly police shootings from 2017 to 2018 is because of the magnitude of media attention focused on the Trump presidency. While an immense number of relevant media hits were able to be compiled using the search engines Nexis Uni and the Media Cloud, time limitations preclude the ability to read or watch every data hit completely in order to observe the extent of bias or opinions presented. Article titles in the Media Cloud results which did not show prima facie relevance to the shooting were opened on a hyperlink to ensure that they were not false positives. Only two dozen false positives were found among the results, however some hyperlinks no longer existed, so those articles could not be verified. Time limitations also drove the decision to review the front page of only one newspaper for relevant stories. *USA Today* was chosen for this because it has the largest distribution in the US. Though they may have the widest of reach among people, the stories chosen by *USA Today* may not be reflective of the newspaper industry as a whole.

RESULTS

QUANTITATIVE ANALYSIS OF USA TODAY

The quantitative analysis of the front-page cover stories and teasers in the *USA Today* newspaper, US edition from 2015 to 2018 performed to test hypothesis 1 and subhypotheses 1a and 1b revealed the following findings:

| Year | Deadly Police Shooting | | | Black on Black Crime | | Line of Duty Killing | | Positive Police Stories |
	Stories	Named Black Subjects	Named White Subjects	Stories	Named Black Victims	Stories	Named Officers	
2015	29	33	0	6	1	7	7	0
2016	29	14	1	7	4	8	13	1
2017	10	3	0	1	2	5	2	1
2018	14	7	0	10	7	4	5	0
TOTAL	82	57	1	24	14	24	27	2

Figure 1 USA Today front-page cover stories and teasers from 2015 to 2018.

Hypothesis 1 and subhypothesis 1a were confirmed: The coverage of deadly police shootings of Black subjects consisted of 82 stories naming 57 separate individuals and far exceeded the coverage of non-Black subjects. Since many stories included more than one black subject, those 57 Black subjects were referenced a total of 132 times in the 82 stories while a lone White subject was named once in a story published a week after his death, which was about the recent shootings of two Black men. There were no stories or mentions of deadly police shootings of subjects belonging to Asian, Hispanic, Native American, or other races.

Subhypothesis 1b was confirmed: The coverage of deadly police shootings of Black subjects consisted of 82 stories. This number was 3.4 times greater than the 24 stories each for both Black-on-Black crime and line-of-duty (LOD) shooting murders of police; and 41 times more than the two positive stories on policing.

	Asian	Black	Hispanic	Native	Other	White	Total	None
2015	14	262	172	9	15	503	975	29
2016	15	234	160	16	11	465	901	61
2017	16	223	179	22	6	461	907	81
2018	21	229	165	15	4	451	885	107
TOTAL	66	948	676	62	36	1,880	3,668	278

Figure 2 Washington Post data base of deadly police shootings by race of subjects killed.

To put *USA Today* coverage tested in sub-hypothesis 1a into perspective, Figure 2. shows how many subjects by race were fatally shot by police from 2015 to 2018, as documented by *The Washington Post* database on Fatal Police Encounters. With 57 separate people named out of a total of 948 over those four years, a black subject had a 6% chance of *USA Today* making their death by police-involved shooting front-page material. Meanwhile a white subject had only a .05% chance of getting mentioned in such coverage, which is more than the 0% chance that all other races had. The centerpiece of media stories alleging racially biased policing has been that while only 13% of the population, Blacks are approximately 26% of the victims of deadly police shootings. Meanwhile, this analysis showed that Black subjects were named in 100% of the reporting in *USA Today* stories on deadly police shootings. By the standard of proportionality used to judge police shootings, *USA Today's* reporting is 120x more racially biased than police.

Consistent with Zuckerman's findings of more than one victim being mentioned in stories on deadly police shootings after that of Michael Brown, there were 27 such stories naming more than one subject, when examined over the four years. It was in one such 2016 story on the deaths of Philando Castile and Alton Sterling by deadly police shooting, that the lone non-Black subject, Dylan Noble, was mentioned[102]. In all there were 56 different Black males and 1 Black female named subjects of deadly police shootings. The names of any of the subjects of the shootings were mentioned several times, with Michael Brown and the Ferguson incident referenced in 39 separate stories. One story about Ferguson mentioned the names of 30 separate Black subjects that had been killed in the past year. Stories about police body cameras and military equipment, urban violence, gun violence, gang violence, TV dramas, church attendance, NFL fans, and even Starbucks anti-bias training for employees–all found a way to include the name of a Black subject of a deadly police shooting, and thus keep the national conversation going.

Contrasting the emphasis that media coverage put on Black subjects of police shootings is the lack of stories for the exponentially greater number of Blacks murdered during Black-on-Black crime. According to the FBI's 2016 crime statistics, there were 2,570 Blacks murdered by other blacks, which is 89.5% of the 2,870 blacks murdered that year[103]. Assuming a similar amount for the other three years, there were approximately 10,280 blacks murdered by fellow blacks during 2015 to 2018. With only fourteen named victims of Black-on-Black crime out of the 10,280 total, these victims had a .14% chance of their murder making the front page of *USA Today*. These Black victims would be 43 times more likely to have their death make the front page of *USA Today* if it instead came at the hands of the police.

For the line-of-duty murders, eight of the stories and eleven of the police officers named were related to murders committed in revenge for the highly publicized deadly police shootings of Black subjects that recently occurred. The lone two positive police stories were how the federal authorities locked up 8,000 violent offenders and an article lamenting how the hero cop of the Orlando Pulse shooting was being laid off before he qualified for his pension in years 2016 and 2017, respectively. The NFL protests started by Colin Kaepernick; arrest of two Black males at Starbucks; and increases in crime raising the question of a "Ferguson effect" upon policing made significant contributions to 50 stories critical of policing, many of which alleged police brutality and biased policing against African Americans. Names of fourteen victims were included in the stories regarding Black-on-Black crime. It is clear from this quantitative analysis that reporting is not being conducted equally on deadly police shootings across races, Black-on-Black crime, and the killing of police officers. The numbers show that the media has an obvious preference to covering deadly police shootings when the subjects are Black over police shootings involving the subjects of any of the other races, Black-on-Black violence, or police-related stories. To paraphrase the modern activist's lingo, based on the complete absence of media coverage, when it comes to deadly police shootings of minorities, it appears that only Black lives matter.

QUANTITATIVE ANALYSIS OF LEGACY AND CABLE NETWORKS

The quantitative analysis of television and online coverage by ABC, CBS, NBC, CNN, FNC and MSNBC performed to test hypothesis 1, and subhypotheses 1c and 1d revealed the following findings:

Hypothesis 1 and subhypothesis 1c were confirmed: The overall coverage of deadly police shootings with 2,666 stories on Black subjects by ABC, CBS, NBC, CNN, and MSNBC was over eight times more than their 330 stories on white subjects of similar shootings, and almost six times more than their 471 stories on police officers fatally shot in the line of duty.

The networks together averaged 533 stories on the Black subjects, 66 stories on the White subjects, and 94 stories on the officers shot dead in the line of duty. Looking at it in another way, among the five networks, each Black subject averaged 667 stories, each White subject averaged 83 stories, and each police officer averaged 118 stories. Broken down even further, when it came to individual media outlet's coverage of deadly police shootings, each Black subject averaged 133 stories, each White subject averaged 17 stories and each police officer averaged 24 stories. Per individual shooting subject, the networks' top two story drivers were on black males Castile and Sterling. Keith Lamont Scott generated the third most stories for each network except ABC, which dedicated 12 more stories to White female Damond than to Scott. Excluding CNN, Damond was mentioned in more stories over these networks than Black subject Gurley was. Among police officers, Wenjian Liu received the most media attention across all networks and was named in more stories than all White subjects, but still had less media hits than all Black subjects, with the exception of Gurley.

Among the Black subjects of deadly police shootings, Akai Gurley was clearly the outlier when it came to generating media attention. Unlike the incidents of intentional use of deadly force, such as those of Sterling, Castile, and Scott, all of which occurred within a few months of each other in 2016, the Gurley incident happened in 2014, and it involved an Asian rookie

Black Subject	ABC	CBS	NBC	CNN	FNC	MSNBC	TOTAL
Akai Gurley	57	15	26	23	40	30	191
Alton Sterling	275	189	187	210	136	162	1,159
Philando Castile	284	185	178	211	186	155	1,199
Keith Lamont Scott	106	80	101	83	66	109	545
Total	722	469	492	527	428	456	3,094

White Subject	ABC	CBS	NBC	CNN	FNC	MSNBC	TOTAL
Dillon Taylor	0	0	1	3	0	2	6
Daniel Shaver	4	14	4	6	8	2	38
Dylan Noble	5	3	1	2	4	1	16
Justine Damond (Rusczcyk)	118	53	58	19	114	34	396
Total	127	70	64	30	126	39	456

Total Stories B&W Subjects	849	539	556	557	554	495	3550

Police Officer	ABC	CBS	NBC	CNN	FNC	MSNBC	TOTAL
Wenjian Liu	95	68	28	56	83	67	397
Liquori Tate	14	7	2	8	14	5	50
Montrell Jackson	28	20	12	14	17	8	99
Miosotis Familia	15	5	8	2	37	9	76
Total	152	100	50	80	151	89	622

Total Stories Subjects & POs	1,001	639	606	637	705	584	4,172

Figure 3 Media coverage of subjects of deadly police shootings and officers fatally shot.

officer's accidental discharge that ricocheted and ultimately killed Akai. Even given those circumstances, Gurley received more media coverage than three of the white subjects (Taylor, Shaver, and Noble) who were intentionally killed by police as well as three of the police officers (Liquori Tate, Montrell Jackson, and Miosotis Familia) who were intentionally murdered. Notably, Castile and Scott were also killed by non-White police officers yet the shootings of both of them had substantially more media coverage than all of the White subjects and police officers analyzed here.

Justine Damond stood out among the White subjects for receiving more media coverage than three of the police officers and all of the other White subjects combined. The only police officer she had less media attention than was Wenjian Liu. Several factors made Damond's deadly police shooting a topic of intense interest for the media. Besides Damond's Australian citizenship making it an international story, the cop who killed her was a Somali American who had already received a well-publicized welcoming to the Minneapolis Police Department by Mayor Betsy Hodges[104]. The Somali ethnicity of the police officer who shot Damond opened a new angle of racism to report on, especially once he was convicted for killing Damond while the officer involved in the nearby Castile shooting was acquitted.

The line-of duty-shooting death of PO Wenjian Liu received four times more coverage than any one of the other three police murders, and more than those three combined. Three reasons for the marked interest in media coverage of his shooting was it was believed to be a revenge killing for the recent police shooting deaths of blacks[105]; his partner NYPD PO Rafael Ramos was also killed in the ambush; and a law named in their honor was signed by President Obama[106]. Despite Miosotis Familia being the first female NYPD officer killed in the line of duty since 9/11; a single mother raising three children; and executed point blank "for her uniform and for the responsibility she embraced"[107], three armed black subjects justifiably shot by police received 38 times more media coverage than her murder.

Hypothesis 1 was confirmed, subhypothesis 1d was not: FNC coverage of shootings where police are the victims did not exceed their coverage of deadly police shootings, and their coverage of deadly police shootings was not equal among black and white subjects. FNC's 554 stories on deadly police shootings were 3.7 times more than the 151 stories they ran about police officers being murdered. Fox News coverage of black subjects of deadly police shootings numbered 428, vastly more than the 126 stories of such shootings with white subjects.

While this method does not analyze the substance of the coverage, based on the number of stories FNC published, there is no indication as suggested in the literature review of a pro-White or anti-Black bias in bringing attention to the issue of deadly police shootings. FNC's 151 stories on LOD shootings exceeded their 126 media pieces on deadly police shootings of white subjects, but that was not unique since all networks except NBC did that as well. Besides the Damond shooting, the three remaining White subjects averaged four stories on FNC, 27 times less than the 107 stories averaged by the Black subjects on the network.

This quantitative analysis showed that the legacy networks and left- and right-leaning cable networks all exhibited the same bias in reporting about the black subjects of deadly police shootings exponentially more than they did when the subjects were White–thereby unanimously confirming hypothesis 1. In the national conversation about policing and race, the networks' preferred topic was deadly police shootings involving Black subjects. Based upon the standard of proportionality of Blacks being victimized twice their rate of population used to label the police as racist, by giving Black victims 6.8 times more coverage than White ones, these networks displayed exponentially more racial bias than the police. Overall, left or right bias had no bearing on networks preferring to report line-of-duty deaths of minority officers over stories of White subjects of deadly police shootings with all but NBC doing so. In comparing the three cable networks, right-leaning FNC had three times more stories on deadly police shootings involving White subjects than did either left-leaning CNN or MSNBC.

CASE STUDY (MICHAEL BROWN VERSUS JUSTINE DAMOND)

The case studies comparing the deadly police shootings of two black subjects to that of two white subjects were conducted by looking at the pre-incident circumstances, actions of subjects during the shooting, police officer's culpability, and media coverage with special attention to social justice activism and political statements.

PRE-INCIDENT CIRCUMSTANCES

Michael Brown. Around noon on August 9, 2014, while driving his marked Ferguson Police Department patrol sport utility vehicle (SUV), Police Officer Darren Wilson encountered two males walking in the middle of the street who were obstructing vehicle traffic. After advising the subjects to walk on the sidewalk, PO Wilson continued driving, but then he noticed that the larger male, Michael Brown, was holding cigarillos that matched with the description of suspects involved in a crime that had just occurred at a nearby store[108]. At that point PO Wilson stopped his vehicle in front of Brown and his friend, Dorian Johnson, as a radio call was put out for back-up units.

Justine Damond (Ruszczyk). Just before 11:30 p.m. of July 15, 2017, Justine Damond called 911 to report hearing a woman in distress in the alley behind her house. Continuing to hear the woman's screams, Damond called 911 again around eight minutes later to report that she feared a woman was being attacked outside her house. Shortly after Damond's second 911 call, a marked Minneapolis Police Department SUV with PO Matthew Harrity at the wheel and PO Mohamed Noor in the passenger seat responded to the alleyway behind Damond's house[109]. After driving through the back alley for a couple of minutes and not seeing or hearing anything concerning, PO Harrity stopped the police vehicle near the end of the alley[110].

DEADLY POLICE SHOOTING

Michael Brown. As PO Wilson tried to exit his vehicle to interview the two men, the approximately 6'5", 289-pound[111] Brown pushed and closed Wilson's door and then physically assaulted the officer as he was confined in the vehicle. After being struck in the face several times by the larger, violent Brown, not armed with a taser and mace not being practical in the closed space, PO Wilson unholstered his gun and threatened Brown with it in hopes of stopping his attack[112]. Instead, Brown grabbed the gun and struggled for control over it with Wilson. When Officer Wilson was finally able to orient the gun away from pointing at himself and instead toward Brown, he pulled the trigger several times. After a few misfires, Wilson successfully fired a round that went into the driver's side door, temporarily stopping Brown's attack[113]. Brown recovered quickly and resumed his attack, at which point Wilson fired again, this time striking Brown's right thumb and causing him to take off running. Yelling multiple times for Brown to stop, Wilson chased after him with his gun drawn but not shooting it. After a few hundred feet, inexplicably to Wilson, Brown turned around and started charging toward the officer. While backing up and fearing that Brown would overpower him and take his weapon as he tried to do just seconds earlier, Officer Wilson fired several volleys of shots as Brown aggressively ran at him. Brown was shot between six and eight times, with the final kill shot to the top of his skull, bringing him down within mere feet of Wilson[114].

Justine Damond. As Officers Harrity and Noor came to a stop in the alleyway behind Justine Damond's house, they heard a loud noise, possibly a result of her hitting the car, before Damond suddenly appeared in her pajamas by the driver's side of their police SUV. Already startled by

Damond's appearance near the car and fearing an ambush when she raised her arm, PO Noor fired one shot across the inside of the vehicle past his partner, through the open driver's side window and into Damond's body. Damond died shortly after, bleeding out from the artery struck by PO Noor's bullet[115].

OFFICER CULPABILITY

Michael Brown. Within two days of the shooting of Michael Brown, the investigation was turned over to the "Criminal Section of the Department of Justice Civil Rights Division, the United States Attorney's Office for the Eastern District of Missouri, and the Federal Bureau of Investigation (FBI)"[116]. The investigation determined that Officer Wilson's statements, the forensic evidence, and witness' statements were consistent with his use of deadly force being reasonable. Therefore, the investigation concluded that there was no basis for charging Officer Wilson for any crime and the incident should be closed[117].

Justine Damond. After many months of investigation by the Minnesota State Bureau of Criminal Apprehension (BCA), it was announced on March 20, 2018, that PO Noor was charged with "third-degree murder and second-degree manslaughter" for abusing "his authority to use deadly force"[118]. On April 30, 2019, a grand jury determined that PO Noor was guilty of both charges[119].

MEDIA COVERAGE

The earlier analysis of legacy and cable media showed a combined total of 396 stories on the Justine Damond shooting. In comparison, by using the same search parameters for Michael Brown, those same networks ran 7,059 stories (ABC 1,565; CBS 1,067; NBC 537; CNN 1,411; FNC 1,069; and MSNBC 1,410). Similar lopsided results were found in a Nexis Uni media search from the day of incident through December 31, 2019, with 2,447 reports on the Michael Brown shooting by the Associated Press, State and Local Wires, when compared to those of Justine Damond being only 224.

Michael Brown: Coverage of the Michael Brown shooting by legacy networks, cable, AP, NPR, and the multitude of smaller networks was intense, with each development related to the incident itself; federal government involvement; grand jury decision; social justice activism; and statements by politicians prompting a story. In the reporting it was common among all the networks to include the races of Michael Brown and Officer Wilson along with discussing tangential issues of other shootings or deadly incidents of black subjects with the police; racism within America's criminal justice system; and Black-on-Black crime. With over 7,000 related stories by just the six legacy and cable networks, it would be impossible within the space of this study to adequately analyze the way each new fact, protest, and quote was presented. However, in looking at key events such as the first few days after the shooting, release of vital evidence, the grand jury and DOJ decisions–a clear distinction could be seen between the framing of coverage among different networks.

Initially all the networks were operating off the few eyewitnesses who had come forward to the press, interviews with concerned members of the community, and what little information was released from the department. The first story by Fox News the day after the shooting did not use the word Black to describe Brown, but his race was clear from the interview of John Gaskin, a local NAACP member concerned the shooting was like "all the other African-American young men that have been killed by police officers"[120]. ABC used this same quote in its August 11 coverage[121]. During the initial reports, other recent, newsworthy, and violent deaths of Black men were mentioned, such as Eric Garner's police-involved death and the "2012 racially charged shooting of 17-year-old Trayvon Martin"[122]. CNN's contribution to the narrative that police were systemically killing Black people was the example of VonDerrit Myers Jr., a black male shot by police in nearby St. Louis[123]. A "related video" link titled "Spike Lee: There's a war on black males"[124] in another CNN Ferguson article showed the magnitude of racial victimization associated with the shooting of Michael Brown.

Early reporting in the Ferguson shooting indeed portrayed Michael Brown as an innocent victim. Included in an FNC story announcing that the FBI would be investigating the shooting were statements from Brown's friend Dorian Johnson about how he was with Michael and saw him put his hands up to surrender but was instead gunned down by the officer[125]. A favorable Michael Brown headline run by FNC the next day was the AP story: "Family and neighbors describe Missouri teenager fatally shot by police as quiet, respectful"[126]. In one of its first reports, ABC had a quote from another eyewitness, Piaget Crenshaw, that she saw Brown "turn around with his arms up in the air and they shot him in his face and chest, and he went down unarmed"[127]. CNN mentioned this account from Crenshaw, as well as similar ones from witnesses Tiffany Mitchell and Dorian Johnson in its August 11 reporting[128]. The first indication that Michael Brown was not an innocent victim "on his way to his grandmother's apartment"[129] who was indiscriminately shot by a police officer came from August 10 reporting on St. Louis County Police Chief Jon Belmar's statement. Chief Belmar indicated that thus far the investigation had revealed that while Officer Wilson was still in his police vehicle, he was assaulted by Brown, who then tried to take his gun from him[130].

A second indication there was more to the Brown shooting than claims of police brutality or racial bias was when, due to numerous Freedom of Information Act (FOIA) requests, Ferguson PD released video footage showing that Brown was involved in a strong-arm robbery just minutes before the shooting incident. The ABC article titled "Ferguson Cop Reports Called "Character Assassination" by Slain Teen's Family"[131] that was reporting this development captured the family's reaction. ABC returned to the narrative of Michael Brown being an ordinary young man a few days later with a story titled "A Different Look at Fergusons Michael Brown Just Days Before His Death." In the article, offered as a "sharp contrast" to the video showing him in a strong-arm robbery, is a video of 18-year-old Brown "seen waiting to join the procession of graduates for Normandy High School in early August, just days before his controversial death on Aug. 9"[132]. Questioning the integrity of the investigation, the release of the robbery video prompted a CNN story titled "Are the police selectively releasing evidence in the Michael Brown investigation?" As an AP story run on FNC showed, some prominent black politicians already questioned St. Louis County Prosecutor Bob McCulloch's integrity, saying that he would "favor the officer"[133] merely because they were both White.

It was within a few days when more evidence of the incident started being revealed that a notable difference in the coverage emerged. When the autopsy results came out, within the ABC report was a statement from Brown's family lawyer insisting that the path of one of the bullets showed "a back-to-front motion"[134], supporting the allegation that Brown was executed from behind. The same day, FNC released a story titled "Lawyers for Michael Browns family say private autopsy backs witness accounts." The difference is that the title is refuted as readers are reminded that Dr.

Michael Baden, whom the family hired to perform the autopsy, had "earlier told *The New York Times* it could be consistent with either surrender or charging at the officer"[135]. Another FNC story run that day reported how additional evidence from the autopsy showed that Brown was shot six times, all from the front[136].

Since all witnesses until that point alleged that Brown was shot as he was running away and/or surrendering, it was breaking news when FNC published a story titled "YouTube video purportedly captures witness backing police version in Ferguson shooting." Included in the story was the link to a YouTube video revealing for the first time an eyewitness supporting Officer Wilson's claims of being attacked, and refuting the "Hands up, don't shoot" narrative that Dorian Johnson had been repeating[137]. In the 21 stories run by ABC, 22 by CBS, 18 by CNN, 26 by MSNBC, and 8 by NBC on August 18, there was no headline of such a key witness supporting the officers' testimony. A CNN story the next day gave eyewitness testimony from Tiffany Wilson, Piaget Crenshaw, and Michael Brady, all of whom supported Dorian Johnson's claims about Brown being shot from behind, without mentioning the witness who was heard on the YouTube video supporting Wilson's narrative. After including Mitchell's quote that "(Brown's) body jerked as if he was hit from behind, and he turned around," the article cites how the autopsy showed that "Brown had been shot at least six times, including twice in the head"[138]. The article never informed how based on that autopsy report, the family hired medical examiner concluded that all shots were from the front.

ABC's first report of the grand jury decision not to indict PO Wilson told how the prosecuting attorney "McCulloch went on to detail the events of Aug. 9, laying out the most explicit and detailed account of events given by a government or law enforcement official in this case"[139]. CNN reported McCullough's statement that "the physical and scientific evidence examined by the grand jury, combined with the witness statements, supported and substantiated by that physical evidence, tells the accurate and tragic story of what happened"[140]. Neither of those stories indicates how PO Wilson was being attacked in his police car, struggled to keep Brown from taking his gun from him, tried to get Brown to surrender, only ultimately shooting Brown in self-defense and out of fear for his own life. Fox News reporting on the grand jury decision made Wilson's innocence clear. Besides citing Wilsons' account of Brown attacking him while still in the police vehicle and then again out in the street, FNC included the impartial eyewitness testimony that "Brown stopped and turned but never raised his hands" as he "ran towards the officer full charge"[141]. It was already apparent a month earlier from a newspaper article published on October 23, 2014, that besides "more than a half-dozen unnamed black witnesses"[142] testimony, forensic evidence provided to the grand jury supported PO Wilson's claims. Had this information been more widely reported, the grand jury's ultimate decision would not have been as big a surprise, and perhaps it would not have provoked such violent protests.

In reporting the results of the Justice Department's investigation of Officer Wilson, ABC's first story noted that testimony alleging that Brown had his hands up were "inaccurate because they are inconsistent with the physical and forensic evidence"[143]. Attorney General Holder is quoted saying that he concurs with the findings before announcing how the parallel investigation into the Ferguson Police Department "found a pattern and practice of discriminatory policing" including "seven racist emails sent by Ferguson officers"[144]. Fox headlined two stories on the racial bias found within the Ferguson PD before announcing the breaking news with the story titled "Federal report backs Ferguson police officer's account in fatal shooting of Michael Brown"[145]. What followed was an AP article reporting the detailed and relevant evidence of: Wilson linking Brown to the earlier robbery; Brown attacking Wilson as he was still in the car, trying to take his gun; and then Brown not trying to surrender, but instead charging toward Wilson. There was no mention of the other DOJ report on biased policing. CNN ran five stories headlining the DOJ report finding systemic discrimination within the Ferguson Police Department before announcing Wilson's innocence on March 5. In that first CNN story announcing the DOJ findings, it is noted that PO Wilson did not commit any violations of the law and the evidence did not "disprove Wilson's stated subjective belief that he feared for his safety"[146]. CNN then devoted 1,026 words to the report finding systemic racial discrimination by the Ferguson Police with 152 words about various witness testimony supporting and refuting Wilson's account sandwiched in between. Among those 152 words was the CNN author pointing out "several witnesses claimed that Brown had his hands up, signaling surrender, when Wilson shot him"[147].

Even after the DOJ report revealed the truth about the Michael Brown shooting incident, Brown's death continued to be referenced in stories alleging police wrongdoing in other deadly incidents involving Black people, as well as by social justice activists. One such story was told a year after the Ferguson shooting as CBS highlighted how the BLM movement grew from the outrage over Michael Brown's death. A tool central to BLM activism is websites dedicated to tracking "police killings" such as "Mapping Police Violence," whose founder was inspired by the Michael Brown shooting and has since concluded that "Ferguson is everywhere"[148]. Another example is a July 2017 ABC story about the Democratic National Convention (DNC) inviting selected mothers of black children killed by police, known as "Mothers of the Movement," to address the audience. The article described the women as mothers who lost "their children to gun violence or excessive use of force by police" in one sentence and "seven mothers who lost their children to gun violence and police brutality"[149] in another. Lesley McSpadden, mother of Michael Brown, was one of those women. FNC's story a day later about the same news was titled "Mothers of the Movement' Mix Righteous Rage and Myth." Making clear the innocence of Michael Brown is one of those myths, the article (also published in the *New York Post*) stated that "the Justice Department found that the evidence supported the officer, Darren Wilson, who said Brown punched him and tried to grab his gun"[150].

Justine Damond. While media coverage of the Damond shooting was only around 5% of that of Browns in the legacy and cable networks, there was still a sizable amount and like that of Browns, it typically referenced other deadly police incidents of Black subjects and racism within America's criminal justice system. Similar to that of Michael, the stories on Justine's shooting grouped around key events, which in her case were the initial incident, announcements of charges against PO Noor, and the final month of his criminal trial.

Initial reporting of the Damond shooting did neither mention the race of the victim nor that of the police officer, though her picture was shown, and within a couple of days when PO Noor was identified as the officer, photos of him in his police uniform typically accompanied the story. It was common for the story to identify Damond's Australian ancestry just as Noor's Somali heritage was. The references to other deadly police incidents involving black subjects started immediately with FNC and ABC News on their first day covering the shooting, both of them mentioning how only a year earlier in the same state, "police officer Jeronimo Yanez, who is Latino, shot Philando Castile, a 32-year-old black man, several times during a traffic stop"[151]. ABC again referenced Castile as "an

African-American man …shot and killed by a police officer one year ago"[152] when reporting that to honor Justine, Valerie Castile attended the march held in a neighborhood park.

CNN too quickly referred to the Castile shooting by using the vigil held for Damond shortly after her killing as the premise. After noting how Damond's death elicited a vigil and not "protest marches, like the ones Black Lives Matter held last year after Philando Castile's shooting death", CNN contributor David Love theorized that it was because America had not "reckoned with our history"[153]. Love went on to compare the lack of protests on Damond's behalf to the lack of media coverage given to the murders during the 1960's in the South, unless the victims as in the 'Mississippi Burning' were white. John Jay College Criminal Justice Professor, Phillip Goff, was then similarly quoted, saying, "The different reaction to the shooting also proves that America is still learning how to deal with its tortured racial past"[154].

With most of her family still living in Australia, Justine's death quickly became an international story with articles in America showing reports of her family's stunned reaction[155] and Australian Prime Minister Malcolm Turnbull "demanding answers" for the "inexplicable"[156] shooting. Another international element was added early on when Mohammed Noor was identified as the police officer who took the shot that killed Damond. ABC's first story identifying Noor was a very favorable one that showed a ceremony of the Minneapolis Mayor welcoming him to the police department and noting how his "arrival had been highly celebrated by the Somali community"[157]. In another Somali-centric story, FNC reported that besides considering PO Noor a "great guy" and "good example,"[158] the Somali community feared retribution since one of its community leaders received threatening emails and phone calls. The story then pivots to tell how the Somali community was upset when Minneapolis cops "fatally shot a machete-wielding Somali man"[159] back in 2002. More modern resentment within the community toward the police is then mentioned with the deadly police shootings of Philando Castile and Jamar Clark.

The Castile and Clark incidents were again referenced in another FNC story that was posted on the same day where BLM organizer Chauntyll Allen is quoted saying that the Damond shooting "shows that police violence has become an endemic problem" and "the militarized police state…shoots first and asks questions later"[160]. In their reporting on illegal street signs saying "Warning: Twin Cities police easily startled" posted in reaction to Damond's shooting, both FNC and NBC referenced the community's past anger from the police shooting deaths of Castile and Clark[161]. CNN used its story announcing the resignation of the Minneapolis Chief of Police to again highlight the deadly police shootings of Black subjects. After referencing Philando Castile, the article notes "Jamar Clark, a 24-year-old African American, was killed in a scuffle with white Minneapolis officers"[162].

Regarding the coverage about Noor specifically, along with ABC, both CNN and FNC reported that he was not cooperating with the investigation by refusing to give a statement[163]. FNC ran a story critical of Noor's training with one expert saying how some "believe the fast-track program could leave officers ill prepared to handle real-world police scenarios,"[164] while the Police Chief is quoted commending Noor's training and ability to do the job. An AP article ran by FNC and ABC quotes Noor's lawyer referring to the recent murder of NYC PO Miosotis Familia as why "it's certainly reasonable to assume any officer would be concerned about an ambush"[165]. The article makes no reference to the race of Noor, Damond, or Alexander Bonds, the Black male who ambushed PO Familia.

As the investigation into the Damond shooting progressed, ABC and CBS mentioned that Noor's personnel records were being scrutinized, but it was an AP article reported by FNC that detailed three critical pieces of information resulting from that scrutiny. First, "a court filing from prosecutors also says that Mohamed Noor pointed a gun at a motorist's head just two months before he fatally shot Justine Damond," second, "two of his training officers had doubts about his ability to be a cop," and third, "psychiatrists said he seemed unable to handle the stress of regular police work"[166]. NBC was the only other network to run the AP story showing the psychiatrist's remarks and officers' criticism, but the part about Noor pointing the gun at the motorist was omitted[167].

Both ABC and CBS used the same AP story of breaking news in September 2017 that PO Noor might be charged in the shooting death of Justine Damond. In that article, references to the police-involved deaths of Jamar Clark, and the " high-profile deaths of blacks in other cities"[168] such as Tamir Rice, Michael Brown, Eric Garner and Philando Castile were included. Though "black" was commonly referenced in the prior police incidents, the race of Noor and Damond was still not usually mentioned in the reporting. While CNN did not report on the possible charges, FNC used part of the AP story. The only previous incident about which the FNC-run story referred to was that of Jamar Clark, while adding the additional element about Noor's accelerated police training program[169].

Five months after Damond's death, coverage turned to criticism of the investigation when a video of the County Attorney admitting to activists that "he didn't have enough evidence to charge Noor because investigators 'haven't done their job'"[170] leaked. In reporting this development, ABC reminded to the readers that Noor still had not cooperated with the investigation. Fox News ran a similar AP story quoting a local activist from the Communities United Against Police Brutality who considered it outrageous that the Damond family had not received justice yet[171]. Unlike the Brown shooting, no allegations of racism were made regarding the investigator's lack of progress, alleged incompetence, or Noor's lack of cooperation.

Though race became an issue again after the grand jury indicted Noor as evidenced by FNC and ABC running an AP story titled "The Latest: Noor jury seated; 6 people of color on panel"[172]. With the trial getting underway, the emphasis on race quickly escalated to racism as apparent in ABC's April 13 story titled "Activists: Cop's shooting of white woman treated differently". After acknowledging that Damond was in fact "a peaceful woman who was trying to help someone else by calling 911," it was noted by activists "that while Damond is seen as an innocent victim, black people shot by police are often made to look like villains"[173]. After BLM activist Shaun King is quoted saying that "it's hard for a jury to identify with an immigrant, Muslim, black man"[174], the article continues with references to the deadly police shootings of Antwon Rose II, Philando Castile, and the off duty shooting of Botham Jean, all Black men. One of ABC's follow-up articles expressed concern that the police officers' code of silence was at play in the Damond shooting. Claiming that cops have been protecting "each other for years," the "1991 police beating in Los Angeles" of Rodney King is referenced before using the more modern example of "a cover up in the 2014 fatal shooting of 17-year-old Laquan McDonald"[175].

Critical evidence reported during the trial announced that investigators found no forensic evidence that Damond smacked the police car[176]; the homicide detective testified that the "alley lighting was bright"[177], and officers had told dispatch that they heard fireworks in the area[178]. After years of silence, the biggest news was PO Noor's testimony. ABC and FNC both ran stories of Noor describing how after "hearing a loud bang on the officer's squad car," "he saw a woman in a pink shirt with blond hair at his partner's window, raising her right arm, and fired his gun to stop the threat"[179]. ABC's story added that Noor "saw his partner go for his gun," and said that he saw "fear in his eyes"[180] before firing his gun.

After the prosecution rested and the trial neared an end, ABC and FNC ran a piece completely favorable toward Noor detailing how he "fled Somalia's civil war as a child"[181] and lived in a refugee camp before his family moved to Minnesota. Noor then spoke of the difficulties he faced in Minnesota since he could tell that Somali's were not well liked, before ending on a positive note about how welcomed he was to the police department. CBS ran a similar positive story about Noor's special welcoming to the police force and how beloved he was in the local Somali community[182].

The jury verdict finding Officer Noor guilty of third-degree murder and second-degree manslaughter was instantly framed more about race than about the unique circumstances of the case. ABC's first story published the day after the April 30 verdict was titled "Conviction for Minneapolis cop prompts questions about race." In the article, noting Damond's whiteness and Noor's blackness, law professor Mark Osler said, "We can't deny that there is implicit racial bias in our society at large"[183]. A similar statement is given by the Minnesota-based Somali American Police Association alleging that Noor was found guilty because of "institutional prejudice"[184]. Local Congresswoman Ilhan Omar referenced recent shootings of black subjects where police were acquitted, as a prelude to stating, "We must have the same level of accountability and justice in all officer-involved killings"[185]. ABC's article then mentions *The Washington Post* data shows American police averaged 900 to 1,000 people shot and killed each year since 2015 before noting the officer who killed "black motorist Philando Castile"[186] was acquitted. Rather than any bias or prejudice, one juror explained how they reached their decision. Stating that "he respects the Somali community and Noor seemed like a good guy," the juror told reporters, "but we determined he committed a crime. And in the end, no one is above the law"[187].

While excluding the juror's comments, FNC's first day of reporting the guilty verdict included the same story authored by Forliti with the slightly different title of "Rare conviction of officer in shooting spurs race concerns." Also referring to the Castile shooting, the FNC article included a statement from Castile's friend that "Officer Noor was going to jail no matter what because he's a black man who shot a white woman"[188]. Another story about the guilty verdict run by both ABC and FNC included allegations that Noor was convicted because of institutional racism. This AP story published by both networks included local Minneapolis Congresswoman Ilhan Omar's tweeted remarks heralding police being held accountable for their actions before "reminding that Noor is Somali" and his conviction "comes after acquittals nationwide for officers who killed people of color"[189]. CBS, too, used an AP story for its first day of reporting the verdict. The CBS story also mentioned the concerns of community leaders that because Damond was White and Noor was Somali, his case was not "treated the same as police shootings involving black victims"[190].

CNN's one and only story about Noor's conviction titled "Mohamed Noor's sentence raises uncomfortable questions about race" expresses similar concerns since "police are seldom if ever indicted, much less convicted, for shooting African American men"[191]. Referring to the Damond shooting, the article then points out "yet, where the victim here is a white woman and the police officer is black, he gets the book thrown at him," calling Noor's sentence of 12.5 years "outrageous and disturbing"[192]. The shootings of Laquan McDonald and Walter Scott are then offered up as "false examples" of cops being held accountable for killing blacks. Using the Castile shooting as an example where the police were not held accountable, the article describes that Philando was shot even though he "specifically told the officer that he had a weapon"[193]. If CNN's Legal Analyst Joey Jackson were interested in educating readers on the truth instead of inflammatory rhetoric, his article would have informed that the reason Castile was shot was because against Officer Yanez's explicit order of not doing so, Castile moved his hand toward the gun about which he had just informed Yanez[194]. Jackson could have then continued to inform that Philando was high at the time of the incident[195], which may explain why, if there is an epidemic of cops murdering black subjects, Castile would give Officer Yanez a legally justified reason to do so.

A week after the verdict came down, the Damond shooting was referenced in a CNN story that new video emerged in the four-year-old death of Sandra Bland in police custody. The opinion piece author, journalist David Love critiqued how the cops who killed Castile and Brown "claimed they feared for their lives–and avoided punishment," "however, a black Minneapolis police officer Mohamed Noor was convicted for murdering a white victim named Justine"[196]. Love goes on to suggest that by claiming that Damond did not appear threatening, the prosecutor meant "white women are not threatening, and that black people are," thereby reinforcing "assumptions about race and criminality that have been an American reality since the days of slavery"[197].

SOCIAL JUSTICE ACTIVISM

Michael Brown. Allegations by neighborhood local Dorian Johnson that Michael Brown was killed by the police as he tried to surrender with his hands up coupled with Brown's lifeless body lying in the street as the crime scene was processed, quickly led to an angry crowd. Within hours that crowd numbered in the hundreds, shots were fired, and by the next day businesses were looted, and cars, including over a dozen police vehicles were destroyed[198]. Protests spread to the national stage in the first week with public displays by students at Howard University[199] and the NFL Washington Redskins players[200] putting their hands up in solidarity with Michael Brown. Among the hundreds of people that showed up for Brown's funeral were civil rights leader Reverend Jesse Jackson and celebrities Sean Combs, MC Hammer, and Spike Lee[201].

After the grand jury's decision to not indict PO Wilson, the protests became more widespread and destructive. In the Ferguson area alone, there were hundreds of arrests, over 100 gunshots, and 25 buildings looted and destroyed, causing damage of approximately $4.6 million[202]. The protests spread past Ferguson and into major cities in New York, California, Texas, Georgia, and Massachusetts[203]. AFL-CIO union workers walked off of jobs while students at universities such as Harvard, Yale, Wheaton, and Stanford staged walkouts or other types of protest[204]. Professional football players from another team, this time the St. Louis Rams entered the playing field with their hands up in the symbolic protest associated with Ferguson[205]. Scores of famous people offered their opinion, epitomized by Chris Rock's tweet quoting W.E.B. DuBois, "A system cannot fail those it was never meant to protect"[206]. In a rare statement to the contrary, Charles Barkley said that the grand jury made the right decision as he then "accused the press of using dubious information to inflame passions"[207].

Barkley's accusation was prognostic as just a few weeks later, angered over the deadly police shooting of Michael Brown, Ismaaiyl Brinsley killed two NYPD officers as they sat in their marked police vehicle. Brinsley's Instagram post shortly before executing POs Ramos and Liu was "I'm putting wings on pigs today. They take 1 of ours, let's take 2 of theirs," with "#Shootthepolice #RIPErivGardner (sic) #RIPMikeBrown"[208]. Even years later, the Michael Brown shooting impassions social justice activism. At the 2016 MTV Video Music Awards, Beyoncé "was accompanied on the red carpet by four Mothers of the Movement"[209]. Lesley McSpadden, mother to Michael Brown was one of those four women. Released shortly before the five-year anniversary of the shooting, Michigan State University associate professor in the School of Criminal Justice, Jennifer E. Cobbina, wrote a book about America's historical and modern racially biased criminal justice system titled *Hands Up, Don't Shoot*[210]. As recently as January 2020, at an event titled "1619: 400 Years of Slavery in America," keynote speaker and John Jay College Constitutional Law Professor Gloria Browne-Marshall lamented how it was "taken for granted that Michael Brown lies in the street of Ferguson, Missouri in the hot sun"[211].

Justine Damond. The first vigil honoring Justine Damond was held the day after her death and consisted of "about 50 friends and neighbors"[212] holding hands with hundreds more looking on at the site near where she had been shot. Tributes to Justine were written in chalk on the street, candles were lit, and flowers were placed "at a makeshift memorial"[213]. Hundreds more people paid tribute to Justine at a beach in her native Sydney, Australia, on July 18 [214]. Two days later activist groups such as March for Healing and Justice, Women's March MN, and "members from the Twin Cities chapter of BLM"[215] joined Damond's family and neighbors in a march through the streets. Philando Castile's mother was also at the march where some people "called for then-Mayor Betsy Hodges to resign"[216]. Calls for Mayor Hodges to resign were heard again the next day as "chaos erupted" at her press conference announcing her nomination of "a new police chief"[217] to replace the chief fired after the outcry over Damond's shooting. Ten days after the unarmed, pajama-clad Damond was shot, protestors put up two street signs with images "of a panicked officer firing off pistols," ridiculing the police for being "easily startled"[218].

Mainstream reporting on Damond's shooting did not show any statements from celebrities or athletes. Former president of the Minneapolis NAACP, Nekima Levy Armstrong was quoted saying, "Race and affluence has played a role in terms of how" Damond's shooting was handled, while BLM activist Shaun King said, "We want black and Latino and native victims of police violence to be treated like"[219] Damond. A memorial of a framed portrait, candles, roses, and signs reading "United We Stand" was put up outside a police station by "the northern California hate group called Identify Evropa"[220]. The police quickly removed the memorial which the city's Mayor-elect Jacob Frey called "disgusting," as he condemned Evropa's "tactics" and said, "Hate has no place in Minneapolis"[221].

POLITICAL STATEMENTS

Michael Brown. The Michael Brown shooting inspired as strong a reaction from politicians as it did from social justice activists. Within a day of the shooting State Senator Jamilah Nasheed, D-St. Louis told the press that she wanted the DOJ to investigate[222]. Nasheed's wish was granted as President Obama offered his condolences to the Brown family the next day before announcing that the DOJ would investigate the shooting[223]. Obama's Attorney General Eric Holder flew to Ferguson where he met with Michael Brown's family, assigned dozens of agents to the case, and penned an op-ed piece pledging a full, fair, and independent investigation[224]. The Obama administration outreach was further reinforced by sending two officials and a third representative to attend Michael Brown's funeral. Also in attendance at the funeral was the Governor of Missouri, along with Senator Claire McCaskill and Congressman William Lacy Clay. Somewhat surprisingly, in his address to the United Nations the next month, President Obama cited the Ferguson shooting as he spoke about America's "racial and ethnic tensions"[225].

The grand jury and Justice Department findings regarding PO Wilson's innocence did not calm the politician's rancor over the Brown shooting. Congressional Black Caucus Chair, Congresswoman Marcia Fudge, said that the grand jury decision exemplified "an unwritten rule that black lives hold no value; that you may kill black men in this country without consequences or repercussions"[226]. Chair of the Senate Judiciary Subcommittee on the Constitution, Civil Rights, and Human Rights, Senator Dick Durbin said that the outcome showed that "racial disparities persist at many stages of the criminal justice system"[227] as he vowed to hold a special hearing on the issue. Following the decision by his DOJ not to prosecute PO Wilson, President Obama said, "We may never know exactly what happened" in the Michael Brown shooting, but what is "very clear"[228] is the Ferguson Police Departments' racial bias. Missouri Congressman Clay made his opinion on the matter clear when he approved displaying a painting of the Ferguson unrest depicting a police officer as a pig "aiming guns at protestors carrying signs saying 'History' and 'Racism Kills' "[229] in the US Capitol.

In contrast to the Democrats, Republicans were neither as quick to judge nor inclined to ignore Brown's culpability in the incident. When asked about the shooting while it was still in the early stages of investigation, New Jersey Governor Chris Christie blamed the media for "making a spectacle out of the situation" and said, "It's too soon to draw conclusions about the situation in Ferguson"[230]. After the grand jury decision was released, former Arkansas Governor and future Republican Presidential candidate Mike Huckabee said that the shooting was a tragedy, "but this is a young man that just roughed up a store owner, just robbed a store, and now he's going after a cop's gun"[231]. Huckabee's fellow former Governor and another Republican Presidential candidate Jeb Bush responded that "the police shooting of unarmed black males … it is very small"[232] when asked about the federal government's role of overseeing police shootings of black males such as happened in Ferguson. During a visit to Ferguson while campaigning for the 2016 Republican Presidential nomination, Ben Carson said, "I think a lot of people understood that he had done bad things, but his body didn't have to be disrespected"[233].

With the 2020 election, several Democrats vying to be the Presidential nominee made unsolicited comments on the Michael Brown shooting. Former San Antonio Mayor and Obama's Housing and Urban Development (HUD) Secretary, Julián Castro said if the police can arrest a mass murderer like Dylan Roof "without hurting him,"[234] then they could have done the same to Michael Brown and several other blacks who were instead killed by the police. Two other candidates competing for the nomination tweeted remarks on the fifth anniversary of the Ferguson shooting, describing it as a murder instead of the justifiable use of deadly force that it was deemed to be. Senator Elizabeth Warren tweeted "5 years ago Michael Brown was murdered by a white police officer in Ferguson,"[235] while Senator Kamala Harris tweeted "Michael Brown's murder forever changed Ferguson and America"[236]. Both Senators promised to fight for racial equity in the criminal justice system.

Justine Damond. Just as happened after the Michael Brown shooting, the nation's most powerful political leader quickly commented on the police shooting death of Justine Damond, only in Damond's case the nation that leader came from was Australia. Four days after Damond was killed, Australian Prime Minister (PM) Malcom Turnbull called the shooting "shocking" and "inexplicable," before asking "How can a woman out in the street in her pajamas seeking assistance from the police be shot like that"[237]. A review of hundreds of stories run by the legacy and cable networks plus a google search reveals neither reported remarks in response to PM Turnbull nor of any kind from the Trump administration. The most senior, active elected official remarking on Damond's shooting was Democratic Representative Ilhan Omar, who used it as a pretext to mention prior police shootings of Blacks. At the city level, Minneapolis Mayor Betsy Hodges commented that she was "sad, disturbed, and looking for more answers, like many of you, including as to why the police body cameras were not on"[238].

A former Republican presidential candidate and Minnesota Congresswoman remarked on both Mayor Hodges and the Damond shooting while giving the guest of honor speech at a Republican forum in Waconia. During her speech, former U.S. Representative Michele Bachmann called Mohamed Noor an "affirmative-action hire by the hijab-wearing mayor of Minneapolis, Betsy Hodges," and then "insinuated that Noor may have shot Damond for 'cultural reasons' "[239]. Bachmann's statements did neither appear to make it into the legacy nor cable networks reporting but were apparent in local and less mainstream stories.

ANALYSIS

The case study comparing the deadly police shootings of Michael Brown/Justine Damond showed that the two were treated dramatically differently. Hypothesis 2 was confirmed as the case studies detailed that besides being greater in volume, media coverage overwhelmingly framed the Brown shooting as being racially biased and used many key words in doing so. Subhypothesis 2a was only partially confirmed because although some networks (CBS and ABC) did, but FNC did not continue framing the Michael Brown shooting as racially biased policing after the DOJ report was released. While FNC did continue using racialized key words and references to other Blacks shot by police, it started framing Brown's shooting as justified after the grand jury decision was made. Although not part of subhypothesis 2a, the social justice activism and even political statements from select Democrats continued to frame Brown's shooting along racial lines even after the DOJ report showed that Brown was the aggressor and PO Wilson simply defended himself.

When PO Wilson shot and killed Michael Brown as the latter charged at him, Brown had already assaulted Wilson and had tried to take his gun. Justifiably fearing for his life, Wilson treated Brown fairly and equally as the social justice contract describes. There was neither reason nor evidence to suggest that PO Wilson would have acted any differently had a 300-pound enraged White man charged at him in the same circumstances. As seen from the lack of focus on it in media reporting, the context of Brown's aggressive and criminal actions to elicit Wilson's response was irrelevant. Also, obviously irrelevant from the amount of criticism it provoked was the context of why Brown's body laid in the street for hours. As the DOJ report noted, within minutes of Brown being killed, a hostile crowd responded and the "crime scene detectives had to stop processing the scene"[240] several times because of gunfire in the area along with threats against the police.

What was not irrelevant to the critics but was instead considered the most important detail of the Michael Brown shooting is that Brown was Black, and PO Wilson was White. Given the priority put on race and ample reporting on the Black community's distrust of police, it is odd that news of the testimony from more than a half-dozen Black witnesses corroborating PO Wilson's story did not generate an avalanche of reporting. References to other unrelated police shootings of blacks were mentioned more in the reporting on the Michael Brown shooting than such relevant, non-biased information. Unfortunately for PO Wilson, only the reporting on other police shootings of black subjects fit the racialized narrative that had taken over the Ferguson incident. Though acknowledged for his six years of unblemished police service before the Brown shooting for which he was found justified, PO Wilson so feared for his safety that he had to quit the force and move his family out of state. Even after the report revealed that the Obama Justice Department found Wilson innocent of any wrongdoing, Wilson continued to be maligned by the press, protestors, and politicians. If anyone was not treated fairly or equally, it was PO Darren Wilson, because his reasonable actions were committed against a Black man.

Ironically, although Noor was a Black officer who shot Damond, a White woman, the only allegations of racism in that deadly police shooting incident were that he would not receive a fair trial or treatment. Reporting on Damond's shooting did not include references to the number of unarmed White women that had been killed by the police in the prior year. Nor, given the importance of racial crime statistics when the officers are White, did any of the stories about PO Noor mention how at just 13% of the population, Blacks murdered more than twice as many Whites in 2016 than Whites murdered Blacks. Neither media coverage nor activism were framed around the possibility that Noor shot an obviously innocent and helpless White woman because he was racist, or worse yet, because of his Muslim religious beliefs. Such a claim was made by former Representative Bachmann, and it was not included in mainstream reporting. Bachmann's remarks did not even result in coverage discussing the historical background of Muslim honor killings of women, whereas allegations of racism in the Brown shooting elicited references to America's history of slavery and lynching.

Somehow instead of being vilified, PO Noor who killed an unarmed woman because she raised her arm by the police car, was portrayed more favorably in the media than PO Wilson who had been physically assaulted by a violent, larger man. The media found it important to speak to members of the Somali community about what a great guy PO Noor was, but in PO Wilson's case, the media did no such investigative work in reporting on the Black witnesses who saw what really happened and were afraid to testify to that truth. To his fortune, PO Noor was treated fairly and equally in the criminal justice system. Regrettably for him, PO Noor did not act reasonably for the context of the situation, and therefore he was found guilty of murder. The possibility that PO Noor was treated differently because he was Black overshadowed the fact that an innocent woman died because of his incompetence.

CASE STUDY (ALTON STERLING VERSUS DANIEL SHAVER)

PRE-INCIDENT CIRCUMSTANCES

Both the Shaver and Sterling shootings were similar in that they started with 911 calls of a man with a weapon. Where they differed was that on January 18, 2016, the 911 caller in the Shaver case was a hotel clerk relaying that two guests saw a man with a rifle through his window five floors above them, whereas with Sterling the 911 caller on July 5, 2016, had actually been threatened by the man with a gun just a few feet away[241]. Both 911 calls resulted in multiple officers responding, six for Shaver and two for Sterling, and doing so with the belief that the subject was armed. There is no similarity in the incidents when comparing the initial contact between the officers and the subjects. Where Shaver was compliant and is seen on the video lying face down and trying to follow the officer's verbal commands, Sterling did not comply with the officer's verbal commands and physically resisted once the two officers tried to gain control over him.

DEADLY POLICE SHOOTING

Alton Sterling. After being unable to physically restrain Sterling, Baton Rouge Police Department Officer Howie Lake tased Sterling, momentarily putting him down to a knee. PO Lake tried tasing Sterling again as the latter stood up but to no avail. So fellow Baton Rouge Police Officer Blane Salamoni tackled Sterling to the ground. Bystander video shows the officer on top of Sterling, with Sterling's right side and arm slightly under a parked car and out of view of the camera. As Officer Salamoni was kneeling on Sterling and struggling to get control of him, he was the only person with a view of Sterling's right hand and right pocket, where the loaded gun was–something which none of the five released videos could capture due to lack of a good angle. On the videos, Officer Salamoni can be heard yelling, "He's got a gun!"[242] and can be seen shooting Sterling three times with his duty gun shortly thereafter, before rolling off of him. Fearful Sterling's continued movements were another attempt to get the gun out of his pocket, Officer Salamoni shot him three more times, killing him[243].

Daniel Shaver. Unlike the Sterling shooting that occurred in an outdoor public area and was over in less than two minutes, the Shaver shooting took place in a hotel hallway that the police controlled for nearly twenty minutes before the fatal shots were fired. Concerned that someone in that fifth-floor room had a rifle, with weapons trained on Shaver's hotel room, the officers ordered the people in the room to exit. First a female came out, followed by Shaver. Both the female and Shaver were ordered by Mesa Police Dept. Sergeant (Sgt.) Charles Langley to lie with his face down in the hallway. After directing the female to push herself up into a kneeling position and crawl toward the officers with her hands in the air, the same instructions were given to Shaver once the female was taken into custody. Shaver uncrossed his legs after pushing himself up into a kneeling position and was yelled at for it. While apologizing and correcting that mistake, Shaver put his hands behind his back. The officers warned Shaver that if he put his hands behind his back again, he would be shot, prompting Shaver to cry, and plead with them not to shoot him. On his hands and knees, Shaver, still crying, crawled towards the officers, and, after a few feet, lifted his right elbow up, bringing his right hand to his right side. At about the same time as Shaver's right hand came back down in front of him and into view of the officer's bodycam, PO Brailsford shot him five times with his AR-15 rifle, killing him[244].

OFFICER CULPABILITY

Officer Salamoni was never charged as the DOJ reported on May 3, 2017, and Louisiana Attorney General Jeff Landry reported on March 27, 2018[245], that both found insufficient evidence to prosecute him for the shooting of Alton Sterling. Officer Brailsford was acquitted on December 7, 2017, in his trial for second-degree murder and reckless manslaughter, and he is being investigated by the DOJ for possible civil-rights violation. However, both officers were fired, Salamoni for his profanity, violating the departments use of force policy[246] and Brailsford for violating departmental policy by etching "You're Fucked"[247] into his AR-15.

MEDIA COVERAGE

Quantitatively, a Nexis Uni media search from the day of incident through December 31, 2019 shows the Associated Press, State and Local Wires ran 39 stories about the Shaver shooting incident and 321 about that of Sterling. Qualitatively the differences between the media coverage of the two shootings was just as dramatic.

Daniel Shaver. An AP piece was the first story broadcast by ABC on Shaver's death, five days later. From ABC's story, it is clear that Shaver was unarmed, a run-in with the police was not typical for him, the police feared that Shaver's hand was going for a gun in his waistband, and an officer's bodycam captured the incident. Despite the shock and irregularity of hearing her law-abiding, "people-pleasing" husband was just killed by the police, and rather than rushing to judgment against the officer, Shaver's wife said, "Until we know the facts, we won't know what happened"[248]. The article about Shaver ended with a reference to the shooting of an unarmed fugitive that happened the previous month in Las Vegas "after officers mistook the cellphone he was carrying for a weapon"[249]. A simple google search reveals that fugitive was Keith Childress, a man that author Shaun King stresses in the *Daily News* article, was killed by police because he was Black[250]. Childress, who was reported to be wanted for armed robbery, had just fled from a car with a gun in it while being chased by the US Marshalls, and as seen on the bodycam video, ignored over twenty commands from the officers to halt as he walked toward them with what they feared was his hand on a gun in his pocket[251]. The Clark County District Attorney's Office investigation cleared the police officers involved of any wrongdoing[252].

CBS ran its first story on the Shaver incident seven weeks later, using a 522-word, sterile AP piece on Officer Brailsford being charged with second-degree murder for the shooting. Along with informing how Shaver was unarmed, the article states that the officer shot Shaver because he "allegedly made a motion with his right hand toward his waistline"[253]. The majority of press on the Shaver shooting came when Brailsford was found not guilty of any criminality in the incident. CBS included the graphic video in its story titled, "Mesa Police shooting: Daniel Shaver seen crawling, begging in disturbing video". The article has quotes from Brailsford's lawyer, no statements from Shaver's family members, and a quote from Brailsford's trial testimony that he "he felt 'incredibly sad' for Shaver"[254].

A much more critical piece was written by CNN's law enforcement (LE) analyst James Gagliano; it was titled "Daniel Shaver's shooting by police officer was an avoidable execution". In this opinion essay, the expert analyst describes the shooting as a "slaughter" and the bodycam video of it as "horrifying"[255]. While Gagliano concedes that the jury may have gotten the acquittal correct on technicalities, he is convinced that a "confluence of interrelated errors by the tactical team transpired to cause this tragedy, and it was entirely preventable"[256]. Citing the "officer's unprofessional conduct, seeming inexperience, and the confusing commands,"[257] Gagliano believed that Shaver would still be alive had the tactical team followed protocol and kept Shaver covered with a weapon as an officer handcuffed him while he was face down on the floor. The online article included links to two articles about the police shooting of a Black male with each link accompanied by a photo of North Charlotte Police Officer Michael Slager and Walter Scott. The titles of those two related articles were "Ex-South Carolina cop Michael Slager gets 20 years for Walter Scott killing" and "Why partial justice for Walter Scott isn't nearly enough." Ironic to have such related articles, considering the 20-year sentence Walter Scott's guilty killer got was considerably more justice than the officer who "slaughtered" Daniel Shaver received.

CNN was not alone in using the Shaver shooting as a pretext for reporting on the Walter Scott shooting. *The New York Times* story about Officer Brailsford's acquittal also informed readers how on that same day the PO found guilty of killing Scott had just been sentenced. The story goes on to note that "the South Carolina case was one of a number of fatal police shootings, often of black men, that have set off outrage in recent years. In Arizona, both the officer and the man who was killed were white"[258]. Just as in the Shaver shooting, there is no evidence that race had any relevance in the shooting of Scott, yet this article that is supposed to be about Daniel Shaver diverts to the fatal police shooting of a black man.

Fox News put out four stories on the Shaver shooting after Brailsford was acquitted, with the first one announcing the verdict. In it, the detective investigating the shooting acknowledged that Shaver's movement could have looked like he was going for a gun, just as it "also looked as though Shaver was pulling up his loose-fitting basketball shorts that had fallen down as he was ordered to crawl toward officers"[259]. Similar to CNN's LE analyst, the detective said that "he did not see anything that would have prevented officers from simply handcuffing Shaver as he was on the floor"[260]. The next article FNC published was from a TMZ report which rehashed some of the same facts from the shooting while appearing to ridicule Officer Brailsford for being a "failed actor"[261] before becoming a cop. FNC's two other articles were about Shaver's wife, Laney Sweet, expressing how she felt betrayed by the verdict and called her husband's shooting an execution. Laney placed the blame for Daniel Shaver's killing on the training provided by the Mesa Police Department, for which along with Shaver's parents, she filed a wrongful death suit against the city[262].

Alton Sterling. Compared to the Shaver shooting, news of Sterling's shooting came out quicker; numbered in the hundreds and was full of extraneous statements framing the shooting along racial lines. National Public Radio (NPR) which boasts a monthly audience of 120 million informed the public about the Sterling incident in an article two days later in which it was put side by side with the police shooting of another black male, Philando Castile. The article included the following statements by family, friends and various journalists: "a lot of our African-American men, women and children are being executed by the police. And there are no consequences"; "extrajudicial killing of black people by the police"; "watching time and time again as black people are killed on camera by police"; "We have to bear witness and resist numbness and help the children of the black people who lose their lives to police brutality"; "Alton Sterling is one of 122 black Americans shot and killed by police so far in 2016"; "Again, a black man has been shot to death by a white police officer"; and "video footage of police violence against black people … that are foreign to many white people but all too familiar to people of color"[263]. Nowhere in the article is it explained how Alton's color has any bearing on why the officers used deadly force on him and whether they were justified in doing so. The article does not even mention that according to the same *The Washington Post* database it referenced, 254 white Americans (one of which was the unarmed Daniel Shaver) had been shot and killed by police so far in 2016.

The AP story that was published three days after the Sterling shooting was similar to that of NPR. Along with statements about the "drumbeat of minority death at the hand of law enforcement in the United States," the story framed Sterling's shooting in the historical context of oppression of blacks by police, and it did so by linking despair of minorities with police shootings and "the long history of violence in America"[264]. This historical connection was solidified by including NFL Quarterback Colin Kaepernick's social media post about the Sterling shooting being "what lynchings look like in 2016!"[265]. The only information given about Sterling is "one black man is shot dead by police while selling CDs outside of a convenience store in Louisiana"[266]. There is no discussion about the fact that Sterling had a loaded gun in his right pocket, he refused to comply with officer's orders, physically resisted them, and was shot as his hand was reaching into his right pocket. Instead, the article is full of interviews with various Black people representing all types of Americana voicing their fear and distrust of racially biased policing. While those Black people may have valid reasons for their personal fear or distrust, their statements are completely unrelated and in fact contrary to the evidence of the Sterling shooting on which they commented.

Like the Shaver case, news coverage increased around that of Sterling when judgment was passed on the officer involved. CNN ran five separate stories within two days of the DOJ's announcement that it was not going to charge Officer Salamoni for the shooting death of Alton Sterling, and 22 stories shortly after the Louisiana AG's similar announcement. True to its title, "Why the feds did not file charges in Alton Sterling's death,"[267] Emanuella Grinberg's article walked readers through the legal process used by the DOJ to conclude that Officer Salamoni reasonably feared for his life from Sterling's actions. Statutes of the law and a link to the video of the shooting were included so the readers could comprehend why the officer justifiably used deadly force. Among the many CNN stories covering the Louisiana's AG's decision, Hanna detailed the escalating use of force used by the officers; the fact that Sterling was armed and had displayed the weapon, prompting the 911 call; and even how Sterling's large size and altered mental state from the drugs in his system all played a role in the shooting being justified. But the story also included extraneous comments from Sterling's aunt that "They're not going to bring charges on anybody. Why would they do that? This is white America,"[268]. The Sterling family attorney too invoked racism, calling it "a biased decision"[269] and urged people to get rid of the AG in the next election.

For its part, Fox News published four related stories in the week when Louisiana's AG announced that no charges would be filed against PO Salamoni in the Sterling shooting. The first was an AP story briefly describing the shooting and how the officers would not be charged[270]. While the short story mentioned three times that Sterling was black, there was no mention of him being armed during the incident. The next story is a more detailed one from AP, which hits upon all the relevant facts making the Sterling shooting justified. Both sides of racial tensions are addressed in mentioning the retaliatory killing of three police officers in Baton Rouge and the Sterling family lawsuit claiming that "the shooting fit a pattern of racist behavior and excessive force by the Baton Rouge police"[271]. FNC's third story was prompted by the firing of Officer Salamoni. As the firing is the only new information, most notable about the article is the hyperlink to a story of another black man killed by police titled "STEPHON CLARK'S INDEPENDENT AUTOPSY RESULTS REVEAL HE WAS SHOT SEVEN TIMES, OFFICIALS SAY"[272] in the middle of it. FNC's final story was about the National Association for the Advancement of Colored People (NAACP)-led protest outside the AG's office, calling for a special prosecutor to review the Sterling shooting[273].

SOCIAL JUSTICE ACTIVISM

Alton Sterling. The 35-person NAACP-led sit-in was one of the first examples of peaceful protest, soon to follow were the Minnesota Lynx Women's NBA team who had Alton Sterling's name adorned on the back of their "black warmup shirts that said on the front, 'Change starts with us. Justice & Accountability'"[274]. On the men's side, NBA Star Chris Paul mentioned Alton Sterling in the opening of the 2016 ESPY's[275]. Months later, a youth football team in Texas inspired by Sterling's death, started protesting the national anthem at their games as Kaepernick had been doing in the NFL[276]. Eric Reid, the San Francisco 49'ers safety also found inspiration from Sterling's death and joined Kaepernick in protesting the issues of "police brutality, [and the] systemic oppression of black and brown people"[277].

From the entertainment world, Beyoncé displayed Sterling's name on the screen during a "moment of silence to remember the victims of police brutality"[278] at her concert in Scotland shortly after his death. Around the same time, back in the Los Angeles, rappers "Snoop Dogg and The Game, led a peaceful march"[279] to police headquarters. A week later, a scholarship fund started by Actress Issa Rae "raised more than $700,000 … for Sterling's children"[280]. Rae's fellow Hollywood stars were quick to blame racism for Sterling's shooting death by a cop. Actor Jesse Williams called it "white mass murders"; Actresses Rashida Jones said "I can't wake up to another innocent black man gone. Police reform NOW"; and Olivia Wilde tweeted "He had a right to sell CDs, and a right to due process, but he was shot for being a black man"[281].

Sadly, these symbolic protests by athletes and actors were small and meek compared to other acts of social justice activism carried out in reaction to the Alton Sterling shooting. Within days after Sterling was killed, "protestors marched in the streets and blocked intersections in Los Angeles, St. Paul, Atlanta and New York City"[282]. Bystander video of the Sterling shooting inspired protestors as far away as Europe and Africa. In Ireland, London, Amsterdam, Berlin, and South Africa, demonstrators marched in solidarity with the calls for racial justice taking place in America[283]. In America "intense and sometimes violent clashes erupted in several major cities,"[284] with nearly 50 protestors being arrested at ground zero in Baton Rouge. During one of the protests in Baton Rouge, where members of the New Black Panther Party were seen demonstrating, an officer had a tooth knocked out by a violent protestor[285]. It was at a protest in Dallas where the violence reached its peak as one protestor, Micah Xavier Johnson, was so enraged by the deadly police shootings of black men like Sterling just three days earlier that he opened fire on police, killing five of them[286].

Daniel Shaver. A search of the legacy and cable news network's yields zero coverage of such protests or violence inspired over the deadly police shooting of Daniel Shaver, the fact it took nearly two years to release the bodycam video, or the acquittal of Officer Brailsford. There was a distinct absence of such coverage because aside from about a dozen peaceful protestors calling for "Justice" in downtown Mesa after Brailsford was found not guilty[287], there was a distinct lack of activism of any kind resulting from the Shaver shooting. As one story succinctly pointed out, before the footage was released "the [Shaver] shooting, unlike other high-profile police shootings captured on video, didn't prompt local protest like in other cities"[288].

Things changed after the footage was released, as another article on Shaver's shooting stated that the "reactions to the Arizona video were swift and furious"[289]. Entertainer Nancy Sinatra tweeted, "I don't think I have ever been this angry. What happened to justice?"[290]. NFL player

Dominique Hamilton tweeted, "Out of all the videos of a cop murdering an unarmed person, in the history! of cops murdering an unarmed person, this absolutely has to be #1 or number two. This idiot walked free"[291]. Where thousands took to the streets for Sterling in nationwide BLM protests, BLM activists and others upset with the video showing what looked like an execution sent out some angry tweets in Shaver's case[292]. The biggest groundswell of activism was the 35,000 likes a Facebook page titled "Justice for Daniel Shaver" received. Such Likes and Tweets are all Shaver's death warranted when it came to the athletes, actors, and other people of fame that were so vocal about the Sterling shooting. The profound lack of public outrage to Shaver's killing compared to what has been commonly seen after shootings of black subjects brought a small media outlet to ask, "Why are the people who constantly campaign against 'police abuse' suddenly silent?"[293]. Part of the answer to that question in the cases of Sterling and Shaver can be found in what politicians did or did not say about a particular shooting.

POLITICAL STATEMENTS

Alton Sterling. When it came to the deadly police shooting of Alton Sterling, America's top politician, President Obama had a lot to say. Two days after the Sterling shooting, the President posted on Facebook, "All Americans should be deeply troubled by the fatal shootings of Alton Sterling in Baton Rouge, Louisiana and Philando Castile in Falcon Heights, Minnesota"[294]. In his posting, Obama then wrote "these fatal shootings are not isolated incidents … they are symptomatic of the broader challenges within our criminal justice system, the racial disparities that appear across the system year after year"[295]. Later that day, President Obama again mentioned Sterling's shooting while addressing the North Atlantic Treaty Organization (NATO) summit in Warsaw, Poland, saying "We have seen too many tragedies like this." Obama then said, "These are not isolated incidents," before citing statistical data from *The Washington Post* that "last year, African-Americans were shot by police at more than twice the rate of whites"[296]. In the press conference afterward, in response to a question, Obama said that all Americans were angered about Sterling's death and "about the larger, persistent problem of African Americans and Latinos being treated differently in our criminal justice system"[297].

Days later, while heading to Dallas for the funerals of five officers killed in retaliation for the deadly police shootings of black men, Obama called Sterling's family "to offer his and the first lady's condolences on behalf of the American people"[298]. Additional condolences were offered from the White House as "two of President Barack Obama's senior advisers, Roy Austin and Stephanie Young"[299] attended Sterling's funeral. The President also personally addressed Sterling's 15-year-old son Cameron at a Presidential town hall on race relations, telling Cameron, "The history of this country and the legacy of race and all the complications involved in that"[300] will take some time to work through. A month later Obama met with Sterling's family for a lengthy discussion with them and the families of cops killed in a recent ambush attack[301].

The top two candidates for the 2016 Democratic nomination for President also remarked on Sterling's death. Former Secretary of State Hillary Clinton quickly put out a statement after Sterling's shooting, that, "From Staten Island to Baltimore, Ferguson to Baton Rouge, too many African-American families mourn the loss of a loved one from a police-involved incident"[302]. In a later interview, Clinton called Sterling's shooting "tragic" and said, "We need to listen to

African-Americans who say they feel on edge all the time"[303]. Fellow competitor for the Presidential nomination, Vermont Senator Bernie Sanders tweeted, "The violence that killed Alton Sterling ... has become an all too common occurrence for people of color and IT. MUST. STOP," and "Enough is enough of our police officers targeting people of color"[304].

Congressional Democrats also sounded off on Sterling's death. One day after Sterling was shot, Louisiana Rep. Cedric Richmond said, "There are a number of unanswered questions surrounding Mr. Sterling's death, "including ... the level of force used by officers, the verbal and physical altercation, and the response of the officers after he was shot"[305]. Talking to CNN, Minnesota Rep. Keith Ellison said Sterling's shooting was not an "isolated" incident before naming "Eric Garner, Mike Brown, Tamir Rice, Sandra Bland" as he claimed, "There is a systematic targeting of African-Americans"[306]. Louisiana Governor John Bel Edwards quickly expressed his concern over Sterling's shooting and the video as he announced that the federal government was taking over the investigation[307]. A few weeks later, Democratic State Party Chairwoman Karen Carter Peterson called out "the fatal shooting of Alton Sterling during a struggle with two Baton Rouge Police officers"[308] while reading the roll call in Philadelphia at the 2016 DNC. Over a year later, when Louisiana AG Jeff Landry announced, like the DOJ, that his office would not be charging the officers involved in the Sterling shooting, Democratic State Representative C. Denise Marcelle said, "Landry's decision means the family will not get any justice"[309].

Statements on Sterling's shooting from the other side of the political aisle were less numerous and more tempered. In a statement put out after the ambush attack on the Dallas police, Republican Presidential candidate Donald Trump called Sterling's shooting a "senseless, tragic death" that "reminds us how much more needs to be done"[310]. A few weeks later, for their calls of peace during the protests over his death, Alton Sterling's family was recognized at the 2016 Republican National Convention by former candidate for the Republican Presidential nomination, Senator Ted Cruz[311].

Daniel Shaver. Even though PO Brailsford was "one of the few police officers in the U.S. to be charged with murder for shooting someone while on duty"[312], Daniel Shaver's family received no condolences or pledges of justice from the Obama administration. Former Republican and Democratic presidential candidates were equally mute on Shavers shooting, and his family was not mentioned at either of the party's national conventions.

ANALYSIS

The case study comparing the Alton Sterling/Daniel Shaver deadly police shootings showed that the disparities revealed in the first case study were not an anomaly. Here, once again, the subjects were treated differently because of their race, with the White victim Shaver receiving less coverage, less social justice activism, and less statements from political leaders. Hypothesis 2 was again confirmed as the case study detailed that besides the media coverage being greater in volume, it also strongly framed the Sterling shooting along racial lines with numerous key words. On the other hand, the Shaver shooting was portrayed as justified but troubling due to problematic police procedures. It bears mentioning that even though both the officer and victim in the Shaver shooting were White, coverage of the incident included ample references to previous police shootings of Black subjects.

Between the Sterling/Shaver deadly police shootings, Shaver was the only of the two men who was in fact unarmed, compliant with police, and innocent of committing any crimes during the incident. Multiple LE experts agreed that the police tactics in the killing of Shaver were wrong. The video showed that Shaver was frightened, and he was trying to follow the officer's instructions during an incredibly stressful situation. According to the context of this incident, Shaver was neither treated fairly by the police nor by the criminal justice system. As a White victim though, Shaver's preventable death by questionable police tactics did not even register on the scale of modern social justice activism. The paucity of media coverage or political outrage related to Shaver's "execution" showed in the realm of deadly police shootings that White lives do not matter.

Paucity is not a word that could properly be used to describe the outrage, coverage, and rhetoric exhibited in reaction to Alton Sterling's fatal incident with the police. Video of Alton Sterling's last minutes showed that he had a loaded gun in his pocket and while resisting the officer's attempts to control him, Alton intentionally moved his hand toward that pocket. Had PO Salamoni not shot Sterling, it is reasonable to believe there would have been two more officers killed in the line of duty that fateful night. In the context of a very real life-or-death situation, Sterling was treated quite fairly. Yet context had no relevance when compared to the importance modern social justice activism placed upon Sterling's Black race as being the paramount detail of his shooting. Because Sterling was Black, Officers Lake and Salamoni were not given the same fair and equal treatment for which the media coverage depicted them as denying Alton Sterling.

RESEARCH STUDY CONCLUSIONS

THE QUANTITATIVE AND QUALITATIVE METHODS USED IN THIS STUDY CONCLUSIVELY SHOWED THAT THE media are guilty of racial bias in deadly police shootings. Mainstream media demonstrated hyper attentiveness to select police shootings of Black subjects and a corresponding lack of attention when those shootings involved other races. During the investigation in the controversial deadly police shootings that became national stories, the press either minimized or ignored evidence produced that showed that the officers were justified. Media reporting was also rife with unfounded race-based generalizations about the police officers' actions when those shot were Black. Along with framing the fatal incidents as racially biased when the subjects were Black, the media also used the shootings of White subjects to advance that same narrative. Unlike the prior research, this study finds that the media portrayal of deadly police shootings would more likely prejudice the public to blame the police instead of the criminals involved.

Contrary to allegations that the police shoot Black people out of racial bias or animus, the case studies showed that police use deadly force on both whites and blacks, and for a variety of reasons. Police shoot subjects to defend themselves from violent assaults; to prevent criminals from accessing a deadly weapon; out of fear that a person is trying to access a deadly weapon; and on rare occasions, because of the officer's incompetence or unsuitability for the police profession. Yes, the police make mistakes, and they make them when dealing with subjects of all races, not just when they are Black. Some of those mistakes could have been prevented by more rigorous hiring standards. On the unusual occasions, where the officers violated procedures and broke the law, they were punished accordingly. Besides PO Noor, the police officers who killed unarmed and fleeing Walter Scott[313] and Jordan Edwards[314] in separate incidents, were both convicted of murder and sentenced to fifteen years or more in prison. Like the Damond shooting, those incidents were heat of the moment, adrenaline induced situations where the officers made split-second decisions that were wrong and illegal.

MEDIA BIAS

Though there was no proof of racial animus in those fateful decisions, the media sensationalized them to at least appear as if there was. This proclivity to racialize events without any evidence was demonstrated in the coverage of the deadly police shootings of Brown and Sterling. The difference between the officer's split-second decisions and the press stories put out about them is that the press was not operating under any such stress-induced, immediate life-or-death situation. The press instead made conscious decisions, even in the presence of facts indicating otherwise, to paint deadly police shootings of Blacks as racial.

It was acknowledged in the research how influential social media was in social justice activism in the post-Ferguson atmosphere. The power of social media was further validated in the case studies discussing BLM's rise and continued efforts since then for police accountability. But social media does not equate to professional media. Any and every person with an opinion can use social media to voice their opinion, express outrage, and make whatever statements they want, regardless of whether they are true or biased. Professional journalists, broadcasters, and editors representing the "fourth estate" can either give a platform to those social media activists and legitimize them or expose the outright lies which some of them so emotionally advocate. Just as former Representative Bachmann's vile comments were blacklisted from the media, the same could be done to many of the baseless remarks made by activists and politicians associating the police shooting with racism. This is especially true for celebrities whose popularity overshadows how uninformed they may be on the actual facts. If mainstream media outlets want to differentiate themselves from such "fake news," they must start reporting on police shootings in an unbiased way that is distinguishable from that of known race grievance provocateurs like activist turned MSNBC analyst Al Sharpton.

By sensationalizing deadly police shootings of Black subjects compared to those of Whites or any other race, and by perpetually insinuating the race is somehow a factor in those shootings, the professional media contributes to the social justice activism seen thereafter. This study reveals that when it comes to deadly police shootings in America, the media is guilty of the very racial bias it purports to be reporting on. The coverage of deadly police shootings was shown to be almost exclusively of Black subjects in *USA Today* while legacy and cable networks had six times more stories about Black subjects than corresponding White ones. Moreover, the media used tangential issues in the economy, arts, finance, and sports to keep the national conversation focused on racial policing. Perhaps the question the media should be asking in that conversation is: If there really is such an epidemic of racially targeted killings of innocent Black people by the police, why are there not better examples to use than the likes of Brown and Sterling who as Dukes caveated– "really are to blame"[315]?

A more diligent effort on investigative reporting of the deadly police shootings as well as covering the ones involving races other than just Black subjects could lessen the physical conflicts with police and enhance cooperation in communities of color. Such cooperation would enhance safety and reduce crime in the communities' officers are sworn to protect but have been wrongly portrayed as racists while doing so. If anything, the shootings analyzed in the case studies revealed how the media helped fuel the fire of racism. As seen in the research, when the subjects of police shootings were Black, the mitigating factors involved were glanced over in the reporting and race was instead made the dominating feature.

With such biased reporting, it is no wonder that Black people continue to mistrust the police even in this modern era of professional, standardized policing that emphasizes community outreach. A mistrust which was documented with numerous anti-police protests during four years of coverage by *USA Today's* front pages as well as by both of the case studies. This mistrust was also apparent in the DOJ report on the Brown shooting, where a hostile crowd quickly gathered at the crime scene. Another aspect of Black culture present in both the *USA Today* front-page stories on inner-city crime and the DOJ's Ferguson investigation was the "snitches get stitches" attitude regarding cooperation with the police.

Several black witnesses who saw what happened during the Brown shooting told the police that they were either afraid or unwilling to testify. A bi-racial witness who told two black women among the angry crowd that he saw what happened and the Officer was justified, was called "racial slurs," including "white motherfucker"[316]. Somehow impartial witnesses like him never became the centerpiece of the reporting on the Brown case, not even after they were revealed in the St. Louis grand jury evidence and the DOJ report. Out of the legacy and cable networks examined in this study, FNC came the closest to presenting both sides of the story in the Ferguson shooting. Some researchers blamed Fox News for "victim blaming" for simply reporting the truth about Brown's actions. As the facts showed, FNC's contributors were correct- "Hand's Up, Don't Shoot" was a lie, one of the biggest of the year according to *The Washington Post* fact-checking[317]. It was more convenient and better fit the racial narrative for most of the media to instead use those witnesses/activists who lied about what happened and made Brown appear innocent. Furthermore, as the case studies demonstrated, the media and social justice activists created their own echo chamber over the Brown and Sterling deadly police shootings, taking incidents that had nothing to do with racial bias and spinning them to fit into a national conversation on racially biased policing.

RESTORATIVE JUSTICE ACTIVISTS

Those social justice activists who target racially biased policing would be more aptly termed as restorative justice activists. When the perpetrators were Black, these so-called activists ignored, or excused outright violence and criminality committed against society and society's protectors. In the name of those Black "victims," these activists referenced slavery, lynchings, and White supremacy. Worse yet, in the name of those "victims," businesses were looted and burned. Reporting on Brown's stepfather, Louis Head, who, in the aftermath of the grand jury decision, vehemently called for the angry mob to "Burn this bitch down," which they did, informed readers, "Don't condemn them for being human"[318] instead of why Head and the rest of them should be charged criminally. Many of those businesses that were burned down were owned by minorities. During other protests, police officers were ambushed and killed. Several of those officers were minorities themselves. As Head was not charged criminally, an area for future research is how much destruction and violence does it take to qualify "justified demonstrators" as being properly called "troublemakers" or "criminals"?

Civil society and police officers were the true victims of deadly police shootings turned into excuses for mob violence in the name of racial justice. For the sins of the two-tiered system of justice decades ago, when blacks were held to a higher standard in society, modern activists are punishing those in uniform who have no connection to slavery and likely grew up during the civil rights era of equality. But it is not equality that these restorative justice activists seek. They want a two-tiered system of justice in which blacks are held to a lower standard. To them, anything less justifies boycotts, protests, and even riots.

DEMOCRAT'S RACIAL PANDERING

Besides the link between blacks and protests, the research also proved to be correct about the different attitudes that America's two main political parties have toward deadly police shootings. When the subjects shot by the police were White, party leadership on both sides were relatively silent. When Republicans commented on deadly police shootings involving Black subjects, it was typically, and as it turned out correctly, how we should see what the investigation uncovers before immediately casting judgment. Although painted as pro-White supremacist by some in the research, Republican leadership demonstrated compassion to Brown's and Sterling's families, yet they legitimately pointed out how Brown was wrong in attacking PO Wilson.

Regretfully, Democrats pandered to the Black community about non-existent racial bias instead of the imminent deadly threats that both Brown and Sterling actually were, as the evidence showed. Rather than promoting temperance, Democrats added to the community's frustration by feeding them false outrage and giving them false hope for justice, when justice had already been served the moment police justifiably used lethal force in self-defense. Together, the Democrats, activists, and an all-too-complicit media pushed a narrative of those two men, and many others like them, as helpless victims killed by a racist police force. Nowhere was that more evident than from the Obama White House. In spite of evidence showing that both Michael Brown and Alton Sterling posed deadly threats to the police involved, President Obama paid tribute to their lives as if they were righteous soldiers killed in combat. The most powerful man in America made sure that everyone knew he believed that the lives of Michael Brown and Alton Sterling mattered. Neither Daniel Shaver nor his family received any such acknowledgment from Obama about Daniel's life. Damond's family did not receive it either from a Republican-led White House administration. Considering the lack of political response when the subjects of deadly police shootings are White, an area for future research is: Why White lives seem to not matter as much?

THE COWARDS

In 2021, over a decade later and after eight years of an Obama administration that was hoped would help America heal its racial divide, AG Holder's quote that we are "a nation of cowards" in discussing racial issues continues to hold true. While the quote does not apply to the entire nation, it surely does apply to the mainstream media. Their minimization of facts, repeated allegations of racial bias, and singular focus on only the deadly police shootings involving black subjects is no better than the racial propaganda used by ISIS or Russia. Despite many accusations of racial bias against the police in the national conversation, the bias evident in this study is by the media. There remains no proof of any racial bias by the police that warrants legislative changes to the criminal justice system. The press, protestors, and liberal politicians repeatedly claim that America is stuck in the 1960's south or worse yet 1800's slave trade, but it is they who are not applying equality and fairness to all races and people within America. These institutions and individuals purporting to care about equal rights in America are too cowardly to hold black people to the same standard against which other minorities and white people are held when interacting with the police. As the good citizens of Ferguson who testified to the truth of the Brown shooting demonstrated, justice is colorblind. Too bad that the media, social justice activists, and Democrats referenced in this study are not.

PART 2.

JUSTIFIED DEADLY FORCE OF UNARMED SUBJECTS, 2019 TO 2020

ONE OF THE DEFINING HALLMARKS OF A CIVILIZED FIRST WORLD SOCIETY IS THE GOVERNMENT'S MONOPOLY on the use of justifiable deadly force against violent and dangerous citizens. This is an awesome power given to agents of the government to maintain order while protecting innocent lives. Two elements are crucial for the government to maintain legitimacy while exercising this power. First, deadly force must be used only as a last resort and with extreme restraint. Second, the citizens must believe that the government is not using deadly force arbitrarily or callously. In the 18,000 law enforcement agencies across the United States, the approximately 800,000 officers who had sworn to support and defend the Constitution of the United States are authorized to use justifiable deadly force while carrying out their duties to the public. Since the Fourth Amendment of the US Constitution enshrines, "The right of the people to be secure in their persons, houses, papers, and effects against unreasonable searches and seizures shall not be violated," there must be a significant reason for any agents of the State to permanently "seize" someone's life by exercising that authority.

Consistent with Federalism and States rights, law enforcement agencies across America are not subject to a national use of deadly force policy, but the federal government will step in and investigate when concerns arise that a citizen's civil rights were violated in a deadly force incident. The agency conducting these investigations as well as allegations of excessive or unreasonable force is the FBI. Such violations are rare as for most agencies, the policies regarding the use of deadly force are formed around adherence to two US Supreme Court decisions providing the standards on what conditions must exist for deadly force to be justified.

In the 1985 *Tennessee v. Garner* landmark case ruling on the "constitutionality of the use of deadly force to prevent the escape of an apparently unarmed suspected felon," the Supreme Court concluded that "such force may not be used unless it is necessary to prevent the escape and the officer has probable cause to believe that the suspect poses a significant threat of death or serious physical injury to the officer or others"[319]. While the Garner ruling dealt only with dangerous fleeing felons, four years later in the *Graham v. Connor* case of 1989, the Supreme Court institutionalized the objectively reasonable standard upon which deadly force incidents must be judged in general. As Chief Justice William Rehnquist stated in the decision, *"The reasonableness of a particular use of force must be judged from the perspective of a reasonable officer on the scene, rather than with the 20/20 vision of hindsight. The calculus of reasonableness must embody allowance for the fact that police officers are often forced to make split-second judgments—in circumstances that are tense, uncertain, and rapidly evolving—about the amount of force that is necessary in a particular situation. The test of reasonableness is not capable of precise definition or mechanical application"*[320].

Using these two landmark cases, eleven of the most significant law enforcement leadership and labor organizations in the United States developed the National Consensus Policy on Use of Force. This policy states: "An officer is authorized to use deadly force when it is objectively reasonable under the totality of the circumstances. Use of deadly force is justified when one or both of the following apply: a. to protect the officer or others from what is reasonably believed to be an immediate threat of death or serious bodily injury; or b. to prevent the escape of a fleeing subject when the officer has probable cause to believe that the person has committed, or intends to commit a felony involving serious bodily injury or death, and the officer reasonably believes that there is an imminent risk of serious bodily injury or death to the officer or another if the subject is not immediately apprehended"[321]. Police departments in cities on the east coast like NYC, on the West Coast such as LA, and across the nation including Chicago, Atlanta, Dallas, and Minneapolis mirror this guidance. As its manual shows, even the federal agency that investigates local police officers use of deadly force provides similar guidance to its officers: "FBI special agents may use deadly force only when necessary—when the agent has a reasonable belief that the subject of such force poses an imminent danger of death or serious physical injury to the agent or another person"[322].

Understanding that situations are indeed evolving, and reasonableness is not capable of precise definition, some agencies detail extenuating factors which could play into an officer's decision to justifiably use deadly force. Chicago PD, for instance, includes the factors of the "level of threat or resistance presented by the subject; and the subject's proximity or access to weapons"[323]. NYPD and LAPD also consider "the seriousness of the crime or suspected offense; the training and experience of the officer; officer versus subject factors such as age, size, relative strength, skill level, injury/exhaustion, and number of officers versus subjects; subject's violent history, if known; presence of hostile crowd or agitators; subject apparently under the influence of a stimulant/narcotic which would affect pain tolerance or increase the likelihood of violence; and other exigent circumstances"[324],[325].

Since 95% of the subjects killed in deadly force incidents are armed with either a handgun, knife, or other dangerous instrument, the benefit of the doubt for it being "reasonably necessary" to use such force in those cases must go to the police unless there is clear and convincing evidence showing otherwise. It would suffice to say that if someone presents a firearm at or motions toward an officer in a threatening manner with a weapon of any kind in their hand–they should expect to have deadly force used against them. With that in mind, it is those remaining 5% of cases where subjects are unarmed, and deadly force is used which elicits the greatest outrage among the public and which will be scrutinized here.

As the data in Part 1 showed overwhelmingly, the systemic racism exhibited in justifiable deadly police shootings from 2015 to 2018 was by the press, protestors, and politicians. Despite that same data being available to each of those entities, they again sounded the alarm of systemic racism in the Breonna Taylor and George Floyd incidents. What happened in 2014 after the Michael Brown shooting happened once again in 2020. LEOs across the nation were considered guilty of institutional racism for an incident that 99.9% of them had nothing to do with. And once again disregarding the objectively reasonable standard, the determination of guilt and racism were both made before all the facts were known and solely on the basis that those killed were Black. In Floyd's case, the initial contact officer was clearly fearful until he was able to see both of Floyd's hands and remove him from the vehicle to be handcuffed. Since once he was handcuffed Floyd did not present a deadly threat to the officers, they used the minimal amount of physical force possible, including a department authorized restraint technique to control him as he resisted. When on April 20th, 2021, a jury decided that Floyd died because of that less than lethal restraint technique observed during the video, they convicted Chauvin of murder. However, the jury in Louisville, Kentucky found that the officers justifiably used deadly force while executing a knock and announce warrant at Breonna Taylor's apartment because they reasonably feared for their lives after being shot at from inside the target location. Despite the officers being fired upon and one being hit before returning fire into Taylor's apartment, any fear for survival that the officers felt was dismissed as their use of force continued to be loudly condemned in the media and calls for their prosecution continued.

Nothing illustrates the double standard toward these officers more starkly than the reactions expressed from a politician who recently perceived a deadly threat to her life. When a democratic socialist Congresswoman recited her "near-death" experience during the riot at the Capitol building on January 6, her sympathizers in politics and the media quickly came to her rescue pointing out that her fear was real. Defending Congresswoman Ocasio Cortez, CNN Chris Cuomo said, "I lived a situation like that, and it doesn't have to be real, the threat, for you to believe it's imminent," as his colleague Don Lemon added, "it's what you believe"[326]. Though the reality ended up being that the Congresswoman was not even in the Capitol building that was under attack and was never in any imminent danger, she was convinced, as she told to her many social media sycophants that she "was going to die"[327]. Unlike the Congresswoman from Queens whose feared assailants never even entered her building, the officers in the Taylor shooting as well as those in the following fatal uses of force were mere feet away from violent criminals and often in split-second, life-or-death situations.

With very few exceptions, the following LEOs and the incidents in which they were compelled to use deadly force were the direct result of a very real threat to their lives or the lives of innocent civilians. Far from a simple sentence describing the subjects age, race, and city the shooting occurred, critical facts regarding the subject's actions and officer's reactions are what is needed to understand why deadly force was used. In the following pages 90 officer-involved shootings of unarmed subjects from 2019 to 2020 are analyzed according to fifteen (1-15) different relevant criteria. And since shootings can be more than just justified or not, they are judged by six (16-21) possible findings. The beauty of these objective criteria is that they can be used to examine past, present, and future deadly force incidents in a uniform manner. An additional seven incidents including five unarmed subjects, a subject erroneously reported as being killed by LE, and George

Floyd are also examined but not included in the statistics. To demonstrate that all the relevant information about these incidents are readily available for the general public, only open-source materials available free of charge were used. While this approach left a few criteria unanswered (annotated by a question mark), it shows that those who politicize such incidents could easily know the critical facts if they actually cared about them.

Rather than let those with an agenda tell you what a great person the subject killed was and how upset their loved ones are, educate yourself on what they did in those last crucial seconds to make officers believe that they posed a mortal threat. Then decide for yourself whether the officers pulled the trigger because of the color of someone's skin, as is often alleged; the subject's violent actions, as is often the case; or a tragic mistake made under intense circumstances, as sometimes happens. As you will see, many of these officers faced threats much more "real" than those experienced by the Queens "drama queen,"[328] who, three weeks later, was still ranting about how Senator Cruz almost had her murdered at the Capitol[329].

INCIDENTS IN 2019:

Name: Dimas Diaz Jr.
Date: 1/12/2019   **Location:** Calabasas, CA
FACTORS (1,2,3,5,8,9,10,12,14,19)

Criminal History/Involved: Yes, pled "guilty to making criminal threats and violating a protective order on Nov. 21, 2016, and was paroled from prison on Dec. 15, 2017"[330]./Yes, Diaz was a parolee who was wanted in another state. He was "considered armed and dangerous"[331] and had just committed domestic assault and grand larceny of an automobile.

Mental Illness: Unknown

Substance Abuse History/Involved: Unknown/Yes, Diaz was "under the influence of methamphetamine and marijuana"[332] at time of incident.

Race/Sex/Age: Latino/Male/43

Officer(s) Involved: California Highway Patrol Officer Brian Green and Ventura County Deputy Sheriff Noel Juarez.

What prompted the initial contact with police? During the morning of January 12, Officers responded to a 911 call of domestic violence against a woman perpetrated by a man she was dating-Dimas Diaz Jr.

Actions taken by subject toward police: Upon the officers' arrival, Diaz stole a vehicle, fled the scene of the domestic violence incident, and crashed on the freeway. During a one-hour standoff with the police, Diaz threatened to "come out shooting,"[333] refusing to comply with the police orders to surrender. Ultimately, Diaz picked up a black object that looked like a knife (ended up being an automobile part) and charged at the officers.

Reactions by the police: After pursuing Diaz onto the freeway, the officers shut it down after he crashed and tried for an hour to get Diaz to surrender. First, the officers used less than lethal rounds to get Diaz to surrender, but to no effect. When Diaz picked up what looked to be a knife and charged at them, they escalated to lethal force and shot him dead.

Outcome of investigation into the fatal police incident: Justified deadly force "in self-defense and in defense of others,"[334] determined by the prosecutors.

What could the subject have done that day to still be alive today? He should have refrained from assaulting his girlfriend and then stealing a car and fleeing the scene; complied with the officers, and peacefully surrendered, instead of charging at them with a weapon.

Justified use of deadly force? YES, the officer's had reasonable cause to believe that Diaz intended to make good on his promise to mortally harm the officer's when he picked up an object and charged at them.

Name: Amiliano Antonio Apodaca
Date: 1/14/2019   **Location:** Pueblo, CO
FACTORS (1,2,8,11,13,14,20)

Criminal History/Involved: Not Applicable (NA)/Yes, by the driver of the vehicle prior to the shooting.

Mental Illness: NA

Substance Abuse History/Involved: NA

Race/Sex/Age: Latino/Male/18

Officer(s) Involved: Canon City Police and Pueblo County Sheriff's Office

What prompted the initial contact with police? Apodaca was a passenger in a vehicle driven by Alicia Antonia Martinez. While fleeing from police in Fremont County on January 13, Martinez struck a Fremont County Sheriff's Office car and then fled into Pueblo County. Pueblo County Deputy Sheriff's attempted to stop the vehicle by using stop sticks and then by executing a Pursuit Intervention Technique (PIT) unsuccessfully in a field before a second successful attempt brought the vehicle to a stop on a front lawn[335].

Actions taken by subject towards police: Martinez drove the vehicle at the deputies as they approached her stopped vehicle[336].

Reactions by the police: Fearing for his life, one of the Deputy Sheriff's shot at the car, seriously injuring Martinez and killing Apodaca.

Outcome of investigation into the fatal police incident: Incident is being investigated by the Tenth Judicial District's Critical Incident Team, led by the Pueblo Police Department.

Miscellaneous: For her actions in the fatal police incident Martinez was later arrested "on a warrant for second-degree assault on a peace officer, as well as four counts of vehicular eluding and a restraining order violation"[337].

What could the subject have done that day to still be alive today? Apodaca lost his life due to the actions of the driver, Alicia Martinez. Press reports do not have information on their relationship, Martinez's drug/mental history, or what led up to her fleeing from the police.

Justified use of deadly force? YES, a vehicle being driven at a law enforcement officer constitutes a deadly threat, and therefore, anyone doing so should expect to have deadly force used against that vehicle and the operator to stop the threat. Martinez should be charged with murder for Apodaca's death.

Name: Shawn Joseph Billinger
Date: 1/16/2019   **Location:** Fort Lupton, CO
FACTORS (1,2,3,4,5,8,12,19)

Criminal History/Involved: Unknown/Yes, reckless endangerment and fleeing from the police.

Mental Illness: None reported, however, Billinger's actions were not normal.

Substance Abuse History/Involved: Yes, Billinger was known to use methamphetamine/Yes, Billinger was upset that he was not able to get methamphetamine.

Race/Sex/Age: White/Male/46

Officer(s) Involved: Fort Lupton Police Officer Zachary Helbig

What prompted the initial contact with police? At approximately 1:45 p.m. on January 16, a female called 911 to report that her friend, Shawn Billinger, had knives and almost made her crash by grabbing the steering wheel as she was driving. The caller claimed that Billinger was "on a death mission" and was upset when she refused to get him some meth. PO Helbig responded to the scene, that was a gas station[338].

Actions taken by subject toward police: As Officer Helbig arrived at the gas station, Billinger fled in a vehicle which he then ditched and ran away from PO Helbig on foot. When Helbig caught up to Billinger in a backyard, Billinger turned around and started walking aggressively towards the officer, angrily telling him, "Kill me!"[339].

Reactions by the police: After yelling at Billinger numerous times to stop, PO Helbig fired one shot fatally hitting Billinger in the chest.

Outcome of investigation into the fatal police incident: Officer Helbig was charged with manslaughter and ultimately found not guilty by a jury trial.

Miscellaneous: Body camera video available at: Kestling and Sylte 2020.

What could the subject have done that day to still be alive today? Billinger could have remained at the gas station and answered whatever questions the officer had to ask. He should have complied with Helbig's commands and stopped advancing toward him.

Justified use of deadly force? YES, Officer Helbig had reasonable fear to believe if Billinger was crazy enough to aggressively advance on him while his firearm was pointed at Billinger, then if Billinger were able to overpower or knock him out, Billinger would take that weapon and use it against him.

Name: Matthew Neil Tuhkanen
Date: 1/19/2019   **Location:** St. Louis Park, Minn
FACTORS (1,2,4,5,10,14,19)

Criminal History/Involved: Yes, Tuhkanen had three active warrants for "trespassing, assault and disorderly conduct"[340]./Yes, he was evading arrest for his active warrants when police responded for the domestic incident.

Mental Illness: None reported, but Tuhkanen's actions were irrational and suicidal.

Substance Abuse History/Involved: Unknown

Race/Sex/Age: White/Male/35

Officer(s) Involved: St. Louis Park Police Officers Samuel Heffernan, Troy Peek and Anthony Pacholke, Smith

What prompted the initial contact with police? During the evening of January 19, 2019, police responded to a 911 call from a woman reporting that Matthew Tuhkanen, the man she had a child in common with, had warrants and was arguing with her in her apartment. Upon arriving at the apartment, police advised Tuhkanen that he was under arrest and ordered him to show his hands. Officer Pacholke pointed his taser at Tuhkanen before holstering it so he could handcuff him[341].

Actions taken by subject toward police: Tuhkanen disregarded the orders and kept moving "his left hand in and out of his pocket". After being warned that he would be shot if he kept disobeying the police orders to show his hands, Tuhkanen ""crouched down, turned toward the dresser and made a jerking motion with his left hand towards an area officers couldn't see"[342].

Reactions by the police: Fearing Tuhkanen was accessing a gun in the dresser, Officer Heffernan shot him four times, twice in the body and twice in the arm.

Outcome of investigation into the fatal police incident: Hennepin County Attorney Mike Freeman announced on Friday that he will not file criminal charges against a St. Louis Park police officer who shot and killed a man who resisted arrest in January 2019. Officer Heffernan was found to have acted, "within the law"[343].

What could the subject have done that day to still be alive today? Should have not violated parole and thus have warrants out for his arrest. Should have complied with the officer's lawful commands to keep his hands visible. Should not have made a furtive movement that a reasonable person would fear was an attempt to access a weapon.

Justified use of deadly force? YES, on the basis of Tuhkanen's non-compliance with their verbal orders, officers had reasonable cause to believe that he was attempting to access a deadly weapon in order to use it against them.

Name: Horacio Ruiz-Rodriguez
Date: 1/21/2019   **Location:** Las Vegas, NV
FACTORS (1,2,4,5,8,10,19)

Criminal History/Involved: Yes, prostitution, narcotics and providing false statement to police./ Yes, he had just kidnapped and sexually assaulted a woman.

Mental Illness: None reported; however, his actions appear to be suicide by cop.

Substance Abuse History/Involved: Yes, Ruiz-Rodriguez had a prior narcotics arrest./None stated.

Race/Sex/Age: Latino/Male/37

Officer(s) Involved: North Las Vegas Police Officers Anthony Watkins; Robert Knickerbocker; Edwin Corales; and Tanner McAninch.

What prompted the initial contact with police? At approximately 8:19 p.m. on January 21, 2019, a woman called 911 reporting that she was sexually assaulted and kidnapped by Horacio Ruiz-Rodriguez. The woman reported that she had just escaped Ruiz-Rodriguez's residence and informed the operator that Ruiz-Rodriguez had told her that there was a dead woman's body underneath his bed. She also told police that he might have a gun. Police responded to Horacio's address and found him sitting in a car nearby[344].

Actions taken by subject toward police: Ruiz-Rodriguez ignored the officers commands and told them he had a gun. After officers tried negotiating with Ruiz-Rodriguez, he reached into his waistband[345].

Reactions by the police: Fearing Ruiz-Rodriguez was reaching for the gun he claimed to have, the four officers fired 19 shots at him, killing him.

Outcome of investigation into the fatal police incident: The North Las Vegas Police Department is investigating the shooting.

Miscellaneous: There was no video of the shooting. "Had Ruiz-Rodriguez survived the shooting, he would have faced charges of murder, kidnapping, sexual assault and obstructing"[346].

What could the subject have done that day to still be alive today? Should not have murdered one woman and sexually assaulted and kidnapped another. Should have complied with the officers to peacefully surrender and not reach into his waistband as if to get a weapon.

Justified use of deadly force? YES, given the totality of the circumstances, officers had reasonable cause to believe that Ruiz-Rodriguez had the means and motive to cause them harm and not be taken without a deadly fight.

Name: Jimmy Atchison
Date: 1/22/2019   **Location:** Atlanta, GA
FACTORS (1,2,21)

Criminal History/Involved: Yes, Atchison had a prior arrest for armed robbery./Yes, resisting arrest by fleeing.

Mental Illness: Unknown

Substance Abuse History/Involved: Unknown/None stated.

Race/Sex/Age: Black/Male/21

Officer(s) Involved: Atlanta Police Officer Sung Kim

What prompted the initial contact with police? On January 22, the Federal Task Force of FBI and Atlanta Officers received information about an apartment in which Atchison was staying. Task Force members including Atlanta PO Sung Kim went to the apartment to serve Atchison with a warrant for armed robbery.

Actions taken by subject toward police: Upon being aware the agents and officers were closing in on him, "Atchison jumped out of a window and fled into another apartment"[347] where he hid in a closet.

Reactions by the police: PO Kim and another Task Force member tracked Atchison down to that other apartment. It is alleged that "Atchison was given two conflicting commands as he hid in a closet. One Task Force member told him to come out with his hands up. Another member told him not to move. As Atchison stepped out of the closet with his hands up, Kim fatally shot Atchison once in the face"[348].

Outcome of investigation into the fatal police incident: The Fulton County District Attorney is still investigating the incident.

Miscellaneous: Atchison's family "plans to file multi-million-dollar lawsuits against the city and the U.S. government"[349]. Since the officer involved was also from a minority group, this incident was not made into one for the social justice activists to rally around.

What could the subject have done that day to still be alive today? He should not have committed an armed robbery that would generate a warrant. He should have peacefully surrendered instead of running from the apartment and hiding in a closet from where the police would be fearful that he could shoot at them.

Justified use of deadly force? If Atchison was unarmed as is reported and did in fact comply with the officer's commands and step out of the closet with his hands up, then it was not a justified shooting. What also remains to be known is whether PO Kim had an accidental discharge or if he intentionally pulled the trigger because he was startled by Atchison's exit from the closet despite being ordered to not move. Until further information becomes available, it remains **UNDETERMINED**.

Name: Preston Oszust
Date: 1/23/2019   **Location:** Flagstaff, AZ
FACTORS (1,2,3,8,9,13,15,20)

Criminal History/Involved: Yes, he was on probation and had an active felony warrant/ Yes, he was fleeing from the police and attempted murder of police during the incident.

Mental Illness: Unknown

Substance Abuse History/Involved: Yes, Oszust had cocaine and fentanyl in his system at time of death[350].

Race/Sex/Age: White/Male/20

Officer(s) Involved: Arizona Department of Public Safety (AZDPS) Troopers and Flagstaff Police Department Officers

What prompted the initial contact with police? At approximately 7:42 p.m. on January 23, upon seeing a traffic violation committed, AZDPS attempted to pull over the vehicle driven by Marcus Gishal, in which his friend Preston Oszust was a passenger.

Actions taken by subject toward police: Gishal made it appear as if he was pulling over in a gas station before accelerating and taking the police on a high-speed pursuit. Gishal and Oszust ditched the vehicle in a nearby residential area and fled on foot. The police set up a perimeter and approximately an hour later, thanks to a 911 caller placing them in the area, the police found them in front of a residence. "As troopers approached both suspects, 20-year-old Marcus Gishal, of Flagstaff, pointed a handgun towards the troopers and fired, striking one of them in the left hand"[351].

Reactions by the police: Troopers returned fire and struck Gishal, who died at the scene, and Oszust who died later from his injuries[352].

Outcome of investigation into the fatal police incident: AZDPS is investigating the incident.

Miscellaneous: During a previous encounter with the AZDPS, Gishal fought with the Trooper and "had a handgun in his waistband as well as marijuana and dangerous drugs for sale in his possession"[353].

What could the subject have done that day to still be alive today? Should not have been a passenger in a car driven by a friend who had marijuana, cocaine, and fentanyl in his system; dealt with drugs; and had previously fought with the police. Should not have run from the police with Gishal after the latter stopped the car. Should not have stood next to Gishal as he shot at the police.

Justified use of deadly force? YES, lethal force was used against the police by Oszust's accomplice, and, reasonably fearing for their lives, the officers responded in kind with justifiable deadly force. Due to his close proximity to his accomplice Gishal, Oszust was killed in the firefight.

Name: Katlyn Alix
Date: 1/24/2019   **Location:** St. Louis, MO
FACTORS (2,3,4,9,13,18)

Criminal History/Involved: No./Yes, Russian roulette and using drugs/alcohol with a loaded weapon is at least a reckless endangerment.

Mental Illness: None reported, however, playing Russian roulette with a loaded weapon is suicidal, as demonstrated by Officer Hendren, who was playing with her and was documented with mental illness.

Substance Abuse History/Involved: Unknown./Yes, alcohol and a powdered substance were found at the scene[354].

Race/Sex/Age: White/Female/24

Officer(s) Involved: St. Louis Police Officers Nathaniel Hendren and Patrick Riordan

What prompted the initial contact with police? On January 24, while she was off duty from her job as a St. Louis Police Officer, Alix was at Officer Nathaniel Hendren's apartment with him and his on-duty partner Patrick Riordan. Allegedly Alix and Hendren were playing a game of Russian roulette. After putting one round in a revolver, spinning the chamber, and firing without it going off, Hendren gave the gun to Alix who pointed it at Hendren and fired with the gun not going off. After getting the gun back, Hendren pointed it at Alix and pulled the trigger, and the live round was struck and hit her in the chest, killing her[355].

Actions taken by subject toward police: NA.

Reactions by the police: NA.

Outcome of investigation into the fatal police incident: Hendren was charged with "first-degree involuntary manslaughter and armed criminal action"[356] and was sentenced to seven years in prison.

Miscellaneous: Hendren was reportedly suicidal and had "complicated psychiatric history, including…anxiety and depression, post-traumatic stress disorder from his time with the Marines"[357].

What could the subject have done that day to still be alive today? Should not have played Russian roulette with a fellow police officer or depending on what is the truth-should not have hung out with an armed psycho.

Justified use of deadly force? NO, regardless of whether Hendren shot Alix in cold blood as her family suggests or he really did so while playing Russian roulette—what Hendren did was outside the scope of normal police duties and he is a disgrace to the profession.

Name: Christian Albarran
Date: 1/24/2019   **Location:** Ehrenberg, AZ
FACTORS (1,2,4,5,8,10,19)

Criminal History/Involved: Yes, Albarran had previous felony arrests for "corporal punishment/ spousal abuse and credit card fraud"[358]./Yes, Albarran had active felony warrants and had been unlawfully fleeing from police.

Mental Illness: None reported but his actions appearing to access a gun while officers had their weapons pointed at him is not normal.

Substance Abuse History/Involved: Unknown/None stated

Race/Sex/Age: Male/Latino/26

Officer(s) Involved: California Highway Patrol (CHP), La Paz County Sheriff's Deputies and Arizona Department of Public Safety (AZDPS) Troopers

What prompted the initial contact with police? At approximately 1 p.m. on January 24, CHP tried to conduct a vehicle stop, but the driver, Christian Albarran refused to pull over and drove across the border into Arizona. They alerted Arizona law enforcement and warned them that Albarran was on his way into their state. AZDPS Troopers were already familiar with Albarran from previous crimes, and they were told earlier that day that he was armed with a gun. AZDPS Troopers and a deputy stopped Albarran in his vehicle just east of the state border. They tried to negotiate with Albarran and repeatedly ordered him to show his hands and keep them where the officers could see them[359].

Actions taken by subject toward police: Albarran ignored the lawful commands of the police and instead "made a rapid and furtive movement indicating a lethal threat to the troopers and the deputy"[360].

Reactions by the police: Justifiably fearing that Albarran was about to pull out a concealed weapon and shoot them, the troopers and deputy shot him multiple times.

Outcome of investigation into the fatal police incident: Arizona law enforcement authorities are investigating the incident.

What could the subject have done that day to still be alive today? Should not have committed previous crimes to generate warrants. Should not have fled from CHP officers who were trying to pull him over. Should have complied with the AZDPS officers' orders to show his hands and be peacefully taken into custody.

Justified use of deadly force? YES, the officers had reasonable cause to believe that Albarran was armed, and his furtive movement was an attempt to gain access to that weapon and use it against them.

Name: Rhogena Nicholas
Date: 1/28/2019   **Location:** Houston, TX
FACTORS (3,9,13,15,20)

Criminal History/Involved: No./No.

Substance Abuse History/Involved: Yes, amounts of marijuana and cocaine for personal use were found at the scene.

Race/Sex/Age: White/Female/58

Officer(s) Involved: Houston Police Department Detectives and Police Officers including Narcotics Officers Gerald Goines and Steven Bryant

What prompted the initial contact with police? Before 5 a.m. on January 28, nine narcotics detectives and six officers conducted a no-knock drug raid on a suspected heroin-trafficking house in which Rhogena Nicholas lived with her husband Dennis Tuttle[361].

Actions taken by subject toward police: The first officer to enter the house reported being shot in the shoulder by Tuttle after he killed Tuttle's charging pit bull. Allegedly, Rhogena made a move for the injured officer's shotgun that had fallen to the floor, prompting other officers to shoot and kill her. Tuttle continued shooting at the officers who had entered the house, hitting three more of them as they retreated from the house[362].

Reactions by the police: As Tuttle continued firing at the officers, the officers returned fire and killed him.

Outcome of investigation into the fatal police incident: The 911 caller prompting the investigation "lied when she implicated Dennis Tuttle and Rhogena Nicholas in drug dealing"[363]. Officer Goines "made numerous materially false statements in the state search warrant" and "repeatedly lied about the circumstances of the raid"[364]. Officer Bryant falsely claimed they recovered "two small packets of heroin"[365] in the raid. No heroin was found in the house, only personal use amounts of marijuana and cocaine were. Forensics experts found evidence Nicholas was shot by an officer outside the house who could not have seen her[366]. A grand jury indicted six of the officers involved on 17 counts: Goines-two counts of felony murder and four counts of tampering with a government record; Bryant-one count aggregate theft by a public servant and two counts of tampering with a government record[367].

Miscellaneous: Since the officers had not announced themselves and were not in uniform, and because neither Tuttle nor Nicholas were running a criminal enterprise, Tuttle likely thought they were the victims of an armed home invasion-just as Breonna Taylor's boyfriend did.

What could the subject have done that day to still be alive today? NA, Nicholas and her husband were the victims of a fraudulent no-knock plainclothes search conducted on the basis of false information.

Justified use of deadly force? NO, in that the raid should never have happened since it was conducted based upon false statements. For those officers involved who believed that it was a lawful raid and came under fire from Tuttle, **YES,** they were justified in returning fire into the house and toward where they believed the shooting was coming from.

THIS IS NOT AN UNARMED SUBJECT SO FACTORS (1,2,8,9,12,13,19) ARE NOT INCLUDED IN STATISTICS

Name: Gregory Griffin

Date: 1/28/2019   **Location:** Newark, NJ

Criminal History/Involved: Yes, Griffin had "previous drug related arrests"[368]./Yes, unlawful fleeing, menacing with a deadly weapon.

Mental Illness: Unknown.

Substance Abuse History/Involved: Yes, previous drug-related arrests./None stated.

Race/Sex/Age: Black/Male/46

Officer(s) Involved: Newark Police Officers Jovanny Crespo and Hector Cruz

What prompted the initial contact with police? At approximately 11:20 p.m. on January 28, while a Newark Police Officer was approaching Griffin's vehicle during a traffic stop, Griffin hit the gas and fled. The officer conducting the stop reported to dispatch that she saw a gun in the car before Griffin drove away[369].

Actions taken by subject toward police: Griffin again refused to pull over when successive police officers attempted to get him to stop the car. Either Griffin or his passenger, Andrew Dixon, is reported to have pointed a gun at responding officers several times during the pursuit.

Reactions by the police: PO Cruz was driving one police vehicle with PO Crespo in the passenger seat. As PO Cruz pursued Griffin's vehicle, PO Crespo jumped out of the vehicle on several occasions to shoot at Griffin's car when it slowed down or was stopped. Griffin was shot in the head and died; his passenger was shot and seriously injured.[370]

Outcome of investigation into the fatal police incident: A grand jury indicted PO Crespo for aggravated manslaughter and a few other charges. Besides aggravated murder, Crespo had been charged with aggravated assault, "two counts of possession of a weapon for an unlawful purpose and two counts of official misconduct"[371].

Miscellaneous: Officers bodycam video of the incident is available for viewing on YouTube at the following link: https://www.youtube.com/watch?v=VULSkQ4YPV0&feature=youtu.be

What could the subject have done that day to still be alive today? Should not have fled from a lawful traffic stop. Should have pulled over and surrendered with his hands up and out of the vehicle. Should not have illegally carried a weapon in his car. Should not have pointed a firearm at the police or have a passenger point it at the police.

Justified use of deadly force? YES, a gun was found in the car, and according to Officer Crespo, one of the occupants of the vehicle pointed a gun at him. The threat of deadly force to officers justified their use of such force toward the vehicle's occupants. This incident should not be described in any database tracking as a fatal police shooting involving unarmed subjects.

Name: Morgan Shane West
Date: 2/7/2019   **Location:** Snyder, TX
FACTORS (1,12,19)

Criminal History/Involved: Unknown./None stated.

Mental Illness: Unknown.

Substance Abuse History/Involved: Unknown./None stated.

Race/Sex/Age: White/Male/38

Officer(s) Involved: Snyder Police Officer Whitney Merket

What prompted the initial contact with police? At approximately 6:35 p.m. on February 7, Officer Merket responded to a 911 call of a suspicious person. Upon arriving at the incident location, Officer Merket encountered Morgan West[372].

Actions taken by subject toward police: There was an altercation between West and Merket.

Reactions by the police: Officer Merket fired her weapon at West, killing him.

Outcome of investigation into the fatal police incident: The Texas Rangers are investigating.

Miscellaneous: Morgan was a black belt in Taekwondo[373].

What could the subject have done that day to still be alive today? Should have complied with the officer's commands and should not have presented a threat to her.

Justified use of deadly force? Not enough information available about the incident to make a definitive conclusion. However, if the officer was being physically threatened and/or attacked as an "altercation" suggests, **YES**, deadly force is considered reasonable because if West gained possession of the officers' firearm, he may have used it against her.

Name: Aaron Allen Przekop
Date: 2/8/2019   **Location:** Bakersfield, CA
FACTORS (1,4,5,8,10,19)

Criminal History/Involved: Yes, arrested April 14, 2018, for unknown crimes[374]./No.

Mental Illness: None reported, but his actions make him appear emotionally disturbed at the time of the incident, and/or he wanted suicide by cop.

Substance Abuse History/Involved: Unknown./None reported.

Race/Sex/Age: White/Male/25

Officer(s) Involved: California Highway Patrol (CHP)

What prompted the initial contact with police? At approximately 4:42 a.m. on February 8, CHP received a 911 call of a motor vehicle accident on the interstate. CHP officers responded to the location of the accident and found a single vehicle occupied by the driver; Aaron Przekop who had crashed into a light pole[375].

Actions taken by subject toward police: Przekop told the police that he was armed which caused them to back away from his vehicle. Przekop then exited his vehicle with a hand hidden from the officer's view as he advanced toward them, against their commands to stop and show his hands.

Reactions by the police: Fearing for their safety based upon Przekop's statement about possessing a gun and his aggressive actions toward them with a concealed hand possibly containing a gun, the officer's fired at Przekop, killing him.

Outcome of investigation into the fatal police incident: There is a multi-agency investigation being conducted by the Kern County Sheriffs Officer, Kern County District Attorney's Office, and CHP.

What could the subject have done that day to still be alive today? Should not have told the officers that he was armed and then approached them with a concealed hand. Should have followed the officers' lawful commands and showed his hands.

Justified use of deadly force? YES, the subject gave officer's the impression he was armed and willing to use lethal force against them, thereby giving them reasonable cause to believe that their lives were in imminent danger.

Name: Eric Young
Date: 2/11/2019   **Location:** Montgomery, W.VA
FACTORS (1,4,5,21) 9?,12?,14?

Criminal History/Involved: Unknown./No criminality involved in incident.

Mental Illness: Yes, Young's mother had reported that he had paranoid schizophrenia and delusions.

Substance Abuse History/Involved: Unknown./None stated.

Race/Sex/Age: White/Male/34

Officer(s) Involved: Montgomery Police Officer Roger King

What prompted the initial contact with police? Shortly after 4:00 a.m. on February 11, Officer King heard noises coming from the area where police cars are parked behind city hall. King reports that the noises were Young yelling to himself. King apparently was not one of the many officers who were aware of Young and his mental illness[376].

Actions taken by subject toward police: Officer King reports that when he told Young to get on the ground, he ignored him and walked away.

Reactions by the police: King reports following Young and tasering him, but to no effect. When Young advanced toward King, telling him "Just shoot me." King felt threatened and "fired five shots, killing Young"[377].

Outcome of investigation into the fatal police incident: The Kanawha County Sheriff's Office is investigating. So far there is no indication that Young was tased, and King reports not having his baton on him and admits not considering using his pepper spray. Forensics shows Young was "30 to 50 feet away" from King, not the "8 to 10 feet"[378] claimed by King when he shot Young. There are also discrepancies with King's statement about where Young's pocketknife was during the shooting.

Miscellaneous: This is an unfortunate example of what happens when emotionally disturbed people who should be committed to an institution or at the very least be kept under supervision, are not.

What could the subject have done that day to still be alive today? Should have been on proper medication for his condition and not been outside at 4:00 a.m. making suspicious noises near police vehicles. Should have complied with the officer's commands to get down on the ground. Should not have aggressively advanced at the officer.

Justified use of deadly force? YES, if Young was in fact advancing aggressively and the officer felt mortally threatened, deadly force is technically justified. Ideally an officer should at least attempt using defensive tactics to control/arrest a subject before resorting to deadly force, but circumstances, proximity, physical size and/or altered mental status of a person can increase an officer's threat perception. NO, if Officer King lied about the details and Young did not present an imminent threat to him. Due to the conflicting evidence, a definitive determination cannot be made, therefore it remains **UNDETERMINED**.

Name: Delmar Espejo

Date: 2/18/2019   **Location:** Honolulu, HI

FACTORS (1,2,3,4,12,14,19)

Criminal History/Involved: Yes, Espejo had prior convictions for drinking alcohol in public and DWI./Yes, Espejo was drinking in public at the time of incident, and then he assaulted an officer.

Mental Illness: None reported, however, Espejo's drinking problems and physical assault of a law enforcement officer are not normal behavior.

Substance Abuse History/Involved: Yes, his prior arrests were alcohol related./Yes, alcohol involved in this incident.

Race/Sex/Age: Latino/Male/28

Officer(s) Involved: Hawaii Department of Public Safety Sheriff's Deputy

What prompted the initial contact with police? At approximately 8:20 p.m. on February 18, while patrolling the capitol, the deputy observed Espejo with an open container of alcohol that he told Espejo to dispose of several times.

Actions taken by subject toward police: Espejo ignored the deputy's lawful order and instead engaged in a physical confrontation with him, wrapping "his arms around the law enforcement officer's head and torso"[379].

Reactions by the police: Fearing that Espejo was posing a lethal threat by his violent physical attack, the Deputy shot Espejo, killing him.

Outcome of investigation into the fatal police incident: The shooting has been reclassified as a second-degree murder and referred to the Honolulu Prosecutor's Office, which will determine if charges should be brought against the deputy. The deputy was immediately put on restrictive duty where he remains[380][381].

What could the subject have done that day to still be alive today? Should have complied with the deputy's lawful order and disposed of the alcohol. Should not have physically attacked the deputy, making him fear for his life.

Justified use of deadly force? YES, when a subject is the aggressor and attacks a law enforcement officer, there is a very credible reason for the officer to fear that the subject will try to disarm the officer and use his weapon against him.

Name: Maurice Arrisgado
Date: 3/1/2019   **Location:** Honolulu, HI
FACTORS (1,2,19)

Criminal History/Involved: Yes, while on probation, Arrisgado was arrested for first-degree attempted murder of a law enforcement officer./Yes, he was attempting to break out of jail when shot.

Mental Illness: Unknown.

Substance Abuse History/Involved: Unknown./None stated.

Race/Sex/Age: Latino/Male/47

Officer(s) Involved: Oahu Correctional Center Guard

What prompted the initial contact with police? At approximately 6:10 p.m. on March 1, Arrisgado was being processed into the Oahu Correctional Center for attempted murder of a law enforcement officer, resisting arrest, and criminal contempt for his actions earlier in the week when he stabbed an officer while being arrested for an outstanding warrant[382].

Actions taken by subject toward police: While in the intake area of the Oahu Correctional Center, Arrisgado managed to escape by going "through a secure door and the front gate as well as the perimeter towers and ran across Kamehameha Highway into a nearby residential area"[383].

Reactions by the police: Upon becoming aware of Arrisgado's escape, corrections officers chased after him, yelling for him to "stop and surrender"[384]. As Arrisgado ignored their commands and continued to flee, a corrections officer fatally shot him in the back.

Outcome of investigation into the fatal police incident: Honolulu Prosecutor's Office is in charge of the investigation and is considering whether to bring charges against the officers.

What could the subject have done that day to still be alive today? Should not have broken the law and have a warrant for his arrest. Should not have stabbed the police officer arresting him for a warrant. Should not have broken out of jail. Should have complied with the corrections officers' commands and stopped running away and escaping the prison.

Justified use of deadly force? YES, Arrisgado proved himself to be a danger to the public and he was attempting to escape the jail he was being lawfully held in for previous violent crimes. As stated by the Hawaii Department of Public Safety Director Nolan Espinda, "deadly force is authorized by law as needed to stop a fleeing inmate"[385].

Name: Eduardo Munoz

Date: 3/1/2019   **Location:** Fairfield, TX

FACTORS (1,2,12,14,19)

Criminal History/Involved: Unknown./Yes, harassment and possible assault during a domestic dispute.

Mental Illness: Unknown.

Substance Abuse History/Involved: Unknown./None stated.

Race/Sex/Age: Latino/Male/29

Officer(s) Involved: Fairfield Police Officer

What prompted the initial contact with police? During the morning of March 1, a Fairfield police officer responded to a 911 call of a domestic dispute where a woman was being harassed and/or attacked by a male acquaintance while they were on the highway[386].

Actions taken by subject toward police: Disregarding the officer's presence and commands, Munoz threatened to harm the woman involved in the domestic dispute[387].

Reactions by the police: The officer first tased Munoz in order to get him under control, but after that failed, deadly force was used.

Outcome of investigation into the fatal police incident: Texas Rangers are investigating.

What could the subject have done that day to still be alive today? Should not have harassed or attacked a woman. Should have complied with the officer's lawful orders and peacefully surrendered. Should not have resisted/fought with the officer.

Justified use of deadly force? YES, the subject was violent, first with a female and then by resisting the officer's non-lethal attempts to control and arrest him. Fearing Munoz presented a deadly threat to the woman and/or the officer himself, the officer justifiably used deadly force to stop Munoz.

Name: Tyler J. Meier
Date: 3/2/2019   **Location:** Fairchild, WI
FACTORS (1,2,4,5,12,14,19)

Criminal History/Involved: Yes, Meier had a prior conviction for felony murder./Yes, he was creating a disturbance and assaulting a police officer.

Mental Illness: None reported, however, Meier's actions were completely irrational and suicidal.

Substance Abuse History/Involved: Unknown/ None stated

Race/Sex/Age: White/Male/46

Officer(s) Involved: Augusta Police Officer Levi M. Stumo and Eau Claire County Sheriff's Deputy Patrolmen Daniel T. Eaton

What prompted the initial contact with police? At around noon on March 2, Sheriff's Deputy Eaton responded to a 911 call of a suspicious person, and Officer Stumo went to assist him. The farmer who called 911 reported that Tyler Meier came naked to his farm and was acting very strange. When the two officers arrived at the farm, they tried to talk to Meier[388].

Actions taken by subject toward police: Meier stripped off his clothing again and told the officers, "You're going to have to shoot me"[389] before physically attacking Officer Stumo. Quickly Meier managed to get on top of Officer Stumo and started strangling him.

Reactions by the police: Deputy Eaton tasered Meier twice and pepper sprayed him in an attempt to get him off of Officer Stumo. Neither the taser nor pepper spray had any effect, so Eaton physically took Meier off of Stumo. At that point Meier again directed his rage at Stumo and charged at him. Fearing for his life, and already seeing the taser and pepper spray were ineffective, Officer Stumo shot Meier, killing him.

Outcome of investigation into the fatal police incident: The officer's actions were deemed justified by the Eau Claire County District Attorney.

What could the subject have done that day to still be alive today? Should not have gone to another person's private property and acted so strangely that they become fearful. Should not have attacked the officers when they tried talking to him.

Justified use of deadly force? YES, Meier was the aggressor and gave the officers reasonable cause to believe that he would kill them if given the opportunity with either his hands or by taking one of their duty weapons.

Name: Stephanie Areanda Quiroz
Date: 3/5/2019   **Location:** Bakersfield, CA
FACTORS (1,2,8,13,20)

Criminal History/Involved: Yes, found not guilty of attempted robbery and kidnapping in 2019./ Yes, in the company of Gavino Castro, a parolee fleeing from the U.S. Marshals.

Mental Illness: Unknown.

Substance Abuse History/Involved: Unknown./None stated.

Race/Sex/Age: Latina/Female/21

Officer(s) Involved: U.S. Marshals Apprehension Task Force

What prompted the initial contact with police? At approximately 4 p.m. on March 5, a U.S. Marshals Task Force apprehension team attempted to arrest parolee Gavin Castro at a motel[390].

Actions taken by subject toward police: Castro ran from the Marshals, got into a vehicle occupied by his brother and Stephanie Quiroz, and drove away with the Marshals in hot pursuit.

Reactions by the police: The Marshal's shot at Castro while he fled from them. During the car pursuit, Castro crashed into another car, injuring his brother and himself. The coroner determined that Quiroz was killed by a gunshot to the chest[391].

Outcome of investigation into the fatal police incident: None reported.

Miscellaneous: "Quiroz was acquitted last year of using Facebook to lure men to locations where they were kidnapped and robbed. She was alleged to have set up the victims by contacting them through Facebook Messenger, according to court documents"[392].

What could the subject have done that day to still be alive today? Should not have been in the company of a fugitive wanted by the U.S. Marshals.

Justified use of deadly force? YES, against Castro. The Marshals were not targeting Quiroz; her death is the unfortunate collateral damage of Castro's unlawful fleeing–he should be charged with murder for her death occurring during his commission of a crime.

Name: Henry Wayne Rivera
Date: 3/13/2019   **Location:** Phoenix, AZ
FACTORS (1,2,8,14,19)

Criminal History/Involved: Yes, Rivera had active warrants for burglary and credit card theft./Yes, Rivera unlawfully fled from the police and stole a car while doing so.

Mental Illness: Unknown.

Substance Abuse History/Involved: Unknown./None reported.

Race/Sex/Age: Latino/Male/30

Officer(s) Involved: Phoenix Police Officers Andrew Carlsson and Kyle Fricke.

What prompted the initial contact with police? On the morning of March 13, while the police were searching a motel for a suspect wanted for recent shootings of three people and kidnapping of a woman, fearing that they were looking for him–Rivera jumped out of a motel window and ran from them. Rivera's attempt to escape and the fact he resembled the wanted suspect made police think he was the man they were looking for, so they chased after him[393].

Actions taken by subject toward police: Rivera stole a car from a nearby business, driving it a short distance before police confronted him. Rivera failed to comply with the officer's commands while he was in the vehicle and again after he exited the vehicle[394].

Reactions by the police: Officer's fired tear gas and less-than-lethal rounds at Rivera to get him to comply but he still resisted their orders. So, the officers used lethal rounds and killed him[395].

Outcome of investigation into the fatal police incident: Not reported.

What could the subject have done that day to still be alive today? Should not have committed previous crimes which would generate warrants. Should not have run from the police when he thought they found him. Should have complied with their orders and peacefully surrendered.

Justified use of deadly force? YES, the police believed that Rivera was the suspect involved in the recent shootings of three people, thereby making him armed and dangerous. Rivera's failure to comply with their orders and the failure of less-than-lethal attempts to stop him left police with no other option when he made a furtive movement for what they reasonably feared may be a weapon.

Name: Kevin Bruce Mason
Date: 3/24/2019   **Location:** Baltimore, MD
FACTORS (1,2,4,10,19)

Criminal History/Involved: Yes, Mason had prior convictions for assault of a civilian and shooting a police officer./Yes, Mason "threatened to kill the responding police officers if they came any closer to his house"[396].

Mental Illness: None reported, however, Mason's actions were irrational.

Substance Abuse History/Involved: Unknown./None reported.

Race/Sex/Age: Black/Male/57

Officer(s) Involved: Baltimore Police Officers John Johnson and numerous others at the scene.

What prompted the initial contact with police? At approximately 11:40 p.m. on March 24, Baltimore Police responded to a domestic-violence call from a woman at Kevin Mason's house.

Actions taken by subject toward police: Mason repeatedly claimed to have a gun and threatened to shoot the police if they approached his house. At 11:53 p.m., as the officers were outside his house, Mason called 911 and threatened to kill them.

Reactions by the police: When Mason exited his house a second time to threaten the officers, PO John Johnson shot at him twice, and Mason retreated inside the house where he was later discovered dead[397].

Outcome of investigation into the fatal police incident: Incident is still under investigation.

Miscellaneous: Several officer bodycam videos are available. The officer who shot Mason is also black so the incident could not be made into one about race. One of the officers can be heard alerting the other officers that Mason had already come to the door with a gun in his hand.

What could the subject have done that day to still be alive today? Should not have caused the woman in his house to fear for her safety and call 911 on him. Should not have told the police that he is armed and will kill them. Should have complied with their lawful orders.

Justified use of deadly force? YES, the officers followed protocol for what was reasonably believed to be an armed and dangerous subject who threatened to have a weapon and the desire to use it against them.

Name: Andrew John Mason
Date: 3/30/2019   **Location:** Watauga County, NC
FACTORS (1,2,3,4,12,14,15,19)

Criminal History/Involved: Unknown./Yes, assaulted a police officer during the incident.

Mental Illness: Not reported, however, Mason was in an altered mental state during the time of incident, but it is unclear if that was because he had ingested a chemical substance and/or because he had a mental illness.

Substance Abuse History/Involved: Unknown./Yes, photographic and text evidence shows that he had ingested some kind of blue pill, characterized as acid by him, just hours before the incident.

Race/Sex/Age: White/Male/22

Officer(s) Involved: Watauga County Sheriff's Deputy Adam Gragg

What prompted the initial contact with police? On the night of March 30, Sheriff's Deputy Gragg responded to multiple 911 calls from residents claiming that a man was making noises in the street and banging on people's doors trying to gain access after 11 p.m. After interviewing some of the residents, Deputy Gragg patrolled the area and encountered Mason walking in the street in his pajamas and with no shoes on.

Actions taken by subject toward police: Disregarding Gragg's orders to stop, Mason advanced toward Gragg, lunging at him as Gragg deployed his taser, causing it to miss. Mason then struck Gragg in the face, kicked him, and reached for Gragg's duty weapon[398].

Reactions by the police: All alone, injured from the strike to the face and having heard Mason say "die," "jail," and "let's go,"[399] Deputy Gragg feared for his life as Mason attacked him after smacking the taser out of his hand. As a last resort, Gragg fired one shot into Mason chest, killing him.

Outcome of investigation into the fatal police incident: It was determined to be a lawful shooting by Watauga County District Attorney Seth Banks.

Miscellaneous: Officer's bodycam video footage is available.

What could the subject have done that day to still be alive today? Should not have taken a mind-altering substance. Should not have wandered around the neighborhood yelling, knocking doors, and scaring people. Should have complied with the deputy's orders. Should not have physically attacked the deputy.

Justified use of deadly force? YES, the deputy was physically attacked, he had tried to use less-than-lethal options, and when he feared that the subject was trying to gain access to his weapon, he justifiably used deadly force to stop him.

Name: Donnell James Lang
Date: 4/2/2019   **Location:** Redding, CA
FACTORS (1,4,5,10,14,19)

Criminal History/Involved: No./No.

Mental Illness: Yes, Lang suffered from post-traumatic stress disorder, possibly from his 17-year military service, and he did appear to be emotionally disturbed during the incident.

Substance Abuse History/Involved: Unknown./None reported.

Race/Sex/Age: White/Male/48

Officer(s) Involved: Redding Police Officer Brett Leonard

What prompted the initial contact with police? On April 2, police responded to Lang's block because of a 911 caller who stated that Lang was walking in the street, "acting strangely," and "appeared to have a small gun in his waistband that he also took out at times"[400]. Upon arriving in the area of the call, police spoke to another person who had also been watching Lang and thought that he had a gun. When the officers confronted Lang, they repeatedly ordered him to show his hands and keep them away from his waistband area for fear that he had a gun hidden there.

Actions taken by subject toward police: Lang repeatedly ignored the officer's orders and moved his hands toward his waistband several times. When one of the officers attempted to gain physical control over him and put handcuffs on, Lang "broke free and quickly thrust his right hand toward his waistband"[401].

Reactions by the police: Fearing that Lang's sudden attempt to put his hand in his waistband was to grab the gun that numerous witnesses had stated seeing him carry, Officer Leonard fired his patrol rifle at Lang, killing him.

Outcome of investigation into the fatal police incident: The shooting was determined to be lawful by the Shasta County District Attorney's Office[402].

Miscellaneous: Land ended up being unarmed, the only objects in his pockets were his wallet, keys, and a key fob. This was not the first time the police were called by neighbors thinking that Lang was acting suspiciously. It appears that he did have mental illness and would have been safer being under some kind of supervision.

What could the subject have done that day to still be alive today? Should not have been outside, acting strangely and causing his neighbors to fear that something was wrong. Should have complied with the officers' orders and kept his hands where they could see them. Should not have resisted the officers' attempts to peacefully take him into custody.

Justified use of deadly force? YES, officers had reasonable cause to believe that Lang was armed. Lang's resisting of arrest and sudden reaching to an area typically used to hide a gun made the officers reasonably fear for their lives, thereby meriting lethal force.

Name: Thomas Verile, Jr.
Date: 4/4/2019   **Location:** Kalamazoo, MI
FACTORS (1,2,4,5,10,19)

Criminal History/Involved: Yes, Verile had prior convictions for burglary, and felony possession of a firearm; he also had active warrants for another weapon's charge and child neglect./Yes, Verile unlawfully fled and resisted arrest.

Mental Illness: Yes, Verile's wife stated, "He had all sorts of demons in him that he was fighting,"[403] and his actions were highly irrational and suicidal.

Substance Abuse History/Involved: Unknown./None stated.

Race/Sex/Age: White/Male/37

Officer(s) Involved: U.S. Marshal Tony Casper, Michigan State Police Detective Sgt. Kevin Conklin, Michigan Department of Corrections Investigator Thomas Johnson, and Battle Creek Police Department Officer Andrew Horn.

What prompted the initial contact with police? The Michigan State Police (MSP) Fugitive Team were looking for Verile because he had violated parole, and when they attempted to arrest him on April 2, he nearly ran the officers over as he escaped. On April 4, the MSP team tracked Verile down to a house.

Actions taken by subject toward police: Verile refused to comply with the officers' orders, instead threatening to kill them and himself with a gun that he claimed to have. While arguing with the officers, Verile moved his arms and "hands in a way that appear to the officers that he is pointing a firearm at them, and they then shot in self-defense"[404].

Reactions by the police: Believing Verile's claims to have a gun and fearing that his furtive movement was an attempt to point it at them from under the shelf in the small basement room he was hiding in, all four officers fired at Verile, hitting him with 13 out of 17 shots.

Outcome of investigation into the fatal police incident: Kalamazoo County Prosecutor Jeff Getting concluded that the officers had reasonable cause to believe that Verile Jr. posed a lethal threat to their lives and therefore reacted accordingly. No charges were filed against the officers.

What could the subject have done that day to still be alive today? Should not have violated his parole. Should not have fled from officers when they found him earlier in the week. Should have complied with the officers' lawful commands. Should not have told the officers that he had a gun and will kill them. Should not have made a sudden movement that could be construed as pointing a weapon at the officers.

Justified use of deadly force? YES, Verile was a known violent criminal who had just recently attempted to run over two police officers and was now threatening to have a gun which he simulated using. Officers reasonably believed that their lives were in imminent danger from Verile and justifiably used deadly force against him.

Name: Marzues Scott

Date: 4/7/2019   **Location:** Blytheville, AR

FACTORS (1,2,4,12,15,19)

Criminal History/Involved: Unknown./Yes, Scott had just viciously assaulted a store clerk.

Mental Illness: Not reported, however, Scott's lack of affect suggested some type of mental illness.

Substance Abuse History/Involved: Unknown./None reported.

Race/Sex/Age: Black/Male/35

Officer(s) Involved: Blytheville Police Officer Leann Norman

What prompted the initial contact with police? Around 11:30 p.m. on April 7, Officer Norman responded to a 911 call of a disturbance at a convenience store. Surveillance video from that store shows Marzues Scott brutally and without provocation beat the store clerk. That clerk lost a tooth and sustained head injuries from the beating Scott gave him. Upon arriving on the scene, Officer Norman canvassed the area and confronted Scott as he was walking away across the street from the store, telling him, "You just assaulted somebody at Dodge Store. Go to my car. Go to my car. Don't get near me. Go to my car now. Go to my car. I need some back up. Go to the car. Get back don't come near me. Get back"[405].

Actions taken by subject toward police: Scott attacked Officer Norman, hitting her several times in the head, knocking her to the ground and injuring her[406].

Reactions by the police: Fearful Scott was going to kill her, PO Norman shot Scott twice, killing him.

Outcome of investigation into the fatal police incident: Prosecutors and the Blytheville PD announced that Officer Norman will neither be prosecuted nor departmentally charged for the shooting.

Miscellaneous: Video from the convenience store and from the officer's body cam show that Scott was a ruthless and violent aggressor.

What could the subject have done that day to still be alive today? Should not have assaulted and injured a store clerk, prompting a 911 call. Should have obeyed the lawful commands of the officer to peacefully be arrested. Should not have physically attacked the officer, injuring her and causing her to fear for her life.

Justified use of deadly force? YES, Scott had already assaulted and injured one person and after disobeying Officer Norman's commands he assaulted her as well. Fearing that she was no match for the much larger and stronger Scott's violent attack, Officer Norman reasonably believed that her life was in danger and justifiably used lethal force.

Name: Marcus McVae
Date: 4/11/2019   **Location:** Boerne, TX
FACTORS (1,2,8,12,14,19)

Criminal History/Involved: Yes, McVae was out on bond for charges of felony possession of controlled substances, prior arrests for armed robbery, pled guilty to organized crime, prior convictions for aggravated robbery and assault of a public servant./Yes, he unlawfully fled arrest.

Mental Illness: Unknown.

Substance Abuse History/Involved: Unknown./None stated.

Race/Sex/Age: Black/Male/34

Officer(s) Involved: Texas Department of Public Safety (DPS) Trooper

What prompted the initial contact with police? During the afternoon of April 11, a Texas DPS Trooper attempted to conduct a vehicle and traffic stop on the car being driven by Marcus McVae[407].

Actions taken by subject toward police: Likely because McVae was out of jail on $150K bond and wanted on charges of drug dealing, he fled on foot after pulling his vehicle over for the trooper.

Reactions by the police: The trooper caught up to McVae in the woods and gave him several commands to peacefully surrender but instead McVae assaulted the trooper. Alone in a rural area with no backup nearby and fearing for his life from the wanted criminal physically assaulting him, the trooper fired his weapon one time, killing McVae[408].

Outcome of investigation into the fatal police incident: Texas Rangers are investigating.

What could the subject have done that day to still be alive today? Should not have unlawfully fled from the DPS Trooper on the traffic stop. Should have complied with the trooper's orders to peacefully surrender. Should not have physically attacked the trooper, making him fear for his life.

Justified use of deadly force? YES, McVae was a violent person who fled from the trooper on a traffic stop, and then rather than be arrested, he physically assaulted the trooper. Given McVae's violent attack, the trooper reasonably feared for his life and justifiably used lethal force.

Name: Isaiah Lewis
Date: 4/29/2019   **Location:** Edmond, OK
FACTORS (1,2,3,4,12,14,15,19)

Criminal History/Involved: Unknown./Yes, Lewis had just been involved in a violent domestic dispute and had broken into a house before assaulting the responding officers.

Mental Illness: Lewis' girlfriend reported that he was acting paranoid and delusional, likely due to the drugs he was on.

Substance Abuse History/Involved: Yes, his friends say that Lewis regularly smoked marijuana./ Yes, a toxicology report showed that Lewis had "diphenhydramine (Benadryl) and tetrahydrocannabinol (THC)"[409] in his system during the time of his death.

Race/Sex/Age: Black/Male/17

Officer(s) Involved: Edmond Police Dept. Sgt. Milo Box and Police Officer Denton Scherman

What prompted the initial contact with police? At approximately 1 p.m. on April 29, police responded to a 911 call of a violent domestic dispute involving a girl who had just got assaulted by her boyfriend. Another 911 caller reported that a naked black male was running around the neighborhood[410].

Actions taken by subject toward police: When Lewis saw the police arrive, he ran naked through the neighborhood and forced his way into a stranger's home to hide from the cops. When confronted by Police Sgt. Box in the house, Lewis ignored his orders to put his hands up and instead charged the Sgt. Lewis punched Sgt. Box in the head and was unphased by the Sgt's attempt to dry-stun him with the taser, nearly beating him unconscious[411].

Reactions by the police: Aware that the taser had no effect on Lewis and fearing that he would access the injured officer's firearm or violently attack him next, PO Denton Scherman shot Lewis dead. Sgt. Box was treated at the hospital for his injuries.

Outcome of investigation into the fatal police incident: Oklahoma County DA's office determined that the officers were justified in their actions and will not be charged for the shooting of Lewis.

Miscellaneous: Neither officer was wearing bodycam. One of the officers sustained a head injury and was treated at a local hospital.

What could the subject have done that day to still be alive today? Should not have taken an illegal substance and acted violently toward his girlfriend. Should not have fled from police. Should have complied with the officers' lawful orders to peacefully surrender. Should not have broken into someone's house to hide from the police. Should not have violently attacked the police when they tracked him down to the house he just burglarized.

Justified use of deadly force? YES, the officers tried to physically subdue Lewis and also used non-lethal weapons, but neither had any effect in stopping the violent attack upon them by Lewis. Reasonably fearing that Lewis was going to knock one of them unconscious and kill them, Officer Scherman justifiably used lethal force and shot Lewis dead.

Name: David Wayne West
Date: 5/2/2019   **Location:** Glenwood, GA
FACTORS (1,2,8,12,14,15,19)

Criminal History/Involved: Yes, West had a warrant for prior crimes of aggravated assault, domestic violence, and drugs./Yes, West unlawfully fled from the police and then assaulted an officer.

Mental Illness: Unknown.

Substance Abuse History/Involved: Yes, West had a prior arrest for methamphetamine./ None stated.

Race/Sex/Age: White/Male/52

Officer(s) Involved: Oconee Drug Task Force Police Officer Jeff Deal

What prompted the initial contact with police? At approximately 1:15 p.m. on May 2, deputies and officers with the Oconee Drug Task Force went to a location they believed West would be at to serve him with a warrant for "charges related to aggravated assault, domestic violence, and methamphetamine"[412].

Actions taken by subject toward police: Upon seeing the Task Force Officers, West fled the area on an all-terrain vehicle (ATV). When Officer Deal caught up to West shortly after, the latter fought with the officer[413].

Reactions by the police: During the fight with West, Officer Deal fired his weapon, killing West[414].

Outcome of investigation into the fatal police incident: Georgia Bureau of Investigation has the lead.

Miscellaneous: Officer Deal suffered minor injuries.

What could the subject have done that day to still be alive today? Should not have committed prior crimes that would cause a Drug Task Force to look for him to serve him warrants. Should not have fled from the police when they found him. Should have complied with Officer Deal's lawful orders and peacefully surrendered. Should not have fought with the officer, causing him to fear for his life.

Justified use of deadly force? YES, West had shown himself to be violent in the past and continued that violence when, first, by putting officers' lives in danger by fleeing from them, and, then again, by physically fighting with Officer Deal. Fighting a violent criminal by himself in the woods, Officer Deal had reasonable cause to believe that if West got the better of him by a lucky punch or submission hold, he would kill him with his duty weapon.

Name: Ethan Austin Murray
Date: 5/4/2019   **Location:** Spokane, WA
FACTORS (1,2,3,4,12,19)

Criminal History/Involved: Yes, Murray has spent time in jail /Yes, he was unlawfully fleeing from police.

Mental Illness: Yes, Murray was diagnosed with schizophrenia.

Substance Abuse History/Involved: Yes, Murray struggled with drug addiction./Yes, witnesses reported that Murray had appeared to be high on drugs and was acting irrationally.

Race/Sex/Age: White/Male/25

Officer(s) Involved: Spokane's Sheriff Deputy Joseph Wallace.

What prompted the initial contact with police? At approximately 5:20 p.m. on May 4, officers responded to an apartment complex where numerous 911 calls had reported that a person was acting strangely and running around shirtless in the vicinity of children[415].

Actions taken by subject toward police: Upon seeing two deputies arrive, Ethan Murray took off running to the nearby woods. When Deputy Wallace caught up to him, Murray cursed at the Deputy and refused Wallace's lawful orders to show his hands[416].

Reactions by the police: Fearing that the uncooperative Murray was reaching for a weapon when he put his hand in his pocket against the Deputy's orders to not do so, Wallace shot Murray six times, killing him.

Outcome of investigation into the fatal police incident: A joint investigation is being done by the Spokane Investigational Regional Response Team and Spokane Police Department.

Miscellaneous: A witness reported seeing Murray take "something out of his pocket before the deputy fired his weapon," and hearing a deputy repeatedly say, "Put it down."[417] Murray's mother recounted his issues with mental illness, drug addiction, and homelessness. This is what happens when mentally ill people are not confined for their own protection and the safety of others.

What could the subject have done that day to still be alive today? Should have been on proper medication in a mental institution or been properly supervised. Should not have acted strangely around children, causing people to call 911. Should not have run from the responding law enforcement officers. Should have complied with the deputy's commands to peacefully surrender. Should not have made a furtive movement with his hand to his pockets.

Justified use of deadly force? YES, Deputy Wallace warned Murray numerous times to show his hands and peacefully surrender. Instead, Murray made a furtive movement to an area typically used to hide a weapon, causing the deputy to reasonably fear for his own safety and justifiably use lethal force.

Name: Luke H. Patterson
Date: 5/23/2019   **Location:** Montgomery, NY
FACTORS (1,4,8,19)

Criminal History/Involved: Unknown./No.

Mental Illness: None reported, however Patterson did act irrationally in this incident, so possibly he had a mental illness or was under the influence of alcohol/drugs.

Substance Abuse History/Involved: Unknown./None reported.

Race/Sex/Age: White/Male/41

Officer(s) Involved: New York State Police troopers

What prompted the initial contact with police? At approximately 2 a.m. on May 23, two troopers responded to a call of an abandoned vehicle blocking the highway. After spotting the vehicle, the troopers found Luke Patterson walking less than a mile away so one of the troopers exited the police vehicle to talk with Patterson and find out what happened[418].

Actions taken by subject toward police: Patterson refused to comply or cooperate with the troopers as they questioned him[419].

Reactions by the police: When Patterson attempted to get into the troopers' vehicle, one of the troopers shot him multiple times, killing him.

Outcome of investigation into the fatal police incident: NY State Attorney General Letitia James presented the shooting to a grand jury. The grand jury did not indict the officers involved.

Miscellaneous: "Patterson was a restaurant owner and community activist"[420].

What could the subject have done that day to still be alive today? Should have complied with the lawful orders of the troopers and cooperated with their questioning. Should not have attempted to get into the troopers' vehicle.

Justified use of deadly force? Patterson acted irrationally and uncooperatively when confronted by the trooper. So, when he attempted to get into the troopers' vehicle, it was reasonable to fear that he did so for nefarious reasons. Given the confined space and vulnerability of the trooper driving the vehicle, **YES**, Patterson was justifiably shot before he could harm the trooper.

Name: Jesse Sarey
Date: 5/31/2019   **Location:** Auburn, WA
FACTORS (1,2,3,4,12,14,15,19)

Criminal History/Involved: Yes, subject had multiple previous arrests and a current warrant for "escape from community custody and failing to register as a sex offender"[421]./Yes, disorderly conduct and resisting arrest.

Mental Illness: Yes, Sarey had been involuntarily committed for psychiatric evaluation numerous times in the past, and one witness thought he was "having a breakdown"[422].

Substance Abuse History/Involved: Unknown./Yes, toxicology from autopsy showed that Sarey had methamphetamines in his system[423].

Race/Sex/Age: Asian/Male/26

Officer(s) Involved: Auburn Police Officer Jeff Nelson

What prompted the initial contact with police? During the evening of May 31, police responded to a 911 call of a man who was creating a disturbance outside a store by "throwing items at vehicles, hitting and kicking walls, creating havoc"[424]. Upon arriving in the area, Officer Nelson encountered Sarey and can be seen on his dashcam video telling Sarey that he was under arrest for disorderly conduct.

Actions taken by subject toward police: Sarey refused to put his hands behind his back to be arrested and instead fought with Officer Nelson. During the scuffle Sarey reached around Nelson, unsuccessfully attempting to grab his gun, but he managed to dislodge Nelson's knife out of his uniform pocket.

Reactions by the police: Fearing that Sarey had gained control of his knife and was going to stab him, Nelson shot Sarey twice, killing him.

Outcome of investigation into the fatal police incident: King County Prosecutor Dan Satterberg charged Nelson with second-degree murder and first-degree assault, alleging that Nelson rushed into the situation causing it to escalate. Video evidence and eyewitness testimony both refute Nelson's account[425].

Miscellaneous: Audio and dashcam video show the officer struggling to control Sarey. Officer Nelson was injured in the incident.

What could the subject have done that day to still be alive today? Should not have created a disturbance and caused people to call 911 on him. Should have complied with the officer's lawful commands and peacefully be arrested. Should not have fought with the officer, injured him, and attempted to gain control of his gun and/or knife.

Justified use of deadly force? YES, Sarey physically resisted Officer Nelson's efforts to arrest him and then escalated the situation by trying to grab the officers' duty weapon. When Nelson became fearful that Sarey had taken his knife he had reasonable cause to believe that Sarey was going to use it against him. It sounds bad that Nelson's knife which Sarey knocked off his uniform was placed upon a car by a witness two seconds before the first shot, however when physically fighting with Sarey, Nelson could have been unaware that Sarey did not have it. Ultimately, Sarey should have peacefully complied and remained alive.

Name: Thomas Goodeyes Gay
Date: 6/1/2019   **Location:** Bartlesville, OK
FACTORS (1,2,3,4,12,14,19)

Criminal History/Involved: Yes, Gay had recently violated a protection order put in place by his wife./No, Gay's actions were paranoid and delusional, but not criminal, until he threatened the officers.

Mental Illness: Yes, family members said Gay was acting erratic and paranoid.

Substance Abuse History/Involved: Yes./Yes, autopsy showed that Gay had methamphetamine in his system.

Race/Sex/Age: Native American/Male/35

Officer(s) Involved: Bartlesville Police Officers Pitts and Lewis.

What prompted the initial contact with police? Around 8 p.m. on June 1, officers responded to a 911 call from Thomas Gay's father requesting his son be removed from the house because he was acting strangely and was possibly on something. Gay's father and brother waited outside the house for the police to arrive[426].

Actions taken by subject toward police: Upon seeing the police enter his house along with his father, Gay retreated back to a bedroom while holding something in his hand. Gay refused to comply with the officer's orders and acted belligerent.

Reactions by the police: The officers ordered Gay not to go to the bedroom and tased him several times to stop him from doing so. The tase had no effect and the officers ended up in the bedroom with Gay where he grabbed an object and appeared ready to use it as a weapon-prompting one of the officers to shoot him in the leg. When Gay again tried to use the object as a weapon, the officer shot him again, killing him[427].

Outcome of investigation into the fatal police incident: Oklahoma State Bureau of Investigation provided a 130-page report to the Washington County District Attorney's office which subsequently cleared the officers involved in the shooting.

Miscellaneous: Gay was a large man, and his brother was so alarmed by his erratic behavior on that night that he had armed himself with a knife for fear that Gay may try to hurt him or their father.

What could the subject have done that day to still be alive today? Should not have acted so strangely that his family becomes afraid of him and calls the police to have him leave the house. Should have complied with the officers' lawful orders. Should not have run away from the officers, grabbed an object, and tried to use it as a weapon on the officers.

Justified use of deadly force? YES, Gay failed to comply with the officers' lawful orders and instead grabbed an object that they feared could be used as a weapon. Despite numerous attempts to get Thomas to cooperate, including the use of less-than-lethal force, Gay attempted to use an object as a weapon, thereby making the officers reasonably fear for their safety and justifiably shoot him.

THIS IS NOT AN UNARMED SUBJECT SO FACTORS (1,2,3,8,9,11,13,20) ARE NOT INCLUDED IN STATISTICS

Name: Kevin Pudlik

Date: 6/3/2019   **Location:** Detroit, MI

Criminal History/Involved: Unknown./Yes, two loaded handguns, cocaine, and MDMA (Ecstasy/Molly) pills were found in the vehicle Pudlik was in.

Mental Illness: Unknown.

Substance Abuse History/Involved: Unknown./Yes, cocaine and MDMA were found in the vehicle.

Race/Sex/Age: Black/Male/41

Officer(s) Involved: Three Detroit police officers and one Michigan State Police trooper.

What prompted the initial contact with police? On the afternoon of June 3, Detroit Police attempted to pull over a vehicle with no license plate and which was involved in a shooting the previous weekend. The driver, Christopher Lee Cavin refused to pull over and took his passenger, Kevin Pudlik, and the police on a dangerous vehicle pursuit[428].

Actions taken by subject toward police: During the chase, both Pudlik and Cavin made gestures trying to get something at their feet. When an officer went to arrest the men as the car stopped after spinning out of control, Cavin accelerated and almost pinned the officer against a wall as he tried to escape again.

Reactions by the police: Fearing one of the Detroit officers was about to get run over, the other officers and trooper shot into the car, killing Pudlik and injuring Cavin.

Outcome of investigation into the fatal police incident: Shooting was determined to be justified.

Miscellaneous: Two loaded handguns were found on the floorboard of the passenger side, exactly where police saw Pudlik reaching-so this is not an "unarmed" incident." Cavin was charged with "second-degree murder, assault with intent to murder, two counts of fleeing and eluding police officers, two counts of possession of a controlled substance, two counts of carrying a concealed weapon, and five counts of felony firearm"[429].

What could the subject have done that day to still be alive today? Should not have been in a car that was linked to a previous shooting or with a driver who fled from the police. Should not have made attempts to access a weapon.

Justified use of deadly force? YES, a motor vehicle was being used as a deadly weapon against one of the officers who had exited his vehicle to arrest the two men who he believed were boxed in. Given the driver's exhibited disregard for human life during the high-speed pursuit and ramming of the police vehicles, the officers had reasonable cause to believe that officers' life was in danger.

Name: Ryan Twyman

Date: 6/6/2019   **Location:** Los Angeles, CA

FACTORS (1,2,8,11,19)15?

Criminal History/Involved: Yes, Twyman had previous weapons convictions; he was on felony probation, and weapons were found in his house during a search two months earlier./Yes, he was wanted on weapons charges and had attempted assault on a law enforcement officer.

Mental Illness: Unknown.

Substance Abuse History/Involved: Unknown./None stated.

Race/Sex/Age: Black/Male/24

Officer(s) Involved: Two Los Angeles Sheriff's Department deputies

What prompted the initial contact with police? On June 6, two deputies approached Twyman while he sat in his car parked in an apartment building parking lot. The deputies intended on arresting Twyman for weapons charges related to the firearms found during a search of his residence[430].

Actions taken by subject toward police: Twyman used his car as a weapon, reversing from the parking spot at which time the open car door struck the deputy who was standing near it, briefly dragging him.

Reactions by the police: As Twyman's vehicle was used as a deadly instrument against the deputy, both deputies opened fire roughly 34 times on the vehicle, killing Twyman. The passenger in the vehicle was unharmed[431].

Outcome of investigation into the fatal police incident: The incident is still under investigation.

Miscellaneous: Video of the shooting is available online.

What could the subject have done that day to still be alive today? Should not have committed prior weapons crimes and been on probation. Should not have had weapons discovered in his house while on felony probation. Should have complied with the deputy's commands and peacefully surrendered. Should not have attempted to flee from the police as they approached his vehicle. Should not have used his vehicle as a weapon against the deputy.

Justified use of deadly force? YES, the deputy reasonably feared for his life when Twyman struck him with the vehicle while trying to escape lawful arrest. Exposed out in the open and with no place to hide from the vehicle, the deputy and his partner were justified in using lethal force to stop Twyman from running the deputy over again.

Name: Juan Manuel Moreno Jr.

Date: 6/12/2019   **Location:** Dallas, TX

FACTORS (1,2,8,17)

Criminal History/Involved: Yes, Moreno had prior charges for drugs and theft[432]./Yes, Moreno was driving a stolen vehicle and fleeing from police.

Mental History: Unknown.

Substance Abuse History/Involved: Yes, Moreno had a prior drug-related arrest./None stated.

Race/Sex/Age: Latino/Male/35

Officer(s) Involved: Farmers Branch Police Officer Michael Dunn

What prompted the initial contact with police? At approximately 7 p.m. on June 12, several Farmers Branch police officers were surveilling a suspected stolen truck parked in a lot[433].

Actions taken by subject toward police: As the officers approached the truck in a marked police vehicle, Moreno moved the truck out of its parked position and quickly drove past the officers with his passenger side door still open and debris flying into the street as he tried to speed away[434].

Reactions by the police: As Moreno drove the truck past him, Officer Dunn fired at Moreno, killing him.

Outcome of investigation into the fatal police incident: Dallas County grand jury indicted Farmers Branch Police Officer Michael Dunn for murder. The indictment and investigation was completed in just over a week while 40 other murders are still without any indictments[435].

Miscellaneous: Video of the incident is available[436].

What could the subject have done that day to still be alive today? Should not have been in a stolen vehicle. Should not have driven away from uniformed police officers attempting to stop him.

Justified use of deadly force? Looking at the video it does not appear that the truck was being driven at the officer. **NO,** unless Moreno posed a deadly threat to someone else if he escaped, the officer was not justified to shoot him at that time. If the officer reasonably feared that the truck was being used as a weapon and driven at him, or it appeared that Moreno was pointing a gun at the officer as he drove by, then Dunn would have been justified in using deadly force. But it did not appear so on the video. Either way, if Moreno did not attempt to flee in a stolen vehicle, he would still be alive. Instead, Moreno is dead regardless of whether Officer Dunn is found to be justified or not.

THIS IS NOT AN UNARMED SUBJECT SO FACTORS (1,2,8,9,12,14,15,19) ARE NOT INCLUDED IN STATISTICS

Name: Paul David Rea

Date: 6/27/2019   **Location:** Los Angeles, CA

Criminal History/Involved: Unknown./Yes, criminal possession of a weapon and assaulting a police officer.

Mental Illness: Unknown.

Substance Abuse History/Involved: Unknown./None stated.

Race/Sex/Age: Latino/Male/18

Officer(s) Involved: Two Los Angeles County Sheriff's deputies

What prompted the initial contact with police? Around 11 a.m. on June 27, deputies stopped a vehicle in which Paul Rea was a passenger after observing a traffic infraction[437].

Actions taken by subject toward police: Upon the deputy's instructions, Rea exited the vehicle to be searched, but then physically assaulted that deputy, giving him a concussion and temporarily dazing him.

Reactions by the police: Upon being struck in the face by Rea so hard, he blacked out. The deputy reacted in survival mode and grabbed Rea in a bearhug, at which point he felt a gun in Rea's waistband. At that point, Rea broke free of the deputy. Then the deputy, fearing that Rea was going to access that gun and kill him, fired his duty weapon at Rea, killing him[438].

Outcome of investigation into the fatal police incident: Los Angeles District Attorney's Office determined that the officer acted lawfully.

Miscellaneous: Upon searching Rea as he lie on the ground, a loaded, Glock 40 caliber handgun was found on him–so this is not really an "unarmed" incident.

What could the subject have done that day to still be alive today? Should not have physically assaulted a law enforcement officer during a traffic stop. Should not have illegally possessed a weapon that a deputy could find, and fear would be used against him. Should have complied with the deputy's lawful orders.

Justified use of deadly force? YES, Rea was the aggressor, physically assaulting a deputy, causing him significant temporary injury. In that injured state, having just discovered a gun on Rea, the deputy reasonably feared that Rea was going to use that gun as soon as he broke free of his bear hug–so he justifiably shot Rea.

Name: Li Xi Wang
Date: 7/3/2019   **Location:** Chino, CA
FACTORS (1,2,3,16)

Criminal History/Involved: Unknown./Yes, he was involved in illegal marijuana trafficking.

Mental Illness: Unknown.

Substance Abuse History/Involved: Unknown./None stated, but incident involved marijuana trafficking.

Race/Sex/Age: Asian/Male/49

Officer(s) Involved: Chino Police officers

What prompted the initial contact with police? On July 3, police conducted a raid on a house suspected of illegally running a "marijuana trafficking operation"[439]. After confirming with a woman taken out of the house that nobody else was inside, the police conducted a search.

Actions taken by subject toward police: Wang hid behind a door until he was spotted and instructed to put his hands up.

Reactions by the police: One of the officers shot Wang just as another was ordering him to put his hands up[440].

Outcome of investigation into the fatal police incident: Incident is being investigated by the San Bernardino County Sheriff's Office and District Attorney.

Miscellaneous: The bodycam video shows that one officer was approaching the door as another officer is seen walking past it. The officer who shoots can be seen pulling the trigger and saying, "Oh shit!" almost simultaneously. It looked like it was an accidental discharge, not an intentional shooting. During the raid, "nearly 1,500 marijuana plants, $35,000 in cash" and grand theft of electricity "in excess of $105,000"[441] was discovered.

What could the subject have done that day to still be alive today? Should not have been inside a house that was part of an illegal marijuana trafficking operation. Should have peacefully surrendered and not have hidden from the police.

Justified use of deadly force? NO, while Wang was hiding, he did not pose a threat, as evidenced in the bodycam video. It appears that the officer shot him due to an **accidental discharge** which is an issue of proper weapons discipline. The officer should have kept his trigger finger out of his trigger guard until he had it aimed at a threat which he intended to shoot.

Name: Joshua Ortiz

Date: 7/5/2019   **Location:** Oak View, CA

FACTORS (1,2,4,12,14,15,19)

Criminal History/Involved: Unknown./Yes, Ortiz assaulted a police officer.

Mental Illness: None reported, but Ortiz was homeless and walking in and out of traffic–two indications that he might have had a mental illness.

Substance Abuse History/Involved: Unknown./None stated.

Race/Sex/Age: Latino/Male/21

Officer(s) Involved: California Highway Patrol (CHP) officer

What prompted the initial contact with police? At approximately 6 a.m. on July 5, a CHP officer responded to a 911 call of a man posing a safety hazard by walking in and out of traffic on the highway[442].

Actions taken by subject toward police: When verbally confronted by the CHP officer, Ortiz physically assaulted him[443].

Reactions by the police: Alone and fearing for his life from the physical attack by the subject along the side of a highway, the CHP officer fired one shot at Ortiz, killing him.

Outcome of investigation into the fatal police incident: CHP and the local Sheriff's office are investigating the incident.

Miscellaneous: The officer suffered minor injuries during the fight with Ortiz and was treated at a local hospital.

What could the subject have done that day to still be alive today? Should not have walked into an active highway, causing citizens to call 911 out of fear that someone was going to get hurt. Should have obeyed the officer's lawful orders. Should not have physically attacked the officer.

Justified use of deadly force? YES, Ortiz physically assaulted the CHP officer. Already injured by the attack, the CHP officer reasonably feared that Ortiz would knock him out or gain control of his duty weapon and kill him, so the officer preemptively used lethal force.

Name: Derek Luis Antonio Sanchez
Date: 7/14/2019   **Location:** Kirkland, WA
FACTORS (1,2,4,19)

Criminal History/Involved: Unknown./Yes, domestic incident involving endangering a child.

Mental Illness: Sanchez was at a homeless camp and acting erratic, two indicators linked with mental illness.

Substance Abuse History/Involved: Unknown./None stated.

Race/Sex/Age: Latino/Male/35

Officer(s) Involved: Kirkland police officers

What prompted the initial contact with police? During the morning of July 14, Police responded to a 911 call about a domestic dispute at a homeless camp between a woman and her ex-boy-friend, Derek Sanchez. Sanchez reportedly grabbed the 18-month-old son they had in common and refused to give him back to the concerned mother. The officers spoke with Sanchez for an hour, trying to get him to release the toddler[444].

Actions taken by subject toward police: Sanchez acted erratically and ignored the officer's lawful commands to hand the toddler over to the mother[445].

Reactions by the police: When it appeared that Sanchez was beyond reasoning with and the young boy's life was in danger, one of the officers shot Sanchez in the head, killing him.

Outcome of investigation into the fatal police incident: The King's County Sheriff Office is investigating.

What could the subject have done that day to still be alive today? Should not have taken his son away from the mother against her wishes. Should have complied with the officer's lawful commands to surrender the boy to his mother. Should not have acted irrationally, causing the officers to fear for the young child's safety.

Justified use of deadly force? YES, based on Sanchez's erratic behavior and refusal to peacefully surrender the delicate young child to the mother or the police, the officer justifiably used deadly force out of a reasonable fear that Sanchez was imminently going to hurt the child.

Name: Josef Delon Richardson
Date: 7/25/2019　　**Location:** Port Allen, LA
FACTORS (1,2,3,12,14,19)

Criminal History/Involved: Yes, Richardson had at least 31 prior arrests, including charges for drug possession and intent to sell the same, resisting arrest, obstructing justice, battery of an officer, and robbery. He was on probation at the time of the incident./Yes, Richardson was actively selling drugs out of the motel room.

Mental Illness: Unknown.

Substance Abuse History/Involved: Yes, Richardson had prior drug arrests./Yes, toxicology reports showed that Richardson had illegal substances including methamphetamine, THC, and cocaine in his system at the time of the incident.

Race/Sex/Age: Black/Male/38

Officer(s) Involved: West Baton Rouge Parish Sheriff's Office (WBRSO) Deputies Matranga, Brett Cavaliere, Thomas Carpenter, and James Woody

What prompted the initial contact with police? On July 25, deputies served a no-knock warrant at the hotel room where an informant had recently bought drugs from Josef Richardson. Also in the room with Richardson was his girlfriend who would be arrested for drug possession (marijuana, methamphetamine, and two digital scales). Upon seeing Richardson in the room and thrusting his left hand into his waistband, Deputy Cavaliere grabbed Richardson to gain control over him in case he had just accessed a weapon. An informant told the deputies that Richardson was armed[446].

Actions taken by subject toward police: Richardson physically struggled with Deputy Cavaliere, breaking his hand free from his waistband, and turned toward Cavaliere.

Reactions by the police: Fearing that Richardson had a gun in his hand that he was about to shoot Cavaliere with, Deputy Matranga shot Richardson in the back of his head, killing him.

Outcome of investigation into the fatal police incident: Louisiana State Police (LSP) investigators and legal analysts with the Louisiana Department of Justice determined that Richardson's actions and prior violent history justified Deputy Matranga's use of lethal force[447].

What could the subject have done that day to still be alive today? Should not have been taking drugs or dealing them in a hotel. Should have complied with the deputy's lawful commands and efforts to peacefully arrest him. Should not have physically struggled with a deputy and made the deputies fear for their own lives.

Justified use of deadly force? YES, Richardson was believed to be armed, had a history of violence toward police, and was physically resisting the deputy's efforts to peacefully put him in custody. When Richardson made a furtive movement with his hand from his waistband and toward the deputy he was struggling with, Deputy Matranga reasonably feared for the safety of that deputy's life and used deadly force.

Name: Margarita Victoria Brooks
Date: 8/1/2019   **Location:** Arlington, TX
FACTORS (13,20)

Criminal History/Involved: Unknown./None.

Mental Illness: None reported, however, Brooks was homeless which is a key indicator associated with mental illness.

Substance Abuse History/Involved: Unknown./None stated.

Race/Sex/Age: White/Female/30

Officer(s) Involved: Arlington Police Officer Ravi Singh

What prompted the initial contact with police? During the afternoon of August 1, Police received a 911 call that a woman passed out on the grass in a commercial business area. Officer Singh responded to the area and called out to that woman, Ms. Brooks, upon seeing her at a distance, asking if she was okay[448].

Actions taken by subject toward police: Brooks told the officer that she was fine, but her dog took off running at the officer.

Reactions by the police: Officer Singh started yelling at the dog to stop as he simultaneously retreated and fired three shots at it. One of those shots hit Brooks in the stomach, killing her[449].

Outcome of investigation into the fatal police incident: Officer Singh's shooting was brought before a grand jury, and he was indicted for criminally negligent homicide[450].

Miscellaneous: Officer Singh resigned from the police department three months after the shooting[451].

What could the subject have done that day to still be alive today? Should not have been passed out in public, causing citizens to be concerned for her welfare and call the police. Should have had her dog on a leash. Noting that these two things should not be confused with placing blame on the victim, Ms. Brooks clearly did not deserve to have lethal force used against her.

Justified use of deadly force? NA, this was not a case of deliberate deadly force being used against the victim. Officer Singh was lawfully using deadly force at a loose dog that was charging at him. Unfortunately, one of the three bullets Officer Singh fired at the dog ended up hitting Ms. Brooks. It was a tragic accident directly caused by the actions of Brook's canine companion.

Name: David Ingle
Date: 8/13/2019   **Location:** Joplin, MO
FACTORS (1,2,4,12,14,15,19)

Criminal History/Involved: Unknown./Yes, Ingle resisted arrest and attempted to assault an officer.

Mental Illness: Yes, Ingle was diagnosed with schizophrenia and "prone to episodes of paranoia and delusion"[452]

Substance Abuse History/Involved: Unknown./None. Toxicology report showed that he did not have any illegal substances in his system at the time of incident. Ingle's father thinks that he was not taking his prescribed medications for mental illness.

Race/Sex/Age: White/Male/31

Officer(s) Involved: Joplin Police Officers Laken Rawlins (F) and Grant Meador

What prompted the initial contact with police? At approximately 9:20 p.m. on August 13, Officers Rawlins and Meador responded to a 911 call of a "suspicious male" in the street "screaming and hollering and cussing"[453]. Upon arrival, Officer Rawlins saw Ingle shirtless lying face down in the street, yelling to himself. Officer Rawlins instructed Ingle not to move, and he complied. When Officer Meador arrived, both officers walked over to Ingle and told him not to move, so they could handcuff him.

Actions taken by subject toward police: Ingle did not comply with the officers' orders, instead he tried to get up even as the officers tased him. Despite being tased, Ingle stood up and went after Officer Rawlins who had just been hit in the hand with a taser prong, possibly by Meador.[454]

Reactions by the police: As Ingle went to attack the injured Officer Rawlins, Officer Meador shot Ingle, killing him.

Outcome of investigation into the fatal police incident: Joplin Police Department as well as the Missouri State Highway Patrol concluded that the officers acted lawfully and did not violate any departmental polices.

Miscellaneous: Videos from the dashcam and both officers' bodycams are available from the Joplin Police Department[455]. Time from police contact with Ingle on the ground to his being shot was 30 seconds.

What could the subject have done that day to still be alive today? Should have taken his prescribed psychological medications or been supervised. Should not have been in the street, causing a disturbance and scaring his neighbors so badly that they called 911. Should have complied with the officers' lawful commands. Should not have resisted officers' efforts to handcuff him. Should not have gotten up from the prone position and tried to attack Officer Rawlins.

Justified use of deadly force? YES, Ingle presented a deadly threat to the officers. Observing that Ingle was having a psychotic episode, was unaffected by the taser, and was about to attack the already-injured Officer Rawlins, Officer Meador reasonably feared for her life and justifiably used deadly force to stop Ingle.

Name: Riley Eugene Peay

Date: 8/22/2019   **Location:** Glennville,GA

FACTORS (1,2,4,12,14,15,19)

Criminal History/Involved: Unknown./Yes, Peay was trespassing by entering the pawn shop since years before they filed a trespass complaint against him. While inside the pawn shop, Peay assaulted an officer[456].

Mental Illness: Unknown, however, Peay exhibited unprovoked violence and was suicidal.

Substance Abuse History/Involved: Unknown./None stated.

Race/Sex/Age: White/Male/39

Officer(s) Involved: Georgia Department of Community Supervision Probation Officer

What prompted the initial contact with police? At around 4:30 p.m. on August 22, a probation officer was in the pawn shop waiting for another probation officer to arrive[457].

Actions taken by subject toward police: Peay entered the pawn shop, and, without provocation, he attacked the probation officer, spitting on him and punching him several times in the face[458].

Reactions by the police: The officer retreated from Peay, yelling at him to stop. Peay ignored his commands and continued to attack the officer, at which point the officer shot him in the shoulder. Wounded, Peay continued to attack the officer, prompting a second and lethal shot.

Outcome of investigation into the fatal police incident: Georgia Bureau of Investigations has the lead.

What could the subject have done that day to still be alive today? Should not have physically assaulted an officer. Should have complied with the officer's lawful commands to stop assaulting him. Should have stopped attacking the officer after he was shot the first time.

Justified use of deadly force? YES, Peay assaulted a law enforcement officer and continued that assault even after being warned and then shot. The officer was injured by Peay's attack and had reasonable cause to fear Peay would kill him if he gained control of his weapon.

Name: Chad Michael Breinholt
Date: 8/23/2019   **Location:** West Valley City, UT
FACTORS (1,2,3,4,5,10,12,14,19)

Criminal History/Involved: Unknown./Yes, public intoxication and driving while intoxicated.

Mental Illness: None reported, however, Breinholt was clearly in an altered mental state.

Substance Abuse History/Involved: Yes, Breinholt had a history of drug addiction./Yes, Breinholt was intoxicated at time of incident.

Race/Sex/Age: White/Male/31

Officer(s) Involved: West Valley City Police Officers

What prompted the initial contact with police? At approximately 7 p.m. on August 23, officers responded to a 911 call for a man causing a disturbance at a business. That man ended up being Chad Breinholt, and, upon interviewing him, the officers determined that he was drunk and had been driving while intoxicated so they arrested him. While Breinholt was being processed at the police station, he informed the officers that he had a gun in his shoe[459].

Actions taken by subject toward police: When two of the officers tried to take Breinholt's shoe, Breinholt refused to cooperate, started grappling with them, and was able to get his hands on one of their guns.

Reactions by the police: After failing to be able to pull Breinholt's hands off the officers' gun and after warning him to do so before shooting, one of the officers shot Breinholt in the head, killing him[460].

Outcome of investigation into the fatal police incident: The Salt Lake County District Attorney's Office is investigating the shooting.

Miscellaneous: Breinholt did not actually have a gun in his shoe. Bodycam video shows the incident inside the DUI processing room[461].

What could the subject have done that day to still be alive today? Should not have caused a disturbance at a business that caused people to call 911. Should not have driven while intoxicated, leading to his arrest. Should have complied with the officers and peacefully given up the shoe in which he alleged to have a gun. Should not have physically fought with the officers and grabbed one of their guns.

Justified use of deadly force? YES, the officers had reasonable cause to fear that Breinholt would use lethal force against them if he gained control over the officer's weapon and was able to take it out of the holster.

Name: Channara Tom Pheap
Date: 8/26/2019   **Location:** Knoxville, TN
FACTORS (1,2,3,8,9,12,14,15,19)

Criminal History/Involved: Yes, Pheap had prior arrests for first-degree robbery, convictions for driving with a suspended license, and evading arrest[462]./Yes, Pheap had cocaine on him, was driving while under the influence, involved in a hit-and-run, and assaulted an officer.

Mental Illness: Unknown.

Substance Abuse History/Involved: Unknown./Yes, the toxicology report showed Pheap had cocaine in his system at the time of the incident.

Race/Sex/Age: Black/Male/33

Officer(s) Involved: Knoxville Police Department Officer Dylan Williams

What prompted the initial contact with police? On August 26, using information gained from witness statements, PO Williams tracked down a vehicle that had just been involved in a hit-and-run. Upon finding out that Channara Pheap was the registered owner of the vehicle, Williams approached Pheap in his apartment complex[463].

Actions taken by subject toward police: While being questioned by PO Dylan Williams for his involvement in a hit-and-run, Pheap attacked the officer. Pheap choked PO Williams, grabbed his taser, and used it on him during the fight[464].

Reactions by the police: Fearful Pheap was going to disarm and kill him after incapacitating him with Williams' own taser, Officer Williams shot and killed Pheap in self-defense.

Outcome of investigation into the fatal police incident: Knox County District Attorney General Charme Allen determined that it was a justified shooting.

Miscellaneous: Audio and video footage of most of the incident is captured[465].

What could the subject have done that day to still be alive today? Should not have fled from the scene of an accident. Should not have physically assaulted the officer questioning him about the accident. Should have complied with the officer's commands and peacefully surrendered. Should not have taken the officer's taser and shot him with it.

Justified use of deadly force? YES, Officer Williams had been assaulted, choked, and shot with his own taser. Unable to reach his K9 partner, Officer Williams had reasonable cause to believe that Pheap meant to inflict lethal harm on him and shooting Pheap was his only recourse to survive.

Name: John J. Carras
Date: 9/5/2019   **Location:** Hartford, CT
FACTORS (1,2,12,14,15,19)

Criminal History/Involved: Unknown./Yes, domestic violence assault and assault of an officer.

Mental Illness: Unknown

Substance Abuse History/Involved: Unknown./None stated.

Race/Sex/Age: White/Male/43

Officer(s) Involved: East Hartford Police Officers Andre Lyew and Daniel Zaleski

What prompted the initial contact with police? Officers responded to a 911 call of domestic violence at a residence around 6 :15 p.m. on September 5. Upon arriving at the residence, the officers encountered Carras choking his wife in the kitchen. The officers ordered Carras, "Get off her!"[466] and pointed their gun or taser at him according to a neighbor who had gone over to help at the pleading of Carras' young children.

Actions taken by subject toward police: Carras let go of his wife and left the kitchen as ordered by the officers, but then returned to the room and started fighting with the officers[467].

Reactions by the police: While being physically assaulted by Carras in the small confines of a kitchen full of readily available improvised weapons, the officers shot Carras, killing him.

Outcome of investigation into the fatal police incident: The shooting is being investigated by the Windham State Attorney's Office and CT State Police.

Miscellaneous: No videos of the incident are available, but ample witness testimony is. The officers sustained minor injuries from Carras' assault on them.

What could the subject have done that day to still be alive today? Should not have physically assaulted his wife, causing his children to seek help from the neighbors. Should have complied with the officer's lawful orders and peacefully surrendered. Should not have physically attacked the officers.

Justified use of deadly force? YES, having choked his wife into unconsciousness, Carras demonstrated a violent disregard for human life, which he then directed at the two officers. Fearing for their lives from his physical attack, they justifiably used lethal force before it could be used against them.

Name: Melvin Watkins
Date: 9/14/2019   **Location:** Baton Rouge, LA
FACTORS (1,2,3,8,11,19)

Criminal History/Involved: Unknown./Yes, disorderly conduct, criminal mischief, and attempted assault of an officer.

Mental Illness: Unknown.

Substance Abuse History/Involved: Unknown./Yes, Watkins had been drinking.

Race/Sex/Age: Black/Male/54

Officer(s) Involved: Baton Rouge Sheriff's Deputy James Hammet

What prompted the initial contact with police? A Sheriff's deputy responded to a 911 call of a man creating a disturbance at a house party around 5:30 p.m. on September 14. Melvin Watkins had crashed the party, argued with some guests, and became violent, hitting a door with a screwdriver. Watkins was asked to leave, and the police were called. Upon arriving, the deputy parked his car in the middle of the street and got out on foot asking where the man was[468].

Actions taken by subject toward police: Watkins, already in his vehicle as the deputy arrived, hit the gas, and drove his vehicle at Deputy Hammett who was on foot.

Reactions by the police: As Watkins accelerated his car at the deputy, Hammett had nowhere to run, so he shot at Watkins twice through his windshield in self-defense[469].

Outcome of investigation into the fatal police incident: Preliminary findings by the Sheriff's Office are that the deputy was justified in his use of lethal force.

Miscellaneous: Testimony of numerous witnesses support the officer's actions.

What could the subject have done that day to still be alive today? Should not have crashed a party and created a disturbance, causing the people to call 911. Should have kept the car parked and should have peacefully cooperated with the responding law enforcement officer. Should not have used the vehicle as a weapon and tried to run the deputy over.

Justified use of deadly force? YES, when Watkins ignored Deputy Hammet's verbal commands to stop the car as he accelerated toward him, the deputy was left with no option except lethal force to protect himself from being run over.

Name: Dewayne Morgan
Date: 9/29/2019   **Location:** Longview, TX
FACTORS (1,2,3,12,14,15,19)

Criminal History/Involved: Yes, Morgan spent 12 years in prison for aggravated assault with a deadly weapon[470]./Yes, burglary and assault of an officer.

Mental Illness: Unknown.

Substance Abuse History/Involved: Unknown./Yes, the police report indicates that Morgan appeared intoxicated or on drugs.

Race/Sex/Age: White/Male/37

Officer(s) Involved: Gregg County Sheriff's Deputy Logan Joines

What prompted the initial contact with police? During the night of September 29, Deputy Joines attempted to detain Morgan for questioning involving an attempted burglary that had just occurred.

Actions taken by subject toward police: Morgan ignored Joines' commands to stop as he ran from the officer and crossed over a highway on foot. When the deputy caught up to Joines on the side of the interstate, Morgan assaulted the deputy, pinning him to the ground, and started choking him to death.[471]

Reactions by the police: Fearing that he was about to go unconscious from being strangled by Morgan, Deputy Joines fired one shot into Morgan's upper body, killing him.

Outcome of investigation into the fatal police incident: The Texas Rangers are investigating the incident.

What could the subject have done that day to still be alive today? Should not have been suspected of attempting to burglarize a house. Should have complied with Deputy Goines' lawful orders and be questioned and/or detained. Should not have run from the deputy. Should not have assaulted and strangled the deputy.

Justified use of deadly force? YES, alone, on the side of the highway and being choked out by a violent criminal, Deputy Joines had reasonable cause to believe that he was going to be killed by Morgan unless he used lethal force.

INCIDENT GARNERING NATIONAL MEDIA ATTENTION AND PROTESTS

THIS IS NOT AN UNARMED SUBJECT SO FACTORS (1,9,12,19) ARE NOT INCLUDED IN STATISTICS

Name: Atatiana Jefferson
Date: 10/12/2019   **Location:** Fort Worth, TX

Criminal History/Involved: NA.

Mental Illness: NA.

Substance Abuse History/Involved: NA..

Race/Sex/Age: Black/Female/28

Officer(s) Involved: Fort Worth Police Officer Aaron Dean

What prompted the initial contact with police? Around 2:30 a.m. on October 12, while searching the outer perimeter of a house that a neighbor had called 911 to report was possibly being burglarized, PO Aaron Dean saw someone inside when he shone his flashlight in the window. Dean yelled, "Put your hands up–show me your hands"[472].

Actions taken by subject toward police: It was Atatiana Jefferson who was inside, and rightfully so, since it was her mother's house. Not realizing that it was the police outside her window and fearing for her safety, Atatiana took out her gun and pointed it at the window (not technically unarmed, though Atatiana did nothing wrong).

Reactions by the police: Upon seeing the gun in her hand, PO Dean shot and killed Atatiana[473].

Outcome of investigation into the fatal police incident: Officer Dean has been charged with murder by Tarrant County DA's office, mainly because he did not identify himself as a cop before shooting Jefferson[474].

Miscellaneous: Footage from the officer's bodycam is available at FOX 4 Staff[475].

What could the subject have done that day to still be alive today? Nothing, Atatiana bears no fault for legally arming herself within her house, believing that a possible intruder was outside in the middle of the night. This is not an "unarmed subject" who was shot by the police.

Justified use of deadly force? YES, in this case of tragic circumstances Atatiana did not deserve to be shot, but the officer was justified in using deadly force based upon his belief at that moment that the house was being burglarized and then seeing a gun in the hand of a subject inside the house on the other side of the window pointed toward him. For "police and city leaders" to say Jefferson's possession of a firearm at that moment "was not relevant to her death" shows how far political correctness has infiltrated this shooting and the mentality associated with police use of force when the subjects are black. This sentence from an article updating the public on the delays in Officer Dean's trail that does not even mention Jefferson holding and pointing a gun shows the media bias and lack of truthful reporting in such incidents: "When Jefferson heard some noise outside, she looked out of a bedroom window and Dean fired a shot, killing her, police have said"[476].

Name: Christopher Whitfield
Date: 10/14/2019   **Location:** Ethal, LA
FACTORS (1,2,4,12,14,16)

Criminal History/Involved: Yes, Whitfield had prior criminal convictions and had been arrested for previously breaking into the same gas station./Yes, Whitfield had just broken into a gas station and stolen raw chicken from it[477].

Mental Illness: Yes, Whitfield had a diagnosed mental illness.

Substance Abuse History/Involved: Unknown./None stated.

Race/Sex/Age: Black/Male/31

Officer(s) Involved: East Feliciana Parish Sheriff's Deputy Glenn Sims, Sr.

What prompted the initial contact with police? Upon responding to a 911 call about a break-in at a Texaco gasoline station at approximately 2:20 a.m. on October 14, Deputy Sims confronted Whitfield at the scene. Whitfield took off running from the store and the older Deputy fired a warning shot as he chased Whitfield[478].

Actions taken by subject toward police: Whitfield stopped running, but he physically attacked the deputy instead of peacefully surrendering.

Reactions by the police: As Whitfield attacked him, Deputy Sims' firearm was struck and accidentally discharged, killing Whitfield[479].

Outcome of investigation into the fatal police incident: A grand jury returned no true bill; the shooting was ruled as an accidental discharge.

Miscellaneous: It was discovered during the investigation that Deputy Sims had a criminal record, with convictions for "illegal discharge of a weapon, simple battery, and resisting an officer"[480]. Since Deputy Sims was also black, the incident was not able to be racialized by social justice activists.

What could the subject have done that day to still be alive today? Should not have committed a commercial burglary that would alert law enforcement to respond. Should have complied with the deputy's lawful order to stop. Should not have fled from the deputy. Should not have physically attacked the deputy.

Justified use of deadly force? NO, Deputy Sims did not intentionally use lethal force against Whitfield. This accidental discharge was a tragic accident that could have been prevented if Whitfield had immediately complied and if Sims exercised better handling of his weapon and kept his trigger finger out of the trigger guard.

Name: Cameron Ely

Date: 10/15/2019   **Location:** Hope Ranch, CA

FACTORS (1,2,4,5,10,19)

Criminal History/Involved: Unknown./Yes, Ely had just murdered his mother.

Mental Illness: None reported, however, Ely's actions were highly irregular and suicidal.

Substance Abuse History/Involved: Unknown./None stated.

Race/Sex/Age: White/Male/30

Officer(s) Involved: From Santa Barbara County Sheriff's Office: Sergeant Desiree Thome; Sheriff's Deputy Special Duty Jeremy Rogers; Sheriff's Deputy Phillip Farley; and Sheriff's Deputy John Gruttadaurio[481].

What prompted the initial contact with police? At around 8 p.m. on October 15, the deputies responded to a 911 call made by Cameron Ely from his house after he murdered his mother. Upon arrival, the deputies observed the dead woman and were told by Ely's father that his son had murdered her. The deputies encountered the younger Ely outside the house[482].

Actions taken by subject toward police: When confronted by the deputies, Ely told them that he had a gun. He moved toward them and "pretended to draw a weapon"[483].

Reactions by the police: Believing that Ely was armed and drawing his weapon to shoot them, the four officers fired 24 shots at Ely, killing him.

Outcome of investigation into the fatal police incident: The Santa Barbara District Attorney's Office found that the officer's acted reasonably given the circumstances and were justified in using deadly force[484].

Miscellaneous: Dashcam video of the incident can be seen and heard at *Law Enforcement Today*[485].

What could the subject have done that day to still be alive today? Should not have murdered his mother. Should not have called 911 to inform law enforcement of the murder. Should have complied with the lawful orders of deputies to peacefully surrender. Should not have told the deputies that he was armed and then motioned as if he was accessing that weapon to shoot them.

Justified use of deadly force? YES, the deputies were dealing with a violent man who had just killed his mother, told them he was armed with a deadly weapon, and motioned to access that weapon–making them each reasonably fear that they were in mortal danger from him.

Name: Robert S. Sikon III
Date: 11/16/2019   **Location:** Alliance, OH
FACTORS (1,2,3,8,14,17)

Criminal History/Involved: Yes, Sikon had previous convictions for aggravated menacing, theft, forgery, breaking and entering, and receiving stolen property./Yes, Sikon had active warrants and had unlawfully fled from the officer[486].

Mental Illness: Unknown

Substance Abuse History/Involved: Yes, the deputy was aware that Sikon was wanted for a drugs-related warrant./Yes, toxicology report showed that Sikon had methamphetamine in his system at the time of incident[487].

Race/Sex/Age: White/Male/41

Officer(s) Involved: Carroll County Sheriff's Deputy Jacob Baker

What prompted the initial contact with police? Around noon on November 16, Deputy Baker observed Sikon sitting in the passenger seat of a vehicle that drove by him. Recognizing Sikon and aware he had active warrants, Baker conducted a traffic stop of the vehicle to arrest him. During the stop Deputy Baker ordered Sikon out of the vehicle and grabbed him to put handcuffs on[488].

Actions taken by subject toward police: Sikon resisted Baker's efforts to handcuff him, and breaking free from Baker's grasp, he took off running.

Reactions by the police: Baker warned Sikon to stop running or he would be shot. When Sikon continued fleeing, Baker shot at him several times, hitting him in the back four times killing him[489].

Outcome of investigation into the fatal police incident: A grand jury indicted Deputy Baker for voluntary manslaughter on August 12, 2020[490].

Miscellaneous: No dashcam or bodycam video exists.

What could the subject have done that day to still be alive today? Should not have been wanted for warrants. Should have complied with the deputy's lawful order and be peacefully arrested. Should not have pushed past the deputy and fled on foot.

Justified use of deadly force? NO, while Sikon was wanted for warrants and broke the law by fleeing, he did not pose an immediate risk of serious bodily injury to the deputy or anyone else if he escaped. Baker will likely be found guilty … but that does not do any good to either Sikon or the children he left behind … so the moral of the story is–comply with the police, peacefully surrender, and have your day in court.

Name: Eliborio Rodrigues
Date: 11/20/2019   **Location:** Eugene, OR
FACTORS (1,2,3,4,9,12,14,15,19)

Criminal History/Involved: Yes, in 2018 Rodrigues was arrested for interfering with a police officer, escaping from custody, and resisting arrest. Earlier in 2020 Rodrigues was arrested for menacing and second-degree disorderly conduct when he threatened the foster family with whom his children were living[491] [492]./Yes, in assaulting an officer and robbery.

Mental Illness: None reported, but Rodrigues "struggled with homelessness"[493] which is linked with mental illness.

Substance Abuse History/Involved: Unknown./Yes, the toxicology report showed that Rodrigues had methamphetamine, amphetamine, opioids, and marijuana in his system at the time of incident[494].

Race/Sex/Age: Latino/Male/40

Officer(s) Involved: Eugene Police Officer Sam Tykol

What prompted the initial contact with police? Officer Tykol observed a suspicious male, Eliborio Rodrigues, in dark clothing, walking on the road around 12:30 a.m. on November 20. Since there had been several recent burglaries and car break-ins nearby, Tykol stopped to question him. Tykol asked to see his identification, and then told Rodrigues that he was being detained and was not free to go.

Actions taken by subject toward police: Rodrigues refused to provide Tykol with identification and physically struggled with him when Tykol tried to take him into custody. After being taken down to the ground by Tykol, Rodrigues got back up, ran away, and was again taken down by Tykol, who tased him, but to no effect. Rodrigues punched Tykol repeatedly, grabbed the taser from Tykol, and used it against him[495].

Reactions by the police: Fighting for his life against a drugged man who was 50 pounds heavier than him, and no longer able to use his legs after being tased, Officer Tykol shot Rodrigues three times in the stomach as Rodrigues was on top of Tykol punching him.

Outcome of investigation into the fatal police incident: Lane County District Attorney Patty Perlow announced that the shooting was justified.

Miscellaneous: When Rodriguez was arrested in April, it took three officers to do so. Officer Tykol suffered injuries to his head and knees.

What could the subject have done that day to still be alive today? Should not have been walking in the street after midnight and going through people's garbage. Should have complied with the officer's commands to see his identification and then to peacefully surrender. Should not have physically assaulted the officer with his hands and then with the officer's stolen taser.

Justified use of deadly force? YES, Tykol was tased and beaten, and he had reasonable cause to believe that he would be killed by Rodrigues if he were not stopped. So he justifiably used deadly force to stay alive.

Name: Michael Lorenzo Dean
Date: 12/2/2019   **Location:** Temple, TX
FACTORS (8,16)

Criminal History/Involved: NA.

Mental Illness: NA.

Substance Abuse History/Involved: NA.

Race/Sex/Age: Black/Male/18

Officer(s) Involved: Temple Police Officer Carmen DeCruz

What prompted the initial contact with police? On December 2, PO Carmen DeCruz pulled Michael Dean over for speeding. Officer DeCruz approached Dean's vehicle with his gun drawn, telling Dean to turn the car off and give him the keys[496].

Actions taken by subject toward police: Dean complied with the officer's commands.

Reactions by the police: Officer DeCruz reached into the car for the keys and as he pulled the keys toward him with his left hand, his right hand pulled back and the gun went off–hitting Dean in the head, killing him[497].

Outcome of investigation into the fatal police incident: DeCruz has been charged with second-degree felony manslaughter[498].

Miscellaneous: Video from the officer's body cam contributed to the charges against him. Since Officer DeCruz is Latino and American Indian, the social justice activists could not racialize this tragic shooting.

What could the subject have done that day to still be alive today? Nothing, since everyone commits minor traffic infractions while driving. Michael Dean shares no blame for this tragic incident.

Justified use of deadly force? NO, this is a tragic example of an accidental discharge due to the bad tactics exhibited by Officer Cruz. As taught from day one in the police academy, officers must keep their trigger finger out of the trigger guard unless and until they are about to intentionally pull the trigger.

Name: Matthew Jonathan Kruper
Date: 12/11/2019   **Location:** League City, TX
FACTORS (1,2,4,12,14,15,19)

Criminal History/Involved: Yes, Krupar was out on bail from a November felony DWI arrest. He also had an earlier conviction for intoxicated assault with a vehicle and charge for possession of LSD./Yes, creating a disturbance and then assaulting an officer.

Mental Illness: None reported, but Kruper's exhibited behavior was not that of a sane person.

Substance Abuse History/Involved: Yes, Kruper had previous alcohol- and drug-related arrests./ None stated.

Race/Sex/Age: White/Male/31

Officer(s) Involved: League City Police Officer Patrick Bradshaw

What prompted the initial contact with police? Police officers responded to a 911 call about a disturbance at a house around 5 p.m. on December 11. Multiple callers reported a man, Kruper, who was "running around the Bay Colony Neighborhood, hands covered in blood and screaming"[499]. Upon arriving at the house, the officers were met by the woman, a neighbor of Krupar who had made the call[500].

Actions taken by subject toward police: While the officers spoke with the woman, Kruper came out of the house and started arguing and then fighting with the officers[501].

Reactions by the police: While being assaulted by Kruper, fearing for his life, Officer Bradshaw shot Kruper with his duty weapon, killing him.

Outcome of investigation into the fatal police incident: Galveston County Sheriff's Office is investigating.

What could the subject have done that day to still be alive today? Should not have created a disturbance in his house and the neighborhood prompting people to call 911 about him. Should have complied with the officer's lawful commands. Should not have physically assaulted a police officer.

Justified use of deadly force? YES, given the little information available, Officer Bradshaw was being physically assaulted by a violent man who had attacked the officer without provocation. Officer Bradshaw was injured in the attack. So if he feared that he might be seriously injured or knocked out by Kruper, who could then use his weapon against him, then Bradshaw had reasonable cause to fear for his life and use lethal force.

ANALYSIS OF THE 51 UNARMED FATAL POLICE SHOOTINGS IN 2019

Subject's race: White: 24(47%) Black: 11(22%) Latino: 13(25%) Asian: 2 (4%) Native-American: 1(2%)

1. Subject failed to comply: 47 (92%)
2. Subject was a wanted criminal, or a crime was involved: 43 (84%)
3. Alcohol or drugs were involved: 19 (37%)
4. Subjects displayed or described having mental illness: 26 (51%)
5. Subjects' words and/or actions appeared to be suicide by cop: 12 (24%)
6. Officers voiced racist rhetoric: 0 (0%)
7. Officers outright ambushed the subject: 0 (0%)
8. Vehicle was involved (car stop, disabled motorist, accident): 17 (33%)
9. Subject's accomplice possessed a weapon: 7 (14%)
10. Subject faked having a gun: 10 (20%)
11. A vehicle was driven at an officer: 3 (6%)
12. Subject/accomplice, threatened/assaulted officer with personal weapon/object: 26 (51%)
13. Accomplices' actions justified deadly force: 5(10%)
14. Less-than-lethal force alternatives failed: 27 (53%)
15. Officer(s) sustained injuries: 15 (29%)
16. Accidental discharges: 3 (6%)
17. Unjustified intentional and targeted use of deadly force: 2 (4%)
18. Not conducting official police duties: 1 (2%)
19. Justified deadly force used: 38 (75%)
20. Justified deadly force used, but wrong target was hit: 5 (10%)
21. Undetermined whether justified or not: 2 (4%)

INCIDENTS IN 2020:

Name: Clando Anitok
Date: 1/10/2020   **Location:** Spokane, WA
FACTORS (1,2,3,4,5,8,10,12,14,19)

Criminal History/Involved: Yes, Anitok had prior charges for attempted rape, strangulation, burglary and ten counts of violating a no-contact order[502]./Yes, driving while intoxicated, unlawful fleeing from an officer, reckless driving, and an attempted home invasion.

Mental Illness: None reported, however Anitok was clearly in an altered mental state.

Substance Abuse History/Involved: Unknown./Yes, Anitok's blood alcohol level was .17.

Race/Sex/Age: Asian/Male/25

Officer(s) Involved: Spokane County Sheriff's Deputy Brent Miller

What prompted the initial contact with police? While on patrol, just before 4:00 a.m. on January 10, Deputy Miller observed that Anitok's vehicle had a defective headlight and initiated a vehicle and traffic stop on him. Anitok refused to pull over, instead he sped up, drove onto the sidewalk, and crashed into a fence. Deputy Miller caught up to Anitok after he crashed and ordered him out of the car and onto the ground[503].

Actions taken by subject toward police: Anitok refused to comply with Millers orders and attacked the deputy.

Reactions by the police: Deputy Miller tried tasing Anitok twice, but the taser did not have any effect. Miller then chased Anitok to a house that Anitok was attempting to break into and possibly take hostages. Miller ordered Anitok to the ground. Anitok disregarded Millers orders and reached toward his waistband, causing Miller to shoot him once in the head, killing him[504].

Outcome of investigation into the fatal police incident: Spokane County Prosecutor's Office deemed it a justified shooting and declined to file charges against Deputy Miller.

What could the subject have done that day to still be alive today? Should not have been driving a car with defective equipment. Should have complied with the deputy's lawful orders and pulled over. Should not have fled from the deputy and then assaulted him. Should not have attempted to break into someone's house. Should have complied with the deputy's orders to peacefully surrender. Should not have made a furtive movement toward his waistband.

Justified use of deadly force? YES, Deputy Miller unsuccessfully used physical force and the less-than-lethal taser to subdue Anitok. When Anitok then attempted to conduct a home invasion and made a furtive movement toward his waistband, Miller had reasonable cause to believe that Anitok posed a lethal threat to Miller and/or the occupants of the house and justifiably used lethal force.

Name: William Howard Green

Date: 1/27/2020   **Location:** Temple Hills, MD

FACTORS (8,17) 2?,3?

Criminal History/Involved: Unknown./Unknown, the toxicology results will show if Green was high/drunk when crashing into the vehicles.

Mental Illness: Unknown.

Substance Abuse History/Involved: Unknown./Unknown as the toxicology results have not been reported.

Race/Sex/Age: Black/Male/43

Officer(s) Involved: Prince George's County Police Cpl. Michael Owen Jr.

What prompted the initial contact with police? At around 7:20 p.m. on January 27, officers responded to a 911 call about a traffic accident in which Green was alleged to crash into several vehicles. Two officers found Green nearby, behind the wheel of his damaged vehicle. Believing that Green was under the influence of drugs, possibly PCP, Officer Owen arrested Green and placed him in his patrol vehicle[505].

Actions taken by subject toward police: Green complied with the Cpl. Owen's commands, he peacefully surrendered, was handcuffed, and placed in the officer's vehicle, awaiting the arrival of a drug recognition expert to test him.

Reactions by the police: Inexplicably, Cpl. Owen shot Green seven times as he sat, handcuffed, in the front seat of the police vehicle, killing him[506].

Outcome of investigation into the fatal police incident: Cpl. Michael Owen Jr. was indicted by a grand jury for "second-degree murder, manslaughter, assault, use of a handgun and misconduct in office"[507].

Miscellaneous: Green's family "reached a $20 million settlement with Prince George County"[508]. Since Cpl. Owen is Black, the incident could not be racialized by social justice activists.

What could the subject have done that day to still be alive today? Should not have crashed into multiple vehicles and given police reason to believe that he was driving under the influence of drugs–this in no way is meant to suggest that Green should have been shot. The point is, for people who believe the police are bad, and for the rare cases where police actually are bad–the best way to minimize your chances of being killed by such bad police are to not break any laws so as to not have any interactions with them.

Justified use of deadly force? NO, Green had peacefully complied and posed no threat to Cpl. Owen or anyone else as he was handcuffed behind-the-back, in the police car.

Name: Jaquyn O'Neill Light
Date: 1/28/2020   **Location:** Graham, NC
FACTORS (1,2,16) 12?

Criminal History/Involved: Yes, Light had a 2017 arrest for attempted armed robbery and more recently for communicating threats and an assault[509]./Yes, Light had active arrest warrants and had attempted to flee from the officers.

Mental Illness: Unknown

Substance Abuse History/Involved: Unknown./None reported.

Race/Sex/Age: Black/Male/20

Officer(s) Involved: Graham Police Officers Marcus Pollock, N. Scoggins, and B. Land

What prompted the initial contact with police? At around 11:30 p.m. on January 28, the officers responded to a residence upon the basis of an anonymous tip that Light was hiding out there. After entering the house through the backdoor, Officers Scoggins and Land searched through to the front of the house[510].

Actions taken by subject toward police: As the officers were getting close to finding him, Light fled out from the front of the house and "accidentally collided with"[511] Officer Pollock. Because the front was under construction and covered in dark plastic, Light and Officer Pollock did not see each other until the collision.

Reactions by the police: During a short struggle between Officer Pollock and Light, Pollock's gun discharged one time into Light's stomach. The officers rendered medical care to Light, and he was transported to a hospital where he died from his wounds.

Outcome of investigation into the fatal police incident: In clearing Officer Pollock of any charges, Sean Boone, the Alamance County District Attorney stated, "In my opinion, the evidence most strongly supports that of accidental discharge caused by an unintentional collision between Pollock and Light,"[512] said Boone. Additionally, Boone stated that if it was not accidental, then it was "in self-defense"[513].

What could the subject have done that day to still be alive today? Should not have committed prior crimes that would generate arrest warrants and should not have the police looking for him. Should not have unlawfully fled from the officers and should have peacefully complied with their service of the warrants upon him.

Justified use of deadly force? As described by the DA it was an **accidental discharge**. Given that there was a collision between Officer Pollock and Light, it cannot even be ascertained if Pollocks finger was improperly on the trigger and if he squeezed the trigger during the collision, or he did so while trying to regain his weapon when it was knocked out of his hands. Neither of these are an intentional use of deadly force. If there was a physical struggle in which Officer Pollock reasonably feared that Light was attempting to take his firearm from him then **YES**, that would have justified his use of deadly force.

Name: Lindy Bowie
Date: 2/21/2020   **Location:** Phoenix, AZ
FACTORS (1,2,12,19)

Criminal History/Involved: Yes, the subject had prior drug and firearm charges./Yes, assault of a federal law enforcement officer attempting to effect a lawful arrest.

Mental Illness: Unknown.

Substance Abuse History/Involved: Yes, Bowie had prior drug charges./None stated.

Race/Sex/Age: White/Female/30

Officer(s) Involved: United States Marshal's Fugitive Task Force

What prompted the initial contact with police? The US Marshals were attempting to arrest a female fugitive at a hotel around 12:30 p.m.[514].

Actions taken by subject toward police: The fugitive assaulted one of the Marshals[515].

Reactions by the police: The Marshal's shot the fugitive, killing her[516].

Outcome of investigation into the fatal police incident: No further details have been released.

Miscellaneous: There is a distinct lack of information and reporting over the incident.

What could the subject have done that day to still be alive today? Should not have been a fugitive wanted by the US Marshals. Should have complied with the Marshals and peacefully surrendered. Should not have physically assaulted the Marshal.

Justified use of deadly force? YES, a violent fugitive physically assaulting a Marshal would give the Marshal's reasonable cause to believe that a Marshal's life and/or their lives could be in mortal danger if the fugitive were armed or able to disarm the Marshal.

Name: Stephen O'Brien

Date: 2/24/2020   **Location:** Floresville, TX

FACTORS (1,2,4,5,10,19)

Criminal History/Involved: Unknown./Yes, falsely reporting an incident.

Mental Illness: Yes, O'Brien had a history of mental illness, and his actions were suicidal.

Substance Abuse History/Involved: Unknown./None stated.

Race/Sex/Age: White/Male/20

Officer(s) Involved: Wilson County Sheriff's Deputy Ronald Broom, another deputy, and a Texas Department of Public Safety Trooper

What prompted the initial contact with police? O'Brien called 911 shortly after midnight on February 24 from a Walmart parking lot and reported that there was a man with a gun and described a man that resembled himself. Upon arriving at the parking lot, the law enforcement officers confronted O'Brien, believing that he was the man with a gun since he fit the description and was the only person there. The deputies can be seen in the bodycam video out in the open of the empty parking lot just feet away from O'Brien telling him to take his hands out of his pockets.

Actions taken by subject toward police: O'Brien told the deputies "Y'all are going to have to shoot me"[517] before pulling his right hand quickly out of his pocket and simulating it being a weapon, pointing it at the officers.

Reactions by the police: As O'Brien quickly drew his right hand out of the pocket with what they believed contained a gun, the deputies shot O'Brien, killing him.

Outcome of investigation into the fatal police incident: Wilson County grand jury did not indict Deputy Broom, and considered it a justified shooting.

Miscellaneous: Video of the shooting taken by the deputy's bodycam is available at FOX San Antonio[518].

What could the subject have done that day to still be alive today? He should have been on the properly prescribed psychological medications, in a mental institution, or properly supervised. Should not have called 911 and reported about a man fitting his description having a gun. Should have complied with the officer's commands and peacefully surrendered. Should not have abruptly simulated drawing a weapon out of his pocket to shoot the officers.

Justified use of deadly force? YES, while the deputies should have used better tactics and taken cover behind their vehicle instead of confronting a suspected armed person out in the open. Given their belief O'Brien was armed, his verbal statement, and his simulated drawing of a weapon, the deputies reasonably believed that he posed a deadly threat and were justified in using lethal force.

Name: Unidentified
Date: 2/26/2020   **Location:** Garden Grove, CA
FACTORS (1,2,8,12,14,15,19)

Criminal History/Involved: Unknown./Yes, operating a stolen vehicle, assaulting an officer.

Mental Illness: Unknown.

Substance Abuse History/Involved: Unknown./ Unknown.

Race/Sex/Age: Unknown/Male/Unknown

Officer(s) Involved: Garden Grove Police Officer

What prompted the initial contact with police? At around 1:30 a.m. on February 26, officers observed a vehicle crash into a pole. A Garden Grove Officer responded to the scene to investigate and see if anyone was injured[519].

Actions taken by subject toward police: One of the occupants of the crashed car that was reported stolen, physically assaulted the officer[520].

Reactions by the police: Fearing for his/her life from the unprovoked attack, the officer shot the suspect, killing him.

Outcome of investigation into the fatal police incident: Orange County District Attorney's Office and Garden Grove police are investigating.

Miscellaneous: The officer suffered minor injuries and was hospitalized[521].

What could the subject have done that day to still be alive today? Should not have been in a stolen vehicle that crashed and drew the attention of the police. Should have complied with officer's commands and cooperate with the investigation. Should not have physically attacked the officer.

Justified use of deadly force? YES, while sustaining injuries from the suspect's physical assault, the officer reasonably feared for his/her life and justifiably used deadly force to stop the violent attack.

Name: Christopher Palmer

Date: 3/3/2020   **Location:** Manila, AR

FACTORS (1,2,4,9,12,14,19)

Criminal History/Involved: Unknown./Yes, robbery (He had stolen the officer's taser).

Mental Illness: Yes, Palmer was a diagnosed schizophrenic[522].

Substance Abuse History/Involved: Unknown./None stated.

Race/Sex/Age: White/Male/37

Officer(s) Involved: Manila Police Department Sgt. Mike Shively

What prompted the initial contact with police? On the night of March 3, Sgt. Shively responded to a 911 call regarding a domestic disturbance at Palmer's house. Upon arriving, the Sgt. was informed by Palmer's brother that Christopher was "out of his head, acting crazy"[523]. Sgt. Shively tried talking to Palmer, but he was uncooperative, and he cursed at Shively. When Palmer aggressively advanced on Shively and got in his face in a threatening manner, Shively told him he was under arrest.

Actions taken by subject toward police: Palmer refused to obey Shively's commands and when Shively threatened to tase him, Palmer ripped the taser off Shively's tactical vest.

Reactions by the police: Fearing that erratic and violent Palmer would use the taser to incapacitate him and then take his duty weapon to kill him, Sgt. Shively shot Palmer point-blank several times, killing him.

Outcome of investigation into the fatal police incident: Second Judicial Prosecuting Attorney Scott Ellington deemed it a justified shooting[524].

What could the subject have done that day to still be alive today? Should not have acted erratic, scaring his family into calling 911 for help. Should have complied with the officer's commands and peacefully surrendered. Should not have threatened the officer and robbed him of his taser.

Justified use of deadly force? YES, once Palmer ripped the taser off Shively's vest he had the means to incapacitate the Sgt. and then use Shively's duty weapon on him or Palmers own family. Shively had a duty to ensure that did not happen, and, therefore, he was justified in using deadly force.

Name: Kenneth Wayne Mullins
Date: 3/5/2020   **Location:** Edison, CA
FACTORS (1,2,4,5,19)

Criminal History/Involved: Yes, Mullins had previous arrests for shoplifting, obstructing a public officer, violating probation, possessing a completed check with intent to defraud, receiving stolen property[529]./Yes, commercial burglary.

Mental Illness: Mullins was homeless, a key indicator associated with mental illness.

Substance Abuse History/Involved: Unknown./None stated.

Race/Sex/Age: White/Male/32

Officer(s) Involved: Fresno County Sheriff's Deputies

What prompted the initial contact with police? Around 5 p.m. on March 5, deputies responded to a 911 call of a commercial burglary at an auto shop that the owner advised contained firearms he worried the burglar may have accessed. Fearing Mullins was armed and waiting to ambush them inside, the deputies tried for a half hour to get Mullins to peacefully exit the building before finally sending in a police robot to see where he was in the building.[530]

Actions taken by subject toward police: Mullins threw the police robot at the deputies and then came out of the building, ignoring their orders to stop and confronted them.[531]

Reactions by the police: Concerned that Mullins was armed when he refused to follow their commands and made a furtive movement, the deputies opened fire and killed him.

Outcome of investigation into the fatal police incident: Fresno County Sheriff's Office is investigating.

What could the subject have done that day to still be alive today? Should not have committed burglary, prompting the store owner to call 911. Should have complied with the lawful orders of the deputies and peacefully surrendered. Should not have confronted the deputies and made a sudden movement that would have made the deputies think he was about to access a weapon.

Justified use of deadly force? YES, the deputies had reasonable cause to believe that Mullins was armed, so when he disobeyed their lawful orders, confronted them, and made a furtive movement that they believed was an attempt to access a weapon, they justifiably used lethal force.

Name: Barry Gedeus

Date: 3/8/2020   **Location:** Fort Lauderdale, FL

FACTORS (1,2,3,12,14,15,19)

Criminal History/Involved: Yes, Gedeus had prior arrests for felony grand theft of firearm, carrying a concealed firearm, and misdemeanor possession of marijuana[525]./Yes, Gedeus had just committed a sexual assault (rape).

Mental History: Unknown.

Substance Abuse History/Involved: Yes, Gedeus had a prior arrest for marijuana./Yes, the woman sexually assaulted by Gedeus that day said that he had drugs on him[526].

Race/Sex/Age: Black/Male/27

Officer(s) Involved: Fort Lauderdale Police Officer Robert Morris

What prompted the initial contact with police? Around 9 p.m. on March 8, officers responded to a 911 call for a "black man with dreads on a bicycle"[527] who had committed a sexual assault on a woman. Upon arriving in the area, Officer Morris saw a man, Barry Gedeus fitting that description and attempted to stop him for questioning.

Actions taken by subject toward police: Gedeus ignored the officer's commands and took off running.

Reactions by the police: Officer Morris managed to catch up to Gedeus. Gedeus struggled with the officer, who ultimately ended up shooting him ten times, with three hitting him in the back, killing him.

Outcome of investigation into the fatal police incident: Florida Department of Law Enforcement (FDLE) is investigating.

Miscellaneous: Officer Morris underwent several surgeries to repair the serious injuries he had received while struggling with Gedeus[528]. DNA evidence confirmed that Gedeus was the perpetrator of the sexual assault.

What could the subject have done that day to still be alive today? Should not have committed sexual assault of a woman that would cause her to call the police on him. Should have complied with the officer's lawful orders and peacefully surrendered for questioning and/or arrest. Should not have fled on foot from the officers and then physically fought with them.

Justified use of deadly force? YES, barring further information, Gedeus fled from and then fought with the officer, causing him severe injuries that gave the officer reasonable cause to believe that his life was in mortal danger if he did not escalate to using lethal force and kill Gedeus.

THIS SUBJECT WAS NOT SHOT BY THE POLICE　　　　**FACTORS (NA)**

Name: Brian Marksberry

Date: 3/8/2020　　**Location:** Humble, TX

Criminal History/Involved: NA.

Mental Illness: NA.

Substance Abuse History/Involved: NA.

Race/Sex/Age: White/Male/31

Officer(s) Involved: NA—officers did not shoot Mr. Marksberry

What prompted the initial contact with police? Humble police officers responded to a domestic disturbance in a mall parking lot and arrived to find an armed man who had just threatened his girlfriend[532].

Actions taken by subject toward police: When the suspect took off running from the police, Marksberry, an innocent bystander, got involved and chased the suspect, however, the suspect shot and killed him[533].

Reactions by the police: Officers were also chasing the suspect, and upon seeing him shoot Marksberry, they shot and killed him[534].

Outcome of investigation into the fatal police incident: NA.

Miscellaneous: Fatalencounters.org and WashingtonPost.com police shootings database both include this incident even though Marksberry was not shot by the police. Mappingpoliceviolence. com at least got it right and listed Zachary Anderson Jr. as the armed man shot dead by police that day.[535]

What could the subject have done that day to still be alive today? Marksberry died a hero that day trying to protect a helpless woman and help the police capture an armed criminal.

Justified use of deadly force? NA.

Name: Aaron Tolen

Date: 3/8/2020   **Location:** Wasilia, AK

FACTORS (1,2,12,14,15,19)

Criminal History/Involved: Yes, Tolen had at least 35 previous cases including nearly 200 offenses and convictions for armed robbery of children in 2007, possession of stolen property, and another armed robbery in 2003[536]./Yes, assault of an officer.

Mental Illness: Unknown.

Substance Abuse History/Involved: Unknown./None stated.

Race/Sex/Age: White/Male/37

Officer(s) Involved: Alaska State Troopers Amy Nelson and Chris Russell

What prompted the initial contact with police? Officer Nelson responded to a 911 call by Tolen's family around 7:15 p.m. on March 8 regarding domestic disturbance. Upon arriving at the Tolen residence, Trooper Nelson encountered Tolen[537].

Actions taken by subject toward police: Tolen refused to comply with the trooper's lawful commands and ended up fighting with her. Despite the trooper deploying her taser, Tolen continued his attack upon Nelson[538].

Reactions by the police: Trooper Russell arrived at the house and saw Trooper Nelson being assaulted by Tolen and shot him.

Outcome of investigation into the fatal police incident: The incident is under investigation.

Miscellaneous: Tolen had a history of violent crimes, and he again exhibited his proclivity for violence by fighting with a female trooper.

What could the subject have done that day to still be alive today? Should not have had a domestic disturbance with his family, prompting them to call the police for help. Should have complied with the trooper's lawful commands. Should not have physically resisted and assaulted the trooper.

Justified use of deadly force? YES, Tolen was attacking a law enforcement officer, giving the back-up trooper reasonable cause to believe that Tolen might access Trooper Nelson's weapon and use it on her. The back-up trooper justifiably used deadly force to stop Tolen's violent attack upon Trooper Nelson.

Name: Pablo Elias
Date: 3/10/2020   **Location:** Bell Gardens, CA
FACTORS (1,2,21)

Criminal History/Involved: Unknown./Yes, domestic violence, robbery, and carjacking[539].

Mental Illness: Unknown.

Substance Abuse History/Involved: Unknown./None stated.

Race/Sex/Age: Latino/Male/44

Officer(s) Involved: Bell Gardens police officers

What prompted the initial contact with police? Officers responded to a 911 call about a domestic disturbance on the morning of March 9. The call was made Elias' mother after Elias robbed her and carjacked her vehicle. Elias was home, but he managed to escape when the officer's tried to arrest him. The police responded back to the house around 9:30 p.m. after being alerted that Elias had returned[540].

Actions taken by subject toward police: Elias barricaded himself in the house overnight and finally exited around 5 a.m. on March 10.

Reactions by the police: When Elias came out of the house he was shot and killed by the officer's surrounding the house.

Outcome of investigation into the fatal police incident: Los Angeles County Sheriff's Department Homicide Squad is investigating.

What could the subject have done that day to still be alive today? Should not have robbed and carjacked his mother, prompting her to call 911. Should have complied with the officers and peacefully surrendered when they arrived the first time and he was inside the house. Should not have made whatever furtive motion he did upon exiting the house to cause the officers to fear for their lives.

Justified use of deadly force? UNDETERMINED, there is too little information about the subject's actions while exiting the house to definitively say whether the shooting was justified.

INCIDENT GARNERING NATIONAL MEDIA ATTENTION AND PROTESTS

Name: Breonna Taylor
Date: 3/12/2020   **Location:** Louisville, KY
FACTORS (1,2,3,9,12,13,15,20)

Criminal History/Involved: Unknown./Yes, evidence used to get the warrant showed that Taylor was in regular contact with a known drug-dealer, her ex-boyfriend Jamarcus Glover who used her house for deliveries.

Substance Abuse History/Involved: Unknown./None stated.

Race/Sex/Age: Black/Female/26

Officer(s) Involved: Louisville Metropolitan Police Department Sgt. Jonathan Mattingly, Officers Brett Hankison and Myles Cosgrove

What prompted the initial contact with police? Police were conducting a knock and announce drug warrant at Taylors residence around 12:40 a.m. on March 12 based upon evidence linking Taylor's drug dealing ex-boyfriend Jamarcus Glover to the location[541].

Actions taken by subject toward police: Taylor's current boyfriend Kenneth Walker thought it was a home invasion. (Who could blame him with Breonna's ex-boyfriend still coming around?!) Kenneth fired at what ended up being the police conducting a raid.

Reactions by the police: After Sgt. Mattingly was struck in the leg by the bullet fired from inside the residence, Mattingly, and Officers Hankison and Cosgrove returned fire into the house at least 22 times, killing Taylor.

Outcome of investigation into the fatal police incident: Hankison, was fired for "blindly" firing 10 rounds into Taylor's apartment and was indicted by a grand jury for "wanton endangerment"[542] for wildly firing his weapon into a nearby apartment. Sgt. Mattingly and Officer Cosgrove were found to have justifiably used deadly force in self-defense.

Miscellaneous: Court documents show that Glover and Taylor were still in contact. Glover used Taylor's address when registering his bank account and her phone number when filing a police report. Taylor rented a car which Glover used and was linked to a murder with. Mail addressed to Glover was found in Taylor's home in the aftermath of the shooting, and she was overheard discussing trap houses and drug proceeds on a tapped call[543].

What could the subject have done that day to still be alive today? Should not have been in close contact with a drug dealer who was being investigated by the police. Jamarcus Glover should be charged with the murder of Taylor, it was his criminality that led to the unfortunate circumstances of an unarmed woman being killed.

Justified use of deadly force? YES, the police were executing a high-risk warrant when they came under fire from inside the residence with one officer being shot. Fearing that it was the subject of the warrant firing at them and having reasonable cause to believe that he would fire more shots, they used lethal force and returned fire in that direction. Tragically Ms. Taylor was fatally hit by the officers' return fire.

Name: Donnie Sanders

Date: 3/12/2020   **Location:** Kansas City, MO

FACTORS (1,2,4,5,8,10,12,19)

Criminal History/Involved: Unknown./Yes, unlawful fleeing from police.

Mental Illness: None reported, however Sanders actions of making it appear that he was holding a weapon and refusing to drop it when ordered to do so by the officer is suicidal.

Substance Abuse History/Involved: Unknown./None stated.

Race/Sex/Age: Black/Male/47

Officer(s) Involved: Kansas City police officer

What prompted the initial contact with police? After observing a traffic violation around 11:15 p.m. on March 12, an officer attempted to pull over a vehicle being driven by Donnie Sanders[544].

Actions taken by subject toward police: Sanders refused to pull over, instead, he drove away before stopping in an alley where he and the passenger both fled on foot. When the officer caught up to Sanders, the latter disobeyed the officer's orders to get on the ground. When Sanders raised his arms, it appeared that he was holding a weapon, so the officer repeatedly ordered him to drop the weapon, but Sanders did not drop whatever was in his hand[545].

Reactions by the police: Fearing that Sanders was armed and pointing a gun at him as Sanders intentionally made it appear, the officer shot Sanders, killing him.

Outcome of investigation into the fatal police incident: Jackson County Prosecutor's Office concluded its investigation and the officer involved has returned to work[546].

What could the subject have done that day to still be alive today? Should not have committed a traffic infraction and gotten pulled over by the police. Should have peacefully pulled over and let the officer conduct a traffic stop. Should not have fled from the police on foot into a dark alley. Should have complied with the officer's lawful commands to peacefully surrender. Should not have positioned his arms in a manner that resembled holding a weapon pointed at the officer.

Justified use of deadly force? YES, the officer was alone in a dark alley and confronted with an armed uncooperative subject who refused to drop what looked like a gun which was pointed at him. Given that set of circumstances the officer reasonably believed that he was in mortal danger and appropriately used lethal force.

Name: Mycael Johnson
Date: 3/20/2020   **Location:** Tallahassee, FL
FACTORS (1,2,8,12,14,15,19)

Criminal History/Involved: Yes, Johnson had multiple prior charges for drugs (marijuana and cocaine), robbery, possessing a weapon as a felon, and fleeing from police./Yes, grand larceny of motor vehicle, fleeing from police, and an attempted carjacking.

Mental Illness: Unknown.

Substance Abuse History/Involved: Yes, Johnson had prior drug arrests. None stated.

Race/Sex/Age: Black/Male/31

Officer(s) Involved: Tallahassee Police Officers Zackri Jones and Justin Davidson

What prompted the initial contact with police? Around 7:30 p.m. on March 20, Tallahassee officers were alerted about a stolen vehicle and attempted to pull it over. The driver fled from the officers, but a police helicopter spotted the suspect, Mycael Johnson, unsuccessfully attempt a carjacking in order to change vehicles. After getting back in the stolen car, Johnson was pursued by a police vehicle until he crashed and tried to carjack another vehicle. Officer Davidson caught up to Johnson at that point and tased Johnson twice in an effort to take him into custody[547].

Actions taken by subject toward police: Johnson ignored Officer Davidson commands and was unaffected by the taser, as he physically assaulted Davidson and was on top of Davidson trying to remove his duty weapon from its holster[548].

Reactions by the police: Catching up to see Davidson struggling for his life against the violent criminal and hearing him say "My gun" indicating that Johnson was trying to take Davison's gun, Officer Jones shot Johnson once in the head, killing him[549].

Outcome of investigation into the fatal police incident: The grand jury presented No True Bill, meaning Officer Jones actions were considered reasonable and the shooting was considered justified[550].

What could the subject have done that day to still be alive today? Should not have stolen a car. Should have complied with the officers and peacefully pulled over and be arrested. Should not have attempted to carjack two vehicles while trying to escape the police. Should have complied with the officer's commands to peacefully surrender. Should not have physically assaulted the police officer.

Justified use of deadly force? YES, Johnson was a violent felon who endangered the lives of civilians and officers during the car pursuit, attempted carjacking, and finally when assaulting an officer. Officer Jones had reasonable cause to believe that Johnson's assault would cause serious physical injury to Officer Davidson or enable him to access the officer's gun and use it against both officers.

Name: John Mark Hendrick Jr.
Date: 3/26/2020   **Location:** Linwood, NC
FACTORS (1,2,8,11,13,20)

Criminal History/Involved: Yes, Hendrick had prior arrests for felony larceny of a firearm, possession of stolen goods, and conspiring to commit felony larceny[551]./Yes, Hendrick was a passenger in a stolen vehicle.

Mental Illness: Unknown.

Substance Abuse History/Involved: Unknown./None stated.

Race/Sex/Age: White/Male/32

Officer(s) Involved: Davidson County Sheriff's deputies

What prompted the initial contact with police? A Forsyth County Sheriff's deputy tried to pull over a vehicle for speeding around 3:00 a.m. on March 26 when the driver sped off and crossed over several counties. Davidson County Sheriff's deputies managed to stop the vehicle in their county.

Actions taken by subject toward police: Rather than surrender, the driver of the stolen vehicle, Charles Justin Boothe, accelerated and tried to run over the deputies.

Reactions by the police: Fearing for their life from the oncoming speeding stolen vehicle, the deputies opened fire, accidentally killing the passenger John Mark Hendrick Jr.[552]

Outcome of investigation into the fatal police incident: State Bureau of Investigations has the lead.

Miscellaneous: Hendrick's friend Booth had prior arrests for drug (heroin) possession with intent to sell.[553] For his actions in this incident, Booth was charged with "assault with a deadly weapon on a law-enforcement officer and fleeing to elude"[554].

What could the subject have done that day to still be alive today? Should not have been in a stolen vehicle with a violent felon who fled from law enforcement officers and then tried to run them over.

Justified use of deadly force? YES, the officers had reasonable cause to believe that their lives were in imminent danger from the stolen vehicle being driven at them by a criminal who had already demonstrated a clear disregard for human life during the car pursuit. Unfortunately, the justified use of deadly force used against the driver Booth, fatally hit the passenger Hendrick instead.

Name: Jose Soto

Date: 4/2/2020   **Location:** Manchester, CT

FACTORS (1,2,4,5,10,19)

Criminal History/Involved: Yes, Soto was on parole for a prior robbery./Yes, obstructing governmental administration.

Mental Illness: Yes, Soto had mental illness, including PTSD[555].

Substance Abuse History/Involved: Unknown./None stated.

Race/Sex/Age: Latino/Male/27

Officer(s) Involved: Parole officers with the Connecticut Department of Correction, Parole Division, and officers with the Capital Region Emergency Service Team (CREST)

What prompted the initial contact with police? Parole officers called the CREST after Soto acted erratic, gave officers the impression that he was armed, and refused to come out of the house when they went there around 7:30 p.m. on April 2 to take him into custody for violating his parole for an earlier robbery conviction. The team responded and negotiators tried for hours to get Soto to exit the house and peacefully surrender.[556]

Actions taken by subject toward police: Soto confronted the officers when he suddenly "burst out the home holding what police thought was a gun in a "firing" position. It turned out to be a cell phone"[557].

Reactions by the police: Four CREST officers (Manchester PD Sgt. Shawn Krom, PO David Williams, Enfield Officer Matthew Alexander, and Wethersfield PD PO Shane Murphy) shot Soto, killing him.

Outcome of investigation into the fatal police incident: Office of Tolland State's Attorney Matthew C. Gedansky lead the investigation. Gedansky has said "Mr. Soto manifested an intent to emerge from the residence in a manner which rejected the negotiator's advice to surrender peacefully"[558]. It was determined to be a justified shooting.

Miscellaneous: CREST Team officers do not have bodycams and a dashcam failed to capture the shooting. It was determined that Soto was not armed.

What could the subject have done that day to still be alive today? Should not have committed a prior robbery and violated his parole. Should have complied with the parole officers and peacefully surrendered when they initially showed up at his house. Should not have told the police that he was armed and made a furtive movement upon exiting his house.

Justified use of deadly force? YES. Soto, a known violent felon who violated parole had just intimated to officers that he was armed and unwilling to come peacefully. Upon exiting his house, Soto made a furtive movement that gave officers reasonable cause to believe that he was going for a weapon, for which they justifiably used deadly force.

Name: Zachary Shane Gifford
Date: 4/9/2020   **Location:** Brandon, CO
FACTORS (1,2,3,8,12,14,21)

Criminal History/Involved: Unknown./Yes, Gifford was unlawfully fleeing from police.

Mental Illness: Unknown.

Substance Abuse History/Involved: Unknown./Yes, autopsy report showed that Gifford had methamphetamine in his system[559].

Race/Sex/Age: White/Male/39

Officer(s) Involved: Kiowa County Undersheriff Tracy Weisenhorn and Sheriff's Deputy Quentin Stump.

What prompted the initial contact with police? When the deputies pulled over a pickup truck for a traffic violation around 3:00 p.m. on April 9, the driver and passenger took off running. The deputies caught up to the passenger Zachary Gifford and attempted to detain him for questioning[560].

Actions taken by subject toward police: Gifford refused to comply with the commands of the deputies to peacefully surrender, and he physically struggled with them.

Reactions by the police: One of the deputies deployed a taser to stop Gifford's violent resistance, but it failed to do so. The deputies escalated to lethal force and shot Gifford at least three times in the back, killing him[561].

Outcome of investigation into the fatal police incident: Upon conclusion of the investigation of the shooting, the Kiowa County District Attorney's Office charged Deputy Stump with criminal attempt to commit murder in the second degree and reckless endangerment[562]

Miscellaneous: Gifford's relatives' comments about him having struggles, coupled with his appearance and methamphetamine in his system gives the impression that he had a substance-abuse problem and likely criminal and or mental health history. People do not run from the police for no reason, they typically do so because they are wanted for a previous crime or are in possession of an illegal substance.

What could the subject have done that day to still be alive today? Should not have fled from the deputies during the traffic stop. Should have complied with the lawful commands of deputies and peacefully surrendered. Should not have physically struggled with the deputies.

Justified use of deadly force? Autopsy by the Kiowa County coroner showed that Gifford had lacerations consistent with a physical struggle with the deputies as well as punctures from a taser. If Gifford was shot at close range while fighting with the deputy's then **YES**, it was justified. If however Gifford was shot while running away and not presenting an immediate threat of danger to the deputy's or anyone else, then **NO** the shooting was not justified.

Name: Giuseppe Particianone
Date: 4/10/2020   **Location:** Philadelphia, PA
FACTORS (1,2,9,13,20)

Criminal History/Involved: Unknown./Yes, unlawfully discharging firearm in city limits.

Mental Illness: Unknown.

Substance Abuse History/Involved: Unknown./None stated.

Race/Sex/Age: White/Male/33

Officer(s) Involved: Philadelphia Police Officers Bradford Conlon and Antoine Hayes

What prompted the initial contact with police? Officers were investigating reports of gunfire around midnight on April 10 when they observed two people in a backyard. The two uniformed officers moved a piece of wood, entered the yard, and confronted the two people, Giuseppe Particianone and Kaitlynn Tugliese.

Actions taken by subject toward police: Upon seeing the officers, Tugliese pointed a weapon at them.

Reactions by the police: Officers Conlon and Hayes opened fire at Tugliese, firing multiple rounds, injuring her, and killing Particianone. The officers observed Tugliese throw her weapon on the kitchen floor as she ran away from them. The officers recovered multiple weapons from the scene, "including a .380-caliber pistol, a shotgun, a semiautomatic handgun (.45 caliber), a revolver (.38 caliber), a .22-caliber rifle, multiple fired shotgun shells, multiple fired cartridge casings, and multiple live rounds of ammunition"[563].

Outcome of investigation into the fatal police incident: The incident is under investigation.

Miscellaneous: Tugliese has been charged with assault and numerous other offenses[564].

What could the subject have done that day to still be alive today? Should not have been shooting a weapon or with his friend who was shooting a weapon in a residential neighborhood. Should not have been next to his friend as she pointed a weapon at uniformed police officers.

Justified use of deadly force? YES, the officers were investigating possible gunfire when they encountered a woman who pointed a firearm at them, giving them reasonable cause to believe that their lives were in imminent danger and warranted their use of deadly force to end that threat.

Name: Fred Brown
Date: 4/23/2020   **Location:** North Las Vegas, NV
FACTORS (1,2,12,14,15,19)

Criminal History/Involved: Unknown./Domestic violence, assault of an officer.

Mental Illness: Unknown.

Substance Abuse History/Involved: Unknown./None stated.

Race/Sex/Age: Black/Male/34

Officer(s) Involved: North Las Vegas Police Officer Alexander Cuevas

What prompted the initial contact with police? At about 6 a.m. on April 23, officers responded to a 911 call regarding a domestic disturbance where they were told by the woman that her boyfriend, Fred Brown, had physically abused her[565].

Actions taken by subject toward police: When the officers arrived and told Brown that they could arrest him, Brown attacked the officers, grabbing Cuevas from behind and choking him[566].

Reactions by the police: Officer Cuevas broke free from the chokehold and shot Brown several times, killing him.

Outcome of investigation into the fatal police incident: Investigation is ongoing.

Miscellaneous: One officer suffered minor injuries from the assault by Brown.

What could the subject have done that day to still be alive today? Should not have physically abused his girlfriend, causing her to call the police. Should have complied with the officer's commands and peacefully surrendered. Should not have physically attacked an officer and choked him.

Justified use of deadly force? YES, Brown violently attacked a police officer, putting him in a chokehold. Although the officer managed to break free from the chokehold, Brown's violent assault gave Cuevas reasonable cause to believe that his life was in imminent danger from Brown.

Name: Michael Ramos
Date: 4/24/2020   **Location:** Austin, TX
FACTORS (1,2,8,14,19) 3?,11?

Criminal History/Involved: Yes, Ramos had two previous convictions for stealing vehicles and fleeing police./Yes, the vehicle Ramos was in was reportedly stolen.

Mental Illness: Unknown.

Substance Abuse History/Involved: Unknown./Yes, Ramos was reportedly doing drugs in the car.

Race/Sex/Age: Latino/Male/42

Officer(s) Involved: Austin Police Officers Mitchel Pieper, Christopher Taylor, Darrell Cantu-Harkless, Benjamin Hart, James P. Morgan, Karl Krycia, Valerie Tavarez, and Katrina Ratcliff

What prompted the initial contact with police? Around 6:35 p.m. on April 24, eight officers responded to a 911 call of a Hispanic man and woman "smoking crack and cooking meth" inside a car parked in an apartment complex lot. The caller repeatedly said that the man "has a gun" and he was holding it to the woman. Upon entering the parking lot, the officers took up tactical positions around the suspect's vehicle and ordered the man out. Ramos eventually complied and exited his vehicle but still refused to comply with the officer's commands to come toward them with his hands up. After several minutes of noncompliance and warnings that they would do so, Officer Pieper shot Ramos with a less-than-lethal round[567].

Actions taken by subject toward police: Ramos got back into the vehicle and attempted to drive away, causing officers to scramble for safety[568].

Reactions by the police: Fearing that Ramos was going to run over the officers surrounding his vehicle, Officer Taylor fired three rounds into the vehicle, killing Ramos[569].

Outcome of investigation into the fatal police incident: On March 11, 2021, a grand jury indicted Officer Christopher Taylor for first-degree murder[570].

Miscellaneous: Dashcam and bodycam video of the incident can be seen at *The Texas Tribune*[571].

What could the subject have done that day to still be alive today? Should not have made it appear as if he was doing drugs with or pointing a gun at a woman in a parked car in an apartment complex. Should have complied with the officers' lawful commands and peacefully surrendered to them. Should not have continued stalling which is typically a tactic used by criminals as they consider how they can escape or access a weapon. Should not have gotten back in the car and driven through a parking lot full of cops who were afraid that he may be trying to run them over.

Justified use of deadly force? YES, Officer Taylor reasonably believed that he and other officers surrounding Ramos were in danger of being run over by Ramos as he attempted to flee.

Name: Nicholas Bils
Date: 5/1/2020   **Location:** San Diego, CA
FACTORS (1,2,4,17)

Criminal History/Involved: Yes, Bils had prior warrant arrests and had just been arrested for assault with a deadly weapon./Yes, in escaping custody and unlawful fleeing.

Mental Illness: Yes, Bils was mentally ill; he suffered from paranoid schizophrenia and was very fearful of police.

Substance Abuse History/Involved: Yes, Bils had a history of drug use./Unknown.

Race/Sex/Age: White/Male/36

Officer(s) Involved: Sheriff's Deputy Aaron Russell

What prompted the initial contact with police? While speaking to Bils about his illegally unleashed dog in the park on May 1, Bils became violent and assaulted two State Park Rangers with a golf club. The rangers arrested Bils and were driving him to the jail for processing[572].

Actions taken by subject toward police: Bils managed to get out of the handcuffs, open the back door of the Ranger vehicle, and escape just before getting to the jail[573].

Reactions by the police: Deputy Russell, off-duty at the time, observed Bils escape from the Ranger vehicle and take off running. Russell chased Bils for a block before opening fire and killing Bils from approximately 15 to 20 feet away.

Outcome of investigation into the fatal police incident: San Diego DA charged Russell with second-degree murder.

Miscellaneous: Videos of the incident were captured by cameras on the jail and another building.

What could the subject have done that day to still be alive today? Should have had his dog on a leash so he is not questioned by Park Rangers. Should not have assaulted the Park Rangers, causing them to arrest him. Should not have escaped from the Park Ranger vehicle as it pulled into the jail. Should not have fled from the deputy.

Justified use of deadly force? Under the new California law (AB392) which took effect January 1, 2020, officers may not use deadly force unless it is necessary (standard used to be "reasonable") and may not shoot a fleeing felon if they do not pose an immediate danger[574]. **NO,** unless Russell can articulate how it was necessary to shoot Bils, or how Bils posed an immediate danger to someone else by escaping, the shooting was not justified.

Name: Shaun Lee Fuhr
Date: 5/1/2020   **Location:** Seattle, WA
FACTORS (1,2,19)

Criminal History/Involved: Yes, Fuhr had four previous convictions for fourth-degree domestic violence assault and unlawful possession of a firearm. He also had seven protection orders against him by three different people[575]./Yes, Fuhr had just committed domestic assault, menacing with a weapon, kidnapping, endangering the welfare of a child, attempted burglary, and unlawful fleeing.

Mental Illness: Unknown.

Substance Abuse History/Involved: Unknown./None stated.

Race/Sex/Age: Black/Male/24

Officer(s) Involved: Seattle Police SWAT Officer Noah Zech

What prompted the initial contact with police? At around 2:15 p.m. on May 1, Seattle Police officers responded to a 911 call by a woman reporting that the father of her child had just shot a gun at her and abducted their infant daughter. Officers observed that the woman had clearly been beaten, but the man, Shaun Fuhr, was gone. A half hour later, a report of a burglary-in-progress alerted officers, and they responded there to find Fuhr and the girl[576].

Actions taken by subject toward police: Disregarding the officer's orders to stop, Fuhr took off running while still holding his daughter.

Reactions by the police: When police caught up to Fuhr trapped in a fenced-in area, SWAT Officer Zech fired one shot from his duty rifle at Fuhr's head, killing him.

Outcome of investigation into the fatal police incident: King County Sheriff's Office's Major Crimes Unit, the Inspector General, and the Office of Professional Accountability are investigating.

Miscellaneous: Video from one of the officer's bodycams is available at *KOMO News*[577].

What could the subject have done that day to still be alive today? Should not have severely beaten the mother of his child, shot a gun at her, and abducted their child. Should have complied with the officer's lawful orders and peacefully surrendered. Should not have endangered the welfare of the child and fled from the police.

Justified use of deadly force? YES, Fuhr was a dangerous criminal who kidnapped and severely beat a woman, shot a gun at her in the presence of their infant child, and then abducted the child against her will. Officers had reasonable cause to believe that the child's life was in imminent danger from Fuhr by using the weapon that officers believed he had or even using his hands since she was an infant and very delicate.

Name: Tyler Hays
Date: 5/19/2020   **Location:** Sale Creek, TN
FACTORS (1,2,8,12,14,15,19)

Criminal History/Involved: Yes, Hays had prior seven arrests, mostly for drugs. He was arrested less than 2 weeks earlier for possession with intent to sell methamphetamine, heroin, LSD, and pills[578]./Yes, unlawful fleeing and assault of an officer.

Mental Illness: Unknown.

Substance Abuse History/Involved: Yes, he was a drug addict[579]./None stated.

Race/Sex/Age: White/Male/29

Officer(s) Involved: Hamilton County Sheriff's Deputy Jordan Long

What prompted the initial contact with police? While conducting a vehicle stop for a traffic violation around 2 a.m. on May 19, Deputy Long observed the driver, Tyler Hays, run from the car. The deputy chased him, ultimately catching up to Hays.

Actions taken by subject toward police: Hays refused to peacefully surrender and instead got into a physical altercation with the deputy. Hays elbowed Deputy Long in the stomach, managed to get on Long's back, and choked Long with his forearm[580].

Reactions by the police: Deputy Long tried to use his personal weapons and a taser to control and subdue Hays, but to no effect. Long shot Hays one time in the back, killing him[581].

Outcome of investigation into the fatal police incident: Tennessee Bureau of Investigations completed their investigation and the Hamilton County District Attorney cleared Officer Long in the shooting and will not be charging him[582].

Miscellaneous: According to the autopsy, the taser penetrated the clothing of Hays but not his skin. The single gunshot killing Hays was shot from "intermediate-range"[583] and hit him in the center of his back.

What could the subject have done that day to still be alive today? Should have peacefully complied with the deputy and pulled over and remained in the vehicle during the traffic stop. Should not have fled from the vehicle and then physically assaulted the deputy. Should have complied with the deputy and have been peacefully arrested.

Justified use of deadly force? YES, Deputy Long was physically attacked and injured by Hays in the middle of the night, and with no backup. Alone, exhausted and having tried unsuccessfully to use his hands and nonlethal means to arrest Hays, Long reasonably feared for his life and used deadly force.

Name: Maurice S. Gordon

Date: 5/23/2020   **Location:** Bass River, NJ

FACTORS (1,2,4,8,12,14,19)

Criminal History/Involved: Unknown./Yes, speeding, attempted grand theft of a police vehicle and assaulting an officer.

Mental Illness: Yes, Gordon was on medication for mental illness and his friends were concerned because he was "talking about being possessed and having paranormal experiences"[584].

Substance Abuse History/Involved: Unknown./None stated.

Race/Sex/Age: Black/Male/28

Officer(s) Involved: New Jersey State Trooper Sgt. Randall Wetzel

What prompted the initial contact with police? Trooper Wetzel pulled over Gordon for driving at the speed of 110 mph on the Garden State Parkway around 6:30 a.m. on May 23. Upon stopping, Gordon's vehicle was unable to be restarted and safely moved out of the traffic lane, so Wetzel ordered a tow truck and permitted Gordon to wait in the police cruiser, where he would be safe.

Actions taken by subject toward police: Gordon became combative with the trooper, got out of the back-seat of the trooper's vehicle, and attempted to get into the front driver's side. He also fought with the trooper along the side of the road as traffic was going by at high rates of speed.

Reactions by the police: Trooper Wetzel pulled Gordon out of the driver's side of the police vehicle. The trooper can be seen on video struggling to detain Gordon on the side of the parkway where he also unsuccessfully used pepper spray to get Gordon to peacefully comply. When Gordon attempted to take Wetzel's weapon, Wetzel shot Gordon at close range, killing him[585].

Outcome of investigation into the fatal police incident: NJ State Attorney General's office is investigating.

Miscellaneous: Dashcam and video of a backward facing camera inside the vehicle of the incident are available at *WHYY*[586].

What could the subject have done that day to still be alive today? Should have been on his proper medications, confined to an institution or properly supervised for his own safety. Should not have been driving over 100 mph, thus gaining the attention of a State Trooper. Should have remained in the trooper's vehicle until the tow truck arrived. Should not have tried to steal the trooper's vehicle. Should have complied with the trooper and peacefully surrendered. Should not have assaulted the trooper and attempted to take his duty weapon.

Justified use of deadly force? YES, Trooper Wetzel tried through physical force and less-than-lethal pepper spray to stop Gordon from attacking him, endangering his life on the side of a busy parkway. When Gordon attempted to take Wetzel's gun, Wetzel had reasonable cause to believe that his life was in danger and used deadly force to stop the imminent threat posed by Gordon.

INCIDENT GARNERING NATIONAL ATTENTION BUT DOES NOT INVOLVE INTENTIONAL DEADLY FORCE

Name: George Floyd

Date: 5/25/2020   **Location:** Minneapolis, MN

FACTORS (1,2,3,4,8,14) NOT INCLUDED IN STATISTICS

Criminal History/Involved: Yes, Floyd had prior convictions for assault and armed robbery, theft, and possession of cocaine[587] [588]./Yes, Floyd used a $20 counterfeit bill.

Substance Abuse History/Involved: Yes, Floyd has numerous prior drug-related arrests./Yes, Floyd told the officers, "I was just hooping earlier"[589]. Additionally, the autopsy showed that Floyd had 11 ng/mL of fentanyl along with 19 ng/mL 5 of meth in his system[590].

Race/Sex/Age: Black/Male/46

Officer(s) Involved: MPLS Police Officers Derek Chauvin, Thomas Lane, J. Alexander Kueng and Tou Thao

What prompted the initial contact with police? At 8:08 p.m. on May 25, MPLS officers responded to a 911 call from a store clerk reporting a forgery in progress. Upon arriving at the scene, the officers were told that the man with the fake money was in a car outside the store. The officers approached the vehicle and encountered George Floyd in the driver's seat[591].

Actions taken by subject toward police: Floyd immediately acted irrational, failed to comply with the officer's commands, and prompted Officer Lane to draw his gun. After Floyd showed his hands, Officer Lane holstered his weapon and handcuffed Floyd as he exited the vehicle. Before the officers used any force on him, Floyd complained seven times that "he couldn't breathe" and twice he said that he was "going to die"[592]. When the officers put Floyd in the patrol car, he climbed out the other side, complained about being claustrophobic, and asked to lie down.

Reactions by the police: The officers let Floyd lie down on the ground as he requested with Officer Chauvin keeping control of Floyd using the department authorized "maximal restraint technique"[593]. As Floyd split his head on the patrol car, the officers requested rescue to respond. When the officers became concerned about Floyd's odd behavior that was indicating possible excited delirium, they requested a rush on advanced medical personnel, but Floyd died before they arrived.

What could the subject have done that day to still be alive today? Should not have ingested more than three times the lethal amount of fentanyl. Should not have committed the crime of forgery. Should have complied with police.

Outcome of investigation into the fatal police incident: On April 20, 2021, a jury found Chauvin guilty of second-degree murder, third-degree murder, and second-degree manslaughter. The other three officers are charged with aiding and abetting both murder and manslaughter in the second-degree[594].

Justified use of deadly force? NO, deadly force was not justified. Once Floyd stopped resisting and especially when he became lifeless, the restraint technique should have been terminated and CPR initiated. The jury has ruled but that does not change the fact that Floyd may have died after 8 minutes 46 seconds even if he had been in the back of the patrol car or at the police precinct. As Dr. Baker told police, with Floyd's blood level of fentanyl at 11 ng/mL, "If he were found dead at home alone and no other apparent causes, this could be acceptable to call an overdose. Deaths have been certified with levels of 3. That is a fatal level of fentanyl under normal circumstances"[595].

Name: Channing Lamar Spivey
Date: 5/27/2020   **Location:** Luverne, AL
FACTORS (1,2,4,12,14,19)

Criminal History/Involved: None stated./Yes, while it was a 911 call for a medical check on the welfare, Spivey acted violently toward the first responders and broke a window in the ambulance.

Mental Illness: Spivey recently had a brain surgery to remove a cancerous tumor. Since the surgery, he had been "irritable, confused and behaving erratically," and his symptoms resembled "schizophrenia"[596].

Substance Abuse History/Involved: None stated./Spivey was on prescription medications.

Race/Sex/Age: White/Male/34

Officer(s) Involved: Luverne Assistant Police Chief Mason Adcock and Crenshaw County Sheriff's Deputy Brent Penny

What prompted the initial contact with police? During the afternoon of May 27, Sheriff's Deputy Penny responded along with emergency medical personnel to a 911 call requesting a check on the welfare of Channing Spivey because he "became irrational, argumentative, and belligerent"[597] toward his family.

Actions taken by subject toward police: Despite the deputy and medical personnel's efforts to restrain him, Spivey punched out a window in the ambulance. Spivey was also unaffected by Penny's use of the taser and advanced aggressively toward Penny who retreated toward Chief Adcock who lived nearby and was asked to intercede by Spivey's family. Even with Deputy Penny and Chief Adcock pointing their weapons at him, Spivey continued to advance toward them.

Reactions by the police: Fearing for his life from Spivey's irrational advancement toward him, Chief Adcock fatally shot Spivey five times.

What could the subject have done that day to still be alive today? Spivey was not in control of his mental facilities due to his medical condition, so he should have been confined to a house or facility where he would be safe from being harmed. His brother and friend could have tried to subdue him instead of calling 911–the fact that they did not initially shows they feared him as well. Should have complied with the deputy and medical personnel.

Outcome of investigation into the fatal police incident: State Bureau of Investigation is conducting the investigation.

Miscellaneous: Any officer would be justifiably fearful someone in Spivey's emotionally disturbed state could overpower them and do them mortal harm.

Justified use of deadly force? YES, but a tragic one. Considering that a taser had already proven ineffective, an earlier attempt to subdue Spivey failed, and Spivey demonstrated that he was oblivious to pain by punching through a glass window. His aggressively walking toward the officers despite the threat of their firearms pointed at him shows that he was acting irrationally and violently-therefore causing Chief Adcock to reasonably fear for his life if Spivey was able to engage him or Deputy Penny physically.

Name: Hannah R. Fizer
Date: 6/13/2020   **Location:** Sedalia, MO
FACTORS (1,2,4,5,8,10,19)

Criminal History/Involved: Unknown./Yes, Fizer threatened an officer.

Mental Illness: None reported, however, Fizer's actions were irrational and suicidal.

Substance Abuse History/Involved: Unknown./None stated.

Race/Sex/Age: White/Female/25

Officer(s) Involved: Pettis County Sheriff's deputy

What prompted the initial contact with police? A deputy pulled over Fizer for a traffic infraction at approximately 10 p.m. on June 13[598].

Actions taken by subject toward police: When the deputy approached her vehicle and asked for identification, Fizer refused to identify herself. Fizer then threatened that she had a gun and was going to shoot the deputy before reaching down into the grabbable area by her feet as if to get a weapon[599].

Reactions by the police: Fearing Fizer was going to follow through on her threat and was accessing a weapon with which to shoot him, the deputy shot Fizer five times, killing her.

Outcome of investigation into the fatal police incident: Missouri Office of Prosecution Services announced that the shooting was deemed justified based on the evidence.

Miscellaneous: There was no officer bodycam or police vehicle dashcam. Surveillance camera from a nearby business captured the incident, but without any sound. The actions by Fizer who had no weapon in the car make no sense to her family/friends, but the deputy did not know Fizer, all he could go on is how she presented herself to him during that stop.

What could the subject have done that day to still be alive today? Should have complied with the deputy's commands, properly identified herself and accepted whatever summons she was issued. Should not have told the deputy that she was armed, was intending to kill him, and then simulate reaching for a weapon.

Justified use of deadly force? YES, the deputy was told by Fizer that she intended to shoot him before she attempted to access an object at her feet, something that is confirmed by the video showing her movements within the vehicle and the audio from the dispatch since her phone was still connected to 911 during the stop. The deputy had reasonable cause to believe that Fizer was grabbing for a gun to shoot him with, thereby justifying his preemptive use of deadly force.

THIS IS NOT AN UNARMED SUBJECT SO FACTORS (1,2,3,8,9,12,19) ARE NOT INCLUDED IN STATISTICS

Name: Robert D'Lon Harris

Date: 6/25/2020   **Location:** Vinita, OK

Criminal History/Involved: Yes, Harris was a known gang member and convicted felon./Yes, Harris was illegally in possession of a 9-mm handgun and cocaine during the time of the traffic stop[600].

Mental Illness: Unknown.

Substance Abuse History/Involved: Unknown./Yes, Harris had PCP in his system.

Race/Sex/Age: Black/Male/34

Officer(s) Involved: Oklahoma State Highway Patrol Trooper Caleb Cole

What prompted the initial contact with police? Just before 9 a.m. on June 25, Trooper Cole stopped a vehicle in which Robert Harris was a passenger because its rear temporary license plate was illegible. During the traffic stop Trooper Cole noticed that Harris was nervous so after talking with the driver he questioned Harris. Trooper Cole told Harris to exit the vehicle, advising Harris that he would be searched for weapons[601].

Actions taken by subject toward police: After exiting the vehicle, Harris ignored Trooper Cole's orders to turn around to be searched and instead sat back down in the car, put his hands behind his back and accessed a handgun which he then quickly pulled out and pointed at the trooper.

Reactions by the police: Seeing the gun in Harris' hand, Trooper Cole shot Harris one time in the face killing him.

Outcome of investigation into the fatal police incident: District 12 District Attorney Matt Ballard concluded Trooper Cole's actions were "justified and appropriate under the law and facts"[602].

Miscellaneous: *The Washington Post's* Police Shootings Database description of this incident is "Robert D'Lon Harris, an unarmed 34-year-old Black man, was shot on June 25, 2020, in a vehicle in Vinita, Okla."[603].

What could the subject have done that day to still be alive today? Should not have been illegally in possession of a gun. Should not have disobeyed the trooper's orders. Should not have pulled a gun out and pointed it at the trooper.

Justified use of deadly force? YES, Trooper Cole justifiably feared for his life when he saw that Harris possessed a handgun and had pointed it at him during the traffic stop. This is as basic as it gets when it comes to justifiable use of deadly force, yet *The Washington Post* database as of 2020 made it appear as if Harris was unarmed–thus feeding into the narrative of unarmed Black males being killed by White officers.

Name: David James Pruitte
Date: 8/4/2020   **Location:** Port Orchard, WA
FACTORS (1,3,4,5,10,19)

Criminal History/Involved: None reported./None stated.

Mental Illness: Yes, Pruitte struggled with mental health issues, had threatened suicide earlier in the year, and had a prior incident in 2016 where a responding officer said that it appeared Pruitte was going to jump off the bridge.

Substance Abuse History/Involved: Yes, Pruitte's family said that he struggled with drug addiction./Yes, Pruitte had alcohol in his system at the time of the shooting.

Race/Sex/Age: White/Male/36

Officer(s) Involved: Kitsap County Sheriff's Deputies Andrew Hren and Josh Puckett

What prompted the initial contact with police? At 7:23 p.m. on August 4, two Kitsap County Sheriff's deputies responded to a 911 call to check the welfare of a man sitting on a highway overpass with his legs dangling above the passing traffic[604].

Actions taken by subject toward police: Deputy Hren said "Pruitte took a "'fighting stance,' threatened to kill the deputies and demanded they shoot him"[605]. Numerous witnesses who observed the incident gave statements supporting Deputy Hren's account, adding that "Pruitt appeared to be armed or arming himself as he approached responding deputies"[606].

Reactions by the police: Fearing that Pruitte was armed with a concealed gun, less than 15 feet away, and about to shoot at Deputy Puckett and himself, Deputy Sheriff Hren fatally shot Pruitte in the chest.

Outcome of investigation into the fatal police incident: Investigation was conducted jointly by the Washington State Patrol, Port Orchard Police, and Bremerton Police Departments, and it is being reviewed by the county prosecutor.

What could the subject have done that day to still be alive today? Should not have been sitting on an overpass causing those passing by to be concerned that he might be looking to commit suicide. Should have complied with the officers' lawful commands. Should not have given the officers the false impression that he was armed. Should not have aggressively advanced toward the officers.

Justified use of deadly force? YES, Pruitte motioned to be holding a weapon in his pocket when confronted by the deputies, giving them reasonable cause to believe that their life was in imminent danger and prompting their justified use of deadly force. Tragically for all involved, it appears that Pruitte changed his original plans of committing suicide from jumping off the overpass to suicide by cop.

Name: Jeffrey Scott Haarsma
Date: 8/7/2020   **Location:** St. Petersburg, FL
FACTORS (1,2,4,12,14,15,19)

Criminal History/Involved: Yes, Haarsma had unknown priors./Yes, larceny and assaulting an officer.

Mental Illness: Yes, Haarsma had a history of mental illness, was being treated by psychotherapist for at least the past ten years, and neighbors feared him[607].

Substance Abuse History/Involved: Unknown./None stated.

Race/Sex/Age: White/Male/55

Officer(s) Involved: St. Petersburg Police Officer Allison Savarese

What prompted the initial contact with police? Officer Savarese responded to a condo complex around 9 p.m. on August 7 for a neighbor dispute where a man, Jeffrey Haarsma had reportedly stolen his neighbor's furniture[608].

Actions taken by subject toward police: Upon seeing the officer coming up the exterior stairs to talk to him, Haarsma physically assaulted her. During the assault, Haarsma grabbed Officer Savarese by the throat and started choking her[609].

Reactions by the police: While being choked by the much larger and stronger Haarsma, Officer Savarese feared that she would be choked to death. Savarese fired two shots into Haarsma at close range, killing him.

Outcome of investigation into the fatal police incident: Pinellas County Sheriff Bob Gualtieri announced the officer was justified in shooting Haarsma.

Miscellaneous: During a 2017 incident, it took two officers and the use of a taser to gain control of Haarsma. The officer's statement of the incident is backed up by a neighbor who observed it and said Haarsma left Savarese no choice[610].

What could the subject have done that day to still be alive today? Should have been on the proper psychological medication, confined to an institution, or properly supervised for his own safety. Should not have gotten in a dispute and stolen from his neighbors. Should not have attacked the police officer sent to investigate the incident. Should have complied with the officer and peacefully surrendered.

Justified use of deadly force? YES, Officer Savarese was violently attacked by Haarsma, a mentally unstable and much larger man. Savarese had reasonable cause to believe Haarsma would continue choking her until she was dead, or unconscious, at which point he could access her weapon and shoot her.

Name: Julian Edward Roosevelt Lewis
Date: 8/7/2020   **Location:** Sylvania, GA
FACTORS (1,2,3,8,17)

Criminal History/Involved: Unknown./Yes, unlawful fleeing.

Mental Illness: Unknown.

Substance Abuse History/Involved: Unknown./Possibly, a beer was found in the center console of the vehicle.

Race/Sex/Age: Black/Male/60

Officer(s) Involved: Georgia State Trooper Jacob Gordon Thompson

What prompted the initial contact with police? Trooper Thompson attempted to pull over a vehicle being operated by Lewis around 9:20 p.m. on August 7 for having an equipment violation.

Actions taken by subject toward police: Lewis refused to pull over, forcing the Trooper to pursue his vehicle for approximately 2.5 miles.

Reactions by the police: To safely end the pursuit, Thompson conducted a PIT maneuver on Lewis' vehicle, sending it into a ditch. Stopping his patrol car next to that of Lewis, Thompson exited it and alleged that Lewis was revving the engine and maneuvering the steering wheel as if to run him over. Fearing that he was about to get run over, Thompson fired one shot into the vehicle, striking Lewis in the face and killing him[611].

Outcome of investigation into the fatal police incident: Thompson was fired from the State Troopers, charged with aggravated assault and felony murder, and held without bail. A review of the dashcam and forensics disputes Thompson's account. According to the dashcam video and examination of the vehicle, Lewis' vehicle was "rendered inoperable by the crash" and the "car wheels were turned away from the trooper"[612]. Additionally, Thompson fired the shot within a second of stopping his patrol vehicle.

What could the subject have done that day to still be alive today? Should have complied with the trooper and pulled his vehicle over. Should not have fled and caused the trooper to have to conduct a dangerous PIT technique to stop Lewis' vehicle. These actions do not justify Lewis getting shot, but they highly likely would have prevented it from happening in the first place.

Justified use of deadly force? If the facts supported Thompson's statement, then yes it would have been justified. Since the facts do not, and Thompson did not have reasonable cause to believe that his life was in imminent danger from Lewis and/or his vehicle, **NO**, he was not justified in using deadly force.

Name: Jonathan Price
Date: 10/3/2020   **Location:** Wolfe City, TX
FACTORS (1,2,12,14,19) 3?

Criminal History/Involved: No./Yes, Price resisted arrest/obstructed governmental authority.

Mental Illness: Unknown.

Substance Abuse History/Involved: No./The officer thought that he was drunk, toxicology reports are awaited to confirm or deny that.

Race/Sex/Age: Black/Male/31

Officer(s) Involved: Wolfe City PD Officer Shaun David Lucas

What prompted the initial contact with police? At 8:24 p.m. on October 3, Officer Lucas responded to a 911 call of a disturbance, "possible fight in progress" at a convenience store. Upon arriving, Officer Lucas was greeted by Jonathan Price who "apologized for broken glass on the ground, saying that someone tried to "wrap me up"" [613]. Thinking that Price was intoxicated and somehow involved in the fight, Officer Lucas attempted to detain Price.

Actions taken by subject toward police: Price refused to comply with the officer, telling him "I can't be detained"[614]. When Officer Lucas then grabbed Price's arm, issued verbal commands, and warned Price that he was going to be tased, Price rebuffed his efforts and started walking away.

Reactions by the police: Officer Lucas tased Price, but it failed to gain his compliance, and instead, Price then walked toward Lucas and "appeared to reach out and grab the end of Officer Lucas' Taser"[615]. At that point Officer Lucas fatally shot Price four times in the upper body.

Outcome of investigation into the fatal police incident: Officer Lucas was fired, arrested, and charged with murder. According to the Texas Department of Public Safety, the "preliminary investigation indicates that the actions of Officer Lucas were not objectionably reasonable"[616].

What could the subject have done that day to still be alive today? Should have complied with Officer Lucas' initial orders to detain him, not have walked away, and not have attempted to grab the taser.

Justified use of deadly force? News reports and statements about Mr. Price make him sound like a remarkable man. Unfortunately, Officer Lucas did not personally know Mr. Price the way so many others did, so he had to act upon the facts presented to him, which were that he just arrived at a 911 call of a possible fight where Price, by apologizing for the broken glass gives the impression that he was involved in. Given the additional impression that Price was drunk, Officer Lucas tried to detain Price. Had Price just complied and been detained, the facts could have been worked out. Unfortunately, Price refused and tried to walk away, prompting Officer Lucas to use force and a taser, both of which failed. When Price attempted to grab the taser, Officer Lucas feared for his safety and **YES**, he justifiably used deadly force. It is a tragic incident that could have easily been avoided, yet if Price were White, it is doubtful Lucas would have been fired or arrested. For comparison, there were no such actions taken against the officers involved in the recent fatal police shootings of Channing Spivey and David Pruitte.

Name: Juan Adrian Garcia
Date: 10/5/2020   **Location:** Napa, CA
FACTORS (1,2,3,4,5,8,10,19)

Criminal History/Involved: Yes, Garcia has three previous arrests for DWI, the most recent being 2019./Yes, Garcia was DWI when observed driving by Sgt. Ackman.

Mental Illness: None reported, however, Garcia was clearly in an altered mental state and his actions were suicidal.

Substance Abuse History/Involved: Yes, Garcia had previous DWI arrests./Yes, toxicology shows Garcia's blood alcohol content was .33%, more than four times the legal limit in California.

Race/Sex/Age: Latino/Male/47

Officer(s) Involved: Napa County Sheriff's Deputy, Sergeant David Ackman

What prompted the initial contact with police? At approximately 10:10 p.m. on October 5, Sgt. Ackman pulled over a vehicle operated by Juan Garcia for driving without the headlights on at night[617] [618].

Actions taken by subject toward police: Without being told to exit his vehicle by the Sgt, Garcia threw his cellphone out of the window and got out of the car, putting his hands behind his back. After first being concerned by the erratic behavior of him throwing the phone and getting out of the car, Sgt. Ackerman holstered his weapon when it looked like Garcia was prepared to be arrested. Far from being cooperative, Garcia then started aggressively walking toward the Sgt. while maintaining one hand behind his back the entire time in defiance of the sergeant's verbal orders for him to stop[619].

Reactions by the police: Contrary to the lawful orders to stop and show both his hands, Garcia kept his right hand behind his back and increased his advance toward Sgt. Ackerman. Fearing for his life from what he perceived as an imminent deadly threat, Sgt. Ackerman shot Garcia six times, killing him[620].

What could the subject have done that day to still be alive today? Should have had his headlights on and should not have been driving while intoxicated. Should have complied with the officers' orders; shown both his hands and stopped aggressively walking toward the deputy.

Outcome of investigation into the fatal police incident: The Napa County Major Crimes Task Force is conducting the investigation.

Justified use of deadly force? YES, the bodycam video shows that this is a clear case where the subject refused to comply with the deputy's orders and instead chose to exhibit aggressive behavior causing that deputy to reasonably fear that the subject was armed and intending to use lethal force.

Name: Anthony Michael Legato
Date: 10/9/2020   **Location:** Pine County, MN
FACTORS (1,2,3,8,11,19)

Criminal History/Involved: Yes, Legato had prior felony convictions for burglary, fraud, and possession of stolen property.[621] /Yes, Legato had several active warrants including those for domestic assault and burglary. He possessed a stolen firearm. He was driving while impaired by drugs down the wrong side of the highway and fleeing from police.

Mental Illness: Unknown.

Substance Abuse History/Involved: Unknown./Yes, Legato possessed meth on his person and in his system according to the toxicology report.

Race/Sex/Age: White/Male/25

Officer(s) Involved: Pine County Sheriff's Deputy Joshua Pepin

What prompted the initial contact with police? At approximately 1:45 p.m. on October 9, Pine County deputies responded to a 911 call about a domestic incident involving Anthony Legato at a nearby Casino when they spotted a vehicle matching that of Legato and began pursuing it[622].

Actions taken by subject toward police: With the deputies' vehicle behind his, Legato entered Interstate 35 by driving south into the northbound lanes of traffic and then shortly after he pulled over and got out of his car. Legato then got back into his car and started driving into oncoming traffic when Deputy Pepin exited his patrol car after stopping it south of and facing head on to Legato's vehicle[623].

Reactions by the police: When Legato started driving toward him, Deputy Pepin opened fire on Legato in his vehicle, fatally shooting him.

What could the subject have done that day to still be alive today? Should not have been involved in a domestic incident, prompting his partner to call 911. Should have immediately pulled over when he saw the Deputy Sheriff's vehicle behind his. Should not have entered into the interstate on the wrong side, driving into oncoming traffic. Should have remained outside of his vehicle and complied with Deputy Pepin's orders instead of getting back into his vehicle and driving toward the deputy and oncoming traffic.

Outcome of investigation into the fatal police incident: Following the investigation by the Minnesota Bureau of Criminal Apprehension, Pine County Attorney Reese Frederickson determined Deputy Pepin was justified in using deadly force to stop Legato from potentially killing Pepin or other nearby motorists.[624]

Miscellaneous: There is bodycam and dashcam video of the incident, but they have not been released to the public yet.

Justified use of deadly force? YES. Upon seeing Deputy Pepin exit his vehicle, Legato purposefully re-entered his and started driving it southbound into northbound traffic toward Deputy Pepin. Reasonably fearing for his safety and the safety of the motorists due to Legato's driving toward him and into oncoming highway traffic, Pepin justifiably used deadly force.

Name: Anthony Jones
Date: 10/12/2020   **Location:** Bethel Springs, TN
FACTORS (1,2,4,8,10,12,14,19)

Criminal History/Involved: Unknown./Yes, Jones was driving a stolen vehicle, and he drove recklessly at high rates of speed while trying to flee from the police.

Mental Illness: None reported, however, Jones' actions of pretending to have a firearm and refusing to comply after being tasered were irrational and suicidal.

Substance Abuse History/Involved: Unknown./None stated.

Race/Sex/Age: Black/Male/24

Officer(s) Involved: Henderson Police Department Officers Kyle Carter and Danielle Cook

What prompted the initial contact with police? At approximately 1:15 a.m. on October 12, Henderson Police Officers responded to a 911 call of a possible drunk driver. The officers identified the vehicle which was driven by Anthony Jones on Highway 45 and attempted to pull it over[625].

Actions taken by subject toward police: Jones refused to pull over and instead took the officers on a high-speed chase reaching speeds over 100 mph which ended when Jones crashed his vehicle in Bethel Springs. After crashing, Jones exited his vehicle and made it appear to the officers that he was armed with a gun[626].

Reactions by the police: Fearing that Jones was armed with a gun as he said but not seeing one, the officers tased him. The taser proved ineffective and did not get Jones to comply and be peacefully arrested. As Jones continued to be combative with the officers, one of them shot Jones twice, killing him.

What could the subject have done that day to still be alive today? Should not have stolen a vehicle. Should not have driven as if he was impaired, prompting concerned motorists to call 911. Should have immediately pulled over for the officers. Should have complied with the officers' commands and not threatened/fought with them.

Outcome of investigation into the fatal police incident: Investigation by the Tennessee Bureau of Investigation is ongoing.

Miscellaneous: Quotes from a protest organizer that "We are trying to understand why these police officers took it upon themselves to cross county lines to subdue an individual,"[627] and from Jones Aunt that "He used to bring strays home, and he used to play with his toys, and I still remember and envision him as that same lovable little boy"[628] are indicative of the biased reporting on such incidents.

Justified use of deadly force? YES, the officers were justified to use deadly force when Jones exited his vehicle and made it appear through his words and actions that he was armed with a gun. The officers showed extreme restraint (and bad tactics) by not taking that threat seriously and instead tasing Jones. When the taser proved ineffective and Jones actions caused the officers to reasonably fear for their own safety from the irrational and violent subject, deadly force was justified.

Name: Marcellis Stinnette
Date: 10/20/2020   **Location:** Waukegan, IL
FACTORS (1,2,8,11,13,20)

Criminal History/Involved: Yes, Stinnette had a probation violation and warrant in Florida./Yes, Stinnette was wanted for a warrant and his girlfriend Tafara Williams fled from police and drove recklessly in doing so.

Mental Illness: Unknown.

Substance Abuse History/Involved: Unknown. / None stated.

Race/Sex/Age: Black/Male/19

Officer(s) Involved: Waukegan Police Department, Police Officers Dante Salinas and James Keating

What prompted the initial contact with police? At just before midnight on October 20, Officer Keating approached a suspicious vehicle with an expired registration and recognized the passenger Marcellis Stinnette who he knew had a warrant.

Actions taken by subject toward police: After Officer Keating told Stinnette that he was under arrest, Williams hit the gas and drove away from Keating while he was leaning against the vehicle, prompting Keating to broadcast over the radio that the car hit him. Officer Salinas was nearby and caught up to the vehicle after it fled from Keating and slid off the road shortly after. As Salinas exited his patrol car, Williams again hit the gas, this time driving the car in reverse toward the officer[629].

Reactions by the police: Fearing that he was about to be run over just as he believed Officer Keating had been moments earlier, Officer Salinas opened fire on the vehicle causing Williams to miss him but continue driving in reverse until crashing into a building. Salinas and other responding officers then arrested Williams and Stinnette and rendered medical care after ensuring that they were not armed[630].

What could the subject have done that day to still be alive today? Stinnette should have complied with Officer Keating instead of arguing with him before his girlfriend decided to drive away. Williams should have turned the vehicle off and complied with Officer Keating instead of driving away. Williams should have exited the vehicle after it slid off the road instead of reversing towards Officer Salinas.

Outcome of investigation into the fatal police incident: Officer Salinas was promptly fired for failing to abide by department policies, including not immediately activating his body camera[631]. The Illinois State Police is conducting a joint investigation with the FBI[632].

Justified use of deadly force? YES, Salinas was justified in using deadly force against the vehicle as it was being driven at him while he was out in the open and could possibly be crushed between it and his patrol car. It is unfortunate that Stinnette was struck instead of the driver, but the fact "there were no bullet holes in the windshield, only in the driver's door"[633] shows that Officer Salinas was using deadly force against the proper target, the driver. It is Ms. Williams fault that Stinnette bore the tragic consequences of her actions, not Officer Salinas.

Name: Emmett Cocreham
Date: 10/20/2020   **Location:** Phoenix, AZ
FACTORS (1,2,4,9,13,20)

Criminal History/Involved: None stated, however, Emmett had a history of domestic violence and previous dealings with the police./Yes, Emmett's violent words and actions made his mother fear for her safety.

Mental Illness: Statements made by Emmett's mother calling police because he was "acting strangely"[634] and his uncle, Bill Martinez, saying Emmett "was upset because he didn't understand what was going on"[635] raises the likelihood he was mentally ill.

Substance Abuse History/Involved: Unknown./None stated.

Race/Sex/Age: Black/Male/44

Officer(s) Involved: Phoenix Police Officer Adrian Juarez and an unnamed Phoenix police officer

What prompted the initial contact with police? At approximately 8:45 p.m. on October 20, two Phoenix police officers responded to a domestic 911 call to check on the welfare of a woman who was scared by her son's (Emmett Cocreham) strange behavior. Upon arriving at the incident location, the woman told the officers that Emmett, and his brother George were armed and may become violent with them. The brothers were observed through the window holding weapons, and when officers went to the back of the house, George was seen with a weapon. Additional officers responded, surrounded the house, and issued commands for the brothers to disarm and peacefully surrender.

Actions taken by subject toward police: The brothers disregarded the officers' commands and continued arguing with each other at the back of the house and then returned inside only for George to come out of the back door and point his rifle at Emmett and the officers[636].

Reactions by the police: Fearing that George was going to start firing at any one of the officers posted around the backyard, Officer Adrian Juarez fired multiple rounds from his patrol AR-15 rifle from behind a fence approximately 50 feet away at George, fatally striking him. Emmett was also hit, but since George had fired his rifle, it has not been officially reported yet from which weapon Emmett was struck. Another unidentified officer also fired one shot at George[637].

What could the subject have done that day to still be alive today? Emmett and his brother George could both have been alive today if they had not caused their mother to fear for her life and call 911, and if they had obeyed the officers' lawful orders and peacefully surrendered.

Outcome of investigation into the fatal police incident: The Maricopa County Attorney's Office and Phoenix Police Department Professional Standards Bureau are investigating the incident[638].

Justified use of deadly force? YES, when George pointed his rifle at the officers, they were presented with a deadly threat and justified to use deadly force. If Emmett was not shot by George, then he was tragically caught in the crossfire.

Name: David Angel Villalobos-Baldovinos
Date: 10/23/2020   **Location:** San Ysidro, CA
FACTORS (1,2,4,12,15,19)

Criminal History/Involved: Unknown./Yes, Baldovinos attempted to illegally cross the border into the USA.

Mental Illness: Baldovinos is reported as being "developmentally delayed"[639].

Substance Abuse History/Involved: Unknown./None stated.

Race/Sex/Age: Latino/Male/30

Officer(s) Involved: U.S. Border Patrol Agent Ryan Gonsalves

What prompted the initial contact with police? At approximately 5:45 p.m. on October 23, Agent Gonsalves responded to the San Ysidro border crossing to apprehend a Mexican national (David Villalobos-Baldovinos) reportedly trying to illegally enter the U.S[640].

Actions taken by subject toward police: Instead of complying with Agent Gonsalves, Baldovinos fought with the agent causing him to suffer minor injuries[641].

Reactions by the police: Alone, injured, and being attacked by the violent man, Agent Gonsalves drew his weapon and shot Baldovinos once in the body which proved fatal.

What could the subject have done that day to still be alive today? Baldovinos should have simply complied with Agent Gonsalves lawful orders and be peacefully arrested, processed, and, no doubt, released soon after to attempt another illegal border crossing on another day.

Outcome of investigation into the fatal police incident: The San Diego Police Department Homicide Unit is investigating the incident.

Miscellaneous: Since it is reported that Baldovinos "spent most of his life in California with his mother and five younger siblings"[642], this was not his first time of illegally crossing the border.

Justified use of deadly force? YES, the extenuating circumstances of Agent Gonsalves being alone, injured, and fighting off a violent border crosser who had already shown complete contempt for the law, all add up to the agent reasonably fearing that his life was in danger and justifiably used deadly force to prevent Baldovinos from overpowering him and using his weapon against him.

Name: John Pacheaco Jr.
Date: 10/31/2020   **Location:** Denver, CO
FACTORS (1,2,8,11,14,15,19)3?

Criminal History/Involved: Yes, Pacheaco served jail time for prior arrests including illegal possession of guns, drugs, aggravated (armed) motor vehicle theft, and escape[643] [644]./Yes, the pickup truck Pacheaco was driving was reported stolen, and he was possibly under the influence of alcohol or drugs while behind the wheel.

Substance Abuse History/Involved: Yes, Pacheaco was a known drug addict with multiple attempts at rehab[645]./Pacheaco's passing out behind the wheel in the middle of the roadway suggests that he was on some kind of illegal substance or DWI. Toxicology results are awaited.

Race/Sex/Age: White/Male/36

Officer(s) Involved: Glendale Police Officer Chandler Phillips

What prompted the initial contact with police? At shortly before 10:00 p.m. on October 31, a Glendale police officer in an unmarked police SUV came upon a Dodge pickup truck operated by John Pacheaco that was stopped in the right lane of traffic on Colorado Blvd forcing vehicles to drive around it. The officer activated his emergency lights, went up to the vehicle to check on the driver, and observed that he was unresponsive. Additional officers arrived with one pulling up head-to-head and effectively boxing Pacheaco's truck in and another trying unsuccessfully to break the window on a passenger side window[646].

Actions taken by subject toward police: Surveillance video shows the pickup truck suddenly moved forward striking the police car in front of it and then shifting into reverse and barely missing the officer crossing over behind it after trying to break the passenger window[647].

Reactions by the police: After the truck nearly hit the cop moving behind it, the officers opened fire on the truck, shooting through the windshield, and fatally hitting Pacheaco as he reversed into the occupied unmarked police SUV.

What could the subject have done that day to still be alive today? Pacheaco should have not stolen a vehicle and driven it under the influence of narcotics or alcohol to the point that he passed out while on an active roadway, thereby impeding traffic and drawing an officer's attention. Should have complied with the officers to shut the vehicle off and exit it (if he was awake to hear/understand the orders). Should have not been so high/drunk that he unintentionally drove into the police car in front of his, then unintentionally switched to reverse, and almost ran over an officer before crashing into another police vehicle and injuring that officer.

Outcome of investigation into the fatal police incident: The Denver Police Department, Denver District Attorney's Office and Aurora Police Department are investigating the incident.

Justified use of deadly force? YES, when Pacheaco drove the truck into one police vehicle and then nearly ran over an officer on foot while reversing toward a second occupied police vehicle, the officers had reasonable cause to believe that Pacheaco intended to use the truck to inflict lethal injury upon an officer and justifiably used deadly force to stop him.

Name: Dylan Ray Scott
Date: 12/8/2020   **Location:** Riverview, FL
FACTORS (1,2,4,5,8,10,19)

Criminal History/Involved: Yes, Scott served time in state prison for convictions including aggravated assault, burglary, fleeing from law enforcement, methamphetamine possession, resisting a law enforcement officer with violence, battery on a law enforcement officer, and driving with a suspended license./Yes, Scott was wanted for active warrants for grand theft and resisting arrest.

Mental Illness: Yes, earlier in the year, Scott communicated to his mom that he wanted "suicide by cop"[648].

Substance Abuse History/Involved: Yes, Scott had a prior drug-related arrest./Unknown.

Race/Sex/Age: White/Male/27

Officer(s) Involved: Hillsborough County Sheriff's Office, Sgt. Michael Hannaford, Deputy Timothy Miskell, Deputy Devin Wooden, and Corporal Steven Schneider.

What prompted the initial contact with police? At approximately 10:08 p.m. on December 8, Hillsborough County Sheriff's deputies made contact with Dylan Scott after observing him in his pickup truck parked at McDonalds. The deputies knew that Scott had active warrants and a violent history, so they approached his vehicle from both sides and ordered him to show his hands[649].

Actions taken by subject toward police: Scott ignored the officer's orders and drove his truck over the curb, across the multi-lane roadway and into another vehicle. While some deputies assisted the motorist he struck, other deputies repeatedly ordered and even pleaded with Scott to show his hands. Scott continued ignoring the deputies and kept his hands in his waistband where he told the officers he had a gun. Despite the best efforts of deputies to get Scott to peacefully comply, he made a quick motion with his hands as if he were pulling a gun from his waistband and motioned at the officers[650].

Reactions by the police: Fearing that Scott was pulling out the gun he warned them about, the four deputies surrounding his vehicle shot him multiple times, killing him.

What could the subject have done that day to still be alive today? Scott should have not committed crimes that would generate warrants and have law enforcement looking for him. Should have complied during the initial stop and not dangerously drove off into traffic. Should not have told the deputies that he was armed and made them think that he was drawing out a weapon to shoot them with.

Outcome of investigation into the fatal police incident: Florida Department of Law Enforcement (FDLE) is investigating the incident[651].

Justified use of deadly force? YES, the deputies had reasonable cause to believe that Scott was armed and about to shoot them, so they were justified in using deadly force to stop what Scott led them to believe was an imminent deadly threat.

Name: Andre Maurice Hill
Date: 12/22/2020   **Location:** Columbus, OH
FACTORS (1,19)

Criminal History/Involved: Unknown./None stated.

Mental Illness: Unknown.

Substance Abuse History/Involved: Unknown./None stated.

Race/Sex/Age: Black/Male/47

Officer(s) Involved: Columbus Police Officer Adam Coy and a female Columbus police officer

What prompted the initial contact with police? At approximately 1:37 a.m. on December 22, Columbus police officers responded to a 911 call called in by a neighbor alarmed over an SUV parked outside occupied by a man who was repeatedly running it on and off. Upon responding to the location dispatched, the officers observed an open garage with a man, Andre Hill inside[652] [653].

Actions taken by subject toward police: Hill came around the vehicle and walked toward the officers, at least one of which had his gun drawn. As he approached the officers at the front of the garage, Hill held a cellphone in his left hand and his right hand was in his pocket and not visible to the officers.

Reactions by the police: Believing he observed one, Officer Coy "yelled that he saw a weapon in Hill's hand"[654] and then opened fire, fatally shooting Hill several times.

What could the subject have done that day to still be alive today? Upon seeing the officers coming toward him, at least one of which with a gun pointed at him, Hill should have simply put his hands in the air and followed the officers' directions.

Outcome of investigation into the fatal police incident: Officer Coy was fired within days for violating the rules and policies of the police department by not immediately activating his bodycam. Along with murder, felonious assault and two charges dereliction of duty, Coy has been indicted by a grand jury for reckless homicide[655] [656].

Justified use of deadly force? A lot is being made of the officers not activating their body cams, but as the investigation of the incident details, the dashcams in the police cars were not on either because it was a nonemergency 911 call, so the emergency lights were not activated. Upon arrival, the two officers thought that it was a nonsense, nuisance call until they observed an open garage with a man inside it, immediately raising their suspicions and fear as Coy drew his gun and pointed it at him. While Mr. Hill knew that he was not a bad guy with bad intentions, the officers had no way of knowing that. So, Hill should have immediately stopped and put his hands up. Instead, when Hill continued moving toward the officers with his right hand hidden from their view, Coy was forced to make a split-second decision that he perceived to be a matter of life or death. Convinced in the poor lighting that he had seen a weapon in Hill's hand when Hill did not stop and raise his hands as a reasonable person would, Coy shot him. While Hill was not committing a crime, based upon the officers' reasonable perception of the circumstances, **YES**, the use of deadly force was justified even though the officer ended up being wrong.

ANALYSIS OF THE 39 UNARMED FATAL POLICE SHOOTINGS IN 2020

Subject's race: White: 17(44%) Black: 15(38%) Latino: 5(13%) Asian: 1(3%) Unknown: 1(3%)

1. Subject failed to comply: 38 (97%)
2. Subject was a wanted criminal, or a crime was involved: 36 (92%)
3. Alcohol or drugs were involved: 8 (21%)
4. Subject displayed or described having mental illness: 17 (44%)
5. Subjects' words and/or actions appeared to be suicide by cop: 9 (23%)
6. Officers voiced racist rhetoric: 0 (0%)
7. Officers outright ambushed the subject: 0 (0%)
8. Vehicle was involved (car stop, disabled motorist, accident): 18 (46%)
9. Subject's accomplice possessed a weapon: 4 (10%)
10. Subject faked having a gun: 9 (23%)
11. A vehicle was driven at an officer: 4 (10%)
12. Subject/accomplice, threatened/assaulted officer with personal weapon/object: 18 (46%)
13. Accomplices' actions justified deadly force: 5 (13%)
14. Less-than-lethal force alternatives failed: 16 (41%)
15. Officer(s) sustained injuries: 9 (23%)
16. Accidental discharges: 1 (3%)
17. Not justified intentional and targeted use of deadly force: 3 (8%)
18. Not conducting official police duties: 0
19. Justified deadly force used: 28 (72%)
20. Justified deadly force used, but wrong target was hit: 5 (13%)
21. Undetermined whether justified or not: 2 (5%)

ANALYSIS OF THE 90 UNARMED FATAL POLICE SHOOTINGS IN 2019-2020

Subject's race: White: 38(42%) Black: 26(29%) Latino: 18(20%) Asian: 3(3%) Native-American: 1(1%)

1. Subject failed to comply: 85 (94%)
2. Subject was a wanted criminal, or a crime was involved: 79 (88%)
3. Alcohol or drugs were involved: 27 (30%)
4. Subject displayed or described having mental illness: 43 (48%)
5. Subjects' words and/or actions appeared to be suicide by cop: 21 (23%)
6. Officers voiced racist rhetoric: 0 (0%)
7. Officers outright ambushed the subject: 0 (0%)
8. Vehicle was involved (car stop, disabled motorist, accident): 35 (39%)
9. Subject's accomplice possessed a weapon: 11 (12%)
10. Subject faked having a gun: 19 (21%)
11. A vehicle was driven at an officer: 7 (8%)
12. Subject/accomplice, threatened/assaulted officer with personal weapon/object: 44 (49%)
13. Accomplices' actions justified deadly force: 10 (11%)
14. Less than lethal force alternatives failed: 43 (48%)
15. Officer(s) sustained injuries: 24 (27%)
16. Accidental discharges: 4 (4%)
17. Not Justified intentional and targeted use of deadly force: 5 (6%)
18. Not conducting official police duties: 1 (1%)
19. Justified deadly force: 66 (73%)
20. Justified deadly force used but wrong target was hit: 10 (11%)
21. Undetermined whether justified or not: 4 (4%)

ANALYSIS

THE DETAILS AND STATISTICS OF THESE 90 SHOOTINGS FROM 2019 TO 2020 DEMONSTRATE THAT RACE HAS absolutely nothing to do with why and when officers use deadly force. Despite all the vitriol regularly spewed after fatal police incidents about how the officer's actions were racist or making it appear like officers are just assassinating good everyday citizens peacefully going about their business, analysis of these 90 shootings shows the truth. In not one of the shootings reviewed was there any reporting of an officer voicing racist rhetoric or ambushing the subject who was killed. Rather than race, violent criminal behavior is what explains the disparities between why 29% of those unarmed subjects fatally shot by the police are black and 42% were white despite blacks being only 13.4% of the population and whites making up 60.1%. That violent behavior will be discussed in Part 3 since the felonious murder of LEOs is one such behavior that more closely parallels with the racial demographics of the unarmed subjects than their population percentages.

Police deadly force incidents of Black subjects continue to be racialized by the press, but their reporting consistently fails to show any relevance of that person's black race. It is hard to believe that it is merely coincidental that of the five subjects mistakenly labeled as unarmed by *The Washington Post* database, all five are people of color with four being black and a lone Latino, Paul David Rea. While not incorporated in the statistics, those five incidents were included here to expose the fallibility of a press which demonizes officers for making mistakes under extreme duress. The media bias exhibited in reporting on fatal police incidents is further demonstrated by the magnitude of reporting on the 90 incidents, 87 of which most people have never heard of before. Besides that of George Floyd, if you noticed which incidents have the heading indicating that they gained nationwide attention, the only other two that did are the shootings of Atatiana Jefferson and Breonna Taylor. The criterion used to determine whether a fatal police incident gained nationwide attention was the major network stations generating five hundred or more stories about it. Using the same Media Cloud research tool as in Part 1, a search for news stories by the US National Media, ABC, NBC, CBS, CNN, FNC, MSNBC, and FB was conducted of each "unarmed" subject killed by police during 2019 to 2020 using the parameters of their "name" and "police," from the date of incident through March 1, 2021.

With 78,811 stories, the George Floyd incident was by far the most widely reported, and with the Chauvin trial underway as this book is being written, that number continues to increase exponentially. Breonna Taylor's shooting easily took the second spot with 16,423 stories. Even though she was armed, Atatiana Jefferson's incident was third with 790 press pieces. To provide context, the next seven incidents with the most national media coverage were: Andre Hill, 291; Rhogena Nicholas, 214; Marcellis Stinnette, 176; Jonathan Price,169; Katlyn Alix,110; Michael Dean, 85; and William Green, 63. With the exception of Nicholas and Alix, all the other subjects are black, which to the media and those pushing a racial agenda appears to be the only prerequisite for any such story. Which is not to say that there are not very valid reasons for stories, especially fatal police shootings, to get nationwide attention. For example, the Katlyn Alix shooting, though not related to the conduct of any official police duties, has many elements likely to arouse the attention of readers and therefore be circulated. There was the outlandish game of Russian roulette being played by two police officers, coupled with intimations of a workplace romance, extra-marital affair, plus the side story of a mentally ill combat veteran ending up in law enforcement. The senseless death of a young female officer had numerous angles to pique the interests of different segments of the population.

Less like bad reality TV or a b-rated movie plot, Rhogena Nicholas' death also had elements making it worthy of the national spotlight. Initially the Nicholas shooting made national news because four police officers were shot in the incident. Months later the shooting was again right-fully in the media crosshairs when the detectives involved were arrested for falsifying evidence to get the search warrant approved. Extraordinary circumstances such as multiple officers getting shot and several detectives getting arrested in a fatal use of force incident are valid reasons for a story to "have legs" and stretch across the country over several days. Such validity is absent when the newsworthiness is based primarily upon the Black race of the subject and White race of the officer. This paradoxically only goes one way as evidenced by the fact that even though the lead detective who lied to get the warrant leading to Nicholas' death was Black and she was White, the press reports were not at all focused on their race.

Another paradox observed with rare female subjects such as Alix and Nicholas is the disparity between the two sexes being involved in such fatal police incidents. Though making up only 49% of the population, males were the subjects of 92% of deadly police shootings studied in 2019 to 2020. Despite that easily identifiable disparity, each time a male is killed by law enforcement, there are none of the accusations that police are sexist or discriminatory that are regularly made regard-ing race when the subject is Black or Brown.

While the critics selectively focus on race, examining these 90 shootings shows what factors are correlated with being the subject of a fatal shooting by the police. The single biggest action taken by 85 of the 90 subjects' shot were their failure to simply comply with the officer's lawful com-mands and be peacefully arrested. With a rare exception in the January 2020 shooting of William Howard Green where Police Corporal Owen Jr. is being prosecuted for second-degree murder, had those subjects complied with the arrest and been processed in the criminal justice system, they would have survived the incident without any injury at all. For those wondering how the deadly shooting of a compliant, handcuffed Black male sitting peacefully in the police car did not go viral and provoke nationwide protests claiming that racism was involved, the answer is that the officer involved is also Black. Just imagine how different the media coverage and reactions would have been had Corporal Owen Jr. been a White male. Aside from that inexplicable anomaly, linked to 94% of the shootings, a subject's failure to comply is the single greatest determining factor associated with being on the receiving end of targeted lethal police force and something which those shot completely control.

The second greatest contributing factor and something also controlled by the subject is the nexus to crime. Involved in 88% of all the fatal shootings, 79 of the 90 subjects killed were either wanted for previous crimes and/or killed during the active commission of crime. Far from the innocent average joe citizens peacefully going about their day suddenly being murdered by rogue police officers, the overwhelming majority of those killed are hardcore and/or violent criminals. Their violent actions frightened, endangered, and injured law-abiding citizens, prompting 911 calls for officers to respond and take immediate action. Ultimately, the same violent criminal actions which brought those subjects to the attention of the police also brought them into the officer's crosshairs.

Such violent actions include 49% of the incidents where 44 of the subjects and/or their accomplices threatened or assaulted the officers or someone else with their hands or a weapon. Officers are given basic defensive tactics training in the police academy, but they are far from being as proficient as Mixed Martial Arts fighters who, despite their expertise, even still get caught with a lucky knockout blow. While such a knockout may hurt the fighter's ego and chances at a title fight, for a police officer the consequences can be deadly. On April 25, 2021, that tragically was the reality for Delmar Police Officer Corporal Keith Heacook. Upon responding to a 911 call about a fight-in-progress[657], Cpl. Heacook was attacked by the perpetrator, career criminal, and emotionally disturbed Randon Wilkerson. After knocking Cpl. Heacook to the ground with his blows, Wilkerson literally stomped the officer to death. A beloved husband and father, Cpl. Heacook's life mattered!

Besides the danger of being beaten to death, there is a saying among the police that because of their duty weapon, every call is a "gun call", and in five of the shootings during 2019 to 2020, the subjects did indeed reach for or tried to get control over the officers' duty gun. Officers cannot take the chance of being knocked out by such violent criminals, because their duty weapon could then be used against themselves as you will read in Part 2 happened to Deputy Sheriff James Blair, other responding officers, or innocent bystanders. In 43 of the incidents, the officers' use of less-than-lethal alternatives such as their hands, physical force, or tasers failed to stop the violent criminals, compelling them to use deadly force before being overpowered. The injuries sustained to 24 of the officers, comprising 27% of the shootings is a testament to the gravity of the situations they encountered. If all lives truly matter, then that includes police lives as well, so anyone attacking and endangering an officer's life should do so with the expectation that the officer will use every means possible, including deadly force to protect themselves.

Another factor prevalent in nearly half of the fatal incidents is that 43 of the subjects killed had either a previous diagnosis of mental illness or exhibited an altered mental state at the scene. Some of these subjects had seen mental health professionals for issues including depression, bipolar disorder, and addictions. Besides those with longstanding mental illnesses, 27 subjects of these 90 police shootings were in an altered mental state during those final moments because of alcohol and/or drugs. As the push to legalize various drugs becomes more mainstream, those numbers should be expected to rise as increasing numbers of people high on drugs encounter LEOs. Further complicating matters is how whether because of the illicit substances or mental illness, 21 of the 90 subjects' words or actions appeared like they wanted suicide by cop, with 19 of the subjects faking possession of a gun. It is indeed sad when those who are mentally ill and in need of professional help end up forcing officers to use deadly force out of fear for their own lives. The resulting deadly force not only leaves behind grieving family members and loved ones, but it also traumatizes the officer(s) involved as well. The effective though unpopular way to minimize such incidents is to keep those with such severe mental illness properly medicated, institutionalized, or under constant adult supervision. The failing of the mental health system and society's reluctance to institutionalize those with severe psychological diagnoses are too often thrust upon the police who do their best to peacefully resolve the situation, yet unfortunately, on occasion, have to resort to deadly force.

Playing a role in 39% of the deadly police shootings, motor vehicles are used by people to commit crimes, evade the authorities, and in extreme cases, try to kill the police. Guidance of many police agencies on the deadly use of force states officers shall not fire upon a vehicle unless deadly force other than the vehicle is being threatened toward the officer. Typically included in that same guidance is a caveat that nothing shall preclude the officer from using deadly force if it is the only option available to prevent an imminent threat to their life. Seven subjects during 2019 to 2020 used a vehicle to present such a deadly imminent threat to officers, and they paid with their lives for it. Subjects such as Twyman, Watkins, and Hendrick may not have been armed in the traditional sense, but the steering wheel in their hands made those two tons of steel under their control every bit the deadly weapon. The officers involved in these incidents are the lucky ones, eleven of their fellow officers were not so lucky as they died during 2019 to 2020 from being run down by such murdering motorists.

A final factor leading to some of these 90 subjects being shot by the police was the company they kept. In 12% of the shootings, the subject that was shot was accompanied by someone who possessed a weapon. The proximity of the subject and the armed accomplice exposes the incident being categorized under the shooting of an unarmed subject as technically correct, but ultimately misleading. It is especially disingenuous considering that nine of the incidents involved accomplice's actions such as shooting at or driving a vehicle toward the LEO's. Whether an unarmed co-conspirator or the unfortunate passenger at the wrong time, the subjects killed in these incidents died because of the deadly threats their accomplices posed to the officer.

After reviewing all the relevant facts involved in the 90 incidents, they can be judged to fit in one of six categories. Consisting of two categories, the most prevalent outcome is shootings where the officers are judged to have justifiably used deadly force. Overall, with 76 of the 90 shootings being justified, this accounts for 84% of the "unarmed" incidents during 2019 to 2020. In 66 of the shooting, the perpetrator threatening or attacking the officers was accurately targeted with the remaining ten tragically receiving the bullets that were justifiably intended for their violent accomplices. Such misfortunes are what happens when violence, weapons, and split-second deadly situations are combined. It was only a matter of seconds after Officer Singh located Miss Brooks before her dog was running toward him intent on attacking him. Singh's reaction to shoot at the dog was completely justified, unfortunately one of his shots missed and fatally hit the owner of the dog instead. These tragedies are compounded when they are racialized and politicized at the expense of the officers who had already been through a traumatic ordeal. The armed accomplices of both Breonna Taylor and Preston Oszust shot at and struck the police officers confronting them. Ms. Taylor and Mr. Oszust were both killed in the ensuing return gunfire from the police, yet the Arizona Troopers rightfully remain unknown while Sgt. Mattingly and Officer Cosgrove continue to be disparaged in the name of racial justice. Neither incident had anything to do with race and everything to do with the simple survival instinct of the officers involved wanting to end the deadly threat.

Perhaps even more tragic are the four subjects killed by accidental discharges, because simple adherence to proper tactics would have prevented them. The most fundamental firearms-handling skill taught to police recruits is to keep the trigger finger out of the trigger guard unless they are intentionally firing at a target. Firearms training is done under the most controlled conditions to ensure the safety of the new officers and range staff, and still every once in a while, an accidental discharge occurs. Taking into consideration the volatile circumstances of two of the shootings where subject Whitfield fought with the officer and subject Light either ran into or fought with the officer, it is possible the officer's fingers entered the trigger guard during the ensuing struggle. The accidental shootings of subjects Dean and Wang are unforgiveable since neither of those officers had a justifiable reason to have their fingers on the trigger. With his finger improperly on the trigger, the officer who shot Wang could have just as easily shot a fellow cop had he tripped while searching the house.

Those incidents which happened outside of the conduct of official police duties encapsulate the rare occasions when a rogue officer does something egregious or off-duty. Nothing can be further from acting in official police capacity then playing a drunken/drug fueled game of Russian roulette with another officer/romantic interest. The deadly shooting of Katlyn Alix in no way reflects upon the profession of policing. It does, however, open the department up to fair criticism on how such a psychologically unstable person as former Officer Hendren managed to slip through the hiring cracks.

Straddled between the justified uses of deadly force and those which are clearly not are incidents whose lack of available details makes an educated determination impossible. If Jimmy Atchison was unarmed and complying with an officer's commands to exit the closet, then his shooting was clearly not justified. What is not clear is whether Officer Kim squeezed the trigger accidentally as happened in the Wang incident or intentionally because he thought Atchison exited the closet to attack them rather than complying with one of the conflicting commands. According to the statistics the officers involved in the other three incidents were most probably justified, but rather than be hypocritical and pass judgment before sufficient facts are known (as those who immediately condemn the police do), these shootings are considered undetermined until further conclusive information becomes available. Statements from the lone officer involved in the Eric Young shooting conflict with the physical evidence, making it difficult to know what transpired. In the Pablo Elias shooting, there were multiple officers on a perimeter dealing with a barricaded, violent criminal, so that incident is more likely a matter of him making a furtive movement when finally exiting the house. Likewise, Zachary Gifford being shot in the back can be the result of one deputy shooting Gifford from behind as he was attacking the other deputy, however until that is confirmed, it remains possible that he was shot as an unarmed fleeing felon, and hence it remains undetermined.

Among the remaining 6% of the 90 shootings are five unarmed subjects for whom the use of deadly force by police was not justified. Already touched upon was the William Green shooting for which Officer Owen will stand trial for murder charges. Subjects Robert Sikon and Nicholas Bils were both fleeing police when they were shot in the back. Deputy Baker has already been indicted for voluntary manslaughter by a grand jury for shooting Sikon and Deputy Russell was charged with second-degree murder for shooting Bils. For shooting Juan Moreno as he drove by but not at him, Officer Dunn was indicted for murder. The final subject, Julian Lewis was shot while seated in his car after his vehicle became inoperable during a pursuit. Since neither Lewis nor his inoperable vehicle posed a threat to Trooper Thompson when he shot Lewis, Thompson was charged with felony murder. Contrary to those who say the police have an unfettered license to kill and are never held accountable for their mistakes or misdeeds, the prosecution of the officers involved in all five of the shootings deemed not justified proves such criticism to be another unsubstantiated lie.

What a review of these 90 shootings also proves is how exceedingly rare, unarmed subjects are justifiably or even unjustifiably shot. The five unjustified shootings over two years average out to 2.5 per year which is roughly one every five months. The 90 shootings come out to an average of 45 each year and nearly once per week. Though that may sound common, when those 45 shootings are put in the context of overall annual police contacts and citizen's criminal behavior, their likelihood of occurrence are infinitesimally rare. According to research by Stanford University and the National Emergency Number Association (NENA), in a typical year, America's LEOs respond to 240 million 911 calls[658] and conduct 20 million traffic stops[659]. Additionally, as the FBI's Uniform Crime Report shows that in 2019, officers effected 10,085,207 arrests, of which 495,871 were for violent crimes[660]. During those contacts, traffic stops, and arrests, 56,034 officers were assaulted with 17,188 officers sustaining physical injuries[661]. As reporting from just half of the nation's law enforcement agencies reveals, 25% of those officers injured were by an unarmed subject's personal physical weapons like their hands, fist, or feet.

All total then out of approximately 270+ million documented contacts with the public in an average year, there are only 45 incidents where officers intentionally used deadly force against an unarmed subject, who, it is now clear includes people in the presence of armed subjects, using vehicles as a weapon, or attacking officers with their personal physical weapons. This comes out to mean that in a typical year, in only .000017% of police interactions is deadly force used and just .0000009% of such interactions in which officers use lethal force that was not justified. To put that into perspective, with the odds of being struck by lightning being 1 in 500,000[662], the average person of any race is 222 times more likely to be struck by lightning than unjustifiably killed by the police.

The fact deadly force was used only approximately 1,000 times out of the 56,000 times the officers were assaulted by armed and unarmed subjects, is a true testament to LEOs restraint and proclivity to use less than lethal force. Further testament to the policing profession is the 100% accountability of officers in those incredibly rare instances that were not justified in shooting unarmed subjects. Most readily apparent and something that should make everyone happy is that although officers are judged based upon the race of the people they shoot, officers DO NOT shoot people based upon their race. Those facts all add up to confirm that America's LEOs are completely opposite from the trigger-happy, racist, and unaccountable police that are portrayed in the media or claimed by social justice warriors looking to defund, reinvent or reimagine them.

PART 3.

FELONIOUS LINE OF DUTY MURDERS OF LAW ENFORCEMENT OFFICERS, 2019 TO 2020

THE PUNDITS AND PROFESSIONAL PROTESTORS HAVE A LOT TO SAY WHEN THE POLICE ARE INVOLVED IN A deadly force incident, but those same critics are not nearly as vocal or passionate when the police themselves are victims of cold-blooded murder. A typical refrain for the outrage when an officer is perceived to have unlawfully used lethal force is that the public entrusts great responsibility in the officers and therefore demands accountability. Just as the nation should be outraged when an officer abuses his/her authority in unjustifiably using deadly force, all Americans should be equally incensed when an officer's life is taken during their service to protect society. Aside from the military, law enforcement is the only profession where its members are purposely targeted and murdered because of the profession they represent and the job they are trying to accomplish.

According to FBI Uniform Crime Reports, 511 LEOs were feloniously murdered from 2010 to 2019. Thankfully due to the advancements in policing including the implementation of body armor, these numbers are much lower than previous decades like the 1970s when an average of 127 officers were annually shot to death. As reported by the Law Enforcement Officers Killed and Assaulted (LEOKA) Program[663], roughly 68 officers' lives have been saved by their body armor each year since 2010. Officers are ambushed while sitting in their patrol cars doing paperwork, approaching houses to diffuse a domestic situation, or fatally assaulted while trying to take a criminal into custody. Since many such instances get scant media attention, those officers are paid tribute here. Let their last moments serve as an education to the citizens who question why officers appear so on edge when dealing with situations and are so adamant about seeing a suspect's hands. In those occasions where the officers made mistakes, which all humans do, hopefully their last moments will serve as lessons for other officers to learn from and ensure they safely finish their tour.

Like how the shootings of unarmed subjects were presented, the felonious murders of America's LEO's are provided here in a standardized format, making it easy to compare among and against each other. 108 officers' final moments are documented, of which eight were injured years ago, decades for some, but since they ultimately died during 2019 to 2020, they are included here and paid their proper respects alongside other recently fallen officers. Relevant factors such as whether a vehicle, alcohol/drugs, or mental illness were involved are highlighted to demonstrate how often they play a role in officers being murdered. Most importantly, the perpetrator's criminal activity, actions toward the officers and officers' reactions are noted. Unlike the justified uses of deadly force by police, those pulling the trigger or running over the officers are not doing so out of self-defense or defense of others. The perpetrators of the murders of America's LEO's committed their violent acts out of pure self-interest, most typically to stay out of prison or some other kind of controlled institutionalized setting. It is sadly unnecessary given how quickly many criminals are released early from their sentences anyway.

As you read about the last moments of America's brave men and women on the front lines in the war on crime, try to remember if you heard about their murders. Is there one of them whom you know as much about as you have learned of George Floyd and Breonna Taylor? Undoubtedly the incident made the local news and possibly even national news for a day, but assuredly there were no nationwide protests, no statements condemning the murderer's family for raising such an animal, no calls to remove the lenient judges and bleeding-heart parole boards that allowed the super-predator back into the public, and no petitions to oust the politicians that changed the laws to make it impossible to legally confine these career criminals. Read on and ponder how many of these officers' deaths were preventable if America's criminal justice system would hold its violent criminals accountable. Finally, imagine how many of these officers might still be alive today if they had not been more fearful of being portrayed as the next Officer Darren Wilson than they were of the violent criminal that ended up taking their lives.

INCIDENTS IN 2019:

Officer: Provo Police Department Master Police Officer Joseph William Shinners
Date: 1/5/2019   **Location:** Orem, UT
FACTORS (1,2,8,9,11,13,14,15,17)
Perpetrator(s) Involved: Matt Frank Hoover

Criminal Activity History/Involved: Yes, Hoover had convictions for drug distribution, felony drug possession, attempted forgery, retail theft, failing to respond to an officer's commands, and theft and burglary./Yes, Hoover was wanted for two active warrants at the time.

Mental Illness: Hoover made remarks about wanting to get killed shooting it out with the police and he was homeless at the time of the crime.

Substance Abuse History/Involved: Yes, Hoover had numerous prior drug arrests./Unknown.

Race/Sex/Age: White/Male/40

What prompted the initial contact with the murderer? On January 5, officers spotted Matt Hoover in a vehicle parked in a shopping center. The officers knew that Hoover had active warrants and wanted to shoot it out with the police, so they carefully surrounded his vehicle. Some officer's approached Hoover's vehicle on foot and attempted to get him to exit and surrender peacefully[664].

Actions taken by subject toward police: Hoover did not comply with their lawful orders. As an officer attempted to pull him out through the driver's side window, Hoover hit the gas, backing into a police vehicle and then drove across the parking lot and stopped.

Reactions by the police: Officer Shinners and another officer approached Hoover's vehicle on foot and attempted to pull him out from the passenger side of the car. While the officers tried to pull him out, Hoover accessed a hidden gun and fatally shot Shinners.

How murdered? Officer Shinners was shot through the unprotected space in his bulletproof vest while trying to arrest a violent subject with active warrants.

What could have been done differently for the officer to still be alive? Stay behind cover and make Hoover exit the vehicle with his hands up.

Would the officer(s) had been justified to use deadly force before being murdered? Yes, officers could have justifiably shot Hoover when he used his vehicle as a weapon while they tried to pull him out.

Outcome for the cop-killer: Before dying, Officer Shinners managed to return fire and shoot Hoover once in the stomach, wounding him. He was charged with aggravated murder, assault on a police officer, theft by receiving stolen property, possession of a firearm by a restricted person, failing to stop for an officer's commands, and two counts of drug possession[665].

Officer: Davis Police Department Police Officer Natalie Becky Corona
Date: 1/10/2019   **Location:** Davis, CA
FACTORS (1,2,4,5,7,15)
Perpetrator(s) Involved: Kevin Douglas Limbaugh

Criminal Activity History/Involved: Yes, Limbaugh was convicted in 2018 for battery./Yes, Limbaugh illegally possessed a firearm.

Mental Illness: Yes, Limbaugh left a note saying "The Davis Police department has been hitting me with ultra-sonic waves meant to keep dogs from barking … I am highly sensitive to its effect on my inner ear. I did my best to appease them, but they have continued for years, and I can't live this way anymore"[666].

Substance Abuse History/Involved: Unknown./None stated.

Race/Sex/Age: White/Male/48

What prompted the initial contact with the killer? NA, Officer Corona was ambushed by Limbaugh.

Actions taken by subject toward police: While Officer Corona was investigating a traffic accident around 6:45 p.m. on January 10, Limbaugh shot and killed her as he was concealed from her view[667].

Reactions by the police: Officer Corona was ambushed by Limbaugh for no apparent reason, and she never had a chance to defend herself.

How murdered? Officer Corona was shot from behind and then again while she was down on the ground.

What could have been done differently for the officer to still be alive? NA, Officer Corona was doing her job and investigating an accident, she had no way of knowing a random uninvolved madman would shoot her.

Would the officer had been justified to use deadly force before being murdered? N/A, Officer Corona never engaged with the murderer.

Outcome for the cop-killer: While in his house surrounded by officer's a few hours after killing Officer Corona, Limbaugh took his own life with a self-inflicted gunshot to the head[668].

Miscellaneous: Limbaugh was not allowed to legally possess firearms because of his prior conviction[669].

Officer: Birmingham Police Department Sergeant WyTasha Lamar Carter
Date: 1/13/2019   **Location:** Birmingham, AL
FACTORS (1,2,8,9,12,13,14,15,21)
Perpetrator(s) Involved: Jeremy Elwin Owens

Criminal Activity History/Involved: Yes, Owens was convicted in 2012 for first-degree robbery (which he pled to in order to have the attempted murder charge dropped), and he was sentenced to 20 years in prison, but released in 2015. Arrested again in Nov 2018 for drug possession, illegally possessing three firearms, and reckless driving-he was arraigned and released in two days. He had an active warrant./Yes, Owens was casing vehicles to break into before shooting at the officers.

Substance Abuse History/Involved: Yes, Owens had prior drug-related arrests./None stated.

Race/Sex/Age: Black/Male/31

What prompted the initial contact with the killer? Sgt. Carter responded to assist an undercover officer, Aaron Smith who observed a group of subjects casing cars around 2 a.m. on January 13 in an area with recent break-ins. Upon seeing marked police cars, Owens returned to his vehicle which is where Sgt. Brown and Officer Allums confronted him and his passenger. Sgt. Brown had Owens exit the vehicle, patted him down (during which time she felt something in his right front pocket), and ordered him to keep his hands on the hood. Owens kept disobeying her commands and taking his hands off the hood so Sgt. Brown warned Owens that he would be tased by Allums[670].

Actions taken by subject toward police: When Officer Allums holstered his taser to hand Sgt. Brown handcuffs to put on Owens, Owens broke free of her grip and tried to run.

Reactions by the police: Brown and Allums managed to stop Owens from running, but, during the struggle, Owens accessed the firearm in his pants and shot at them, critically wounding Allums and killing Carter. Allums, Brown, and Smith all returned fire at Owens, seriously wounding him.

How murdered? Sgt. Carter was fatally shot in the head while assisting officers with a traffic stop related to an investigation.

What could have been done differently for the officer to still be alive? Once Owens exhibited non-compliance and took his hands off the hood of the car, officers could have tased Owens and handcuffed him as he was on the ground. They should have gained positive control over Owens and handcuffed him as soon as Sgt. Brown felt that something was in his right front pocket. They should have shot Owens when he broke free from Sgt. Brown and put his hand into his pants.

Would the officer had been justified to use deadly force before being murdered? Yes, as soon as Owens reached into his pants after breaking free from Sgt. Brown, the officers had reasonable cause to believe that he was going for a weapon with which to kill them.

Outcome for the cop-killer: Owens was shot and seriously wounded by one of the officer's returning gunfire at him. He was indicted on capital murder, attempted murder (2 counts), felon in possession of a firearm, receiving stolen property (third-degree) and possession of marijuana (first-degree).

Officer: Mobile Police Department Police Officer Sean Paul Tuder
Date: 1/20/2019   **Location:** Mobile, AL
FACTORS (1,2,9,13,14,15,21)
Perpetrator(s) Involved: Marco Perez

Criminal Activity History/Involved: Yes, Perez was arrested for more than a dozen car break-ins, had active warrants for firearms charges, and was wanted for probation violation by the federal government./Yes, Perez was evading law enforcement and believed to be conducting burglaries.

Mental Illness: None reported, but Perez was homeless[671].

Substance Abuse History/Involved: Unknown/None stated

Race/Sex/Age: Latino/Male/19

What prompted the initial contact with the killer? Officer Tuder was investigating the whereabouts of Perez because earlier in the month, Perez had faked his own kidnapping and more recently, he was linked to a stolen vehicle. At around 3 p.m. on January 20, Tuder was looking for Perez at an apartment complex where he was suspected in a number of burglaries. Upon finding Perez outside, Officer Tuder initially held him at gunpoint but then holstered his weapon to take Perez into custody[672].

Actions taken by subject toward police: When Officer Tuder holstered his weapon, Perez took out his and shot Tuder[673].

Reactions by the police: Officer Tuder was alone and incapacitated by his injuries, dying shortly afterward.

How murdered? Officer Tuder was shot at close range while trying to effect an arrest on a wanted subject.

What could have been done differently for the officer to still be alive? Work with a partner so one officer could cover Perez as the other handcuffed him. Prone Perez out on the ground when he had him at gunpoint, and then wait for backup or handcuff him from a position of strength.

Would the officer had been justified to use deadly force before being murdered? Yes, as soon as Perez reached into his pants, the officer could have reasonably believed that Perez was reaching for a gun and shot him.

Outcome for the cop-killer: Perez was captured, and he is facing numerous charges including capital murder and possession of a stolen firearm[674].

Master Police Officer Joseph William Shinners

Provo Police Department, Utah

End of Watch Saturday, January 5, 2019

Police Officer Natalie Becky Corona

Davis Police Department, California

End of Watch Thursday, January 10, 2019

Sergeant WyTasha Lamar Carter

Birmingham Police Department, Alabama

End of Watch Sunday, January 13, 2019

Police Officer Sean Paul Tuder

Mobile Police Department, Alabama

End of Watch Sunday, January 20, 2019

Officer: Susquehanna Township Police Department Lt. Robert Earl "Bo" McCallister
Date: 1/20/2019   **Location:** Susquehanna, PA
FACTORS (1,2,15,19)
Perpetrator(s) Involved: Unknown, the perpetrator was never captured or identified.

Criminal Activity History/Involved: Unknown./Yes, the perpetrator was involved in a bank robbery.

Mental Illness: Unknown.

Substance Abuse History/Involved: Unknown.

Race/Sex/Age: Unknown.

What prompted the initial contact with the killer? Sgt. McCallister responded to an alarm call at a bank on February 19, 1981[675].

Actions taken by subject toward police: A suspected bank robber engaged Sgt. McCallister in a gun battle as he tried to flee the scene.

Reactions by the police: Sgt. McCallister chased and shot at the suspect until he himself was seriously wounded.

How murdered? Nearly 40 years later, Lt. McCallister died from the gunshot wound that he suffered that day.

What could have been done differently for the officer to still be alive? This is an unfortunate but acknowledged part of being a police officer, responding to and confronting deadly criminals. While all officers can always improve upon tactics, criminals do have a say and whether by skill or luck sometimes their shots hit the officers first.

Would the officer had been justified to use deadly force before being murdered? Sgt. McCallister was using deadly force at time of incident. It is exceedingly difficult to accurately engage a moving target shooting back at you while running after it.

Outcome for the cop-killer: The perpetrator escaped and has never been identified.

Officer: Clermont County Sheriff's Office Detective William Lee Brewer, Jr.
Date: 2/2/2019   **Location:** Cincinnati, OH
FACTORS (1,2,3,4,5,7,15,19)
Perpetrator(s) Involved: Wade Edward Winn

Criminal Activity History/Involved: Yes, Winn had previous marijuana convictions; and arrests for carrying a concealed weapon, drug possession, and operating a motor vehicle with a suspended license./Yes, Winn lured officers into a deadly ambush.

Mental Illness: Yes, Winn is bipolar, has dealt with mental health problems for years, and is currently on anti-psychotic medication[676].

Substance Abuse History/Involved: Yes, previous marijuana convictions./Yes, Winn took large amounts of LSD and cocaine prior to the incident.

Race/Sex/Age: White/Male/23

What prompted the initial contact with the killer? Around 10:30 p.m. on February 2, Detective Brewer and other officers responded to a 911 call about a suicidal subject barricaded in his apartment[677].

Actions taken by subject toward police: Upon seeing the Hostage and Rescue Team arrive, Winn faked his own suicide, firing one shot and making noises simulating that he was injured.

Reactions by the police: Fearing that Winn had just shot himself, officers left protective cover and rushed into the apartment to render medical aid. Winn then opened fire on the responding officers, killing Det. Brewer and injuring Lt. DeRose.

How murdered? Detective Brewer was fatally shot by a suicidal subject who set up an ambush while being barricaded in his apartment.

What could have been done differently for the officer to still be alive? Retired SWAT Commander, Lt. Doug Ventre said, "There wasn't anything else they could do short of just saying, "We're not going in""[678].

Would the officer had been justified to use deadly force before being murdered? No, they were dealing with a suicidal subject and had not yet been given reasonable cause to believe their lives were in imminent danger.

Outcome for the cop-killer: After an exchange of gunfire with Winn and SWAT trucks were used to break down the walls to his apartment, a fire started in Winn's apartment. Winn leapt from his apartment, clearly unarmed, and was taken into custody. Winn was charged with aggravated murder and attempted aggravated murder, to avoid the death penalty he pled guilty to one count of aggravated murder and six counts of attempted aggravated murder. Winn was sentenced to life plus 115 years in prison with no chance of parole[679].

Officer: Virginia State Police Trooper Lucas Bartley Dowell
Date: 2/4/2019   **Location:** Farmville, VA
FACTORS (1,2,3,7,15,17)
Perpetrator(s) Involved: Corey Johnson

Criminal Activity History/Involved: Yes, Johnson was convicted in 1994 for attempted murder, robbery, and firearms charges. Johnson was sentenced to 23 years in prison and then did more time after violating his parole in 2008[680]./Yes, Johnson illegally possessed a firearm and was in a residence suspected of drug trafficking.

Mental Illness: Unknown

Substance Abuse History/Involved: Unknown./Yes, the incident was spurred by a search warrant related to a drug investigation.

Race/Sex/Age: Black/Male/44

What prompted the initial contact with the killer? A Virginia State Police Tactical Team was assisting with executing a search warrant connected to a narcotics investigation at a residence around 10 p.m. on February 4[681].

Actions taken by subject toward police: As the officers entered the residence, the lone suspect in the house, Corey Johnson, opened fire on them, killing Trooper Dowell.

Reactions by the police: Officers returned fire, killing Johnson.

How murdered? Trooper Dowell was killed by gunfire during a narcotics search warrant.

What could have been done differently for the officer to still be alive? Nothing, Trooper Dowell was part of a tactical team executing a dangerous search warrant. One of the inherent dangers involved is being ambushed by a subject at the location before officers see him/her.

Would the officer had been justified to use deadly force before being murdered? The officers were ambushed in the house and did not appear to have a chance to use deadly force before it was used against them.

Outcome for the cop-killer: Johnson was justifiably shot and killed by two other tactical officers who returned fire.

Officer: Milwaukee Police Department Police Officer Matthew John Rittner
Date: 2/6/2019   **Location:** Milwaukee, WI
FACTORS (1,2,3,7,15,17)
Perpetrator(s) Involved: Jordan Fricke

Criminal Activity History/Involved: Yes, Fricke had prior arrests for underage possession of alcohol and driving while under the influence./Yes, Fricke was the subject of a search warrant because of his prior sales of drugs and guns to a confidential informant.

Mental Illness: Unknown

Substance Abuse History/Involved: Yes, Fricke had prior alcohol-related arrests./Yes, Fricke was dealing in narcotics.

Race/Sex/Age: White/Male/25

What prompted the initial contact with the killer? As part of the Milwaukee PD Tactical Enforcement Unit, Officer Rittner was executing a 'no-knock' search warrant at a residence shortly after 9 a.m. on February 6 for suspected drug and gun sales. After the unit used a battering ram to make entry into Fricke's building, Officer Rittner hit the front door to Fricke's apartment while the team was announcing "Police!"[682].

Actions taken by subject toward police: Even though his girlfriend said it was clear that it was the police breaking down the door, Fricke fired four military grade rounds of a shortened AK-47 through the front door, striking Officer Rittner in his upper chest and shoulder area that was unprotected by his body armor. Fricke then put his weapon down and brought his hands up as he surrendered.

Reactions by the police: A tactical officer sighted his weapon through the hole in the front door and saw the unarmed Fricke surrendering. Officers entered the residence and arrested the unarmed Fricke.

How murdered? Officer Rittner was killed by a high-powered rifle round while conducting a high-risk narcotics/gun search warrant.

What could have been done differently for the officer to still be alive? Nothing, Officer Rittner was assigned the battering ram position executing a high-risk warrant and came under fire from a high-powered rifle with armor piercing ammunition.

Would the officer had been justified to use deadly force before being murdered? No, officers could not have opened fire into the apartment until they were fired upon by somebody from within the apartment.

Outcome for the cop-killer: Fricke was found "guilty of first-degree intentional homicide, recklessly endangering the safety of another officer, and maintaining a drug trafficking place"[683] and sentenced to life in prison with no chance of parole.

Miscellaneous: The search warrant uncovered "at least 8 firearms, a taser, parts for assault rifles … $3,000 cash … and two digital scales"[684].

Lieutenant Robert Earl "Bo" McCallister

Susquehanna Township PD, Pennsylvania

End of Watch Sunday, January 20, 2019

Detective William Lee Brewer, Jr.

Clermont County Sheriff's Office, Ohio

End of Watch Saturday, February 2, 2019

Trooper Lucas Bartley Dowell

Virginia State Police, Virginia

End of Watch Monday, February 4, 2019

Police Officer Matthew John Rittner

Milwaukee Police Department, Wisconsin

End of Watch Wednesday, February 6, 2019

Officer: NYPD Detective Brian P. Simonsen
Date: 2/12/2019   **Location:** Richmond Hill, NY
FACTORS (1,2,4,5,10,16,19)
Perpetrator(s) Involved: Christopher Ransom and Jagger Freeman

Criminal Activity History/Involved: Yes, Ransom was a career criminal with numerous prior arrests for petit larceny, grand larceny, and criminal impersonation of a police officer, violating an order of protection and resisting arrest./Yes, Ransom was in the midst of robbing a T-Mobile store with an imitation handgun while Freeman served as lookout outside.

Mental Illness: Yes, Ransom was committed to a psych ward when he was a teenager and had committed numerous erratic acts that got him arrested. Additionally, Ransom stated that he was trying to commit "suicide by cop"[685] by charging at the officers.

Substance Abuse History/Involved: Unknown./None stated.

Race/Sex/Age: Ransom: Black/Male/27; Freeman: Black/Male/25

What prompted the initial contact with the killer? On February 12 at approximately 6 p.m., Detective Simonsen and at least six other officers responded to a 911 call about an armed robbery at a T-Mobile store. Officers flanked the outside of the store from both sides[686].

Actions taken by subject toward police: The suspect inside, Christopher Ransom, advanced at the officers as he simulated firing a realistic-looking imitation handgun at them.

Reactions by the police: Reasonably believing Ransom was pointing a real gun at them as he simulated firing it, seven officers surrounding the store opened fire on him with at least 42 rounds. Ransom was struck by eight rounds and seriously injured but survived. Detective Simonsen was caught in the crossfire of friendly fire, fatally struck once in his chest.

How murdered? Det. Simonsen was killed by friendly fire while responding to a 911 call of an armed robbery of a business.

What could have been done differently for the officer to still be alive? A bulletproof vest may have saved Det. Simonsen's life. Better tactics and communication among the officers might have prevented the deadly crossfire.

Would the officer had been justified to use deadly force before being murdered? Officers justifiably used deadly force as soon as they were presented with what they believed was a deadly threat.

Outcome for the cop-killer: Ransom was charged with "murder, robbery, assault, aggravated manslaughter and menacing" and Freeman was charged with "murder and a dozen other offenses"[687].

Officer: Puerto Rico Police Department Agent Alfred Sanyet-Perez
Date: 2/15/2019   **Location:** San German, Puerto Rico
FACTORS (1,7,8,15)
Perpetrator(s) Involved: Unknown, no subject has been identified.

Criminal Activity History/Involved: Unknown./Unknown.

Mental Illness: Unknown.

Substance Abuse History/Involved: Unknown./Unknown.

Race/Sex/Age: Unknown.

What prompted the initial contact with the killer? On February 15, Agent Sanyet-Perez was outside a store working an undercover narcotics assignment[688].

Actions taken by subject toward police: An unknown subject shot at Perez from a passing automobile.

Reactions by the police: Perez was fatally wounded by the gunfire.

How murdered? While working undercover, Agent Sanyet-Perez was ambushed in a drive-by shooting.

What could have been done differently for the officer to still be alive? Nothing, Perez was in plainclothes, undercover, and not in a confrontation with any subject before the shooting.

Would the officer had been justified to use deadly force before being murdered? Had Agent Perez seen the gunman pointing the gun at him, Perez would have been justified in shooting first.

Outcome for the cop-killer: The murderer has yet to be brought to justice.

Officer: Sullivan County Sheriff's Office Sergeant Steven Billie Hinkle
Date: 2/26/2019   **Location:** Sullivan County, TN
FACTORS (1,4,5,13,15,19)
Perpetrator(s) Involved: Jackie Scott Pendergrass

Criminal Activity History/Involved: Yes, Pendergrass had prior convictions for arson and aggravated burglary in 1993[689]./None reported, this was a mental illness call.

Mental Illness: Yes, Pendergrass had threatened to hurt himself, and he ended up committing suicide.

Substance Abuse History/Involved: Unknown./None stated.

Race/Sex/Age: White/Male/44

What prompted the initial contact with the killer? On the morning of February 23, Sgt. Hinkle and other officers responded to a 911 call to check upon the welfare of Jackie Pendergrass. A family member had called for police because Pendergrass was threatening to hurt himself. When approaching the house, the officers were fired upon by Pendergrass, so they fell back and tried communicating with him as he barricaded himself inside the house[690].

Actions taken by subject toward police: At some point Pendergrass again opened fire at the officers surrounding his house, and one of those bullets fatally wounded Sgt. Hinkle.

Reactions by the police: Officers on the scene returned fire at Pendergrass, but he ultimately ended up committing suicide before they made entry into his house[691].

How murdered? Sgt. Hinkle was fatally shot in the head with a .22-caliber firearm by the barricaded suspect while outside his house[692].

What could have been done differently for the officer to still be alive? After coming under fire upon arrival at Pendergrass' house, the officers should have stayed behind cover until SWAT officers with armored trucks and shields were able to respond.

Would the officer had been justified to use deadly force before being murdered? Yes, once Pendergrass fired the first round at the officers, they were justified to use deadly force until he was neutralized. The officers ceased fire in hopes of negotiating Pendergrass' peaceful surrender.

Outcome for the cop-killer: Pendergrass committed suicide before the officers were able to make entry into his house.

Officer: Midland Police Department Police Officer Nathan Hayden Heidelberg
Date: 3/5/2019   **Location:** Midland, TX
FACTORS (16,19)
Perpetrator(s) Involved: David Charles Wilson

Criminal Activity History/Involved: NA./No.

Mental Illness: NA.

Substance Abuse History/Involved: NA.

Race/Sex/Age: White/Male/37

What prompted the initial contact with the killer? Officers responded to a silent residential burglar alarm dispatched through 911 around 1 a.m. on March 5. Upon searching the property with his partner, Officer Heidelberg noticed the front door was ajar. Heidelberg carefully entered through the front door and then announced that it was the Police, an announcement verified by other officers who had arrived at the scene[693].

Actions taken by subject toward police: Awoken by his wife who heard the front door chime, David Wilson feared that their home was being invaded by criminals, so he grabbed his gun and went toward the front door and fired one shot in that direction[694].

Reactions by the police: Officer Heidelberg was fatally wounded as the bullet struck him in an area not protected by his vest. Other officers tried to render aid to Officer Heidelberg and arrested Wilson.

How murdered? Officer Heidelberg was shot in an area unprotected by his body armor[695].

What could have been done differently for the officer to still be alive? Nothing, it was a freak accident, Heidelberg had his vest on, had other officers there backing him up, and had found an "open door". Erring on the side that it was a home invasion in progress, the officers had stealthily searched the perimeter and entered the house rather than have lights and sirens and making loud announcements.

Would the officer had been justified to use deadly force before being murdered? It sounds like the homeowner blindly fired his weapon without seeing the officer, so Heidelberg likely never saw Wilson, nor he had an opportunity to engage him.

Outcome for the cop-killer: Wilson was arrested at the scene and was charged with second-degree manslaughter. Wilson alleges that he did not hear the officer announce his presence and feared that he was the subject of a home invasion, firing once he saw the flashlight pointed at him[696].

Miscellaneous: This is a tragic incident that shows the unintended consequences of false alarms and 911 calls of concerned citizens such as happened in the shooting of Atatiana Jefferson in what police thought was a burglary/home invasion as well.

Detective Brian P. Simonsen

New York City Police Department, New York

End of Watch Tuesday, February 12, 2019

Agent Alfred Sanyet-Pérez

Puerto Rico Police Department, Puerto Rico

End of Watch Friday, February 15, 2019

Sergeant Steven Billie Hinkle

Sullivan County Sheriff's Office, Tennessee

End of Watch Tuesday, February 26, 2019

Police Officer Nathan Hayden Heidelberg

Midland Police Department, Texas

End of Watch Tuesday, March 5, 2019

Officer: McHenry County Sheriff's Office, Deputy Sheriff Jacob Howard Keltner
Date: 3/7/2019   **Location:** Rockford, IL
FACTORS (1,2,8,13,15,17,21)
Perpetrator(s) Involved: Floyd E. Brown

Criminal Activity History/Involved: Yes, Brown had prior felony convictions for residential burglary and forgery. (He had received a 13-year prison sentence in 2013, so this murder was preventable if he had been kept in prison.)/Yes, Brown had active warrants for burglary, failure to appear in court and violating parole which the fugitive team was looking to execute on him[697].

Mental Illness: Unknown.

Substance Abuse History/Involved: Unknown./None stated.

Race/Sex/Age: Black/Male/41

What prompted the initial contact with the killer? On the morning of March 7, 2019, Deputy Keltner's assigned fugitive apprehension unit was working with the U.S. Marshals Fugitive Task Force to arrest a wanted fugitive who had been spotted at an area motel. The team surrounded the motel while an officer knocked on the door to Floyd Brown's room, announcing himself as police[698].

Actions taken by subject toward police: Using a high-powered rifle, Brown opened fire from the room toward the door and then from a third-floor window through which he escaped. Brown then managed to shoot Deputy Keltner in the parking lot as Brown moved to his vehicle and then fled the scene.

Reactions by the police: Officers took cover from the gunfire, rendered aid to Deputy Keltner, and pursued Brown in their vehicles. After a few hours of the deadly shooting of Deputy Keltner, federal agents caught up with Brown, and after a brief standoff, he surrendered[699].

How murdered? Deputy Keltner was shot in the head with a high-powered rifle while apprehending a wanted fugitive.

What could have been done differently for the officer to still be alive? The team could have positioned members behind cover, with rifles trained at the front door and windows of the hotel room in case the fugitive came through them with a weapon as he did.

Would the officer had been justified to use deadly force before being murdered? Brown fired through a closed door so those officers could not target him before he started firing at them. Officers could have justifiably shot Brown if given the opportunity after he climbed out the window and ran to the parking lot.

Outcome for the cop-killer: Brown has since been indicted on charges of first-degree murder, criminal possession of a weapon, "attempting to kill a deputy marshal and two special deputy marshals, use of a deadly and dangerous weapon to forcibly assault Keltner and three other officers, discharge of a firearm during a crime of violence, causing Keltner's death, discharge of a firearm during the assault and attempted murder of three officers"[700].

Officer: Kittitas County Sheriff's Office, Deputy Sheriff Ryan Shane Thompson
Date: 3/19/2019   **Location:** Kittitas, WA
FACTORS (1,2,3,4,8,13,15,19,21)
Perpetrator(s) Involved: Juan Manuel Flores Del Toro

Criminal Activity History/Involved: Yes, Del Toro was an illegal alien since April 2017 when he overstayed his H-2A visa and earlier that day he menaced his girlfriend with a weapon./Yes, Del Toro was driving recklessly and unlawfully fleeing from the officers.

Mental Illness: Yes, Del Toro was "prone to bouts of paranoia and rage," and a girlfriend described him as "delusional"[701].

Substance Abuse History/Involved: Yes, Del Toro frequently used methamphetamine./Yes, an autopsy showed Del Toro had meth in his system at the time of the incident and drug paraphernalia were found on him.

Race/Sex/Age: Latino/Male/29

What prompted the initial contact with the killer? On March 19, Deputy Thompson attempted to stop a vehicle that fit the description from a 911 call at 7:35 p.m. of a car being driven erratically[702].

Actions taken by subject toward police: Juan Manuel Flores Del Toro, the operator of that vehicle refused to pull over. Instead, Del Toro took Deputy Thompson on a brief pursuit which was joined in by Deputies Chavez and Goeman. Del Toro stopped at a trailer park where he exited his vehicle and opened fire on the deputies who had stopped their vehicles behind his[703].

Reactions by the police: Caught in the open, Deputy Thompson was struck by the bullets before he could shoot Del Toro. Deputy Chavez, too, was seriously wounded before having a chance to fire, while Deputy Goeman fired five rounds, killing Del Toro.

How murdered? Deputy Thompson was fatally shot while conducting a traffic stop on an erratically driven vehicle.

What could have been done differently for the officer to still be alive? They could have remained behind cover and ordered the driver out of his vehicle at gunpoint.

Would the officer had been justified to use deadly force before being murdered? The deputies would have been justified to use deadly force as soon as they saw a weapon in Del Toro's hand or reasonably believed that he was accessing one as he exited his vehicle and went towards theirs.

Outcome for the cop-killer: Del Toro was shot dead at the scene by Deputy Goeman, who with his partner, Deputy Chavez, was backing up Deputy Thompson on the stop.

Officer: El Paso County Sheriff's Office, Deputy Sheriff Peter John Herrera
Date: 3/24/2019   **Location:** San Elizario, TX
FACTORS (1,2,7,8,9,15)
Perpetrator(s) Involved: Facundo Chavez

Criminal Activity History/Involved: Yes, Chavez had prior arrests for marijuana, possession of a controlled substance (heroin), and distribution of a controlled/counterfeit substance, and he had a pending charge for domestic assault in 2018[704]./Yes, Chavez had three active warrants, and he illegally possessed a firearm when stopped.

Mental Illness: Unknown.

Substance Abuse History/Involved: Yes, Chavez has prior drug related arrests./None stated.

Race/Sex/Age: Latino/Male/27

What prompted the initial contact with the killer? At approximately 1:50 a.m. on March 22, Deputy Herrera conducted a vehicle and traffic stop on a vehicle for a headlight violation. While interviewing the driver, Facundo Chavez, Deputy Herrera asked him to step out of the vehicle[705].

Actions taken by subject toward police: While exiting his car, Chavez accessed a gun hidden in his waist and fired it at Deputy Herrera at least 15 times, fatally striking him several times in the vest and unprotected parts of his body. Chavez got back in his car and drove away before his car stalled forcing him and his girlfriend, Arlene Pina, to flee on foot[706].

Reactions by the police: Deputy Herrera did not even have a chance to unholster his weapon before being shot. When officers responded to the scene, they rendered medical aid to Herrera and started a manhunt for Chavez and Pina. Within a couple of hours, the two suspects were caught hiding in a shed[707].

How murdered? Deputy Herrera was shot point-blank during a traffic stop for an equipment infraction, he died from his wounds two days later.

What could have been done differently for the officer to still be alive? It is extremely difficult for an officer to react fast enough to a subject pulling a gun on them when exiting the car since it is nearly impossible to see the subject's hands the whole time. At best, an officer can step back to the rear of the car so if the subject exits with a gun in hand the officer has cover behind the rear of the car.

Would the officer had been justified to use deadly force before being murdered? Had Deputy Herrera reasonably believed that Chavez was accessing a weapon in his waistband or seen Chavez holding the weapon he could have justifiably used deadly force.

Outcome for the cop-killer: Chavez was charged with capital murder and unlawful possession of a firearm by a felon.

Miscellaneous: Arlene Pina, girlfriend of Chavez, who was in the vehicle during the incident and can be heard on Herrera's bodycam video telling him to hit the fallen deputy, was charged with capital murder as well.

Officer: Cowlitz County Sheriff's Office, Deputy Sheriff Justin Richard DeRosier
Date: 4/14/2019   **Location:** Kalama, WA
FACTORS (1,8,15,19) 7?,9?,13?
Perpetrator(s) Involved: Brian Dellaann Butts

Criminal Activity History/Involved: Yes, Butts had numerous prior arrests and convictions including second-degree robbery, assault, obstructing law enforcement, several charges for possession of controlled substances, including intent to distribute meth, hit-and-run, operating a motor vehicle with a suspended license, and possessing marijuana[708]./No, not until Butts shot Deputy DeRosier without provocation.

Mental Illness: Unknown.

Substance Abuse History/Involved: Yes, Butts had numerous prior drug-related arrests./ None stated.

Race/Sex/Age: White/Male/33

What prompted the initial contact with the killer? Shortly after 10 p.m. on April 14, Deputy DeRosier responded to a 911 call of a mobile home parked blocking the roadway[709].

Actions taken by subject toward police: The man, Brian Butts, who last had possession of the mobile home shot Deputy DeRosier within two minutes of the deputy's arrival.

Reactions by the police: After being shot, Deputy DeRosier radioed in that he was shot and provided a description of the subject. DeRosier was flown to a hospital where he died shortly after. A manhunt ensued and within 24 hours with the help of a 911 call about a suspicious person fitting the shooters description, the armed suspect Brian Butts was shot dead in a shoot-out with two police officers from Kelso[710].

How murdered? Deputy DeRosier was shot in the chest within two minutes of arriving at the scene of the mobile home blocking the roadway.

What could have been done differently for the officer to still be alive? That 911 call was not one that is typically considered high risk, so the deputy was likely not expecting an armed confrontation and let his guard down just as most officers have done during such calls countless times before, or he was ambushed.

Would the officer had been justified to use deadly force before being murdered? Since Deputy DeRosier would have been justified shooting Butts as soon as he saw Butts with a weapon in his hand or making a furtive movement to get one, it appears DeRosier did not see either until it was too late.

Outcome for the cop-killer: Butts was justifiably shot and killed the next day by two police officers involved in the manhunt for him.

Deputy Sheriff Jacob Howard Keltner

McHenry County Sheriff's Office, Illinois

End of Watch Thursday, March 7, 2019

Deputy Sheriff Ryan Shane Thompson

Kittitas County Sheriff's Office, Washington

End of Watch Tuesday, March 19, 2019

Deputy Sheriff Peter John Herrera

El Paso County Sheriff's Office, Texas

End of Watch Sunday, March 24, 2019

Deputy Sheriff Justin Richard DeRosier

Cowlitz County Sheriff's Office, Washington

End of Watch Sunday, April 14, 2019

Officer: Montgomery County Police Department Police Officer Kyle David Olinger
Date: 4/18/2019   **Location:** Silver Spring, MD
FACTORS (1,2,4,8,13,15)
Perpetrator(s) Involved: Terrence A. Green

Criminal Activity History/Involved: No. According to his brother, Mickey Green who is a police officer./Yes, he had an illegally procured handgun.

Mental Illness: Green's attorney stated that he suffers from "several mental afflictions, including depression, paranoia and post-traumatic stress disorder"[711].

Substance Abuse History/Involved: Unknown./None stated.

Race/Sex/Age: Black/Male/19

What prompted the initial contact with the killer? During a traffic stop of a suspicious vehicle on August 13, 2003, Officer Olinger approached the passenger's side and observed Terrence Green reach to the floorboard for a chrome-plated handgun. Olinger drew his weapon and pointed it at Green's head while commanding all occupants in the vehicle to put their hands up where he could see them[712].

Actions taken by subject toward police: Green did not comply with Olinger's commands and did not show the officer his hands. While the other occupants put their hands up, Green shot Officer Olinger in the neck.

Reactions by the police: Officer Olinger went down to the ground and Green took off running. Police eventually tracked Green down and arrested him[713].

How murdered? Officer Olinger died 16 years later from complications arising from the bullet that severed his spinal cord on April 13 while conducting a traffic stop.

What could have been done differently for the officer to still be alive? Officer Olinger should have justifiably shot Green when he saw him reaching for the chrome-plated pistol by his feet on the floorboard[714].

Would the officer had been justified to use deadly force before being murdered? Yes, Olinger would have been justified shooting Green when he initially reached toward the weapon and again when Green did not comply to put his hands up and kept them out of Olinger's view.

Outcome for the cop-killer: Green was found guilty of attempted first-degree murder, assault, and using a handgun during a violent crime, he was sentenced to life in prison plus 20 years.

Miscellaneous: Since the shooting, Olinger has voiced that "fear of shooting a young black man–and igniting tensions–might have played a role in his decision not to use force"[715] immediately on Green, which unfortunately gave Green the opportunity to shoot him.

Officer: Mooresville Police Dept., K9 Officer Jordan Harris Sheldon
Date: 5/4/2019   **Location:** Mooresville, NC
FACTORS (1,2,4,5,8,9,15)
Perpetrator(s) Involved: Michael Yovany Aldana

Criminal Activity History/Involved: Unknown./Yes, Aldana was driving with a suspended license.

Mental Illness: Aldana's girlfriend stated that he had talked about killing himself and a police officer, he ended up doing both[716].

Substance Abuse History/Involved: Unknown./None stated.

Race/Sex/Age: White/Male/28

What prompted the initial contact with the killer? Around 10:15 p.m. on May 4, Officer Sheldon conducted a car stop on a subject he believed had a suspended driver's license. After talking with the driver, Michael Aldana, Officer Sheldon took Aldana's paperwork back to his patrol vehicle to run through the system. The system check confirmed that Aldana was driving with a suspended license, which Sheldon then returned to Aldana's car and relayed[717].

Actions taken by subject toward police: After Officer Sheldon informed Aldana about his suspended license, Aldana gave the officer some additional documentation to look at. While Sheldon was reviewing the paperwork, Aldana accessed a handgun and shot Sheldon, killing him.

Reactions by the police: Officer Sheldon never saw the gun nor the shots coming as evidenced by the video on his bodycam and the fact he did not try to release his K9 from the patrol vehicle. Aldana fled the scene and was found dead by a self-inflicted gunshot wound when officers tracked him down at his residence[718].

How murdered? Officer Sheldon was shot point-blank for no apparent motive during a traffic stop.

What could have been done differently for the officer to still be alive? As the Mooresville Police Chief Ron Campurciani described after seeing the bodycam video, Officer Sheldon was essentially ambushed while looking over the paperwork, he "didn't have any time to react"[719]. Had Officer Sheldon insisted Aldana keep his hands on the steering wheel where they could be seen, it would have been harder for Aldana to ambush him.

Would the officer had been justified to use deadly force before being murdered? Aldana did not give the officer any reason to believe that deadly force was necessary before he shot Sheldon as Sheldon was distracted looking at the paperwork.

Outcome for the cop-killer: Aldana fled the scene and took his own life with a self-inflicted gunshot shortly after.

Miscellaneous: This incident shows why officers always appear to be on guard and are so insistent on seeing a person's hands when dealing with them. Aldana did not have a violent criminal history and did not give any indications that he was going to be violent with Sheldon.

Officer: Biloxi Police Department Police Officer Robert Stanton McKeithen
Date: 5/5/2019   **Location:** Biloxi, MS
FACTORS (1,4,6,7,15)
Perpetrator(s) Involved: Darian Tawan Atkinson

Criminal Activity History/Involved: Atkinson had no prior convictions, but he received a three-day school suspension for threatening to conduct a school shooting like that of Parkland[720]./No, not before Atkinson murdered Officer McKeithen.

Mental Illness: Atkinson's mother reported that he had recently started exhibiting signs of mental illness[721].

Substance Abuse History/Involved: Unknown./None stated.

Race/Sex/Age: Black/Male/19

What prompted the initial contact with the killer? Atkinson walked approximately eight miles from his home to a Biloxi police station. After going inside the station behind a couple around 10:00 p.m., Atkinson followed the couple out as they went to the parking lot to speak with Officer McKeithen who had just pulled in. While discussing the domestic incident with the couple, McKeithen asked Atkinson if he was involved in it[722].

Actions taken by subject towards police: Atkinson told McKeithen to leave him alone and walked away. After briefly waiting near a tree, Atkinson walked up behind McKeithen, pulled out a 40-caliber handgun from his waistband and shot him six times.

Reactions by the police: Officer McKeithen was unaware that Atkinson had returned and ambushed him. Before he could have realized it, McKeithen was fatally struck outside his protected vest area several times and was pronounced dead within an hour. A manhunt was conducted, and Atkinson was captured within 24 hours after being spotted by an off-duty police officer[723].

How murdered? Officer McKeithen was ambushed in cold blood while filling out domestic incident paperwork for a couple in the police station parking lot.

What could have been done differently for the officer to still be alive? At that moment, though Atkinson may have appeared weird, Officer McKeithen had no reason to believe that he was a violent murderer and meant him any harm.

Would the officer had been justified to use deadly force before being murdered? No, while strange or rude for standing nearby as the couple spoke with McKeithen about their domestic incident, Atkinson presented no visible threat or aggressive behavior toward the officer before walking away.

Outcome for the cop-killer: Atkinson has been indicted by a grand jury on the charge of capital murder.

Miscellaneous: Psychiatrist, Dr. Chris Lott testified that "Atkinson said he shot the officer because black people have been oppressed and he had the right to bear arms and act"[724]. Besides this incident showing the effect of constant demonization of police as racist, it also demonstrates why officers have shot people as they make furtive movements toward their waist, because that is typically where they are hiding a deadly weapon.

Officer: Savannah Police Department Sergeant Kelvin Bernard Ansari
Date: 5/11/2019   **Location:** Savannah, GA
FACTORS (1,2,3,7,8,15,19)
Perpetrator(s) Involved: Edward Fuller III

Criminal Activity History/Involved: Yes, Fuller was a career criminal. He had over 30 arrests for the crimes of robbery, armed robbery, DUI, carrying a concealed weapon, possession of cocaine with intent to distribute, obstruction, aggravated assault, simple battery, and numerous parole/probation violations./Yes, Fuller had just committed a violent robbery and he had substantial amounts of heroin, meth, and hydrocodone in his vehicle before the shooting.

Mental Illness: Unknown.

Substance Abuse History/Involved: Yes, Fuller had previous drug- and alcohol-related offenses./Yes, the autopsy showed that Fuller had cocaine and alcohol in his system during the time of the incident.

Race/Sex/Age: Black/Male/49

What prompted the initial contact with the killer? Sgt. Ansari and Officer Douglas Thomas responded to a 911 call of an armed robbery at approximately 8:10 p.m. on May 11. While investigating what happened, Sgt. Ansari walked near a vehicle in which the perpetrator, Edward Fuller III was hiding[725].

Actions taken by subject toward police: Without provocation, Fuller got out of the vehicle and started shooting at Sgt. Ansari and Officer Thomas as they neared his vehicle.

Reactions by the police: Sgt. Ansari was shot in the leg, severing his femoral artery, and died shortly thereafter. Officer Thomas too was shot in the leg, and as he tended to their wounds, Fuller took off running. Two other officers tracked Fuller down to a nearby backyard. As Fuller attempted to flee from the officers while still holding a gun in his hand, Officer Foraker shot him several times, killing him[726].

How murdered? Sgt. Ansari was ambushed and shot dead while investigating a robbery.

What could have been done differently for the officer to still be alive? Neither Sgt. Ansari nor Officer Thomas had a chance to draw their weapons. Both were unaware of Fuller's presence in the car and neither had any reason to believe that their life was in imminent danger as they conducted a field investigation into the robbery. The officers would have had to look closely at each vehicle they walked by to prevent it.

Would the officer had been justified to use deadly force before being murdered? No, Sgt. Ansari did not appear to see Fuller or the threat he presented until the moment he turned the corner and was being shot at by Fuller.

Outcome for the cop-killer: Fuller pointed his weapon at and was justifiably shot dead by, the officers who tracked him down.

Police Officer Kyle David Olinger

Montgomery County PD, Maryland

End of Watch Thursday, April 18, 2019

K9 Officer Jordan Harris Sheldon

Mooresville Police Department, North Carolina

End of Watch Saturday, May 4, 2019

Police Officer Robert Stanton McKeithen

Biloxi Police Department, Mississippi

End of Watch Sunday, May 5, 2019

Sergeant Kelvin Bernard Ansari

Savannah Police Department, Georgia

End of Watch Saturday, May 11, 2019

Officer: Auburn Police Division, Police Officer William Ray Buechner, Jr.
Date: 5/19/2019   **Location:** Auburn, AL
FACTORS (1,2,7,15,18,19)
Perpetrator(s) Involved: Grady Wayne Wilkes

Criminal Activity History/Involved: No, Wilkes was not known to the local police[727]./Yes, Wilkes had just assaulted his live-in girlfriend and threatened to kill her.

Mental Illness: Unknown, and it is noted that Wilkes had never been deployed into combat operations.

Substance Abuse History/Involved: Unknown./None stated.

Race/Sex/Age: White/Male/29

What prompted the initial contact with the killer? Shortly after 10 p.m. on May 19, Officer Buechner and several other officers responded to a 911 call about domestic violence phoned in by a woman about her boyfriend assaulting her[728].

Actions taken by subject toward police: As the officers approached the door to the residence, Grady Wilkes, a military-trained infantryman, shot at them through the door with his rifle[729].

Reactions by the police: Officer Buechner was mortally wounded by the bullet and Officers Elliott and Sistrunk also sustained gunshot wounds. Elliot, Sistrunk, and a fourth officer who was not shot, all tended to Officer Buechner and their injuries as Wilkes escaped from the scene. Law enforcement agencies started searching for Wilkes and with the help of citizens calling 911, they captured and arrested Wilkes the next day.

How murdered? Officer Buechner was shot with a rifle when responding to a domestic incident.

What could have been done differently for the officer to still be alive? Officers are taught not to stand in the fatal funnel that is the doorway, but eventually if they are to enter a residence they need to be in the doorway. If the officers were told that the subject was armed with a rifle, they should have taken up positions behind cover and had the suspect exit the residence with his hands up.

Would the officer had been justified to use deadly force before being murdered? With Wilkes shooting his high-powered rifle at the officers from inside his home, they would not have had an opportunity to use deadly force on him before he opened fire.

Outcome for the cop-killer: Wilkes has been charged with "capital murder, three counts of attempted murder, and second-degree domestic violence"[730].

Officer: Manati Municipal Police Department, Police Officer Jesus Abner Marrero-Martinez
Date: 5/25/2019   **Location:** Manati, Puerto Rico
FACTORS (1,2,8,15,20)
Perpetrator(s) Involved: Jose Edgardo Berrios Colon, Giovannie Oquendo Guevarez and Kelvin Joel Melendez Colon

Criminal Activity History/Involved: Yes, Guevarez was already wanted for his role in prior "armed robberies and carjackings"[731]./Yes, the suspects were conducting an armed robbery/carjacking.

Mental Illness: Unknown.

Substance Abuse History/Involved: Unknown./None stated.

Race/Sex/Age: J.Colon: Latino/Male/21; Guevarez: Latino/Male/25; K.Colon: Latino/Male/Unknown

What prompted the initial contact with the killer? On May 25, Officer Martinez was with a friend while off-duty on vacation outside of a club that ended up being closed. While in the parking lot, Martinez and his friend were approached by three masked men who told them to give up their car keys. Instead of giving his keys, Martinez presented his weapon at the trio and told them he was a police officer[732].

Actions taken by subject toward police: The trio did not peacefully surrender to Officer Martinez and a gunfight ensured.

Reactions by the police: Officer Martinez shot and killed one of the perpetrators, Jose Colon, and then retreated to his vehicle as the remaining two suspects fled the area.

How murdered? While Officer Martinez was in his vehicle, one of the two remaining suspects shot him twice from behind, fatally wounding him.

What could have been done differently for the officer to still be alive? Tough to second guess as it is possible that the trio would have shot both men upon finding out Martinez was an officer, or for no reason at all.

Would the officer had been justified to use deadly force before being murdered? Yes, Martinez was justified and did use deadly force successfully on one of the perpetrators.

Outcome for the cop-killer: Jose Colon was killed in the shootout with Officer Martinez. The two remaining suspects, Guevarez and Kelvin Colon, have been identified and are being pursued for justice.

Officer: Racine Police Department Patrol Officer John David Hetland
Date: 6/17/2019   **Location:** Racine, WI
FACTORS (1,2,14,15,20,21)
Perpetrator(s) Involved: Dalquavis Ward

Criminal Activity History/Involved: Yes, Ward had prior convictions for armed robbery, disorderly conduct on two separate occasions, and possession of a firearm by a felon./Yes, Ward was committing an armed robbery at a bar and grill.

Mental Illness: Unknown

Substance Abuse History/Involved: Yes, addicted to marijuana./None stated.

Race/Sex/Age: Black/Male/26

What prompted the initial contact with the killer? While off-duty, Officer Hetland was at a local bar and grill around 9:40 p.m. on June 17 when Dalquavis Ward entered the establishment, went to the bar, and pointed a gun at the bartender, demanding the money from the cash register. As the bartender was handing over the money to Ward, Hetland took police action, jumped over the bar, and started grappling with Ward for control of his firearm.[733]

Actions taken by subject toward police: During the struggle, Ward managed to push Hetland away from him and fired one shot into his chest, striking Hetland's heart and quickly killing him[734].

Reactions by the police: Once shot, Officer Hetland was out of the fight and there were no other officers around to assist him or arrest Ward. Through surveillance video and eyewitness testimony, police identified Ward and arrested him within days of the shooting[735].

How murdered? Officer Hetland was killed trying to stop an armed robbery while off-duty.

What could have been done differently for the officer to still be alive? Officer Hetland could have chosen to not get involved since he was off-duty and presumably unarmed since it is a violation of most department's policy for officers' to be armed while drinking alcohol. Had Officer Hetland been armed, he could have shot Ward while Ward was distracted taking the money from the bartender during the robbery, though Hetland would likely have been scrutinized for being armed while drinking.

Would the officer had been justified to use deadly force before being murdered? Yes, if Hetland had been armed, he would have been justified to shoot Ward as soon as he saw him pointing his handgun at the bartender.

Outcome for the cop-killer: Ward was found guilty by a jury trial of "first-degree intentional homicide, armed robbery, and possession of a firearm by a felon"[736].

Miscellaneous: Ward had just gotten out of federal prison four days before the shooting and was on supervised release from his last armed robbery conviction. Had the criminal justice system kept Ward imprisoned to serve his full sentence, Officer Hetland could still be alive today.

Officer: Sacramento Police Department, Police Officer Tara Christina O'Sullivan
Date: 6/19/2019   **Location:** Sacramento, CA
FACTORS (1,2,4,7,15,18,19)
Perpetrator(s) Involved: Adel Sambrano Ramos

Criminal Activity History/Involved: Yes, Ramos had prior convictions for DUI, petty theft, domestic violence, and battery, and he had an active warrant for a battery charge involving a minor./Yes, while Ramos was involved in what was only considered a domestic disturbance, he had an active warrant and was in possession of illegal firearms in his residence.

Mental Illness: Yes, Ramos had once threatened to "blow up my family with a bomb"[737] and he was kept in a psychiatric unit because he had inflicted self-harm on himself while in jail.

Substance Abuse History/Involved: Unknown./None stated.

Race/Sex/Age: Latino/Male/45

What prompted the initial contact with the killer? Officer O'Sullivan and several other officers responded around 5:40 p.m. on June 19 to a 911 call from a woman who was the victim of a domestic disturbance asking for a police presence as she gathered some of her belongings from the house. While waiting outside the house for nearly 30 minutes, officers had announced themselves and informed Ramos he was not in trouble[738].

Actions taken by subject toward police: Without provocation, from inside the house Ramos unleashed a barrage of bullets from his high-powered rifle through the house toward the officers, fatally striking Officer O'Sullivan.

Reactions by the police: Officers scrambled for cover from the bullets and used an armored vehicle to exfiltrate the wounded O'Sullivan to get her medical attention, but she succumbed to her wounds shortly after. After hours of negotiations while barricaded and continuing to occasionally shoot at officers, Ramos surrendered around 2 a.m. the next day and was arrested[739].

How murdered? Officer O'Sullivan was ambushed during a domestic disturbance by a man with a high-powered rifle.

What could have been done differently for the officer to still be alive? Nothing, Officer O'Sullivan was doing her job by responding to a 911 call and assisting a woman get her belongings. Officer O'Sullivan was standing outside of the house and could not have seen the suspect holding a weapon or preparing to shoot through the walls at her and her fellow officers.

Would the officer had been justified to use deadly force before being murdered? No, Officer O'Sullivan had never seen her killer.

Outcome for the cop-killer: Ramos has been charged with murder with special circumstances, several counts of attempted murder, and several more counts of illegal manufacture of firearms.

Police Officer William Ray Buechner, Jr.

Auburn Police Division, Alabama

End of Watch Sunday, May 19, 2019

Police Officer Jesus Abner Marrero-Martínez

Manatí Municipal PD, Puerto Rico

End of Watch Saturday, May 25, 2019

Patrol Officer John David Hetland

Racine Police Department, Wisconsin

End of Watch Monday, June 17, 2019

Police Officer Tara Christina O'Sullivan

Sacramento Police Department, California

End of Watch Wednesday, June 19, 2019

Officer: Mission Police Department, Corporal Jose Luis "Speedy" Espericueta, Jr.
Date: 6/20/2019   **Location:** Mission, TX
FACTORS (1,2,4,9,13,15,18)
Perpetrator(s) Involved: Juan Carlos Chapa Jr.

Criminal Activity History/Involved: Yes, Chapa had prior arrests for drug possession, DWI, trespassing, twice for evading arrest, and, most recently, for resisting arrest[740]./Yes, Chapa had just shot at his mother with a gun.

Mental Illness: Yes, Chapa's family reported that he suffered from depression.

Substance Abuse History/Involved: Yes, Chapa had numerous prior drug-related arrests and his family had tried to get him help for his addiction./None stated.

Race/Sex/Age: Latino/Male/33

What prompted the initial contact with the killer? Shortly after 8 p.m. on June 20, Corporal Espericueta responded to assist another officer who had been flagged down by a woman reporting her son, Juan Carlos Chapa Jr. had just shot at her with a handgun. Upon arriving at the scene, Espericueta observed Chapa and went to interview him[741 742].

Actions taken by subject toward police: Upon seeing Corporal Espericueta try to engage with him, Chapa took off running, shooting at, and fatally hitting Espericueta as he did so[743].

Reactions by the police: Corporal Espericueta and other officers at the scene returned fire at Chapa, killing him.

How murdered? Corporal Espericueta died from the gunshot received from pursuing a violent subject who had just shot at his own mother.

What could have been done differently for the officer to still be alive? Nothing, Corporal Espericueta observed and attempted to contact a subject he believed was involved in the violent domestic disturbance. Chapa got a lucky shot off as he ran from Espericueta who was doing his job and pursuing him.

Would the officer had been justified to use deadly force before being murdered? Yes, given the totality of the circumstances, as soon as Chapa moved his hand toward his waistband which is a common area to access a weapon, Corporal Espericueta was justified to use deadly force.

Outcome for the cop-killer: Chapa was justifiably shot and killed by officers after he initiated a gun battle with them.

Officer: North County Police Cooperative, Police Officer Michael Vincent Langsdorf
Date: 6/23/2019   **Location:** St. Louis, MO
FACTORS (1,2,9,12,14,15,19)3?13?
Perpetrator(s) Involved: Bonette Kymbrelle Meeks

Criminal Activity History/Involved: Yes, Meeks had prior arrests for gun and drug possession (cocaine and marijuana), as well as drug sales[744]./Yes, Meeks tried to cash approximately $6,000 worth of fake checks and illegally possessed a firearm[745].

Substance Abuse History/Involved: Yes, Meeks had numerous prior drug-related arrests./Unknown, however, witnesses believed that he was on drugs during the incident because of "his mumbling and odd demeanor"[746].

Race/Sex/Age: Black/Male/26

What prompted the initial contact with the killer? Officer Langsdorf responded to a 911 call from a food market around 4:30 p.m. on June 23 about a man attempting to cash bogus checks. Upon arriving at the store, Langsdorf confronted that man, Bonette Meeks.

Actions taken by subject toward police: Meeks refused to comply and instead physically fought with Officer Langsdorf, with both men ending up on the ground and Officer Langsdorf on top of Meeks. While Langsdorf tried to take Meeks into custody, Meeks managed to pull a handgun from his waistband and struck Langsdorf in the head, dazing him. With Langsdorf dazed and injured on the ground, Meeks got up, stood behind Langsdorf, and shot him in the back of his head, killing him[747].

Reactions by the police: Other officers responding to the scene tracked down Meeks soon after and arrested with the murder weapon still in his possession.

How murdered? Executed after being injured during a physical struggle while trying to arrest a man for attempting to pass bad checks.

What could have been done differently for the officer to still be alive? All indications are that Officer Langsdorf acted properly. He confronted the suspect involved in the crime, and when Meeks became combative, he was able to get him to the ground in a superior position. Until Meeks accessed his hidden firearm, Langsdorf used the proper amount of force to take Meeks into custody. After the fact it is clear Langsdorf should have shot him.

Would the officer had been justified to use deadly force before being murdered? No, until being struck in the head by it, Officer Langsdorf was not aware that Meeks was armed. During the chaos involved during the fight, Meeks was able to pull out a hidden weapon without Langsdorf being able to see it or stop it before it was too late. Had Langsdorf feared that Meeks was armed and that he was attempting to access a weapon, then Yes, Langsdorf could have preemptively used justifiable deadly force.

Outcome for the cop-killer. Meeks has been charged with first-degree murder, armed criminal action, unlawful possession of a weapon, and resisting arrest.

Miscellaneous: This incident is a classic example of why officers escalate up the use of force continuum when suspects fail to comply, physically resist, and especially when they make furtive movements toward their waistband.

Officer: Fulton County Sheriff's Office, Deputy Sheriff Troy Phillip Chisum
Date: 6/25/2019   **Location:** Avon, Illinois
FACTORS (1,2,7,15,18,19)
Perpetrator(s) Involved: Nathan Woodring

Criminal History Activity /Involved: Yes, Woodring's prior arrests included resisting arrest, fleeing, and attempting to elude, along with two felony drug possessions[748]./Unknown; Woodring was reportedly involved in a suspected domestic assault and told a woman in his house that he pistol-whipped someone.

Mental Illness: Unknown.

Substance Abuse History/Involved: Yes, Woodring had prior drug arrests./None stated.

Race/Sex/Age: White/Male/42

What prompted the initial contact with the killer? Deputy Chisum responded to a 911 call about a disturbance at Nathan Woodring's home around 2 p.m. on June 25. Upon arriving at the scene, Deputy Chisum saw a car preparing to leave and spoke with the two occupants, one of whom reported that Woodring had a shotgun and an assault-type rifle. After speaking with Chisum the car drove away and Chisum approached the house to talk to Woodring who was already familiar to the deputies[749].

Actions taken by subject toward police: After Chisum knocked on Woodring's door, Woodring fired his shotgun at Chisum from inside the house. The first shot apparently missed but the second shot hit and killed Chisum as he was running away from the door[750].

Reactions by the police: The other deputies maintained a perimeter and negotiated a peaceful surrender by Woodring after nearly 20 hours of him barricading himself inside his house.

How murdered? Deputy Chisum was shot in the back by a shotgun while outside a subject's house that was involved in a 911 disturbance call.

What could have been done differently for the officer to still be alive? Given that the other three deputies were putting on their body armor when Chisum arrived and the woman he interviewed reported that Woodring was armed, it would have been prudent and more tactical for Chisum to take cover with the other deputies and have Woodring exit the house with his hands up.

Would the officer had been justified to use deadly force before being murdered? Deputy Chisum would have been justified in shooting Woodring once he saw the shotgun or was shot at by it; however, it is likely that with Woodring inside the house and Chisum outside, Chisum did not clearly see Woodring or the fact he was armed.

Outcome for the cop-killer: After surrendering, Woodring was arrested and has been charged with two counts of first-degree murder.

Officer: Hall County Sheriff's Office, Deputy Sheriff Nicolas Blane Dixon
Date: 7/8/2019   **Location:** Gainesville, GA
FACTORS (1,2,8,13,15)
Perpetrator(s) Involved: Hector Garcia-Solis, Brayan Omar Cruz, London Clements, Eric Edgardo Velasquez

Criminal Activity History/Involved: Yes, the suspects had a criminal history with Garcia-Solis in particular having just got out of jail earlier in the week after being arrested for "DUI, driving on a suspended license, possession of an open container, striking a fixed object and felony obstruction of an officer"[751]./Yes, the subjects were in possession of stolen goods in a stolen car which they were using during the commission of residential and commercial burglaries.

Substance Abuse History/Involved: Unknown./None stated.

Race/Sex/Age: All four subjects were Latino/Male/17

What prompted the initial contact with the killer? When around 11 p.m. on July 8, deputies attempted to stop a stolen vehicle suspected to be used in numerous recent burglaries, the driver Hector Garcia-Solis, one of four Latino males, refused to comply and tried to flee. After crashing the vehicle, the perpetrators took off on foot with Deputy Dixon and another deputy catching up to the driver as both sides exchanged gunfire. With nobody hit after the first volley, the deputies ordered Garcia-Solis to surrender and put up his hands[752].

Actions taken by subject toward police: Garcia-Solis refused to comply with the deputy's commands, ducked behind a house, and then popped out, again shooting at them and striking Deputy Dixon under his body armor, fatally wounding him.

Reactions by the police: Both deputies returned fired at Garcia-Solis, hitting him several times. Deputy Dixon was then rushed for emergency medical care, but the one gunshot proved to be fatal.

How murdered? Deputy Dixon was fatally shot while pursuing an armed burglary suspect.

What could have been done differently for the officer to still be alive? Deputy Dixon performed admirably, courageously pursuing a subject suspected in numerous felonies and exchanging gunfire with him. Dixon and the other deputy gave Garcia-Solis a chance to peacefully surrender even after being shot at. It is unclear if Garcia-Solis was in the open and the deputies had a clear shot at him at that point. If Garcia-Solis were and if either of the deputies did, they would have been completely justified in taking the shot when he moved to get behind cover again.

Would the officer had been justified to use deadly force before being murdered? Yes, and Deputy Dixon did use deadly force in the initial gunfight and could have again when Garcia-Solis refused to surrender.

Outcome for the cop-killer: Garcia-Solis was treated for his wounds and was arrested the night of the incident, while his accomplices were captured by the next day. All four have been charged with "malice murder, felony murder, aggravated assault on a police officer and conspiracy to commit robbery and burglary"[753].

Corporal Jose Luis "Speedy" Espericueta, Jr.

Mission Police Department, Texas

End of Watch Thursday, June 20, 2019

Police Officer Michael Vincent Langsdorf

North County Police Cooperative, Missouri

End of Watch Sunday, June 23, 2019

Deputy Sheriff Troy Phillip Chisum

Fulton County Sheriff's Office, Illinois

End of Watch Tuesday, June 25, 2019

Deputy Sheriff Nicolas Blane Dixon

Hall County Sheriff's Office, Georgia

End of Watch Monday, July 8, 2019

Officer: Stone County Sheriff's Office, Sergeant Michael David Stephen, Sr.
Date: 7/18/2019   **Location:** Leslie, AR
FACTORS (1,2,13,15,18,19)
Perpetrator(s) Involved: Samuel Fullerton

Criminal Activity History/Involved: Yes, the previous year Fullerton was arrested by Sgt. Stephen and charged with "terroristic threatening, aggravated assault, and battery in the second degree"[754]./ Yes, Fullerton had just assaulted his girlfriend and had active warrants for the prior charges from 2018.

Mental Illness: Unknown.

Substance Abuse History/Involved: Unknown./None stated.

Race/Sex/Age: White/Male/39

What prompted the initial contact with the killer? Sgt. Stephen and two other deputies arrived at Samuel Fullerton's house around 8:40 a.m. on July 18 in response to a third-party 911 call reporting that Fullerton had just assaulted his live-in girlfriend. Aware of Fullerton's felony warrants and violent behavior, the deputies arranged for two of them to cover the front and back of the house as Sgt. Stephen made contact at the front door. The girlfriend answered the door and was talking with Sgt. Stephen when Fullerton opened the door and was visibly armed, prompting the Sgt. to order him to drop the weapon[755].

Actions taken by subject toward police: In a matter of seconds, Fullerton ignored the Sgt's orders, raised the firearm toward Stephen and started shooting, hitting him several times.

Reactions by the police: Sgt. Stephen and Deputy Johnson, who was covering the front of the house, both opened fire on Fullerton as Fullerton withdrew into the house while still shooting at Stephen.

How murdered? Sgt. Stephen was shot seven times at close range while responding to a domestic violence call. His vest stopped one of the bullets but not the other six. Deputy Johnson was also shot during the incident but survived his wounds.

What could have been done differently for the officer to still be alive? Fullerton's opening the front door and being armed caught the Sgt. off guard. Perhaps the Sgt. ordered Fullerton to drop the weapon because he feared that if he went for his gun, he would be shot so his best bet was to get Fullerton to comply. After the fact it is clear that the Sgt's only chance of coming out of that incident alive was to shoot Fullerton as soon as he saw him holding a gun upon opening the door.

Would the officer had been justified to use deadly force before being murdered? Yes, both Sgt. Stephen and Deputy Johnson could have justifiably used deadly force against Fullerton the moment he opened the door with a gun in his hand.

Outcome for the cop-killer: Fullerton was justifiably shot and mortally wounded by the deputies during the shootout.

Miscellaneous: Video from Sgt. Stephen's bodycam captured the incident.

Officer: Los Angeles Police Department, Police Officer Juan Jose Diaz
Date: 7/27/2019 **Location:** Los Angeles, CA
FACTORS (1,2,8,13,15,20)
Perpetrator(s) Involved: Cristian Facundo, Francisco Talamantes III, and Ashlynn Smith

Criminal Activity History/Involved: Yes, Talamantes was a prior convicted felon./Yes, all three were involved in a crime spree that included vandalism and an attempted murder of an ex-boyfriend[756].

Mental Illness: Unknown.

Substance Abuse History/Involved: Unknown./None stated.

Race/Sex/Age: Facundo: Latino/Male/20; Talamantes III: Latino/Male/24; Smith: White/Female/18

What prompted the initial contact with the killer? While off-duty and out for an evening with his friends around 1 a.m. on July 27, Officer Juan Diaz observed some male gang members tagging graffiti and ordered them to stop. When one of the gang members, Cristian Facundo responded to Diaz's interjection by lifting his shirt to show his handgun, Diaz disengaged and got into his car to leave with his friends[757].

Actions taken by subject toward police: While Diaz and his friends were driving away, Facundo and fellow gang member Francisco Talamantes III ran after the vehicle as Facundo shot at it, fatally hitting Officer Diaz and injuring another occupant.

Reactions by the police: After Diaz and one of the other occupants were shot, the driver flagged down a passing LAPD car and notified them of the incident. After a week-long manhunt, Facundo and Talamantes were captured along with their crime spree accomplice Smith[758].

How murdered? Officer Diaz was killed after taking police action to stop vandalism by some gang members but then leaving to avoid a violent confrontation.

What could have been done differently for the officer to still be alive? Officer Diaz could have drawn his weapon and ordered Facundo at gunpoint to get on the ground with his hands out to his sides after seeing he was armed.

Would the officer had been justified to use deadly force before being murdered? Yes, Officer Diaz could have justifiably shot Facundo when he displayed his firearm since at any moment Facundo could have accessed it and shot Diaz and his friends with it.

Outcome for the cop-killer: Facundo and Talamantes have been "charged with one count of murder and two counts of attempted murder, along with a special circumstance allegation of murder by an active member of a street gang"[759].

Miscellaneous: The shooting was captured by a nearby surveillance camera.

Officer: Atlanta Police Department, Detective James Joseph Biello
Date: 7/28/2019   **Location:** Atlanta, GA
FACTORS (1,2,15,20) 13?
Perpetrator(s) Involved: David Timothy Moore

Criminal Activity History/Involved: Unknown./Yes, Moore was in the middle of an armed robbery.

Mental Illness: Unknown.

Substance Abuse History/Involved: Unknown./None stated.

Race/Sex/Age: Black/Male/17

What prompted the initial contact with the killer? Back on April 15, 1987, while off-duty, Detective Biello saw a suspicious man enter a restaurant and when he went inside to investigate, he interrupted David Moore committing an armed robbery[760].

Actions taken by subject toward police: Moore immediately shot at Det. Biello, hitting him twice.

Reactions by the police: Though injured Det. Biello managed to return fire and hit Moore once before Moore then shot him execution style while he lay injured on the ground. The execution shot left Biello paralyzed for 32 years, and autopsies are being done to see if it eventually led to his death in 2019. Moore was eventually tracked down and arrested[761].

How murdered? Biello was shot while interrupting an armed robbery.

What could have been done differently for the officer to still be alive? Det. Biello was doing good police work and investigating something that appeared suspicious. Biello's hunch was correct, and that put him in a dangerously exposed position.

Would the officer had been justified to use deadly force before being murdered? It appears that the suspect opened fire as soon as Det. Biello interrupted the robbery so Biello may neither have seen Moore's weapon nor had time to shoot before Moore did. Since Biello was investigating suspicious activity that could include a robbery as it turned out, Biello would have been justified to have his weapon out and ready to shoot first.

Outcome for the cop-killer: Moore was convicted of aggravated assault and armed robbery; he is currently serving a 60-year sentence. If Biello's death can be tied to the wounds Moore inflicted upon him, Moore may face new charges of murder.

Officer: California Highway Patrol Officer Andre Maurice Moye
Date: 8/12/2019 **Location:** Riverside, CA
FACTORS (1,2,4,8,9,15)
Perpetrator(s) Involved: Aaron Luther

Criminal Activity History/Involved: Luther had numerous prior violent criminal convictions including attempted second-degree murder (10 years in prison), assault with a deadly weapon against a peace officer, battery, stalking, along with disturbing the peace, vandalism, burglary, and a couple of domestic violence incidents, one of which involved child cruelty[762]./Yes, Luther illegally possessed a weapon during the traffic stop.

Mental Illness: Luther's family stated that he was struggling with depression and that he suggested that he wanted to die by "suicide by cop"[763].

Substance Abuse History/Involved: Luther's family stated that he had a history of drug abuse./ None reported.

Race/Sex/Age: White/Male/49

What prompted the initial contact with the killer? Shortly before 5 p.m. on August 12, Officer Moye pulled over a vehicle operated by Aaron Luther for an observed traffic infraction. Upon conducting the stop, Officer Moye became aware that Luther did not have a valid driver's license and the vehicle was unregistered, so he called for a tow truck to impound it[764].

Actions taken by subject toward police: While Officer Moye was filling out impound paperwork near the tow-truck, Luther reached into his pickup truck, accessed a semiautomatic rifle, and opened fire on Moye, fatally wounding him[765].

Reactions by the police: A back-up CHP Officer along with Riverside Deputy Sheriff's and a Riverside Police Officer dragged Moye to safety for medical attention and engaged Luther in a gun battle. Two of the officers suffered gunshot wounds to their legs while they succeeded in shooting Luther dead.

How murdered? Officer Moye was shot while filling out impound paperwork during a traffic stop.

What could have been done differently for the officer to still be alive? With no knowledge of Luther's violent past and no indication from his brief verbal exchange with Luther during the stop to make him think that Luther may have posed a mortal threat, Officer Moye did not practice the extreme vigilance he likely otherwise would have had.

Would the officer had been justified to use deadly force before being murdered? No, but Officer Moye would have been justified if he had ordered Luther to stay away from his vehicle and reasonably feared that Luther might be attempting to access a weapon when he saw him reaching into his truck.

Outcome for the cop-killer: Luther was killed in the shootout that ensued with Moye's backup officer along with other officers who responded to the emergency radio call of officer's needing assistance.

Sergeant Michael David Stephen, Sr.

Stone County Sheriff's Office, Arkansas

End of Watch Thursday, July 18, 2019

Police Officer Juan Jose Diaz

Los Angeles Police Department, California

End of Watch Saturday, July 27, 2019

Detective James Joseph Biello

Atlanta Police Department, Georgia

End of Watch Sunday, July 28, 2019

Officer Andre Maurice Moye, Jr.

California Highway Patrol, California

End of Watch Monday, August 12, 2019

Officer: Illinois State Police Trooper Nicholas John Hopkins
Date: 8/23/2019   **Location:** East St. Louis, IL
FACTORS (1,2,3,7,15,17)
Perpetrator(s) Involved: Christopher R. Grant and Al Stewart Jr.

Criminal Activity History/Involved: Yes, Grant had multiple prior charges for drug possession and sales (4 years prison), felon in possession of a gun, and two separate times for obstructing justice./Yes, Grant was operating a drug dealing operation out of the incident location, and, as a convicted felon he was illegally in possession of firearms.

Mental Illness: Unknown.

Substance Abuse History/Involved: Yes, Grant had prior drug-related arrests./Yes, Grant was operating a drug-dealing business.

Race/Sex/Age: Grant: Black/Male/45; Stewart Jr.: Black/Male/19

What prompted the initial contact with the killer? Around 5:30 a.m. on August 22, 2019, Trooper Hopkins along with other members of the Illinois State Police SWAT Team executed a high-risk warrant at an East St. Louis drug house occupied by Christopher R. Grant[766].

Actions taken by subject toward police: Grant opened fire on the officers with his illegally possessed 9-mm Glock 19 handgun, mortally wounding Trooper Hopkins.

Reactions by the police: Officers provided emergency medical care to Trooper Hopkins and evacuated him to a hospital while other officers returned fire at Grant. The SWAT Team eventually used an armored vehicle and flash bang grenades to get Grant, Stewart, and a third unidentified suspect to surrender[767].

How murdered? Shot with a handgun while serving a high-risk narcotics warrant.

What could have been done differently for the officer to still be alive? Nothing, Trooper Hopkins was courageously performing his duty as a SWAT Team member by executing a dangerous no-knock warrant.

Would the officer had been justified to use deadly force before being murdered? Unknown if any officer had an opportunity to shoot Grant before Grant started shooting at the officers or if Grant shot through a door before officers had eyes on him[768].

Outcome for the cop-killer: Grant and Stewart were arrested the day of the shooting. Grant was charged with first-degree murder, "three counts distribution of crack cocaine, maintaining a drug house, possession of a firearm in furtherance of a drug trafficking crime, use of a firearm to commit murder in furtherance of a drug trafficking and possession of a firearm of a felon"[769]. Stewart faced charges of "armed violence, obstructing justice and possession with the intent to distribute cannabis"[770].

Officer: Texas Department of Public Safety–Texas Highway Patrol, Trooper Moises Sanchez
Date: 8/24/2019   **Location:** Edinburg, TX
FACTORS (1,2,8,13,15,19) 9?
Perpetrator(s) Involved: Victor Alejandro Godinez

Criminal Activity History/Involved: Yes, Godinez was involved in an earlier hit-and-run accident, and he had a pending court date before this shooting[771]./Yes, Godinez was just involved in an accident and fled the scene[772].

Mental Illness: Unknown.

Substance Abuse History/Involved: Unknown./None stated.

Race/Sex/Age: Latino/Male/24

What prompted the initial contact with the killer? On April 6, 2019, at approximately 8:45 p.m., Trooper Sanchez responded to a motor vehicle accident[773].

Actions taken by subject toward police: One of the vehicle operators, Victor Godinez, fled the scene, causing Trooper Sanchez to pursue him. As Trooper Sanchez was catching up to him, Godinez fired at the Trooper with his .357 revolver, hitting him in the head and shoulder[774].

Reactions by the police: Edinburg Police Officer Sandra Tapia and Jessie Moreno joined in the pursuit and shot at Godinez, wounding him. Despite his injury, Godinez managed to escape and eluded capture until the following morning[775].

How murdered? Trooper Sanchez was shot in the head and shoulder with a .357 handgun while chasing a hit-and-run suspect. Despite numerous surgeries and rehabilitation efforts, the trauma from those injuries ultimately killed Trooper Sanchez four months later.

What could have been done differently for the officer to still be alive? Trooper Sanchez was rightly pursuing a fleeing suspect who opened fire on him. Officers are vulnerable when pursuing someone on foot or in a car, which is why extra criminal penalties should be levied against those who flee instead of complying.

Would the officer had been justified to use deadly force before being murdered? There are not enough details known about whether Trooper Sanchez could see that Godinez was armed while running or if Godinez reached into his waistband while being pursued. Seeing Sanchez already armed or reach toward his waistband while running would have justified Sanchez to shoot Godinez first.

Outcome for the cop-killer: After an overnight manhunt for him, Godinez was captured and has been charged with three counts of attempted capital murder, one of which was supposed to be upgraded to murder after the death of Trooper Sanchez.

Officer: Tuscaloosa Police Department, Investigator Dornell Cousette
Date: 9/16/2019   **Location:** Tuscaloosa, AL
FACTORS (1,2,15,17)
Perpetrator(s) Involved: Luther Watkins, Jr.

Criminal Activity History/Involved: Yes, Watkins had a felony warrants and was out on bail from armed robbery and assault charges[776] [777]./ Yes, Watkins was "avoiding a lawful arrest and disrupting law enforcement operations"[778].

Mental Illness: Unknown./None stated.

Substance Abuse History/Involved: Unknown./None stated.

Race/Sex/Age: Black/Male/20

What prompted the initial contact with the killer? Around 6:20 p.m. on September 16, Investigator Cousette was actively looking for and spotted a suspect, Luther Watkins, Jr. who was wanted for active felony warrants. Upon seeing Watkins, Cousette quickly exited his vehicle and yelled "Luther," "Don't you run!"[779].

Actions taken by subject toward police: Watkins refused to comply with Cousette's lawful orders and instead took off running into his grandmother's house. When Investigator Cousette ran after Watkins into the house, a gunfight ensued in which Watkins shot at Cousette several times with a 9-mm handgun.

Reactions by the police: From witness accounts, Investigator Cousette fired first and hit Watkins soon after following him into the house. According to that witness, Watkins almost immediately returned fire, mortally wounding Cousette. Watkins escaped but officers tracked him down and arrested him soon after when he was getting treatment for his gunshot wound[780].

How murdered? Inv. Cousette was fatally shot after pursuing a wanted suspect into his house.

What could have been done differently for the officer to still be alive? Cousette managed to shoot first and strike Watkins, but not fatally, demonstrating why officers are taught to shoot until the threat is neutralized, typically with two shots to the body and one to the head. Had Cousette shot Watkins in the head in the initial volley, then perhaps that would have ended the gunfight before it started.

Would the officer had been justified to use deadly force before being murdered? Yes, according to the eyewitness, Inv. Cousette did use deadly force before he was shot by Watkins.

Outcome for the cop-killer: Watkins was indicted for capital murder.

Officer: Milwaukee Police Department Officer Mark Lentz
Date: 9/18/2019   **Location:** Milwaukee, WI
FACTORS (1,2,7,8,11)
Perpetrator(s) Involved: Sirantoine Powell

Criminal Activity History/Involved: Unknown./Yes, Powell was conducting armed robberies that day.

Mental Illness: Unknown

Substance Abuse History/Involved: Unknown./None stated.

Race/Sex/Age: Black/Male/17

What prompted the initial contact with the killer? On August 3, 2017, while conducting patrol as a motorcycle police officer, Lentz attempted to pull over a speeding vehicle. As the investigation revealed, the vehicle Lentz tried pulling over was working in tandem with a second vehicle to commit armed robberies[781].

Actions taken by subject toward police: Sirantoine Powell was driving that second vehicle, an SUV which he intentionally drove into Officer Lentz's motorcycle causing serious physical injuries to Lentz[782].

Reactions by the police: Officers tracked down Powell, arresting him and his accomplice.

How murdered? Officer Lentz was intentionally struck by a vehicle while on his police motorcycle. Lentz suffered a traumatic brain injury and nerve damage from the vehicular assault which is believed to have resulted in his death two years later.

What could have been done differently for the officer to still be alive today? Nothing; Officer Lentz was performing his sworn duties and enforcing the rules of the road.

Could the officer have used justified deadly force before being murdered? No, Officer Lentz was ambushed on his motorcycle by Powell while attempting to stop Powell's accomplice. Lentz never had a chance to confront his killer.

Outcome for the cop-killer: Powell was found guilty and sentenced to 6 years in prison. Now that Officer Lentz likely died from that vehicular assault, Sirantoine may face new charges.

Miscellaneous: A Google search for "Sirantoine Powell convicted" generates a total of one media story, making it difficult to find updated information on the case while making it clear that according to the media, justice for Milwaukee Police Officer Mark Lentz does not matter.

Trooper Nicholas John Hopkins

Illinois State Police, Illinois

End of Watch Friday, August 23, 2019

Trooper Moises Sanchez

Texas DPS - Texas Highway Patrol, Texas

End of Watch Saturday, August 24, 2019

Investigator Dornell Cousette

Tuscaloosa Police Department, Alabama

End of Watch Monday, September 16, 2019

Police Officer Mark Lentz

Milwaukee Police Department, Wisconsin

End of Watch Wednesday, September 18, 2019

Officer: Mandeville Police Department, Captain Vincent Nat Liberto
Date: 9/20/2019   **Location:** Mandeville, LA
FACTORS (1,2,8,15)13?
Perpetrator(s) Involved: Mark E. Spicer, Jr.

Criminal Activity History/Involved: None is reported, but Spicer was in possession of stolen firearms./Yes, Spicer was unlawfully fleeing from the police while possessing stolen firearms.

Mental Illness: Unknown.

Substance Abuse History/Involved: Unknown./None stated.

Race/Sex/Age: Black/Male/21

What prompted the initial contact with the killer? Around 2 a.m. on September 20, an unidentified police officer attempted to conduct a vehicle and traffic stop on a car operated by Mark Spicer. When Spicer refused to pull over, a pursuit ensued, and Captain Liberto joined in to assist[783].

Actions taken by subject toward police: The pursuit ended when Captain Liberto's unmarked vehicle, the original marked police vehicle, and Spicer's vehicle collided. Spicer immediately exited his vehicle upon the crash and fired into both occupied police vehicles, injuring the unidentified officer with a grazing headshot and killing Captain Liberto[784].

Reactions by the police: Additional officers responded to the scene, provided medical care to the two injured officers, and started a manhunt for Spicer, eventually arresting him nearby.

How murdered? CPT Liberto was mortally shot while assisting with a traffic stop.

What could have been done differently for the officer to still be alive? Since Captain Liberto is not reported to have fired at Spicer, it is possible that Liberto was injured during the crash and either did not see or could not react to Spicer exiting his vehicle and pointing a gun at the two occupied police vehicles. This incident is a classic example of why there must be enhanced criminal charges for anyone fleeing from the police–it puts the public and our officers at enhanced risk of injury or death.

Would the officer had been justified to use deadly force before being murdered? If Captain Liberto were in fact not seriously injured during the crash and able to, he would have been justified in shooting Spicer as soon as he saw Spicer exit his vehicle with a weapon.

Outcome for the cop-killer: Spicer was arrested soon after shooting the officers and was indicted by a grand jury on charges of "first degree murder, attempted first degree murder, aggravated flight from an officer, obstruction of justice by tampering with evidence, and illegal possession of stolen firearms"[785].

Officer: Harris County Sheriff's Office, Deputy Sheriff Sandeep Singh Dhaliwal
Date: 9/27/2019   **Location:** Houston, TX
FACTORS (1,2,8,9,15,21)
Perpetrator(s) Involved: Robert Solis

Criminal Activity History/Involved: Yes, Solis had two prior felony convictions for shooting a man and then using his toddler son as a shield. After serving 12 years of a 20-year sentence, Solis was paroled in 2014. In 2017, after Solis violated his parole and illegally possessed a weapon, a warrant was put out for him./Yes, Solis had an active felony warrant, and he illegally possessed a firearm at the time of the traffic stop.

Mental Illness: Unknown.

Substance Abuse History/Involved: Unknown./None stated.

Race/Sex/Age: White/Male/47

What prompted the initial contact with the killer? Deputy Dhaliwal conducted a "routine traffic stop"[786] on a vehicle operated by Robert Solis around 12:45 p.m. on September 27. After speaking with Solis, Deputy Dhaliwal turned and walked back toward his patrol vehicle.

Actions taken by subject toward police: Dashcam video shows that as Deputy Dhaliwal returned to his car, Solis exited his and shot the deputy from behind with what ended up being a .45-caliber handgun[787].

Reactions by the police: Responding officers took Dhaliwal to a hospital where he died from the gunshots. A manhunt was conducted using video from Dhaliwal's dashcam and bodycam. Deputies tracked Solis down to a shopping center and peacefully arrested him as he left one of the stores[788].

How murdered? Deputy Dhaliwal was shot in the back while conducting a traffic stop.

What could have been done differently for the officer to still be alive? Law enforcement officers are taught that there is no such thing as a routine traffic stop and this incident cements that fact. Even though Dhaliwal likely was not aware of Solis' criminal history and active warrants, he should have kept his body bladed and looked over his shoulder at Solis' vehicle as he returned to his patrol car.

Would the officer had been justified to use deadly force before being murdered? No, because the Deputy never saw the suspect exit the vehicle and point a firearm at him. If the Deputy had seen Solis exit his vehicle while holding a weapon, then yes, he would have been completely justified to shoot first.

Outcome for the cop-killer: Solis was quickly captured after an intense manhunt and was charged with capital murder[789].

Miscellaneous: If Solis had been kept in prison for his full sentence, Deputy Dhaliwal could still be alive.

Officer: NYPD Detective Brian Charles Mulkeen
Date: 9/29/2019   **Location:** Bronx, NY
FACTORS (1,2,10,16,21)
Perpetrator(s) Involved: Antonio Lavance Williams

Criminal Activity History/Involved: Yes, Williams was convicted of burglary in 2011, had received a 42-month sentence, and had been paroled in 2015; felony drug arrest in 2018, was put on probation until 2022; most recently arrested for harassment./Yes, Williams was a felon in possession of a loaded handgun, and he resisted arrest.

Mental Illness: Unknown.

Substance Abuse History/Involved: Prior drug-related arrest./None stated.

Race/Sex/Age: Black/Male/27

What prompted the initial contact with the killer? As part of a street-crime unit, around 12:30 a.m. on September 29, Det. Mulkeen approached Antonio Williams, a suspected gang member[790].

Actions taken by subject toward police: Rather than be questioned by the police, Williams took off running. Detective Mulkeen chased, caught up to Williams and struggled to gain control over him. While grappling on the ground, Mulkeen could be heard yelling "he's reaching for it,"[791] suggesting he was aware Williams was armed and attempting to access that weapon.

Reactions by the police: In response to the immediate deadly threat posed by an armed suspect, who was physically resisting arrest, Det. Mulkeen fired five shots at Williams. In the confusion of the two men struggling against each other on the ground and fearing that Williams had accessed his weapon and just shot Mulkeen, the other officers on the scene opened fire, fatally striking both Mulkeen and Williams.

How murdered? Det. Mulkeen was mortally wounded by friendly fire while wrestling with an armed suspected gang member.

What could have been done differently for the officer to still be alive? Nothing. Det. Mulkeen bravely pursued, physically fought with, and shot a violent armed suspect. Through no fault of his own, Det. Mulkeen was killed by friendly fire striking his head and body.

Would the officer had been justified to use deadly force before being murdered? Yes, Det. Mulkeen did justifiably use deadly force before he was accidentally killed by friendly fire.

Outcome for the cop-killer: Williams was shot and killed by Det. Mulkeen and the other officers at the scene[792].

Miscellaneous: If Williams were in jail instead of being out free on probation, Det. Mulkeen could still be alive.

Officer: El Dorado County Sheriff's Office, Deputy Sheriff Brian David Ishmael
Date: 10/23/2019   **Location:** Somerset, CA
FACTORS (1,2,3,7,15,19,21)
Perpetrator(s) Involved: Juan Carlos Vasquez-Orozco (illegal alien, Mexican); Ramiro Bravo Morales (illegal alien, Mexican); Chris Ross.

Criminal Activity History/Involved: The criminal history of two subjects is unknown prior to their illegally entering the US./Yes, both men were illegal aliens involved in an illegal marijuana business, and they illegally possessed a firearm[793].

Mental Illness: Unknown.

Substance Abuse History/Involved: Unknown./A marijuana grow business was central to the incident.

Race/Sex/Age: Vasquez-Orozco: Latino/Male/20; Morales: Latino/Male/22; Ross: White/Male/47

What prompted the initial contact with the killer? Around 12:30 a.m. on October 23, Deputy Ishmael and an off-duty deputy conducting a "ride-along" responded to a 911 call about petty theft from Chris Ross stating that people were stealing plants from a marijuana farm. Upon arrival at Ross' location, the deputies were directed to the nearby grow site[794].

Actions taken by subject toward Police: When Deputy Ishmael yelled for anyone hiding among the brush to come out, Juan Vasquez-Orozco opened fire with a handgun from his hiding spot in the dark among the marijuana plants. Deputy Ishmael was fatally shot in the foot and upper chest area that was unprotected by his bulletproof vest[795].

Reactions by the police: Despite both being wounded by the armed ambush, both deputies returned fire and injured one of the suspects. Law enforcement officers arrested Ross, Vasquez-Orozco and his accomplice Ramiro Morales.

How murdered? Deputy Ishmael was shot and killed while handling a 911 call about petty theft.

What could have been done differently for the officer to still be alive? Nothing; Deputy Ishmael wore his vest and could not have anticipated being ambushed by an unseen subject who was willing to use deadly force over a mere petty theft incident.

Would the officer had been justified to use deadly force before being murdered? No, the deputies did not even see the suspects before they were fired upon, and Ishmael was fatally shot.

Outcome for the cop-killer: The shooter, Juan Vasquez, has been indicted for murder and weapons charges; his partner Ramiro Morales was indicted as an accessory to murder and weapons charges; and for failing to inform 911 or Deputy Ishmael that he leased the grow property to the suspects and called because he feared they were going to take the harvest without paying him, Ross was indicted for murder.

Captain Vincent Nat Liberto, Jr.

Mandeville Police Department, Louisiana

End of Watch Friday, September 20, 2019

Deputy Sheriff Sandeep Singh Dhaliwal

Harris County Sheriff's Office, Texas

End of Watch Friday, September 27, 2019

Detective Brian Charles Mulkeen

New York City Police Department, New York

End of Watch Sunday, September 29, 2019

Deputy Sheriff Brian David Ishmael

El Dorado County Sheriff's Office, California

End of Watch Wednesday, October 23, 2019

Officer: Lemoore Police Department, Officer Elmer Jonathan Diaz
Date: 11/2/2019   **Location:** Hanford, CA
FACTORS (1,2,3,5,15,18,20)
Perpetrator(s) Involved: Ramiro Trevino Jr.

Criminal Activity History/Involved: Unknown./Yes, Trevino had just committed domestic assault upon his pregnant wife.

Mental Illness: Unknown.

Substance Abuse History/Involved: Unknown./Trevino was drinking at the time[796].

Race/Sex/Age: Latino/Male/32

What prompted the initial contact with the killer? While off-duty on November 2 at a birthday party for the father of Ramiro Trevino Jr., Officer Elmer Diaz took police action to safely remove Trevino's girlfriend from the house after Trevino verbally and physically assaulted her. Along with Trevino's father Ramiro Trevino Sr., Officer Diaz then returned to the house to check on Trevino as they heard a gunshot come from inside the residence[797].

Actions taken by subject toward police: Trevino Jr. shot and killed Officer Diaz and wounded Trevino Sr. before turning the gun on himself and committing suicide[798].

Reactions by the police: NA.

How murdered? Officer Diaz was fatally shot checking on the welfare of a domestic-violence suspect.

What could have been done differently for the officer to still be alive? Officer Diaz's close personal involvement in the situation with an apparent friend, further exacerbated by the father's likely desire to go check on his son, understandably caused him to act emotionally and enter the house rather than tactically and wait outside after hearing the gunshot. Officer Diaz would have been better off staying outside behind cover, calling 911, and let the on-duty officers do their job while wearing body armor.

Would the officer had been justified to use deadly force before being murdered? It is not known if Officer Diaz was armed and if he saw Trevino Jr. pointing the gun at him before he was shot. However, given the violent domestic disturbance that just occurred, knowing that Trevino Jr. was armed due to his employment, and the gunshot that was heard, yes, Diaz would have been justified to use deadly force if he felt threatened by Trevino Jr. upon returning inside the house.

Outcome for the cop-killer: Trevino Jr. killed himself shortly after shooting Diaz.

Officer: Dayton Police Department, Detective Jorge Rene Del Rio
Date: 11/4/2019   **Location:** Dayton, OH
FACTORS (1,2,3,7,15,17)
Perpetrator(s) Involved: Nathan Goddard, Jr.; Cahke Cortner; Lionel Combs III

Criminal Activity History/Involved: Goddard had previous convictions for felony assault with a deadly weapon (2002); assault (2011 and 2013); resisting arrest, drug possession, obstructing official business and numerous traffic violations[799]./Yes, illegal weapons, armor piercing ammo, drugs and criminal proceeds were discovered at the target house.

Mental Illness: Unknown.

Substance Abuse History/Involved: Yes, Goddard had numerous prior drug-related arrests./Yes, Goddard was the ringleader of a drug-trafficking network.

Race/Sex/Age: Black/Male/39; Black/Male/39; Black/Male 40

What prompted the initial contact with the killer? At approximately 7 p.m. on November 4, 2019, Detective Del Rio and other officers on a DEA/Dayton Police Joint Task Force conducted a search warrant at a house known to be used by a drug-trafficking network[800].

Actions taken by subject toward police: As the officers announced themselves and entered the house, Goddard Jr. hid down in the basement, waiting. When Detective Del Rio was descending the stairs into the basement, Goddard opened fire, hitting Del Rio twice in the face[801].

Reactions by the police: Other officers rushed Del Rio to a nearby hospital, where he was on life support for three days before dying from his wounds. Within hours the authorities arrested Goddard and his accomplices.

How murdered? Det. Del Rio was shot in the head while conducting a search warrant on a known drug house.

What could have been done differently for the officer to still be alive? Det. Del Rio was shot while descending stairs by a gunman hiding in wait, short of having a full shield in front of him while clearing the house, there was nothing Del Rio could have done.

Would the officer had been justified to use deadly force before being murdered? Yes, if Det. Del Rio had seen Goddard before being shot by him, which is not likely.

Outcome for the cop-killer: Goddard was indicted on nine counts, including murder, assault, narcotics distribution, felony possession of a weapon. For their part, Cortner and Combs III, were both indicted on five counts, narcotics possession/distribution and discharging a firearm resulting in death by murder during and in relation to a drug trafficking crime[802].

Officer: Richmond County Sheriff's Office, Investigator Cecil Dwayne Ridley
Date: 11/19/2019   **Location:** Augusta, GA
FACTORS (1,2,3,9,15,21)
Perpetrator(s) Involved: Alvin Theodore Hester Jr.

Criminal Activity History/Involved: Yes, Hester was on probation for a prior conviction for possession with intent to distribute cocaine and obstructing justice in 2017./Yes, Hester was in possession of a firearm as a felon along with marijuana and narcotics during the time of the incident[803].

Mental Illness: Unknown.

Substance Abuse History/Involved: Yes, Hester had prior marijuana- and cocaine-related arrests./ Yes, Hester possessed marijuana and cocaine at the time of arrest.

Race/Sex/Age: Black/Male/24

What prompted the initial contact with the killer? As part of a narcotics investigation, Investigator Ridley and several other officers confronted some subjects outside a convenience store around 8:30 p.m. on November 19. Disregarding the officer's instructions, Alvin Hester Jr. walked away from them and entered the store[804].

Actions taken by subject toward police: As Investigator Ridley entered the store to assist another officer who was already inside, Hester went up to Ridley and shot him.

Reactions by the police: After Ridley was fatally shot, other officers both inside the store and out in the parking lot returned fire at Hester, wounding him. Hester was arrested and transported to the hospital for medical care[805].

How murdered? Investigator Ridley was shot point-blank while conducting a narcotics investigation.

What could have been done differently for the officer to still be alive? Focus on Hester's hands, though since Hester is reported to be carrying a sizable bag containing several weapons and drugs, he most likely hid his armed hand behind that bag until the fateful moment he shot Ridley. This is a good example of why officers handcuff suspicious subjects first to search them for their own safety, and then conduct a field investigation.

Would the officer had been justified to use deadly force before being murdered? No, because it appears that Investigator Ridley did not see Hester holding or pointing a weapon at him. If Ridley had seen that Hester was armed, then yes, he would have been justified to shoot first.

Outcome for the cop-killer: Hester was arrested at the scene and has been indicted on 16 charges including malice murder, possession of a firearm during commission of a felony, and possession of cocaine with intent to distribute.

Miscellaneous: Hester was released in June 2018, after serving just seven months of a two-year sentence, "had he served his entire time; we likely wouldn't be discussing the death of Cecil Ridley"[806].

Officer: Detroit Police Department, Sergeant Rasheen Phillipe McClain
Date: 11/20/2019   **Location:** Detroit, MI
FACTORS (1,2,4,7,15,18,19,21)
Perpetrator(s) Involved: Jujuan Parks

Criminal Activity History/Involved: Yes, Parks had prior convictions for weapons, assault, and home invasions, for which he served eight years in prison and was on parole./Yes, Parks was burglarizing the home of a former girlfriend.

Mental Illness: Park's brother voiced concerns about Jujuan's mental health.

Race/Sex/Age: Black/Male/28

What prompted the initial contact with the killer? Around 7:30 p.m. on November 20, Detroit Police Sgt. McClain and Officer Phillippe Batoum-Bissel responded to a 911 call from a woman who had broken off a relationship with Jujuan Parks and feared that he had broken into her house and was armed with a rifle. Aware of the potentially armed and dangerous subject inside, McClain requested backup, and when two officers arrived, McClain led them into the house to search for Parks. After searching the first two levels and not finding Parks, the officers proceeded to the only lit area of the house, the basement[807].

Actions taken by subject toward police: As the officer's descended the stairs into the basement, Parks shot his assault-style rifle, fatally striking McClain in the neck and hitting Battoum-Bissel in the ankle.

Reactions by the police: The two backup officers retreated from the stairs but managed to shoot Parks in the arm as he ran by them to get out of the house. Officers arrested Parks about a block away and brought him to a hospital[808].

How murdered? McClain was murdered while searching for a domestic-violence suspect.

What could have been done differently for the officer to still be alive? McClain understood the danger, called for backup, and led the search like a courageous officer. The only way he could still be alive was if he maintained a perimeter and had a SWAT team conduct the search since their shields may have stopped the bullet when McClain's regular body armor would not.

Would the officer had been justified to use deadly force before being murdered? Yes, Officer McClain would have been justified shooting Parks on sight if Parks were holding the rifle. McClain's bodycam video showed that Parks jumped out of hiding to shoot the officers as they came down the stairs, so for any officer in that position, it would be too late to react and defend themselves.

Outcome for the cop-killer: Parks' charges include, "murder of a police officer, three counts of assault with intent to murder, one count of resisting and obstructing a police officer causing death, one count of felon in possession of a firearm and eight felony firearm violations"[809].

Miscellaneous: After being released on parole in December 2015, Parks was arrested and imprisoned in 2016 for domestic assault only to be paroled again in 2019, 4 months before this incident. Parks is also likely responsible for a November 18 murder[810].

Police Officer Elmer Jonathan Diaz

Lemoore Police Department, California

End of Watch Saturday, November 2, 2019

Detective Jorge Rene DelRio

Dayton Police Department, Ohio

End of Watch Thursday, November 7, 2019

Investigator Cecil Dwayne Ridley

Richmond County Sheriff's Office, Georgia

End of Watch Tuesday, November 19, 2019

Sergeant Rasheen Phillipe McClain

Detroit Police Department, Michigan

End of Watch Wednesday, November 20, 2019

Officer: Lowndes County Sheriff John Arthur "Big John" Williams, Sr.
Date: 11/23/2019   **Location:** Hayneville, AL
FACTORS (1,2,8,9,15,19)
Perpetrator(s) Involved: William Chase Johnson

Criminal Activity History/Involved: Yes, Johnson had prior arrests for alcohol and weapons possession[811]./Yes, the vehicle Johnson was in during the incident was allegedly stolen[812].

Mental Illness: Unknown

Substance Abuse History/Involved: Johnson had a prior alcohol-related arrest./None stated.

Race/Sex/Age: White/Male/18

What prompted the initial contact with the killer? While responding to complaints of excessive noise from an automobile at a gas station on November 23, Sheriff John Williams approached the vehicle in question and asked the driver, William Johnson, why he was playing the music so loud[813].

Actions taken by subject toward police: Without provocation, in response to Sheriff Williams' reasonable question, Johnson shot the Sheriff point-blank, killing him. Johnson then took off running, only to peacefully surrender to authorities four hours later with the murder weapon in his possession.

Reactions by the police: There were no other officers involved in the incident. Responding officers searched for the suspect and arrested Johnson when he turned himself in.

How murdered? Sheriff Williams was shot point-blank while questioning a suspect for a petty noise complaint.

What could have been done differently for the officer to still be alive? This is yet another example of how no police interaction can be considered routine. Officers are taught to be vigilant on every interaction but thinking every petty interaction such as this one for a noise complaint would result in lethal force could make officers hypervigilant. While hypervigilance would lead to burnout, officers should follow their training and always insist on seeing the subject's hands. At such a close range though, if Sheriff Williams did tell Johnson to show his hands, it is possible that he could not have reacted in time anyway.

Would the officer had been justified to use deadly force before being murdered? As witnesses were shocked at how the Sheriff's question over the noise was met with lethal force, it appears the Sheriff did not observe a weapon before it was used against him, so no.

Outcome for the cop-killer: Johnson is in custody and charged with murder.

Officer: United States Navy Security Forces, Master-at-Arms Oscar J. Temores
Date: 11/30/2019   **Location:** Virginia Beach, VA
FACTORS (1,2,8,11,13)
Perpetrator(s) Involved: Nathaniel Lee Campbell

Criminal Activity History/Involved: Yes, Campbell had prior convictions for reckless handling of a firearm, domestic assault and battery, and felony strangling. In 2015 he was given four years' probation after a 90-day sentence. Additionally, he had arrests for numerous traffic violations and one for public intoxication in 2015 which violated his probation./Yes, Campbell recklessly and illegally entered a military installation without authorization.

Mental Illness: Unknown.

Substance Abuse History/Involved: Yes, Campbell had prior alcohol-related arrests./Authorities report that alcohol was not a factor in this incident.[814]

Race/Sex/Age: White/Male/38

What prompted the initial contact with the killer? Around 7:30 p.m. on November 30, Master-at-Arms Temores responded in his marked police vehicle to a radio report that a pickup truck had illegally entered Joint Expeditionary Base Fort Story by driving through the exit lane of the base checkpoint[815].

Actions taken by subject toward police: At over three times the base speed limit of 25 mph, Nathaniel Campbell drove his Chevy pickup truck 81 mph head-on into Temores US Navy police cruiser[816].

Reactions by the police: Responding officer's transported Temores and Campbell to the hospital where Temores died from his injuries.

How murdered? Temores was killed by a suspect who intentionally crashed into his vehicle head-on in an excessive rate of speed.

What could have been done differently for the officer to still be alive? Nothing, Master-at-Arms Temores was responding to a base intruder and possible threat to service members. At the high rate of speed Campbell was driving, it was likely impossible for Temores to avoid being struck by Campbell's vehicle.

Would the officer had been justified to use deadly force before being murdered? Yes, Temores would have been justified in using deadly force against Campbell's oncoming deadly use of a motor vehicle, but that was not an option as Temores was driving a smaller vehicle and could not accurately use a weapon even if he could access one in the short amount of time before his vehicle was struck. Guards stationed at the gate would have been justified to use deadly force upon seeing the pickup truck illegally enter the military base.

Outcome for the cop-killer: Campbell was charged with involuntary manslaughter.

Officer: Huntsville Police Department, Agent Billy Fred Clardy, III
Date: 12/6/2019   **Location:** Huntsville, AL
FACTORS (1,2,3,9,15,21)
Perpetrator(s) Involved: LaJeromeny Brown

Criminal Activity History/Involved: Yes, Brown is the epitome of "career criminal" with over 25 arrests spanning multiple states over the past 30 years. Back in 2013, the feds called Brown a "major player in Chattanooga's drug trade"[817]. He had arrests and convictions for drug sales, assaulting an officer, impersonating an officer, attempted murder, kidnapping, and just a year prior to this shooting for felony weapon possession. Brown was classified as a "flight risk and danger to his community"[818] by a federal prosecutor. But despite his repeated violations of the terms of his early release, the feds did not put him back in prison./Yes, the incident involved a drug buy during which Brown illegally possessed a weapon as well.

Substance Abuse History/Involved: Yes, Brown had previous drug-related arrests./Yes, this incident was drug related.

Race/Sex/Age: Black/Male/41

What prompted the initial contact with the killer? After buying three pounds of marijuana from LaJeromeny Brown the previous month, an Alabama multi-agency Strategic Counterdrug Team targeted him for a larger buy and bust operation. Agent Billy Clardy was one of three officers who were to buy 100 pounds of marijuana from Brown when he arrived at the pre-arranged drug house on December 6. As one of the two officers inside the house, Clardy's job was to make the arrest and take Brown into physical custody. When Brown arrived with several large bags and opened the door to enter, Clardy stepped out to arrest him while wearing a tactical vest with the word "Police" on it[819].

Actions taken by subject toward police: Without even saying a word, Brown shot at Clardy eight times with an illegally modified 9-mm handgun, striking him twice before taking off running[820].

Reactions by the police: While some officers on the scene rendered medical aid to Clardy before getting him to a hospital, others chased Brown and captured him moments later. Unfortunately, Clardy's vest failed to stop one bullet which went through it and into his heart, proving fatal[821].

How murdered? Agent Clardy was shot at close range when he was about to arrest a suspect involved in a targeted drug buy at a house.

What could have been done differently for the officer to still be alive? Brown had a record of illegal weapons possession and violence, so it would not have been inappropriate for Clardy to tactically wait inside the house, behind cover, and greet Brown at gunpoint as he entered.

Would the officer had been justified to use deadly force before being murdered? Since Clardy was intent on arresting Brown, not shooting him, he did not have his weapon out and pointed at Brown, so Clardy did not have an opportunity to use deadly force, which he would have been justified in doing.

Outcome for the cop-killer: Brown was arrested near the scene and was charged with capital murder.[822]

Officer: Fayetteville Police Department, Officer Stephen Paul Carr
Date: 12/7/2019   **Location:** Fayetteville, AR
FACTORS (1,2,7,15)
Perpetrator(s) Involved: London T. Phillips

Criminal Activity History/Involved: Yes, Phillips was arrested for a domestic assault in Florida after threatening to burn his mother./Yes, though it was purchased legally, Phillips illegally possessed the handgun since he had a medical marijuana card[823].

Mental Illness: Unknown.

Substance Abuse History/Involved: Unknown./None stated,

Race/Sex/Age: White/Male/35

What prompted the initial contact with the killer? At approximately 9:45 p.m. on December 7, 2019, Officer Stephen Carr was completing paperwork while sitting in his marked police vehicle in the parking lot of the police station[824].

Actions taken by subject toward police: Surveillance video from the building shows, and for no apparent reason, before Officer Carr could react, London Phillips walked up to the police car and fired his 9-mm handgun into it, striking Carr in the head ten times[825].

Reactions by the police: After hearing the gunshots in the police station parking area, Fayetteville Police Officers Seay Floyd and Natalie Eucce ran out and confronted Phillips, eventually chasing him a short distance and shooting him dead during a gun battle for which they were found to be justified[826].

How murdered? Officer Carr was ambushed and executed while doing paperwork in his parked patrol car.

What could have been done differently for the officer to still be alive? Officers have been told to do their paperwork while parked in the safety of their precinct parking lots due to previous ambushes upon officers parked in public areas, so Officer Carr was exhibiting smart tactics in that regard. Acknowledging how quickly this ambush took place, the only thing Carr could have done was to literally have his head on a swivel and look up every few seconds from doing his paperwork.

Would the officer had been justified to use deadly force before being murdered? Officer Carr was ambushed from behind, and he never saw his attacker.

Outcome for the cop-killer: Phillips was justifiably shot and killed during a gun battle with other responding officers.

Sheriff John Arthur "Big John" Williams, Sr.

Lowndes County Sheriff's Office, Alabama

End of Watch Saturday, November 23, 2019

Master-at-Arms Oscar J. Temores

U.S. Navy Security Forces, U.S. Government

End of Watch Saturday, November 30, 2019

Agent Billy Fred Clardy, III

Huntsville Police Department, Alabama

End of Watch Friday, December 6, 2019

Police Officer Stephen Paul Carr

Fayetteville Police Department, Arkansas

End of Watch Saturday, December 7, 2019

Officer: Houston Police Department, Sergeant Christopher Charles Lewis Brewster
Date: 12/7/2019   **Location:** Houston, TX
FACTORS (1,2,4,13,15,18,19)
Perpetrator(s) Involved: Arturo Solis

Criminal Activity History/Involved: Yes, Solis was a repeat offender with arrests for domestic assault and burglary of a motor vehicle./Yes, Solis just assaulted his girlfriend and due to his prior domestic violence conviction, he was in illegal possession of a weapon[827].

Mental Illness: Yes, Solis' father believed that his son has been mentally ill since he was a teenager.

Substance Abuse History/Involved: Unknown./None stated.

Race/Sex/Age: Latino/Male/25

What prompted the initial contact with the killer? At approximately 6 p.m. on December 7, Sgt. Brewster responded to a 911 call of a woman being assaulted by her armed boyfriend, Arturo Solis. After discovering that they were no longer at the location stated in the 911 call, Brewster drove around the area searching for them. Upon spotting the couple walking nearby, Sgt. Brewster exited his patrol vehicle and approached them[828].

Actions taken by subject toward police: Solis opened fire on Sgt. Brewster with his handgun, penetrating Brewster's body armor and fatally wounding him[829].

Reactions by the police: Though mortally wounded, Sgt. Brewster managed to put out a radio description of Solis. Responding officers rushed Brewster to a hospital but he died shortly after. Solis was still armed with a pistol when officers arrested him after a short foot pursuit[830].

How murdered? Sgt. Brewster was shot and killed while handling a domestic-violence incident.

What could have been done differently for the officer to still be alive? Given the 911 call mentioned the subject was assaulting his girlfriend and he was armed with multiple handguns, Sgt. Brewster would have been tactically justified to use cover and have Solis in his crosshairs before attempting to speak with him.

Would the officer had been justified to use deadly force before being murdered? Yes, given the nature of the call and knowledge Solis was armed, Sgt. Brewster could have justifiably shot Solis as soon as he made a furtive movement toward a weapon or as soon as he saw Solis in possession of that weapon.

Outcome for the cop-killer: Solis has been charged with capital murder.

Officer: Jersey City Police Department, Detective Joseph Alan Seals
Date: 12/10/2019   **Location:** Jersey City, NJ
FACTORS (1,2,7,8,15)
Perpetrator(s) Involved: David Anderson; Francine Graham

Criminal Activity History/Involved: Yes, Anderson had an extensive criminal history, including numerous arrests/convictions for illegal weapons and domestic violence, spending several stints in prison before being paroled in 2011. This was several years prior to fulfilling a five-year sentence[831] [832]./Yes, Anderson and Graham were in a stolen vehicle when they killed Det. Seals before embarking on an anti-Semitic inspired domestic terror attack.

Mental Illness: Unknown.

Substance Abuse History/Involved: Unknown./None stated.

Race/Sex/Age: Anderson: Black/Male/47; Graham: Black/Female/50

What prompted the initial contact with the killer? Around noon on December 10, Detective Seals noticed a parked U-Haul truck that was wanted in connection with a murder just days earlier.[833]

Actions taken by subject toward police: When Det. Seals approached the truck to get a closer look at it and any possible occupants, David Anderson or Francine Graham fired one shot from one of their many firearms, hitting Seals in the head, killing him. Anderson and Graham then carried out their planned terrorist attack on a Jewish grocery store, killing three more people.

Reactions by the police: Police officers responded to the grocery store attack and engaged the domestic terrorists in an extended gun battle, ultimately killing them both[834].

How murdered? Det. Seals was murdered with a single shot to the head while investigating a suspicious vehicle.

What could have been done differently for the officer to still be alive? Aware that the vehicle he was investigating was involved in a recent murder, Det. Seals was likely already on high alert as he approached it. Given the distance and shadows, Seals probably could neither see the occupants in the truck nor that they had a weapon trained on him. Ninety-nine out of one hundred times, when an officer approaches such a vehicle, it ends up being unoccupied or uneventful which is why it is not standard operating procedure (SOP) to call for SWAT.

Would the officer had been justified to use deadly force before being murdered? Det. Seals was essentially ambushed, shot from inside the vehicle which he could not see into, so no, he had no chance to use justified deadly force.

Outcome for the cop-killer: Both perpetrators were killed in the shootout with police.

Miscellaneous: Anderson is a follower of the Black Supremacist group, the Black Hebrew Israelite movement and is believed to have social media posts on prior highly publicized police shootings such as in Ferguson and Baton Rouge[835].

Officer: Nassau Bay Police Department, Sergeant Kaila Marie Sullivan
Date: 12/10/2019   **Location:** Nassau Bay, TX
FACTORS (1,2,8,11,12,13,14)
Perpetrator(s) Involved: Tavores D. Henderson

Criminal Activity History/Involved: Yes, besides having a warrant for a prior domestic assault, Henderson had been arrested for misdemeanor domestic assault, felony theft, marijuana possession, and unlawful possession of a weapon[836]./Yes, Henderson resisted arrest and was unlawfully fleeing from the police during this incident.

Mental Illness: Unknown.

Substance Abuse History/Involved: Yes, Henderson had a prior marijuana-related arrest./ None stated.

Race/Sex/Age: Black/Male/21

What prompted the initial contact with the killer? At approximately 8:30 p.m. on December 10, Sgt. Sullivan responded to an apartment complex to assist other officers on a traffic stop arrest of Tavores Henderson, who had an active felony warrant for domestic assault[837].

Actions taken by subject toward police: When the officers tried to take Henderson into custody, he physically fought with them, broke free, and got back into his car. Henderson then drove his vehicle at Sgt. Sullivan, striking her before driving away.

Reactions by the police: The other officers on the scene rushed Sgt. Sullivan to a nearby hospital instead of chasing after Henderson. Tragically Sgt. Sullivan died shortly afterward. After an intense manhunt, officers tracked down Henderson at a house within a couple of days and arrested him[838].

How murdered? Sgt. Sullivan was run over by a suspect fleeing the police during a traffic stop.

What could have been done differently for the officer to still be alive? Sgt. Sullivan or another officer could have shot Henderson as soon as he started driving toward any of the officers that were out of their vehicles and vulnerable to being run over.

Would the officer had been justified to use deadly force before being murdered? Yes, Sgt. Sullivan would have absolutely been justified shooting Henderson as he drove at her.

Outcome for the cop-killer: Henderson was charged with capital murder.

Miscellaneous: This is a textbook example of why no traffic stop is routine; why officers want people to simply comply; and why officers are justified in using deadly force when a subject uses a vehicle as a weapon to assault/kill them.

Officer: Panola County Constable Eula Ray Hawkins
Date: 12/12/2019   **Location:** Batesville, MS
FACTORS (1,2,8,11,13)
Perpetrator(s) Involved: Darion Dogan; Johnathan Taylor

Criminal Activity History/Involved: Unknown, given their juvenile age any arrests they have are likely sealed./Yes, Dogan and Taylor were driving a stolen vehicle which precipitated the entire incident.

Mental Illness: Unknown.

Substance Abuse History/Involved: Unknown./None stated.

Race/Sex/Age: Dogan: Black/Male/16; Taylor: Black/Male/15

What prompted the initial contact with the killer? At approximately 2:30 p.m. on December 12, officers in a neighboring county attempted to pull over a stolen vehicle driven by Darion Dogan and Johnathan Taylor. Hearing over the radio those subjects refused to pull over and were headed toward Panola County, Constable Eula Hawkins drove his marked patrol vehicle in their direction[839].

Actions taken by subject toward police: As Constable Hawkins was driving south on Mississippi 35, Dogan and Taylor, who were driving northbound, drove right into Hawkins at such a high rate of speed that their stolen Chevy Colorado crushed his patrol car, killing him[840].

Reactions by the police: The other officers involved in the pursuit arrested the two at the scene.

How murdered? Constable Hawkins was murdered by two youths driving a stolen vehicle, who purposely crashed into his patrol car at a high rate of speed.

What could have been done differently for the officer to still be alive? As the district attorney handling the case said, "The speed we believe the vehicle was going there was nothing he could do. They crashed right into him and crushed him under the vehicle"[841].

Would the officer had been justified to use deadly force before being murdered? Yes, the perpetrators were using the vehicle as a deadly weapon by driving directly toward the constable so he could have justifiably shot them before they crashed into him.

Outcome for the cop-killer: Both young men have been charged with felony murder and will be tried as adults.

Sergeant Christopher Charles Lewis Brewster

Houston Police Department, Texas

End of Watch Saturday, December 7, 2019

Detective Joseph Alan Seals

Jersey City Police Department, New Jersey

End of Watch Tuesday, December 10, 2019

Sergeant Kaila Marie Sullivan

Nassau Bay Police Department, Texas

End of Watch Tuesday, December 10, 2019

Constable Eula Ray "Raye" Hawkins

Panola County Constable's Office, Mississippi

End of Watch Thursday, December 12, 2019

Officer: San Antonio Independent School District PD, Detective Clifton John Martinez
Date: 12/21/2019   **Location:** San Antonio, TX
FACTORS (1,2,8,11,12,13,14,20)
Perpetrator(s) Involved: Jorge Amado Lopez; Alfredo Martinez-Contreras

Criminal Activity History/Involved: Unknown./Yes, the subjects were involved in disturbance at a restaurant before assaulting and killing Detective Martinez[842] **843**.

Mental Illness: Unknown.

Substance Abuse History/Involved: Unknown./None stated.

Race/Sex/Age: Lopez: Latino/Male/23; Martinez-Contreras: Latino/Male/29

What prompted the initial contact with the killer? Around 4 a.m. on December 21, Detective Martinez was in his police uniform working an off-duty security job at an IHOP restaurant when a fight broke out among customers[844].

Actions taken by subject toward police: When Detective Martinez tried to break up the fight, Alfredo Martinez-Contreras stopped fighting with the other subject and pushed the detective. Exercising his sworn duties as an officer, Det. Martinez tried to arrest Martinez-Contreras and was assaulted by him and Jorge Lopez. After Martinez-Contreras pushed the detective to the ground outside the restaurant, he got into a vehicle driven by Lopez who then ran Martinez over twice, before both men fled the scene on foot as Martinez was left pinned under the car[845] [846].

Reactions by the police: Additional officers arrived on scene and tried to save Det. Martinez, but it was too late, he died from the injuries sustained from the vehicle. With the help of a public tip and good police work, both Lopez and Martinez-Contreras were arrested later on that day[847].

How murdered? Det. Martinez was assaulted and then run over by two subjects after he broke up a fight at a late-night diner.

What could have been done differently for the officer to still be alive? Det. Martinez could have shot at Lopez as he drove the vehicle at him.

Would the officer had been justified to use deadly force before being murdered? Yes, while Det. Martinez had no reason to believe that he was in mortal danger by being pushed to the floor, once a vehicle was driven at him, he could have justifiably used deadly force to stop the men driving at him.

Outcome for the cop-killer: Lopez and Martinez-Contreras have been indicted for capital murder of a police officer[848].

Miscellaneous: This is yet another example of why officers are justified in using deadly force to stop a subject driving a vehicle at them or another officer.

Officer: Camden Police Department Lieutenant Leroy G. Palmer
Date: 12/24/2019   **Location:** Camden, NJ
FACTORS (1,2,3,9,13,15)
Perpetrator(s) Involved: Unnamed in the reporting of the incident.

Criminal Activity History/Involved: Unknown./Yes, the killer was unknowingly conducting a drug deal during an undercover narcotics sting.

Mental Illness: Unknown.

Substance Abuse History/Involved: Unknown.

Race/Sex/Age: Unknown.

What prompted the initial contact with the killer? On February 13, 1998, Lt. Palmer was assisting on a narcotics operation. State Trooper Joe Badecki attempted to arrest a suspect who was observed buying drugs[849].

Actions taken by subject toward police: Refusing to comply, the suspect pulled out a gun and shot at the trooper, hitting him twice.

Reactions by the police: Dave Lick of the county prosecutor's office and Lt. Palmer exchanged gunfire with the suspect. The gunfight left the suspect dead, Lick injured with two gunshot wounds, and Palmer paralyzed.

How murdered? Lt. Palmer was paralyzed after being shot during an undercover drug deal. More than 20 years later he died as a result of complications from that shooting[850].

What could have been done differently for the officer to still be alive today? Undercover drug deals are inherently an extremely dangerous operation. There is no indication the officers should have done anything differently.

Would the officer had been justified to use deadly force before being murdered? Yes, given the totality of the circumstances including an undercover drug buy with a combative subject, once that subject made a furtive motion that a reasonable officer would have believed was to access a weapon, justified deadly force could have been used.

Outcome for the cop-killer: The unidentified cop-killer was killed during the shootout.

Officer: Panola County Sheriff's Office, Deputy Sheriff William Christopher Dickerson
Date: 12/31/2019   **Location:** Panola County, TX
FACTORS (1,2,3,8,13,15)
Perpetrator(s) Involved: Gregory Dewayne Newson

Criminal Activity History/Involved: Yes, Newson has been a career criminal since he was 17, with arrests/convictions for possession of cocaine, felony possession of a firearm, attempted armed robbery, DUI, possession of marijuana and cocaine with intent to sell and aggravated flight from an officer[851]./Yes, Newson had over a pound of marijuana, and, as a felon, he was in illegal possession of a firearm when Deputy Dickerson pulled him over[852].

Mental Illness: Unknown.

Substance Abuse History/Involved: Yes, Newson's previous arrests include possession of cocaine, marijuana, and a DUI./Yes, more than a pound of marijuana was found in Newson's vehicle upon arrest.

Race/Sex/Age: Black/Male/47

What prompted the initial contact with the killer? At approximately 2 a.m. on December 31, Deputy Sheriff Dickerson stopped a Chevy Tahoe driven by Gregory Newson[853].

Actions taken by subject toward police: Dashcam and bodycam videos show that before Deputy Dickerson could even get to Newson's vehicle, Newson jumped out of it and started shooting Dickerson with a semiautomatic rifle, hitting him six times. Though injured, Deputy Dickerson managed to return fire and shot Newson three times in his leg. Despite his injuries, Newson managed to get back into his car and drive off, while Dickerson was found by civilians who alerted the authorities[854].

Reactions by the police: Paramedics were able to get Dickerson to a hospital, but his injuries were fatal, and he died shortly after. A Shreveport Police Officer heard the description put out over the radio of Newson's Tahoe and spotted it enter his jurisdiction. After a short chase in which Newson crashed, the officer arrested the cop-killer without further incident[855].

How murdered? Deputy Dickerson was shot by a high-powered rifle while approaching the driver during a traffic stop.

What could have been done differently for the officer to still be alive? Deputy Dickerson approached the vehicle as any officer would. Short of approaching with his weapon out which is against most department's policy, Dickerson reacted as quickly as he could when Newson essentially ambushed him before he could reach the car.

Would the officer had been justified to use deadly force before being murdered? Yes, as soon as Newson exited his vehicle, he presented a threat. Upon seeing Newsom with something in his hand resembling a weapon and/or raising it toward him, that threat became deadly, and Deputy Dickerson would have been justified to use deadly force.

Outcome for the cop-killer: Newson was captured shortly after murdering Deputy Dickerson and was charged with capital murder.

Detective Clifton John Martinez

San Antonio Ind. School District PD, Texas

End of Watch Saturday, December 21, 2019

Lieutenant Leroy G. Palmer

Camden Police Department, New Jersey

End of Watch Tuesday, December 24, 2019

Deputy Sheriff William Christopher Dickerson

Panola County Sheriff's Office, Texas

End of Watch Tuesday, December 31, 2019

ANALYSIS OF THE 55 LAW ENFORCEMENT OFFICERS FELONIOUSLY KILLED IN 2019

Killer's race: White: 16 (29%); Black: 23 (42%); Latino: 13 (24%); Unknown: 3 (5%)

1. Subject failed to comply: 54 (98%)
2. Subject was a wanted criminal, or a crime was involved: 50 (91%)
3. Alcohol or drugs were involved: 13 (24%)
4. Subjects' actions displayed or were described having mental illness: 13 (24%)
5. Subjects' words and/or actions appeared to be suicidal and/or suicide by cop: 6 (11%)
6. Subjects' actions fueled by recent anti-police rhetoric: 1 (2%)
7. Subject ambushed the officer: 18 (33%)
8. Vehicle was involved (car stop, disabled motorist, accident): 25 (45%)
9. Subject accessed a hidden/concealed weapon before the LEO could react: 13 (24%)
10. Officer killed by friendly fire: 2 (4%)
11. A vehicle was used as a weapon to kill the officer: 6 (11%)
12. Subject attacked/threatened officers with personal weapons or an object: 4 (7%)
13. Officer could have justifiably shot subject first but did not: 19 (35%)
14. Less-than-lethal force alternatives failed: 7 (13%)
15. Officer was intentionally shot: 47 (85%)
16. Officer was accidentally killed: 3 (5%)
17. Officers were serving a warrant: 7 (13%)
18. Domestic incident was involved: 8 (15%)
19. Incident originated from a 911 call: 18 (33%)
20. Officer was killed taking police action while off-duty: 6 (11%)
21. Subject could have still been in jail, prison, or deported: 11 (20%)

INCIDENTS IN 2020:

Officer: Florence Regional Airport Dept. of Public Safety, Officer Jackson Ryan Winkeler
Date: 1/5/2020   **Location:** Florence, SC
FACTORS (1,2,8,15)7?13?
Perpetrator(s) Involved: James Edward Bell

Criminal Activity History/Involved: Yes, Bell was a career criminal with convictions dating back to 1998 for burglary and grand theft of a motor vehicle and 1999 for a strong-armed robbery[856]. In 2001 he was again convicted for fleeing the police, violently resisting an officer, and battery on a first responder (two counts). In 2002, Bell was charged with aggravated assault with a firearm and resisting a police officer, but it was charges of third-degree grand theft of a motor vehicle (four counts), fleeing from a police officer, and burglary of an occupied structure that got him 15 years in prison from 2002 to 2017[857]./Yes, earlier that same morning Bell had just committed an armed robbery and he was a felon in illegal possession of a firearm when Winkeler pulled him over.

Race/Sex/Age: Black/Male/37

What prompted the initial contact with the killer? At approximately 6 a.m. on January 5, Officer Winkeler conducted a traffic stop on the airport property of a vehicle operated by James Edward Bell[858].

Actions taken by subject toward police: Bell caught Winkeler off guard, shooting at him over 30 times with his 9-mm handgun, killing him mere feet away from his police vehicle[859].

Reactions by the police: Responding officers found that Winkeler had already died from his wounds and put out a description on the vehicle he had stopped. A nearby deputy pulled over Bell shortly after and arrested him without further incident. In Bell's possession was Winkeler's duty weapon along with a magazine from the handgun left at the scene that Bell used to kill the officer.

How murdered? Officer Winkeler was killed without provocation while conducting an early morning traffic stop.

What could have been done differently for the officer to still be alive? Officers are taught to approach all vehicles as if the subject could be armed so Winkeler was likely on guard, but when a subject starts shooting and hitting an officer, that officer will always be a step behind and reacting, so shooting Bell as soon as his vehicle stopped is the only tactic Winkeler could have used to ensure his own safety.

Would the officer had been justified to use deadly force before being murdered? Given the proximity of Winkeler's body to his own patrol vehicle and the 30+ rounds Bell was able to fire without Winkeler landing a shot on him, most probably Winkeler was ambushed during the stop and did not have a chance to use deadly force before he was shot.

Outcome for the cop-killer: Bell was arrested and was charged with murder of a police officer, discharging of a firearm into a vehicle, and possession of a weapon during a violent crime[860].

Officer: Honolulu Police Department, Officer Tiffany-Victoria Bilon Enriquez
Date: 1/19/2020   **Location:** Waikiki, HI
FACTORS (1,2,4,5,7,15,19)
Perpetrator(s) Involved: Jerry Hanel

Criminal Activity History/Involved: Yes, Hanel had several temporary restraining orders against him./Yes, Hanel had just assaulted his landlord and illegally possessed a firearm.

Mental Illness: Yes, Hanel did have mental health issues as reported by his lawyer and evidenced by the restraining orders against him by several neighbors who feared his volatile behavior[861].

Substance Abuse History/Involved: Unknown./None stated.

Race/Sex/Age: White/Male/69

What prompted the initial contact with the killer? At approximately 9:40 a.m. on January 19, Officer Enriquez responded with other officers to a 911 call of a woman being stabbed in a house. Upon arriving at the scene, Officer Enriquez encountered the injured woman outside of the house, rendered first aid to the stab wounds in the woman's leg and assisted her in walking back to the house[862].

Actions taken by subject toward police: The man, Jerry Hanel, who had just stabbed the woman, whom was his landlord, fired an illegally possessed weapon at the officers as they approached the house. Hanel's shot struck Officer Enriquez above her bulletproof vest, killing her.

Reactions by the police: Additional officers arrived and were also met with lethal gunfire. The officers took up defensive positions on the perimeter of the house and observed it go up in flames after the shooter set fire to it from inside.

How murdered? Officer Enriquez was shot and killed from a distance during an ambush while she assisted an injured woman during a 911 call.

What could have been done differently for the officer to still be alive? Considering the woman had just been stabbed and the person who did it was possibly still in the house, rather than return to the house, the officers could have taken the woman to another location to await an ambulance. However, given that the injury was a stabbing and not a gun shot, the officers did not have immediate reason to believe that they were in danger of an ambush attack with a firearm.

Would the officer had been justified to use deadly force before being murdered? Officer Enriquez was ambushed and did not have an opportunity to see her murderer and use deadly force on him first.

Outcome for the cop-killer: Hanel died in the building to which he had set fire while he barricaded from the police.

Miscellaneous: Hanel "is a really good example of somebody who fell in that gap where previously he had never, as far as we can tell, he had never risen to the level where he appeared to be imminently dangerous in his previous contacts with police." "But all the warning signs and all the risks were there"[863].

Officer: Honolulu Police Department, Officer Kaulike Kalama
Date: 1/19/2020   **Location:** Waikiki, HI
FACTORS (1,2,4,5,15,19)
Perpetrator(s) Involved: Jerry Hanel

Criminal Activity History/Involved: Yes, Hanel had several temporary restraining orders against him./Yes, Hanel had just assaulted his landlord and illegally possessed a firearm.

Mental Illness: Yes, Hanel did have mental health issues as reported by his lawyer and evidenced by the restraining orders against him by several neighbors who feared his volatile behavior[864].

Substance Abuse History/Involved: Unknown./None stated.

Race/Sex/Age: White/Male/69

What prompted the initial contact with the killer? At approximately 9:40 a.m. on January 19, Honolulu Police Officers responded to a 911 call of a woman being stabbed in a house. Upon arriving at the scene and rendering first aid to the woman outside the house, those officers came under deadly fire by the perpetrator of the initial assault, Jerry Hanel. One of several officers, Kalama, arriving as backup to the deadly ambush, was armed with his patrol rifle to engage the killer[865].

Actions taken by subject toward police: From the cloak of shadows in the house, Hanel shot and killed Kalama while he was in the open and unable to see the threat inside the house[866] [867].

Reactions by the police: The remaining officers took up defensive positions on the perimeter of the house and observed it go up in flames after the shooter set fire to it from inside.

How murdered? Officer Kalama was shot and killed from a distance while attempting to shoot a man who had just assaulted his landlord and killed a police officer.

What could have been done differently for the officer to still be alive? Officer Kalama bravely attempted to find and engage a deadly shooter who had the advantage of cover and concealment within his house while Kalama was outside and without cover. Considering fellow Officer Enriquez had just been shot, Kalama may have been trying to distract the shooter so she could be attended to, or other officers could get to cover. If no other officers were in immediate danger from the shooter, Officer Kalama may have been better off hiding behind cover and maintaining the perimeter until SWAT officers could respond.

Would the officer had been justified to use deadly force before being murdered? Officer Kalama knew that he was in a deadly force scenario as a fellow officer was just killed, but he never got a chance to get Hanel in his sights before Hanel shot him.

Outcome for the cop-killer: Hanel died in the building to which he had set fire while he barricaded from the police.

Miscellaneous: Hanel "is a really good example of somebody who fell in that gap where previously he had never, as far as we can tell, he had never risen to the level where he appeared to be imminently dangerous in his previous contacts with police." "But all the warning signs and all the risks were there"[868].

Officer: Newport News Police Department, Police Officer Katherine Mary Thyne
Date: 1/23/2020   **Location:** Newport News, VA
FACTORS (1,2,3,8,11,13,19,21)
Perpetrator(s) Involved: Vernon Evander Green

Criminal Activity History/Involved: Yes, Green had felony convictions in 2003 for cocaine sales and weapons possession. More recently in 2016 he had committed an armed bank robbery in North Carolina and was indicted by the state (but not the feds) for "robbery with a dangerous weapon and possession of a firearm as a convicted felon"[869]. Since it was only a state indictment, Green posted bond and was not prohibited from interstate travel./Yes, Green possessed marijuana, and, as a felon, was illegally in possession of a firearm when Officer Thyne and her partner questioned him.

Mental Illness: None stated.

Substance Abuse History/Involved: Yes, Green had prior drug-related arrests./Yes, this incident started on the basis of a complaint of suspected drug activity.

Race/Sex/Age: Black/Male/38

What prompted the initial contact with the killer? At approximately 6:30 p.m. on January 23, Officer Thyne and her partner responded to a complaint of possible drug activity in a parked car. The officers asked the driver, Vernon Green, and his female passenger to exit the vehicle. While the woman complied and exited the car, Green refused, prompting Officer Thyne who was standing near Green's open car door to order him several times to get out of the car.

Actions taken by subject toward police: Green refused to comply with Thyne's lawful orders and instead turned the car on and sped off, dragging Officer Thyne along for a block and pinning her against a tree before crashing into a brick wall.

Reactions by the police: Officers provided medical care to Thyne and arrested Green shortly after.

How murdered? Officer Thyne died of "multiple blunt trauma"[870] after being dragged during a traffic stop and pinned against a tree.

What could have been done differently for the officer to still be alive? Officer Thyne might still be alive if she was able to access her gun while being dragged and use it to shoot Green, or if her partner did so.

Would the officer had been justified to use deadly force before being murdered? Yes, Thyne or her partner could have justifiably used deadly force and shot Green the moment he drove off and dragged Officer Thyne along as he attempted to escape.

Outcome for the cop-killer: Green was arrested soon after murdering Officer Thyne and is facing charges for felony murder, felony possession of a firearm, possession of marijuana, failing to stop after a crash, and attempting to evade and elude law enforcement[871].

Miscellaneous: If the federal government had chosen to prosecute Green under federal charges for the robbery, "he would likely have been locked up awaiting trial"[872]–and Officer Thyne would still be alive.

Public Safety Officer Jackson Ryan Winkeler

Florence Regional Airport DPS, South Carolina

End of Watch Sunday, January 5, 2020

Officer Tiffany-Victoria Bilon Enriquez

Honolulu Police Department, Hawaii

End of Watch Sunday, January 19, 2020

Officer Kaulike S. G. Kalama

Honolulu Police Department, Hawaii

End of Watch Sunday, January 19, 2020

Police Officer Katherine Mary Thyne

Newport News Police Department, Virginia

End of Watch Thursday, January 23, 2020

Officer: Liberty County Sheriff's Office, Deputy Sheriff Richard Edward Whitten
Date: 2/3/2020   **Location:** Liberty, TX
FACTORS (1,2,4,5,8,9,13,15,20)
Perpetrator(s) Involved: Pavol Vido

Criminal Activity History/Involved: Yes, Vido had prior arrests for DWI, unlawfully possessing a weapon, aggravated assault, deadly conduct, and evading arrest[873]./Yes, Vido had just murdered two people and shot another at a business over an ongoing eviction issue. He was driving a stolen vehicle while confronted by Deputy Whitten[874].

Mental Illness: None reported; however, his ultimate suicide is indicative of mental illness.

Race/Sex/Age: White/Male/65

What prompted the initial contact with the killer? On May 29, 2019, while off-duty, Deputy Whitten observed a man, Pavol Vido, suspected of having just committed multiple murders at a local business. After pursuing Vido's vehicle into an alley, Deputy Whitten exited his vehicle with his gun drawn to engage Vido. Fearing that nearby civilians would be hit if he fired, Whitten refrained from shooting and just kept Vido in his sights[875].

Actions taken by subject toward police: About the same time Whitten exited his patrol vehicle, Vido opened his car door, planted his feet outside the car, and turned toward Whitten while keeping his right hand hidden. Vido ignored several commands by Whitten to show his hands before suddenly bringing his right hand up and shooting Whitten without aiming, striking Whitten in the neck, instantly paralyzing him[876].

Reactions by the police: Another officer on the scene shot at Vido, causing him to flee, while a different responding officer rendered emergency trauma care to Whitten before he was taken to a hospital. After six months of surgeries and physical therapy, Whitten died of a heart attack from complications of that gunshot.

How murdered? Deputy Whitten was shot in the neck after confronting a murder suspect on a vehicle stop.

What could have been done differently for the officer to still be alive? Deputy Whitten recognized a wanted suspect and bravely confronted him. As the Deputy recounts, he did not immediately open fire on Vido for fear of hitting innocent bystanders in the background. Given how Vido shot Whitten soon after being confronted, Whitten would have had to disregard the public and immediately opened fire on Vido.

Would the officer had been justified to use deadly force before being murdered? Yes, Vido was a suspected murderer armed with a deadly weapon who disregarded Whitten's lawful orders to show his hands.

Outcome for the cop-killer: Vido killed himself later that day before authorities could take him into custody.

Miscellaneous: This is a unique incident where the officer lived long enough to be able to describe the incident and his thought process of not immediately shooting at Vido for concern of bystanders, and Vido's ability to accurately shoot him without taking aim.

Officer: Kimberly Police Department, Police Officer Nick O'Rear
Date: 2/5/2020   **Location:** Warrior & Liberty, AL
FACTORS (1,2,8,14,15,21)
Perpetrator(s) Involved: Preston Chyenne Johnson

Criminal Activity History/Involved: Yes, Johnson was a career criminal with convictions dating back to 2001 for possession forged instrument and second-degree forgery; a 2006 conviction for first-degree theft, then two separate drug possessions, a felony possession of weapon conviction; and most recently in 2019 he was arrested for possession with intent to sell narcotics, possession of a stolen motor vehicle, and felony possession of a weapon[877]./Yes, as a felon, Johnson was illegally possessing the gun and AK-47 in his vehicle at the time of the incident, along with unlawful fleeing.

Substance Abuse History/Involved: Yes, Johnson had prior drug-related arrests and was a known methamphetamine user./None stated.

Race/Sex/Age: White/Male/37

What prompted the initial contact with the killer? On February 5, Warrior Police Officer Lee Glenn attempted to pull over a vehicle driven by Preston Johnson after it appeared that Johnson got nervous upon seeing the police. When Johnson refused to pull over and a pursuit was put over the radio, Kimberly Police Officer O'Rear responded to assist Glenn[878].

Actions taken by subject toward police: As Officer O'Rear pulled his vehicle in front of Johnson and braked in an attempt to slow Johnson's vehicle down, Johnson shot through his own windshield and into O'Rears' vehicle, fatally striking him in the head.

Reactions by the police: After being shot at himself and seeing Officer O'Rear crash after being shot, Officer Glenn stopped the chase to render first aid to O'Rear. Johnson escaped and was picked up by his associates, but he was captured soon after, when one of their relatives called 911 and alerted authorities.

How murdered? Officer O'Rear was shot in the head by a perpetrator in a moving vehicle as O'Rear drove in front of his vehicle attempting to slow it down.

What could have been done differently for the officer to still be alive? Nothing, vehicle pursuits are a common occurrence in law enforcement as criminals continue to flee to escape arrest and/or tickets. A perpetrator shooting at the police during such pursuits are not common and there is no way O'Rear could have known or protected himself once Johnson started shooting at him while Johnson's vehicle was behind his own.

Would the officer had been justified to use deadly force before being murdered? No, before Johnson shot at and killed Officer O'Rear, he was only wanted for suspicious behavior and fleeing the police, there was no commission of a violent crime that warranted deadly force.

Outcome for the cop-killer: Johnson was arrested shortly after the incident and was charged with capital murder, attempted murder of a police officer, and felony possession of a weapon.

Miscellaneous: Despite numerous criminal sentences including 15 years in 2011, Johnson was out of prison and free to reign havoc on the American public and kill a sworn officer.

Officer: Florida Highway Patrol, Trooper Joseph Jon Bullock
Date: 2/5/2020 **Location:** Palm City, FL
FACTORS (1,4,5,7,8,9,15,19)
Perpetrator(s) Involved: Franklin Reed III

Criminal Activity History/Involved: No, Reed was reported as not having a criminal history in Florida. Although the day before this incident, he had stolen a gold pendant from a pawn shop./No, at the time of the incident, Reed was a disabled motorist and legally in possession of his firearm.

Mental Illness: None reported; however, killing a police officer over his car being towed and then shooting himself in the head are not the actions of a normal man.

Substance Abuse History/Involved: Unknown./None stated.

Race/Sex/Age: Black/Male/30

What prompted the initial contact with the killer? At 10:12 a.m. on February 5, in response to a 911 call of a possible accident, Trooper Bullock returned to the median where an hour earlier he had spoken with Franklin Reed III, whose vehicle was disabled. The trooper called a tow truck to take Reed's vehicle, but after it was towed out of the ditch it rolled into, Reed did not want to pay. After advising Reed that he had ten minutes to either pay the tow-truck operator or his vehicle would be towed away, Bullock returned to his patrol vehicle to fill out paperwork related to the incident[879].

Actions taken by subject toward police: As Bullock sat in his car doing paperwork, Reed casually walked up to the police car, pulled out a .40-caliber Glock handgun and shot the trooper point-blank in the head. Reed then turned toward the tow truck operator to shoot him, but the gun jammed, so the driver ran off and called 911[880].

Reactions by the police: No other officers were present, but an off-duty detective stopped upon seeing something suspicious about the trooper's vehicle and ended up in a gunfight with Reed, shooting him twice[881].

How murdered? Trooper Bullock was ambushed while sitting in his vehicle filling out paperwork at a disabled motorist call.

What could have been done differently for the officer to still be alive? It is commonplace for motorists to walk up to patrol cars while officers are filling out accident or disabled motorist reports so Trooper Bullock, or any officer, would not have expected that ambush attack. For officer's safety, however, officers are instructed to exit their vehicle to engage with any subject approaching them, even for simple questions on directions.

Would the officer had been justified to use deadly force before being murdered? No, prior to being ambushed, Trooper Bullock had no justifiable reason to use deadly force on Reed.

Outcome for the cop-killer: Reed killed himself with a shot to the head before dying from the lethal wounds sustained in a gunfight with an off-duty officer at the scene.

Officer: White Mountain Apache Tribal Police Department, Officer David Kellywood
Date: 2/17/2020   **Location:** Pinetop, AZ
FACTORS (1,2,15,18,19) 9?,13?
Perpetrator(s) Involved: Jeremy Dewey

Criminal Activity History/Involved: Internet search shows a Jeremy Cruz Dewey with date of birth 8/20/1992 was arrested for possession of dangerous drugs in June 2019 and in 2018 for two warrants for shoplifting and falsely reporting[882] [883]./Yes, Dewey had just fired his gun during a domestic dispute before physically assaulting the responding police officer[884].

Mental Illness: Unknown

Substance Abuse History/Involved: Yes, Dewey had a previous drug-related arrest./None stated.

Race/Sex/Age: Latino/Male/27

What prompted the initial contact with the killer? Officer Kellywood and another officer responded to a 911 call about a domestic dispute involving gunfire at the Hon-Dah Resort and Casino around 1 a.m. on February 17. Upon arriving at the scene, Kellywood located Jeremy Dewey, the man suspected to be involved.

Actions taken by subject toward police: Dewey "immediately engaged in a violent, physical altercation"[885] with Officer Kellywood and fatally shot the officer.

Reactions by the police: Another officer who responded to the incident shot and killed Dewey[886].

How murdered? Officer Kellywood was physically attacked and shot while handling a 911 call of domestic violence.

What could have been done differently for the officer to still be alive? With neither dashcam or bodycam available nor any information coming from the FBI on the incident, it is difficult to know exactly how the altercation with and shooting by Dewey took place.

Would the officer had been justified to use deadly force before being murdered? Given Officer Kellywood responded to a domestic incident involving shots fired, he would have been justified in drawing his gun immediately upon contacting the suspect to get compliance and ensure his own personal safety.

Outcome for the cop-killer: Dewey was justifiably shot and killed by the other responding Officer after Dewey killed Officer Kellywood[887].

Deputy Sheriff Richard Edward Whitten

Liberty County Sheriff's Office, Texas

End of Watch Monday, February 3, 2020

Police Officer Nicholas D. O'Rear

Kimberly Police Department, Alabama

End of Watch Wednesday, February 5, 2020

Trooper Joseph Jon Bullock

Florida Highway Patrol, Florida

End of Watch Wednesday, February 5, 2020

Officer David W. Kellywood

White Mountain Apache Tribal PD, Tribal Police

End of Watch Monday, February 17, 2020

Officer: Sumter County Sheriff's Office, Corporal Andrew J. Gillette
Date: 2/25/2020   **Location:** Dalzell, SC
FACTORS (1,2,9,13,14,15)
Perpetrator(s) Involved: Terry Hasty

Criminal Activity History/Involved: Unknown./Yes, Hasty was illegally presiding at the residence and was served an eviction notice which he failed to comply with. He then resisted the officer's efforts to arrest him.

Mental Illness: Unknown

Substance Abuse History/Involved: Unknown./None stated.

Race/Sex/Age: Black/Male/56

What prompted the initial contact with the killer? At approximately 11:30 a.m. on February 25, Corporal Gillette and several other deputies were serving an eviction notice to Terry Hasty, which was the culmination of a year-long legal battle between Hasty and the landowner. When Hasty refused to comply with the order and leave the premises, the deputies informed him he was under arrest. When Hasty ignored the orders of deputies to peacefully comply, Gillette drew his taser and pointed it at Hasty to gain compliance[888].

Actions taken by subject toward police: Perhaps thinking the taser was a gun, Hasty told the deputy to "put that gun down" as he pulled out a .44 Magnum hidden in his waistband. Upon seeing Hasty pull out a gun, Gillette shot the taser at Hasty, but it failed to incapacitate Hasty who then shot Gillette point-blank in the chest several times[889].

Reactions by the police: One deputy fired back at Hasty five times and despite being mortally wounded, Corporal Gillette also managed to shoot fifteen rounds at Hasty. Hasty ran into his trailer to reload but died from his injuries before he could return to the door and fire again[890].

How murdered? Corporal Gillette was shot point-blank while serving a subject with an eviction notice.

What could have been done differently for the officer to still be alive? As the bodycam and testimony show, Gillette and his fellow deputies "did everything right"[891]. Gillette used less-than-lethal force until a lethal threat was presented. Unfortunately, the taser failed to stop Hasty from utilizing that lethal threat. The only possible way Gillette could have survived the incident is if another deputy were in position to see Hasty pull the gun out and shoot him before Hasty could use it.

Would the officer had been justified to use deadly force before being murdered? Yes, the deputies were justified to shoot Hasty as soon as he made a furtive movement to his waistband which is where he retrieved the gun from.

Outcome for the cop-killer: Hasty died at the scene from the gunshots sustained from Gillette and his fellow deputy.

Officer: Hot Springs Police Department, Corporal Brent William Perry Scrimshire
Date: 3/10/2020   **Location:** Hot Springs, AR
FACTORS (1,2,8,9,12,13,14,15)
Perpetrator(s) Involved: Kayvon Moshawn Daking Ward; Coriama Hernandez

Criminal Activity History/Involved: Yes, Ward had active felony warrants for a shooting involving first-degree battery in August 2019 and misdemeanor third-degree battery occurring in July 2019./Yes, during the car stop, Ward illegally possessed a defaced firearm, then resisted arrest and unlawfully fled, while Hernandez also assaulted the officers and then fled as well.

Mental Illness: Ward's lawyer was arguing that his client's defense was "innocent by reason of mental disease or defect"[892].

Substance Abuse History/Involved: Unknown./None stated.

Race/Sex/Age: Ward: Black/Male/21; Hernandez: Latina/Female/20

What prompted the initial contact with the killer? On March 10 at approximately 6:30 p.m., Corporal Scrimshire conducted a traffic stop on a vehicle operated by Kayvon Ward for running a stop sign. During the car stop, besides having an underage child in the car without the proper safety seat, Ward failed to provide his driver's license and gave a false name. When Ward's girlfriend, Coriama Hernandez arrived with the proper baby seat, she too failed to cooperate with providing Wards real name. As Scrimshire and backup officer Larkin questioned Hernandez, Ward kept trying to exit the vehicle against the officer's orders. As the officer's then tried to arrest Ward, he assaulted them and was assisted by Hernandez who "began pulling and pushing on the officers" to get off him[893].

Actions taken by subject toward police: When the officers pushed Hernandez away, Ward broke free from them and ran into a backyard where he then turned on the pursuing officers and shot at them, fatally striking Scrimshire above his vest.

Reactions by the police: Larkin and the injured Scrimshire returned fire, striking Ward. Scrimshire and Ward were transported to a hospital, but Scrimshire died from his wound.

How murdered? Corporal Scrimshire was shot chasing a subject from a car stop into a yard.

What could have been done differently for the officer to still be alive? Scrimshire used good tactics in getting back-up and was looking out for the toddler in asking for a car seat, but another person friendly to the suspect should not be brought to a scene until the suspect is in custody as experiences at domestic calls have shown, loved ones can act very unpredictably as Hernandez did.

Would the officer had been justified to use deadly force before being murdered? When Ward resisted arrest and assaulted the officers, if they feared he was trying to access a gun on his own person or one of theirs then yes, they would have been. Likewise, when he turned his hand toward them while holding an object, they reasonably feared was a weapon, the officers were justified to use deadly force.

Outcome for the cop-killer: Ward was charged with capital murder, aggravated assault on a LEO and possession of a defaced firearm, while Hernandez faces charges of accomplice to capital murder and aggravated assault on a LEO.

Officer: Philadelphia Police Department, Sergeant James R. O'Connor, IV
Date: 3/13/2020   **Location:** Philadelphia, PA
FACTORS (1,2,7,15,17,21)
Perpetrator(s) Involved: Hassan Elliot; Bilal Mitchell; Khalif Sears

Criminal Activity History/Involved: Yes, Elliot pled to a lesser charge for an illegal weapons possession arrest in 2018; was arrested for criminal possession of a controlled substance in January 2019; and generated a felony warrant for a March 2019 robbery and murder. Mitchell had several recent drug-related arrests[894]. Sears was also wanted for the same March-2019 robbery/murder as Elliot./Yes, Elliot had an active felony warrant and was illegally in possession of a weapon; Bilal and Sears faced conspiracy charges with Elliot during the shooting because the three were "part of a street gang and they conducted a lot of illegal activity that supported each other,"[895] including Sgt. O'Connor's murder.

Mental Illness: Unknown.

Substance Abuse History/Involved: Unknown./None stated.

Race/Sex/Age: Elliot: Black/Male/21; Mitchell: Black/Male/19; Sears: Black/Male/18

What prompted the initial contact with the killer? On March 13 at approximately 5:40 a.m., Sgt. James O'Connor and other members of a Philadelphia Police SWAT team made entry into an apartment building to arrest Hassan Elliot for a felony murder warrant[896].

Actions taken by subject toward police: As O'Connor and the officers made their way up to the second floor, Elliot shot at them from behind a closed door at least 20 times from a .22-caliber rifle, striking O'Connor in his arm and shoulder[897].

Reactions by the police: Officers returned fire, striking two other men hiding behind closed doors in that second-floor apartment while O'Connor was rushed to a hospital where he died from his wounds.

How murdered? Sgt. O'Connor was fatally shot while conducting a SWAT raid to arrest a suspect for a felony murder warrant.

What could have been done differently for the officer to still be alive? Short of blindly shooting through each door O'Connor and the other officers observed as they entered the house, there was nothing he could have done to stop from being ambushed that way by Elliot.

Would the officer had been justified to use deadly force before being murdered? O'Connor or the other officers had never seen Elliot or a lethal threat before Elliot opened fire at them from behind a closed door.

Outcome for the cop-killer: Elliot and his accomplices are being charged with murder and several other weapons and drug-possession related crimes.

Miscellaneous: U.S. Attorney William M. McSwain said Philadelphia DA "Krasner's radical decarceration policies led directly to the murder of Cpl. O'Connor"[898].

Officer: Springfield Police Department, Police Officer Christopher Ryan Walsh
Date: 3/16/2020   **Location:** Springfield, MO
FACTORS (1,2,4,5,7,8,15,19)
Perpetrator(s) Involved: Joaquin S. Roman

Criminal Activity History/Involved: None reported./Yes, Roman was on a shooting spree, having just shot from his vehicle at other moving vehicles before crashing into the storefront and shooting four people inside.

Mental Illness: None reported; however, his erratic behavior and ultimate suicide are indicative of mental illness.

Substance Abuse History/Involved: Unknown./None stated.

Race/Sex/Age: Latino/Male/21

What prompted the initial contact with the killer? On the night of March 15, there were several 911 calls of an active shooter in Springfield, first on the roadways and then at a shopping center. At approximately 11:45 Officers Ryan Walsh and Josiah Overton responded to the Kum and Go store where the shooter, Joaquin S. Roman, had crashed into the store before going into it and shot the innocent people inside[899].

Actions taken by subject toward police: Roman opened fire on the officers as they arrived at the store, hitting them both.

Reactions by the police: A SWAT entry team arrived minutes later to pull Walsh and Overton away from Roman's line of fire and transported them to a hospital. Overton recovered from his injuries, but Walsh died at the hospital. When the entry team went into the building, they found that Roman had killed himself[900].

How murdered? Officer Walsh was ambushed by a suspect shooting from inside a building as Walsh arrived at the scene.

What could have been done differently for the officer to still be alive? Fighting their instinct to get inside as fast as possible to stop Roman from shooting any more innocent civilians, the officers would have had to park outside the line of sight of the Kum and Go store and then tactically make entry.

Would the officer had been justified to use deadly force before being murdered? The officers were justified to use deadly force as soon as they saw Roman, since he was an active shooter, but from outside the store, they were unable to see Roman before he shot them from the cover of being inside.

Outcome for the cop-killer: Roman killed himself with a self-inflicted gunshot at the scene.

Miscellaneous: Although it is the deadliest shooting "in recent southwest Missouri history"[901], there is a distinct lack of reporting about the shooter, and his motive remains unknown.

Corporal Andrew J. Gillette

Sumter County Sheriff's Office, South Carolina

End of Watch Tuesday, February 25, 2020

Corporal Brent William Perry Scrimshire

Hot Springs Police Department, Arkansas

End of Watch Tuesday, March 10, 2020

Sergeant James R. O'Connor, IV

Philadelphia Police Department, Pennsylvania

End of Watch Friday, March 13, 2020

Police Officer Christopher Ryan Walsh

Springfield Police Department, Missouri

End of Watch Friday, March 16, 2020

Officer: Springdale Police Department, Police Officer Kaia LaFay Grant
Date: 3/21/2020   **Location:** Springdale, OH
FACTORS (1,2,4,5,8,11,13,17)
Perpetrator(s) Involved: Terry Blankenship

Criminal Activity History/Involved: Yes, besides previous arrests for domestic violence and assault, Blankenship had an active felony warrant for an aggravated burglary he committed just two days earlier./Yes, Blankenship was unlawfully fleeing from the police, likely because of his active warrant.

Mental Illness: Unknown.

Substance Abuse History/Involved: Unknown./None stated.

Race/Sex/Age: White/Male/42

What prompted the initial contact with the killer? On March 21 at approximately 8 p.m., Elmwood police officers tried to pull over Terry Blankenship as he drove his pickup truck so they could arrest him for a felony armed burglary warrant from an incident two days before[902].

Actions taken by subject toward police: Blankenship refused to pull over and was pursued at speeds up to 60 mph by the officers into nearby Springdale where Officer Grant and Sgt. Andrew Davis were setting up stop sticks in the road to incapacitate Blankenship's truck. The officers never got a chance to lay out the sticks as Blankenship turned toward them and struck them as well as their police cruisers. After the crash which killed Officer Grant, Blankenship shot himself once in the face with his .45-caliber handgun[903].

Reactions by the police: Officer Grant was declared dead at the hospital while Sgt. Davis was treated and released, and Blankenship was hospitalized for his injuries.

How murdered? Officer Grant was purposely run over by a motor vehicle by a subject fleeing from police trying to arrest him for a felony warrant.

What could have been done differently for the officer to still be alive? Police were notified that Blankenship was considered armed and dangerous; however, the officers did not anticipate Blankenship using his vehicle as a weapon the way he did. Had Officer Grant remained in her vehicle, there is still a possibility that Blankenship would have rammed it or used his .45-caliber gun to shoot at the officers.

Would the officer had been justified to use deadly force before being murdered? Yes, Officer Grant would have been justified to use deadly force when she saw Blankenship turn his vehicle toward her to use it as a deadly weapon.

Outcome for the cop-killer: Blankenship has been indicted for aggravated murder of Officer Grant and nine other counts including aggravated vehicular homicide, failure to comply, felonious assault, and aggravated burglary[904].

Officer: Washington State Patrol, Trooper Justin R. Schaffer
Date: 3/24/2020   **Location:** Chehalis, WA
FACTORS (1,2,3,4,8,11,13,17)
Perpetrator(s) Involved: William D. Thompson

Criminal Activity History/Involved: Yes, Thompson has been charged with first-degree assault for a March-18 road-rage incident and was wanted for larceny and other charges for a shoplifting incident on March 23./Yes, Thompson was unlawfully fleeing and recklessly endangering the public as he fled from law enforcement.

Mental Illness: Thompson was deemed temporarily mentally incompetent to stand trial and was diagnosed with mental health issues including hallucinations, as he mentioned, "that command him to harm President Donald Trump"[905].

Substance Abuse History/Involved: Unknown./Yes, investigation of the incident revealed that Thompson was "high or drunk"[906] at the time of the incident.

Race/Sex/Age: Black/Male/39

What prompted the initial contact with the killer? At approximately 4 p.m. on March 24, Trooper Schaffer responded to assist officers from a nearby municipality pursuing a wanted suspect, William D. Thompson. Thompson was heading toward Trooper Schaffer's location, so Schaffer was putting down spike strips to incapacitate Thompson's vehicle[907].

Actions taken by subject toward police: Thompson intentionally swerved toward Schaffer while going over 100 mph, hitting Schaffer, and launching his body 120 feet. Instead of stopping then, Thompson intentionally drove into a patrol car, injuring another trooper before continuing down the highway[908].

Reactions by the police: While some officers rushed Trooper Schaffer to the hospital, where he was officially declared dead, others continued pursuing Thompson until he crashed on the side of the road.

How murdered? Trooper Schaffer was hit by a wanted suspect fleeing police, who intentionally swerved into him as he was lying down spike strips.

What could have been done differently for the officer to still be alive? Short of not showing up to work or assisting his fellow officers in trying to capture the wanted subject, there is nothing Schaffer could have done when Thompson decided to intentionally drive towards him at such a high rate of speed.

Would the officer had been justified to use deadly force before being murdered? Yes, legally Schaffer was justified to shoot at Thompson as soon as Schaffer saw the vehicle turn towards him, especially at such a high rate of speed.

Outcome for the cop-killer: Thompson was arrested following a long standoff after crashing his vehicle into a light post on the highway. He faced multiple charges including murder of a law enforcement officer, robbery, and assault.

Officer: Nevada Highway Patrol, Sergeant Ben Jenkins
Date: 3/27/2020   **Location:** Elko, NV
FACTORS (1,2,4,7,8,9,15,21)
Perpetrator(s) Involved: John Dabritz

Criminal Activity History/Involved: Yes, "Dabritz has an extensive criminal history dating back to 1973"[909]./Yes, Dabritz was illegally in possession of possible explosives and weapons when his vehicle broke down.

Mental Illness: Yes, Dabritz had a history of paranoia, was diagnosed with Type 1 bipolar disorder, and spent a week in a mental institution before being released on March 20 and killing Sgt. Jenkins a week later[910].

Substance Abuse History/Involved: Yes, Dabritz's ex-wife describes him as "a mentally ill man with a history of alcoholism"[911]./None reported.

Race/Sex/Age: White/Male/65

What prompted the initial contact with the killer? At approximately 6 a.m. on March 27, Sgt. Jenkins stopped to help a motorist, John Dabritz, whose vehicle appeared to be broken down in a very rural area of Nevada[912].

Actions taken by subject toward police: Without warning or provocation, Dabritz shot and killed Sgt. Jenkins as he tried to render assistance to Dabritz. Dabritz then stole Sgt. Jenkins uniform and drove away in his police vehicle[913].

Reactions by the police: Within hours, other officers tracked down the stolen police vehicle, found Dabritz, and arrested him.

How murdered? Sgt. Jenkins was ambushed and fatally shot by a suspect he mistakenly, though reasonably, believed was a disabled motorist and had stopped on the side of the road to assist.

What could have been done differently for the officer to still be alive? Unfortunately, while Sgt. Jenkin's intentions to assist a disabled motorist were admirable, police officers are taught to treat each encounter with an unknown person as a potentially dangerous situation, and this is a clear example of why.

Would the officer had been justified to use deadly force before being murdered? Not realistic given Jenkin's belief that Dabritz needed help. Jenkins likely never had a chance to access his weapon by the time Dabritz was fatally shooting him.

Outcome for the cop-killer: Dabritz was arrested around four hours later and 100 miles from where he had killed Sgt. Jenkins. He faced "numerous charges, including open murder and third-degree arson"[914].

Officer: Phoenix Police Department, Commander Greg Carnicle
Date: 3/29/2020   **Location:** Phoenix, AZ
FACTORS (1,4,5,7,15,19)
Perpetrator(s) Involved: Jacob Emry Mcilveen

Criminal Activity History/Involved: Yes, Mcilveen was arrested for DUI and criminal possession of drugs in 2016[915]./No, not until Mcilveen fired upon the officers.

Mental Illness: This incident started because Mcilveen's roommates were afraid of his erratic behavior. Mcilveen's actions at the end were clearly suicidal.

Substance Abuse History/Involved: Yes, Mcilveen had a prior arrest for DUI and possession of drugs./None stated.

Race/Sex/Age: White/Male/22

What prompted the initial contact with the killer? During the afternoon of March 29, Phoenix Officers responded to multiple 911 calls of an armed man, Jacob Mcilveen, acting so erratic that his roommates were afraid and wanted him to leave. The initial officers on scene patiently tried to get Mcilveen to leave but as they walked out in front of him, Mcilveen closed the door on them and went back into the house, locking himself in his upstairs bedroom. After several hours of attempting to get Mcilveen to come out of his room and down the stairs, Sgt. Carnicle and Officers Alicia Hubert and Marissa Dowhan started walking up the stairs toward Mcilveen's room[916].

Actions taken by subject toward police: As the officers approached his room, Mcilveen shot at them through his closed door, fatally wounding Sgt. Carnicle, and wounding Officers Hubert and Dowhan[917].

Reactions by the police: A fourth officer shot back at Mcilveen's room and then other officers went into the house to remove the three injured officers and get them medical attention. Once the officers were safely out of the house, a perimeter was set up and officers negotiated for Mcilveen's peaceful surrender.

How murdered? Sgt. Carnicle was ambushed by an erratic subject who shot him from behind a closed door during a 911 call to have him removed from the house.

What could have been done differently for the officer to still be alive? Since the initial 911 caller had stated Mcilveen was armed with a gun and acting erratically, the responding officers should have immediately searched Mcilveen and his room for that weapon and secured it before letting him access his room to retrieve his belongings.

Would the officer had been justified to use deadly force before being murdered? No, up until Mcilveen shot at the officers ascending the stairs, he had not presented a deadly threat. However, he did disobey the officers' lawful orders and stall for over half an hour while they were telling him to leave the apartment so they could have physically taken him into custody and prevented the entire incident from escalating so badly.

Outcome for the cop-killer: After being barricaded inside the house for several hours, Mcilveen came out of the house with a gun in his hands and was justifiably shot dead by the police at the scene.

Police Officer Kaia LaFay Grant

Springdale Police Department, Ohio

End of Watch Saturday, March 21, 2020

Trooper Justin R. Schaffer

Washington State Patrol, Washington

End of Watch Tuesday, March 24, 2020

Sergeant Benjamin M. Jenkins

Nevada Highway Patrol, Nevada

End of Watch Friday, March 27, 2020

Commander Greg S. Carnicle

Phoenix Police Department, Arizona

End of Watch Sunday, March 29, 2020

Officer: Indianapolis Metropolitan Police Department, Officer Breann Leath
Date: 4/9/2020   **Location:** Indianapolis, IN
FACTORS (1,4,7,15,19)
Perpetrator(s) Involved: Elliahs Lamar Dorsey

Criminal Activity History/Involved: No, Dorsey did not have a criminal record./No, Dorsey was acting erratically but had not broken any laws before shooting through the door.

Mental Illness: The incident started because Dorsey's girlfriend reported that he was acting paranoid about someone being out to get him, so the 911 call was dispatched as a possible mentally ill man involved. Dorsey reportedly did not believe that it was really the police at the door.

Substance Abuse History/Involved: Unknown./None stated.

Race/Sex/Age: Black/Male/27

What prompted the initial contact with the killer? At approximately 3 p.m. on April 9, Officer Leath and several others responded to a 911 call about a disturbance in an apartment. A woman reported the erratic behavior of her boyfriend, Elliahs Dorsey was frightening her. Upon arriving at the address, Officer Leath knocked on the apartment door to investigate the situation[918].

Actions taken by subject toward police: Without warning, from behind the closed door, Dorsey fired several shots from his KelTec PLR-16 handgun, fatally striking Officer Leath as well as hitting his girlfriend four times[919].

Reactions by the police: The other officers on scene carried Leath's limp body away from the door and to an ambulance which transported her to a hospital where she was declared dead. None of the officers fired back at the door. A perimeter was set up and Dorsey eventually peacefully surrendered without further fatalities[920].

How murdered? Officer Leath was ambushed and shot by a subject on the other side of a closed front door as she investigated a domestic disturbance 911 call.

What could have been done differently for the officer to still be alive? Officer Leath was capably performing her job in answering a 911 call and investigating the situation. Though described as mentally ill, there was no indication that the subject was armed and there was no reason to believe that he would blindly shoot through the front door.

Would the officer had been justified to use deadly force before being murdered? No, Officer Leath and the other officers on the scene had not made visual contact with the subject, Dorsey, before he fired at them from the other side of the apartment door. Once Dorsey did shoot through the door, the officers were justified to shoot back through the door to neutralize the deadly threat.

Outcome for the cop-killer: Dorsey was arrested and faced charges of misdemeanor battery, criminal confinement, and four counts of attempted murder and murder.

Officer: San Marcos Police Department, Police Officer Justin Putnam
Date: 4/18/2020   **Location:** San Marcos, TX
FACTORS (1,2,3,4,5,7,15,18,19,21)
Perpetrator(s) Involved: Jose Alfredo Perez DeLaCruz

Criminal Activity History/Involved: Yes, DeLaCruz was an illegal alien who had been in the US since the 1990s. DeLaCruz used numerous aliases, and the media does not seem especially curious about his criminal history with those aliases./Yes, DeLaCruz's assault upon his wife precipitated the deadly shooting.

Mental Illness: None reported; however, suicide is indicative of an emotionally disturbed person.

Substance Abuse History/Involved: Unknown./Yes, alcohol was involved in the domestic assault.

Race/Sex/Age: Latino/Male/46

What prompted the initial contact with the killer? At slightly after 6 p.m. on April 18, Officers Justin Putnam, Franco Stewart, and Justin Mueller responded to an apartment for a 911 call of domestic violence. Jose DeLaCruz's wife reported that he was drinking and had assaulted her[921].

Actions taken by subject toward police: As the officers approached the apartment, DeLaCruz, already clad in body armor and lying-in wait, opened fire on them with his rifle, fatally striking Officer Putnam and injuring Officers Stewart and Mueller[922].

Reactions by the police: Officers Stewart and Mueller's lives were saved by the paramedics, but Putnam's wounds were fatal. Officers arrived from multiple jurisdictions and eventually made entrance into the apartment only to find DeLaCruz dead with a self-inflicted gunshot wound[923].

How murdered? Officer Putnam was ambushed by a domestic violence suspect as the officer approached his apartment to investigate the 911 call from his wife.

What could have been done differently for the officer to still be alive? NA. Officer Putnam was performing his job in responding to a 911 call of domestic violence and properly wearing his body armor.

Would the officer had been justified to use deadly force before being murdered? NA. The officers were ambushed and shot before they even saw the threat. Once DeLaCruz shot at them from the apartment, they were justified to use deadly force and shot back into the apartment.

Outcome for the cop-killer: DeLaCruz killed himself shortly after shooting at the three officers and before he could be taken into custody[924].

Officer: San Diego Police Officer Dan Walters
Date: 4/23/2020   **Location:** San Diego, CA
FACTORS (1,2,8,13,14,15,18)
Perpetrator(s) Involved: Jaime Contreras

Criminal Activity History/Involved: Unknown./Yes, Contreras was committing a violent domestic incident against his wife and children on the roadway when Officer Ingram came across him.

Mental Illness: Unknown.

Substance Abuse History/Involved: Unknown./None stated.

Race/Sex/Age: Latino/Male/26

What prompted the initial contact with the killer? At approximately 10:30 p.m. on November 12, 2003, Officer Walters and his partner pulled up on another SD Police Officer, Henry Ingram, involved in a traffic stop. Unbeknownst to Walters, Ingram had stumbled across a violent domestic dispute, and the perpetrator, Jaime Contreras had just shot at Ingram forcing Ingram to the ground to take cover. Walters had not heard any gun shots but saw Ingram's look of fright and gun drawn as Walters jumped out of his patrol car to assist him[925].

Actions taken by subject toward police: Walters was immediately confronted by an armed Contreras who was pointing his gun at Walters face as he advanced toward him. Since Walters weapon was still holstered and Contreras moved within arm's reach, he unsuccessfully tried to wrestle Contreras weapon away from him. Contreras reached his arm around Walters and shot him in the neck, paralyzing Walters and sending him to the ground, where he was then run over by a passing motorist.

Reactions by the police: Officer Walters' partner shot Contreras dead and then assisted giving Walters medical attention at the scene before Walters was rushed to the hospital for what would be 17 years of medical treatment.

How murdered? Officer Walters was shot in the neck and then run over by a passing motorist while assisting another officer on a violent domestic dispute in the roadway. The incident left Walters paralyzed and in terrible pain for 17 years, eventually killing him[926].

What could have been done differently for the officer to still be alive? As Officer Walters himself recounts, upon pulling up to the traffic stop he saw a frightened officer taking cover with his gun drawn so Walters knew there was a threat somewhere, but not having seen the threat himself he did not draw his weapon out when he stepped out of the patrol car and was quickly attacked by Contreras.

Would the officer had been justified to use deadly force before being murdered? Yes, upon seeing Contreras point a gun at him from 15 feet away, Walters would have been justified to immediately shoot Contreras.

Outcome for the cop-killer: Contreras was justifiably shot and killed by Officer Walters' partner shortly after Contreras ambushed Walters[927].

Officer: Baton Rouge Police Department, Lieutenant Glenn Dale Hutto, Jr.
Date: 4/26/2020   **Location:** Baton Rouge, LA
FACTORS (1,2,6,7,15,17,18)
Perpetrator(s) Involved: Ronnie DeWayne Kato, Jr.

Criminal Activity History/Involved: Yes, Kato had two prior arrests for drug possession in 2001 and 2010./Yes, just hours before killing Officer Hutto, Kato had assaulted his girlfriend and murdered her stepfather.

Mental Illness: None stated.

Substance Abuse History/Involved: Kato had prior drug-related arrests./None stated.

Race/Sex/Age: Black/Male/36

What prompted the initial contact with the killer? At approximately 12:30 p.m. on April 26, Lt. Hutto and Corporal Derrick Maglone were assisting investigators looking for Ronnie Kato, Jr. to arrest him for a domestic assault and homicide that he had committed just hours earlier a few miles away at his girlfriend's house. Hutto and Maglone went to the backyard of the house to prevent Kato from trying to escape from the backdoor as the investigators knocked on the front door[928].

Actions taken by subject toward police: Kato was clearly waiting for the officers as he ambushed them with a rifle before they could react. Evidence shows that Kato stood over Lt. Hutto after the initial shots and continued shooting him point-blank, before running back into and barricading himself in the house.

Reactions by the police: A perimeter was formed, and SWAT responded while officers rushed Hutto and Maglone to the hospital where Hutto was declared dead and Maglone was in critical condition but would eventually recover.

How murdered? Hutto was ambushed and murdered by a domestic-violence subject wanted for a murder perpetrated earlier in the day.

What could have been done differently for the officer to still be alive? If Hutto came face to face with Kato without his weapon at the ready, that would prove to be a fatal mistake, but if Hutto was shot and killed by Kato as Kato was inside the house and Hutto could not even see him, then there is nothing he could have done. Approaching a house or location with an armed murderer is extremely dangerous and a testament to any officer's bravery when they do so.

Would the officer had been justified to use deadly force before being murdered? No, Hutto was ambushed and killed before having a chance to confront Kato and use deadly force against him.

Outcome for the cop-killer: After an approximate four-hour standoff with officers in which he was barricaded in the house and exchanging fire with them, Kato surrendered without anybody else being injured. Kato was charged with aggravated battery, five counts of home invasion, six counts of attempted murder, and two counts of murder[929].

Miscellaneous: During a 2017 domestic incident, Kato threatened to "Gavin Long" any responding officers. Gavin Long is the black anti-government group shooter who ambushed and killed three Baton Rouge Officers in 2016 in a "targeted attack on law-enforcement"[930].

Officer Breann R. Leath

Indianapolis Metropolitan PD, Indiana

End of Watch Thursday, April 9, 2020

Police Officer Justin R. Putnam

San Marcos Police Department, Texas

End of Watch Saturday, April 18, 2020

Police Officer Daniel G. Walters

San Diego Police Department, California

End of Watch Thursday, April 23, 2020

Lieutenant Glenn Dale Hutto, Jr.

Baton Rouge Police Department, Louisiana

End of Watch Sunday, April 26, 2020

Officer: Overland Park Police Department, Police Officer Michael S. Mosher
Date: 5/3/2020   **Location:** Overland Park, KS
FACTORS (1,2,3,8,9,13,15,20)
Perpetrator(s) Involved: Phillip Michael Carney

Criminal Activity History/Involved: Yes, Carney had a substantial history of violence and crime including arrests for burglary, criminal damage to property, domestic battery and battery, and aggravated assault of a police officer[931] [932]./Yes, Carney was DWI and had just fled the scene of an accident.

Mental Illness: Unknown.

Substance Abuse History/Involved: Yes, Carney was a drug addict and alcoholic./Yes, the post-mortem toxicology showed that Carney had prescription drugs and cocaine in his blood at the time of the incident.

Race/Sex/Age: White/Male/38

What prompted the initial contact with the killer? At around 6 p.m. on May 3, while driving his personal vehicle in uniform for his next shift, Officer Mosher followed a driver, Phillip Carney, whom he had just observed committing a hit-and-run[933].

Actions taken by subject toward police: At some point while being followed by Mosher, Carney stopped his vehicle, got out, and went toward Mosher's vehicle to confront him. Officer Mosher called for backup officers on his handheld radio when Carney refused to return to his car. As Mosher made the call, Carney took out a concealed gun and shot Mosher point-blank.

Reactions by the police: Though injured, Mosher managed to unholster his weapon and shoot Carney back, killing him. Responding units rushed Mosher to the hospital where he died from his injuries.

How murdered? Officer Mosher was shot and killed by a subject who had just committed a hit-and-run and confronted Mosher for following him.

What could have been done differently for the officer to still be alive? Officer Mosher was a firearms trainer and an accomplished competition shooter who had earned a valor award for successfully fighting off an ambush just two years earlier[934] [935]. This incident shows that no matter how tactically proficient the police are, since they are reacting to the perpetrator's actions, they are always a second behind. As the Overland Park DA said, "He did everything right and it still wasn't good enough"[936].

Would the officer had been justified to use deadly force before being murdered? Yes, given that Mosher identified himself as an officer and was observed by Carney requesting backup, Mosher could have reasonably assumed Carney's furtive motion was to access a hidden gun.

Outcome for the cop-killer: Carney was justifiably shot and killed by Officer Mosher right after Carney shot him.

Officer: Grand Forks Police Department, Police Officer Cody N. Holte
Date: 5/27/2020   **Location:** Grand Forks, ND
FACTORS (1,2,4,13,15)
Perpetrator(s) Involved: Salamah Pendleton

Criminal Activity History/Involved: Yes, Pendleton's criminal history included numerous arrests for driving with a suspended license and no insurance, as well as more serious charges of domestic assault, assault on a police officer, and fleeing from police officers./Yes, Pendleton refused to comply with the officers who were carrying out a lawful eviction order.

Mental Illness: Pendleton has been "talking crazy"[937] since the COVID pandemic.

Substance Abuse History/Involved: Unknown./None stated.

Race/Sex/Age: Black/Male/41

What prompted the initial contact with the killer? At approximately 2:30 p.m. on May 27, Grand Forks Deputy Sheriff's Cpl. Ron Nord and Sgt. Kelly McLean went to a residence occupied by Salamah Pendleton to enforce a court-ordered eviction on him. When the deputies entered the apartment, Pendleton retreated to a bedroom. After Pendleton disobeyed the sheriff's orders to come out, the deputies went into the room and were immediately fired upon by Pendleton. Pendleton's mother, Lola Moore was killed in this initial shooting. The deputies retreated and waited for backup, which came in the form of Officer Holte and Cpl. Patrick Torok[938].

Actions taken by subject toward police: As the four officers were coming up with a plan in the living room, Pendleton opened the bedroom door and shot at them all with his AK-47 semiautomatic rifle. Holte was hit three times and died from his wounds while Cpl. Nord was shot in the leg and stomach.

Reactions by the police: The officers returned fire, striking Pendleton several times, and incapacitating him so he was arrested, and the injured officers were given medical attention[939].

How murdered? Officer Holte was shot and killed while assisting the deputy sheriffs evict a subject.

What could have been done differently for the officer to still be alive? Given that Pendleton had already fired upon the deputies, inadvertently killing his mother, the deputies and responding officers should have been behind cover and/or had ballistic shields. They should not have been out in the open where Pendleton could just open the door and shoot them.

Would the officer had been justified to use deadly force before being murdered? The deputies were justified to use deadly force when Pendleton shot at them when they initially entered the bedroom. Responding Officers Holte and Torok were justified to use deadly force immediately upon arriving on the scene.

Outcome for the cop-killer: Pendleton was shot in the exchange of gunfire with the officers, so he was transported to a hospital and has since been charged with two counts of murder, three counts of attempted murder, terrorizing, reckless endangerment, and criminal mischief[940].

Officer: Ogden Police Department, Police Officer Nathan James Lyday
Date: 5/28/2020   **Location:** Ogden, UT
FACTORS (1,2,3,7,15,18,19)
Perpetrator(s) Involved: John Benedict Coleman

Criminal Activity History/Involved: Yes, besides being arrested as a juvenile in 1986, Coleman had a prior charge for illegally carrying weapons in 1994 and domestic battery in 2000[941]./Yes, Coleman had just assaulted his wife and had illegal drugs in the house.[942]

Mental Illness: Unknown.

Substance Abuse History/Involved: Unknown./Yes, Coleman's wife claimed in the 911 call that he had drugs in the house.

Race/Sex/Age: Unknown/Male/53

What prompted the initial contact with the killer? On May 28, Officer Lyday and another Ogden Police Officer responded to a 911 call from John Coleman's wife claiming that Coleman beat her and threatened to kill her. Immediately, upon arrival the officers were met with noncompliance by Coleman who refused to open the storm door, speaking to the officers outside his house while he remained in it. After being confrontational with the officers, Coleman shut that door in their face as well and the officers could be seen on their bodycam discussing their next move[943].

Actions taken by subject toward police: While the officers contemplated what to do next and were not paying attention to the door, Coleman opened the inside door again and shot at them point-blank with a semiautomatic rifle, striking Lyday in the head, killing him instantly.

Reactions by the police: The other officer immediately returned fire at Coleman, forcing him further back into the house. Two nearby adult parole and probation officers responded, and the three officers together engaged Coleman in a gun battle until he stopped shooting[944].

How murdered? Lyday was shot while investigating a domestic-violence call.

What could have been done differently for the officer to still be alive? Given that the officers had reason to believe that Coleman had committed violence against his wife, and she may be inside the house, the officers could have forced their way through the storm door and into the house when the interior door was open while Coleman spoke to them. At the very least, considering the nature of the call, the officers should have kept their eyes on the door and/or retreated to cover while contemplating how to proceed.

Would the officer had been justified to use deadly force before being murdered? The officers were justified to use force to gain compliance from Coleman but were not justified to use deadly force until it was too late, and Coleman preemptively targeted them with his rifle.

Outcome for the cop-killer: Coleman was fatally shot in the gun battle with the officers and was found dead when SWAT searched the house.

Miscellaneous: There is remarkably little reported on Coleman.

Officer: Fort Bend County Constable's Office, Deputy Constable Caleb Daniel Rule
Date: 5/29/2020   **Location:** Sugar Land, TX
FACTORS (10,16,19)
Perpetrator(s) Involved: Fort Bend County Sheriff's Deputy Chadwick Devin McRae

Criminal History/Involved: NA.

Mental Illness: NA.

Substance Abuse History/Involved: NA.

Race/Sex/Age: Black/Male/49

What prompted the initial contact with the killer? At approximately 1:45 a.m. on May 28, Deputy Constable Rule, Deputy Sheriff McRae and two other deputies responded to a 911 call of suspicious activity at a vacant house. Upon finding the back door to the house open, the four officers entered and began clearing the house room by room[945].

Actions taken by subject toward police: While searching the house, Deputy McRae heard a sound that he thought was a prowler and opened fire in that direction. The prowler ended up being Deputy Constable Rule who despite wearing a bulletproof vest, was fatally struck in the chest by McRae's bullet[946].

Reactions by the police: Rule was medically evacuated to a hospital where he died.

How murdered? Rule was inadvertently shot by a fellow law enforcement officer who mistook Rule for a burglar but did not visually identify him before firing his weapon.

What could have been done differently for the officer to still be alive? NA. Rule could not account for McRae blindly discharging his weapon without seeing an actual physical threat. Aware that he was not the only officer searching the house, McRae should have kept his trigger finger out of the trigger guard and been much more restrained in firing his weapon at the mere sound of a suspicious noise.

Would the officer had been justified to use deadly force before being murdered? NA.

Outcome for the cop-killer: Deputy McRae was fired and had subsequently been indicted by a grand jury for criminally negligent homicide. The indictment states that McRae caused the death of Caleb Rule by "firing a deadly weapon, namely a firearm, in the direction of the complainant without visually checking the area where he was firing"[947].

Police Officer Michael S. Mosher

Overland Park Police Department, Kansas

End of Watch Sunday, May 3, 2020

Police Officer Cody N. Holte

Grand Forks Police Department, North Dakota

End of Watch Wednesday, May 27, 2020

Police Officer Nathan James Lyday

Ogden Police Department, Utah

End of Watch Thursday, May 28, 2020

Deputy Constable Caleb Daniel Rule

Fort Bend County Constable's Office - Pct 4, TX

End of Watch Friday, May 29, 2020

Officer: Detroit Police Department, Police Officer Waldis "Jay" Johnson
Date: 5/31/2020   **Location:** Detroit, MI
FACTORS (1,7,9,14,15,19)
Perpetrator(s) Involved: James Edward Ray

Criminal Activity History/Involved: Yes, Ray had 2009 DWI conviction[948]./No, Ray was not involved in the 911 call or wanted for a crime until he attacked the officers during this incident.

Mental Illness: Unknown.

Substance Abuse History/Involved: Unknown./None stated.

Race/Sex/Age: Black/Male/46

What prompted the initial contact with the killer? At approximately 11:45 p.m. on April 30, 2017, Officer Johnson and his partner Darren Weathers responded to a 911 call about a domestic incident at an apartment building. Since the common access door to the building was locked, the officers knocked and kicked the door to get the callers attention[949].

Actions taken by subject toward police: James Ray, also a tenant in the building but not involved in the 911 call, heard the officer's trying to get in. Ray opened the common door for them and unexpectedly pointed a .380-caliber handgun at Officer Johnson. After initially struggling over control for Ray's gun, Johnson let go to access his duty weapon and Ray seized the moment and shot Johnson in the head[950].

Reactions by the police: Simultaneously as he was being shot, Officer Johnson succeeded in shooting Ray twice. Johnson's partner, too, fired and fatally struck Ray, ending the surprise attack.

How murdered? Officer Johnson was ambushed and shot point-blank by a subject uninvolved with a domestic incident Johnson was responding to.

What could have been done differently for the officer to still be alive? Officer Johnson was attacked by someone it looked like was helping the police gain access to the building. When that perpetrator unexpectedly pulled a gun on Johnson, Johnson was able to at least grab it and fight for control. Johnson made a judgment call that he was better off letting go of Ray's gun to access his own weapon. The only possible way it could have ended differently is if Officer Meadows had a clean shot at Ray, but that is not likely since Ray and Johnson were engaged in a physical struggle.

Would the officer had been justified to use deadly force before being murdered? No, prior to Ray pointing a gun at Officer Johnson, Johnson had no reason to believe that Ray was a threat.

Outcome for the cop-killer: Ray was justifiably shot and killed by Johnson's partner, Officer Darren Weathers[951].

Miscellaneous: Johnson and his family endured three years of rehabilitation and medical treatment for the traumatic brain injury sustained in the shooting.

Officer: Moody Police Department, Lieutenant Stephen P. Williams
Date: 6/2/2020   **Location:** Moody, AL
FACTORS (1,2,3,6,7,15,19)
Perpetrator(s) Involved: Tapero Corlene Johnson; Marquisha Annissa Tyson

Criminal Activity History/Involved: None reported./Yes, the two perpetrators set up an ambush for responding police officers.

Mental Illness: None stated.

Substance Abuse History/Involved: Unknown./Yes, marijuana was found at the scene[952].

Race/Sex/Age: Johnson: Black/Male/27; Tyson: Black/Female/28

What prompted the initial contact with the killer? At approximately 9:30 p.m. on June 2, Lt. Williams and a trainee officer responded to a motel to investigate a 911 call from a woman, Marquisha Tyson, in room 222 saying that she was fearful of some men outside the room[953].

Actions taken by subject toward police: Surveillance video and the trainee officer's testimony illustrate that as soon as Lt. Williams knocked on the door to room 222, he was shot by someone inside the room. That someone was Tapero Johnson[954].

Reactions by the police: Though his wounds proved fatal, Lt. Williams managed to return fire through the door after being shot. Numerous officers responded and an hours-long standoff ensued during which more than 40 shots came from inside the motel room.

How murdered? Lt. Williams was ambushed by a man who shot him from inside a motel room while Williams responded to the fake 911 call placed by a woman to set up the ambush[955].

What could have been done differently for the officer to still be alive? NA, Lt. Williams was conducting his job and investigating a 911 call from a complainant who had asked for police assistance. The only thing Lt. Williams could have done that might have prevented him from being shot is to stand to the side of the door when/after he knocked.

Would the officer had been justified to use deadly force before being murdered? No, Lt. Williams was shot by Johnson while Johnson was inside the motel room, and Williams knocked on the door to investigate the 911 call placed from Johnson's room. Williams never saw a threat until he was shot.

Outcome for the cop-killer: After an hours-long exchange of gunfire and standoff, Johnson and Tyson were taken into custody and both face charges of capital murder.

Miscellaneous: Alabama Attorney General Steven Marshall (R) was quick to state, "At this point, we have no reason to believe that Sergeant Williams's shooting is related to the unrest we're witnessing across the nation"[956]. This remark flies in the face of the level of anti-police rhetoric in America a week after the Floyd incident, the fact that neither of the subjects are reported as having a criminal record, and their premeditated ambush on the officers.

Officer: Alexander Police Department Officer Scott Hutton
Date: 6/3/2020   **Location:** Alexander, AR
FACTORS (7,10,16)
Perpetrator(s) Involved: Calvin Nicholas "Nick" Salyers

Criminal Activity History/Involved: Unknown./None prior to the shooting.

Mental Illness: None reported.

Substance Abuse History/Involved: Unknown./None reported.

Race/Sex/Age: White/Male/33

What prompted the initial contact with the killer? At approximately 7:09 p.m. on June 3, Officer Hutton went to off-duty Alexander Police Officer Calvin Salyers' house to retrieve a patrol vehicle for his upcoming shift. Getting no response from calling and texting Salyers, Officer Hutton walked up to Salyers' front door and knocked on it.

Actions taken by subject toward police: Given the anti-police violence since George Floyd's death, and concerned the person at his door was there to do him harm, Salyers answered the door with his Glock .40-caliber pistol in hand. After seeing a person wearing a gun through his door's peephole, Salyers "transferred his weapon from his right hand into his left hand and reached for the doorknob and, as he opened the door, the gun went off, firing a round through the front door"[957]. Officer Hutton was struck in the chest by that bullet and fell to the ground.

Reactions by the police: After seeing the man fall to the ground, Salyers recognized him to be his fellow officer, Scott Hutton and called 911. The medical personnel responded, but they could not save the mortally wounded Hutton.

How murdered? Officer Hutton was fatally shot by a coworker while picking up his patrol car.

What could have been done differently for the officer to still be alive today? Nothing, whether it was an accidental discharge or something more sinister, there is nothing officer Hutton should have done differently.

Would the officer had been justified to use deadly force before being murdered? No, Officer Hutton was for all intents, ambushed while contacting a "friendly".

Outcome for the cop-killer: Though Salyers claimed that it was an accidental discharge, forensic evidence of gunpowder burns, and residue showed that "Salyers had his Glock pressed against the door when he fired it"[958]. Additionally, prior to this shooting when Salyers said he would ""shoot through the door" if any protesters showed up at his home," a supervisor reprimanded him and advised that would be "reckless and negligent"[959]. Salyers was arrested and charged with felony manslaughter.

Officer: Santa Cruz County Sheriff's Office, Sergeant Damon Gutzwiller
Date: 6/6/2020   **Location:** Santa Cruz, CA
FACTORS (1,2,6,7,8,15,19)
Perpetrator(s) Involved: Steven Carrillo

Criminal Activity History/Involved: Yes, Carrillo was charged with the murder of Federal LEO Patrick Underwood on May 29, 2020[960]./Yes, Carrillo ambushed officers responding to a 911 call of his suspicious van containing illegal explosives.

Race/Sex/Age: Latino/Male/32

What prompted the initial contact with the killer? At approximately 1:30 p.m. on June 6, Sgt. Gutzwiller and other LEO's responded to a 911 call about a suspicious van with firearms and bomb-making devices inside it. Upon arriving at the location, officers observed a man, Steven Carrillo, in the van who then drove away so they followed[961].

Actions taken by subject toward police: Carrillo drove the van to his house and then ambushed the officers as they arrived in his driveway, throwing improvised explosive devices at them, and shooting Sgt. Gutzwiller and Deputy Alex Spencer in the chest and another officer in the hand with a semiautomatic rifle. Carrillo then drove off in another vehicle, striking Deputy Spencer as he did so[962].

Reactions by the police: One of the officers managed to shoot Carrillo in the leg. As medical attention was rendered to the injured officers, other LEOs searched for the injured Carrillo and found him being subdued by a nearby civilian.

How murdered? Sgt. Gutzwiller was ambushed when following a subject operating a suspicious vehicle.

What could have been done differently for the officer to still be alive? Given the nature of the call about the van the officers had to pursue it. It is a judgment call to follow into the driveway and hope to catch the subject before he can run in and set up in the house or stop on the street and make a perimeter.

Would the officer had been justified to use deadly force before being murdered? Since the 911 call stated there were firearms and bomb-making devices in the vehicle, responding officers had reasonable cause to believe that they were facing a deadly threat and were therefore justified to use deadly force at the slightest provocative motion by the driver–but they were ambushed and did not get the chance to.

Outcome for the cop-killer: Injured during the initial ambush on the officers, Carrillo was subdued until police arrived by a local resident he tried to carjack. Carrillo faced numerous felony charges including murder, attempted murder, and carjacking[963].

Miscellaneous: Carrillo's Facebook posts showed that the recent George Floyd incident made him upset at "racist" white people and the "fascist" police, posting on May 31, "I'll never let racist white people make me forget about the dope white people I know exist. I love y'all" and then on June 5, "Who need antifa to start riots when you have the police to do it for you…" Upon arrest, Carrillo shouted "This is what I came here to fight. I'm sick of these goddamn police"[964]. Carrillo is reportedly connected to the right wing "Boogaloo Boys" who "believe in armed insurrection and include attacks on the police"[965].

Police Officer Waldis V. "Jay" Johnson

Detroit Police Department, Michigan

End of Watch Sunday, May 31, 2020

Lieutenant Stephen P. Williams

Moody Police Department, Alabama

End of Watch Tuesday, June 2, 2020

Police Officer Scott Hutton

Alexander Police Department, Arkansas

End of Watch Wednesday, June 3, 2020

Sergeant Damon C. Gutzwiller

Santa Cruz County Sheriff's Office, California

End of Watch Saturday, June 6, 2020

Officer: Simpson County Sheriff's Office, Deputy Sheriff James H. Blair
Date: 6/12/2020   **Location:** Mendenhall, MS
FACTORS (1,4,12,14,15)
Perpetrator(s) Involved: Joaquin Steven Blackwell

Criminal Activity History/Involved: Unknown./None stated.

Mental Illness: Yes, Blackwell's family said that he had mental issues. Blackwell was being transported back from a court mandated psychiatric evaluation when he attacked Deputy Blair[966].

Substance Abuse History/Involved: Unknown./None stated.

Race/Sex/Age: Black/Male/22

What prompted the initial contact with the killer? At approximately 3:30 p.m. on June 12, Deputy Blair was transporting Joaquin Blackwell to and from an involuntary psychiatric evaluation[967].

Actions taken by subject toward police: While being escorted back to the deputy's car after the evaluation, Blackwell overpowered Blair, pushing him to the ground, and took his duty weapon and shot him dead before running into the nearby woods[968].

Reactions by the police: Officers were called to the scene of the reported shooting and found Blair on the ground dying from his wounds. Blair was immediately transported to a hospital as other officers started a manhunt for Blackwell[969].

How murdered? Deputy Blair was attacked, disarmed, and murdered with his own weapon while transporting a subject for psychiatric evaluation.

What could have been done differently for the officer to still be alive? Deputy Blair was 77 years old and only still working because he was raising his three grandchildren from his deceased daughter[970]. Even if Deputy Blair exercised good tactics, he was still no match for a younger, stronger, mentally imbalanced subject. Perhaps it was a standard operating procedure, but if Blackwell was not handcuffed–he should have been.

Would the officer had been justified to use deadly force before being murdered? It appears that the older deputy was not able to physically defend himself against the younger aggressor, so no, Deputy Blair never had a chance to use deadly force once Blackwell attacked him.

Outcome for the cop-killer: After an intense manhunt, Blackwell surrendered to authorities the next day and was charged with capital murder.

Officer: Florida Fish and Wildlife Conservation Commission Wildlife Officer Julian Keen, Jr.
Date: 6/14/2020   **Location:** Labelle, FL
FACTORS (1,2,3,8,9,15,20)7?,13?
Perpetrator(s) Involved: Eliceo Hernandez

Criminal Activity History/Involved: No, Hernandez is only reported to have traffic violations in the past three years[971]./Yes, it was Hernandez's unlawful flight from a motor vehicle accident that led to the shooting incident.

Mental Illness: Unknown.

Substance Abuse History/Involved: Unknown./Yes, Hernandez possessed synthetic cannabis upon arrest.

Race/Sex/Age: Latino/Male/20

What prompted the initial contact with the killer? On the morning of June 14, Officer Keen observed a driver, Eliceo Hernandez, drive recklessly and unlawfully flee from a motor vehicle accident. Even though he was off-duty, Officer Keen followed Hernandez's vehicle[972].

Actions taken by subject toward police: At some point both Hernandez and Keen stopped their vehicles and when Keen confronted Hernandez, Hernandez shot him dead[973].

Reactions by the police: Sheriff's deputies responding to 911 calls of the shooting incident arrived at the scene to find Keen dead and the perpetrator gone. An investigation revealed that Hernandez was that perpetrator, and a manhunt was immediately started to find him.[974]

How murdered? Officer Keen was shot and killed when confronting a subject who had just left the scene of an accident.

What could have been done differently for the officer to still be alive? Officer Keen was upholding his oath to serve and protect even while off-duty so he is commended for acting even when he could have turned a blind eye. Keen would have had to have his gun out and ready as well as keep his eyes on Hernandez's hands in order to have reacted swiftly enough once Hernandez went for a gun.

Would the officer had been justified to use deadly force before being murdered? No, Keen was only justified to use the force required to keep Hernandez from leaving until an on-duty officer could arrive and handle the hit-and-run, so without further details it is difficult to know if Keen had a chance to see Hernandez accessing a gun or if he was ambushed at the start.

Outcome for the cop-killer: Hernandez was tracked down and arrested early the next morning. He was charged with second-degree murder with a firearm, attempted second-degree murder discharging a firearm, leaving the scene of an accident, and possession of synthetic cannabis[975].

Officer: Tulsa Police Department, Sergeant Craig Vincent Johnson
Date: 6/30/2020   **Location:** Tulsa, OK
FACTORS (1,2,3,8,9,13,14,15)
Perpetrator(s) Involved: David Anthony Ware

Criminal Activity History/Involved: Yes, Ware was a career criminal with numerous arrests and convictions since his teenage years, including felony burglary, larceny, concealing a weapon, possession of drug paraphernalia, possession of burglars' tools, public intoxication, and domestic assault and battery[976]./Yes, Ware was illegally operating an unregistered motor vehicle and in felony possession of a weapon when stopped.

Substance Abuse History/Involved: Yes, Ware had prior drug-related arrests./Yes, Ware was in possession of illegal drugs during the shooting incident.

Race/Sex/Age: White/Male/32

What prompted the initial contact with the killer? At approximately 3:20 a.m. on June 29, Tulsa Police Officer Aurash Zarkeshan pulled over a vehicle operated by David Ware for an observed traffic infraction and expired plates. Shortly after Sgt. Johnson arrived to assist, both he and Officer Zarkeshan ordered Ware out of the vehicle so it could be towed[977].

Actions taken by subject toward police: Ware refused to exit his vehicle and argued with the officers for nearly ten minutes before Sgt. Johnson finally tased him through the passenger side window. Ware was unaffected by the taser and continued disobeying the officer's commands, so Johnson went around to the driver's side and pepper sprayed Ware, again to no avail. When both officers then tried to physically pull Ware out of the vehicle, Ware grabbed a gun from under the steering wheel area and shot Johnson and then Zarkeshan point-blank several times before taking off running. At least one of the bullets went through Johnson's body armor and into his chest. Zarkeshan was critically injured, and Johnson died from his wounds the next day[978].

Reactions by the police: Responding officers immediately started searching for Ware and were able to take him into custody the next day without further bloodshed.

How murdered? Sgt. Johnson was shot and killed while assisting on a traffic stop.

What could have been done differently for the officer to still be alive? Sgt. Johnson ran through the use of force continuum using the taser, pepper spray and physical force to try and remove Ware from the vehicle. The only thing Johnson and Zarkeshan did not do that may have prevented the shooting would have been to strike Ware in the head with their flashlight to knock him out and drag him out of the car.

Would the officer had been justified to use deadly force before being murdered? Yes, either of the officers could have justifiably used deadly force upon seeing Ware reaching around inside his vehicle after refusing to obey with their command's multiple times. The officers also could have used physical force such as strikes to his head with their ASP or flashlight.

Outcome for the cop-killer: Ware was arrested and charged with one count each of murder, shooting with intent to kill, drug possession with intent to distribute, and possession of a firearm after a felony conviction[979].

Officer: Toledo Police Department, Police Officer Anthony Dia
Date: 7/4/2020   **Location:** Toledo, OH
FACTORS (1,2,3,4,5,9,15,19)
Perpetrator(s) Involved: Edward Henry

Criminal Activity History/Involved: Yes, Henry had prior charges of felony assault, felony drug possession, resisting arrest, obstructing police, several DWI's, public intoxication, public indecency, and menacing[980]./Yes, Henry was publicly intoxicated, harassing a group of people in the parking lot and had active warrants[981].

Mental Illness: None reported; however, suicide and substance abuse are key indicators.

Substance Abuse History/Involved: Yes, Henry had previous arrests for public intoxication and DWI./Yes, Henry was reported to be holding a beer and intoxicated at the time of the incident.

Race/Sex/Age: White/Male/57

What prompted the initial contact with the killer? Shortly after midnight on July 4, 2020, Officer Dia responded to a 911 call about an intoxicated man holding a beer and harassing people in the parking lot of Home Depot. Upon arriving at the scene, Dia observed the intoxicated man, Edward Henry, and approached him asking if he was okay[982].

Actions taken by subject toward police: Henry ignored Officer Dia's questions and was reported to be walking away from Dia when he suddenly turned and fired a single shot at Dia, penetrating through his body armor and into his chest[983].

Reactions by the police: Though fatally wounded, Dia immediately returned fire at Henry who then took off running into a nearby wooded area. Responding officers took Dia to the hospital, where he was declared dead, while other officers set up a perimeter and searched for Henry[984].

How murdered? Officer Dia was ambushed while investigating a simple disturbance call of an intoxicated man harassing people in a parking lot.

What could have been done differently for the officer to still be alive? As Dia's Police Chief, George Kral reiterated, "Officer Dia did everything "perfectly" that night"–Edward Henry's sudden and accurate shot was "dumb luck"[985]. A disturbance call with an intoxicated subject is not likely to escalate from the subject walking away to him quickly turning around and landing a surprise kill shot, and yet here it did. This is another example of why cops may seem on the edge when dealing with what should be a low-threat situation, because the officer never knows when that low-threat situation and seemingly harmless person will be the cause of their death.

Would the officer had been justified to use deadly force before being murdered? No, before Henry turned around and shot Officer Dia, all he had done was act like a stupid drunk, harassing some people in the parking lot and walking away from the officer.

Outcome for the cop-killer: After running into a wooded area nearby the Home Depot parking lot, Henry took his own life with a gunshot to the head as the police searched for him.

Deputy Sheriff James H. Blair

Simpson County Sheriff's Office, Mississippi

End of Watch Friday, June 12, 2020

Wildlife Officer Julian L. Keen, Jr.

Florida Fish &Wildlife Cons. Comm., Florida

End of Watch Sunday, June 14, 2020

Sergeant Craig Vincent Johnson

Tulsa Police Department, Oklahoma

End of Watch Tuesday, June 30, 2020

Police Officer Anthony H. Dia

Toledo Police Department, Ohio

End of Watch Saturday, July 4, 2020

Officer: McAllen Police Department, Police Officer Ismael Chavez, Jr.
Date: 7/11/2020   **Location:** McAllen, TX
FACTORS (1,2,3,4,5,7,15,18,19)
Perpetrator(s) Involved: Audon Ignacio Camarillo

Criminal Activity History/Involved: Yes, Camarillo had prior arrests for assault, fleeing an officer, possession of marijuana, liquor violations, and DWI[986]./Yes, Camarillo's domestic assault of his mother prompted the 911 call.

Mental Illness: None stated, though suicide is a key indicator of mental issues.

Substance Abuse History/Involved: Yes, Camarillo had prior alcohol- and marijuana-related arrests./Yes, Camarillo was reportedly drunk and on drugs during the time of the incident.

Race/Sex/Age: Latino/Male/23

What prompted the initial contact with the killer? At 3:30 p.m. on July 11, Officers Chavez and Garza responded to a 911 call of a man, Audon Camarillo, who was drunk and/or on drugs and had just assaulted his mother. After making contact with the caller outside and away from the incident location, the officers approached the house at 3:51 p.m. to speak with Camarillo[987].

Actions taken by subject toward police: As Officers Chavez and Garza approached the house, waiting for them by the door was Camarillo who opened fire and killed them both before they could access their duty weapons or radios. The officers were both shot at close range above their shoulders.

Reactions by the police: Other officers who responded to the call as backup were shocked to find Officers Chavez and Garza dead in front of the house. Those officers found and confronted an armed Camarillo who they ordered to drop his weapon. Camarillo instead raised it to his head and took his own life[988].

How murdered? Officers Chavez and Garza were ambushed by a domestic violence suspect when approaching the house to speak with him.

What could have been done differently for the officer to still be alive? Besides not performing their duty and answering the call or requesting a SWAT team to assist in what should have been an uneventful domestic violence arrest, as McAllen Police Chief Victor Rodriguez said, "The officers never had a chance to suspect deadly assault on them"[989]. They could have approached the house with weapons drawn and separated, but the public and department policies around the country has made it clear that they do not want officers brandishing their weapons unless facing a known imminent threat.

Would the officer had been justified to use deadly force before being murdered? No, it appears that the officers could not clearly see Camarillo, so they had no idea that he was armed and ready to shoot them as they approached his house.

Outcome for the cop-killer: Camarillo killed himself when confronted by the officers who responded to the scene shortly after he ambushed and killed Officers Garza and Chavez.

Officer: McAllen Police Department, Police Officer Edelmiro Garza, Jr.
Date: 7/11/2020   **Location:** McAllen, TX
FACTORS (1,2,3,4,5,7,15,18,19)
Perpetrator(s) Involved: Audon Ignacio Camarillo

Criminal Activity History/Involved: Yes, Camarillo had prior arrests for assault, fleeing an officer, possession of marijuana, liquor violations, and DWI[990]./Yes, Camarillo's domestic assault of his mother prompted the 911 call.

Mental Illness: None stated, though suicide is a key indicator of mental illness.

Substance Abuse History/Involved: Yes, Camarillo had prior alcohol- and marijuana-related arrests./Yes, Camarillo was reportedly drunk and on drugs during the time of the incident.

Race/Sex/Age: Latino/Male/23

What prompted the initial contact with the killer? At 3:30 p.m. on July 11, Officers Chavez and Garza responded to a 911 call of a son, Audon Camarillo, who was drunk and/or on drugs and had just assaulted his mother. After making contact with the caller outside and away from the incident location, the officers approached the house at 3:51 p.m. to speak with Camarillo.

Actions taken by subject toward police: As Officers Chavez and Garza approached the house, waiting for them at the door was Camarillo who opened fire and killed them both before they could access their duty weapons or radios. The officers were both shot at close range above their shoulders[991].

Reactions by the police: Other officers who responded to the call as backup were shocked to find Officers Chavez and Garza dead in front of the house. Those officers found and confronted an armed Camarillo who they ordered to drop his weapon. Camarillo instead raised it to his head and took his own life[992].

How murdered? Officers Chavez and Garza were ambushed by a domestic violence suspect when approaching the house to speak with him.

What could have been done differently for the officer to still be alive? Besides not performing their duty and answering the call or requesting a SWAT team to assist in what should have been an uneventful domestic violence arrest–as McAllen Police Chief Victor Rodriguez said, "The officers never had a chance to suspect deadly assault on them"[993]. They could have approached the house with weapons drawn and separated, but the public and department policies around the country has made it clear that they do not want officers brandishing their weapons unless facing a known imminent threat.

Would the officer had been justified to use deadly force before being murdered? No, it appears that the officers could not clearly see Camarillo, so they had no idea that he was armed and ready to shoot them as they approached his house.

Outcome for the cop-killer: Camarillo killed himself when confronted by the officers who responded to the scene shortly after he ambushed and killed Officers Garza and Chavez.

Officer: Bothell Police Department, Police Officer Jonathan Shoop
Date: 7/13/2020   **Location:** Bothell, WA
FACTORS (1,2,3,4,6,8,10,13,16)
Perpetrator(s) Involved: Henry Eugene Washington

Criminal Activity History/Involved: Yes, Washington's criminal history spreads over three states and goes back to 1997. Between Texas, Kansas, and Arizona, Washington had convictions and charges for assault, domestic violence, evading arrest, possession of marijuana, felony drug possessions, criminal threat causing terror, assault of a LEO, eluding police, violation of a protective order, interference with law enforcement, stalking, aggravated intimidation of a witness, and disorderly conduct[994]./Yes, Washington illegally possessed a firearm and marijuana.

Mental Illness: Yes, Washington's mother claims that he had a history of mental illness and had probably not been taking his medication. Washington "rambled about voices in his head"[995] and is reportedly homeless.

Substance Abuse History/Involved: Yes, Washington had prior drug arrests./Yes, Washington feared that the officers would take the weed he had in the car.

Race/Sex/Age: Black/Male/37

What prompted the initial contact with the killer? At 9:40 p.m. on July 13, Officer Jonathan Shoop and Training Officer Mustafa Kumcur initiated a traffic stop on a vehicle operated by Henry Washington for not having a license plate. After initially stopping for the officers, as Shoop approached his vehicle, Washington drove off, striking a man driving a scooter, breaking his leg, and then crashing into a median. As Washington paced outside his vehicle, the officers caught up to him[996].

Actions taken by subject toward police: Upon seeing the officers patrol SUV, Washington cursed "Come on Pigs!,"[997] advancing toward their SUV as he fired two rounds, one of which struck Kumcur in the arm and head.

Reactions by the police: Taking fire from Washington while in their SUV, both officers returned fire, shooting at least nine times at Washington. Washington took off running and hid out for five hours before becoming trapped between two buildings and getting arrested when he called 911 for help. None of the bullets hit Washington but Shoop was caught in the crossfire and died when one of Kumcur's bullets struck his head[998].

How murdered? Officer Shoop was killed by friendly fire when his patrol SUV came under fire from a motorist he attempted to pull over for a minor traffic infraction.

What could have been done differently for the officer to still be alive? Nothing, Officer Shoop did everything right; he could not have protected himself from his partner's friendly fire.

Would the officer had been justified to use deadly force before being murdered? Yes, upon seeing Washington holding a gun outside his vehicle, they would have been justified.

Outcome for the cop-killer: Washington was charged with aggravated first-degree murder, attempted first-degree murder, assault, resisting arrest, and vehicular assault.

Officer: Puerto Rico Police Department, Sergeant Ricardo Perez-Ortiz
Date: 8/24/2020   **Location:** San Juan, Puerto Rico
FACTORS (1,2,7,8,11,13,15,20)
Perpetrator(s) Involved: Unknown.

Criminal Activity History/Involved: Unknown./It appears numerous weapons and motor-vehicle related laws were broken during the commission of this assassination.

Mental Illness: Unknown.

Substance Abuse History/Involved: Unknown./Unknown.

Race/Sex/Age: Unknown.

What prompted the initial contact with the killer? At approximately 11:50 p.m. on April 30, 2020, while in uniform and on his way to work at police headquarters, Sgt. Perez-Ortiz's personal car was surrounded by a "gang of people riding off-road vehicles and motorcycles"[999]. The gang of vehicles forced Sgt. Perez to bring his vehicle to a complete stop.

Actions taken by subject toward police: As Sgt. Perez's vehicle was boxed in and at a standstill, at least one of the riders shot him four times with a .40-caliber gun[1000].

Reactions by the police: Officers arriving to the scene rushed Sgt. Perez to a hospital where he suffered for nearly four months before dying from his gunshot wounds on August 24.

How murdered? Sgt. Perez was boxed in on a highway and assassinated by a gang of motorists.

What could have been done differently for the officer to still be alive? Being in a larger, more powerful motor vehicle, Sgt. Perez could have refused to slow down and stop for the motorcycles and ATV's that boxed him in. Undoubtedly if Sgt. Perez did this, he would face media scrutiny, and possible departmental and/or criminal charges, though, in hindsight it is clear that his actions would have been justified.

Would the officer had been justified to use deadly force before being murdered? Yes, as those who have served overseas in combat can attest, motorists trying to box in a vehicle is a technique used to ambush or kidnap public figures so deadly force would be justified to prevent from being boxed in.

Outcome for the cop-killer: The identified suspect is still at large.

Miscellaneous: During the few months Sgt. Perez was in critical condition in the hospital, he provided homicide investigators enough information for them to identify a suspect who authorities are currently searching for.

Police Officer Ismael Z. Chavez

McAllen Police Department, Texas

End of Watch Saturday, July 11, 2020

Police Officer Edelmiro Garza, Jr.

McAllen Police Department, Texas

End of Watch Saturday, July 11, 2020

Police Officer Jonathan P. Shoop

Bothell Police Department, Washington

End of Watch Monday, July 13, 2020

Sergeant Ricardo Perez-Ortiz

Puerto Rico Police Department, Puerto Rico

End of Watch Monday, August 24, 2020

Officer: Tohono O'odham Nation Police Department, Police Officer Bryan Brown
Date: 8/27/2020   **Location:** Why, AZ
FACTORS (1,2,3,8,11,12,13,19)
Perpetrator(s) Involved: Carlos Maximilliano Galvan

Criminal Activity History/Involved: Yes, Galvan has a prior DUI conviction./Yes, Galvan was DUI of illegal drugs and he had stolen an official police vehicle.

Mental Illness: Unknown.

Substance Abuse History/Involved: Yes, Galvan had a prior DUI arrest./Yes, Galvan admitted to being high on methamphetamine at the time of the incident.

Race/Sex/Age: Native American/Male/39

What prompted the initial contact with the killer? At around 9 a.m. on August 27, Officer Brown responded to a 911 call of an erratic and possibly armed motorist. Brown stopped and exited his police vehicle upon arriving and observing a man, Carlos Galvan, on the side of the road and out of his vehicle[1001]. When Brown realized that Galvan was holding a broken bottle in his hand, Brown started backing away from Galvan.

Actions taken by subject toward police: As Officer Brown backed away from his own police cruiser and Galvan, Galvan jumped into the police vehicle and drove off. Rather than simply drive away, Galvan turned around and drove straight at Brown causing Brown to fire several shots at him before Galvan ran him over[1002].

Reactions by the police: Nearby Border Patrol Agents and another Nation's Police Officer took Galvan into custody after he rammed their vehicles and finally came to a stop.

How murdered? Officer Brown was intentionally run over by the suspect while investigating a 911 call of an erratic driver on the highway.

What could have been done differently for the officer to still be alive? As a LEO, Officer Brown did not have a duty to retreat, and, as such, when Galvan approached him with a broken bottle in his hand, Brown should have warned him to stop, and if Galvan did not stop, Brown should have shot Galvan until he no longer posed a threat.

Would the officer had been justified to use deadly force before being murdered? Yes, Brown justifiably shot at Galvan as he was driving toward him, but this is a clear case where Brown could have justifiably used deadly force even earlier than that, thereby preempting the subsequent robbery of his patrol vehicle and his own death.

Outcome for the cop-killer: Galvan was arrested by border patrol agents and faced charges of premeditated murder, felony murder, carjacking resulting in a death, assault on a federal officer, and robbery[1003].

Officer: St. Louis Metropolitan PD, Police Officer Tamarris Leon-Wesley Bohannon
Date: 8/30/2020   **Location:** St. Louis, MO
FACTORS (1,2,7,15,19,21)
Perpetrator(s) Involved: Thomas Kinworthy, Jr.

Criminal Activity History/Involved: Yes, Kinworthy is a career criminal with numerous drug-related convictions in the early 90s; had served 6.5 years for an aggravated battery with firearm conviction in 1998; and had a conviction for exposing himself in 2009. More recently, Kincaid was charged in 2020 in Florida with attempted sexual battery, kidnapping, and aggravated assault with a firearm. He received additional charges after firearms and ammunition were discovered during the execution of a search warrant[1004][1005]./Yes, Kinworthy had an active felony warrant from Florida, and either fired the shots prompting the 911 call or made the call to ambush responding officers.

Substance Abuse History/Involved: Yes, Kinworthy had prior drug-related arrests./None.

Race/Sex/Age: White/Male/43

What prompted the initial contact with the killer? At about 6 p.m. on August 29, Officers Bohannon and Arlando Bailey were searching for an injured man reported by a 911 caller of a shooting that just occurred[1006].

Actions taken by subject toward police: Observing the officers arrive while they were unaware of his presence hidden inside a house he had just taken over in a home invasion, Thomas Kinworthy gunned them down through a window, fatally striking Officer Bohannon in the head and Officer Bailey in the leg[1007].

Reactions by the police: Patrol and SWAT officers surrounded the house, exchanged gunfire with Kinworthy and shot tear gas into the house before he eventually surrendered without any other officers being injured. Officers Bohannon and Bailey were both rushed to the hospital where Bohannon died the next day and Bailey was released[1008].

How murdered? Officer Bohannon was ambushed and murdered by a gunman hidden inside a house while Bohannon searched the area for a victim of a 911 call reporting a shooting.

What could have been done differently for the officer to still be alive? Nothing, Officer Bohannon was doing his job, and there was no way for him or Officer Bailey to know that a gunman was hiding inside a house, targeting them as they were outside and looking to help a possible gunshot victim.

Would the officer had been justified to use deadly force before being murdered? NA, Officer Bohannon never saw Kinworthy.

Outcome for the cop-killer: After a 12-hour standoff while being barricaded inside a house he took over; Kincaid surrendered and was arrested. Kincaid has been charged with first-degree murder, first-degree-assault of a law enforcement officer, first-degree burglary, three counts of armed criminal action, resisting/interfering with arrest, and unlawful possession of a firearm[1009].

Miscellaneous: Florida Law Enforcement warned that Kinworthy was a dangerous man, but after a judge released him on $15,000, he fled from Florida and brought his carnage to Missouri.

Officer: Cleveland Division of Police, Detective James M. Skernivitz
Date: 9/3/2020   **Location:** Cleveland, OH
FACTORS (1,2,7,8,9,15)
Perpetrator(s) Involved: David McDaniel; Kevin Robinson; Unnamed juvenile

Criminal Activity History/Involved: Yes, the teens had prior "traffic cases and other minor crime"[1010]./Yes, the teens were attempting an armed robbery before they opened fire on Det. Skernivitz.

Mental Illness: Unknown.

Substance Abuse History/Involved: Unknown./None stated.

Race/Sex/Age: McDaniel: Black/Male/18; Robinson:Black/Male/17; Unnamed: Unknown/Male/15

What prompted the initial contact with the killer? At approximately 10 p.m. on September 3, while Detective Skernivitz sat in his unmarked police car with an informant preparing to conduct an undercover drug deal, three young males approached the vehicle[1011].

Actions taken by subject toward police: In an apparent attempted robbery gone badly, the three youths opened fire on Det. Skernivitz and his informant, killing them both. The suspects "knew or had reasonable cause to know [James Skernivitz] was a law enforcement officer"[1012].

Reactions by the police: There were no other officers in the area, so when it was discovered that Det. Skernivitz was shot, he was rushed for medical attention while other officers reviewed surveillance video and canvassed the area[1013].

How murdered? Det. Skernivitz was ambushed and shot in his chest while sitting in an unmarked police car as part of an undercover drug operation.

What could have been done differently for the officer to still be alive? While engaged in an undercover drug operation Det. Skernivitz was extremely vulnerable, because to have backup nearby could have given away his cover. Skernivitz would have had to profile the behavior of the three teenagers and had his gun discretely pointed at the youths, so he was ready to fire as soon as he saw them pull out a gun.

Would the officer had been justified to use deadly force before being murdered? NA, Det. Skernivitz was essentially ambushed and unable to return fire.

Outcome for the cop-killer: McDaniel was indicted on four counts of aggravated murder, two counts each of murder, aggravated robbery, and felonious assault. Robinson and the 15-year-old have been charged with 11 counts, including aggravated murder, aggravated robbery, and felonious assault[1014] [1015].

Officer: Lincoln Police Department, Investigator Luis "Mario" Herrera
Date: 9/7/2020   **Location:** Lincoln, NE
FACTORS (1,2,13,15,17)
Perpetrator(s) Involved: Felipe Vazquez

Criminal Activity History/Involved: Yes, besides a lengthy juvenile record, in 2020, Vazquez was involved in commercial burglaries in February and a murder in March./Yes, Vazquez had a felony assault warrant, and he illegally possessed the firearm used to shoot Inv. Herrera[1016].

Mental Illness: None stated.

Substance Abuse History/Involved: Unknown./None stated.

Race/Sex/Age: Latino/Male/17

What prompted the initial contact with the killer? At approximately 11:30 a.m. on August 26, Lincoln PD Officers went to the residence of Felipe Vazquez to arrest him for a second-degree assault warrant. The officers were given consent to search the house by Vazquez's parents and located Felipe hiding inside a bedroom with a locked door. For 25 minutes the officers tried to negotiate with Vazquez for a peaceful surrender[1017].

Actions taken by subject toward police: As the officers tried to negotiate with him, Vazquez escaped through a bedroom window he broke and took off running down the street, firing his stolen handgun at the officers stationed in the street. Investigator Herrera was one of those officers and he was struck in the chest by one of the .45-caliber bullets. Herrera was rushed to the hospital, where for 12 days he underwent numerous surgeries before dying from the gunshot wound on September 7.

Reactions by the police: Another officer returned fire at Vazquez but did not hit him. Officers searched the area and found Vazquez hiding in a stranger's house. The .45-caliber gun he used was also recovered[1018].

How murdered? Inv. Herrera was shot and killed by a teenage career criminal who was fleeing his house as officers tried to arrest him for a warrant.

What could have been done differently for the officer to still be alive? Had Inv. Herrera been wearing body armor while executing that warrant, it might have stopped the bullet. It is unknown whether Inv. Herrera was able to see that Vazquez possessed a firearm as he went running from the house and fired at Herrera and his fellow officers. This incident illustrates the importance of cover as well as why officer's demand to see subject's hands.

Would the officer had been justified to use deadly force before being murdered? Vazquez was armed, had a violent felony warrant, and was attempting to escape, so officers would have been justified in using deadly force as soon as he tried to escape. No doubt that the officers did not pre-emptively use deadly force because it would not look good, and now one of their own is dead.

Outcome for the cop-killer: Vazquez was captured shortly afterward trying to hide at another house and faced charges of first-degree murder, use of a firearm to commit a felony, first-degree assault of an officer, possessing a firearm by a fugitive of justice, and escape using force or deadly weapon[1019].

Police Officer Bryan Brown

Tohono O'odham Nation PD, Tribal Police

End of Watch Thursday, August 27, 2020

Police Officer Tamarris Leon-Wesley Bohannon

St. Louis Metropolitan PD, Missouri

End of Watch Sunday, August 30, 2020

Detective James M. Skernivitz

Cleveland Division of Police, Ohio

End of Watch Thursday, September 3, 2020

Investigator L. Mario Herrera

Lincoln Police Department, Nebraska

End of Watch Monday, September 7, 2020

Officer: Henderson County Sheriff's Office, Deputy Sheriff Ryan Phillip Hendrix
Date: 9/10/2020   **Location:** Mountain Home, NC
FACTORS (1,2,8,9,13,15,19,21)
Perpetrator(s) Involved: Robert Ray Doss Jr.

Criminal Activity History/Involved: Yes, Doss' criminal history included drug offenses, larceny, and arson and felony theft in South Carolina, Georgia, Maryland, and Virginia. Doss was currently wanted for a probation and parole violation in South Carolina[1020]./Yes, Doss had just burglarized a car and violently threatened a homeowner with a crowbar and firearm.

Mental Illness: Unknown.

Substance Abuse History/Involved: Yes, Doss had prior drug-related arrests./None stated.

Race/Sex/Age: White/Male/Unknown age

What prompted the initial contact with the killer? At approximately 2:50 a.m. on September 10, Henderson County Deputy Sheriffs responded to a 911 call about a vehicle break-in, which escalated into shots fired between the complainant and criminal. Upon arriving at the scene, three deputies were advised by the homeowner that a man, Robert Ray Doss, Jr., had tried to break into his car, then broken his window with a crowbar, and then exchanged gunfire with him by using a gun stolen from the man's vehicle. The deputies observed Doss sitting in a nearby vehicle and approached him, telling him to show his hands[1021].

Actions taken by subject toward police: Doss made it appear that he was going to comply with the deputies' orders, and then "in one rapid movement, he retrieved the gun, firing one round, striking Deputy Hendrix in the face and critically wounding him"[1022].

Reactions by the police: The other two deputies next to Deputy Hendrix immediately returned fire and killed Doss, before getting Hendrix emergency medical care. Hendrix was transported to a hospital and declared dead later that day.

How murdered? Deputy Hendrix was shot in the face by a suspect who had just shot at a homeowner, whose car he broke into.

What could have been done differently for the officer to still be alive? Given that the 911 call involved shots fired and Doss was believed to be armed and dangerous, at least one of the deputies should have had his duty weapon leveled at Doss' head to immediately use lethal force if Doss made one furtive movement, such as he did in reaching for the firearm and shooting Hendrix.

Would the officer had been justified to use deadly force before being murdered? Yes, any of the three deputies would have been justified in shooting Doss as soon as he disobeyed their lawful order to show his hands and made the sudden movement for the handgun in his vehicle.

Outcome for the cop-killer: Doss was justifiably shot dead by two other deputies at the scene.

Officer: Myrtle Beach Police Department, Police Officer Jacob William Hancher
Date: 10/3/2020   **Location:** Myrtle Beach, SC
FACTORS (1,7,9,15,18,19)4?,5?
Perpetrator(s) Involved: John Derek Aycoth

Criminal Activity History/Involved: No, his only prior run-in with law enforcement was a traffic ticket for not wearing a helmet while operating a motorcycle./No, there was no reported violence in the domestic incident.

Mental Illness: Unknown; however, if he did commit suicide, it would indicate a mental illness.

Substance Abuse History/Involved: None./None stated.

Race/Sex/Age: White/Male/20

What prompted the initial contact with the killer? At approximately 10 p.m. on October 3, Myrtle Beach Officers Jacob Hancher and Tom Vest responded to a 911 call about a domestic disturbance between a woman and her boyfriend, John Aycoth, at an apartment complex[1023].

Actions taken by subject toward police: Aycoth had left the scene but returned approximately the same time as the officers arrived. Without provocation or warning, Aycoth opened fire on both officers, fatally striking Officer Hancher and wounding Corporal Vest[1024].

Reactions by the police: Both officers immediately returned fire, causing Aycoth to flee. Medical attention was rendered to the officers as a search began for Aycoth who was found dead from a gunshot wound shortly after.

How murdered? Officer Hancher was shot and killed upon arriving at a domestic dispute.

What could have been done differently for the officer to still be alive? The domestic dispute at which Officer Hancher arrived was not reported as violent or involving a weapon, and the subject involved had no record of violence or reason to shoot at the officers. Both officers were undoubtedly caught by surprise by the deadly attack. It is uncertain if there was anything they could have done differently.

Would the officer had been justified to use deadly force before being murdered? No, prior to Aycoth attacking the officers, they may not have even known that he was involved, and thus had no justifiable reason to use deadly force.

Outcome for the cop-killer: Aycoth was found dead nearby shortly after the shooting. Authorities are not reporting if it was from an officer's bullet or self-inflicted[1025].

Officer: Pine Bluff Police Department, Detective Kevin Dwaine Collins
Date: 10/5/2020   **Location:** Pine Bluff, AR
FACTORS (1,2,8,9,13,15,17)
Perpetrator(s) Involved: Keshone Quantarious Smith

Criminal Activity History/Involved: Yes, Smith was wanted for a robbery homicide committed during the summer in Georgia[1026]./Yes, Smith was actively evading police and was in felony possession of a firearm.

Mental Illness: Unknown.

Substance Abuse History/Involved: Unknown./None stated.

Race/Sex/Age: Black/Male/19

What prompted the initial contact with the killer? Following up on a tip, officers from the Pine Bluff Police Department's Violent Crime Division responded to an Econo Lodge at around 12:05 p.m. on October 5, to look for Keshone Smith, who was wanted for a robbery and murder in Georgia. Upon seeing a vehicle with a suspect matching Smith's description, the officers approached the vehicle and ordered the two suspects out[1027 1028].

Actions taken by subject toward police: Smith refused to comply with the officer's lawful orders and instead opened fire upon them, fatally striking Det. Collins, injuring Lt. Ralph Isaac, and hitting Officer Kelsey Collins, who was spared injury by his bulletproof vest[1029].

Reactions by the police: The officers returned fire, striking Smith, and his accomplice. The officers and suspects were taken for medical care at a hospital where Det. Collins was declared dead.

How murdered? Det. Collins was fatally shot when requesting a wanted murder suspect exit his vehicle.

What could have been done differently for the officer to still be alive? Given that Smith was wanted for a murder, was considered armed and dangerous, and Violent Crime Division Officers were searching for him, Collins and the other officers who approached Smith in the vehicle should have had their weapons pointed at Smith while making the contact and requesting him to exit the vehicle.

Would the officer had been justified to use deadly force before being murdered? Yes, any of the three officers would have been justified to shoot Smith when he made any furtive actions with his hands while in the vehicle after they ordered him to peacefully surrender and exit.

Outcome for the cop-killer: Smith was shot during the gunfight, taken for medical attention, and then charged with capital murder of Det. Collins[1030].

Officer: Houston Fire Marshall's Office, Investigator Lemuel Delray Bruce
Date: 10/16/2020   **Location:** Houston, TX
FACTORS (1,2,4,5,8,9,13,15)
Perpetrator(s) Involved: Joshua Delacerda

Criminal Activity History/Involved: None./Unknown if Delacerda ended up being the subject committing the arsons.

Mental Illness: None stated, however, suicide is clearly a sign of mental illness.

Substance Abuse History/Involved: Unknown./None stated.

Race/Sex/Age: Latino/Male/30

What prompted the initial contact with the killer? At approximately 3:30 a.m. on October 16, Investigator Bruce and several other Fire Marshall Investigators were conducting surveillance in an area that had recently had numerous vehicle arsons. When Investigator Bruce spotted a vehicle matching the description of a suspect vehicle seen in the area of a previous car fire, he informed the other investigators and started following it[1031].

Actions taken by subject toward police: At some point while Inv. Bruce was following the vehicle, a confrontation with the driver, Joshua Delacerda, ensued, and Delacerda shot Inv. Bruce several times in the head and body[1032].

Reactions by the police: When the other investigators pulled up to Bruce's car, they found him seriously injured in his car and transported him to the hospital where he died soon after. Delacerda was found a block away from Bruce's car, dead from a self-inflicted gunshot[1033].

How murdered? Inv. Bruce was shot by a suspect he was following as part of an arson investigation.

What could have been done differently for the officer to still be alive? Since Bruce radioed for backup, he was not trying to engage Delacerda yet, so Delacerda likely engaged him first. It is also likely that Delacerda surprised Inv. Bruce with a firearm and shot Bruce first, though Bruce managed to draw his weapon and return fire.

Would the officer had been justified to use deadly force before being murdered? Inv. Bruce would have been justified to use deadly force as soon as Delacerda ignored his orders to show his hands and made a furtive movement for what ended up being a deadly weapon.

Outcome for the cop-killer: After the shootout with Inv. Bruce, Delacerda drove a block away and killed himself with his firearm.

Deputy Sheriff Ryan Phillip Hendrix

Henderson County Sheriff's Office, NC

End of Watch Thursday, September 10, 2020

Police Officer Jacob William Hancher

Myrtle Beach Police Department, South Carolina

End of Watch Saturday, October 3, 2020

Detective Kevin Dwaine Collins

Pine Bluff Police Department, Arkansas

End of Watch Monday, October 5, 2020

Investigator Lemuel Delray Bruce

Houston Fire Marshal's Office, Texas

End of Watch Friday, October 16, 2020

Officer: Greenville County Sheriff's Office, Sgt. Conley Jumper
Date: 10/20/2020　　　　**Location:** Greenville County, SC
FACTORS (1,2,3,8,11,12,13,14)
Perpetrator(s) Involved: Ray Kelly

Criminal Activity History/Involved: Yes, Kelly had two prior felony drug convictions in New York as well as an open warrant from there for possession of controlled substances[1034]./Yes, Kelly committed numerous traffic infractions, and he illegally possessed narcotics and a firearm at the time of the stop.

Mental Illness: None stated.

Substance Abuse History/Involved: Yes, Kelly had prior narcotics-related arrests./Yes, Kelly possessed crack cocaine in the vehicle.

Race/Sex/Age: Black/Male/37

What prompted the initial contact with the killer? At approximately 3 p.m. on October 20, Greenville deputies pulled over a speeding Nissan Altima on I-85 operated by Ray Kelly. During the traffic stop, Kelly tried to flee from the deputies after he refused to provide them with his driver's license. Sgt. Jumper arrived upon the scene and attempted to help his fellow deputies as they were physically fighting with Kelly outside his vehicle trying to take him into custody[1035].

Actions taken by subject toward police: Kelly managed to fight off the deputies and got back into his vehicle. Sgt. Jumper continued trying to detain Kelly and became trapped on top of Kelly's vehicle as Kelly intentionally drove the vehicle into a tractor trailer, pinning Sgt. Jumper between the Nissan and truck, ultimately killing him[1036] [1037].

Reactions by the police: Deputies managed to take Kelly into custody after his vehicle crashed into the tractor trailer, killing Sgt. Jumper, and injuring two other deputies as well as Kelly and his passenger.

How murdered? Sgt. Jumper was intentionally driven into a tractor trailer by a subject trying to escape a traffic stop.

What could have been done differently for the officer to still be alive? Sgt. Jumper acted honorably by backing up his deputies and continuing to fight to take a wanted criminal into custody. Sgt. Jumper or one of the deputies could have justifiably shot Kelly once he started driving off with Sgt. Jumper trapped on the vehicle.

Would the officer had been justified to use deadly force before being murdered? Yes, as soon as Kelly got back into his vehicle, he could have justifiably been shot because he could either use it as a deadly weapon just as he did or access a deadly weapon which he did have in the vehicle.

Outcome for the cop-killer: Kelly was arrested at the scene, treated at a hospital for his injuries incurred in the accident, and faced charges of murder, trafficking meth and cocaine, possession of a weapon during a violent crime, resisting arrest with assault and injury, assault and battery high and aggravated, and resisting arrest with a deadly weapon.

Officer: Houston Police Department, Sergeant Harold L. Preston
Date: 10/20/2020 **Location:** Houston, TX
FACTORS (1,2,7,15,18,19,21)
Perpetrator(s) Involved: Elmer Manzano

Criminal Activity History/Involved: Yes, Manzano was an illegal alien who had been arrested for unlawful carrying of a firearm in 1994, felony evading of police in 2002, and had several domestic assault arrests, the last of which in 2001 was a felony./Yes, Manzano illegally possessed a firearm and refused to let his wife into their shared apartment.

Mental Illness: None stated.

Substance Abuse History/Involved: Unknown./None stated.

Race/Sex/Age: Latino/Male/51

What prompted the initial contact with the killer? At approximately 7:55 a.m. on October 20, three Houston police officers responded to a 911 call of domestic violence at an apartment complex. The caller stated that her estranged husband, Elmer Manzano locked her out of the house, and she needed to get some belongings so she could move out[1038].

Actions taken by subject toward police: After speaking with the woman in the parking lot for an hour, the officers were informed by the 14-year-old son that he managed to open the door, but his dad had a gun. About that time Manzano opened fire, fatally striking Sgt. Preston several times in the head and wounding Officer Courtney Waller as well as his own son[1039].

Reactions by the police: The officers returned fire and shot Manzano in the stomach, causing him to retreat inside the house and enabling the officers to be taken to the hospital where Sgt. Preston died[1040].

How murdered? Sgt. Preston was shot and killed while assisting his officers handle a domestic disturbance of a man refusing to let his wife gain entry to their apartment.

What could have been done differently for the officer to still be alive? The whole incident could have been avoided if Manzano had been deported, he illegally entered the US in 1989, and was granted temporary protected status and work authorizations that expired in 2000. During one of Manzano's many run-ins with the law since 2000 he should have been deported. Officers responded to a domestic just days earlier where Manzano threatened his wife with a gun and was found to have bullets in his possession, but he was not arrested or turned over to Immigration[1041].

Would the officer had been justified to use deadly force before being murdered? The first opportunity Sgt. Preston had to use deadly force was after being fired upon by Manzano.

Outcome for the cop-killer: About an hour after shooting Sgt. Preston and once his house was fully surrounded by SWAT officers, Manzano peacefully surrendered and was arrested. He faced state charges of capital murder, attempted capital murder, and aggravated assault. And, as an illegal alien, he faces federal charges of an alien in possession of a firearm and felon in possession of a firearm[1042].

Officer: Mangham Police Department, Police Officer Marshall Waters, Jr.
Date:11/5/2020   **Location:** Richland Parish, LA
FACTORS (1,2,7,8,15)
Perpetrator(s) Involved: Hermandus Dashanski Semien

Criminal Activity History/Involved: Yes, Semien is suspected of committing an armed robbery of a pharmacy while wearing a chipmunk costume a month earlier[1043]/Yes, Semien was driving a stolen vehicle when stopped.

Mental Illness: None stated.

Substance Abuse History/Involved: Unknown; however, Semien's prior robbery of prescription drugs from a pharmacy indicates either personal usage or illegal sales./None stated.

Race/Sex/Age: Black/Male/27

What prompted the initial contact with the killer? At around 1 p.m. on October 17, Officer Waters pulled over a vehicle driven by Hermandus Semien on a Louisiana highway near the Franklin and Richard Parish line[1044].

Actions taken by subject toward police: Right after Officer Waters exited his patrol car to approach Semien's vehicle, Semien shot him once in the stomach below Water's body armor. Semien then fled in the vehicle, crashing it approximately 20 miles away[1045].

Reactions by the police: While responding officers attended to Water's injuries and rushed him to a hospital, other police departments started searching for Semien. Within a couple hours Semien was located and though still armed, he was taken into custody without further incident. Officer Waters ended up having five surgeries but ultimately died from the gunshot wound 19 days later in the hospital[1046][1047].

How murdered? Officer Water's was ambushed as soon as he exited his vehicle during a traffic stop.

What could have been done differently for the officer to still be alive? Since Waters was shot as soon as he exited his vehicle, other than keeping his eyes on Semien as he exited the vehicle and possibly alerting him to the weapon Semien must have been pointing out the window, Waters would have had to run for cover behind his vehicle as soon as he exited. That is not something any officer will commonly do without an identified threat.

Would the officer had been justified to use deadly force before being murdered? No since it appears that Officer Waters did not see the deadly threat in the short time span between exiting his vehicle and getting shot.

Outcome for the cop-killer: Upon being captured, Semien was charged with attempted first-degree murder of a police officer, armed robbery, and theft of a motor vehicle.

Officer: Houston Police Department, Sergeant Sean Rios
Date: 11/9/2020   **Location:** Houston, TX
FACTORS (1,2,8,13,15,20,21)
Perpetrator(s) Involved: Robert Soliz

Criminal Activity History/Involved: Yes, Soliz has had numerous arrests as an adult: possession of marijuana, evading arrest, unlawfully carrying a weapon, making a terroristic threat by threatening to kill his girlfriend, and earlier during February 2020 for unlawfully carrying a weapon in a motor vehicle[1048]./Yes, Soliz was suspected of having just shot at another vehicle during a road-rage incident before shooting Sgt. Rios.

Mental Illness: Unknown.

Substance Abuse History/Involved: Yes, Soliz had prior marijuana-related arrests./None stated.

Race/Sex/Age: Latino/Male/24

What prompted the initial contact with the killer? At approximately 1:30 p.m. on November 9, while driving to work to start his shift, Sgt. Rios took police action after seeing a blue Mercedes operated by Robert Soliz and engaged in an armed road-rage incident[1049].

Actions taken by subject toward police: Soliz fired multiple times at Sgt. Rios, fatally striking him as Rios returned fire. Surveillance video shows that Soliz was then picked up by another man in a pickup truck and fled the scene[1050].

Reactions by the police: A manhunt ensued for Soliz, and officers arrested him during a traffic stop around 3:15 p.m. on November 10[1051].

How murdered? Sgt. Rios was murdered while taking police action against an armed subject committing violence during a road-rage incident.

What could have been done differently for the officer to still be alive? Sgt. Rios could have called the incident in over the radio and trailed the Mercedes from a distance. However, if reports are correct and Sgt. Rios feared that innocent lives were in danger by Soliz' reckless shooting, he could not wait and correctly took immediate police action. If Sgt. Rios observed Soliz firing his weapon, then Rios could have shot Soliz immediately, though that is difficult to do with both vehicles moving.

Would the officer had been justified to use deadly force before being murdered? Yes, Soliz presented a deadly threat to the civilians on the road as well as to Sgt. Rios, so Rios could have used lethal force as his first option.

Outcome for the cop-killer: Soliz has been charged with murder.

Miscellaneous: Soliz was out on a mere $100 bond from his February 2020 arrest for unlawfully carrying a weapon in a motor vehicle, the very same crime he committed the day he fatally shot Sgt. Rios.

Sergeant Conley Jumper

Greenville County Sheriff's Office, South Carolina

End of Watch Tuesday, October 20, 2020

Sergeant Harold L. Preston

Houston Police Department, Texas

End of Watch Tuesday, October 20, 2020

Police Officer Marshall L. Waters, Jr.

Mangham Police Department, Louisiana

End of Watch Thursday, November 5, 2020

Sergeant Sean Sebastian Rios

Houston Police Department, Texas

End of Watch Monday, November 9, 2020

Officer: Helena-West Helena Police Department, Police Officer Travis C. Wallace
Date: 11/12/2020   **Location:** Helena-West Helena, AR
FACTORS (1,2,8,9,13,15,17)
Perpetrator(s) Involved: Latarius Howard

Criminal Activity History/Involved: Yes, Howard was wanted for a November 1 shooting[1052]. Additionally, Helena-West Helena Mayor Kevin Smith said Howard "seemed to be on our suspect list for anything gun-related or violence-related in the community"[1053]./Yes, Howard was trying to flee from the officers who tracked him down and opened fire on them.

Mental Illness: None stated.

Substance Abuse History/Involved: Unknown./None stated.

Race/Sex/Age: Black/Male/29

What prompted the initial contact with the killer? At approximately 4:30 p.m. on November 12, Helena-West Helena police officers responded to the Delta Inn acting on a tip that a shooting suspect, Latarius Howard, was there. Upon spotting Howard in the passenger seat of a SUV about to enter the highway from the hotel, Officer Wallace drove his police car in front of it and blocked it from leaving[1054].

Actions taken by subject toward police: Howard quickly exited the SUV and shot Officer Wallace as he moved toward his police car. Officer Wallace managed to return fire before succumbing to his wounds. Howard got back into the SUV and was driven away by an accomplice[1055].

Reactions by the police: Officers rushed Wallace to the hospital where he later died. After a massive multi-agency manhunt, the U.S. Marshals tracked Howard down to an address in Mississippi, where he surrendered without incident around 6 a.m. the next day[1056].

How murdered? Officer Wallace was shot while attempting to stop a wanted shooting suspect from fleeing a motel parking lot.

What could have been done differently for the officer to still be alive? Since Officer Wallace was driving and Howard was a passenger, there was no way Wallace could have exited his vehicle as quickly as Howard exited his. Officer Wallace was at a tactical disadvantage when he necessarily used his patrol car to block the suspect vehicle. Wallace would have had to immediately draw his weapon and get it sighted on Howard before Howard was able to exit his vehicle.

Would the officer had been justified to use deadly force before being murdered? Yes, Howard was wanted for a recent shooting and should have been considered armed and dangerous. As soon as Howard exited the vehicle with a gun in his hand, Officer Wallace or his partner could have used lethal force.

Outcome for the cop-killer: Howard remains in custody and was charged with capital murder.

Miscellaneous: A hotel employee who witnessed the shooting said "I don't think the officer even saw it coming or even had a chance to defend himself"[1057].

Officer: K9 Sjaak
Date: 11/18/2020   **Location:** La Vergne, TN
FACTORS (1,2,7,8,15)
Perpetrator(s) Involved: Javon Brice

Criminal Activity History/Involved: Unknown./None stated.

Mental Illness: Unknown.

Substance Abuse History/Involved: Unknown./None stated.

Race/Sex/Age: Black/Male/39

What prompted the initial contact with the killer? At approximately noon on November 17, La Vergne Police Officer Justin Darby drove his marked K9 police vehicle out of the police station and onto the roadway[1058].

Actions taken by subject toward police: As soon as Officer Darby's vehicle entered Murfreesboro Road, a vehicle operated by Javon Brice pulled alongside his and opened fire on the officer and his police K9 Sjaak, striking the K9 three times but missing Officer Darby[1059].

Reactions by the police: Unscathed by the ambush and unaware that his K9 was hit, Officer Darby then pursued Brice along with other officers who joined in to an apartment complex. Brice exited his vehicle and shot at the responding officers who returned fire. Brice returned to his vehicle, drove a short distance, and crashed. When officers approached Brice's vehicle, they discovered he had been shot and rushed him to the hospital where he died. K9 Sjaak's injuries were realized about that time, and he was rushed for emergency veterinary care, but unfortunately, he died the following day.

How murdered? K9 Sjaak was shot during an ambush while riding along in the police vehicle.

What could have been done differently for the officer to still be alive? Absolutely nothing. When violent criminals feel emboldened either through constant vilification of police as the enemy or by a criminal justice system that does not hold them accountable, there is nothing to stop them from committing such deadly ambushes upon law enforcement officers.

Would the officer had been justified to use deadly force before being murdered? No, it was an ambush and K9 Sjaak's partner Officer Darby first became aware of the deadly threat after the fact.

Outcome for the cop-killer: Brice was killed during the ensuing shootout with the police.

Miscellaneous: There is remarkably little in the reporting about Javon Brice's criminal and mental history for someone who ambushed a police vehicle and killed a K9 officer in cold blood.

Officer: Charleston Police Department, Patrolman Cassie Marie Johnson
Date: 12/3/2020   **Location:** Charleston, WV
FACTORS (1,2,3,8,9,12,13,14,15,19,21)
Perpetrator(s) Involved: Joshua Marcellus Phillips

Criminal Activity History/Involved: Yes, Phillips had previous arrests for brandishing a firearm, DUI, and was out on bond for his most recent arrest for driving with a revoked license[1060]./Yes, Phillips had just bought drugs and was driving with a revoked license.

Mental Illness: None stated.

Substance Abuse History/Involved: Yes, Phillips was reported to have bought drugs in the past./ Yes, Phillips was in possession of 63 Klonopin pills.

Race/Sex/Age: White/Male/38

What prompted the initial contact with the killer? At approximately 2:45 p.m. on December 3, Officer Johnson responded to a 911 call about an unknown man parking his SUV in the complainant's driveway. Upon arriving at the residence, Officer Johnson tracked down that man to a house across the street where she went next and discovered that the man was Joshua Phillips. Johnson asked for Phillips driver's license and she had him accompany her back to his illegally parked vehicle. Phillips now back inside his vehicle still could not produce a license so Officer Johnson told him to put his hands behind his back and attempted to arrest him[1061 1062].

Actions taken by subject toward police: Instead of complying, Phillips took Johnson's handcuffs from her and threw them in the street. Phillips then put his hand over Johnsons' holstered duty gun so she could not draw it out and shot her five times with a gun he pulled from his waistband[1063].

Reactions by the police: Though one of the bullets struck an artery in her neck, Officer Johnson had freed her weapon from Phillip's grasp and managed to shoot him two times before she fell to the ground. Phillips took off in his vehicle and was captured nearby while Johnson was rushed to a hospital, where she held on for two days before dying from the gunshot wounds[1064].

How murdered? Officer Johnson was shot point-blank by a subject refusing to be arrested for a vehicle and traffic infraction.

What could have been done differently for the officer to still be alive? During the initial struggle reported seen on the video, Officer Johnson could have tased Phillips if she had such less-than-lethal means, or she could have drawn her gun and held him at gun point until backup arrived.

Would the officer had been justified to use deadly force before being murdered? Yes, Officer Johnson could have justifiably shot Phillips during the initial struggle solely based on fear that he may overpower her and take her weapon.

Outcome for the cop-killer: Phillips was hospitalized after being arrested and has since been charged and indicted for first-degree murder.

Miscellaneous: Further investigation revealed that Phillips was at the house to illegally buy prescription drugs that were found in his pocket during the search incident to arrest.

Officer: Mount Holly Police Department, Police Officer Tyler Avery Herndon
Date: 12/11/2020   **Location:** Mount Holly, NC
FACTORS (1,2,13,15,19,21)9?
Perpetrator(s) Involved: Joshua Tyler Funk

Criminal Activity History/Involved: Yes, Funk had a previous felony arrest for larceny in October 2020./Yes, Funk was burglarizing a commercial business.

Mental Illness: Unknown.

Substance Abuse History/Involved: Unknown./None stated.

Race/Sex/Age: White/Male/24

What prompted the initial contact with the killer? At around 3:30 a.m. on December 11, police officers from Mount Holly and Gaston responded to a 911 call of a commercial burglary at a car wash and arcade. Upon arrival at the business, the officers were confronted by the suspect, Joshua Funk[1065].

Actions taken by subject toward police: Funk refused to peacefully comply with the officers and instead shot at them, fatally wounding Officer Herndon[1066].

Reactions by the police: The officers returned fire, ultimately arresting Funk who received minor injuries. Officer Herndon was rushed to a nearby hospital, where he died from his injuries.

How murdered? Officer Herndon was shot while confronting a commercial burglary suspect.

What could have been done differently for the officer to still be alive? Unfortunately handling dangerous 911 calls involving armed suspect's intent on using deadly force against police is a hazard of the job and refusing to show up is not an option. Officer Herndon bravely answered the call and tragically was shot before the suspect could be captured or killed. Details on whether the officers were ambushed or had Funk at gunpoint first have not been reported so it is hard to say. It only takes a matter of seconds for a criminal to draw a gun and take unaimed but deadly shots.

Would the officer had been justified to use deadly force before being murdered? The officers would have been justified in drawing their weapons and pointing them at Funk upon contact with him until he showed his hands were empty. If he were seen to be armed or made a furtive movement for a weapon, they would have been justified to shoot him.

Outcome for the cop-killer: Funk has been indicted for first-degree murder[1067].

Miscellaneous: While the scant reporting does not detail any indications of substance abuse, Funk's recent criminal behavior of a larceny and commercial burglary could be to fund a drug addiction.

Police Officer Travis C. Wallace

Helena-West Helena PD, Arkansas

End of Watch Thursday, November 12, 2020

K9 Sjaak

La Vergne Police Department, Tennessee

End of Watch Wednesday, November 18, 2020

Patrolman Cassie Marie Johnson

Charleston Police Department, West Virginia

End of Watch Thursday, December 3, 2020

Police Officer Tyler Avery Herndon

Mount Holly PD, North Carolina

End of Watch Friday, December 11, 2020

Officer: Concord Police Department, Police Officer Jason Shuping
Date: 12/16/2020   **Location:** Concord, NC
FACTORS (1,2,8,9,13,15,19)
Perpetrator(s) Involved: Jeremy Maurice Daniels

Criminal Activity History/Involved: Yes, Daniels has numerous felony convictions including "creating a counterfeit-controlled substance; possession of a stolen vehicle; attempted armed robbery; conspiracy to armed robbery; and four counts of armed robbery"[1068]; and for assaulting a government official in 2017 for which he only got a year probation./Yes, Daniels attempted two carjacking's and was illegally in possession of a firearm.

Mental Illness: Unknown.

Substance Abuse History/Involved: Unknown; though Daniels does have previous drug-related arrests./None stated.

Race/Sex/Age: Black/Male/29

What prompted the initial contact with the killer? At approximately 10:20 p.m. on December 16, officers from the Concord Police and State Alcohol Law Enforcement responded to a 911 call of an attempted carjacking. After getting a description of the male suspect from the complainant the officers broadcasted it and searched the nearby Sonic restaurant parking lot, where they saw a possible suspect, Jeremy Daniels[1069].

Actions taken by subject toward police: As the officers approached him in the Sonic parking lot, Daniels took out a concealed handgun and opened fire, fatally striking Officer Shuping and injuring Officer Kaleb Robinson. Daniels then attempted to carjack a passing motorist[1070].

Reactions by the police: Additional officers who responded to the scene shot and killed Daniels when they observed him attempting to carjack the vehicle and escape[1071].

How murdered? Officer Shuping was ambushed and shot when tracking down a carjacking suspect.

What could have been done differently for the officer to still be alive? It is not detailed if the officers had their weapons drawn as they approached Daniels, but given that he attempted a carjacking, they should have had because of the nature of his attempted crime. Additionally, the officers could have taken cover behind a vehicle and with their guns drawn on him and ordered Daniels onto the ground.

Would the officer had been justified to use deadly force before being murdered? Yes, the moment Daniels made a furtive movement with his hands toward his waistband, the officers could have justifiably shot him. However, they likely did not, because in today's anti-police atmosphere the officers know if they were wrong and Daniels, a black man, was not going for a weapon, they will be on the front-page news and be indicted. Such a hesitation cost Officer Shuping his life, making him an unfortunate casualty of social justice activism.

Outcome for the cop-killer: Daniels was justifiably shot and killed by the officers during the shootout.

INCONCLUSIVE DETAILS AVAILABLE THAT FELONY CRIME LED TO THIS LOD DEATH

Officer: Birmingham Police Department Officer Randall Versie Smith
Date: 12/28/2020   **Location:** Ensley, AL
FACTORS (10,18,19) NOT INCLUDED IN STATS
Perpetrator(s) Involved: Unnamed male.

Criminal Activity History/Involved: Unknown./Unknown.

Mental Illness: None stated.

Substance Abuse History/Involved: Unknown./None stated.

Race/Sex/Age: Unknown/Male/Unknown

What prompted the initial contact with the killer? On March 22, 1995, at around 3 a.m. police responded to a 911 call about domestic violence involving a young child "left inside the house with an angry gunman"[1072]. Officer Smith went into the house, grabbed the young child, and quickly exited.

Actions taken by subject toward police: The subject stood down long enough for Officer Smith to grab the child and quickly exit the house.

Reactions by the police: Smith's partner, Sgt. Ronnie Hull, heard the disturbance going on inside the house and was rushing inside when he nearly crashed into Smith. During the near collision, Sgt. Hull's gun was accidentally fired, striking Officer Smith in the head, leaving him permanently disabled until he died from it 25 years later[1073].

How murdered? Officer Smith was accidentally shot by a fellow officer on a domestic violence 911 call.

What could have been done differently for the officer to still be alive? Officer Smith did a great job of averting a disaster by quickly removing the child from a volatile situation. The only thing that could have been done differently was for Sgt. Hull to have better control over his weapon. Even then, it is possible that Sgt. Hull had his trigger finger out of his trigger guard and the near collision caused his finger to inadvertently get inside the guard and squeeze it.

Would the officer had been justified to use deadly force before being murdered? NA. Officer Smith was killed by accidental friendly fire.

Outcome for the cop-killer: NA. It was an accidental discharge of friendly fire.

Police Officer Jason Nicholas Shuping

Concord Police Department, North Carolina

End of Watch Wednesday, December 16, 2020

Officer Randall Versie Smith

Birmingham Police Department, Alabama

End of Watch Monday, December 28, 2020

Special thanks to the Officer Down Memorial Page from which all the photos of the fallen officers were taken with permission. Please visit them at https://www.odmp.org/

ANALYSIS OF THE 53 LAW ENFORCEMENT OFFICERS FELONIOUSLY KILLED IN 2020

Killer's race: White: 16(30%) Black: 22(42%) Latino: 12(23%) Native-American: 1(2%) Unknown: 2(4%)

1. Subject failed to comply: 51 (96%)
2. Subject was a wanted criminal, or a crime was involved: 45 (85%)
3. Alcohol or drugs were involved: 15 (28%)
4. Subjects' actions displayed or were described having mental illness: 18 (34%)
5. Subjects' words and/or actions appeared to be suicidal and/or suicide by cop: 12 (23%)
6. Subjects' actions fueled by recent anti-police rhetoric: 4 (8%)
7. Subject ambushed the officer: 23 (44%)
8. Vehicle was involved (car stop, disabled motorist, accident): 29 (55%)
9. Subject accessed a hidden/concealed weapon before the LEO could react: 18 (34%)
10. Officer killed by friendly fire: 3 (6%)
11. A vehicle was used as a weapon to kill the officer: 6 (11%)
12. Subject attacked/threatened officer with personal weapons or an object: 5 (9%)
13. Officer could have justifiably shot subject first but did not: 23 (43%)
14. Less-than-lethal force alternatives failed: 9 (17%)
15. Officer was intentionally shot: 45 (85%)
16. Officer was accidentally killed: 3 (6%)
17. Officer was serving a warrant: 7 (13%)
18. Domestic incident was involved: 9 (17%)
19. Incident originated from a 911 call: 25 (47%)
20. Officer was killed taking police action while off-duty: 5 (9%)
21. Subject could have still been in jail, prison, or deported: 11 (21%)

ANALYSIS OF THE 108 LAW ENFORCEMENT OFFICERS FELONIOUSLY KILLED 2019-2020

Killer's race: White: 32(30%) Black: 45(42%) Latino: 25(23%) Native-American: 1(1%) Unknown: 5(5%)

1. Subject failed to comply: 105 (97%)
2. Subject was a wanted criminal, or a crime was involved: 95 (88%)
3. Alcohol or drugs were involved: 28 (26%)
4. Subjects' actions displayed or were described having mental illness: 31 (29%)
5. Subjects' words and/or actions appeared to be suicidal and/or suicide by cop: 18 (17%)
6. Subjects' actions fueled by recent anti-police rhetoric: 5 (5%)
7. Subject ambushed the officer: 41 (38%)
8. Vehicle was involved (car stop, disabled motorist, accident): 54 (50%)
9. Subject accessed a hidden/concealed weapon before the LEO could react: 32 (30%)
10. Officer killed by friendly fire: 5 (5%)
11. A vehicle was used as a weapon to kill the officer: 12 (11%)
12. Subject attacked/threatened officer with personal weapons or an object: 9 (8%)
13. Officers could have justifiably shot subject first but did not: 42 (39%)
14. Less-than-lethal force alternatives failed: 16 (15%)
15. Officer was intentionally shot: 92 (85%)
16. Officer was accidentally killed: 6 (6%)
17. Officer was serving a warrant: 14 (13%)
18. Domestic incident was involved: 17 (16%)
19. Incident originated from a 911 call: 43 (40%)
20. Officer was killed taking police action while off-duty: 11 (10%)
21. Subject could have still been in jail, prison, or deported: 22 (20%)

ANALYSIS

THE 108 OFFICERS FELONIOUSLY KILLED IN THE LINE OF DUTY DURING 2019 AND 2020, AS IN PREVIOUS YEARS, are representative of both sexes as well as the various races and religions common in the United States. Unlike when there is an officer-involved shooting involving a person of color, the race of the officer murdered is not made headline material. Except for rare instances such as the racially motivated targeted assassinations of the Dallas police officers in 2016, most officers are killed feloniously because of the lawful duties they are executing or for what their profession represents, but not for their color.

Since racial and ethnic demographics are omnipresent in any discourse on policing, the demographics of the murderers were compiled, just as they were for the subjects killed by the police. Again, there are striking disparities between the percentage population of both Blacks and Whites with the percentages of officers killed by the two respective races. Though only 13.4% of the population according to the July 1, 2019, US Census[1074], Blacks were responsible for 42% of the officers feloniously killed from 2019 to 2020. At 60.1% in the same census, non-Latino whites were responsible for 30% of those officer's deaths. Since Latinos are now lumped together with Blacks and described as persons of color when making allegations of racially biased policing, it bears noting that while constituting 18.5% of the population, Latinos accounted for 23% of the officers killed. Combined, people of color account for just 31.9% of the population, which is slightly over half that of Whites, yet they were responsible for 65% of the officers murdered, which is more than double the percentage murdered by Whites.

Accusations of racialized police shootings make headlines but rather than race, it is violent criminal actions like murdering police officers that makes people more susceptible to having officers justifiably use deadly force against them. Besides murdering LEOs, other actions that increase violent interactions with police are engaging in violent crimes and carrying weapons. The FBI UCR considers the following as violent crimes: murder and manslaughter, rape, robbery, and aggravated assault. Compared to their 13.4% of the population, in 2019 blacks accounted for 51.2% of recorded murder and manslaughter arrests; 26.7% of the rapes; 52.7% of the robberies; 33.2% of the aggravated assaults; and 41.8% of weapons possessions. Those percentages of criminal arrests range from two to nearly four times greater than their percentage of the population and combine with their 42% of LEO murders for a total of 41.3%. Those statistics are why Blacks are killed by officers at a rate higher than their population share would suggest, though that is still 12% points less than expected according to their rate of violent criminality.

Unarmed Whites were killed by officers during 2019-2020 at a much lower rate than their population share, but markedly higher than their rate of felonious police murders. Along with Whites being responsible for 30% of the officers murdered during 2019-2020 which is half their 60.1% of the population, Whites are also proportionally underrepresented in their commission of violence. In 2019, Whites accounted for 37.4% of those arrested for: murder and manslaughter; 57% of rapes; 36.4% of robberies; 50.4 % of aggravated assaults; and 45.4% of weapons' possessions. Combined with their felonious murders of LEOs, these percentages put Whites at committing 42.8% of the violent crimes that could bring them into lethal encounters with the police and happens to be nearly identical to their representation as 42% of the unarmed subjects killed by LEOs.

At 1.3% of the population, American Indians and Alaskan Natives are the most proportional to their rates of accounting for 1% of the unarmed subjects of police shootings and felonious murderers of police. It is the Asian race that is most typically underreported and disproportionately reflected in these situations. At 5.9% of the population, Asians accounted for 0% of the officers feloniously killed and were 3% of the unarmed subjects shot by officers. Asian's rate of violent criminality are typically less than half that 3% with their representing 1% of murder and manslaughter arrests; 2% of rapes and aggravated assaults; and 1% of robbery and weapons' possession arrests.

All the racial statistics aside, unlike the racialized stereotyping done to the profession of policing, this book neither presumes to generalize all races because of the criminal elements nor actions among them. These statistics were highlighted to show how accusations of police use of deadly force incidents being driven by race are completely unfounded because race is irrelevant. As each incident is detailed in this book, it is the perpetrator, not his White, Black, Native American, or Asian race, who is responsible for his actions, which ultimately resulted in his death or that of an officer. The same goes for gender as the relative absence of females being confirmed killers in any of the felonious murders of LEOs during 2019-2020 is a significant reason why females were so rarely the subjects of deadly police shootings detailed in Part 2. However, if those in the racial grievance industry, politics, and the press want to lionize criminals or refuse to call them criminals because of their race, then they are complicit in perpetuating further violence in those communities.

Moving on to perpetrators actions, the 108 officers feloniously murdered during 2019-2020 will now be analyzed according to the factors that are relevant. As these 108 incidents showed, officers were murdered in situations ranging from high-risk search warrants to seemingly innocuous attempts to render assistance to a disabled motorist. Mirroring the single most common factor present in the police shootings of unarmed subjects and applicable 97% of the time here, the common denominator across 105 of these incidents was the subject's failure to comply with the LEO. This noncompliance was demonstrated by 71 of those murderers who disregarded the officer's lawful orders. The remaining murderers exhibited noncompliance by their blatant contempt for the officer's lawful presence. Mere presence is known in policing to be an effective deterrent because the officers represent the authority of the state's enforcement arm. Officers are strategically assigned to both roving and stationary, foot and vehicle patrols because their presence discourages those in the vicinity from committing criminal acts. Therefore, when an officer is targeted, ambushed, or assassinated before being able to communicate with the offender verbally or visually, that offender still failed to comply because they disregarded the officer's statutory authority. Ultimately, there can be no greater example of failing to comply with a law enforcement officer than feloniously murdering him or her.

Not surprisingly, the second greatest contributing factor that links most officers who are being feloniously killed was interaction with either a wanted criminal or a criminal committing a crime. Demonstrating another shared similarity with unarmed fatal police shootings where this factor also ranked second, those feloniously murdering officers were not typical law-abiding citizens. A nexus to crime was present in 88% of the incidents and accounted for 95 of the officers murdered. Sometimes the officers were aware of the dangerous crime or criminal they were encountering and other times these facts did not become apparent until it was too late. Confirming once again there is no such thing as "routine," 50% of the incidents involved vehicles; 40% were initiated by 911 calls, of which the always emotionally volatile domestic disputes accounted for 16%; and 13% occurred during execution of search and arrest warrants. Exemplifying LEO's commitment to protecting the public, 10% of those who were feloniously murdered happened when officers took official police action while off-duty. The most selfless example of bravery while off-duty being when Racine Patrol Officer David Hetland attempted to stop an armed robbery while he was apparently unarmed. Officer Hetland's life mattered!

Besides bravery, the extraordinary restraint common among officers (though for which they get no credit), was exhibited by 39% of the officers murdered who could have preemptively used justifiable deadly force against their perpetrators but did not. Liberty County Deputy Sheriff Whitten exhibited both bravery and restraint when he chased down and had suspected mass murder Pavol Vidal lined up in the sights of his firearm. Aware Vidal was very violent and possibly armed, Deputy Whitten did not take the shot because he feared for the safety of the civilians nearby if he missed. Criminals like Vidal have no such concerns, so he took advantage of the deputy's hesitation and killed him. Deputy Whitten's life mattered!

In the case of Montgomery County PO Olinger, since he did not die from his injuries until many years later, he was able to recount how he hesitated because of his fear of the ramifications of shooting a person of color. If Officer Olinger felt that way back in 2003 more than a decade before the lambasting of Officer Darren Wilson in 2014 or the 2020/2021 scapegoating of all officers because of the George Floyd incident, imagine how much that must weigh upon the minds of a typical officer today. How many of these LEOs feloniously killed during 2019-2020 feared that they would be judged unfairly if they used deadly force, especially on a person of color, and therefore hesitated? That realistic fear could account for the 13% difference between blacks being 29% of those killed by police and 42% of officers being murdered by black criminals. Those officers and the other 40 will never get to tell their side of the story and we will never know why they did not act sooner or differently. Officer Olinger's life mattered!

It is not coincidental that many of the officers who refrained from immediately using deadly force upon a subject's furtive movement ended up becoming killed by subjects accessing a hidden/concealed weapon. Speed and surprise favor the person who acts first, so when criminals access a hidden weapon and commit to using it, the officer will always be reacting and therefore will be a step behind. This is especially true when officers are justifiably concerned that if they are mistaken, then their reasonable fear will be misconstrued as racist or criminal. Such was the case for 30% of the officers feloniously murdered over the past two years. Officers such as William Shinners of Provo, Utah and Sergeant Craig Johnson of Tulsa, Arizona. Both these officers were murdered when they were trying to physically remove non-cooperative subjects who refused to exit their vehicles. While the officers were focused on removing the subjects from the car using the minimal amount of force possible, the subjects managed to access a gun within arm's reach and kill the officers in the blink of an eye. Officer Shinners and Sgt. Johnson's lives mattered!

Rather than take the chance of being murdered the same way, LEOs justifiably shot the unarmed Christian Albarran in 2019 and Dylan Scott in 2020 when they made furtive movements to their waist as if to access a weapon. Watch the bodycam videos of the shootings involving Sgt. Johnson and Dylan Scott and observe how the officers in both situations did everything they could to avoid using deadly force. The deputies literally begged Scott to show his hands and Sgt. Johnson exhausted the use of force continuum and yet it in the end, it was the perpetrator that controlled the outcome in both incidents. It is very apparent in the video the deputies did not want to kill Dylan Scott, but they could not take the chance of being killed like Sgt. Johnson and so many of their fellow LEOs had been in similar situations.

Next time there is an officer-involved shooting, and the officer is being criticized for shooting what turned out to be an unarmed man, think of these 32 officers who were murdered because they could not react fast enough once the criminal had the gun pointing at them. When subjects disregard an officer's lawful order and run back into their car where they start reaching around or make a furtive movement to their waistband, every officer should reasonably assume that person is trying to access a deadly weapon to kill them with. Period. The end. LEOs are not mind readers. It is the public's responsibility to follow the officer's commands and to act in a way that does not make the officer fear for his/her life. Any law-abiding citizen who does that has nothing to fear from the police. The fact that there are roughly 50 unarmed subjects fatally shot by officers out of the 270+ million encounters each year means that the majority of the public understands this. Somehow though the outrage of that remaining minority gets the media's attention and politician's groveling.

What fails to get the attention of the press or those politicians looking to decriminalize the criminals is the disturbing fact that 20% of the officers murdered could still be alive today if the vile perpetrator they encountered that fateful day was still in prison, jail, a mental institution or deported. Those who argue that the criminal justice system is too harsh are proven absurd by violent recidivist Jeremy Owens. After pleading down to a robbery 1 charge instead of attempted murder, Owens was sentenced to 20 years in prison in 2012 but was released in less than five, only to get arrested for drug and weapons possession in 2018 when he was again released and free to case vehicles before murdering Sgt. WyTasha Carter of Birmingham PD in 2019 with another illegally possessed handgun. Kimberly Police Officer Nick O'Rear was also killed by a perpetrator who was released early from a long prison sentence. Career criminal Preston Johnson had a felony weapons conviction and sentence of 15 years in 2011, yet by 2019 he was free and arrested again for felony weapons possession and intent to sell drugs. Even still, instead of being behind bars, in 2020 Johnson was fleeing from police when he shot Officer O'Rear in the head with an illegally possessed weapon. Sgt. Carter's and Officer O'Rear's lives mattered!

Whereas the state criminal justice systems failed Sgt. Carter and Officer O'Rear, the federal one failed Newport News Police Officer Katherine Thyne. Thyne's assailant, Vernon Green, should have been locked up in North Carolina under federal charges for armed robbery, but since the feds declined prosecuting him, Green only faced state charges and was free on bail to travel to Virginia where he crushed Officer Thyne against a tree with his car. Only 24 years old and leaving behind a two-year-old daughter, Officer Thyne's life mattered!

America's mental health and immigration systems have also failed the public and the officer's sworn to protect them. Nevada Highway Patrol Sgt. Ben Jenkins was murdered while checking up on disabled motorist, John Dabritz. Little did Jenkins know that Dabrtiz had an extensive decades-long criminal history and had just the week before been released from a mental institution. Clearly Dabritz did not have a handle on his bipolar disorder and should have still been under professional mental health care. If he had been, Sgt. Jenkins could still be alive today. Sgt. Jenkins was a father of four children and his life mattered! Kittitas County Deputy Sheriff Ryan Thompson, San Marcos Police Officer Justin Putnam and Houston Police Sgt. Harold Preston should all still be alive as well. Each was murdered by illegal aliens who never should have been in America in the first place. America's open borders and politicized immigration controls failed these fine officers. Deputy Thompson's, Officer Putnam's, and Sgt. Preston's lives mattered!

While it was demonstrated in Part 2 that LEOs are not ambushing and assassinating anybody, more than one-third of the officers who were feloniously murdered never stood a chance as 41 of them were ambushed and murdered in cold blood. Seventeen of those ambushes occurred in 2019 and 22 happened in 2020, 13 of which were after the George Floyd incident put a bull's-eye on every LEO's back. Among the dozens of officers ambushed were these four who never even saw the face of their murderer. Milwaukee Police Officer Mark Lentz was run over while Davis Police Officer Natalie Corona, Puerto Rico Police Agent Alfred Sanyet-Perez and Indianapolis Metro Police Officer Breann Leath were all mercilessly gunned down during the commission of their duties. Corona was a rookie at just 22 years old, Leath was just two years older and a military veteran, and Agent Perez left behind a wife and eight children. Agent Sanyet-Perez's, Officers Lentz, Corona and Leath's lives mattered!

Eight percent of the subjects threatened or assaulted the officers with their hands or a weapon before murdering them. This is roughly five times less than the assault rate experienced by officers in Part 2, contrasting how quickly criminals resort to deadly force to eliminate LEOs while nearly half of the LEOs did not use it until they were threatened with violence or were physically attacked. North County Police Officer Michael Langsdorf was one of the nine officers comprising that 8%. While he was on top of suspected criminal Bonette Meeks trying to arrest him, Meeks accessed a gun hidden in his waist band and struck Langsdorf in the head with it. While the officer was on his knees–dazed, instead of running away, Meeks got up and executed Langsdorf with a shot to the head. Officer Langsdorf's life mattered!

Six brave officers were killed from 2019 to 2020 because of the same volatile circumstances that lead to accidental discharges or confusing duty guns for tasers in deadly police shootings. In two separate incidents, NYPD Detectives Brian Simonsen and Brian Mulkeen were both killed by friendly fire while trying to arrest violent criminals refusing to simply comply. When it is officers who are the ones accidentally shot by fellow officers or law-abiding citizens, the incidents are recognized for the tragic mishaps they are instead of politicized to be about a larger systemic issue. Detective Simonsen and Mulkeen's lives mattered!

During most of 2020, the American public were under lockdowns and constant stress associated with the much-politicized coronavirus pandemic. This stress likely explains at least part of why mental illness (29%) increased from being a factor in 13 incidents in 2019 to 18 in 2020, alcohol and drugs (26%) increased from 13 to 15, and suicidal subjects (17%) doubled from 6 in 2019 to 12 in 2020. Simpson County Deputy Sheriff James Blair was murdered in 2020 by one such mentally ill subject. While taking Joaquin Blackwell for an involuntary psychiatric evaluation, Deputy Blair was overpowered by the much younger man who stole his duty weapon, shot him dead, and ran off. Deputy Blair was 77 years old and was still working, so he could provide for his grandchildren whom he became the legal guardian for when his daughter died. Deputy Blair's life mattered! Notably the transport of nonviolent subjects for psychological evaluations is among the tasks defund the police advocates believe that social workers should take over from law enforcement. By their very nature, those with mental illnesses are remarkably unpredictable, so if armed trained LEOs can be overpowered and killed while transporting them, it is ignorant to purposely put unarmed social workers in such situations.

Also unpredictable are those dealing in or consuming alcohol and drugs. These vices were involved in 28 of the felonious murders of officers during 2019-2020, which is just two more than were a factor in 26 of the unarmed subjects fatally shot during that time. The drunk that Toledo Police Officer Anthony Dia was questioning in 2020 was unpredictable and incredibly accurate. Despite his intoxication, while walking away from Officer Dia, Edward Henry turned around and fatally shot Dia through his vest. Officer Dia managed to make one last radio transmission as he was dying, saying "tell my family I love them". His heart-wrenching quote made headline news, but it did not become a national rallying cry to condemn violence against police. Officer Dia's life mattered!

Further demonstrating the dangers of dealing with mentally unstable subjects are the 18 officers feloniously murdered by people exhibiting suicidal tendencies. In the case of Clermont County Sheriff's Office Detective William Brewer, Jr., he was murdered in 2019 while attempting to render medical aid to suicidal subject Wade Winn. Little could Det. Brewer know that Winn set up an ambush by faking shooting himself to lure the officers in. Killed while trying to save a suicidal subjects life, Det. Brewer's life mattered! Officers are often criticized after using deadly force on suicidal subjects as they had to in the 21 times detailed in Part 2, yet Det. Brewer and the 17% of officers murdered by such subjects during 2019-2020 reinforces the reason why the officers use of such force was justified.

Another remedy commonly promoted by those seeking to reimagine the police is to have unarmed "public safety officers" respond to traffic accidents and disabled motorists. As 54 of these 108 incidents revealed, violent criminals commonly used vehicles to get around. Along with traffic stops, trained officers were also killed by subjects who appeared to be disabled motorists or were involved in ordinary traffic accidents. Besides Sgt. Jenkins, who was highlighted earlier, Florida Highway Patrol Trooper Joseph Bullock was also murdered while assisting a disabled motorist in 2020. Upset that Trooper Bullock told him he either had to pay the tow truck driver or his vehicle would be towed, Franklin Reed III casually walked up to the Trooper's patrol car as he was filling out paperwork and shot him in the head. An Air Force veteran with 19 years of service in the Florida Highway Patrol, Trooper Bullock's life mattered!

Two other officers were killed during 2019-2020 while responding to nonemergency 911 calls of seemingly innocuous parked vehicles in people's driveways. The call of a mobile home parked blocking a driveway in 2019 and an unknown SUV parked in the complainant's driveway seemed innocuous enough. The reality was anything but as Cowlitz County Deputy Sheriff Justin DeRosier was murdered by the mobile home's driver within two minutes of arriving at the scene. And after Charlestown Police Patrolman Cassie Johnson tracked down the SUV's owner, Joshua Phillips, and followed him back to his illegally parked vehicle, Patrolman Johnson was attacked and shot in the face by him. Deputy DeRosier was survived by his wife and five-month-old daughter, while Patrolman Johnson's service continued even in death as her organs were donated. Deputy DeRosiers' and Patrolman Johnson's lives mattered!

A consequence of the daily deluge of hateful lies accusing the police of racial bias against blacks is exhibited in the final analysis of the felonious murders of officers. That consequence is an officer's life and five times during 2019-2020 the circumstances and evidence reveal the perpetrator's violent attack upon the officer was fueled by anti-police rhetoric. There were two such incidents from January 2019 through April 2020 and then three within two months of the Floyd incident and subsequent daily condemnation of police nationwide. Not that there were not enough regular accusations of racism in America before the Floyd incident to provoke impressionable young minds like 19-year-old Darian Atchison. On May 5, 2019, Darian walked eight miles to a police station where he then approached Biloxi Police Officer Robert McKeithen and shot him in the back of the head as he handled a peaceful domestic incident in the parking lot. According to the psychiatrist who examined him, "Atkinson said that he shot the officer because black people have been oppressed"[1075]. Tragically for Officer McKeithen the police have been made out to be the government agent most often associated with racism, so he paid the price for Atchison's perceived oppression. Officer McKeithen's life mattered!

The incident occurring in April 2020 involved a search for domestic homicide suspect Ronnie Kato. Several years earlier during a previous domestic dispute, referring to the anti-police rhetoric which inspired Gavin Long to ambush and murder three Baton Rouge officers, Kato said that he would "Gavin Long"[1076] the responding police officers. On April 26, 2020, Kato made good on that threat and executed Baton Rouge Police Lt. Glen Dale Hutto, Jr. after Hutto came looking for Kato at his house. The lies that inspired Long at that time were that Castile and Sterling were murdered by police because they were Black. Lt. Hutto's life mattered!

There were no such statements of admission to easily link the ambush of Moody Police Lt. Stephen Williams just days after the Floyd incident, but as they say in policing, "if it walks like a duck, looks like a duck, and quacks like a duck ... it's a duck". The Alabama AG's premature statement that there was no reason to believe that the ambush was associated with the unrest after the George Floyd incident did nothing to refute that highly likely possibility. After all, there has been no evidence to suggest the police-involved fatalities of Michael Brown, Alton Sterling, or George Floyd had anything to do with racism and yet the BLM movement has thrived by doing exactly that. As has the nationwide defund the police movement. By contrast, in the ambush of Lt. Williams, there is abundant evidence indicating that anti-police rhetoric was a driving factor. Unless of course you are the Alabama AG and believe it is merely a coincidence that the week after Floyd's much televised death, a young black couple with no reported prior brushes with the law premeditatedly rented a hotel room, called 911 to bring officers to their room, and then shot the officers once they arrived outside their door. Lt. Williams' life mattered!

Another premeditated anti-police-inspired murder was carried out by Steven Carrillo just four days later. Carrillo sped away from responding deputies sent to investigate reports of his vehicle having firearms and bomb-making materials. When the deputies finally caught up to Carillo he was ready, and he ambushed them with small arms fire and IEDs. Carrillo shot Santa Cruz County Sheriff's Office, Sgt. Damon Gutzwiller that day just as he is believed to have done to federal LEO

Patrick Underwood on May 29. Carrillo's anti-police social media posts and statements at the scene made his motive crystal clear for both murders. Santa Cruz County Sheriff's Sgt. Damon Gutzwiller's life mattered!

It is also obvious where Henry Washington derived the lexicon "Come on Pigs!"[1077] which he yelled while advancing at a patrol car and shooting at the Bothell Police Officers inside it on July 13, 2020. A person would have had to been living in a cave since the justified deadly force shooting of Michael Brown to not have seen news stories of BLM rallies with chants such as "Pigs in a blanket, fry'em like bacon"[1078]. As a career criminal with a history of mental illness, Washington was especially prone to acting upon such hateful rhetoric toward the police. Sadly, on the fateful day Washington did so, Officer Jonathan Shoop suffered the consequences, his life mattered!

What bears pointing out is the lack of hate or vengeance responding officers exhibited when encountering the cop-killers highlighted in these 108 very personal incidents for law enforcement. Only 12 of the murderers in 2019 were justifiably killed either during the gun battle with the officer they murdered or by other officers when the perpetrator refused to peacefully surrender. Among those 12 were four white subjects, four black, three Latinos, and one whose race is unknown. The numbers in 2020 were similar with 10 subjects justifiably killed, three of which were white, five were black, and two were Latino. Those 22 fatal shootings are among the statistics used by websites and individuals alleging that police deadly force incidents are excessive or unjustified. Reading the particulars of each incident reveals the lie of such allegations.

Another lie dispelled is that criminals, particularly black ones, are eagerly killed by the police rather than arrested. Of the 55 LEOs killed in 2019, 37 perpetrators were captured alive: nine were white, nineteen were black, and nine were Latino. In 2020, of the 31 cop-killers taken alive, eight were white, seventeen were black, and five were Latino. Far from LEOs using the opportunity to exact revenge or just kill black subjects because of their race as is often alleged, at 53% of those cop-killers captured; blacks were more than twice as likely to be taken alive into police custody then their white counterparts.

The fact is that America's LEOs do not serve, protect, or sacrifice their lives according to race. Although not highlighted, the 108 officers whose murders were detailed in this section included numerous races and ethnicities. Since the law enforcement community is comprised of all races, when it is said Police Lives Matter, it signifies that All Lives Matter. Those LEOs, however, were not listed or described by their race in this book, because they were not defined by their race while executing their duties or living their lives. Those serving and protecting in America are defined by the heroic actions they take each and every day. The rest of America, particularly the press, politicians and protestors should follow the lead of these fine officers and start categorizing people by their personal choices and actions instead of the color of their skin.

CONCLUSION

As promised, this book has provided you, the reader, with the facts about justified deadly force incidents involving law enforcement. Following the science, this book started with a scientific research study demonstrating the racial bias in police deadly force incidents on behalf of the press, protestors, and politicians. Important details then came in the form of over 200 individual encounters involving unarmed subjects killed by police as well as the officers feloniously murdered from 2019 to 2020. The characteristics divulged over these incidents coupled with the numerous statistics derived from them clearly dispel any notion of racism in the use of deadly force by law enforcement. Contrary to popular propaganda, the statistics showed that Blacks are killed by police at a rate disproportionately lower than their commission of violent crime and felonious murder of officers, while Whites are killed by police at nearly the same rate as they commit violent crimes. The desire by those crying out for officers to use lethal force in accordance with population percentages instead of personal actions are antithetical to the principles of America and are the basest kind of racial quotas imaginable.

There was such a time after the Civil War when Blacks were killed simply for the color of their skin. That time is commonly referred to as Jim Crow and it was a dark period, where, among other vile discriminations, "paramilitary violence"[1079] was conducted against Black people. A study by the Equal Justice Initiative calculated from 1877 to 1950 that there were 3,959 Blacks killed by such violence in the form of lynching[1080]. That period is long past, but it continues to be used to frame current events as racist and undesirable. Such was the case when former Democratic Presidential candidate Beto O'Rourke referred to policing in 2018 as "the new Jim Crow"[1081]. Most recently President Biden disingenuously characterized Georgia's legal changes to strengthen election integrity as "Jim Crow on steroids"[1082].

As bad as Jim Crow was, the rate of Blacks being murdered in the twenty-first century is substantially worse. Adding the 2,600 Blacks killed by fellow Blacks in 2018 with the 2,974 similarly murdered in 2019 makes a two-year total of 5,574 and far exceeds the 3,959 murdered during 73 years of Jim Crow. (Intra-racial murders are common among Whites as well with 5,271 whites murdered by fellow whites during 2018-2019, the difference being White murders are not racialized by the press, politicians, and protestors). While those who lynched Black's decades ago during Jim Crow were surely reprehensible, what makes those who kill their own in modern times any less despicable? No longer "paramilitary" mobs or "slave police," Blacks are committing the equivalent of 51 years of Jim Crow lynchings every single year against their own. When will the press, politicians, protestors, and society make it a priority to address the underlying causes behind that conundrum to show that Black lives really do matter to them?

Instead, the priority for these segments is to attack law enforcement over the handful of questionable officer-involved shootings that they portray as controversial solely based upon race. As the incidents in Part 2 detailed, most times the officers were found to have acted reasonably with district attorneys or departmental investigations, concluding that it was a justified shooting with 23 of the 90 unarmed subjects killed. In the name of transparency, despite the clear justification of most shootings, some DA's present all such cases to a grand jury. Of all the armed and unarmed cases of deadly force detailed during 2019-2020, 19 of the incidents resulted in officers either being charged by the DA or indicted by a grand jury. Among those 19 incidents, eight of the subjects killed were Black, eight were White, two were Latino and one was Asian. With many of the cases still going through the legal channels, the seven which have been concluded resulted in five of the officers either found innocent during the trial or not indicted by the grand jury. Two of those incidents involved Black subjects and three involved White ones. Besides the conviction of Derek Chauvin, the other incident where a cop has been found guilty of murder or manslaughter was of a White subject, Katlyn Alix the off-duty police officer. In the Breonna Taylor shooting, the officers involved were found by a jury to be innocent of any murder/manslaughter charges. The reason why Sgt. Cosgrove, Officer Mattingly, and so many of the other LEOs were ultimately not found guilty is because despite the impassioned protests and Monday morning quarterbacking, juries of their peers determined that the officers reasonably feared for their lives and justifiably used deadly force. The officers were not part of a "paramilitary hit squad" or indiscriminately killing Americans of any race.

Those knowledgeable on these facts about fatal police incidents should rightfully be outraged by the wide-sweeping efforts made by groups misrepresenting them to defund, reimagine, and, in some cases, even dismantle America's frontline criminal justice representatives. Convinced that every police encounter with Blacks is based upon racism, the left seized the momentum gained from the Floyd incident and has quickly been deconstructing the rule of law across the country. Such efforts span the nation from coast to coast affecting numerous cities and towns in between.

Within three weeks of Floyd's death, the Minneapolis City Council committee voted unanimously on a resolution to replace the Minneapolis PD "with a community-led public safety system"[1083]. Such a move combines the council's expressed desire to disband the department with the demands of social activist group MPD150 to have "community-based models of safety, support, and prevention"[1084] instead of the police. Over a thousand miles away, a similar fate has been determined for the police department in Ithaca, New York. Though completely uninvolved in the death of George Floyd, Ithaca, like every other NY municipality, was mandated by Gov. Cuomo's Executive Order 203 to partner with community stakeholders to conduct a complete review of their department's policies and procedures. Per EO 203, these "police reform and reinvention collaboratives" had to submit their plans to address identified problem areas such as "any racial bias and disproportionate policing of communities of color"[1085]. Falling short of Ithaca Mayor

Svante Myrick's expressed intention to abolish the police department, the city council's approved plan kept the current officers while adding "unarmed officers to handle nonviolent calls like petty thefts"[1086]. Rather than having an epiphany of common sense, the council's last-minute change to keep the current officers instead of abolishing the entire department was brought about by heavy pressure from the labor movement.

Besides sense, Ithaca's leadership showed a complete lack of decency by giving a convicted cop-killer a seat on their Reimagining Public Safety Collaborative panel. Back in 1981 while taking part in an armed robbery at a bar, Richard Rivera literally executed off-duty NYPD Officer Robert Walsh[1087]. Walsh identified himself as a police officer and tried to stop Rivera and his accomplices, for which he was immediately shot by Rivera. While Walsh was on the ground wounded from Rivera's first bullet, Rivera went over to him, put the gun to Walsh's head and murdered him. Now forty years later and out on parole since 2019, this cold-blooded cop-killer was given a voice in executing an entire police department.

Another suburban New York department where a convicted killer was given a voice was out on Long Island's Suffolk County. Complying with Cuomo's Executive Order 203, Suffolk County developed a Police Reform Task Force which held eight public forums on Zoom where community members voiced their criticisms or support for the police. One of those people was an ex-convict, who used the forum to ask the activist groups for help in battling his latest criminal charges. While the many self-proclaimed socialists and BLM supporters voiced their support for the ex-con on the side chat seen on the screen during the Zoom meetings, those law-abiding citizens speaking in favor of the police were googled and called racists. These accusations of racism in each meeting served as a deterrent to any other citizens who had signed up to voice their support for the police. Achieving their goal, the accusations silenced the majority of Suffolk citizens who appreciate the police and left the police-hating radicals as the overwhelming voice heard by the sympathetic Task Force.[1088]

Illustrating how blinded by race and blind to real predators those calling for police reforms are, for weeks they rallied behind that ex-con who, besides recently starting a riot where a cop's nose was broken[1089], had done something over 99% of police officers never have–he killed a person of color. Back in the 1990s, he was convicted of manslaughter for stabbing another man to death. By comparison, the entire Suffolk PD which were being depicted as violent thugs during these meetings had only two deadly use of force incidents in the previous year, each of which included men who threatened the officers with a handgun. Far from anything to do with Minneapolis, Suffolk County is one of the safest in the nation and its officers are among the most restrained.

Fortunately for the citizens of Suffolk, their County Executive and Legislators could not be bullied by the outspoken socialists and the Task Force was not able to dramatically reimagine or defund policing as the activists hoped for. NYPD, on the other hand, had no such support from their city leadership and suffered the largest defunding of any department in the nation when the city council voted in July 2020 to remove $1 billion from their budget. Though smaller dollar figures, Seattle city council leaders voiced support for defunding their police by up to 50% while Austin's City Council unanimously approved cutting their police budget by 34.5%, or 150 out of $434 million[1090] [1091]. Leaders in Los Angeles voted to defund their police budget by $150 million as San Francisco's Mayor proposed an identical $150 million reduction in funding for the Bay City's police. Portland, Oregon, commissioners removed close to $16 million from their police budget, nearly twice as much as the $9.1 million cut by the Minneapolis City Council.

Even more drastic then multi-million-dollar budget cuts were the passing of radical policies and legislation effectively deterring LEOs from performing their job and policing the criminals among society. On April 10, 2021, Maryland's Democrat-controlled General legislature overrode several of Gov. Larry Hogan's vetoes to drastically change policing in that state. Along with repealing "Maryland's Law Enforcement Officers' Bill of Rights, a 1974 law that guarantees job protections and due process rights for officers"[1092], the legislature replaced the "reasonable" standard under which an officer's use of force is typically based upon. Like California, instead of what officers reasonably believed at the time, Maryland will begin judging use-of-force incidents in hindsight based upon whether the officer's actions were shown after the fact to be "necessary". Maryland's new laws also provided criminals with the comfort of knowing no-knock warrants would typically be restricted to the hours of 8 a.m. to 7 p.m. while affording unrestricted public access to complaints lodged against officers, even those found to be without merit. Proclaiming how it was "fueled by the experiences of those who have lived with police brutality and discrimination," on February 24, 2021, Governor J.B. Pritzker signed off on House Bill 3653 making Illinois "the first in the nation to completely abolish cash bail"[1093]. This legislation will assuredly fuel further victimization of the citizens of Illinois and brutalities against LEOs as their state's courts becomes a revolving door for violent criminals, much as happened after New York's disastrous bail reform law took effect.

Adding to their well-established anti-police agenda, in March 2021, New York's City Council passed a "law that removes qualified immunity from police officers for actions carried out during the course of duty"[1094] making it the first and only city in America to do so. Demonstrating what little regard NYC's city council has for its officers, city leaders opted to remove a basic protection afforded officers carrying out their hazardous duties in good faith since the 1967 Supreme Court ruling of *Pierson v. Ray*. Officers still maintain qualified immunity under state and federal law; however, several social justice warriors of the house and senate have introduced legislation to remove such protections at the federal level as well. Democrat Congresswoman Ayana Pressley and Senators Ed Markey, Bernie Sanders and Elizabeth Warren sponsored the "Ending Qualified Immunity Act" to "abolish legal protections for law enforcement officers from personal lawsuits originating out of their on-duty conduct"[1095]. Despite their legislative actions not being made under the split-second, life-or-death circumstances in which police do, these elected officials exemplified hypocritical elitists by keeping in place their own congressional immunity.

According to NYC Mayor DeBlasio, NYPD officers will not have to personally pay any civil judgments found against them, but if that changes and if it expands across the fifty states–the mass exodus from NYPD and police ranks nationwide will get even worse. As it is, officers in municipalities demonstrably hostile to police are already leaving in droves. Marking a 75% increase compared to 2019 and showing that they were through being "criminalized" by their anti-police city leadership, more than 5,300 officers in NYPD either quit or retired in 2020[1096]. An even larger increase in departures was seen in nearby Philadelphia. Compared to the 135 Philly cops who filed retirement papers in 2020, 114 did so just in the month of January 2021[1097]. Over in Portland, 48 retirements in just the month of August 2020 was more than the Portland Police Bureau had in any calendar year since 2006[1098]. In total, from July 2020 to April 2021, 115 Portland Police Officers blazed a trail off the job by either retiring or resigning[1099]. The 2020 "historic mass exodus" of Seattle Police Officer's left that department with its "lowest number of deployable staff since 1990"[1100]. With over 190 separations and retirements, Seattle lost twice as many officers in 2020 than the previous year and substantially more than any year since at least 2012. Like Portland, many of the officers separating from Seattle PD moved on to departments where officers were still respected, and policing was actually appreciated.

Simultaneously concocting legislation targeting the hundreds of thousands honorable LEOs, politicians have also been busy promoting laws favoring law breakers. Taking swift action post-Floyd to combat systemic racism, "in early 2020, Atlanta instituted a zero-tolerance policy prohibiting police officers from chasing fleeing suspects for even the most vicious crimes"[1101]. Doing their part to "dismantle systemic racism" and "improve policing,"[1102] Illinois passed the SAFE-T (Safety, Accountability, Fairness and Equity–Today) Act in February 2021. Like Atlanta's law, this Act restricts officers from pursuing criminals and "prohibits an officer from making a custodial arrest for Class B misdemeanors"[1103]. Opening up officers to criminal charges and further encouraging criminals to flee, the law also "makes it illegal to shoot a TASER at someone's back, pelvis and head–despite the fact that the back is a recommended target in all of the training"[1104].

Lowering the bar even further than restricting pursuits, New York's chief legal officer wants police to cease attempting to even stop criminals in the first place. As the incidents in this book demonstrated, criminals utilize vehicles to facilitate or even commit many of their heinous crimes. Despite that obvious criminal nexus to car stops, to prevent future deadly officer-involved shootings like that of Allan Feliz (which her office found the cop was justified), New York's AG Letitia James "recommended the New York Police Department (NYPD) no longer conduct traffic stops"[1105]. But if NYPD insists on conducting traffic stops, James' next recommendation for NYPD is to "scrap a policy encouraging police to arrest any motorist they stop who has open warrants"[1106]. While NYPD has yet to be constrained by such inept policy recommendations, Virginia passed a new law starting in March 2021 prohibiting police from conducting traffic stops based upon vehicle's with, "defective and unsafe equipment,"[1107] tinted windows, the smell of marijuana emanating from it, an expired inspection, without brake lights or an adequate muffler. Since driving an automobile is one of the most dangerous activities many American's will ever do, legislation should be focused on ensuring that vehicles are safe for the road rather than preventing criminals from being subjected to traffic stops.

This nightmare of a social justice experiment in protecting criminals and criminalizing police has yielded undeniable results which any competent leader or legislator could have easily forecasted. In New York, car thefts increased 67% in 2020; burglaries increased 42%; with a ten year high of 462, homicides increased 44% in 2020 and were already 12% higher in 2021; shootings increased 97% in 2020 and are 40% higher in 2021[1108] [1109]. Doubling New York's ten-year high, a 59% increase from 99 in 2019 to 157 murders during 2020 made it Atlanta's deadliest in over twenty years[1110]. Already home to the most murders of any city in America, in 2020, Chicago experienced a 53% increase in homicides with a total of 774, and the 2021 numbers were already 16% higher than 2020[1111]. The number of 4,033 shooting victims in Chicago was also greatly increased in 2020, up 55% from 2019[1112]. Homicide rates for San Francisco and Los Angeles in 2020 were both more than 30% above the previous year, and the first few month's of 2021 show that the city of angels' homicides were up another 28%[1113].

Home to Antifa and daily anti-police "protests", Portland has been the epitome of criminality and violence. Marking a 26-year high, Portland's 55 homicides in 2020 represents a 53% increase from 2019[1114]. With 20 murders in less than a quarter into 2021, Portland is on track for another record year as it continues to criminalize policing[1115]. Murders represent just a small fraction of the Portlanders lives touched by violence in 2020 with roughly 900 shootings throughout the city, more than doubling the 393 in 2019[1116]. With three less murders than Portland, Seattle's 52 homicides in 2020 were its highest in 26 years and a 49% increase from the previous year[1117]. Dwarfing both Portland and Seattle, Minneapolis saw murders jump 70% from 48 in 2019 to 82 in 2020. A host of other violent crimes that skyrocketed in Minneapolis in 2020 were aggravated assaults (up 24%); robberies (up 47%); shootings (up 105%); and carjacking's (up 301%) with 405 such incidents[1118].

With murder rates rising an average of 35% in more than 50 cities across America, federal buildings fire-bombed, police precincts overrun, and masked perpetrators with makeshift shields throwing Molotov cocktails at officers, America, at times resembled more a third-world country or a scene out of Mad Max. At the intersection where George Floyd was killed, a complete breakdown of civil order materialized into an "autonomous zone" described by its supporters as "revolutionary space" and by its opponents as a "no-go zone"[1119]. Declared free from government authority, police were not "allowed to go in" and White people were banned as well[1120]. Still allowed inside though was the senseless violence which escalated from just three fatal and nonfatal shootings the previous year to nineteen in 2020[1121]. Besides denying basic services to the law-abiding citizens living within the zone of this American city, business owners were victimized by robbers, and even more Blacks were murdered.

Another six square block lawless zone, initially called the Capitol Hill Autonomous Zone (CHAZ) and later renamed Capitol Hill Occupation Protest (CHOP) zone was created in Seattle. Beginning with violent protests causing the abandonment of the Capitol Hill police precinct on June 8, 2020, the CHOP zone's three-week existence was fancifully promoted as the "summer of love"[1122] by Seattle Mayor Jenny Durkan. It was a summer that saw residents trapped inside the zone file lawsuits, because they were denied basic public safety services such as from the police who dared not enter except for "an immediate threat to life or safety"[1123]. Two Black teenagers did not make it through the summer, casualties of the five shootings occurring within nine days in Seattle's lawless zone. One of those murdered, 16-year-old Antonio Mays Jr.'s "SUV was riddled with 300 bullet holes"[1124] by the self-proclaimed "security guards" when he drove toward the zone's concrete barriers.

Let that sink in. Armed criminals guarding an illegally barricaded six block "no-go zone," shot at young Antonio Mays at least 300 times, killing him for merely trying to enter a neighborhood here in America, not 1998 Somalia, 2012 Iraq, or 2020 Venezuela. Was Mayor Durkan held responsible for the murders occurring during her city's "summer of love"? Did the media cover Mays death nonstop for days? Were there nationwide protests in Mays' name? Does anybody even remember his name? As expected, since Mays was not killed by police, a simple internet search shows the answer to all those questions is no. Antonio Mays was just another casualty of the war against policing.

DEMONIZING POLICE WHEN EXERCISING OBVIOUS SELF-DEFENSE:

Exhibiting further hypocrisy of the social justice war against policing, those so enraged by the Floyd video, attacked officers for incidents where videos clearly showed them defending themselves against armed and aggressive perpetrators. During the 100 plus nights of riots where Antifa and associates "broke windows, set small fires, punctured police car tires, and pelted officers with rocks and frozen water bottles"[1125], police used chemical spray to protect themselves and disperse the anarchists. Caving to outrage over the use of such irritants against "protestors," Mayor Wheeler banned them from being used anymore, removing an effective nonlethal tool to prevent officers from being hit with projectiles and eye-damaging lasers. Funny enough, just a few months later, Wheeler found it necessary to employ such nonlethal means when he pepper-sprayed a man outside a restaurant merely because "he remained at close distance"[1126].

There was nothing funny in Pennsylvania where police were forced to shoot men charging at them with a knife in two separate incidents. Already facing charges for stabbing four people in 2019, Ricardo Munoz was fatally shot on September 13, 2020, when he charged at a Lancaster City Police Officer with ... you guessed it, a knife! With a prior conviction in 2013 for putting a gun to a woman's head during a robbery[1127], on October 26, 2020, the choice of weapon for Walter Wallace Jr. was a knife. Despite the officers begging him to drop the knife as they backed away from him, Wallace continued to advance toward them with knife in hand and was justifiably shot dead. Though videos showed that the officers faced imminent mortal danger, violent protests ensued in which dozens of cops were injured and government property was destroyed[1128] [1129].

In Atlanta on the night of June 12, 2020, rather than be arrested for DWI and processed in the police precinct like millions before him have been, Rayshard Brooks assaulted the cops, forcibly stole Officer Devin Brosnan's taser, and then attempted to immobilize Officer Garrett Rolfe by shooting that taser at him.[1130] Reasonably fearing for his life and that of his partner from the now-armed Brooks, Officer Rolfe justifiably shot Brooks dead. Just two weeks prior, Fulton County DA Paul Howard charged six officers for assault, classifying tasers– "a deadly weapon under Georgia law"[1131] and citing the officer's tasing of two college students as deadly force. Quixotically that same DA charged Officer Rolfe with murder and aggravated assault for defending himself against the deadly force presented by Brooks.

While DA Howard played politics with the rule of law, lawlessness already played out in the makeshift autonomous zone set-up around the Wendy's where Brooks' fatal encounter took place. As they had in Seattle's CHOP zone, self-proclaimed armed guardians of Atlanta's "no-go zone" set-up barriers, banned officers from entering, and claimed to be policing their own streets. What they actually did though was shake down law-abiding residents and murder an eight-year-old Black girl. Young Secoriea Turner was shot dead when the car she was in was riddled with bullets by the armed insurgents because the driver tried to enter a parking lot within their autonomous zone[1132]. It was only after the killing of this innocent young girl that Mayor Keisha Lance Bottoms gained the political courage to have law enforcement officials put an end to the illegal no-go zone she had thus far tolerated in her city.

When officers are demonized and criminalized for acting in self-defense as the officers in the preceding incidents did, it makes others more susceptible to attacks and more reluctant to aggressively defend themselves. Positive proof of this concept was caught on video for all to see on March 12, 2021, as Metro Nashville Police Officer John Baker was shot while conducting a traffic stop.[1133] Officer Baker could have justifiably used deadly force once the combative woman, Nika Nicole Holbert, got back into her car as he was tasing her to stop her from doing so. Justified because rather than try to drive away, Holbert was reaching around for something in her car that Baker could have reasonably assumed was a weapon. Understandably in today's atmosphere,

Officer Baker was not going to take the chance that Holbert might have been reaching around for keys, so he did not shoot. Even when Baker realized his mistake as Holbert found that something and pointed a gun at him, Baker still did not act as he was trained. Officer Baker should have immediately drawn his weapon and shot Holbert until she no longer presented a deadly threat. Instead, Baker ordered Holbert to drop the weapon, and he nearly paid with his life for it. An officer has no duty to warn in such a situation! There was no way for Officer Baker to react fast enough once Holbert acted first and shot at him. It is out of fear of being criminalized that Officer Baker did not act appropriately and only by luck that he is not being added to the 2021 Officer Down Memorial Page.

DEMONIZING POLICE WHEN DEFENDING OTHERS:

Proving that George Floyd was just another Black pawn used by the press, politicians, and protestors to advance the agenda which the Michael Brown shooting failed to do, their next false idol was already making headlines the same day Derek Chauvin was found guilty. On April 20, just minutes before it was announced that the jury convicted Chauvin on all three charges, Columbus Ohio police responded to a 911 call about an attempted stabbing between girls fighting. PO Nicholas Reardon arrived at the scene to see Ma'Khia Bryant push one female to the ground before turning around to attack another female backed up against a car. Observing the knife in Bryant's right hand, Officer Reardon yelled at Bryant to "Get down, Get down!"[1134]. Bryant ignored Reardon's commands and swung the knife toward the helpless female, forcing Officer Reardon to shoot Bryant and stop her deadly attack. The victim whose life was saved corroborated this story at the scene, as did a neighbor's surveillance video. Due to the growing outrage, within 24 hours the police released the bodycam video clearly showing Bryant about to stab the unarmed girl dressed in pink trapped against the car. Instead of a story about police saving the life of an unarmed Black girl within nine seconds of arriving on scene, the press, politicians, and protestors made up lies and ignored details to make it one of a White cop shooting a teenage Black girl.

Along with emphasizing the races of the officer and Bryant, numerous press outlets including *The New York Times*, *The Daily Beast*, *HuffPost*, *The Washington Post*, *NPR*, and *AJ+* left out the critical detail of the knife in their initial reporting[1135]. NBC edited out the part of the 911 call where the caller exclaimed, "It's these grown girls over here trying to fight us, trying to stab us, get here now!"[1136] just as they edited out the moments in the video showing Bryant about to stab the real victim of this story. MSNBC's Joy Reid[1137] and CNN's Brianna Keilar[1138] both downplayed the involvement of the knife while using the incident to criticize police. Outspoken activist Lebron James quickly took to twitter, sending out a picture of Officer Reardon, accompanied by "YOU'RE NEXT" and "#ACCOUNTABILITY"[1139]. Naturally, BLM got involved, with over 100 activists marching through Columbus and protesting outside of Police HQ[1140]. Hundreds of students at The Ohio State University marched to the Ohio Statehouse, demanding the university to sever ties with the Columbus Police Department[1141].

Even more disappointing was the rhetoric coming from American's political leaders. A day after the shooting, Ohio's Democratic Senator Sherrod Brown tweeted, "Columbus police shot and killed a sixteen-year-old girl. Her name was Ma'Khia Bryant. She should be alive right now"[1142]. Congressional Democrats, squad members Ilhan Omar[1143] and Ayanna Pressley both made their own statements by criticizing police or making it appear that the shooting was an act of police violence toward Blacks. But it was none other than the Biden White House that pushed the party line of systemic racism onto an incident where a Black life was saved. In calling the recent shooting a "tragedy," Biden's Press Secretary, Jen Psaki went on to say, "We know that police violence disproportionately impacts Black and Latino people and communities and that Black women and girls like Black men and boys experience higher rates of police violence"[1144]. Like Michael Brown, Philando Castile, Breonna Taylor, Rayshard Brooks, and so many others, Ma'Khia Bryant's death will be used to scapegoat police and further divide America upon racial lines by manipulating feelings over facts.

CANCEL CULTURE CLAIMING PRO-POLICE SYMBOLS ARE SYMBOLS OF WHITE SUPREMACIST HATE:

As violent criminals assaulted America's LEOs, their sympathetic social justice comrades targeted pro-police symbols like the blue line flag with lies about racism. On January 17, 2021, the Santa Rosa Police Department posted a positive, feel-good community story. Two anonymous citizens presented the department with a blue line flag, adorned with the words "Heroes Work Here" written across it. With all the anti-police sentiment and outright violence against law enforcement, this was a nice moment where the residents showed support for their local officers. The Chief himself acknowledged how the flag represented "the courage and the bravery that our staff show every single day"[1145]. Yet, after others expressed how they saw the flag as an expression of "white supremacy" and as the local NAACP chapter claimed the flag "means stay in your place"[1146] to certain people, the Chief apologized to the public and removed the flag from the building. Cowering to the "woke" mob as this chief did will only inspire the mob to find and protest against future contrived injustices.

When a similar attack upon the blue line flag occurred on Long Island a month later, the silent majority showed what happens when people speak up against the woke mob. It all started when Newsday stirred the racial pot and ran a news story about one person complaining to the Smithtown Fire Department that they were offended by the blue line flag displayed on their fire truck[1147]. The "offensive" flag was put on the truck in honor of NYPD Officers Wenjian Liu and Rafael Ramos after they were murdered by Ismaaiyl Abdullah Brinsley on December 20, 2014, and had been there ever since. One complaint does not typically make for a news story, unless of course it stokes the flames of racial divisiveness which the media regularly does. As typically happens in such incidents, in response to the offense claimed and media attention, the FD announced on Facebook that it removed the flag. This did not sit well with the Smithtown community that knew the history of the flag in question, so they flooded the FD with ridicule and complaints for removing the symbol memorializing two fallen officers. Empowered by the flag's overwhelming support by the community, the FD announced they made a mistake and put it back on their truck[1148].

Only in America 2021 could a flag honoring two minority police officers be construed to be a symbol of white supremacy, but such facts seldom stop the social justice warriors from calling for a protest. Except in this case when activists arrived to protest in Smithtown, they were outnumbered around ten to one. In America, everyone has an equal right to protest, but that by no means signifies a moral equivalency among each side of an issue. Marching in what is best described as a "participation trophy protest," with fists in the air and carrying flags representing BLM and the United Nations, those claiming racism against the blue line flag chanted "Fuck Donald Trump" and "Black Lives Matter". Standing in opposition to that protest were over 100 Smithtown residents chanting such racist things as, "Back the blue," "All Lives Matter," and "Say their names, Ramos and Liu". The radical left mob can be overcome, it just takes the rational right to stand up to the lefts' lies and the fake news accompanying them.

TEACHING CHILDREN IN PUBLIC SCHOOLS THAT THE POLICE ARE RACIST.

More discretely than protests, activist administrators are using benign sounding equity programs in elementary schools to wage war against police on another front. Copying the Marxist indoctrination seen in American universities, Public School boards are promoting materials describing the police as racist oppressors, thereby ensuring the cycle of hatred toward the police will continue well into the future. Contributing their part to the nationwide conversation on racism after Floyd's death, Long Island's Smithtown Central School Board sent a letter to families in the district soliciting input for their Equity Team. Additionally, the letter included links to *Child Mind Institute* and *Parent Toolkit* for resources to help parents speak to their children about issues like racial violence. Among the resources found searching through *Child Mind Institute* were articles titled, "TELLING MY WHITE FOUR-YEAR-OLD ABOUT ALTON STERLING AND PHILANDO CASTILE,"[1149] and "7 Tips for White Parents Talking to Kids About Police Murders of Black People"[1150]. As antagonistic and untruthful as these two articles were, and there were many more like them, the worst display of hypocrisy was the one about the Dallas police shooting of 2016.

The unprovoked murder of five Dallas police officers on July 7, 2016, was the deadliest day for law enforcement since 9/11, and it was causally related to racism as Micah Xavier himself told the negotiators that he wanted to "kill white people, especially white officers" since he was "upset about Black Lives Matter and recent police shootings"[1151]. Micah's FB page showed he supported the New Black Panther Party (NBBP), which even the left leaning Southern Poverty Law Center describes as, "a virulently racist and anti-Semitic organization whose leaders have encouraged violence against whites, Jews and law enforcement officers"[1152]. And that is exactly what Xavier did when he assassinated five Dallas POs as they provided security for BLM activists during a protest. Yet, the article linked through *Child Mind Institute* titled, "How to Talk to Your Kids About the Dallas Shooting, Because It Shouldn't be Ignored" does not make one mention of Micah Xavier, his support of the NBBP, nor his expressed desire to kill White officers. What the article does do is use the murder of five officers to portray the police as the racists with this pivot: "And as was certainly the case with the Dallas shooting, police officers are there to keep the public safe (though that discussion is clearly a complex one, given what happened to Alton Sterling and Philando Castile earlier this week)"[1153].

Once again, the good citizens of Smithtown stepped up and did not let the false narrative against policing go unanswered. Since the anti-police materials promoted by the Smithtown Board were part of a larger effort of their Equity Team to bring critical race theory into the classrooms, a group of concerned parents determined they needed new leadership on the board. Officers living in Smithtown outraged by the anti-police propaganda being put out by their children's school district informed their union and set in motion a truly grass-roots effort among various local entities. The Suffolk County Police Benevolent Association (PBA) teamed up with Save our Schools–Smithtown, Long Island Loud Majority, and local radio show "In the Ring with Captain C", and together they challenged the school board with three pro-equality (not equity), and pro-police candidates in the election. The school board race received national press from Fox News[1154] and the election had a historic turnout[1155]. Ultimately the people of Smithtown voted for equality over equity and elected the three challengers. In a positive sign moving forward, the school board has already partnered with the Suffolk County Police Department and Suffolk PBA to bring the police officers and pro-police programs back into Smithtown schools.

THE WAY FORWARD:

Hopefully now, after becoming educated on the dire reality of the propaganda being used to curtail law enforcement's noble efforts of keeping citizens of every race, color, and creed safe to pursue their American dream, you, the reader, are now courageous enough to take a stand. In the schools just as in the city and state legislatures, the reason damaging anti-American policies have been pushed through is because small groups of very vocal radicals pressured their elected representatives to do so. These representatives lacked the courage to stand up to the mob and make policies based off facts instead of emotions. When these officials only hear from the social justice warriors, then that is who they fear, who they respond to, and who their legislation ends up best representing the values of. This is not conjecture, the politician's themselves admit it. For example, while speaking to the NYS Public Employees Conference at its annual meeting, a powerful Democrat State Senator told the audience that the most effective way to influence change among your elected representatives is to call them out on twitter. According to the seasoned Senator, and as observed by how powerful people cave to the twitter mob, the thing politicians most feared was being attacked on social media. It is high time the silent majority that does not agree with the anti-police, anti-American agenda goes on the attack before it becomes too late.

For all you patriots, fed up with small groups of radicals attacking your values and the country you love, add this book and www.JDFinformation.com to your arsenal to fight the lies being spread in your hometown or DC.

- Link an example of the many violent criminals justifiably killed by the police and send them to any politician, celebrity, or activist falsely claiming that the police are systemically killing innocent minorities.
- Link to an example of a career criminal that should have been behind bars but was instead free and killed a cop, and email/tweet/message it to your local politician or any federal level politician or cabinet member pushing for early releases.
- Likewise, send to those politicians the links to examples of criminals who should still be behind bars, but were recently released as part of the reimagining of the criminal justice system. Criminals like Brandon Elliot who murdered his mother, spent 17 years in jail before being released in 2020 on lifetime parole, and went on to attack a 65-year-old defenseless Asian woman in the streets of NYC.

- Or link to an example of the many officers and civilians killed by illegal aliens and send them to the next politician, celebrity, or globalist organization calling for amnesty, open borders, an end to border enforcement.

Finally, escalate it to the next level and truly take matters into your own hands by stepping into the arena and running for office. Whether it be for your city council, county legislature, or at the grassroots level of your local school board–put those elected officials on notice that their anti-American policies will not go unchallenged, because proud Americans will take their job. Every elected person who chooses to defund, dismantle, or reimagine the very law enforcement agencies that keep everyone safe must themselves be reimagined out of office. America's great strength of being a nation governed by the people and for the people has been hijacked by the woke mob. It is time for the silent majority to take it back before America resembles more a third-world hellhole than the land of freedom and opportunity. Become that next great patriot today whom young Americans will learn about in their history books a hundred years from now! Otherwise, those books will feature BLM and Antifa as the good guys.

REFERENCES

Blackstone, Ginger E., Holly S. Cowart, and Lynsey M. Saunders. 2017. "TweetStorm in #ferguson: How News Organizations Framed Dominant Authority, Anti-Authority, and Political Figures in a Restive Community." *Journal of Broadcasting & Electronic Media* 61 (3): 597–614. Accessed January 18, 2020. doi:10.1080/08838151.2017.1344670.

Cruz, Jose Miguel. 2015. "Police Misconduct and Political Legitimacy in Central America." *Journal of Latin American Studies* 47 (2): 251–83. Accessed January 3, 2020. doi:10.1017/S0022216X15000085.

Dukes, Kristin Nicole, and Sarah E. Gaither. 2017. "Black Racial Stereotypes and Victim Blaming: Implications for Media Coverage and Criminal Proceedings in Cases of Police Violence against Racial and Ethnic Minorities." *Journal of Social Issues* 73 (4): 789–807. Accessed January 7, 2020. doi:10.1111/josi.12248.

Fryer Jr., Roland G. 2018. "Reconciling Results on Racial Differences in Police Shootings." *AEA Papers & Proceedings* 108 (May 1): 228–234. Accessed January 20, 2020. https://apus.primo. exlibrisgroup.com/discovery/fulldisplay?docid=bth_137511880&context=Ebsco&vid=01APUS_INST:01APUS&lang=en&search_scope=MyInst_and_CI&adaptor=EbscoLocal&tab=Everything&query=title, contains,Reconciling%20Results%20on%20Racial, AND&query=creator,contains,Fryer,AND&sortby= rank&mode=advanced&offset=0

James, Lois, Stephen M. James, and Bryan J. Vila. 2016. "The Reverse Racism Effect." *Criminology & Public Policy* 15 (2): 457–79. Accessed January 5, 2020. http://web.b.ebscohost.com. ezproxy1.apus.edu/ehost/pdfviewer/pdfviewer?vid=43&sid=5b889c7d-0544-4262-9430-381e7948a3a9%40pdc-v-sessmgr05

Johnson, David J, Trevor Tress, Nicole Burkel, Carley Taylor, and Cesario Joseph. 2019. "Officer Characteristics and Racial Disparities in Fatal Officer-Involved Shootings." *Proceedings of The*

National Academy of Sciences of The United States of America 116:15877-15882. Accessed January 25, 2020. https://www.pnas.org/content/116/32/15877

Jones, James M. 2017. "Killing Fields: Explaining Police Violence against Persons of Color." *Journal of Social Issues* 73 (4): 872–83. Accessed January 6, 2020. doi:10.1111/josi.12252.

Krieger, Nancy, Mathew V. Kiang, Jarvis T. Chen, and Pamela D.Waterman. 2015. "Trends in US deaths due to legal intervention among Black and White men, age 15-34 years, by county income level: 1960–2010." *Harvard Public Health Review*, 3. Accessed February 10, 2020. http://harvardpublichealthreview.org/190/

Lasch, Christopher N. 2016. "Sanctuary Cities and Dog-Whistle Politics." *New England Journal on Criminal & Civil Confinement* 42 (2): 159–90. Accessed January 5, 2020. http://search.ebscohost.com.ezproxy1.apus.edu/login.aspx?direct=true&AuthType=ip&db=i3h&AN=115902672&site=e-host-live&scope=site

Mac Donald, Heather. 2016. *The War on Cops: How the New Attack on Law and Order Makes Everyone Less Safe*. New York: Encounter Books.

Mills, Colleen E. 2017. "Framing Ferguson: Fox News and the Construction of US Racism." *Race & Class* 58, no. 4 (April): 39–56. Accessed January 5, 2020. doi:10.1177/0306396816685030

Nix, Justin, Bradley A. Campbell, Edward H. Byers, and Geoffrey P. Alpert. 2016. "A bird's eye view of civilians killed by police in 2015: Further evidence of implicit bias." *Criminology & Public Policy*, 16 (1): 1-32. Accessed February 10, 2020. https://onlinelibrary.wiley.com/doi/abs/10.1111/1745-9133.12269

Roussell, Aaron, Kathryn Henne, Karen S. Glover, and Dale Willits. 2019. "Impossibility of a 'Reverse Racism' Effect." *Criminology & Public Policy* 18 (1): E5–16. Accessed January 5, 2020. doi:10.1111/1745-9133.12289.

Shjarback, John A., David C. Pyrooz, Scott E. Wolfe, and Scott H. Decker. 2017. "De-Policing and Crime in the Wake of Ferguson: Racialized Changes in the Quantity and Quality of Policing among Missouri Police Departments." *Journal of Criminal Justice* 50 (May): 42–52. Accessed January 9, 2020. doi:10.1016/j.jcrimjus.2017.04.003.

Williamson, Vanessa, Kris-Stella Trump, and Katherine Levine Einstein. 2018. "Black Lives Matter: Evidence That Police-Caused Deaths Predict Protest Activity." *Perspectives on Politics* 16, no. 2: 400-15. Accessed January 5, 2020. doi:10.1017/S1537592717004273.

Zuckerman, Ethan, J. Nathan Matias, Rahul Bhargava, Fernando Bermejo, and Allan Ko. 2019. "Whose Death Matters? A Quantitative Analysis of Media Attention to Deaths of Black Americans in Police Confrontations, 2013–2016" *International Journal of Communication* [Online] 13(September): 4751-4777. Accessed January 30, 2020. https://ijoc.org/index.php/ijoc/article/view/8782/2810

ENDNOTES

1 Quote Investigator. 2018. "The Greatest Trick the Devil Ever Pulled Was Convincing the World He Didn't Exist." *QuoteInvestigator.com*, March 20. Accessed January 22, 2021. https://quoteinvestigator. com/2018/03/20/devil/

2 Bartiromo, Michael. 2020. "Starbucks offering free coffee to front-line responders amid coronavirus outbreak." *Fox News Channel*, March 25. Accessed January 27, 2021. https://www.foxnews.com/ food-drink/starbucks-free-coffee-frontline-responders-coronavirus

3 WPVI-TV. 2020. "'We're here for you.' Wawa offers free coffee to first responders, health care workers during coronavirus pandemic." *6 ABC Action News*, March 26. Accessed January 27, 2021. Wawa offers free coffee for first responders and health care heroes - 6abc Philadelphia

4 Stock, Jeremy. 2020. "George Floyd Death | Full Video | GeorgeFloyd." *YouTube*, May 30. Accessed February 1, 2021. https://www.youtube.com/watch?v=thfNLVvve4A&bpctr=1612233748

5 Smith, Savannah, Jiachuan Wu & Joe Murphy 2020. "Map: George Floyd protests around the world: The protests that started in the U.S. after the death of George Floyd have gone global. Track where they are." *NBC News*, June 9, Accessed February 1, 2021. https://www.nbcnews.com/news/world/ map-george-floyd-protests-countries-worldwide-n1228391

6 Pullman, Joy. 2020. "Study: Up To 95 Percent Of 2020 U.S. Riots Are Linked To Black Lives Matter." *The Federalist*, September 16. Accessed February 2, 2021. https://thefederalist.com/2020/09/16/ study-up-to-95-percent-of-2020-u-s-riots-are-linked-to-black-lives-matter/

7 Phillips, Morgan. 2020. "Damage from riots across US will cost at least $1B in claims: report." *Fox Business*, September 16. Accessed February 2, 2021. https://www.foxbusiness.com/economy/ damage-riots-1b-most-expensive

8 Pavlich, Katie. 2020. "Cost of Recent Riot Damages Are the Worst in U.S. History." *Townhall.com*, September 16. Accessed February 1, 2021. https://townhall.com/tipsheet/katiepavlich/2020/09/16/ the-financial-cost-of-recent-riots-has-been-tabulated-n2576294

9 Bowden, Ebony. 2020. "More than 700 officers injured in George Floyd protests across US." *New York Post*, June 8. Accessed February 2, 2021. https://nypost.com/2020/06/08/ more-than-700-officers-injured-in-george-floyd-protests-across-us/

10 Major Cities Chiefs Association. 2020. "REPORT ON THE 2020 PROTESTS AND CIVIL UNREST." *Major Cities Chiefs Association Intelligence Commanders Group*, October. Accessed February 2, 2021. https://www.majorcitieschiefs.com/pdf/news/mcca_report_on_the_2020_protest_and_civil_unrest.pdf

11 Horowitz, Daniel. 2020. "Horowitz: More than 1,500 buildings, many black-owned businesses, damaged in Twin Cities area as violence continues." *The Blaze*, June 18. Accessed February 2, 2021. Horowitz: More than 1,500 buildings, many black-owned businesses, damaged in Twin Cities area as violence continues - TheBlaze

12 Ibid 6.

13 Rosas, Julio. 2020. "Jaw-Dropping: Police Chief Association Releases Number of Officers Injured During Violent Riots." *Townhall.com*, November 30. Accessed February 1, 2021. https://townhall.com/tipsheet/juliorosas/2020/11/30/police-chief-association-releases-jawdropping-numbers-of-injured-officers-during-n2580844

14 Darrah, Nicole. 2020. "Darrah, Nicole. 2020. "AMERICA ON FIRE Violence spreads to 140 cities as more than 4,100 arrested and cop shot during George Floyd protests." *The U.S. Sun*, June 1. Accessed February 3, 2021. https://www.the-sun.com/news/915025/george-floyd-protests-violent-unrest-thousands-arrested/

15 Oliver, Jay. 2020. "George Floyd Protests In Michigan: Reaction From Across The State." *Patch*, June 1. Accessed January 29, 2021. https://patch.com/michigan/detroit/george-floyd-protests-michigan-reaction-across-state

16 Shaw, Adam. 2020. "Officials who pushed strict lockdowns now argue protesters are an exception." *Fox News*, June 5, Accessed January 28, 2021. https://www.foxnews.com/politics/officials-lockdowns-protesters-exception

17 Saxena, Vivek. 2020. "Uproar when Newsom declares church parishioners are no longer allowed to sing in 14-page mandate." *BizPac Review*, July 3. Accessed February 6, 2021. https://www.bizpacreview.com/2020/07/03/newsom-declares-church-parishioners-are-no-longer-allowed-to-sing-in-14-page-mandate-942500/

18 Newsom, Gavin. 2020. "Twitter Feed @GavinNewsom." *Twitter*, May 30. Accessed January 28, 2021. https://twitter.com/GavinNewsom/status/1266850781090598912

19 Kashiwagi, Sydney. 2020. "Protesters can stay out past curfew, if peaceful, but need to leave when cops tell them to go, mayor says." *silive.com*, June 4. Accessed January 29, 2021. https://www.silive.com/coronavirus/2020/06/protesters-can-stay-out-past-curfew-if-peaceful-but-need-to-leave-when-cops-tell-them-to-go-mayor-says.html

20 Epshteyn, Boris. 2020. "Democrats' Hypocrisy on Riots Reveals Political Nature of Coronavirus Lockdowns | Opinion." *Newsweek*, June 12, Accessed January 28, 2021. https://www.newsweek.com/democrats-hypocrisy-riots-reveals-political-nature-coronavirus-lockdowns-opinion-1510325

21 Ibid 20.

22 Ibid 16.

23 Wetsman, Nicole. 2020. "Blaming protesters for COVID-19 spread ignores the bigger threats to health." *The Verge*, June 3. Accessed January 27, 2021. https://www.theverge.com/2020/6/3/21278340/protestors-coronavirus-spread-police-violence-health-racism

24 Diamond, Dan. 2020. "Suddenly, Public Health Officials Say Social Justice Matters More Than Social Distance." *Politico*, June 4. Accessed January 28, 2021. https://www.politico.com/news/magazine/2020/06/04/public-health-protests-301534

25 Culver, Jordan. 2020. "Republican Sen. Mitt Romney joins George Floyd protest near White House: 'We need to stand up and say that black lives matter'." *USA Today*, June 7.

Accessed February 3, 2021. https://www.usatoday.com/story/news/politics/2020/06/07/george-floyd-mitt-romney-utah-protest-racial-equality/3172595001/

26 Lesniewski, Niels. 2020. "McConnell blasts Bowser for restricting church services but allowing protests." *Roll Call*, June 9. Accessed February 4, 2021. https://www.rollcall.com/2020/06/09/mcconnell-blasts-bowser-for-restricting-church-services-while-allowing-protests-during-covid-19-pandemic/

27 Donaghue, Erin. 2019. "Disturbing video shows Dallas officers joking as they restrain man who died." *CBS News*, August 1. Accessed July 1, 2020. https://www.cbsnews.com/news/tony-timpa-disturbing-video-shows-dallas-officers-joking-as-they-restrain-man-who-died/

28 Aratani, Lauren. 2020. "George Floyd killing: what sparked the protests – and what has been the response?" *The Guardian*, May 29. Accessed February 3, 2021. https://www.theguardian.com/us-news/2020/may/29/george-floyd-killing-protests-police-brutality

29 FBI. 2020. "Crime in the United States, 2019: Expanded Homicide Data Table 6." *FBI Uniform Crime Report*. Accessed February 9, 2021. https://ucr.fbi.gov/crime-in-the-u.s/2019/crime-in-the-u.s.-2019/tables/expanded-homicide-data-table-6.xls

30 Hassett-Walker, Connie. 2019. "The racist roots of American policing: From slave patrols to traffic stops." *The Conversation*, June 4. Accessed February 3, 2021. https://theconversation.com/the-racist-roots-of-american-policing-from-slave-patrols-to-traffic-stops-112816

31 Myers, Amrita Chakrabarti. 2020. "From slave patrol to storm troopers, America's police have an ugly history." *Courier Journal*, July 7. Accessed February 1, 2021. https://www.courier-journal.com/story/opinion/2020/07/10/slave-patrol-storm-troopers-police-have-ugly-history/5399798002/

32 Clooney, George. 2020. "America's Greatest Pandemic Is Anti-Black Racism." *The Daily Beast*, June 1. Accessed February 2, 2021. https://www.thedailybeast.com/george-clooney-on-the-murder-of-george-floyd-americas-greatest-pandemic-is-anti-black-racism

33 Tinney, Don. 2020. "Tinney: 400 years of systemic racism." *The Barre Montpelier Times Argus*, June 6. Accessed February 3, 2021. https://www.timesargus.com/opinion/perspective/tinney-400-years-of-systemic-racism/article_10b7df5e-8c03-5799-9d6a-b6a3218b83a4.html

34 Philimon, Wenei. 2020. "Not just George Floyd: Police departments have 400-year history of racism." *USA Today*, June 7. Accessed February 2, 2021. https://www.usatoday.com/story/news/nation/2020/06/07/black-lives-matters-police-departments-have-long-history-racism/3128167001/

35 Ibid 34.

36 Benson, Guy. 2020. "Gov. Murphy and Mayor De Blasio: Let's Face It, Protesting Police Brutality Is More Important Than Protesting COVID Lockdowns." *Townhall*, June 4. Accessed April 22, 2021. https://townhall.com/tipsheet/guybenson/2020/06/04/nj-governor-look-protesting-police-brutality-is-different-than-protesting-covid-lockdowns-n2569980

37 Re, Gregg. 2020. "Democrats cheering 'Black Lives Matter' protests now say Trump rallies pose coronavirus risk." *Fox News*, June 13. Accessed February 4, 2021. https://www.foxnews.com/politics/democrats-cheering-black-lives-matter-protests-now-say-trump-rallies-pose-coronavirus-risk

38 Yelimeli, Supriyai. 2020. "Rep. Barbara Lee wants to form a racial healing commission to reckon with 400 years of systemic racism". *Berkeleyside*, June 9. Accessed February 3, 2021. https://www.berkeleyside.com/2020/06/09/rep-barbara-lee-wants-to-form-a-healing-commission-to-reckon-with-400-years-of-systemic-racism

39 Associated Press. 2021. "Read Joe Biden's first speech as president." *PBS*, January 20, Accessed February 5, 2021. https://www.pbs.org/newshour/politics/read-joe-bidens-first-speech-as-president

40 Kaufman, Elliot. 2019. "The '1619 Project' Gets Schooled." *Wall Street Journal*, December 16. Accessed February 2, 2021. https://www.wsj.com/articles/the-1619-project-gets-schooled-11576540494

41 Barrett, Devlin. 2009. "Holder: US a nation of cowards on racial matters." *The San Diego Union-Tribune*, February 18. Accessed March 5, 2020. https://www.sandiegouniontribune.com/sdut-holder-race-021809-2009feb18-story.html

42 Khan, Amina. 2019. "Getting killed by police is a leading cause of death for young black men in America." *LA Times*, August 16. Accessed March 3, 2020. https://www.latimes.com/science/story/2019-08-15/police-shootings-are-a-leading-cause-of-death-for-black-men

43 Luibrand, Shannon. 2015. "How a death in Ferguson sparked a movement in America." *CBS News*, August 7. Accessed January 18, 2020. https://www.cbsnews.com/news/how-the-black-lives-matter-movement-changed-america-one-year-later/

44 Gates, John Fitzgerald. 2015. "Institutionalized Racism: National Security Threat and Mental Health Crisis." *Huffington Post*, April 24. Accessed March 3, 2020. https://www.huffpost.com/entry/institutionalized-racism_b_7130822

45 Law Enforcement Today Staff. 2019. "Joe Biden: Cops don't pull over white girls". *Law Enforcement Today*, October 28. Accessed January 5, 2020. https://www.lawenforcementtoday.com/joe-biden-cops-dont-pull-over-white-girls/

46 Ibid 44.

47 Lacour, Greg. 2018. "Clemson Profs Unveil Russian Trolls' Information War, Tweet by Tweet." *Charlotte Magazine*, December 10. Accessed January 7, 2020. https://www.charlottemagazine.com/clemson-profs-unveil-russian-trolls-information-war-tweet-by-tweet/

48 Chabria, Anita. 2019. "Newsom signs 'Stephon Clark's Law,' setting new rules on police use of force." *Los Angeles Times*, August 19. Accessed January 25, 2020. https://www.latimes.com/politics/la-pol-ca-california-police-use-of-force-law-signed-20190711-story.html

49 Ortiz, Jorge L. 2019. "California's new police use-of-force law marks a 'significant' change in law enforcement. Here's why." *USA Today*, August 20. Accessed January 27, 2020. https://www.usatoday.com/story/news/nation/2019/08/20/california-new-police-use-force-law-significant-change/2068263001/

50 Stewart-Cousins, Andrea. 2018. "Senate Democrats Fight To Reform New York's Criminal Justice System." *The New York State Senate*, February 13. Accessed January 17, 2020. https://www.nysenate.gov/newsroom/press-releases/andrea-stewart-cousins/senate-democrats-fight-reform-new-yorks-criminal

51 Robinson, Pam. 2020. "Sheriff Cites Recidivism in Release of Accused Under Bail Reform Laws." *Huntington Now*, January 8. Accessed January 17, 2020. https://huntingtonnow.com/sheriff-cites-recidivism-in-release-of-accused-under-bail-reform-laws/

52 Benjamin, Michael. 2020. "Pols could fix this law…if only they would read it first." *New York Post*, January 31. New York edition.

53 Schow, Ashe. 2020. "Another Bail Reform Fail: Gang Member Released from Prison, Sent Back Same Day For Committing Same Crime." *The Daily Wire*, January 16. Accessed January 27, 2020. https://www.dailywire.com/news/another-bail-reform-fail-gang-member-released-from-prison-sent-back-same-day-for-committing-same-crime

54 Zuckerman, Ethan, J. Nathan Matias, Rahul Bhargava, Fernando Bermejo, and Allan Ko. 2019. "Whose Death Matters? A Quantitative Analysis of Media Attention to Deaths of Black Americans in Police Confrontations, 2013–2016" *International Journal of Communication* [Online] 13(September): 4751-4777. Accessed January 30, 2020. https://ijoc.org/index.php/ijoc/article/view/8782/2810

55 Roussell, Aaron, Kathryn Henne, Karen S. Glover, and Dale Willits. 2019. "Impossibility of a 'Reverse Racism' Effect." *Criminology & Public Policy* 18 (1): E5–16. Accessed January 5, 2020. doi:10.1111/1745-9133.12289.

56 Jones, James M. 2017. "Killing Fields: Explaining Police Violence against Persons of Color." *Journal of Social Issues* 73 (4): 872–83. Accessed January 6, 2020. doi:10.1111/josi.12252.

57 Ibid 54.

58 Williamson, Vanessa, Kris-Stella Trump, and Katherine Levine Einstein. 2018. "Black Lives Matter: Evidence That Police-Caused Deaths Predict Protest Activity." *Perspectives on Politics* 16, no. 2: 400-15. Accessed January 5, 2020. doi:10.1017/S1537592717004273.

59 Ibid 56, page 872.

60 Shjarback, John A., David C. Pyrooz, Scott E. Wolfe, and Scott H. Decker. 2017. "De-Policing and Crime in the Wake of Ferguson: Racialized Changes in the Quantity and Quality of Policing among Missouri Police Departments." *Journal of Criminal Justice* 50 (May): 50. Accessed January 9, 2020. doi:10.1016/j.jcrimjus.2017.04.003.

61 Ibid 55, page E6.

62 Mills, Colleen E. 2017. "Framing Ferguson: Fox News and the Construction of US Racism." *Race & Class* 58, no. 4 (April): 52. Accessed January 5, 2020. doi:10.1177/0306396816685030

63 Nix, Justin, Bradley A. Campbell, Edward H. Byers, and Geoffrey P. Alpert. 2016. "A bird's eye view of civilians killed by police in 2015: Further evidence of implicit bias." *Criminology & Public Policy*, 16 (1): 4. Accessed February 10, 2020. https://onlinelibrary.wiley.com/doi/abs/10.1111/1745-9133.12269

64 Mac Donald, Heather. 2016. *The War on Cops: How the New Attack on Law and Order Makes Everyone Less Safe*. Page 73. New York: Encounter Books.

65 Ibid 64, pages 112, 152.

66 Ibid 64, page 28.

67 Johnson, David J, Trevor Tress, Nicole Burkel, Carley Taylor, and Cesario Joseph. 2019. "Officer Characteristics and Racial Disparities in Fatal Officer-Involved Shootings." *Proceedings of The National Academy of Sciences of The United States of America* 116:15877-15882. Accessed January 25, 2020. https://www.pnas.org/content/116/32/15877

68 Ibid 64.

69 Ibid 64, page 79.

70 Fryer Jr., Roland G. 2018. "Reconciling Results on Racial Differences in Police Shootings." *AEA Papers & Proceedings* 108 (May 1): 229. Accessed January 20, 2020. https://apus.primo.exlibrisgroup.com/discovery/fulldisplay?docid=bth_137511880&context=Ebsco&vid=01APUS_INST:01APUS&lang=en&search_scope=MyInst_and_CI&adaptor=EbscoLocal&tab=Everything&query=title,contains,Reconciling%20Results%20on%20Racial,AND&query=creator,contains,Fryer,AND&sortby=rank&mode=advanced&offset=0

71 James, Lois, Stephen M. James, and Bryan J. Vila. 2016. "The Reverse Racism Effect." *Criminology & Public Policy* 15 (2): 457–79. Accessed January 5, 2020. http://web.b.ebscohost.com.ezproxy1.apus.edu/ehost/pdfviewer/pdfviewer?vid=43&sid=5b889c7d-0544-4262-9430-381e7948a3a9%40pdc-v-sessmgr05

72 Ibid 56, page 873.

73 Ibid 64, page 153.

74 Ibid 73.

75 Ibid 64, page 212.

76 Ibid 71, page 457.

77 Ibid 71, page 472.

78 Ibid 71, page 476.

79 Ibid 67.

80 Ibid 56, page 878.

81 Cruz, Jose Miguel. 2015. "Police Misconduct and Political Legitimacy in Central America." *Journal of Latin American Studies* 47 (2): 251–83. Accessed January 3, 2020. doi:10.1017/S0022216X15000085.

82 Ibid 60, page 44.

83 Ibid 58, page 406.

84 Ibid 70, page 228.

85 Ibid 71, page 476.

86 Blackstone, Ginger E., Holly S. Cowart, and Lynsey M. Saunders. 2017. "TweetStorm in #ferguson: How News Organizations Framed Dominant Authority, Anti-Authority, and Political Figures in a Restive Community." *Journal of Broadcasting & Electronic Media* 61 (3): 610. Accessed January 18, 2020. doi:10.1080/08838151.2017.1344670.

87 Lasch, Christopher N. 2016. "Sanctuary Cities and Dog-Whistle Politics." *New England Journal on Criminal & Civil Confinement* 42 (2): 159–90. Accessed January 5, 2020. http://search.ebscohost.com.ezproxy1.apus.edu/login.aspx?direct=true&AuthType=ip&db=i3h&AN=115902672&site=ehost-live&scope=site

88 Ibid 87, page 174.

89 Ibid 54, page 4755.

90 Ibid 86, page 608.

91 Ibid 90.

92 Ibid 54, page 4759.

93 Dukes, Kristin Nicole, and Sarah E. Gaither. 2017. "Black Racial Stereotypes and Victim Blaming: Implications for Media Coverage and Criminal Proceedings in Cases of Police Violence against Racial and Ethnic Minorities." *Journal of Social Issues* 73 (4): 791. Accessed January 7, 2020. doi:10.1111/josi.12248.

94 Ibid 93, page 802.

95 Ibid 62, page 48.

96 Ibid 56, page 878.

97 Ibid 62, page 49.

98 Carter, Corinthia A. 2017. "Police Brutality, the Law & Today's Social Justice Movement: How the Lack of Police Accountability has Fueled #Hashtag Activism." *CUNY Law Review*, 20 (2): 521-557. Accessed February 1, 2020. https://academicworks.cuny.edu/clr/vol20/iss2/12

99 Rawls, John. 1971. "*A Theory of Justice: Revised Edition.*" Page 10. Massachusetts: Belknap Press of Harvard University Press. Accessed February 1, 2020. https://philosophyintrocourse.files.wordpress.com/2016/05/rawls-theory-of-justice.pdf

100 Ibid 99, page 53.

101 Robinson, Matthew. 2010. "Assessing Criminal Justice Practice Using Social Justice Theory." *Social Justice Research* 23 (1): 82. Accessed January 24, 2020. doi:10.1007/s11211-010-0108-1.

102 Madhani, Aamer. 2016. "Activists cry out on police shootings." *USA Today*, July 8. Accessed February 15, 2020. https://pressreader.com/@nickname14640979/csb_hsSWiZXGehZT9X_loLatwhGisu_kxzUGr 5036jM6TOhJ7LUGwJAMph4kvRPM-oJQ272uYXtF6SSR78V96AlNcQ

103 FBI. 2017. "2016 Crime in the United States: Expanded Homicide Data Table 3." *FBI Uniform Crime Report*. Accessed April 9, 2020. https://ucr.fbi.gov/crime-in-the-u.s/2016/crime-in-the-u.s.-2016/tables/ expanded-homicide-data-table-3.xls

104 Associated Press. 2017. "Who is Mohamed Noor, Minneapolis officer accused in Justine Damond's death?" *CBS News*, July 18. Accessed March 12, 2020. https://www.cbsnews.com/news/ who-is-mohamed-noor-minneapolis-officer-accused-in-justine-damond-shooting/

105 Celona, Larry, Shawn Cohen, Jamie Schram, Amber Jamieson and Laura Italiano. 2014. "Gunman executes 2 NYPD cops in Garner 'revenge'". *New York Post*, December 20. Accessed February 28, 2020. https://nypost.com/2014/12/20/2-nypd-cops-shot-execution-style-in-brooklyn/

106 Korte, Gregory. 2015. "Obama signs 'Blue Alert' law to protect police." *USA Today*, May 19. Accessed February 28, 2020. https://www.usatoday.com/story/news/politics/2015/05/19/ obama-blue-alert-law-bill-signing/27578911/

107 Crane-Newman, Molly, Edgar Sandoval, and Larry McShane. 2017. "NYPD officer assassinated by cop-hating schizophrenic while inside police truck in the Bronx." *New York Daily News*, July 6. Accessed April 30, 2021. https://www.nydailynews.com/new-york/nyc-crime/ police-officer-shot-bronx-suspect-custody-article-1.3301718

108 Department of Justice (DOJ). 2015. "DEPARTMENT OF JUSTICE REPORT REGARDING THE CRIMINAL INVESTIGATION INTO THE SHOOTING DEATH OF MICHAEL BROWN BY FERGUSON, MISSOURI POLICE OFFICER DARREN WILSON." *U.S. DOJ*, March 4. Page 13. Accessed January 27, 2020. https://www.justice.gov/sites/default/files/opa/press-releases/ attachments/2015/03/04/doj_report_on_shooting_of_michael_brown_1.pdf

109 Winsor, Morgan and Julia Jacobo. 2017. "Minneapolis police release 911 transcript in fatal shooting of bride-to-be from Australia." *ABC News*, July 20. Accessed March 12, 2020. https://abcnews.go.com/US/ minneapolis-police-release-911-transcript-fatal-shooting-bride/story?id=48726585

110 Forliti, Amy. 2019. "Officer says partner fired before he could analyze threat." *ABC News*, April 18. Accessed March 12, 2020. https://abcnews.go.com/International/wireStory/ partner-cop-charged-minneapolis-shooting-takes-stand-62486732

111 Ibid 107, page 44.

112 Ibid 107, page 13.

113 Ibid 107, page 14.

114 Ibid 107, page 7.

115 Ibid 108.

116 Ibid 107, page 4.

117 Ibid 107, page 5.

118 Hutchinson, Bill, Julia Jacobo and Alex Perez. 2018. "Police officer charged with murder in killing of Australian woman in Minnesota." *ABC News*, March 20. Accessed March 12, 2020. https://abcnews. go.com/US/police-officer-charged-murder-killing-australian-woman-minnesota/story?id=53882129

119 Francis, Enjoli. 2019. "Police officer gives account on body camera after partner fatally shoots Australian woman: 'She just came up out of nowhere'." *ABC News*, May 24. Accessed March 12, 2020. https://abcnews.go.com/US/911-calls-body-camera-footage-released-police-officers/story?id=63260393

120 FNC. 2014. "Missouri town on edge after 18-year-old fatally shot by police." *Fox News*, August 10. Accessed March 7, 2020. https://www.foxnews.com/us/missouri-town-on-edge-after-18-year-old-fatally-shot-by-police

121 Curry, Colleen. 2014. "What We Know About the Police Shooting of 18-year-old Michael Brown" *ABC News*, August 11. Accessed March 7, 2020. https://abcnews.go.com/US/police-shooting-18-year-michael-brown/story?id=24929276

122 FNC. 2014. "Michael Brown shooting: FBI opens inquiry into case." *Fox News*, August 11. Accessed March 7, 2020. https://www.foxnews.com/us/michael-brown-shooting-fbi-opens-inquiry-into-case

123 Basu, Moni. 2014. "Another lost son, another call for justice." *CNN*, November 24. Accessed March 9, 2020. https://www.cnn.com/2014/11/24/us/ferguson-vonderrit-myers/index.html?utm_source=feedburner&utm_medium=feed&utm_campaign=Feed%3A+rss%2Fcnn_latest+%28RSS%3A+CNN+-+Most+Recent%29

124 CNN Staff. 2014. "Dueling narratives in Michael Brown shooting." *CNN*, August 19. Accessed March 8, 2020. https://edition.cnn.com/2014/08/19/us/ferguson-michael-brown-dueling-narratives/

125 Ibid 121.

126 Associated Press. 2014. "Family and neighbors describe Missouri teenager fatally shot by police as quiet, respectful." *Fox News*, August 12. Accessed March 8, 2020. https://www.foxnews.com/us/family-and-neighbors-describe-missouri-teenager-fatally-shot-by-police-as-quiet-respectful

127 Schabner, Dean. 2014. "Witness Says Missouri Teen's Hands Were Up When Cop Shot Him." *ABC News*, August 10. Accessed March 6, 2020. https://abcnews.go.com/US/witness-missouri-teens-hands-cop-shot/story?id=24920358

128 McLaughlin, Eliott C. 2014. "What we know about Michael Brown's shooting." *CNN*, August 11. Accessed March 8, 2020. https://edition.cnn.com/2014/08/11/us/missouri-ferguson-michael-brown-what-we-know/

129 Ibid 119.

130 Ibid 126.

131 Keneally, Meghan. 2014. "Ferguson Cop Reports Called 'Character Assassination' by Slain Teen's Family." *ABC News*, August 15. Accessed March 6, 2020. https://abcnews.go.com/US/ferguson-police-detail-moments-michael-brown-shot/story?id=24998305

132 Wash, Stephanie and Steven Portnoy. 2014. "A Different Look at Ferguson's Michael Brown Just Days Before His Death." *ABC News*, August 21. Accessed March 10, 2020. https://abcnews.go.com/US/fergusons-michael-brown-days-death/story?id=25077435

133 Associated Press. 2014. "Some residents, politicians question credibility of investigation in Missouri teen's shooting." *Fox News*, August 14. Accessed March 8, 2020. https://www.foxnews.com/us/some-residents-politicians-question-credibility-of-investigation-in-missouri-teens-shooting

134 Curry, Colleen and Sabina Ghebremedhin. 2014. "Michael Brown Could Have Survived First 5 Shots, Last Shot Killed Him, Autopsy Says." *ABC News*, August 18. Accessed March 7, 2020. https://abcnews.go.com/US/michael-brown-shot-times-autopsy-shows/story?id=25017247

135 FNC. 2014. "Lawyers for Michael Brown's family say private autopsy backs witness accounts." *Fox News*, August 18. Accessed March 7, 2020. https://www.foxnews.com/us/lawyers-for-michael-browns-family-say-private-autopsy-backs-witness-accounts

136 FNC. 2014. "Missouri governor orders National Guard to Ferguson after latest night of clashes." *Fox News*, August 18. Accessed March 10, 2020. https://www.foxnews.com/us/missouri-governor-orders-national-guard-to-ferguson-after-latest-night-of-clashes

137 FNC. 2014. "YouTube video purportedly captures witness backing police version in Ferguson shooting." *Fox News*, August 18. Accessed March 7, 2020. https://www.foxnews.com/us/youtube-video-purportedly-captures-witness-backing-police-version-in-ferguson-shooting

138 Ibid 123.

139 Keneally, Meghan. 2014. "Ferguson Grand Jury Does Not Indict Officer Darren Wilson in Death of Michael Brown." *ABC News*, November 24. Accessed March 7, 2020. https://abcnews.go.com/US/ferguson-grand-jury-indict-officer-darren-wilson-death/story?id=27146400

140 Basu, Moni, Holly Yan and Dana Ford. 2014. "Fires, chaos erupt in Ferguson after grand jury doesn't indict in Michael Brown case." *CNN*, November 25. Accessed March 8, 2020. https://www.cnn.com/2014/11/24/justice/ferguson-grand-jury

141 FNC. 2014. "Gunshots, looting after grand jury in Ferguson case does not indict officer in Michael Brown shooting." *Fox News*, November 25. Accessed March 7, 2020. https://www.foxnews.com/us/gunshots-looting-after-grand-jury-in-ferguson-case-does-not-indict-officer-in-michael-brown-shooting

142 Washington Post. 2014. "Witnesses, data are said to back Ferguson cop." *Newsday*, October 23.

143 Levine, Mike, Pierre Thomas, Jack Cloherty and Jack Date. 2015. "Ferguson Report DOJ Will Not Charge Darren Wilson in Michael Brown Shooting." *ABC News*, March 4. Accessed March 6, 2020. https://abcnews.go.com/US/ferguson-report-doj-charge-darren-wilson-michael-brown/story?id=29338078

144 Ibid 142.

145 Associated Press. 2015. "Federal report backs Ferguson police officer's account in fatal shooting of Michael Brown." *Fox News*, March 4. Accessed March 7, 2020. https://www.foxnews.com/us/federal-report-backs-ferguson-police-officers-account-in-fatal-shooting-of-michael-brown

146 Perez, Evan and Wes Bruer. 2015. "CNN Justice Department: No Darren Wilson charges." *CNN*, March 4. Accessed March 14, 2020. https://www.cnn.com/2015/03/04/politics/ferguson-darren-wilson-justice-department-report/index.html?utm_source=feedburner&utm_medium=feed&utm_campaign=Feed%3A+rss%2Fcnn_latest+%28RSS%3A+CNN+-+Most+Recent%29

147 Ibid 145.

148 Ibid 43.

149 Kindelan, Katie. 2016. "Mothers of the Movement to Speak at Democratic National Convention." *ABC News*, July 26. Accessed March 6, 2020. https://abcnews.go.com/US/mothers-movement-speak-democratic-national-convention-speech/story?id=40882052

150 Sullum, Jacob. 2016. "'Mothers of the Moment' mix righteous rage and myth." *NY Post*, July 26. Accessed March 8, 2020. https://nypost.com/2016/07/26/mothers-of-the-moment-mix-righteous-rage-and-myth/

151 Shapiro, Emily. 2017. "Minneapolis man 'devastated' by police shooting of bride-to-be." *ABC News*, July 17. Accessed March 12, 2020. https://abcnews.go.com/US/deadly-police-shooting-bride-minneapolis/story?id=48678930

152 Caplan, David. 2017. "Hundreds attend Minneapolis march in honor of Justine Damond." *ABC News*, July 21. Accessed March 14, 2020. https://abcnews.go.com/US/hundreds-attend-minneapolis-march-honor-justine-ruszczyk/story?id=48764378

153 Criss, Doug. 2017. "There's a predictable pattern to a fatal police shooting. But not in the case of Justine Ruszczyk." *CNN*, July 19. Accessed March 12, 2020. https://www.cnn.com/2017/07/19/us/minneapolis-shooting-upended-outrage-trnd/index.html?utm_source=feedburner&utm_medium=feed&utm_campaign=Feed%3A+rss%2Fcnn_latest+%28RSS%3A+CNN+-+Most+Recent%29

154 Ibid 152.

155 Allen, Karma. 2017. "Sunrise vigil held in Sydney for Australian woman fatally shot by Minn. Officer." *ABC News*, July 19. Accessed March 10, 2020. https://abcnews.go.com/International/family-friends-gather-sydney-honor-woman-fatally-shot/story?id=48716069

156 Helsel, Phil. 2017. "Australian Justine Damond Shot Dead by Minneapolis Officer Called 911 Twice." *NBC News*, July 19. Accessed March 15, 2020. https://www.nbcnews.com/news/us-news/australian-shot-dead-minneapolis-officer-called-911-twice-n784576

157 Allen, Karma. 2017. "What we know about the officer involved in the fatal police shooting in Minneapolis." *ABC News*, July 18. Accessed March 12, 2020. https://abcnews.go.com/US/officer-involved-fatal-police-shooting-minneapolis/story?id=48694855

158 O'Reilly, Andrew. 2017. "Minneapolis Somali community shocked by police killing, worried about backlash." *Fox News*, July 20. Accessed March 13, 2020. https://www.foxnews.com/us/minneapolis-somali-community-shocked-by-police-killing-worried-about-backlash

159 Ibid 157.

160 O'Reilly, Andrew. 2017. "Minnesota police shooting: Justine Damond's family, friends join march." *Fox News*, July 20. Accessed March 13, 2020. https://www.foxnews.com/us/minnesota-police-shooting-justine-damonds-family-friends-join-march

161 FNC. 2017. "Police mocked in fake street signs illegally installed in Twin Cities." *Fox News*, July 25. Accessed March 16, 2020. https://www.foxnews.com/us/police-mocked-in-fake-street-signs-illegally-installed-in-twin-cities

162 Ellis, Ralph. 2017. "Minneapolis police chief resigns in wake of fatal shooting." *CNN*, July 23. Accessed March 12, 2020. https://edition.cnn.com/2017/07/21/us/minneapolis-police-chief-resigns/index.html

163 Winsor, Morgan. 2017. "Key witness identified in fatal Minneapolis police shooting of bride-to-be." *ABC News*, July 22. Accessed March 15, 2020. https://abcnews.go.com/US/key-witness-identified-minneapolis-officer-involved-shooting-killed/story?id=48790698

164 FNC. 2017. "Minnesota cop who fatally shot Australian woman was 'fast-tracked' into the force." *Fox News*, July 24. Accessed March 13, 2020. https://www.foxnews.com/us/minnesota-cop-who-fatally-shot-australian-woman-was-fast-tracked-into-the-force

165 Associated Press. 2017. "The Latest: Lawyer says officer ambush worry was reasonable." *Fox News*, July 19. Accessed March 16, 2020. https://www.foxnews.com/us/the-latest-lawyer-says-officer-ambush-worry-was-reasonable

166 Associated Press. 2018. "Records: Cop accused in Australian's death can't take stress." *Fox News*, September 6. Accessed March 13, 2020. https://www.foxnews.com/us/records-cop-accused-in-australians-death-cant-take-stress

167 Associated Press. 2018. "Minnesota officer involved in Justine Damond's death can't handle stress, records show." *NBC News*, September 6. Accessed March 13, 2020. https://www.nbcnews.com/news/us-news/minnesota-officer-involved-justine-damond-s-death-can-t-handle-n907036?cid=public-rss_20180906

168 Forliti, Amy. 2017. "Prosecutors to consider charges in Australian woman's death." *Associated Press*, September 12. Accessed March 12, 2020. https://apnews.com/7807517b485a48e48ce092370c3ecc7e

169 Fedschun, Travis. 2017. "Minnesota prosecutors to consider charges in case of Australian woman killed by police officer." *Fox News*, September 12. Accessed March 12, 2020. https://www.foxnews.com/us/minnesota-prosecutors-to-consider-charges-in-case-of-australian-woman-killed-by-police-officer

170 Allen, Karma. 2017. "Australian man slams Minnesota investigation of his daughter's killing by police." *ABC News*, December 21. Accessed March 12, 2020. https://abcnews.go.com/US/australian-father-slams-minnesota-investigation-daughters-killing-police/story?id=51926431

171 FNC. 2017. "Relatives of Australian woman killed by Somali-born Minneapolis cop cast doubt on investigation." *Fox News*, December 21. Accessed March 13, 2020. https://www.foxnews.com/us/relatives-of-australian-woman-killed-by-somali-born-minneapolis-cop-cast-doubt-on-investigation

172 Associated Press. 2019. "The Latest: Noor jury seated; 6 people of color on panel." *ABC News*, April 8. Accessed March 12, 2020. https://abcnews.go.com/US/wireStory/latest-noor-jury-seated-people-color-panel-62251512

173 Forliti, Amy. 2019. "Activists: Cop's shooting of white woman treated differently." *ABC News*, April 13. Accessed March 12, 2020. https://abcnews.go.com/International/wireStory/activists-cops-shooting-white-woman-treated-differently-62377028

174 Ibid 172.

175 Forliti, Amy. 2019. "Minnesota cop's trial raises questions about code of silence." *ABC News*, April 16. Accessed March 12, 2020. https://abcnews.go.com/US/wireStory/minnesota-cops-trial-raises-questions-code-silence-62435507

176 Forliti, Amy. 2019. "Officer says partner fired before he could analyze threat." *ABC News*, April 18. Accessed March 12, 2020. https://abcnews.go.com/International/wireStory/partner-cop-charged-minneapolis-shooting-takes-stand-62486732

177 Associated Press. 2019. "The Latest: Detective: Scene of fatal shooting clearly lit." *ABC News*, April 11. Accessed March 12, 2020. https://abcnews.go.com/US/wireStory/latest-detective-scene-fatal-shooting-lit-62344120

178 Joyce, Kathleen. 2019. "Body cam footage shows officers attempting to save Justine Damond after she was shot by officer." *Fox News*, April 12. Accessed March 13, 2020. https://www.foxnews.com/us/body-cam-footage-justine-damond-shooting-shows-officers-trying-save-her

179 Forliti, Amy. 2019. "Ex-Minneapolis officer resumes testimony in woman's death." *FNC*, April 26. Accessed March 13, 2020. https://www.foxnews.com/us/ex-minneapolis-officer-resumes-testimony-in-womans-death

180 Associated Press. 2019. "The Latest: Ex-officer cries in describing woman's death." *ABC News*, April 25. Accessed March 12, 2020. https://abcnews.go.com/US/wireStory/latest-officer-testifies-ambush-training-62635057

181 Baenen, Jeff and Amy Forliti. 2019. "Officer fled civil war as a child, resettled in Minneapolis." *ABC News*, April 26. Accessed March 12, 2020. https://abcnews.go.com/US/wireStory/officer-fled-civil-war-child-resettled-minneapolis-62643897

182 Ibid 104.

183 Forliti, Amy. 2019. "Conviction for Minneapolis cop prompts questions about race." *ABC News*, May 1. Accessed March 12, 2020. https://abcnews.go.com/US/wireStory/black-minneapolis-officers-conviction-surprise-62744353

184 Ibid 182.

185 Ibid 182.

186 Ibid 182.

187 Ibid 182.

188 Forliti, Amy. 2019. "Rare conviction of officer in shooting spurs race concerns." *Fox News*, May 1. Accessed March 13, 2020. https://www.foxnews.com/us/rare-conviction-of-officer-in-shooting-spurs-race-concerns

189 Associated Press. 2019. "The Latest: BCA head: Damond probe thorough, independent." *ABC News*, May 1. Accessed March 12, 2020. https://abcnews.go.com/US/wireStory/latest-somali-american-police-group-pans-noor-verdict-62750985

190 Associated Press. 2019. "Minneapolis paying $20 million to unarmed woman's family over deadly police shooting." *CBS News*, May 3. Accessed March 12, 2020. https://www.cbsnews.com/news/justine-ruszczyk-damond-minneapolis-20-million-family-deadly-police-shooting-today-2019-05-03-live-updates/

191 Jackson, Joey. 2019. "Mohamed Noor's sentence raises uncomfortable questions about race." *CNN*, May 3 (Updated June 8th). Accessed March 12, 2020. https://www.cnn.com/2019/05/03/opinions/mohamed-noor-conviction-justine-ruszczyk-death-raises-questions-jackson/index.html?utm_source=feedburner&utm_medium=feed&utm_campaign=Feed%3A+rss%2Fcnn_latest+%28RSS%3A+CNN+-+Most+Recent%29

192 Ibid 190.

193 Ibid 190.

194 Karnowski, Steve. 2017. "Philando Castile trial: Officer says motorist had hand on gun when shot." *USA Today*, June 9. Accessed April 11, 2020. https://www.usatoday.com/story/news/nation/2017/06/09/philando-castile-trial-officer-says-motorist-had-hand-gun-when-shot/102680818/

195 Horner, Sarah. 2017. "Officer's defense can bring up Philando Castile's marijuana use, judge rules." *Pioneer Press*, May 17. Accessed April 11, 2020. https://www.twincities.com/2017/05/16/judge-assault-charge-pending-against-castiles-girlfriend-not-relevant-to-legal-issues-of-his-death/

196 Love, David. 2019. "Sandra Bland's cellphone video is a disturbing reminder." *CNN*, May 11. Accessed March 12, 2020. https://www.cnn.com/2019/05/11/opinions/sandra-bland-video-disturbing-reminder/index.html?utm_source=feedburner&utm_medium=feed&utm_campaign=Feed%3A+rss%2Fcnn_topstories+%28RSS%3A+CNN+-+Top+Stories%29

197 Ibid 195.

198 McLaughlin, Eliott C. 2014. "Fatal police shooting in Missouri sparks protests." *CNN*, August 10. Accessed March 11, 2020. https://www.cnn.com/2014/08/10/justice/missouri-police-involved-shooting/index.html

199 Curry, Colleen and Andrew Springer. 2014. "Howard Students 'Surrender' in Solidarity with Michael Brown." *ABC News*, August 14. Accessed March 5, 2020. https://abcnews.go.com/US/howard-students-hold-hands-solidarity-michael-brown/story?id=24984573

200 Associated Press. 2014. "Redskins show solidarity with Ferguson protest." *USA Today*, August 19. Accessed March 3, 2020. https://www.usatoday.com/story/sports/nfl/2014/08/19/redskins-show-solidarity-with-ferguson-protest/14284105/

201 Associated Press. 2014. "Celebrities, civil rights leaders at Brown funeral." *Washington Times*, August 25. Accessed March 8, 2020. https://www.washingtontimes.com/news/2014/aug/25/celebrities-civil-rights-leaders-at-brown-funeral/

202 Unglesbee, Ben. 2014. "Buildings destroyed in Ferguson riots worth millions." *St. Louis Business Journal*, December 4. Accessed March 5, 2020. https://www.bizjournals.com/stlouis/news/2014/12/04/buildings-destroyed-in-ferguson-riots-worth.html

203 Wulfhorst, Ellen, Daniel Wallis and Edward McAllister. 2014. "More than 400 arrested as Ferguson protests spread to other U.S. cities." *Reuters*, November 25. Accessed March 6, 2020. https://www.reuters.com/article/us-usa-missouri-shooting/more-than-400-arrested-as-ferguson-protests-spread-to-other-u-s-cities-idUSKCN0J80PR20141126

204 Murray, Rheana. 2014. "People Walk Out of Work, School in Ferguson Protests." *ABC News*, December 1. Accessed March 7, 2020. https://abcnews.go.com/US/people-walk-work-school-ferguson-protests/story?id=27288450

205 Good, Dan. 2014. "Police Officers Association 'Profoundly Disappointed' by St. Louis Rams Players' Display." *ABC News*, December 1. Accessed March 7, 2020. https://abcnews.go.com/Sports/police-officers-association-profoundly-disappointed-st-louis-rams/story?id=27271318

206 Fisher, Luchina. 2014. "Chris Rock on Ferguson, Black Progress and Future for His Kids." *ABC News*, December 2. Accessed March 9, 2020. https://abcnews.go.com/blogs/entertainment/2014/12/chris-rock-on-ferguson-black-progress-and-future-for-his-kids/

207 FNC. 2014. "Charles Barkley says Ferguson grand jury got it right; looters 'scumbags'." *Fox News*, December 1. Accessed March 7, 2020. https://www.foxnews.com/us/charles-barkley-says-ferguson-grand-jury-got-it-right-looters-scumbags

208 FNC. 2014. "Authorities say cop killer wanted retaliation for Michael Brown, Eric Garner deaths." *Fox News*, December 21. Accessed March 7, 2020. https://www.foxnews.com/us/authorities-say-cop-killer-wanted-retaliation-for-michael-brown-eric-garner-deaths

209 Fox News Insider. 2016. "Beyoncé Backup Dancers 'Shot' at VMAs to Make Point About Police & Gun Violence." *Fox News*, August 29. Accessed March 7, 2020. https://insider.foxnews.com/2016/08/29/beyonce-mtv-video-music-awards-performance-gun-violence-police-shootings

210 Cannariato, Nicholas. 2019. "'Hands Up, Don't Shoot' Examines What Led to Ferguson And Baltimore Protests." *NPR*, August 1. Accessed March 10, 2020. https://www.npr.org/2019/08/01/745484653/hands-up-don-t-shoot

211 Olson, David. 2020. "Speakers discuss legacy of slavery after 400 years." *Newsday*, January 12.

212 Shapiro, Emily. 2017. "Minneapolis man 'devastated' by police shooting of bride-to-be." *ABC News*, July 17. Accessed March 12, 2020. https://abcnews.go.com/US/deadly-police-shooting-bride-minneapolis/story?id=48678930

213 McKirdy, Euan and Ralph Ellis. 2017. "Woman killed by Minneapolis police a month before wedding." *CNN*, July 18. Accessed March 12, 2020. https://www.cnn.com/2017/07/18/us/justine-ruszczyk-minneapolis-shooting-australia/index.html

214 Allen, Karma. 2017. "Sunrise vigil held in Sydney for Australian woman fatally shot by Minn. Officer." *ABC News*, July 19. Accessed March 10, 2020. https://abcnews.go.com/International/family-friends-gather-sydney-honor-woman-fatally-shot/story?id=48716069

215 O'Reilly, Andrew. 2017. "Minnesota police shooting: Justine Damond's family, friends join march." *Fox News*, July 20. Accessed March 13, 2020. https://www.foxnews.com/us/minnesota-police-shooting-justine-damonds-family-friends-join-march

216 Forliti, Amy. April 13, 2017

217 Fowler, Tara, Catherine Thorbecke and Julia Jacobo. 2017. "Protesters shout down Minneapolis mayor in wake of fatal shooting of bride-to-be." *ABC News*, July 21. Accessed March 12, 2020. https://abcnews.go.com/US/minneapolis-police-chief-resigns-wake-fatal-shooting-bride/story?id=48783798

218 Ibid 160.

219 Ibid 172.

220 Associated Press. 2017. "Minneapolis police remove Justine Damond memorial created by white nationalists." *CBS News*, December 25. Accessed March 12, 2020. https://www.cbsnews.com/news/minneapolis-police-remove-memorial-to-slain-woman-created-by-white-nationalists/

221 Ibid 219.

222 Ibid 126.

223 Margolin, Josh, Dan Good and Colleen Curry. 2014. "President Obama Calls Shooting of Missouri Teen 'Heartbreaking'." *ABC News*, August 12. Accessed March 5, 2020. https://abcnews.go.com/US/president-obama-calls-shooting-missouri-teen-heartbreaking/story?id=24941866

224 Richey, Warren. 2014. "Eric Holder visits Ferguson. Will US take over Michael Brown case?" *The Christian Science Monitor*, August 20. Accessed March 12, 2020. https://www.csmonitor.com/USA/Justice/2014/0820/Eric-Holder-visits-Ferguson.-Will-US-take-over-Michael-Brown-case

225 FNC. 2014. "Cheney: 'Stunned' over Obama comparison between Mideast, Ferguson unrest." *Fox News*, September 25. Accessed March 7, 2020. https://www.foxnews.com/politics/cheney-stunned-over-obama-comparison-between-mideast-ferguson-unrest

226 FNC. 2014. "Congressional Black Caucus calls Ferguson decision 'slap in the face'." *Fox News*, November 25. Accessed March 7, 2020. https://www.foxnews.com/politics/congressional-black-caucus-calls-ferguson-decision-slap-in-the-face

227 Fischer, Sara. 2014. "Durbin to hold human rights hearing on Ferguson." *CNN*, November 25. Accessed March 9, 2020. https://www.cnn.com/2014/11/25/politics/durbin/index.html?utm_source=feedburner&utm_medium=feed&utm_campaign=Feed%3A+rss%2Fcnn_latest+%28RSS%3A+CNN+-+Most+Recent%29

228 Larotonda Matthew and Chris Good. 2015. "Obama Says 'We May Never Know What Happened' in Ferguson, But Defends DOJ." *ABC News*, March 6. Accessed March 9, 2020. https://abcnews.go.com/Politics/obama-happened-ferguson-defends-doj/story?id=29441456

229 FNC. 2016. "Painting depicting cops as animals displayed on Capitol Hill." *Fox News*, December 30. Accessed March 7, 2020. https://www.foxnews.com/politics/painting-depicting-cops-as-animals-displayed-on-capitol-hill

230 Colvin, Jill. 2014. "Governor Chris Christie won't draw conclusions about Ferguson." *ABC7NY*, August 19. Accessed March 7, 2020. https://abc7ny.com/politics/christie-wont-comment-on-ferguson/271666/

231 Jaffe, Alexandra. 2014. "Huckabee: Michael Brown acted like a 'thug'." *CNN*, December 3. Accessed March 8, 2020. https://www.cnn.com/2014/12/03/politics/ferguson-mike-huckabee-michael-brown-shooting-thug/index.html?utm_source=feedburner&utm_medium=feed&utm_campaign=Feed%3A+rss%2Fcnn_latest+%28RSS%3A+CNN+-+Most+Recent%29

232 Smith, Candace. 2016. "Bush Sweeps Aside Police Violence to Discuss Black-on-Black Crime." *ABC News*, January 13. Accessed March 3, 2020. https://abcnews.go.com/Politics/jeb-bush-cops-build-trust-black-communities/story?id=36271351

233 Rafferty, Andrew. 2015. "Ben Carson Emphasizes Respect During Trip to Ferguson." *NBC News*, September 11. Accessed March 9, 2020. https://www.nbcnews.com/politics/2016-election/ben-carson-emphasizes-respect-during-trip-ferguson-n426021?cid=sm_twitter_feed_politics

234 LET Staff. 2019. "Bernie Sanders: Respect police "so that you don't get shot in the back of the head." *Law Enforcement Today*, October 28. Accessed March 2, 2020. https://www.lawenforcementtoday.com/bernie-sanders-respect-police-so-that-you-dont-get-shot-in-the-back-of-the-head/

235 Nelson, Joshua. 2019. "Former Missouri Dem lawmaker, retired officer blasts Warren for tweet claiming Michael Brown was murdered." *Fox News*, August 12. Accessed March 7, 2020. https://www.foxnews.com/media/cops-blast-elizabeth-warren-claiming-michael-brown-murdered

236 Steinhauser, Paul. 2019. "Harris, Warren fact-checked on claim Michael Brown was murdered." Fox News, August 13. Accessed March 5, 2020. https://www.foxnews.com/politics/harris-warren-fact-checked-on-claim-michael-brown-was-murdered

237 Pestano, Andrew V. 2017. "Australian PM demands answers in police shooting of Justine Ruszczyk." *UPI*, July 19. Accessed March 15, 2020. https://www.upi.com/Top_News/World-News/2017/07/19/Australian-PM-demands-answers-in-police-shooting-of-Justine-Ruszczyk/4861500478932/

238 Ibid 212.

239 Otarola, Miguel. 2017. "Back in spotlight, Michele Bachmann praises Trump, addresses Minneapolis police shooting of Justine Damond." *Star Tribune*, July 20. Accessed March 12, 2020. http://www.startribune.com/bachmann-praises-trump-blasts-political-correctness/435517653/

240 Ibid 107, page 10.

241 Department of Justice (DOJ). 2017. "Federal Officials Close Investigation into Death of Alton Sterling." *Department of Justice Press Release 17-487*, May 3. Accessed February 21, 2020. https://www.justice.gov/opa/pr/federal-officials-close-investigation-death-alton-sterling

242 Donnella, Leah. 2016. "Two Days, Two Deaths: The Police Shootings of Alton Sterling And Philando Castile." *NPR*, July 7. Accessed February 20, 2020. https://www.npr.org/sections/codeswitch/2016/07/07/485078670/two-days-two-deaths-the-police-shootings-of-alton-sterling-and-philando-castile

243 Ellis, Ralph. 2018. "How five videos captured the fatal shooting of Alton Sterling." *CNN*, March 31. Accessed March 1, 2020. https://www.cnn.com/2018/03/31/us/alton-sterling-video-descriptions/index.html

244 Wang, Vivian. 2017. "From 2017: Video Shows Daniel Shaver Pleading for His Life Before Being Shot by Officer." *The New York Times*, December 9. Accessed February 20, 2020. https://www.nytimes.com/2017/12/09/us/police-shooting-video-arizona.html

245 Ortiz, Erik. 2018. "Alton Sterling killing: No state criminal charges against 2 Baton Rouge police officers." *NBC News*, March 27. Accessed February 27, 2020. https://www.nbcnews.com/news/us-news/alton-sterling-killing-no-state-criminal-charges-against-2-baton-n860391

246 Levenson, Eric. 2019. "Baton Rouge police chief apologizes for hiring the officer who killed Alton Sterling." *CNN*, August 1. Accessed March 2, 2020. https://www.cnn.com/2019/08/01/us/alton-sterling-baton-rouge-police/index.html?utm_source=feedburner&utm_medium=feed&utm_campaign=Feed%3A+rss%2Fcnn_latest+%28RSS%3A+CNN+-+Most+Recent%29

247 Garcia, Uriel J. 2018. "Feds investigating Daniel Shaver shooting." *The Republic*, March 9. Accessed February 21, 2020. https://www.azcentral.com/story/news/local/mesa/2018/03/08/mesa-police-confirm-justice-department-investigating-shooting-officer/409331002/

248 Tang, Terry. 2016. "Woman questions husband's shooting by Phoenix-area police." *NY Daily News*, January 23. Accessed March 2, 2020. https://www.nydailynews.com/sdut-woman-questions-husbands-shooting-by-phoenix-area-2016jan23-story.html

249 Ibid 247.

250 King, Shaun. 2016. "KING: Instead of getting the facts, Las Vegas police kill unarmed Keith Childress, Jr., claiming he was wanted for attempted murder." *NY Daily News*, January 12. Accessed March 2, 2020. http://www.nydailynews.com/news/national/king-las-vegas-police-kill-unarmed-black-man-false-facts-article-1.2494201

251 Cruz, Jennifer. 2016. "Body cam footage shows suspect ignored more than 20 commands." *Guns.com*, January 11. Accessed March 18, 2020. https://www.guns.com/news/2016/01/11/body-cam-footage-shows-suspect-ignored-more-than-20-commands-video

252 Clark County District Attorney. 2016. "REPORT ON USE OF FORCE: Legal Analysis Surrounding the Death of Keith Childress on December 31, 2015". *Clark County*, September 22. Accessed March 2, 2020. http://www.clarkcountynv.gov/district-attorney/Documents/OIS%20Report-FINAL%20RELEASED.pdf

253 Associated Press. 2016. "Mesa officer charged with murder in shooting of unarmed man." *CBS News*, March 7. Accessed March 2, 2020. https://www.cbsnews.com/news/mesa-officer-charged-with-murder-in-shooting-of-unarmed-man/

254 Associated Press. 2017. "Mesa Police shooting: Daniel Shaver seen crawling, begging in disturbing video." *CBS News*, December 8. Accessed March 2, 2020. https://www.cbsnews.com/news/mesa-police-shooting-daniel-shaver-seen-crawling-begging-in-disturbing-video/

255 Gagliano, James. 2017. "Daniel Shaver's shooting by police officer was an avoidable execution." *CNN*, December 12. Accessed March 2, 2020. https://www.cnn.com/2017/12/11/opinions/daniel-shaver-shooting-opinion-gagliano/index.html?utm_source=feedburner&utm_medium=feed&utm_campaign=Feed%3A+rss%2Fcnn_latest+%28RSS%3A+CNN+-+Most+Recent%29

256 Ibid 255.

257 Ibid 255.

258 Ibid 244.

259 Billeaud, Jacques. 2017. "Ex-Arizona police officer acquitted in fatal hotel shooting". *Fox News*, December 7. Accessed March 2, 2020. https://www.foxnews.com/us/ex-arizona-police-officer-acquitted-in-fatal-hotel-shooting

260 Ibid 244.

261 FNC. 2017. "Former Arizona cop acquitted in shooting was a failed actor, report says." *Fox News*, December 11. Accessed March 2, 2020. https://www.foxnews.com/us/former-arizona-cop-acquitted-in-shooting-was-a-failed-actor-report-says

262 Joyce, Kathleen. 2017. "Unarmed man's death 'an execution' by Arizona officer, widow says." *Fox News*, December 14. Accessed March 2, 2020. https://www.foxnews.com/us/unarmed-mans-death-an-execution-by-arizona-officer-widow-says

263 Ibid 241.

264 Contreras, Russell. 2016. "Police shootings of black men stir fears, anger among blacks." *Associated Press*, July 8. Accessed March 1, 2020. https://apnews.com/b35b79fbae5d43838026f99fe61dd9c1

265 Ibid 263.

266 Ibid 263.

267 Grinberg, Emanuella. 2017. "Why the feds did not file charges in Alton Sterling's death." *CNN*, May 3. Accessed March 3, 2020. https://www.cnn.com/2017/05/03/us/alton-sterling-death-federal-charges/index.html

268 Hanna, Jason. 2018. "No charges against officers in Alton Sterling death; other videos are coming." *CNN*, March 27. Accessed March 3, 2020. https://www.cnn.com/2018/03/27/us/alton-sterling-investigation/index.html?utm_source=feedburner&utm_medium=feed&utm_campaign=Feed%3A+rss%2Fcnn_latest+%28RSS%3A+CNN+-+Most+Recent%29

269 Ibid 267.

270 Associated Press. 2018. "2 officers in Alton Sterling's fatal shooting won't be charged." *Fox News*, March 27. Accessed March 3, 2020. https://www.foxnews.com/us/2-officers-in-alton-sterlings-fatal-shooting-wont-be-charged

271 Associated Press. 2018. "The Latest: No charges in Alton Sterling's fatal shooting." *Fox News*, March 27. Accessed March 3, 2020. https://www.foxnews.com/us/the-latest-no-charges-in-alton-sterlings-fatal-shooting

272 Zwirz, Elizabeth. 2018. "One officer in Alton Sterling shooting fired, and another suspended, police chief says." *Fox News*, March 30. Accessed March 3, 2020. https://www.foxnews.com/us/one-officer-in-alton-sterling-shooting-fired-and-another-suspended-police-chief-says

273 Associated Press. 2018. "NAACP seeks special prosecutor in black man's shooting death." *Fox News*, April 2. Accessed March 3, 2020. https://www.foxnews.com/us/naacp-seeks-special-prosecutor-in-black-mans-shooting-death

274 CBS. 2016. "Report: Cops furious at WNBA team's social protest walk off job." *CBS News*, July 12. Accessed March 4, 2020. https://www.cbsnews.com/news/report-cops-walk-off-job-minnesota-lynx-black-lives-matter/

275 Messer, Lesley, and David Caplan. 2016. "ESPYS 2016: LeBron James, Dwyane Wade, Chris Paul and Carmelo Anthony Call for an End to Violence." *ABC News*, July 13. Accessed March 4, 2020. https://abcnews.go.com/Entertainment/espys-2016-lebron-james-dwyane-wade-chris-paul/story?id=40563702

276 Hayden, Michael Edison. 2016. "Texas Youth Football Team to Continue Protesting Anthem Despite Death Threats." *ABC News*, September 14. Accessed March 3, 2020. https://abcnews.go.com/US/texas-youth-football-team-continue-protesting-anthem-death/story?id=42082211

277 Yang, Allie. 2017. "49ers' Eric Reid defends taking a knee during national anthem: 'We want to make our country better'." *ABC News*, October 7. Accessed March 4, 2020. https://abcnews.go.com/US/49ers-eric-reid-defends-taking-knee-national-anthem/story?id=50395766

278 Ng, Philiana. 2016. "Beyonce holds moment of silence for shooting victims at her concert." *CBS News*, July 8. Accessed March 4, 2020. https://www.cbsnews.com/news/beyonce-holds-moment-of-silence-for-shooting-victims-at-her-concert/

279 McKenzie, Joi-Marie and Kayna Whitworth. 2016. "Snoop Dogg and The Game Lead Peaceful March to LAPD Headquarters." *ABC News*, July 8. Accessed March 4, 2020. https://abcnews.go.com/Entertainment/snoop-dogg-game-lead-peaceful-march-lapd-headquarters/story?id=40439959

280 Thorbecke, Catherine. 2016. "Baton Rouge in Mourning as Alton Sterling Laid to Rest." *ABC News*, July 15. Accessed March 4, 2020. https://abcnews.go.com/US/mourners-gather-baton-rouge-alton-sterling-laid-rest/story?id=40601972

281 Thorbecke, Catherine. 2016. "'I Have to Wake Up to This' Serena Williams, Celebs React to Two Police Shootings of Black Men One Day Apart." *ABC News*, July 7. Accessed March 4, 2020. https://abcnews.go.com/US/serena-williams-celebrities-react-deadly-24-hours-separate/story?id=40407451

282 McBride, Brian. 2016. "Tipping Point? A Nation on Edge After Days of Protests, Hundreds Arrested." *ABC News*, July 11. Accessed March 3, 2020. https://abcnews.go.com/US/tipping-point-nation-edge-days-protests-hundreds-arrested/story?id=40483629

283 Winsor, Morgan. 2016. "Black Lives Matter Protests Go Global, From Ireland to South Africa." *ABC News*, July 13. Accessed March 3, 2020. https://abcnews.go.com/International/black-lives-matter-protests-global-ireland-south-africa/story?id=40546549

284 Ibid 281.

285 Hayden, Michael Edison, and David Caplan. 2016. "Protests Continue in Baton Rouge and St. Paul Following Night of Arrests." *ABC News*, July 10. Accessed March 3, 2020. https://abcnews.go.com/US/protests-continue-baton-rouge-st-paul-night-arrests/story?id=40467365

286 Winsor, Morgan, and Devin Villacis. 2016. "Dallas Suspect Micah Xavier Johnson Accused of Sexual Harassment in Army Reserve." *ABC News*, July 9. Accessed March 5, 2020. https://abcnews.go.com/News/dallas-shooting-suspect-micah-xavier-johnson-accused-sex/story?id=40456396

287 AZ Family. 2017. "VIDEO: Protesters gather in Mesa in response to deadly police shooting." *AZFamily.com*, December 22. Accessed March 3, 2020. https://www.youtube.com/watch?v=0bgzpQ2dDr8

288 Ibid 246.

289 Ibid 243.

290 Ibid 243.

291 Ibid 243.

292 Conley, Julia. 2017. "Black Lives Matter Supporters Call Attention to Graphic Video of Arizona Shooting." *Common Dreams*, December 9. Accessed March 3, 2020. https://www.commondreams.org/news/2017/12/09/black-lives-matter-supporters-call-attention-graphic-video-arizona-shooting

293 Kangadis, Nick. 2017. "No Protests Scheduled for the White Guy Shot by a Cop." *Media Research Center*, December 8. Accessed March 3, 2020. https://www.mrctv.org/blog/former-ariz-officer-found-not-guilty-shooting-unarmed-white-man-protesters-silent

294 Parkinson, John. 2016. "Obama Reacts on Facebook to Police-Involved Killings of Sterling and Castile." *ABC News*, July 7. Accessed March 4, 2020. https://abcnews.go.com/Politics/obama-reacts-facebook-police-involved-killings-sterling-castile/story?id=40413740

295 Ibid 293.

296 Memoli, Michael A. and Christi Parsons. 2016. "Obama on deadly shootings of black men: 'We can do better'." *Los Angeles Times*, July 7. Accessed March 16, 2020. https://www.latimes.com/nation/la-na-obama-minnesota-louisiana-shootings-20160707-snap-story.html

297 The White House. 2016. "Press Conference by President Obama after NATO Summit." *Office of the Press Secretary*, July 9. Accessed March 17, 2020. https://obamawhitehouse.archives.gov/the-press-office/2016/07/09/press-conference-president-obama-after-nato-summit

298 Boyer, Dave. 2016. "Obama calls the families of two black men shot by police." *The Washington Times*, July 12. Accessed March 4, 2020. https://www.washingtontimes.com/news/2016/jul/12/obama-calls-families-black-men-shot-police/

299 Ibid 279.

300 Chadbourn, Margaret. 2016. "Obama Offers Hope to Alton Sterling's Son Cameron: 'The Country Is Not as Divided as It Seems'." *ABC News*, July 14. Accessed March 4, 2020. https://abcnews.go.com/US/obama-offers-hope-alton-sterlings-son-cameron-country/story?id=40588198

301 Associated Press. 2016. "President Obama meets with Alton Sterling's family, families of slain Baton Rouge officers." *The Advocate*, August 23. Accessed March 4, 2020. https://www.theadvocate.com/louisiana_flood_2016/article_1b352c7a-6962-11e6-9835-f70c9a3f2d8d.html

302 Scott, Eugene. 2016. "Clinton Warren call attention to police shootings." *CNN*, July 7. Accessed March 3, 2020. https://www.cnn.com/2016/07/07/politics/alton-sterling-philando-castile-2016-election/

303 Haskell, Josh and Liz Kreutz. 2016. "Hillary Clinton Calls for 'Greater Respect' for Cops, National Guidelines on Use of Force". *ABC News*, July 8. Accessed March 4, 2020. https://abcnews.go.com/Politics/hillary-clinton-calls-greater-respect-cops-national-guidelines/story?id=40441697

304 Ibid 301.

305 McBride, Brian. 2016. "Baton Rouge Police Investigate Fatal Shooting of Black Man at Convenience Store." *ABC News*, July 6. Accessed March 16, 2020. https://abcnews.go.com/US/baton-rouge-police-investigate-fatal-shooting-black-man/story?id=40365543

306 Ibid 301.

307 Carlson, Adam. 2016. "FBI and Justice Department's Civil Rights Division Take Over Alton Sterling Shooting Investigation from Baton Rouge PD." *People*, July 6. Accessed March 4, 2020. https://people.com/crime/alton-sterling-investigation-handed-over-to-doj-and-fbi/

308 Rainey, Richard. 2016. "Watch Louisiana's 2016 DNC roll call vote: Happy, defiant." *The New Orleans Advocate*, July 27. Accessed March 4, 2020. https://www.nola.com/news/politics/article_ed5d616c-88f7-5db1-8197-4b8de8f47d19.html

309 Ibid 269.

310 Falcone, Michael, and Veronica Stracqualursi. 2016. "Donald Trump Wants to 'Restore Law and Order' After Week of Police-Involved Shootings" *ABC News*, July 8. Accessed March 4, 2020. https://abcnews.go.com/Politics/donald-trump-offers-prayers-condolences-families-shooting-victims/story?id=40429817

311 ABC News. 2016. "FULL TEXT: Ted Cruz's 2016 Republican National Convention Speech." *ABC News*, July 21. Accessed March 4, 2020. https://abcnews.go.com/Politics/full-text-ted-cruzs-2016-republican-national-convention/story?id=40768272

312 Billeaud, Jacques. 2017. "Ex-Arizona police officer acquitted in fatal hotel shooting". *Fox News,* December 7. Accessed March 2, 2020. https://www.foxnews.com/us/ex-arizona-police-officer-acquitted-in-fatal-hotel-shooting

313 Osunsami, Steve and Emily Shapiro. 2017. "Ex-cop Michael Slager sentenced to 20 years for shooting death of Walter Scott." *ABC News*, December 7. Accessed March 21, 2020. https://abcnews.go.com/US/cop-michael-slager-faces-19-24-years-prison/story?id=51595376

314 Karimi, Faith and Emanuella Grinberg. 2018. "Texas ex-officer is sentenced to 15 years for killing an unarmed teen." *CNN*, August 30. Accessed March 21, 2020. https://www.cnn.com/2018/08/29/us/texas-jordan-edwards-death-sentencing-phase/index.html

315 Ibid 93, page 802.

316 Ibid 107, page 28.

317 Marsh, Kristine. 2015. "WaPo Calls 'Hands Up, Don't Shoot' One of 2015's 'Biggest Pinocchios'." *Newsbusters.org*, December 15. Accessed March 10, 2020. https://www.newsbusters.org/blogs/culture/kristine-marsh/2015/12/15/wapo-calls-hands-dont-shoot-one-2015s-biggest-pinocchios

318 ABC News. 2014. "Michael Brown's Stepfather Apologizes for 'Burn' Outburst in Ferguson." *ABC News*, December 3. Accessed March 3, 2020. https://abcnews.go.com/US/michael-browns-stepfather-investigated-ferguson-outburst/story?id=27331195

319 Caselaw.findlaw.com. 2021. "Tennessee v. Garner." Caselaw.findlaw.com. Accessed February 20, 2021. https://caselaw.findlaw.com/us-supreme-court/471/1.html

320 Clark, Mark. 2014. "Understanding Graham v. Connor." *Policemag.com*, October 27. Accessed February 20, 2021. https://www.policemag.com/341717/understanding-graham-v-connor

321 Law Enforcement Organizations. 2020. "National Consensus Policy on Use of Force." *The International Association of Chiefs of Police*, July. Page 4. Accessed February 20, 2021. https://www.theiacp.org/sites/default/files/2020-07/National_Consensus_Policy_On_Use_Of_Force%2007102020%20v3.pdf

322 FBI. 2021. "What is the FBI's policy on the use of deadly force by its special agents?" *FBI.gov*. Accessed February 20, 2021. https://www.fbi.gov/about/faqs/what-is-the-fbis-policy-on-the-use-of-deadly-force-by-its-special-agents

323 Chicago Police Department. 2020. "Use of Force." General Order G03-02, February 28. Page 2. Accessed February 20, 2021. https://home.chicagopolice.org/information/use-of-force-policy/

324 NYPD. 2016. "Force Guidelines." Interim Order, May 31. Page 5. Accessed February 20, 2021. https://www1.nyc.gov/assets/ccrb/downloads/pdf/investigations_pdf/io_34_16-force-guidelines.pdf

325 LAPD. 2020. "Policy on the Use of Force – Revised." *Office of the Chief of Police*, June 29. Accessed February 20, 2021. https://www.lapdonline.org/home/news_view/66709

326 Flood, Brian. 2021. "CNN hosts Chris Cuomo, Don Lemon defend AOC's Capitol riot claim, bash critics of her account." *Fox News*, February 5. Accessed February 9, 2021. https://www.foxnews.com/media/aoc-capitol-riot-account-cnn-don-lemon-chris-cuomo

327 Talmazan, Yuliya. 2021. "AOC says she feared for her life during Capitol riot: 'I thought I was going to die'." *NBC News*, January 13. Accessed February 9, 2021. https://www.nbcnews.com/politics/congress/aoc-says-she-feared-her-life-during-capitol-riot-i-n1254042

328 Vallejo, Vanessa. 2021. "Alexandria Ocasio-Cortez: Congress' Drama Queen." *ElAmerican.com*, February 5. Accessed February 21, 2021. https://elamerican.com/alexandria-ocasio-cortez-the-congress-drama-queen/

329 Curley, Grace. 2021. "Curley: Conservatives need to cut out their thirst for progressive approval." *Boston Herald*, January 30. Accessed February 21, 2021. https://www.bostonherald.com/2021/01/30/curley-conservatives-need-to-cut-out-their-thirst-for-progressive-approval/

330 Marantos, Jeanette. 2019. "The Homicide Report: Dimas Diaz Jr., 43." *Los Angeles Times*, January 14. Accessed September 3, 2020. https://homicide.latimes.com/post/dimas-diaz-jr/

331 ABC7.com Staff. 2019. "Suspect ID'd in chase, fatal officer-involved shooting on 101 in Calabasas." *ABC7.com*, January 19. Accessed September 3, 2020. https://abc7.com/suspect-idd-in-chase-fatal-officer-involved-shooting-on-101-in-calabasas/5077042/

332 Contributing Editor. 2019. "DA Declines to File Charges Involving Two Officer-Involved Shooting Deaths." *MyNewsLA.com*, November 15. Accessed September 3, 2020. https://mynewsla.com/crime/2019/11/15/da-declines-to-file-charges-involving-two-officer-involved-shooting-deaths/

333 Ibid 331.

334 Ibid 331.

335 Case, Angela. 2019. "Sheriff's office arrests woman who was shot after trying to run over Pueblo County deputies." *Fox 21 News*, January 25. Accessed September 4, 2020. https://www.fox21news.com/news/crime/sheriffs-office-arrests-woman-who-was-shot-after-trying-to-run-over-pueblo-county-deputies/

336 Hindi, Saja. 2019. "Man shot by police following Pueblo County chase identified." *The Denver Post*, January 31. Accessed January 7, 2021. https://www.denverpost.com/2019/01/17/pueblo-county-officer-involved-shooting/

337 Roper, Peter, & Zach Hillstrom. 2019. "Pueblo West man charged with vehicular homicide." *The Pueblo Chieftain*, January 25. Accessed September 3, 2020. https://www.chieftain.com/news/20190125/pueblo-west-man-charged-with-vehicular-homicide

338 Kestling, Amanda, & Allison Sylte. 2020. Body cam footage released after Fort Lupton officer acquitted of manslaughter in 2019 shooting." *9 News*, February 18. Accessed September 3, 2020. https://www.9news.com/article/news/investigations/fort-lupton-officer-acquitted-of-manslaughter-in-2019-shooting/73-6f0f444c-2faf-4f72-8c7c-4ffec03b58e6

339 Miller, Blair. 2019. "Fort Lupton police officer indicted on manslaughter charge in deadly January shooting of unarmed man." *The Denver Channel*, April 12. Accessed January 7, 2021. https://www.thedenverchannel.com/news/crime/fort-lupton-police-officer-indicted-on-manslaughter-charge-in-deadly-january-shooting-of-unarmed-man

340 Omastiak, Rebecca. 2019. "Man killed in St. Louis Park officer-involved shooting had prior warrants." *KSTP-TV*, January 21. Accessed September 4, 2020. https://kstp.com/news/matthew-neil-tuhkanen-killed-st-louis-park-officer-involved-shooting-prior-warrants/5217183/

341 Hennepin County Attorney. 2020. "Criminal charges will not be filed against St. Louis Park police officer for fatal shooting." *Hennepin County Attorney*, April 3. Accessed September 4, 2020. https://www.hennepinattorney.org/news/news/2020/April/no-charges-against-st-louis-park-police-officer

342 CBS Minnesota Staff. 2020. "No Criminal Charges For St. Louis Park Police Officer After Fatal Jan. 2019 Shooting." *CBS Minnesota*, April 3. Accessed September 4, 2020. https://minnesota.cbslocal.com/2020/04/03/no-criminal-charges-for-st-louis-park-police-officer-after-fatal-jan-2019-shooting/

343 Ibid 341.

344 Shoro, Mike. 2019. "Man killed by North Las Vegas police had woman's body under bed." *Las Vegas Review-Journal*, January 24. Accessed September 4, 2020. https://www.reviewjournal.com/crime/homicides/man-killed-by-north-las-vegas-police-had-womans-body-under-bed-1580905/

345 Torres-Cortez, Ricardo. 2019. "Police: Officers shoot suspect after kidnapped woman escapes." *Las Vegas Sun*, January 24. Accessed September 5, 2020. https://m.lasvegassun.com/news/2019/jan/24/police-kidnapped-woman-escaped-to-report-captor-sh/

346 Ibid 343.

347 Prince, Chelsea, and John Spink. 2019. "Man dead in federal operation involving Atlanta officer; FBI investigating." *The Atlanta Journal-Constitution*, January 23. Accessed January 7, 2021. https://www.ajc.com/news/crime--law/breaking-atlanta-officer-serving-federal-task-force-involved-shooting-police-say/DpMWYgHxDYLDu75ciNpzuJ/

348 Habersham, Raisa. 2019. "Atlanta cop retires after new details emerge in FBI task force shooting." *The Atlanta Journal-Constitution*, November 1. Accessed September 4, 2020. https://www.ajc.com/news/local/atlanta-cop-retires-after-new-details-emerge-fbi-task-force-shooting/HneBGNgnBKhDdUp26FuNCL/

349 FOX 5 Atlanta Staff. 2019. "Atlanta police officer resigns amid lawsuit." *FOX5 Atlanta*, October 31. Accessed September 4, 2020. https://www.fox5atlanta.com/news/atlanta-police-officer-resigns-amid-lawsuit

350 Buffon, Scott. 2019. "Medical Examiner: Railroad Springs shooting suspects shot total of 10 times." *Arizona Daily Sun*, September 26. Accessed September 7, 2020. https://azdailysun.com/news/medical-examiner-railroad-springs-shooting-suspects-shot-total-of-10-times/article_b1f0a961-faec-549d-a122-eb1900b5555e.html

351 Arizona DPS. 2019. "Arizona Troopers Return Fire Killing Armed Suspect in Flagstaff." *Arizona Department of Public Safety – Arizona State Troopers*, January 23. Accessed September 7, 2020. https://www.azdps.gov/news/ims/30

352 The Republic. 2019. "2nd man involved in DPS shooting in Flagstaff dies." *AZCentral.com*, January 25. Accessed January 7, 2021. https://www.azcentral.com/story/news/local/phoenix-breaking/2019/01/25/dps-shooting-second-man-involved-shootout-flagstaff-dies-preston-oszust-marcus-gishal/2686355002/

353 Ibid 350.

354 Sutton, Candace. 2019. "Stormy love life revealed after cop dies playing Russian roulette." *News.com.au*, February 6. Accessed September 7, 2020. https://www.news.com.au/world/north-america/stormy-love-life-revealed-after-cop-dies-playing-russian-roulette/news-story/6707faba81018713255dc50c21c95b0d

355 Miller, Joshua Rhett. 2020. "Ex-cop gets 7 years for killing fellow officer in Russian roulette shooting." *New York Post*, February 28. Accessed September 8, 2020. https://nypost.com/2020/02/28/ex-cop-gets-7-years-for-killing-fellow-officer-in-russian-roulette-shooting/

356 Ibid 354.

357 Hayes, Chris. 2019. "Lawsuit from Katlyn Alix's family paints frightening picture of officer conduct and supervision." *FOX2 Now*, October 10. Accessed September 7, 2020. https://fox2now.com/news/fox-files/lawsuit-from-katelyn-alixs-family-paints-frightening-picture-of-officer-conduct-and-supervision/

358 KGUN9. 2019. "Arizona DPS involved in shooting with California suspect." *KGUN9. com*, January 26. Accessed October 7, 2020. https://www.kgun9.com/news/local-news/arizona-dps-involved-in-shooting-with-california-suspect

359 De Atley, Richard K. 2019. "Yucca Valley man shot dead during confrontation with Arizona authorities." *The Press-Enterprise*, January 27. Accessed September 7, 2020. https://www.sbsun.com/2019/01/27/yucca-valley-man-shot-dead-during-confrontation-with-arizona-authorities/

360 ABC15.com Staff. 2019. "DPS, La Paz County deputies involved in deadly shooting along I-10." *ABC15.com*, January 26. Accessed October 7, 2020. https://www.abc15.com/news/state/dps-la-paz-county-deputies-involved-in-shooting-along-i-10

361 Carter, Marla. 2019. "What we know about husband and wife killed in Houston officer-involved shooting." *ABC 7 News*, January 30. Accessed January 13, 2021. https://abc7news.com/houston-police-shooting-harding-7800-black-tar-heroin/5110865/

362 Sullum, Jacob. 2019. "Forensic Experts Find 'No Evidence' That Houston Narcs Who Killed Dennis Tuttle and Rhogena Nicholas Encountered Gunfire As They Entered the House." *Reason*, May 14. Accessed 1/29/2020. https://reason.com/2019/05/14/forensic-experts-find-no-evidence-that-houston-narcs-who-killed-dennis-tuttle-and-rhogena-nicholas-encountered-gunfire-as-they-entered-the-house/

363 Sullum, Jacob. 2019. "Federal Indictment Says Deadly Houston Drug Raid Was Based on Lies From Start to Finish." *Reason*, November 20. Accessed January 10, 2021. https://reason.com/2019/11/20/federal-indictment-says-deadly-houston-drug-raid-was-based-on-lies-from-start-to-finish/

364 Ibid 362.

365 Barned-Smith, St. John, & Keri Blakinger. 2019. "Former HPD officer charged with murder in botched raid at Harding Street house." *Houston Chronicle*, August 26. Accessed January 11, 2021. https://www.houstonchronicle.com/news/houston-texas/houston/article/Former-HPD-officer-charged-with-murder-in-botched-14373874.php

366 Martin, Brittney, & Eli Rosenberg. 2019. "Two people were killed in a botched drug raid. Investigators say the official story was a lie." *The Washington Post*, July 26. Accessed January 10, 2021. https://www.washingtonpost.com/nation/2019/07/26/two-people-were-killed-botched-drug-raid-investigators-say-official-story-was-lie/

367 FOX 26 Houston. 2020. "Harris County grand jury indicts six former Houston police officers in deadly drug raid." *FOX 4 News*, July 31. Accessed January 11, 2021. https://www.fox4news.com/news/harris-county-grand-jury-indicts-six-former-houston-police-officers-in-deadly-drug-raid

368 Johnson, Alex. 2019. "N.J. officer charged with manslaughter in shooting death of fleeing motorist." *NBC News*, May 22. Accessed September 8, 2020. https://www.nbcnews.com/news/crime-courts/n-j-officer-charged-manslaughter-shooting-death-fleeing-motorist-n1008626

369 Klefer, Eric. 2019. "Newark Cop Shot 2 Men During Chase, Gun Found In Car: Prosecutor." *Patch*, January 29. Accessed January 7, 2021. https://patch.com/new-jersey/newarknj/newark-cop-shot-2-men-during-chase-gun-found-car-prosecutor

370 Everett, Rebecca. 2019. "Cop who fatally shot fleeing driver is a 'hero,' shouldn't be sitting in jail, his lawyer says." *NJ.com*, May 23. Accessed September 7, 2020. https://www.nj.com/essex/2019/05/cop-who-fatally-shot-fleeing-driver-is-a-hero-who-shouldnt-be-sitting-in-jail-today-his-lawyer-says.html

371 Ibid 367.

372 Gutschke, Laura. 2019. "UPDATE: Man fatally shot by Snyder police officer identified." *Abilene Reporter News*, February 8. Accessed September 8, 2020. https://www.reporternews.com/story/news/crime/2019/02/08/snyder-texas-police-officer-whitney-merket-fatally-shoots-suspect-during-altercation/2812053002/

373 Bell-Cypert-Seale. 2019. "Morgan Shane West of Snyder, Texas | 1980 - 2019 | Obituary." *BCSFH.com*, February 8. Accessed September 8, 2020. https://www.bcsfh.com/obituary/morgan-west?fh_id=14781

374 Crime Informer. 2018. "ELIBORIO RODRIGUES ARRESTED." *Crimeinformer.com*, October 28. Accessed September 15, 2020. https://crimeinformer.com/arrestArticle/Oregon/134217

375 The AV Times Staff, 2019. "Man shot dead by CHP identified as Lancaster man." *The Antelope Valley Times*, February 11. Accessed September 8, 2020. http://theavtimes.com/2019/02/11/man-shot-dead-by-chp-identified/

376 Aaron, Bob, Anna Taylor and Jeff Morris. 2019. "Man killed in officer-involved shooting in Montgomery identified." *WCHS TV*, February 11. Accessed September 8, 2020. https://wchstv.com/news/local/one-dead-after-officer-involved-shooting-in-montgomery

377 Starkey, Jessi. 2019. "iTeam Investigation: Family demands answers after deadly officer involved shooting." *WCHS TV*, August 28. Accessed September 8, 2020. https://wchstv.com/news/local/i-team-family-demands-answers-after-deadly-officer-involved-shooting

378 Ibid 376.

379 Star-Advertiser Staff. 2019. "Medical examiner identifies homeless man fatally shot by deputy sheriff at state Capitol." *Star-Advertiser*, February 22. Accessed September 8, 2020. https://www.staradvertiser.com/2019/02/22/breaking-news/medical-examiner-identifies-man-fatally-shot-by-deputy-sheriff-at-hawaii-state-capitol/

380 Ng, Alexandria. 2019. "Deputy sheriff's shooting of homeless man reclassified as second-degree murder." *Hawaii News Now*, June 28. Accessed January 8, 2021. https://www.hawaiinewsnow.com/2019/06/29/deputy-sheriffs-fatal-shooting-homeless-man-reclassified-second-degree-murder/

381 Lund, Casey. 2019. "Heartbreak, tears: Family of a man shot at the Capitol raises questions over his death." *Hawaii News Now*, February 25. Accessed September 8, 2020. https://www.hawaiinewsnow.com/2019/02/24/heartbreak-tears-family-man-shot-capitol-raises-questions-over-his-death/

382 HNN Staff. 2019. "Man arrested after allegedly trying to stab HPD officer in Manoa." *Hawaii News Now*, February 27. Accessed September 18, 2020. https://www.hawaiinewsnow.com/2019/02/27/police-investigation-ongoing-manoa/

383 Fujimori, Leila. 2019. "Case of Hawaii inmate's shooting by CO reportedly sent to prosecutor's office." *The Honolulu Star-Advertiser*, July 4. Accessed September 18, 2020. https://www.corrections1.com/escapes/articles/case-of-hawaii-inmates-shooting-by-co-reportedly-sent-to-prosecutors-office-l5VLmHLJOq86yTzk/

384 KHON2 Staff. 2019. "How Maurice Arrisgado Jr. escaped OCCC before he was shot." *KHON2.com*, March 2. Accessed September 18, 2020. https://www.khon2.com/news/how-maurice-arrisgado-jr-escaped-occc-before-he-was-shot/

385 Ibid 382.

386 Maya, Taina. 2019. "Officer kills man near area courthouse after domestic incident." *KWTX*, March 1. Accessed September 19, 2020. https://www.kwtx.com/content/news/Officer-Involved-Shooting-near-courthouse-506548031.html

387 Staff Reports. 2019. "Fairfield officer kills man during domestic dispute." *Palestine Herald-Press*, March 1. Accessed September 19, 2020. https://www.palestineherald.com/news/fairfield-officer-kills-man-during-domestic-dispute/article_83a34b36-3c6c-11e9-a92b-c799379cbb18.html

388 News Release. 2019. "UPDATE: Name released of suspect, officers in officer-involved shooting." *WEAU*, March 6. Accessed January 7, 2021. https://www.weau.com/content/news/UPDATE--Name-released-of-suspect-officers-in-officer-involved-shooting-506783501.html

389 Kelley, Stephen. 2019. "Eau Claire County deputy, Augusta officer cleared in officer-involved shooting." *WQOW*, August 15. Accessed September 19, 2020. https://wqow.com/2019/08/15/eau-claire-county-deputy-augusta-officer-cleared-in-officer-involved-shooting/

390 The Bakersfield Californian. 2019. "Coroner: Woman in chase with US. Marshals died of gunshot wound to the chest." *Bakersfield.com*, March 11. Accessed January 8, 2021. https://www.bakersfield.com/news/coroner-woman-in-chase-with-us-marshals-died-of-gunshot/article_51ba1678-4468-11e9-b883-bfbbe7458678.html

391 KGET Staff. 2019. "CAPTURED: Gavino Castro, Golden Empire Most Wanted." *KGET.com*, March 7. Accessed September 19, 2020. https://www.kget.com/most-wanted/captured-gavino-castro-golden-empire-most-wanted/

392 The Bakersfield Californian. 2019. "Woman killed in crash that occurred after officer-involved shooting has been identified." *Bakersfield.com*, March 7. Accessed September 19, 2020. https://www.bakersfield.com/news/breaking/woman-killed-in-crash-that-occurred-after-officer-involved-shooting-has-been-identified/article_8f4e14ac-411c-11e9-aef7-d7d69660dda1.html

393 Crenshaw, Zach. 2019. "Unarmed father shot, killed running from Phoenix police." *ABC15.com*, March 19. Accessed September 19, 2020. https://www.abc15.com/news/region-phoenix-metro/central-phoenix/unarmed-father-shot-killed-running-from-phoenix-police

394 Lollman, Laura, and David Baker. 2019. "Police shoot, kill unarmed man near state Capitol." *AZFamily.com*, March 13. Accessed September 19, 2020. https://www.azfamily.com/news/police-shoot-kill-unarmed-man-near-state-capitol/article_b24a9ffc-45b3-11e9-ae70-473024785cb1.html

395 Shuman, Mackenzie, Nathan J. Fish and Dani Coble. 2019. "Police fatally shoot man while searching for kidnapping suspect near state Capitol." *AZCentral.com*, March 14. Accessed September 19, 2020. https://www.azcentral.com/story/news/local/phoenix-breaking/2019/03/13/officer-involved-shooting-near-arizona-state-capitol-closes-19th-avenue-between-van-buren-and-adams/3152571002/

396 Anderson, Jessica. 2019. "Harrison: No gun recovered at home of Baltimore man found dead after police standoff; family has questions." *The Baltimore Sun*, March 27. Accessed September 19, 2020. https://www.baltimoresun.com/news/crime/bs-md-ci-police-involved-shooting-update-20190327-story.html

397 Anderson, Jessica, and Sarah Meehan. 2019. "Man dies after Baltimore police standoff — the second time he was involved in police shooting." *The Baltimore Sun*, March 25. Accessed September 19, 2020. https://www.baltimoresun.com/news/crime/bs-md-ci-officer-shooting-20190325-story.html

398 Associated Press. 2019. "District Attorney: Deputy Justified in Fatal Shooting." *U.S. News & World Report*, July 11. Accessed January 8, 2021. District Attorney: Deputy Justified in Fatal Shooting | North Carolina News | US News

399 Sherrill, Thomas. 2019. "DA determines WCSO deputy justified in shooting death of Mason." *WataugaDemocrat.com*, July 11. Accessed September 20, 2020. https://www.wataugademocrat.com/news/da-determines-wcso-deputy-justified-in-shooting-death-of-mason/article_7982dd40-11ee-5596-acb1-76d458222d66.html

400 Shulman, Alayna. 2019. "Man Redding police shot after caller said he had gun 'just wasn't that way'." *Record Searchlight*, April 12. Accessed September 20, 2020. https://www.redding.com/story/news/local/2019/04/06/redding-man-police-shot-after-caller-said-he-had-gun-just-wasnt-way/3379909002/

401 Schmieding, Stephanie. 2019. "Shasta County Sheriff's Office identifies man killed in officer-involved shooting." *Action News Now*, April 5. Accessed September 20, 2020. https://www.actionnewsnow.com/content/news/1-dead-in-Redding-officer-involved-shooting-508028981.html

402 Brannon, Matt. 2019. "Family of unarmed man shot by police files lawsuit against city, Redding police." *Record Searchlight*, December 18. Accessed September 20, 2020. https://www.redding.com/story/news/local/2019/11/21/family-donnell-lang-unarmed-man-shot-police-sues-redding-police-city/4255121002/

403 Monacelli, Emily. 2019. "Man shot, killed by police in Kalamazoo 'didn't deserve to die,' ex-wife says." *MLive.com*, April 5. Accessed September 21, 2020. https://www.mlive.com/news/kalamazoo/2019/04/man-shot-killed-by-police-in-kalamazoo-didnt-deserve-to-die-ex-wife-says.html

404 WOODTV.com Staff & Kyle Mitchell. "Prosecutor: 4 officers justified in killing parole absconder." *WOOD TV*, January 17. Accessed September 21, 2020. https://www.woodtv.com/news/kzoo-and-bc/thomas-verile-officer-involved-shooting-decision/

405 WMCAActionNews5.comStaff. 2019. "'Don't come near me:' Blytheville police release details of officer-involved shooting investigation." *WMCA Action News 5*, May 2. Accessed September 21, 2020. https://www.wmcactionnews5.com/2019/05/02/blytheville-police-releasing-details-officer-involved-shooting-investigation/

406 ConcealedPatriot.Net. 2019. "Dramatic Bodycam Shows Man Attacking Female Cop Before She Fires, Killing Him [VIDEO]." *ConcealedPatriot.Net*, May 10. Accessed September 21, 2020. https://concealedpatriot.net/2019/05/09/dramatic-bodycam-shows-man-attacking-female-cop-before-she-fires-killing-him-video/

407 Hyde, Joe. 2019. "Renowned San Angelo Criminal Shot and Killed by a DPS Trooper." *Sanangelolive.com*, April 12. Accessed September 21, 2020. https://sanangelolive.com/news/crime/2019-04-12/renowned-san-angelo-criminal-shot-and-killed-dps-trooper

408 Sabawi, Fares. 2019. "Texas DPS identifies man killed by trooper after chase, fight." *San Antonio Express-News*, April 15. Accessed September 21, 2020. https://www.mysanantonio.com/news/local/crime/article/Texas-DPS-identifies-man-killed-by-trooper-after-13769197.php

409 Douglas, Kaylee. 2019. "Toxicology report for Edmond teen killed in officer-involved shooting released." *KFOR.com*, June 28. Accessed September 22, 2020. https://kfor.com/news/edmond-teen-killed-in-officer-involved-shooting-toxicology-report-released/

410 Nashrulla, Tasneem. 2019. "An Unarmed Teen Was Running Around Naked In An Oklahoma Neighborhood. Then Police Shot And Killed Him." *Buzzfeed News*, May 2. Accessed September 21, 2020. https://www.buzzfeednews.com/article/tasneemnashrulla/oklahoma-police-shooting-naked-teen

411 KFOR-TV & K. Querry. 2019. "District attorney: Edmond officers justified in deadly shooting of Oklahoma teenager." *KFOR.com*, September 24. Accessed September 21, 2020. https://kfor.com/news/district-attorney-edmond-officers-justified-in-deadly-shooting-of-oklahoma-teenager/

412 Whitfield, Jayla. 2019. "'Didn't have to kill him': Family of man killed by Wheeler County officer grieving death." *WXGA TV*, May 2. Accessed September 22, 2020. https://wgxa.tv/news/local/gbi-agents-responding-to-officer-involved-shooting-in-wheeler-county

413 Hansen, Zachary. 2019. "Suspect fled arrest on ATV, fought officer before being fatally shot, GBI says." *The Atlanta Journal-Constitution*, May 6. Accessed September 22, 2020. https://www.wsbtv.com/news/suspect-fled-arrest-on-atv-fought-officer-before-being-fatally-shot-gbi-says/946888403/

41413WMAZ Staff. 2019. "GBI: Task force member fatally shot man while serving warrant in Wheeler County." *5 News Online*, May 2. Accessed September 22, 2020. https://www.5newsonline.com/article/news/crime/gbi-task-force-member-fatally-shot-man-while-serving-warrant-in-wheeler-county/93-6419ec83-44de-4227-8bf8-2957d5d7cb3e

415 KHQ Staff. 2019. "Police: No weapon has been recovered from scene of Spokane Valley officer-involved shooting." *KHQ.com*, May 8. Accessed September 23, 2020. https://www.khq.com/top_story/police-no-weapon-has-been-recovered-from-scene-of-spokane/article_52f3740a-711b-11e9-b578-e3ed1ab27b64.html

416 KREM Staff. 2019. "Spokane Co. deputy who killed man near transient camp identified." *KREM.com*, May 8. Accessed September 23, 2020. https://www.krem.com/article/news/man-killed-in-officer-involved-shooting-in-spokane-valley/293-0d5a923c-7fd6-4213-85f1-6b2cd76fc8a5

417 Earley, Pete. 2019. "Mom Learns Son Was Fatally Shot By Police After "Running around without shirt on and 'acting strange.'" *Official Website of Pete Earley*, May 8. Accessed September 23, 2020. http://www.peteearley.com/2019/05/08/mom-learns-son-was-fatally-shot-by-police-after-running-around-without-shirt-on-and-acting-strange/

418 Yakin, Heather. 2020. "Grand jury clears troopers in 2019 fatal shooting on I-84." *Poughkeepsie Journal*, April 2. Accessed September 23, 2020. https://www.poughkeepsiejournal.com/story/news/local/2020/04/02/new-york-state-police-troopers-cleared-killing-tannersville-man/5110523002/

419 Greenson, Thadeus. 2019. "Former Arcata Restaurant Owner Killed by New York Police." *North Coast Journal*, May 23. Accessed January 8, 2021. https://www.northcoastjournal.com/NewsBlog/archives/2019/05/25/former-arcata-restaurant-owner-killed-by-new-york-police

420 Welber, Bobby. 2019. "Restaurant Owner Identified as Man Fatally Shot by Police on I-84." *Hudson Valley Post*, May 28. Accessed September 23, 2020. https://hudsonvalleypost.com/beloved-restaurant-owner-community-activist-killed-by-police/

421 KIRO 7 News Staff. 2020. "Auburn officer-involved shooting video released." *KIRO 7*, January 2. Accessed September 22, 2020. https://www.kiro7.com/news/local/auburn-officer-involved-shooting-video-released/BJBV7TJXRBHB5M4X6MEUWKNSYQ/

422 Ibid 420.

423 Green, Sara Jean. 2020. "Washington Police Officer Charged With Murder in 2019 Shooting." *The Seattle Times*, August 21. Accessed September 22, 2020. https://www.officer.com/investigations/news/21151177/washington-police-officer-charged-with-murder-in-2019-shooting

424 Whale, Robert. 2019. "Friends, family, supporters gather to remember man lost in police shooting." *Auburn Reporter*, July 18. Accessed September 22, 2020. https://www.auburn-reporter.com/news/friends-family-supporters-gather-to-remember-man-lost-in-police-shooting/

425 Whale, Robert. 2020. "Auburn Police Officer pleads not guilty to second-degree murder and first-degree assault in fatal shooting of Jesse Sarey in 2019." *Auburn Reporter*, August 24. Accessed September 22, 2020. https://www.auburn-reporter.com/news/prosecutor-charges-auburn-police-officer-with-second-degree-murder-and-first-degree-assault-in-fatal-shooting-of-jesse-sarey/

426 Goforth, Dylan. 2019. "Bartlesville family copes with questions, loss, following fatal officer-involved shooting." *The Frontier*, October 21. Accessed September 22, 2020. https://www.readfrontier.org/stories/bartlesville-family-copes-with-questions-following-fatal-officer-involved-shooting/

427 Thompson, Nathan. 2019. "Officers cleared in June 1 incident that left 1 dead." *Bartlesville Examiner-Enterprise*, July 14. Accessed September 22, 2020. https://www.examiner-enterprise.com/news/20190714/officers-cleared-in-june-1-incident-that-left-1-dead

428 Clarke, Kayla. 2019. "Driver charged with second-degree murder after police chase through Southwest Detroit." *Click on Detroit*, June 5. Accessed September 22, 2020. https://www.clickondetroit.com/news/2019/06/06/driver-charged-with-second-degree-murder-after-police-chase-through-southwest-detroit/

429 FOX 2 Detroit. 2019. "Driver involved in Detroit police chase charged with murder." *FOX 2 Detroit*, June 6. Accessed September 22, 2020. https://www.fox2detroit.com/news/driver-involved-in-detroit-police-chase-charged-with-murder

430 Hernandez, Daniel, and Lexis-Olivier Ray. 2019. "Video: Ryan Twyman Threw His Car in Reverse Before Deputies Began Shooting." *L.A. Taco*, June 20. Accessed September 23, 2020. https://www.lataco.com/video-ryan-twyman-shooting-sheriff/

431 Salahieh Nouran, Eric Spillman and Rick Chambers. 2019. Deputies Fired Some 34 Rounds, Killing Man Who Used Car as 'Weapon,' LASD Cmdr. Says as Video Is Released." *KTLA.com*, June 20. Accessed September 23, 2020. https://ktla.com/news/local-news/video-shows-lasd-deputy-involved-shooting-that-killed-unarmed-father-in-willowbrook/

432 Fink, Jack. 2019. "Family Demands Answers After Suspect, Juan Moreno Jr., Killed By Farmers Branch Police Officer." *DFW CBS Local*, June 14. Accessed September 2, 2020. https://dfw.cbslocal.com/2019/06/14/family-demands-answers-juan-moreno-jr-killed-by-farmers-branch-police-officer/

433 NBC DFW Staff. 2019. "1 Dead After Shooting Involving Farmers Branch Police." *NBC DFW*, June 19. Accessed January 9, 2021. https://www.nbcdfw.com/news/local/1-dead-after-shooting-involving-farmers-branch-police/240925/

434 DFW-CBS Local Staff. 2019. "Surveillance Video: Auto Theft Suspect Juan Manuel Moreno Jr. Fatally Shot by Farmers Branch Police." *DFW CBS Local*, June 14. Accessed September 3, 2020. https://dfw.cbslocal.com/2019/06/14/surveillance-video-juan-manuel-marino-jr-shot-farmers-branch-police/

435 Young, Stephen. 2019. "Dallas Police Association Blasts DA Over Handling of Farmers Branch Cop Shooting." *Dallas Observer*, June 28. Accessed September 3, 2020. https://www.dallasobserver.com/news/dallas-cops-angry-after-speedy-murder-indictment-of-farmers-branch-officer-11697103

436 Ibid 433.

437 CBS Los Angeles Staff. 2019. "'You Don't Shoot Them Down Like A Dog': Family Mourns 18-Year-Old Killed in East LA Deputy Shooting." *CBS Los Angeles*, June 28. Accessed September 3, 2020. https://losangeles.cbslocal.com/2019/06/28/suspect-dead-deputy-involved-shooting-in-east-la/

438 Lacey, Jackie, District Attorney. 2020. "Officer Involved Shooting of Paul Rea Los Angeles County Sheriff's Department." *District Attorney Justice System Integrity Division*, May 12. Accessed September 3, 2020. https://da.lacounty.gov/sites/default/files/pdf/JSID-OIS-05-12-2020-Rea.pdf

439 Associated Press & Ralph R. Ortega. 2019. "Chinese immigrant, 49, shot dead by cops during raid on marijuana factory 'didn't speak English so could not understand when police told him to show his hands'." *Daily Mail*, August 29. Accessed September 3, 2020. https://www.dailymail.co.uk/news/article-7407011/Chinese-immigrant-shot-dead-cops-drug-factory-raid-didnt-understand-told-hands.html

440 Gundran, Robert. 2019. "Chino police body camera footage shows moments leading to police shooting that killed Fontana man." *Daily Bulletin*, August 26. Accessed September 3, 2020. https://www.dailybulletin.com/2019/08/23/chino-police-body-camera-footage-shows-moments-leading-to-police-shooting-that-killed-fontana-man/

441 Matkin, Holly. 2019. "VIDEO: 'Oh S–t,' Cop Shoots Alleged Drug Trafficker Hiding Behind Door." *The Police Tribune*, October 25. Accessed November 10, 2020. https://policetribune.com/video-oh-s-t-cop-shoots-alleged-drug-trafficker-hiding-behind-door/

442 Childs, Jeremy. 2019. "Authorities identify man killed in Oak View after CHP officer shooting." *VC Star*, July 9. Accessed September 3, 2020. https://www.vcstar.com/story/news/local/communities/ojai/2019/07/09/chp-officer-involved-shooting-oak-view-authorities-release-name-man-shot-killed/1687444001/

443 Hayes, Rob. 2019. "Suspect killed in officer-involved shooting in Oak View." *ABC 7*, July 5. Accessed September 4, 2020. https://abc7.com/suspect-killed-in-officer-involved-shooting-in-oak-view/5380375/

444 Cornwell, Paige. 2019. "Man killed by Kirkland police had grabbed son during fight with girlfriend." *The Seattle Times*, July 15. Accessed September 4, 2020. https://www.seattletimes.com/seattle-news/crime/man-killed-by-kirkland-police-had-grabbed-son-during-fight-with-girlfriend/

445 McNamara, Neal. 2019. "Man Killed By Kirkland Police Identified." *Patch*, July 15. Accessed September 4, 2020. https://patch.com/washington/kirkland/new-details-kirkland-police-shooting

446 Foster, Kevin. 2020. "In Josef Richardson killing, WBR deputy won't be charged." *WAFB*, March 23. Accessed September 5, 2020. https://www.wafb.com/2020/03/24/josef-richardson-killing-wbr-deputy-wont-be-charged/

447 Rddad, Youssef. 2020. "Deputy cleared after fatal shooting in no-knock drug raid at Port Allen-area motel." *The Advocate*, March 23. Accessed September 2, 2020. https://www.theadvocate.com/baton_rouge/news/communities/westside/article_a710327a-6d1a-11ea-8b37-0fddd831da87.html

448 NewsOne Staff. 2019. "Rookie Texas Cop Shoots Wildly At Dog And Kills Homeless Woman Instead." *NewsOne*, August 3. Accessed September 5, 2020. https://newsone.com/3883484/arlington-texas-cop-margarita-brooks-dog-shooting/

449 Howland, Jack. 2019. "Woman fatally shot by Arlington officer had a dog who 'was her soul,' friend says." *Fort Worth Star-Telegram*, August 6. Accessed September 6, 2020. https://www.star-telegram.com/news/local/arlington/article233438282.html

450 Burke, Minyvonne. 2020. "Ex-officer indicted for fatally shooting Texas woman whose dog ran at him." *NBC News*, September 17. Accessed January 9, 2021. https://www.nbcnews.com/news/us-news/ex-officer-indicted-fatally-shooting-texas-woman-whose-dog-ran-n1240370

451 Smith, LaVendrick. 2019. "Arlington officer quits 3 months after killing woman while shooting at her dog." *The Dallas Morning News*, November 1. Accessed September 6, 2020. https://www.dallasnews.com/news/2019/11/01/arlington-officer-who-fatally-shot-woman-during-august-welfare-check-resigns-police-say/

452 McClintock, Kevin. 2019. "UPDATED: Joplin officers involved in August shooting cleared by internal, Missouri Highway Patrol investigations." *The Joplin Globe*, December 27. Accessed September 7, 2020. https://www.joplinglobe.com/news/updated-joplin-officers-involved-in-august-shooting-cleared-by-internal-missouri-highway-patrol-investigations/article_e45c79d6-2800-11ea-867b-6fe0a606bd21.html

453 Ibid 451.

454 Lehr, Jeff. 2020. "Neighbors viewed David Ingle as a 'harmless' loner, but two Joplin officers say they feared for their lives." *The Joplin Globe*, February 15. Accessed September 7, 2020. https://www.joplinglobe.com/news/local_news/neighbors-viewed-david-ingle-as-a-harmless-loner-but-two-joplin-officers-say-they-feared/article_b3125a86-d814-588e-b10b-a5663161e766.html

455 Joplin Police Department. 2019. "VIDEO: Police release dash, body camera videos of Ingle shooting." *The Joplin Globe*, December 26. Accessed September 7, 2020. https://www.joplinglobe.com/multimedia/videos/video-police-release-dash-body-camera-videos-of-ingle-shooting/video_eb37483e-2824-11ea-8ecf-bb99c7a8195c.html

456 WTOC Staff. 2019. "GBI investigating officer-involved shooting at Glennville pawn shop." *WTOC*, August 23. Accessed September 7, 2020. https://www.wtoc.com/2019/08/22/law-enforcement-investigating-deadly-shooting-glennville/

457 Hansen, Zachary. 2019. "Man shot, killed by probation officer after punching him 'without warning,' GBI says." *The Atlanta Journal-Constitution*, August 23. Accessed January 9, 2021. https://www.ajc.com/news/crime--law/breaking-person-dead-probation-officer-injured-officer-involved-shooting-georgia/WKvDsdAOETZWsWGX5o9ftJ/

458 WJCL Staff Reports. 2019. "GBI: Officer shot attacker in the shoulder but the man wouldn't stop. The next shots were deadly." *WJCL*, August 23. Accessed September 7, 2020. https://www.wjcl.com/article/gbi-probation-officer-shot-attacker-in-the-shoulder-but-the-man-wouldnt-stop-fighting/28799542#

459 Leonard, Wendy. 2019. "Police identify West Valley man who was shot, killed by officer during arrest." *Deseret News*, August 24. Accessed September 7, 2020. https://www.deseret.com/utah/2019/8/24/20831326/police-identify-west-valley-man-shot-killed-by-officer-chad-michael-breinholt

460 Reavy, Pat. 2019. "'Let go of my gun!': Video depicts 6 seconds of chaos before Utah officer fires fatal shot." *Deseret News*, September 6. Accessed

September 7, 2020. https://www.deseret.com/utah/2019/9/6/20853597/let-go-of-my-gun-video-depicts-6-seconds-of-chaos-before-utah-officer-fires-fatal-shot

461 Harkins, Paighten. 2019. "DUI suspect grabbed Utah officer's gun before being shot by police, footage shows." *The Salt Lake Tribune*, September 7. Accessed September 8, 2020. https://www.sltrib.com/news/2019/09/07/dui-suspect-grabbed-utah/

462 Andrade, Kevin G. 2019. "R.I. family mourns man killed by police in Tennessee." *Providence Journal*, September 3. Accessed September 8, 2020. https://www.providencejournal.com/news/20190903/ri-family-mourns-man-killed-by-police-in-tennessee

463 Dorman, Travis. 2019. "Knoxville police officer was justified in killing Channara 'Philly' Pheap, prosecutors say." *Knox News*, November 8. Accessed September 9, 2020. https://www.knoxnews.com/story/news/crime/2019/11/07/knoxville-police-officer-justified-killing-philly-pheap-da-says/2518165001/

464 WATE 6 Staff. 2019. "Statement: KPD officer 'violently' choked, attacked by own Taser before fatally shooting man." *WATE*, September 3. Accessed September 8, 2020. https://www.wate.com/news/statement-kpd-officer-violently-choked-attacked-by-own-taser-before-fatally-shooting-man/

465 Ibid 462.

466 Hartford Courant Staff. 2019. "EAST HARTFORD NEIGHBORHOOD SHATTERED BY DOMESTIC VIOLENCE, DEADLY POLICE SHOOTING." *Hartford Courant*, September 7. Accessed September 10, 2020. https://tarrant.tx.networkofcare.org/dv/news-article-detail.aspx?id=107146

467 Leavenworth, Jessie. 2019. "East Hartford officers involved in fatal police shooting of school psychologist have clean records." *Hartford Courant*, October 9. Accessed September 6, 2020. https://www.courant.com/community/east-hartford/hc-news-east-hartford-officers-records-20191009-7jfku56ecralpgoedcmewuvkwy-story.html

468 DeRobertis, Jaqueline. 2019. "Man fatally shot by East Baton Rouge deputy was unarmed and leaving scene, family says." *The Advocate*, September 16. Accessed September 11, 2020. https://www.theadvocate.com/baton_rouge/news/crime_police/article_29fd8e80-d8d8-11e9-bfbf-5f5fe12b2d13.html

469 WBRZ Investigative Unit Staff. 2019. "Deputy identified in September deadly shooting of man whose family told 911 he may kill someone." *WBRZ*, October 17. Accessed September 10, 2020. https://www.wbrz.com/news/deputy-identified-in-september-deadly-shooting-of-man-whose-family-told-911-he-may-kill-someone/

470 Cunningham, Patrick. 2019. "Gregg County Sheriff's deputy shoots, kills suspect after violent fight on I-20." *KETK*, September 30. Accessed September 9, 2020. https://www.ketk.com/video/gregg-county-sheriffs-deputy-shoots-kills-suspect-after-violent-fight-on-i-20/

471 Greene, Melissa. 2019. "Report: Gregg County deputy shot suspect while being strangled." *KLTV*, October 30. Accessed September 6, 2020. https://www.kltv.com/2019/10/30/report-gregg-county-deputy-shot-suspect-while-being-strangled/

472 FOX 4 Staff. 2019. "Ex-Fort Worth officer who fatally shot Atatiana Jefferson charged with murder." *FOX 13 News*, October 14. Accessed September 12, 2020. https://www.fox13news.com/news/ex-fort-worth-officer-who-fatally-shot-atatiana-jefferson-charged-with-murder

473 Baer, Stephanie K. 2019. "The Fort Worth Cop Who Killed Atatiana Jefferson In Her Home Has Been Indicted For Murder." *BuzzFeed News*, December 20. Accessed January 9, 2021. https://www.buzzfeednews.com/article/skbaer/aaron-dean-atatiana-jefferson-murder-indictment

474 Ortiz, Erik. 2019. "Fort Worth police officer who fatally shot Atatiana Jefferson indicted on murder charge." *NBC News*, December 20. Accessed September 12, 2020. https://www.nbcnews.com/news/us-news/fort-worth-police-officer-who-fatally-shot-atatiana-jefferson-indicted-n1105916

475 Ibid 471.

476 Manna, Nichole. 2020. "COVID delayed Aaron Dean's trial for killing Atatiana Jefferson. When could he see a jury?" *Fort Worth Star-Telegram*, October 12. Accessed December 17, 2020. https://www.star-telegram.com/news/local/crime/article246172495.html

477 WBRZ Staff. 2020. "Grand jury clears East Feliciana deputy who shot and killed fleeing thief." *WBRZ*, March 10. Accessed September 12, 2020. https://www.wbrz.com/news/grand-jury-clears-east-feliciana-deputy-who-shot-and-killed-fleeing-thief/

478 Rddad, Youssef. 2019. "East Feliciana deputy kills man suspected of stealing raw chicken from gas station; deputy on leave." *The Advocate*, October 14. Accessed September 12, 2020. https://www.theadvocate.com/baton_rouge/news/communities/westside/article_fff89b9c-ee7c-11e9-86cb-e3a9aaea84da.html

479 Rddad, Youssef. 2020. "Grand jury declines to charge East Feliciana deputy who fatally shot man stealing chicken, family heartbroken." *The Advocate,* March 10. Accessed January 9, 2021. https://www.theadvocate.com/baton_rouge/news/communities/east_feliciana/article_4a614f6e-f9b6-11e9-b097-5f5251659c80.html

480 Thomas, Rachel. 2019. "Sheriff's office admits shooting death of Christopher Whitfield was accidental; NAACP calls for DOJ to investigate." *WAFB*, October 18. Accessed September 13, 2020. https://www.wafb.com/2019/10/18/family-man-killed-deputy-involved-shooting-calling-officer-responsible-be-fired-arrested/

481 Edhat Staff. 2019. "OFFICERS IDENTIFIED IN SHOOTING OF UNARMED HOPE RANCH MURDER SUSPECT." *Edhat Santa Barbara*, October 29. Accessed September 13, 2020. https://www.edhat.com/news/officers-identified-in-shooting-of-unarmed-hope-ranch-murder-suspect

482 Goldstein, Joelle. 2019. "arzan Actor Ron Ely's Son Cameron Was Shot 24 Times by Police Unarmed After Claiming He Had a Weapon." *People*, October 29. Accessed September 14, 2020. https://people.com/crime/ron-ely-son-cameron-shot-24-times-by-police-unarmed-claiming-he-had-weapon/

483 Ross, Martha. 2019. "Ron Ely mystery deepens: Unarmed son pretended to have a gun when shot by deputies." *Mercury News*, October 31. Accessed September 14, 2020. https://www.mercurynews.com/2019/10/30/ron-ely-mystery-deepens-unarmed-son-pretended-to-have-a-gun-when-shot-by-deputies/

484 Roberto, Melissa. 2020. "Ron Ely challenges Santa Barbara district attorney after fatal shooting of his son deemed 'justifiable'." *Fox News*, October 16. Accessed October 16, 2020. https://www.foxnews.com/entertainment/ron-ely-challenges-santa-barbara-district-attorney-fatal-shooting-son-cameron

485 McKinley, Mitch. 2019. "Cops fatally shoot 'Tarzan' actor's son after he allegedly stabbed his mother to death." *Law Enforcement Today*, December 6. Accessed September 14, 2020. https://www.lawenforcementtoday.com/cops-fatally-shoot-tarzan-actors-son-after-he-allegedly-stabbed-his-mother-to-death/

486 Steineck, Lori. 2019. "Family describes final moments of fatal Carroll County deputy-involved shooting." *CantonRep.com*, November 18. Accessed September 14, 2020. https://www.cantonrep.com/news/20191118/family-describes-final-moments-of-fatal-carroll-county-deputy-involved-shooting

487 River News. 2020. "CARROLL CO. SHERIFF'S DEPUTY UNDER INVESTIGATION." *River News*, January 28. Accessed September 15, 2020. https://rivernewstoday.com/2020/01/28/carroll-co-sheriffs-deputy-under-investigation/

488 Free Press Standard. 2019. "Carroll County sheriff speaks on events that led to deputy-involved shooting death." *Free Press Standard*, November 26. Accessed September 15, 2020. https://freepressstandard.com/carroll-county-sheriff-speaks-on-events-that-led-to-deputy-involved-shooting-death/

489 Gallek, Peggy. 2020. "I-TEAM: Suspect was shot four times in the back by a Carroll County Deputy, lawsuit alleges." *FOX 8*, May 10. Accessed September 15, 2020. https://fox8.com/

news/i-team/i-team-suspect-was-shot-four-times-in-the-back-by-a-carroll-county-deputy-lawsuit-alleges/

490 Balint, Ed. 2020. "Carroll County deputy indicted in Robert Sikon's death." *CantonRep.com*, August 12. Accessed September 15, 2020. https://www.cantonrep.com/story/news/courts/2020/08/12/carroll-county-deputy-indicted-in-robert-sikonrsquos-death/113372120/

491 Crime Informer. 2018. "ELIBORIO RODRIGUES ARRESTED." *Crimeinformer.com*, October 28. Accessed September 15, 2020. https://crimeinformer.com/arrestArticle/Oregon/134217

492 Sevren, Michael. 2019. "FAMILY OF MAN KILLED BY EUGENE POLICE SPEAKS OUT." *KEZI*, December 9. Accessed September 15, 2020. https://www.kezi.com/content/news/Family-of-man-killed-by-police-speak-out-566005261.html

493 KEZI 9 News. 2019. "USE OF DEADLY FORCE BY EUGENE OFFICER WAS LAWFUL, DA SAYS." *KEZI 9*, December 13. Accessed January 9, 2021. https://www.kezi.com/content/news/DA-to-brief-media-on-North-Eugene-shooting---566170601.html

494 Hill, Christian. 2019. "Lane County DA: Eugene officer justified in fatal shooting Nov. 30." *The Register-Guard*, December 13. Accessed September 15, 2020. https://www.registerguard.com/news/20191213/lane-county-da-eugene-officer-justified-in-fatal-shooting-nov-30

495 Koumoue, Christelle, and KVAL.com Staff. "DA: Eugene Police officer justified in shooting, killing man in November." *KVAL*, December 13. Accessed September 15, 2020. https://kval.com/news/local/epd-officer-cleared-by-da-after-shooting-and-killing-man-in-late-november

496 Houmard, Celeste & Lea Wilson. 2020. "Temple cop charged with manslaughter in shooting death of Michael Dean." *KCEN*, February 14. Accessed September 15, 2020. https://www.kcentv.com/article/news/local/temple-officer-charged-with-manslaughter-in-michael-dean-death/500-e304f89f-f5df-48ff-ba2c-4adf8ae86746

497 Miles, Frank. 2020. "Texas officer who shot, killed unarmed man may have fired by accident, officials say." *Fox News*, February 13. Accessed September 15, 2020. https://www.foxnews.com/us/texas-officer-who-shot-killed-unarmed-man-may-have-fired-by-accident-officials-say

498 Isenberg, Sydney. 2020. "Temple officer arrested for manslaughter after death of Michael Dean." *KXXV*, December 1. Accessed December 17, 2020. https://www.kxxv.com/hometown/bell-county/officer-arrested-for-manslaughter-after-death-of-michael-dean

499 deGrood, Matt. 2019. "Bloodied man sparked calls before deadly League City shooting." *Galveston County The Daily News*, December 12. Accessed December 15, 2020. https://www.galvnews.com/news/article_b804b7aa-4e63-54e9-a8b4-fc5e1f152b38.html

500 Powell, Nick. 2019. "League City Police ID's officer who killed suspect." *Chron.com*, December 12. Accessed September 16, 2020. https://www.chron.com/news/houston-texas/houston/article/League-City-Police-ID-s-officer-who-killed-14902019.php

501 McCord, Cory. 2019. "Man dies after being shot during altercation with League City officer, officials say." *KHOU*, December 12. Accessed September 15, 2020. https://www.khou.com/article/news/local/officials-league-city-pd-officer-shoots-man-after-being-attacked/285-29b40d30-2f1c-48e0-9242-18aaa61fb102

502 Epperly, Emma. 2020. "Man killed, Spokane County sheriff's deputy who shot him identified." *The Spokesman-Review*, January 14. Accessed September 16, 2020. https://www.spokesman.com/stories/2020/jan/14/man-killed-by-spokane-county-sheriffs-deputy-durin/

503 Webley, Jared. 2020. "No Criminal Charges in January, 2020 Police Shooting." *Spokane County*, March 31. Accessed September 16, 2020. https://www.spokanecounty.org/CivicAlerts.aspx?AID=2838&ARC=4502

504 Epperly, Emma. 2020. "Prosecutor: Sheriff's Deputy justified in shooting man after car chase." *The Spokesman Review*, March 31. Accessed September 16, 2020. https://www.spokesman.com/stories/2020/mar/31/prosecutor-sheriffs-deputy-justified-in-shooting-m/

505 Bonvillian, Crystal. 2020. "Maryland police officer charged with murder in shooting of handcuffed man." *KIRO 7*, January 29. Accessed September 16, 2020. https://www.kiro7.com/news/trending/maryland-police-officer-charged-with-murder-shooting-handcuffed-man/TAOWMH4GO5BATET4H5EHZW5YOU/

506 Associated Press. 2020. "Bond denied for officer in handcuffed man's fatal shooting." *WBAL*, January 30. Accessed September 16, 2020. https://www.wbaltv.com/article/officer-accused-of-killing-handcuffed-man-charged-with-murder-police-say/30689923

507 Franklin, Jonathan, & Pete Muntean. 2020. "Prince George's County officer indicted on murder charge in fatal shooting of suspect." *WUSA 9*, March 5. Accessed September 16, 2020. https://www.wusa9.com/article/news/crime/prince-georges-county-officer-indicted-on-murder-charge-in-fatal-shooting-of-suspect/65-1b1960ca-92bf-4aad-b672-52b4420c66dc

508 Braine, Theresa. 2020. "Family of handcuffed man shot by Maryland cop reaches $20 million settlement with county." *New York Daily News*, September 28. Accessed December 17, 2020. https://www.nydailynews.com/news/national/ny-settlement-cop-handcuffed-20200929-45mp7ol5erf2xklj6uywrwqa2u-story.html

509 Staff Report. 2017. "2 charged with attempted armed robbery in Burlington." *Greensboro News & Record*, July 21. Accessed December 17, 2020. https://greensboro.com/news/crime/2-charged-with-attempted-armed-robbery-in-burlington/article_976d84bd-1f96-587c-ad4f-d8de2772bdea.html

510 Staff Report. 2020. "Graham police identify officer who fatally shot a 20-year-old man early today while trying to serve arrest warrants." *Greensboro News & Record*, January 29. Accessed December 17, 2020. https://greensboro.com/news/graham-police-identify-officer-who-fatally-shot-a-20-year-old-man-early-today-while/article_20d4fcf1-6162-5519-9316-c966da55bb2c.html

511 Bargebuhr, Tess. 2020. "Officer shot Graham man accidentally or in self-defense, district attorney says; suspect was not armed." *FOX 8*, July 17. Accessed January 10, 2021. https://myfox8.com/news/officer-shot-graham-man-accidentally-or-in-self-defense-district-attorney-says-suspect-was-not-armed/

512 Shrair, Justin. 2020. "Alamance County DA does not charge Graham police officer after shooting in January." *WXII 12*, July 17. Accessed January 10, 2021. https://www.wxii12.com/article/alamance-county-da-does-not-charge-graham-police-officer-after-shooting-in-january/33351505

513 Ibid 510.

514 AZ Family.com News Staff. 2020. "Woman dead after being shot by U.S. Marshals task force at Phoenix hotel." *AZFamily.com*, February 21. Accessed September 15, 2020. https://www.azfamily.com/news/woman-dead-after-being-shot-by-u-s-marshals-task/article_37c78018-54eb-11ea-9ba2-77f44e7bcdf1.html

515 ABC15.com Staff. 2020. "US Marshals shoot, kill arrest warrant suspect near I-17 and Peoria Avenue, FBI says." *ABC15.com*, February 21. Accessed September 16, 2020. https://www.abc15.com/news/region-phoenix-metro/north-phoenix/pd-us-marshals-involved-in-shooting-near-i-17-and-peoria-avenue

516 Weichselbaum, Simone, and Sachi McClendon, The Marshall Project and Uriel J. Garcia. 2021. "US marshals act like local police, but with more violence and less accountability." *USA Today*, February 11. Accessed February 21, 2021. https://www.usatoday.com/in-depth/news/investigations/2021/02/11/investigation-us-marshals-kill-more-people-but-face-less-scrutiny/4397533001/

517 SBG San Antonio. 2020. "'Y'all are just gonna have to shoot me,' man shot by deputies outside Floresville Walmart." *News 4 San Antonio*, February 24.

Accessed December 19, 2020. https://news4sanantonio.com/news/local/yall-are-just-gonna-have-to-shoot-me-man-shot-by-deputies-outside-floresville-walmart

518 Virgin, Yami. 2020. "EXCLUSIVE: Body cam video shows fatal shooting of 20-year-old, family questions training." *Fox San Antonio*, September 14. Accessed September 16, 2020. https://foxsanantonio.com/news/yami-investigates/exclusive-police-body-cam-video-shows-fatal-shooting-of-20-yr-old-family-questioning-training

519 Cheney, Alex, & ABC7.com Staff. 2020. "Rookie officer injured, suspect dead after altercation leads to police shooting in Garden Grove." *ABC7.com*, February 26. Accessed September 16, 2020. https://abc7.com/garden-grove-police-officer-involved-shooting/5968735/

520 Fausto, Alma, & Eric Licas. 2020. "Theft suspect killed by California police; video shows car being stolen just before the shooting." *The Mercury News*, February 27. Accessed December 18, 2020. https://www.mercurynews.com/2020/02/27/suspect-killed-officer-hurt-in-shooting-in-garden-grove/?shared=email&msg=fail

521 Kurzweil, Tony, Christina Pascucci & Ellina Abovian. 2020. "Stolen vehicle suspect fatally shot during altercation with officer in Garden Grove." *KTLA.com*, February 26. Accessed December 19, 2020. https://ktla.com/news/local-news/officer-among-2-hospitalized-when-altercation-led-to-police-shooting-in-garden-grove/

522 Nexstar Inc. 2020. "Deadly officer-involved shooting in Mississippi County." *FOX 16*, March 4. Accessed September 17, 2020. https://www.fox16.com/news/local-news/deadly-officer-involved-shooting-in-mississippi-county/

523 Shameer, Danny. 2020. "Manila officer cleared in fatal shooting." *Arkansas Democrat Gazette*, April 14. Accessed September 17, 2020. https://www.arkansasonline.com/news/2020/apr/14/manila-officer-cleared-in-fatal-shootin/?crime

524 Region 8 Newsdesk. 2020. "Prosecutor clears officer in deadly shooting." *KAIT 8*, April 7. Accessed September 17, 2020. https://www.kait8.com/2020/04/07/prosecutor-clears-officer-deadly-shooting/

525 North Lauderdale News.Net. 2019. "Baked, Beat Up, Arrested...I'm Yours. North Lauderdale Street Crime February 5-11." *NorthLauderdaleNews.net*, February 18. Accessed September 17, 2020. http://northlauderdalenews.net/baked-beat-up-arrestedim-yours-north-lauderdale-street-crime-februa-p472-168.htm

526 DeLuca, Alex. 2020. "New Records Shed Light on Shooting of Black Man by Fort Lauderdale Cop." *Miami News Times*, July 6. Accessed September 17, 2020. https://www.miaminewtimes.com/news/updates-on-shooting-of-barry-gedeus-by-fort-lauderdale-police-11660930

527 DeLuca, Alex. 2020. "Fort Lauderdale Cop in March Shooting Has Long History of Use-of-Force Reviews." *Broward Palm Beach New Times*, June 15. Accessed September 17, 2020. https://www.browardpalmbeach.com/news/fort-lauderdale-officer-robert-morris-investigated-in-shooting-10655830

528 Henry, Carma. 2020. "Fort Lauderdale Cop in March Shooting Has Long History of Use-of-Force Reviews." *Westside Gazette*, June 18. Accessed September 17, 2020. https://thewestsidegazette.com/fort-lauderdale-cop-in-march-shooting-has-long-history-of-use-of-force-reviews/

529 California Mugshots. 2018. "California Mugshots: Kenneth Wayne Mullins." *California Mugshots*, November 3. Accessed September 17, 2020. https://www.californiamugshots.com/inmate/2374684/kenneth-wayne-mullins

530 Granda, Nathalie. 2020. "Suspect identified in deadly officer-involved shooting in Fresno County." *ABC 30*, March 7. Accessed September 17, 2020. https://abc30.com/deputy-involved-shooting-officer-fresno-county-shot-countys-sheriffs-office/5992277/

531 Valenzuela, Larry. 2020. "Homeless man ends up dead in officer-involved shooting in southwest Fresno." *The Fresno Bee*, March 7. Accessed September 17, 2020. https://www.fresnobee.com/news/local/crime/article240982566.html

532 Whitfield, Stephanie. 2020. "Good Samaritan's last words before deadly Deerbrook Mall shooting: 'Someone's got to do something'." *KHOU 11*, March 9. Accessed September 17, 2020. https://www.khou.com/article/news/local/good-samaritans-last-words-before-deerbrook-mall-shooting-someones-got-to-do-something/285-8eebcf4c-18cf-4b82-96fb-9bf7653c39f3

533 Haworth, Jon. 2020. "Good Samaritan shot and killed chasing suspect who held woman at gunpoint." *ABC News*, March 9. Accessed September 17, 2020. https://abcnews.go.com/US/good-samaritan-shot-killed-chasing-suspect-held-woman/story?id=69478551

534 Quinn, Dave. 2020. "Good Samaritan Tx. Dad Is Killed Chasing Suspect Who'd Aimed a Gun at a Woman in Mall Parking Lot." *People*, March 10. Accessed September 17, 2020. https://people.com/crime/good-samaritan-texas-dad-killed-chasing-suspect-pulled-gun-woman-parking-lot/

535 Gill, Julian. 2020. "'He's always been a hero': Father of 2 killed while tackling gunman near Deerbrook Mall." *Houston Chronicle*, March 11. Accessed September 17, 2020. https://www.houstonchronicle.com/news/houston-texas/houston/article/hero-good-Samaritan-gun-death-dad-husband-15121478.php

536 Wickersham's Conscience. 2020. "Tales from Wasilla: Aaron Tolen." *Wickersham's Conscience*, March 13. Accessed September 17, 2020. https://wickershamsconscience.wordpress.com/2020/03/13/tales-from-wasilla-aaron-tolen/

537 Associated Press. 2020. "Troopers release details of fatal officer-involved shooting." *Associated Press News*, March 9. Accessed September 17, 2020. https://apnews.com/article/25598683f7c7e0be7355fb7353c36c41

538 Alaska Department of Public Safety. 2020. "Daily Dispatch: AK20016675." *Alaska DPS, State Troopers Public Information Office*, March 8. Accessed September 17, 2020. https://dailydispatch.dps.alaska.gov/Home/DisplayIncident?incidentNumber=AK20016675

539 Contributing Editor. 2020. "Authorities ID Man Fatally Shot by Bell Gardens Police." *MyNewsLA.com*, March 12. Accessed September 18, 2020. https://mynewsla.com/crime/2020/03/12/authorities-id-man-fatally-shot-by-bell-gardens-police/

540 Quednow, Cindy Von, & Sara Welch. 2020. "Man who allegedly robbed, carjacked mother is fatally shot by police in Bell Gardens." *KTLA*, March 10. Accessed September 18, 2020. https://ktla.com/news/local-news/man-who-allegedly-robbed-carjacked-mother-is-fatally-shot-by-police-in-bell-gardens/

541 Martinez, Natalia, & John P. Wise. 2020. "Warrants issued for arrest of Breonna Taylor's ex-boyfriend amid leaked new documents." *WAVE 3 News*, August 31. Accessed September 19, 2020. https://www.wave3.com/2020/08/26/warrants-issued-arrest-breonna-taylors-ex-boyfriend-amid-leaked-new-documents/

542 BBC News. 2020. "Breonna Taylor: Police officer charged but not over death." *BBC*, September 23. Accessed October 15, 2020. https://www.bbc.com/news/world-us-canada-54273317

543 Malone, Sandy. 2020. "Police Release Almost 5,000-Page Breonna Taylor Investigation File." *The Police Tribune*, October 7. Accessed April 29, 2021. https://policetribune.com/police-release-almost-5000-page-breonna-taylor-investigation-file/

544 Bergan, Shain, & Zoe Brown. 2020. "Unarmed man dies after being shot by KC officer on Thursday night." *KCTV 5*, March 13. Accessed September 19, 2020. https://www.kctv5.com/news/local_news/unarmed-man-dies-after-being-shot-by-kc-officer-on-thursday-night/article_463f6a4c-6531-11ea-bf74-6784429e86d1.html

545 Associated Press. 2020. "Kansas City police shoot, kill man officer thought was armed." *Associated Press News*, March 13. Accessed September 19, 2020. https://apnews.com/article/252b29762228f5d10334041827698feb

546 KCTV. 2020. "Family of man killed by KCPD officers seeking answers after memorial is removed." *KCTV 5*, August 17. Accessed September 19, 2020. https://www.kctv5.com/news/local_news/family-of-man-killed-by-kcpd-officers-seeking-answers-after-memorial-is-removed/article_46aea136-e0d4-11ea-993a-879a77c07ad7.html

547 Davidson-Hiers, CD, & William L. Hatfield. 2020. "Attempted carjacking suspect dead after he 'violently resisted' and was shot by a TPD officer." *Tallahassee Democrat*, March 21. Accessed September 19, 2020. https://www.tallahassee.com/story/news/2020/03/20/tallahassee-police-department-carjacking-leads-officer-involved-shooting/2890027001/

548 Dunmore, Royce. 2020. "Protestors Slam Tallahassee's Past Police Shootings After Black Person Is Killed By Cop." *Newsone*, May 28. Accessed September 19, 2020. https://newsone.com/3949748/protestors-tallahassees-past-police-shootings-after-black-woman-is-killed/

549 Etters, Karl. 2020. "Suspect started fight with officers before fatal shooting, TPD says." *El Paso Times*, March 30. Accessed September 19, 2020. https://www.elpasotimes.com/story/news/2020/03/30/suspect-started-fight-officers-before-fatal-shooting-tpd-says/5088532002/

550 Tallahassee Democrat. 2020. "Read the grand jury findings from the three TPD-involved shootings | Documents." *Tallahassee Democrat*, September 4. Accessed September 19, 2020. https://www.tallahassee.com/story/news/2020/09/04/grand-jury-tony-mcdade-mychael-johnson-findings-tallahassee-police-department-shootings/5709205002/

551 Sheriff Mike Marshall. 2017. "Wanted: John Mark Hendrick Jr." *Stokes County Sheriff's Office*, October 6. Accessed September 20, 2020. http://nixle.s3.amazonaws.com/uploads/pub_media/user35103-1513286764-media1

552 Associated Press. 2020. "Police ID passenger in stolen SUV who was shot by deputies." *Associated Press News*, April 1. Accessed September 19, 2020. https://apnews.com/article/9777da9015575b695ea31fe17bbc230e

553 Stokes County Sheriff's Office. 2015. "News Release." *Stokes County Sheriff's Office*, November 16. Accessed September 19, 2020. http://www.co.stokes.nc.us/sheriff/files/fall2015.pdf

554 Hinton, John. 2020. "Man killed by Davidson County deputies identified. John Mark Hendrick Jr., 32, of Winston-Salem was a passenger in stolen SUV, officials said." *Winston-Salem Journal*, March 31. Accessed September 20, 2020. https://journalnow.com/news/crime/man-killed-by-davidson-county-deputies-identified-john-mark-hendrick-jr-32-of-winston-salem/article_3f635fb2-2f5c-5587-8d64-7ab5a2c889be.html

555 Eaton-Robb, Pat. 2020. "Protesters Spotlight Police Shooting of Latino Parolee." *U.S. News & World Report*, June 16. Accessed September 20, 2020. https://www.usnews.com/news/best-states/connecticut/articles/2020-06-16/protesters-spotlight-police-shooting-of-latino-parolee

556 Connecticut State Division of Criminal Justice. 2020. "Statement of Tolland State's Attorney Matthew C. Gedansky Concerning the Use of Deadly Physical Force on April 2, 2020, in Manchester." *Connecticut State Division of Criminal Justice*, April 3. Accessed September 20, 2020. https://portal.ct.gov/DCJ/Press-Room/Press-Releases/040320-Manchester-Deadly-Force-Jose-Soto

557 Associated Press & Rick Lessard. 2020. "CT state attorney's office says officers justified in fatal April shooting." *FOX 61*, October 26. Accessed February 21, 2021. https://www.fox61.com/article/news/crime/states-attorney-for-the-judicial-district-of-tolland-releases-report-on-manchester-police-shooting/520-8e5927db-840d-4950-99aa-52bb471476f7

558 Frazer, Sklyer, & Erica Purdy. 2020. "Man killed by police showed violent intent, prosecutor says." *Journal Inquirer*, October 26. Accessed December 20, 2020. https://www.journalinquirer.com/

crime_and_courts/man-killed-by-police-showed-violent-intent-prosecutor-says/article_ef4067f0-812d-11ea-b0a5-73e2a57dca18.html

559 Waggoner, Priscilla. 2020. "AUTOPSY REPORT RELEASED IN ZACH GIFFORD SHOOTING." *Kiowa County Independent*, May 20. Accessed September 21, 2020. https://kiowacountyindependent.com/news/1810-autopsy-report-released-in-zach-gifford-shooting

560 Sylte, Allison. 2020. "CBI: Suspect shot, killed by Kiowa County deputies after running away during traffic stop." *9 News*, April 15. Accessed September 21, 2020. https://www.9news.com/article/news/local/kiowa-county-officer-shooting/73-ff5c34e4-c9fc-426f-9f3d-de3a0f7bb909

561 Waggoner, Priscilla. 2020. "TEN WEEKS AFTER: What We Know and Don't Know About the Officer-Involved Shooting of Zachary Gifford." *Kiowa County Independent*, June 17. Accessed September 21, 2020. https://www.kiowacountyindependent.com/news/1839-ten-weeks-after-what-we-know-and-don-t-know-about-the-officer-involved-shooting-of-zachary-gifford

562 Barnett, Betsy. 2021. "One Officer charged in the April 9, 2020 officer-involved shooting of Zachary Gifford." *Kiowa County Independent*, January 22. Accessed July 6, 2021. https://www.kiowacountyindependent.com/news/2069-one-officer-charged-in-the-april-9-2020-officer-involved-shooting-of-zachary-gifford

563 Dean, Mensah M. 2020. "Philly police identify man fatally shot by officers last week." *The Philadelphia Inquirer*, April 13. Accessed September 21, 2020. https://www.inquirer.com/news/police-involved-shooting-south-philadelphia-fatal--20200413.html

564 CBS 3 Staff. 2020. "Police Identify Man Killed, Woman Charged In South Philadelphia Police-Involved Shooting." *CBS Philly*, April 13. Accessed June 2, 2020. https://philadelphia.cbslocal.com/2020/04/13/police-identify-man-killed-woman-charged-in-south-philadelphia-police-involved-shooting/

565 Puit, Glenn. 2020. "Man fatally shot in struggle with police identified." *Las Vegas Review-Journal*, April 27. Accessed September 21, 2020. https://www.reviewjournal.com/crime/homicides/man-fatally-shot-in-struggle-with-police-identified-2015967/

566 Haas, Greg. 2020. "UPDATE: Coroner identifies man shot and killed by North Las Vegas Police." *8 News Now*, April 27. Accessed September 21, 2020. https://www.8newsnow.com/news/local-news/suspect-reported-dead-in-north-las-vegas-officer-involved-shooting/

567 Venkataramanan, Meena. 2020. "Austin police release footage showing the killing of Mike Ramos." *The Texas Tribune*, July 27. Accessed September 21, 2020. https://www.texastribune.org/2020/07/27/mike-ramos-austin-video/

568 Cantu, Tony. 2020. "Austin Officer-Involved Shooting Case Headed To Grand Jury." *Patch*, May 29. Accessed September 21, 2020. https://patch.com/texas/downtownaustin/austin-officer-involved-shooting-case-headed-grand-jury

569 McGlinchy, Audrey. 2020. "Austin Police Report Confirms Michael Ramos Was Fatally Shot, Says Officer Considered Car A Weapon." *KUT 90.5*, May 20. Accessed September 21, 2020. https://www.kut.org/austin/2020-05-20/austin-police-report-confirms-michael-ramos-was-fatally-shot-says-officer-considered-car-a-weapon

570 Sanchez, Ray & Will Brown. 2021. "Austin, Texas, police officer indicted for murder in fatal shooting." *CNN*, March 11. Accessed April 29, 2021. https://www.cnn.com/2021/03/11/us/austin-texas-police-shooting-indictment/index.html

571 Ibid 566.

572 Gotfredson, David. 2020. "Deputy-involved shooting case goes to San Diego DA's office." *CBS 8*, June 22. Accessed September 22, 2020. https://www.cbs8.com/article/news/local/deputy-involved-shooting-case-goes-to-the-das-office/509-baf7d991-31c5-405c-8ea3-c26ba5d0fe9c

573 Rivas, Alexis. 2020. "Man Killed By Deputy Was Shot 3 Times, Including in the Back." *NBC San Diego*, May 7. Accessed September 22, 2020. https://www.nbcsandiego.com/news/local/man-killed-by-deputy-was-shot-3-times-including-in-the-back/2320118/

574 Moran, Greg. 2020. "Ex-deputy's murder charge is first in California under new use-of-force law." *Los Angeles Times*, August 30. Accessed September 22, 2020. https://www.latimes.com/california/story/2020-08-30/murder-charge-san-diego-county-sheriffs-deputy-first-under-new-law

575 Green, Sara Jean. 2020. "Medical Examiner identifies 24-year-old man fatally shot by Seattle police during domestic-violence call." *The Seattle Times*, May 7. Accessed September 22, 2020. https://www.seattletimes.com/seattle-news/crime/medical-examiner-identifies-24-year-old-man-fatally-shot-by-seattle-police-during-domestic-violence-call/

576 Matkin, Holly. 2020. "VIDEO: Police Take Out Armed Suspect Holding Abducted Baby." *The Police Tribune*, May 8. Accessed September 22, 2020. https://policetribune.com/video-police-take-out-armed-suspect-holding-abducted-baby/

577 Moreno, Joel. 2020. "Police release body cam footage in deadly shooting following child abduction." *KOMO News*, May 1. Accessed September 22, 2020. https://komonews.com/news/local/suspect-accused-of-beating-woman-abducting-baby-killed-by-officer-while-holding-infant

578 Parker, Collins. 2020. "Suspect shot by deputy was just arrested on drug charges 11 days ago." *WDEF*, May 18. Accessed September 22, 2020. https://wdef.com/2020/05/18/suspect-shot-deputy-just-arrested-drug-charges-11-days-ago/

579 Hughes, Rosana. 2020. "Medical examiner: Man was shot in back following May pursuit by Hamilton County sheriff's deputy in Sale Creek." *Chattanooga Times Free Press*, July 5. Accessed September 22, 2020. https://www.timesfreepress.com/news/local/story/2020/jul/05/medical-examiner-mwshot-back-following-may-pu/526850/

580 Hughes, Rosana. 2021. "Fatal struggle between man and Hamilton County deputy detailed in newly released TBI records." *Chattanooga Times Free Press*, January 7. Accessed February 21, 2021. https://www.timesfreepress.com/news/local/story/2021/jan/07/tbi-records-detail-fatal-struggle-between-man/539250/

581 Hughes, Rosana. 2020. "Hamilton County sheriff's deputy at center of deadly shooting has previously been accused of assault, unreasonable seizure." *Chattanooga Times Free Press*, May 22. Accessed September 22, 2020. https://www.timesfreepress.com/news/local/story/2020/may/22/deputy-story-rosana/523666/

582 Hughes, Rosana. 2020. "Hamilton County DA announces no charges against sheriff's deputy Jordan Long in May shooting death of 29-year-old." *Chattanooga Times Free Press*, October 5. Accessed February 22, 2021. https://www.timesfreepress.com/news/local/story/2020/oct/05/hamiltcounty-dannounces-no-charges-against-sh/533513/

583 Cummings, Travis, & WRCB Staff. 2020. "UPDATE: Medical Examiner deems Sale Creek shooting involving Hamilton Co. deputy a homicide." *WRCB TV*, July 2. Accessed September 22, 2020. https://www.wrcbtv.com/story/42317180/update-medical-examiner-deems-sale-creek-shooting-involving-hamilton-co-deputy-a-homicide

584 Everett, Rebecca, & Avalon Zoppo. 2020. "Fatal shooting of unarmed man by cop during traffic stop raises questions about mental health training, communication." *NJ.com*, June 17. Accessed September 22, 2020. https://www.nj.com/burlington/2020/06/fatal-shooting-of-unarmed-man-by-cop-during-traffic-stop-raises-questions-about-mental-health-training-communication.html

585 Ibid 583.

586 Hernandez, Joe. 2020. "Dashcam captures shooting of Maurice Gordon by N.J. police, but questions remain." *WHYY*, June 8. Accessed September 22, 2020. https://whyy.org/articles/dashcam-captures-shooting-of-maurice-gordon-by-n-j-police-but-questions-remain/

587 Sheehy, Kate. 2020. "George Floyd had 'violent criminal history': Minneapolis police union chief." *New York Post*, June 2. Accessed February 25, 2021. https://nypost.com/2020/06/02/george-floyd-had-violent-criminal-history-minneapolis-union-chief/

588 Jangra, Sachin. 2020. "George Floyd Criminal Past Record/Arrest History/Career Timeline: Baggie, Gun Pregnant and All Details." *The Courier Daily*, June 11. Accessed February 25, 2021. https://www.thecourierdaily.com/george-floyd-criminal-past-record-arrest/20177/

589 Parry, George. 2020. "Who Killed George Floyd?" *The Spectator*, August 6. Accessed February 16, 2021. https://spectator.org/george-floyd-death-toxicology-report/

590 Bay Area News Group. 2020. "Read: George Floyd autopsy report, with cause of death and other factors." *The Mercury News*, June 5. Accessed December 24, 2020. https://www.mercurynews.com/2020/06/05/read-george-floyd-autopsy-report-with-cause-of-death-and-other-factors/

591 Higham, Aliss. 2020. "George Floyd timeline: The FULL events that led to George Floyd arrest and death." *Express*, June 5. Accessed December 24, 2020. https://www.express.co.uk/news/world/1290302/George-Floyd-timeline-arrest-death-USA-protests-Black-Lives-Matter

592 Law Officer. 2020. "The Big Lie: The Acquittal of Chauvin, Lane, Kueng & Thao." *Lawofficer.com*, August 8. Accessed February 15, 2021. https://www.lawofficer.com/the-big-lie/

593 Raguse, Lou. 2020. "MPD training materials show knee-to-neck restraint similar to the one used on Floyd." *KARE 11*, July 8. Accessed February 16, 2021. https://www.kare11.com/article/news/local/george-floyd/minneapolis-police-training-materials-show-knee-to-neck-restraint-similar-to-used-on-george-floyd/89-9f002e3f-972a-4410-86cb-50a1237fc496

594 Higgins, Tucker. 2021. "Former police officer Derek Chauvin found guilty of murder, manslaughter in the death of George Floyd." *CNBC*, April 20. Accessed April 21, 2021. https://www.cnbc.com/2021/04/20/derek-chauvin-trial-verdict.html

595 Raguse, Lou. 2020. "New court docs say George Floyd had "fatal level" of fentanyl in his system." *KARE 11*, August 26. Accessed February 15, 2021. https://www.msn.com/en-us/news/us/new-court-docs-say-george-floyd-had-fatal-level-of-fentanyl-in-his-system/ar-BB18pb0p

596 Remkus, Ashley. 2020. "Assistant police chief shot and killed his neighbor, who had just survived brain surgery." *AL.com*, August 30. Accessed December 22, 2020. https://www.al.com/news/2020/08/assistant-police-chief-shot-and-killed-his-neighbor-who-had-just-survived-brain-surgery.html

597 Mitchell, Amya. 2020. "Aunt of slain man files suit against off-duty cop." *The Greenville Advocate*, September 3. Accessed December 22, 2020. https://www.greenvilleadvocate.com/2020/09/03/aunt-of-slain-man-files-suit-against-off-duty-cop/

598 Nozicka, Luke, & Anna Spoerre. 2020. "Though possibly avoidable, deputy was justified in shooting Sedalia woman: prosecutor." *The Kansas City Star*, September 14. Accessed September 22, 2020. https://www.kansascity.com/news/local/crime/article245699485.html

599 Geisler, Lucas. 2020. "Search warrant reveals new details in Pettis County deputy shooting." *ABC 17 News*, June 23. Accessed September 22, 2020. https://abc17news.com/news/2020/06/22/search-warrant-reveals-new-details-in-pettis-county-deputy-shooting/

600 Smith, Cory. 2020. "Oklahoma trooper justified in deadly shooting, DA rules." *KTUL*, September 18. Accessed December 22, 2020. https://ktul.com/news/local/oklahoma-trooper-justified-in-deadly-shooting-da-rules

601 Raache, Hicham. 2020. "District Attorney says OHP trooper's fatal shooting of armed vehicle passenger was justified." *KFOR*, September 19. Accessed December 22, 2020. https://kfor.com/news/local/district-attorney-says-ohp-troopers-fatal-shooting-of-vehicle-passenger-was-justified/

602 Eger, Andrea. 2020. "Video released: June shooting by OHP trooper on Will Rogers Turnpike ruled justified." Tulsa World, October 26. Accessed December 22, 2020. https://tulsaworld.com/news/

state-and-regional/crime-and-courts/video-released-june-shooting-by-ohp-trooper-on-will-rogers-turnpike-ruled-justified/article_4cd4bd74-f9f8-11ea-84be-c7c518142d70.html

603 Washington Post. 2020. "Fatal Force: Robert D'Lon Harris." *Washington Post.com*, December 22. Accessed December 23, 2020. https://www.washingtonpost.com/graphics/investigations/police-shootings-database/

604 Binion, Andrew. 2020. "Man shot and killed by Kitsap deputy identified." *Kitsap Sun*, August 5. Accessed December 22, 2020. https://www.kitsapsun.com/story/news/2020/08/05/man-shot-and-killed-kitsap-deputy-identified/3304979001/

605 Binion, Andrew. 2021. "Investigation: Deputy who shot unarmed man said David Pruitte appeared to have gun." *Kitsap Sun*, January 23. Accessed February 22, 2021. https://www.msn.com/en-us/news/crime/investigation-deputy-who-shot-unarmed-man-said-david-pruitte-appeared-to-have-gun/ar-BB1d0Xqg

606 Henry, Chris. 2020. "Man fatally shot by deputy was unarmed, investigators determine." *Kitsap Sun*, August 21. Accessed December 22, 2020. https://www.kitsapsun.com/story/news/local/2020/08/21/man-fatally-shot-deputy-unarmed-investigators-determine/3409404001/

607 McLarty, Christine. 2020. "St. Pete police justify officers actions in shooting death, add new protocols following 'failures'." *WFLA*, September 20. Accessed September 23, 2020. https://www.wfla.com/news/pinellas-county/st-pete-police-justify-officers-actions-in-shooting-death-add-new-protocols-following-failures/amp/

608 Hollenbeck, Sarah. 2020. "Report: Deadly St. Pete officer-involved shooting justified, but raises concerns." *ABC Action News*, September 17. Accessed September 23, 2020. https://www.abcactionnews.com/news/region-pinellas/report-deadly-st-pete-officer-involved-shooting-justified-but-raises-concerns

609 CBS Broadcasting Inc. 2020. "UPDATE: Officer Shoots, Kills Man That Was Choking Her." *CW44 Tampa Bay*, August 8. Accessed September 23, 2020. https://cwtampa.cbslocal.com/2020/08/08/deadly-officer-involved-shooting-following-struggle-in-st-pete-18/

610 O'Donnell, Christopher 2020. "'It shouldn't have ended this way.' Friends, family question St. Pete police shooting of mentally ill man." *Tampa Bay Times*, August 14. Accessed September 23, 2020. https://www.tampabay.com/news/st-petersburg/2020/08/14/it-shouldnt-have-ended-this-way-friends-family-question-st-pete-police-shooting-of-mentally-ill-man/?utm_medium=social&utm_source=facebook&utm_campaign=SocialFlow&utm_content=FBtimes&fbclid=IwAR1Hb-nS7fv0r2HWLVVkgK0riRFZthCCCDxf4X4EJG7xh-Nd-R-kEX_dZnM

611 Bonvillian, Crystal. 2020. "Georgia trooper charged with murder in shooting of Black driver forced into ditch during traffic stop." *FOX 23 News*, August 17. Accessed September 24, 2020. https://www.fox23.com/news/trending/georgia-trooper-charged-with-murder-shooting-black-driver-forced-into-ditch-during-traffic-stop/GHP3NDACC5CVLEEJQDKD6YWG4I/

612 Saxon, Holly Deal. 2020. "GBI: Video disputes former trooper's account in fatal shooting." *Statesboro Herald*, August 25. Accessed September 24, 2020. https://www.statesboroherald.com/local/gbi-video-disputes-former-troopers-account-fatal-shooting/

613 Hernandez, Arelis R, Mark Berman, and Mary Beth Gahan. 2020. "Texas police officer antagonized people in small town prior to shooting, residents say." *The Washington Post*, October 10. Accessed December 22, 2020. https://www.washingtonpost.com/nation/2020/10/10/texas-police-officer-antagonized-residents-small-town-prior-shooting-residents-say/

614 Razek, Raja, and Nicole Chavez. 2020. "A Texas officer charged in Jonathan Price's shooting death has been fired ." *CNN*, October 8. Accessed December 21, 2020. https://www.cnn.com/2020/10/08/us/jonathan-price-shooting-police-officer-fired/index.html

615 Ibid 613.

616 DeMarche, Edmund. 2020. "Texas cop charged with murder in connection to Jonathan Price shooting: reports." *Fox News*, October 6. Accessed October 6, 2020. https://www.foxnews.com/us/texas-cop-charged-with-murder-in-connection-to-jonathan-price-shooting-reports

617 CBS SF Staff. 2020. "Man Shot By Napa County Sheriff's Deputy During Traffic Stop Dies Of His Wounds." *KPIX 5*, October 7. Accessed December 10, 2020. https://sanfrancisco.cbslocal.com/2020/10/07/suspect-in-napa-county-officer-involved-shooting-dies-of-his-wounds/

618 Miller, Joshua Rhett. 2020. "California sergeant fatally shot drunk man who refused to show hands: video." *New York Post*, October 15. Accessed December 22, 2020. https://nypost.com/2020/10/15/california-cop-fatally-shot-man-who-refused-to-show-hands-video/

619 Freedman, Wayne, and Krisann Chasarik. 2020. "Body cam video released in deadly shooting by Napa County deputy." *ABC 7 News*, October 14. Accessed December 22, 2020. https://abc7news.com/body-cam-video-released-in-deadly-shooting-by-napa-co-deputy/7031004/

620 Klearman, Sarah. 2020. "Napa County Sheriff's Office releases body cam footage featuring the shooting of Napa resident Juan Adrian Garcia." *Napa Valley Register*, November 24. Accessed December 22, 2020. https://napavalleyregister.com/news/local/napa-county-sheriffs-office-releases-body-cam-footage-featuring-the-shooting-of-napa-resident-juan/article_79221d22-4d9b-5723-ba27-29527894d5fb.html

621 Arrests.org. 2020. "Anthony Legato." *Minnesota Arrests.org*, June 2. Accessed December 26, 2020. https://minnesota.arrests.org/Arrests/Anthony_Legato_45245552/

622 Griswold, David. 2020. "Suspect, deputy identified in deadly Pine County officer involved shooting." *KARE 11*, October 12. Accessed December 26, 2020. Suspect, deputy identified in deadly Pine County officer involved shooting | kare11.com

623 Gainor, Mike. 2020. "Family demands footage of fatal police shooting." *Kanabec County Times*, December 11. Accessed December 26, 2020. http://www.moraminn.com/news/family-demands-footage-of-fatal-police-shooting/article_1d4f21e6-3a32-11eb-9c99-335cbb7ed033.html

624 Faurie, Kirsten. 2021. "Pine County Attorney: Deputy's use of deadly force justified in shooting." Kanabec County Times, February 14. Accessed April 29, 2021. http://www.moraminn.com/pine-county-attorney-deputy-s-use-of-deadly-force-justified-in-shooting/article_1d787ef4-6bb7-11eb-b459-df2fe6bca445.html

625 Morris, Kevin. 2020. "Henderson Police Department traffic stop results in fatal shooting." *Chester County Independent*, October 14. Accessed December 26, 2020. https://chestercountyindependent.com/2020/10/14/henderson-police-department-traffic-stop-results-in-fatal-shooting/

626 Fernandez, Stephanie. 2020. "Protesters seek answers for West TN man killed in officer-involved shooting." *WBBJ TV*, October 21. Accessed December 26, 2020. https://www.wbbjtv.com/2020/10/21/protesters-seek-answers-for-west-tn-man-killed-in-officer-involved-shooting/

627 Ibid 625.

628 Ewoldt, Julia. 2020. "Family seeks answers following officer-involved fatal shooting." *WBBJ TV*, October 14. Accessed December 26, 2020. https://www.wbbjtv.com/2020/10/14/family-seeks-answers-following-officer-involved-fatal-shooting/

629 Freishtat, Sarah, and Steve Sadin. 2020. "Waukegan releases reasons for firing police officer who killed Marcellis Stinnette ." *Lake County News-Sun*, November 6. Accessed December 26, 2020. https://www.chicagotribune.com/suburbs/lake-county-news-sun/ct-lns-stinnette-williams-police-reports-st-20201107-jva53ruf55c2xnkped3w3fvfni-story.html

630 Hickey, Megan. 2020. "Now-Fired Waukegan Police Officer Dante Salinas, Who Shot And Killed Marcellis Stinnette, Was Never Disciplined In Earlier Disputed Use-Of-Force Incident." *CBS*

Chicago, November 6. Accessed December 26, 2020. https://chicago.cbslocal.com/2020/11/06/now-fired-waukegan-police-officer-dante-salinas-who-shot-and-killed-marcellis-stinnette-was-never-disciplined-in-earlier-disputed-use-of-force-incident/

631 Gunn, Tamantha. 2020. "Dashcam, body cam footage released in police shooting of Marcellis Stinnette." *Revolt*, October 28. Accessed December 26, 2020. https://www.revolt.tv/2020/10/28/21539322/dashcam-body-cam-marcellis-stinnette

632 Pagones, Stephanie. 2020. "Video of Chicago-area police shooting to be released, mayor says." *Fox News*, October 26. Accessed October 26, 2020. https://www.foxnews.com/us/chicago-area-police-shooting-waukegan-mayor

633 McLaughlin, Elliot C. 2020. "Car chase preceded police shooting that killed Marcellis Stinnette in Waukegan, Illinois, video shows." *CNN*, October 29. Accessed December 26, 2020. https://www.cnn.com/2020/10/29/us/waukegan-police-shooting-video-marcellis-stinnette/index.html

634 Cruz, Mike, & Kaila White. 2020. "2 brothers die after family dispute with weapons ends in Phoenix police shooting." *Arizona Republic*, October 21. Accessed December 16, 2020. https://www.azcentral.com/story/news/local/phoenix-breaking/2020/10/21/phoenix-police-shooting-happened-dispute-where-1-person-armed/6005357002/

635 Roman, Anita, Jennifer Martinez , Kenneth Wong and Brent Corrado. 2020. "Phoenix PD: Two suspects shot and killed, no officers hurt." *FOX 10 Phoenix*, November 3. Accessed December 26, 2020. https://www.fox10phoenix.com/news/phoenix-pd-two-suspects-shot-and-killed-no-officers-hurt

636 Blasius, Melissa. 2020. "Phoenix police may have shot unarmed man in welfare check call." *ABC 15*, November 13. Accessed December 26, 2020. https://www.abc15.com/news/local-news/investigations/phoenix-police-may-have-shot-unarmed-man-in-domestic-dispute-call

637 Police Overwatch. 2020. "Bodycam of George and Emmett Cocreham shooting (Viewer Discretion Advised)." *YouTube*, November 3. Accessed December 26, 2020. https://www.youtube.com/watch?v=srWHdXWLLE4

638 Ford, Daniel. 2020. "Police Release Footage Of Officers Fatally Shooting Arguing Brothers." *Zenger*, November 10. Accessed December 26, 2020. https://www.zenger.news/2020/11/10/police-release-edited-footage-of-officers-fatally-shooting-arguing-brothers/

639 Spagat, Elliot, and Christopher Weber. 2020. "Video shows San Diego police shooting man who charged them." *Associated Press*, October 29. Accessed December 26, 2020. https://www.pressdemocrat.com/article/news/video-shows-san-diego-police-shooting-man-who-charged-them/?sba=AAS

640 Ireland, Elizabeth. 2020. "Mexican National Who Was Killed in Border Patrol Shooting ID'd." *Times of San Diego*, October 27. Accessed December 26, 2020. https://timesofsandiego.com/crime/2020/10/27/mexican-national-killed-in-border-patrol-shooting-idd/

641 Riggins, Alex. 2020. "Authorities ID Border Patrol agent who shot, killed man in San Ysidro." *The San Diego Union-Tribune*, November 2. Accessed December 26, 2020. https://www.sandiegouniontribune.com/news/public-safety/story/2020-11-02/authorities-identify-border-patrol-agent-who-fatally-shot-mexican-man-in-san-ysidro

642 Ibid 638.

643 Lynn, Nate. 2020. "Man shot by Glendale police officer dies." *9 News*, November 1. Accessed December 27, 2020. https://www.msn.com/en-us/news/crime/shooting-involving-glendale-police-under-investigation/ar-BB1aAaky

644 Maass, Brian. 2020. "Mother Calls Killing Of John Pacheaco Jr. By Glendale Police 'Like A Firing Squad'." *4 CBS Denver*, November 6. Accessed Decemberr 27, 2020. https://denver.cbslocal.com/2020/11/06/john-pacheaco-jr-glendale-police-shooting-mother-compares-firing-squad/

645 Salinger, Marc. 2020. "Little information released nearly a week after Glendale Police shot and killed a man on Colorado Boulevard." *9 NEWS*, November 6. Accessed December 10, 2020. https://www.9news.com/article/news/crime/little-information-released-nearly-week-after-glendale-police-shot-killed-man/73-ebbd83ca-458a-4670-8c62-719d5a5527da

646 Maass, Brian. 2020. "New Video Emerges of Deadly Glendale Police Shooting; 2 Officers Still Have Not Given Statements." *4 CBS Denver*, November 13. Accessed December 27, 2020. https://denver.cbslocal.com/2020/11/13/new-video-emerges-of-deadly-glendale-police-shooting-2-officers-still-have-not-given-statements/

647 Roberts, John. 2020. "Glendale Cop Turns Controversial Police Killing Into a Joke." *Westworld*, December 9. Accessed December 27, 2020. https://www.westword.com/news/john-pacheaco-glendale-police-shooting-and-joke-gone-wrong-update-11844998

648 Marrero, Tony, and Luis Santana. 2020. "Body cam video shows moments before Hillsborough deputies fatally shoot man." *Tampa Bay Times*, December 9. Accessed December 10, 2020. https://www.tampabay.com/news/hillsborough/2020/12/09/crash-shooting-involving-hillsborough-deputies-in-riverview/

649 Luckey, Skyla. 2020. "Video Shows Officer Shooting Suspect Sitting In Truck: Sheriff." *The Patch*, December 9. Accessed January 5, 2021. https://patch.com/florida/bloomingdale/suspect-killed-officer-involved-shooting-hillsborough-sheriff

650 The Spectator Media. 2020. "A police shooting that shows why we need body cameras." *The Spectator*, December 12. Accessed January 5, 2021. https://thespectator.info/2020/12/12/a-police-shooting-that-shows-why-we-need-body-cameras/

651 Associated Press. 2020. "Florida deputies shoot, kill man who 'motioned for a gun,' sheriff says." *Click Orlando*, December 9. Accessed January 5, 2021. https://www.clickorlando.com/news/florida/2020/12/09/florida-deputies-shoot-kill-man-who-motioned-for-a-gun-sheriff-says/

652 Bruner, Bethany. 2020. "Unarmed Black man fatally shot by Columbus police officer responding to noise complaint." *The Columbus Dispatch*, December 23, 2020. Accessed January 1, 2021. https://www.dispatch.com/story/news/local/2020/12/22/one-killed-after-police-shooting-northwest-side/4004989001/

653 Smith, Mary. 2020. "Community leaders, members outraged over officer-involved shooting in north Columbus." *ABC 6*, December 22. Accessed January 1, 2021. https://abc6onyourside.com/news/local/community-leaders-members-outraged-over-officer-involved-shooting-in-north-columbus

654 Bruner, Bethany. 2020. "What we know about the fatal shooting of Andre Hill, a Black man, by Columbus police." *The Columbus Dispatch*, December 29. Accessed January 1, 2021. https://www.dispatch.com/story/news/local/2020/12/22/what-we-know-fatal-shooting-black-man-columbus-police/4014334001/

655 Deliso, Meredith. 2020. "Columbus, Ohio officer who shot unarmed Black man fired as family demands justice." *6 ABC*, December 29. Accessed January 1, 2021. https://6abc.com/andre-hill-police-shooting-adam-coy-columbus-ohio-killed/9138603/

656 Nexstar Media Inc. 2021. "Adam Coy pleads not guilty to reckless homicide in death of Andre' Hill." NBC4i.com, April 28. Accessed April 29, 2021. https://www.nbc4i.com/news/local-news/court-hearing-for-former-columbus-officer-adam-coy/

657 Chang, David. 2021. "Delaware Police Officer Dies Days After Being Attacked While Responding to Fight." *NBC Philadelphia*, April 29. Accessed May 1, 2021. https://www.nbcphiladelphia.com/news/local/delaware-police-officer-dies-days-after-being-attacked-while-responding-to-fight/2795910/

658 NENA, The 911 Association. 2021. "9-1-1 Statistics." *Nena.org*, February. Accessed March 3, 2021. https://www.nena.org/general/custom.asp?page=911statistics

659 Stanford University. 2021. The Stanford Open Policing Project: Findings." *Stanford.edu*. Accessed March 3, 2021. https://openpolicing.stanford.edu/findings/

660 FBI. 2020. "Crime in the United States, 2019: Arrests." *FBI Uniform Crime Report*, Accessed March 1, 2021. https://ucr.fbi.gov/crime-in-the-u.s/2019/crime-in-the-u.s.-2019/topic-pages/persons-arrested.pdf

661 FBI. 2020. "Law Enforcement Officers Killed and Assaulted, 2019." *FBI Uniform Crime Report*. Accessed March 2, 2021. https://ucr.fbi.gov/leoka/2019/topic-pages/officers-assaulted.pdf

662 CDC. 2021. "Natural Disasters and Severe Weather: Lightning Strike Victim Data." *CDC.gov*. Accessed March 3, 2021. https://www.cdc.gov/disasters/lightning/victimdata.html

663 FBI. 2021. "Law Enforcement Officers Killed and Assaulted (LEOKA) Program." *FBI.gov*. Accessed April 25, 2021. https://www.fbi.gov/services/cjis/ucr/leoka

664 Reavy, Pat. 2019. "Utah man charged with capital offense in killing of Provo officer." *Deseret News*, January 23. Accessed September 21, 2020. https://www.deseret.com/2019/1/23/20663963/utah-man-charged-with-capital-offense-in-killing-of-provo-officer

665 Knox, Annie. 2020. "Hearing set for man charged with killing Provo officer Joseph Shinners." *Deseret News*, June 29. Accessed September 21, 2020. https://www.deseret.com/utah/2020/6/29/21306935/hearing-set-for-man-charged-with-killing-provo-officer-joseph-shinners

666 Rochita, Ananda. 2020. "Parents of fallen Davis Police Officer Natalie Corona remember her one year later." *ABC 10*, January 10. Accessed September 21, 2020. https://www.abc10.com/article/news/local/abc10-originals/remembering-fallen-davis-police-officer-natalie-corona-one-year-later/103-fe34eed0-1c1e-47c1-a8bc-56af855956f1

667 KCRA Staff, 2019. "Chief: Davis officer was ambushed when she was killed." *KCRA 3*, January 12. Accessed September 21, 2020. https://www.kcra.com/article/chief-says-davis-officer-natalie-corona-was-ambushed-when-she-was-killed/25851744#

668 Associated Press. 2019. "Suspect in death of Davis Police Officer Natalie Corona identified." *ABC 30 Action News*, January 12. Accessed September 21, 2020. https://abc30.com/davis-police-officer-killed-involved-shooting-natalie-corona-suspect-kevin-douglas-limbaugh/5063402/

669 Stanton, Sam. 2019. "Exclusive: New details emerge about Kevin Limbaugh, the man who killed Davis Officer Natalie Corona." *The Sacramento Bee*, February 3, 2019. Accessed September 21, 2020. https://www.sacbee.com/news/local/crime/article225054545.html

670 Robinson, Carol. 2019. "Suspect indicted in shooting death of Birmingham police Sgt. Wytasha Carter." *AL.com*, September 24. Accessed September 21, 2020. https://www.al.com/news/birmingham/2019/09/suspect-indicted-in-shooting-death-of-birmingham-police-sgt-wytasha-carter.html

671 FOX 10. 2019. "Mobile DA: suspect in police officer shooting homeless, running from police." *FOX10 TV*, January 21. Accessed September 21, 2020. https://www.fox10tv.com/news/mobile-da-suspect-in-police-officer-shooting-homeless-running-from/article_ccd00b1e-1d77-11e9-9d4c-3be8ba71e379.html

672 Ramey, Andrea. 2019. "The bizarre events leading to Mobile police officer's shooting death." *ABC 3340 News*, January 21. Accessed September 21, 2020. https://abc3340.com/news/nation-world/the-bizarre-events-leading-to-mobile-police-officers-shooting-death

673 Koplowitz, Howard. 2019. "Death penalty sought against suspect accused of killing Mobile Police Officer Sean Tuder." *AL.com*, October 29. Accessed September 21, 2020. https://www.al.com/news/mobile/2019/10/death-penalty-sought-against-suspect-accused-of-killing-mobile-police-officer-sean-tuder.html

674 Carter, Ly'Nita & Chorus Nylander. 2019. "Bond denied for 19-year-old arrested for killing Mobile police officer." *ABC 3 WEAR TV*, January 21. Accessed September 21, 2020. https://weartv.com/news/local/bond-denied-for-19-year-old-arrested-for-killing-mobile-police-officer

675 Czech, Ted. 2019. "Pa. police officer's death - from wounds suffered in 1981 bank robbery - ruled homicide." *York Daily Record*, May 15. Accessed September 21, 2020. https://www.ydr.com/story/news/crime/2019/05/15/pa-police-officer-robert-bo-mccallister-death-1981-wounds-ruled-homicide/3682424002/

676 Knight, Cameron, and Sheila Vilvens. 2019. "Suspect in deadly Clermont County standoff 'struggled with mental health'." *Cincinnati Enquirer*, February 5. Accessed September 22, 2020. https://www.cincinnati.com/story/news/crime/crime-and-courts/2019/02/03/clermont-county-standoff-suspect-wade-winn/2761305002/

677 Shapiro, Emily. 2019. "Prosecutors to seek death penalty against 23-year-old accused of killing Ohio sheriff's detective." *ABC News*, February 4. Accessed September 22, 2020. https://abcnews.go.com/US/23-year-accused-killing-sheriffs-detective-ohio-due/story?id=60828069

678 Knight, Cameron. 2019. "'All hell broke loose': SWAT leader recounts deadly Clermont County standoff." *Cincinnati Enquirer*, February 6. Accessed September 22, 2020. https://www.cincinnati.com/story/news/crime/crime-and-courts/2019/02/06/swat-bill-brewer-nick-derose-doug-ventre-clermont-county-standoff/2784174002/

679 Knight, Cameron. 2019. "Wade Winn, man who killed Clermont County deputy, sentenced to life plus 115 years." *Cincinnati Enquirer*, September 23. Accessed September 22, 2020. https://www.cincinnati.com/story/news/crime/crime-and-courts/2019/09/23/man-who-killed-clermont-county-deputy-plead-guilty-murder/2418173001/

680 Gorman, Sean, and Reid Williams. 2019. "Man suspected of killing state trooper had criminal past in Chesterfield." *Richmond Times-Dispatch*, February 5. Accessed September 22, 2020. https://richmond.com/news/local/crime/man-suspected-of-killing-state-trooper-had-criminal-past-in-chesterfield/article_75f959f1-8ca7-5467-a811-a0f6d5d8a3dc.html

681 Wise, Scott, and Shannon Lily. 2019. "Virginia State Trooper killed during drug investigation." *WTVR*, February 5. Accessed September 22, 2020. https://www.wtvr.com/2019/02/05/lucas-dowell-obit/

682 Vielmetti, Bruce. 2019. "Fricke sentenced to life in prison with no chance of parole in killing of Milwaukee officer Matthew Rittner." *Milwaukee Journal Sentinel*, October 3. Accessed September 22, 2020. https://www.jsonline.com/story/news/crime/2019/10/03/killer-milwaukee-cop-matthew-rittner-gets-life-no-chance-parole/3847377002/

683 Ibid 681.

684 Laviola, Erin. 2019. "Jordan Fricke: 5 Fast Facts You Need to Know." *Heavy.com*, February 10. Accessed September 22, 2020. https://heavy.com/news/2019/02/jordan-fricke/

685 Blau, Reuvan. 2019. "Man charged in detective's death says he wanted to commit 'suicide by cop'." *The City*, April 5. Accessed September 22, 2020. https://qns.com/2019/04/man-charged-in-detectives-death-says-he-wanted-to-commit-suicide-by-cop/

686 Katersky, Anna, and Emily Shapiro. 2019. "What we know about NYPD detective Brian Simonsen, who was slain in friendly fire." *ABC News*, February 14. Accessed September 22, 2020. https://abcnews.go.com/US/nypd-detective-brian-simonsen-slain-friendly-fire/story?id=61045065

687 Brodsky, Robert. 2020. "Pair charged in friendly fire death of NYPD Det. Brian Simonsen to stay in jail." *Newsday*, April 15. Accessed September 22, 2020. https://www.newsday.com/long-island/crime/nypd-friendly-fire-brian-simonsen-1.43890738

688 Llorente, Elizabeth. 2019. "Puerto Rico Police Department Agent Alfred Sanyet-Perez, father of 8, had memorable laugh and work ethic." *Fox News*, September 20. Accessed September 22, 2020. https://www.foxnews.com/us/puerto-rico-police-agent-alfred-zanyet-perez

689 McGee, David. 2019. "Prior convictions: Pendergrass had previous criminal record." *Herald Courier*, April 17. Accessed September 23, 2020. https://heraldcourier.com/news/pendergrass-had-previous-criminal-record/article_3d8325ab-a15f-5f4f-950c-42d60eec9469.html

690 Sorrell, Robert. 2019. "'Lost a hero': Sullivan County officer dies from injuries in shooting." *Herald Courier*, February 26. Accessed September 23, 2020. https://heraldcourier.com/news/sullivan-county-officer-dies-from-injuries-in-shooting/article_c8f5a144-7790-5798-803d-edfdaab33755.html

691 Smith, Rain. 2020. "TBI: Suspect in Sullivan standoff committed suicide." *Times News*, July 6. Accessed September 23, 2020. https://www.timesnews.net/news/crime/tbi-suspect-in-sullivan-standoff-committed-suicide/article_dd771c80-5397-5e47-a432-732d48e0832c.html

692 News Channel 11 Staff. 2019. "Findings of grand jury investigation of deadly Sullivan County officer-involved shooting released." *News Channel 11*, June 26. Accessed September 23, 2020. https://www.wjhl.com/news/local/findings-of-grand-jury-investigation-of-deadly-sullivan-county-officer-involved-shooting-released/

693 Associated Press, 2019. "Midland man charged with manslaughter in death of officer." *Abilene Reporter News*, March 6. Accessed September 25, 2020. https://www.reporternews.com/story/news/crime/2019/03/06/midland-man-david-charles-wilson-charged-manslaughter-death-officer-nathan-heidelberg/3084483002/

694 CBS 7 Staff. 2019. "Attorney for man charged with shooting Midland police officer says alarm system malfunctioned." *CBS 7*, September 19. Accessed September 25, 2020. https://www.cbs7.com/content/news/Attorney-for-man-charged-with-shooting-Midland-police-officer-says--560825911.html

695 Borden, Mitch. 2019. "A Week After A Midland Officer Is Shot And Killed, Questions Remain." *Marfa Public Radio*, March 12. Accessed September 25, 2020. https://marfapublicradio.org/blog/a-week-after-a-midland-officer-is-shot-and-killed-questions-remain/

696 Cleary, Tom. 2019. "David Charles Wilson: 5 Fast Facts You Need to Know." *Heavy*, March 6. Accessed September 26, 2020. https://heavy.com/news/2019/03/david-charles-wilson-midland/

697 Keeperman, Brittanny, 2019. "Suspect who allegedly killed McHenry County Sheriff's deputy had threatened to shoot police before." *Northwest Herald*, March 9. Accessed September 25, 2020. https://www.nwherald.com/2019/03/08/suspect-who-allegedly-killed-mchenry-county-sheriffs-deputy-had-threatened-to-shoot-police-before/aspz2pd/

698 Norman, Greg. 2019. "McHenry County Sheriff's Deputy Jacob Keltner's family says support 'gives you a new respect for humanity'." *Fox News*, September 20. Accessed September 25, 2020. https://www.foxnews.com/us/mchenry-county-illinois-sheriffs-deputy-jacob-keltner

699 Keilman, John, and Amanda Marrazzo. 2019. "'Bad guys even respected Jake': Thousands attend funeral service for slain McHenry County Deputy Jacob Keltner." *Chicago Tribune*, March 13. Accessed September 25, 2020. https://www.chicagotribune.com/news/breaking/ct-met-mchenry-county-deputy-jacob-keltner-funeral-20190313-story.html

700 Smith, Katie. 2020. "Added federal charges filed against man accused of fatally shooting McHenry County Sheriff's deputy." *Northwest Herald*, July 7. Accessed September 25, 2020. https://www.nwherald.com/2020/07/07/added-federal-charges-filed-against-man-accused-of-fatally-shooting-mchenry-county-sheriffs-deputy/az6ddt1/

701 Myers, Donald W. 2019. "Report provides details on man accused of killing Deputy Thompson." *Yakima Herald-Republic*, August 27. Accessed September 25, 2020. https://www.dailyrecordnews.com/news/report-provides-details-on-man-accused-of-killing-deputy-thompson/article_c22f8ba9-ea70-512d-a662-179c866cdb93.html

702 Daily Record Staff, 2019. "Ellensburg Police complete investigation in murder of Kittitas County Sheriff's Deputy Ryan Thompson." *Daily Record*, August 1. Accessed September 25, 2020. https://www.dailyrecordnews.com/news/ellensburg-police-complete-investigation-in-murder-of-kittitas-county-sheriffs-deputy-ryan-thompson/article_21466e77-f7e7-5d79-8bbc-bb4573d47e3b.html

703 Lacitis, Eric. 2019. "Investigators focus on background of suspect in Kittitas County deputy's slaying." *Seattle Times*, March 22. Accessed September 25, 2020. https://www.seattletimes.com/seattle-news/crime/suspect-in-kittitas-county-deputys-slaying-was-in-u-s-on-expired-visa/

704 Martinez, Aaron. 2019. "About Facundo Chavez, accused of killing El Paso deputy: not immigrant, history of crime." *El Paso Times*, March 30. Accessed September 25, 2020. https://www.elpasotimes.com/story/news/crime/2019/03/25/facundo-chavez-man-accused-murder-shooting-el-paso-deputy-peter-herrera/3271862002/

705 Valencia, Jamel. 2019. "Report: Felon armed himself with handgun moments before shooting Deputy Peter Herrera." *KFOX14*, March 25. Accessed September 25, 2020. https://kfoxtv.com/news/local/arrest-report-felon-armed-himself-with-handgun-moments-before-fatal-shooting-of-deputy-pe

706 CBS, 2019. "2nd Suspect Charged In Death Of El Paso County Deputy Peter Herrera." *CBS-DFW*, May 13. Accessed September 25, 2020. https://dfw.cbslocal.com/2019/05/13/2nd-suspect-charged-in-death-of-el-paso-county-deputy-peter-herrera/

707 Borunda, Daniel. 2019. "El Paso County sheriff's deputy, who was shot when driver fired 15 times, has died." *El Paso Times*, March 25. Accessed September 25, 2020. https://www.elpasotimes.com/story/news/crime/2019/03/24/el-paso-county-sheriffs-deputy-shot-peter-herrera-critical-condition/3261686002/

708 Thomas, Keaton. 2019. "Sheriff's office identifies man suspected of shooting, killing Cowlitz County deputy." *KATU News*, April 15. Accessed September 25, 2020. https://katu.com/news/local/sheriffs-office-identifies-man-brian-butts-suspected-of-shooting-killing-cowlitz-county-deputy

709 Bernton, Hal. 2019. "'Shots fired — I'm hit': A southwest Washington county grieves after deputy's deadly encounter." *Seattle Times*, April 24. https://www.seattletimes.com/seattle-news/crime/shots-fired-im-hit-a-southwest-washington-county-grieves-in-the-aftermath-of-a-deadly-encounter-that-takes-the-life-of-a-young-deputy-with-deep-roots-in-the-community/

710 Solomon, Molly. 2019. "Suspect Identified In Killing Of SW Washington Sheriff's Deputy." *OPB*, April 15. Accessed September 25, 2020. https://www.opb.org/news/article/suspect-identified-in-killing-of-sw-washington-officer-cowlitz-county/

711 Klein, Allison. 2005. "Officer's Shooter Gets Maximum Prison Term." *The Washington Post*, January 7. Accessed September 25, 2020. https://www.washingtonpost.com/archive/local/2005/01/07/officers-shooter-gets-maximum-prison-term/d4007287-33a8-4a94-a1ab-1f8d424c6637/

712 Ibid 711.

713 Wright, Charlie. 2019. "County Police Officer, Paralyzed in 2003 Shooting, Dies." *Bethesda Magazine*, April 22. Accessed September 25, 2020. https://bethesdamagazine.com/bethesda-beat/police-fire/county-police-officer-paralyzed-in-2003-shooting-dies/

714 The Washington Times, 2005. "Teen sentenced to life in cop shooting." *The Washington Times*, January 7. Accessed September 25, 2020. https://www.washingtontimes.com/news/2005/jan/07/20050107-120829-2532r/

715 Llorente, Elizabeth. 2019. "Montgomery County Police Officer Kyle Olinger wrote Facebook post reflecting on shooting that paralyzed him." *Fox News*, September 20. Accessed September 25, 2020. https://www.foxnews.com/us/montgomery-county-maryland-police-officer-kyle-olinger

716 Harris, Amanda. 2019. "Man who shot Mooresville officer talked of killing himself, police officer, report says." *The Herald*, May 19. Accessed September 27, 2020. https://www.heraldonline.com/news/local/article230595739.html

717 Lehtonen, Amy, and Sarah French. 2019. "Fallen officer repeatedly complained about faulty equipment, inadequate safety, family says." *WCNC Charlotte*, November 7. Accessed September 27, 2020. https://www.wcnc.com/article/news/investigations/investigators/fallen-officers-family-he-feared-for-his-safety-citing-lack-of-backup/275-86ac960d-e1f6-4cd0-816f-6e9d3ba2defc

718 Price, Mark, and Amanda Harris. 2019. "North Carolina Police Officer Shot and Killed During Traffic Stop." *Officer.com*, May 6. Accessed September 27, 2020. https://www.officer.com/command-hq/news/21079194/mooresville-north-carolina-police-officer-jordan-harris-sheldon-shot-and-killed-during-traffic-stop

719 Ibid 717.

720 Baker, Margaret. 2019. "An 'ambush': New details released in killing of Biloxi police officer Robert McKeithen." *Sun Herald*, May 8. Accessed September 27, 2020. https://www.sunherald.com/news/local/crime/article230164994.html

721 McConnaughey, Janet, and Jeff Amy. 2019. "Mother of man accused in Biloxi cop slaying says her son was troubled." *WDAM*, May 9. Accessed September 27, 2020. https://www.wdam.com/2019/05/09/mother-man-accused-biloxi-cop-slaying-says-her-son-was-troubled/

722 Knowles, Lindsay, and Bill Snyder. 2019. "'Respect the shooter': Accused cop killer demands respect when arrested." *WDAM*, June 19. Accessed September 27, 2020. https://www.wdam.com/2019/06/18/man-accused-gunning-down-biloxi-police-officer-appears-court/

723 Baker, Margaret. 2019. "Grand jury indicts teen in ambush killing of Biloxi police officer Robert McKeithen." *Sun Herald*, November 21. Accessed September 27, 2020. https://www.sunherald.com/news/local/crime/article237617904.html

724 WJTV, 2020. "Mississippi judge: Man can stand trial in officer's death." *WJTV*, May 23. Accessed September 27, 2020. https://www.wjtv.com/news/mississippi-judge-man-can-stand-trial-in-officers-death/

725 Ray, Brittini. 2019. "Suspect in fatal shooting of Savannah Police Sgt. Kelvin Ansari had long criminal history." *Savannah Now*, May 19. Accessed September 28, 2020. https://www.savannahnow.com/news/20190514/suspect-in-fatal-shooting-of-savannah-police-sgt-kelvin-ansari-had-long-criminal-history

726 David, Andrew. 2019. "Savannah Police cleared in shooting of suspect in Sgt. Kelvin Ansari's death." *WSAV*, August 21. Accessed September 28, 2020. https://www.wsav.com/news/developing-savannah-police-cleared-in-shooting-of-the-suspect-in-sgt-kelvin-ansaris-death/

727 Gore, Leada. 2019. "Who is Grady Wayne Wilkes? Police killing suspect is Army veteran, wrote on earlier officer shooting." *Alabama.com*, May 20. Accessed September 28, 2020. https://www.al.com/news/2019/05/who-is-grady-wayne-wilkes-man-suspected-in-death-of-1-auburn-alabama-officer-wounding-2-others.html

728 Opelika-Auburn News. 2020. "ONE YEAR AGO: Auburn police officer William Buechner shot, killed; two other officers injured." *Opelika-Auburn News*, May 20. Accessed September 28, 2020. https://oanow.com/news/local/one-year-ago-auburn-police-officer-william-buechner-shot-killed-two-other-officers-injured/collection_0586576a-96d5-11ea-b708-33b675249d5a.html#1

729 Bryce, Morgan. 2020. "Auburn Police Department Officer William Buechner lost his life in tragic shooting one year ago today." *Opelika Observer*, May 19. Accessed September 28, 2020. https://opelikaobserver.com/auburn-police-department-officer-william-buechner-lost-his-life-in-tragic-shooting-one-year-ago-today/

730 WFSA Staff. 2019. "More details released about slain Auburn officer, suspect." *WFSA12 News*, May 20. Accessed September 28, 2020. https://www.wsfa.com/2019/05/20/suspect-wanted-auburn-manhunt-custody-2/

731 Matkin, Holly. 2019. "Hero Down: Officer Jesus Marrero-Martinez Murdered In Gunfight With Carjackers." *The Police Tribune*, May 27. Accessed September 28, 2020. https://bluelivesmatter.blue/hero-down-officer-jesus-marrero-martinez-murdered-in-gunfight-with-carjackers/

732 Ibid 731.

733 Spicuzza, Mary, John Diedrich, and Bruce Vielmetti. 2019. "Man accused of killing Racine Police Officer John Hetland was released from prison 4 days earlier." *Milwaukee Journal Sentinel*, June 28. Accessed September 28, 2020. https://www.jsonline.com/story/news/crime/2019/06/28/man-accused-killing-racine-cop-released-prison-4-days-earlier/1599222001/

734 Klopf, Rebecca. 2020. "Witnesses testify Racine Police Officer John Hetland died 'seconds' after being shot." *TMJ4*, September 23. Accessed September 28, 2020. https://www.tmj4.com/news/local-news/witnesses-testify-racine-police-officer-john-hetland-died-seconds-after-being-shot#:~:text=Facebook-,Witnesses%20testify%20Racine%20Police%20Officer,died%20'seconds'%20after%20being%20shot&text=An%20early%20and%20abrupt%20end,off%2Dduty%20Racine%20police%20officer

735 Mauk, Alyssa. 2020. "Top stories of 2019 — No. 1: The death of RPD Officer John Hetland." *The Journal Times*, January 1. Accessed September 28, 2020. https://journaltimes.com/news/local/top-stories-of-2019-no-1-the-death-of-rpd-officer-john-hetland/article_d788b168-e45e-5e7a-ba6d-750cb3bee612.html

736 Flores, Christine. 2020. "Jury finds Ward guilty in 2019 homicide of Racine Officer John Hetland." *CBS 58*, September 25. Accessed September 28, 2020. https://www.cbs58.com/news/jury-deliberates-in-ward-homicide-trial-man-accused-of-killing-racine-officer-hetland

737 Stanton, Sam. 2020. "Death penalty sought against suspect in Sacramento Officer Tara O'Sullivan slaying." *The Sacramento Bee*, January 23. Accessed September 30, 2020. https://www.sacbee.com/article239358248.html

738 Estrada, Marie. 2019. "Timeline: Shooting of slain Sacramento Police Officer Tara O'Sullivan." *ABC 10*, June 21. Accessed September 28, 2020. https://www.abc10.com/article/news/crime/timeline-shooting-of-slain-sacramento-police-officer-tara-osullivan/103-b88ffe01-39f9-4799-aca2-1cf2a230abbc

739 Fry, Hannah. 2019. "Chilling body cam video details shooting of Sacramento police Officer Tara O'Sullivan ." *Los Angeles Times*, June 24. Accessed September 28, 2020. https://www.latimes.com/local/lanow/la-me-ln-tara-osullivan-sacramento-police-shooting-20190624-story.html

740 KRGV. 2019. "Suspected Gunman Who Fatally Shot Mission Officer had Lengthy Criminal History." *KRGV.com*, June 21. Accessed September 28, 2020. https://www.krgv.com/videos/suspected-gunman-who-fatally-shot-mission-officer-had-lengthy-criminal-history/

741 Garcia, Berenice. 2019. "'He died a hero': Mission police reveal more details about corporal's shooting death." *The Monitor*, June 21. Accessed September 28, 2020. https://www.themonitor.com/2019/06/21/mission-police-reveal-details-shooting-death-cpl-espericueta/

742 Editor. 2019. "Mission Police Corporal José Espericueta killed last night." *Progress Times*, June 21. Accessed September 28, 2020. https://www.progresstimes.net/2019/06/21/mission-police-corporal-jose-espericueta-killed-last-night/

743 DFW-CBS. 2019. "The Mission Police Officer Killed Thursday Was The Station's First Death In More Than 40 Years." *DFW-CBS local*, June 23. Accessed September 28, 2020. https://dfw.cbslocal.com/2019/06/23/mission-police-officer-killed-stations-first-death-40-years/

744 Cole, Ashley. 2019. "Man confessed to murder of North County Police Cooperative police officer." *WGRZ*, July 1. Accessed September 28, 2020. https://www.wgrz.com/article/news/local/man-confessed-to-murder-of-north-county-police-cooperative-police-officer/63-710095f2-de91-403a-8c06-d414983aec08

745 Murphy, Doyle. 2019. "Second Suspect Kawyn Smith Charged in Officer Michael Langsdorf's Killing." *Riverfront Times*, July 2. Accessed September 28, 2020. https://www.riverfronttimes.com/newsblog/2019/07/02/second-suspect-kawyn-smith-charged-in-officer-michael-langsdorfs-killing

746 Bell, Kim, and Rachel Rice. 2019. "Man with criminal history charged in police officer's shooting death at Wellston market." *St. Louis Post-Dispatch*, June 25. Accessed September 28, 2020. https://www.stltoday.com/news/local/crime-and-courts/man-with-criminal-history-charged-in-police-officers-shooting-death-at-wellston-market/article_057cc14c-84ac-5375-9dd6-1cee406bce67.html

747 Ibid 744.

748 WQAD Digital Team. 2019. "What we know about the man accused in the deadly shooting of Deputy Troy Chisum." *WQAD*, June 26. Accessed September 28, 2020. https://www.wqad.com/article/news/crime/what-we-know-about-the-man-accused-in-the-deadly-shooting-of-deputy-troy-chisum/526-f07b2905-d273-471b-abb5-a6a70ae2d89c

749 Kravetz, Andy. 2019. "Deputy Troy Chisum was backing up when he was shot." *Journal Star*, June 27. Accessed September 28, 2020. https://www.pjstar.com/news/20190627/deputy-troy-chisum-was-backing-up-when-he-was-shot

750 Schrodt, Hannah. 2019. "Judge moves case forward in Fulton County deputy's slaying." *Journal Star*, July 17. Accessed September 28, 2020. https://www.pjstar.com/news/20190717/judge-moves-case-forward-in-fulton-county-deputys-slaying

751 Williams, B.J. 2019. "Suspects in deputy's murder have criminal history." *Access WDUN*, July 9. Accessed October 1, 2020. https://accesswdun.com/article/2019/7/812272/suspects-in-deputys-murder-have-criminal-history

752 Boone, Christian, and Chelsea Prince. 2019. "Family recalls fallen young deputy: 'He loved what he did'." *The Atlanta Journal-Constitution*, July 11. Accessed October 1, 2020. https://www.ajc.com/news/crime--law/breaking-hall-county-deputy-killed-suspects-the-run-after-shootout/ZkQQUy5gy5Mjy3TvkQM7dI/

753 Watson, Nick. 2019. "4 teens indicted in Deputy Dixon's death." *Gainesville Times*, August 20. Accessed October 1, 2020. https://www.gainesvilletimes.com/news/4-teens-indicted-deputy-dixons-death/

754 Burch, Alex. 2019. "Documents reveal fallen deputy may have helped arrest suspect in the past." *KATV*, July 19. Accessed October 1, 2020. https://katv.com/news/local/documents-reveal-fallen-deputy-may-have-helped-arrest-suspect-in-the-past

755 Region 8 Newsdesk. 2019. "Prosecutor: Deputies use of force justified in Stone Co. officer-involved shooting." *KAIT 8*, December 5. Accessed October 1, 2020. https://www.kait8.com/2019/12/05/prosecutor-deputies-use-force-justified-stone-co-officer-involved-shooting/

756 City News Service, 2019. "Reputed gang members charged in off-duty LAPD officer's murder due in court." *Fox 11 LA*, September 11. Accessed October 2, 2020. https://www.foxla.com/news/reputed-gang-members-charged-in-off-duty-lapd-officers-murder-due-in-court

757 Allen, Karma. 2019. "Off-duty LAPD officer was trying to stop vandals when he was fatally shot, sources say." *ABC News*, July 28. Accessed October 2, 2020. https://abcnews.go.com/US/off-duty-lapd-officer-stop-vandals-fatally-shot/story?id=64620262

758 Ortega, Ralph R. 2019. "Two suspected gang members are charged with killing off-duty Los Angeles cop who was shot dead at a late-night taco stand." *DailyMail.com*, August 7. Accessed October 2, 2020. https://www.dailymail.co.uk/news/article-7334297/Suspected-gang-members-charged-killing-duty-Los-Angeles-cop-outside-taco-stand.html

759 Lloyd, Jonathan, and Toni Guinyard. 2019. "LAPD Honors an Officer Killed After Confronting Suspected Gang Members." *NBC Los Angeles*, August 12. Accessed October 2, 2020. https://www.nbclosangeles.com/news/police-officer-lapd-diaz-funeral-memorial-service-los-angeles-shooting/78034/

760 Torpy, Bill. 2019. "J.J. Biello, paralyzed by a bullet in 1987, lived fully for others." *The Atlanta Journal-Constitution*, July 31. Accessed October 2, 2020. https://www.ajc.com/news/local/torpy-large-great-calling-him-cop-cop-doesn-him-justice/bFM9QSbBmUiEekJlsZWcyN/

761 Raymond, Jonathan. 2019. "32 years later: Shooter who left Atlanta detective paralyzed could face murder charge." *11 Alive*, July 30. Accessed October 2, 2020. https://www.11alive.com/article/news/crime/32-years-later-shooter-who-left-atlanta-detective-paralyzed-could-face-murder-charge/85-9b60f5d4-3a28-486e-8b54-0f54ae475394

762 Associated Press. 2019. "CHP officer Andre Moye Jr. and ex-con gang member die in Riverside shootout." *Desert Sun*, August 20. Accessed October 5, 2020. https://www.desertsun.com/story/news/ crime_courts/2019/08/12/two-chp-officers-injured-exchange-gunfire-suspect/1994016001/

763 Wallace, Danielle. 2019. "Violent felon who killed California Highway Patrol officer 'wasn't a monster,' his widow insists." *Fox News*, August 14. Accessed October 5, 2020. https://www.foxnews.com/us/ california-highway-patrol-officer-killed-andre-moye-suspect-aaron-luther-identified

764 Rokos, Brian. 2019. "Killer of CHP officer fired at least 100 times, Riverside police say." *The Press Enterprise*, August 28. Accessed October 5, 2020. https://www.pe.com/2019/08/28/ killer-of-chp-officer-fired-at-least-100-times-riverside-police-say/

765 City of Riverside. 2019. "Murder Investigation of California Highway Patrol Officer Andre Moye Jr." *City of Riverside Press Release*, August 16. Accessed October 5, 2020. https://www.riversideca.gov/press/ murder-investigation-california-highway-patrol-officer-andre-moye-jr

766 Bell, Kim. 2019. "Second man charged in connection with Illinois trooper shooting." *St. Louis Post-Dispatch*, August 27. Accessed October 5, 2020. https://www.stltoday.com/news/local/ crime-and-courts/second-man-charged-in-connection-with-illinois-trooper-shooting/article_18678b94-c4ef-5a8e-b1a8-7215fc3db390.html

767 Smith, Carolyn P., and Mike Koziatek. 2019. "Illinois State Police SWAT trooper dies after being shot in East St. Louis." *Belleville News-Democrat*, August 23. Accessed October 5, 2020. https://www.bnd.com/ news/local/crime/article234308222.html

768 Smith, Carolyn P. 2019. "Family says trooper shooting suspect heard a bang, thought someone was breaking in." *Belleville News-Democrat*, September 1. Accessed October 6, 2020. https://www.bnd.com/ article234474492.html

769 Sanders, Nicole. 2020. "Federal charges filed in Trooper Nick Hopkins' death." *KMOV 4*, March 19. Accessed October 5, 2020. https://www.kmov.com/news/federal-charges-filed-in-trooper-nick-hopkins-death/article_671078c2-c592-11e9-aef2-7fbe3da748bd.html

770 Ibid 766.

771 KRGV. 2019. "Suspected Shooter of DPS Trooper Has Criminal Background." *KRGV.com*, April 7. Accessed October 5, 2020. https://www.krgv.com/news/ suspected-shooter-of-dps-trooper-has-criminal-background/

772 Reagan, Mark. 2019. "DPS: Trooper Sanchez died after April shooting." *Valley Morning Star*, August 24. Accessed October 5, 2020. https://www.valleymorningstar.com/2019/08/24/ dps-trooper-sanchez-died-april-shooting/

773 CBS 4 News. 2019. "Hidalgo County DA to seek capital murder charge for suspect following Trooper's death." *ValleyCentral.com*, August 24. Accessed October 5, 2020. https://www.valleycentral.com/news/ local-news/dps-confirms-death-of-trooper-moises-sanchez/

774 Zazueta-Castro, Lorenzo. 2019. "Suspect in Trooper Sanchez's shooting pleads not guilty." *Valley Morning Star*, October 8. Accessed October 5, 2020. https://www.valleymorningstar.com/2019/10/08/ suspect-in-trooper-sanchezs-shooting-pleads-not-guilty/

775 Ozimek, Tom. 2019. "Suspect Arrested in Shooting of Texas Trooper Fighting for His Life." *The Epoch Times*, April 7. Accessed October 6, 2020. https://www.theepochtimes.com/suspect-arrested-in-shooting-of-texas-trooper-fighting-for-his-life_2869823.html

776 WVTM 13 Digital. 2019. "Tuscaloosa police officer killed in line of duty, 20-year-old charged." *WVTM 13*, September 17. Accessed September 9, 2020. https://www.wvtm13.com/article/ tuscaloosa-police-officer-shot-investigation-underway/29078096#

777 Donley, Andrew. 2019. "Alabama's violent offenders keep bonding out, only to commit more crimes." *ABC 3340 News*, November 7. Accessed October 7, 2020. https://abc3340.com/news/local/violent-offenders-bonding-out-only-to-commit-more-crimes

778 Enfinger, Emily. 2020. "Officer Dornell Cousette's dedication is remembered one year after his death." *The Tuscaloosa News*, September 16. Accessed October 7, 2020. https://www.tuscaloosanews.com/story/news/2020/09/16/officer-dornell-cousette-died-line-duty-last-year/5803270002/

779 Gooden, Ashley. 2019. "Preliminary hearing begins for man accused of killing Tuscaloosa police officer." *ABC 3340 News*, October 4. Accessed October 7, 2020. https://abc3340.com/news/local/preliminary-trial-begins-for-man-accused-of-killing-tuscaloosa-police-officer

780 Gallien, Stephen. 2019. "Luther Watkins indicted for capital murder in death of Police Detective Dornell Cousette." *ABC 3340 News*, December 10. Accessed October 7, 2020. https://abc3340.com/news/local/luther-watkins-indicted-for-capital-murder-in-death-of-police-detective-dornell-cousette

781 Associated Press. 2019. "Police officer dies 2 years after being hit by driver." *WISN*, September 20. Accessed April 18, 2021. https://www.wisn.com/article/police-officer-mark-lentz-dies-2-years-after-being-hit-by-driver/9604643

782 LET Staff. 2019. "Officer Down: Cop dies from injuries after teen intentionally slammed SUV into his motorcycle." *Law Enforcement Today*, September 26. Accessed April 18, 2021. https://www.lawenforcementtoday.com/officer-down-cop-dies-from-injuries-after-teen-intentionally-slammed-suv-into-his-motorcycle/

783 Morgan, Justin. 2019. "Louisiana Man Shoots Police Officers After Car Chase, Killing 1." *NTD.com*, September 21. Accessed October 7, 2020. https://www.ntd.com/louisiana-man-shoots-police-officers-after-car-chase-killing-1_382821.html

784 Malone, Sandy. 2019. "Hero Down: Mandeville PD Captain Vincent 'Vinny' Liberto Murdered By Gunman." *The Police Tribune*, September 23. Accessed October 7, 2020. https://bluelivesmatter.blue/hero-down-mandeville-pd-captain-vincent-vinny-liberto-murdered-by-gunman/

785 District Attorney Montgomery. 2019. "Grand Jury Indicts Covington Man On Murder Charges in Mandeville Police Shooting." *DA Montgomery*, December 5. Accessed October 7, 2020. https://damontgomery.org/2019/12/grand-jury-indicts-covington-man-murder-charges-mandeville-police-shooting/

786 Fernandez, Stacy. 2019. "Sikh Deputy Sandeep Dhaliwal remembered as "all that is good"." *The Texas Tribune*, October 2. Accessed October 8, 2020. https://www.texastribune.org/2019/10/02/sikh-deputy-sandeep-dhaliwal-remembered-all-good/

787 Glenza, Jessica. 2019. "Texas officer who made headlines for his turban and beard killed in traffic stop." *The Guardian*, September 28. Accessed October 8, 2020. https://www.theguardian.com/us-news/2019/sep/28/texas-police-turban-beard-killed-sikh

788 Blakinger, Keri. 2019. "Houston man charged in Harris County deputy slaying to be held without bond." *Chron.com*, October 18. Accessed October 8, 2020. https://www.chron.com/news/houston-texas/houston/article/Man-charged-in-deputy-slaying-scheduled-for-court-14478566.php

789 Barker, Aaron, and Brittany Taylor. 2019. "Authorities identify suspect charged in deadly ambush of Harris County deputy." *Click2Houston.com*, September 27. Accessed October 8, 2020. https://www.click2houston.com/2019/09/27/hcso-deputy-shot-during-traffic-stop-in-northwest-harris-county-sheriff-says/

790 NBC New York. 2019. "NYPD Releases Bodycam Footage from Fatal Shooting of Det. Brian Mulkeen." *NBC New York*, December 14. Accessed October 14, 2020. https://www.nbcnewyork.com/news/local/nypd-releases-bodycam-footage-from-fatal-shooting-of-det-brian-mulkeen/2241734/

791 McDonald, Leah. 2019. "NYPD cop Brian Mulkeen was killed by FRIENDLY FIRE from fellow officers as he fought with gangster for control of his own gun." *Daily Mail*, September 30. Accessed October

14, 2020. https://www.dailymail.co.uk/news/article-7521041/Footage-shows-slain-NYPD-officer-singing-partner-moments-death.html

792 Taranelli, Ryan. 2019. "NYPD officer killed by friendly fire is hailed as a hero." *Daily Herald*, October 4. Accessed October 14, 2020. https://www.dailyherald.com/article/20191004/news/310049856

793 CBS Local. 2019. "4 Suspects Indicted In Death Of El Dorado County Deputy Brian Ishmael." *CBS Sacramento*, November 7. Accessed October 14, 2020. https://sacramento.cbslocal.com/2019/11/07/suspects-indicted-death-deputy-brian-ishmael/

794 McGough, Michael, Sam Stanton, and Molly Sullivan. 2019. "Update: El Dorado County deputy killed responding to call of stolen marijuana, 2 arrested." *The Sacramento Bee*, October 23. Accessed October 14, 2020. https://www.sacbee.com/news/local/article236555138.html

795 Stanton, Sam. 2019. "Fourth man charged in Mexican pot conspiracy that cops say killed El Dorado sheriff's deputy." *The Sacramento Bee*, November 5. Accessed October 14, 2020. https://www.sacbee.com/news/local/crime/article236777383.html

796 McNeff, Jim. 2019. "WELFARE FRAUD INVESTIGATOR KILLS POLICE OFFICER AND SELF, CRITICALLY WOUNDS FATHER AT FAMILY BIRTHDAY PARTY SHOOTING." *Badge145.com*, November 5. Accessed October 15, 2020. https://badge145.com/welfare-fraud-investigator-kills-police-officer-and-self-critically-wounds-father-at-family-birthday-party-shooting/

797 Wagner, Lauren. 2019. "UPDATE: Second victim of murder-suicide dies days after his son shot him, officals said." *The Sentinel*, November 8. Accessed October 15, 2020. https://hanfordsentinel.com/news/local/update-second-victim-of-murder-suicide-dies-days-after-his-son-shot-him-officals-said/article_55b0e2ac-6c44-5b68-95d1-f491acda0836.html

798 Yeager, Joshua. 2019. "Kings County murder-suicide leaves two law enforcement dead, shooter's father critically injured." *Visalia Times-Delta*, November 4. Accessed October 15, 2020. https://www.visaliatimesdelta.com/story/news/2019/11/04/kings-county-murder-suicide-leaves-two-law-enforcement-dead/4153737002/

799 Journal-News Staff. 2019. "Dayton officer shot: 4 men arrested had past drug, violence charges." *Journal-News*, November 9. Accessed October 15, 2020. https://www.journal-news.com/news/crime--law/men-arrested-police-shooting-had-past-drug-violence-charges/f65q67EaRNQ2h5q0PK9KdN/

800 DOJ – Southern District of Ohio. 2019. "Grand jury indicts men allegedly involved in murder of DEA task force officer." *Justice.gov*, November 14. Accessed October 15, 2020. https://www.justice.gov/usao-sdoh/pr/grand-jury-indicts-men-allegedly-involved-murder-dea-task-force-officer

801 Baker, Jennifer Edwards. 2019. "Shooter of Dayton police detective could face death penalty." *FOX19 Now*, November 8. Accessed October 15, 2020. https://www.fox19.com/2019/11/08/shooter-dayton-police-detective-could-face-death-penalty/

802 FOX 19. 2019. "Grand jury indicts 3 men allegedly involved in murder of Dayton police detective." *FOX19.com*, November 14. Accessed October 15, 2020. https://www.fox19.com/2019/11/14/grand-jury-indicts-men-allegedly-involved-murder-dayton-police-detective/

803 Hester, Ceara, and Miya Payton. 2020. "Suspect accused of Inv. Cecil Ridley's murder formally indicted." *FOX54 News Now*, February 25. Accessed October 15, 2020. https://www.wfxg.com/story/41658864/suspect-accused-of-inv-cecil-ridleys-murder-formally-indicted

804 Shapiro, Emily. 2019. "'Cowardly act': Experienced narcotics investigator shot dead on routine patrol in Georgia." *ABC News*, November 20. Accessed October 15, 2020. https://abcnews.go.com/US/narcotics-investigator-shot-dead-routine-patrol-georgia-losing/story?id=67163996

805 CSRA Staff. 2019. "911 call released in shooting death of RCSO Investigator Cecil Ridley." *WJBF.com*, November 20. Accessed October 15, 2020. https://www.wjbf.com/csra-news/911-call-released-in-shooting-death-of-rcso-investigator-cecil-ridley/

806 Hoyt, Gregory. 2019. "Man suspected of murdering officer had been released from prison early, was on probation." *Law Enforcement Today*, November 25. Accessed October 15, 2020. https://www.lawenforcementtoday.com/man-suspected-of-murdering-officer-had-been-released-from-prison-early/

807 Witsil, Frank. 2019. "28-year-old man charged with murder in fatal shooting of Detroit police officer." *Detroit Free Press*, December 5. Accessed October 15, 2020. https://www.freep.com/story/news/local/michigan/detroit/2019/12/03/jujuan-parks-detroit-police-shooting-charges/2594255001/

808 Helsel, Phil. 2019. "Gunman accused of killing Detroit officer appeared to be trying to 'bait' police, chief says." *NBC News*, November 22. Accessed October 15, 2020. https://www.nbcnews.com/news/us-news/gunman-accused-killing-detroit-officer-appeared-be-trying-bait-police-n1089401

809 Bartkowiak Jr., Dave, and Shawn Ley. 2019. "Man arraigned on 16 charges in connection with fatal shooting of Detroit police officer Rasheen McClain." *Click on Detroit*, December 5. Accessed October 15, 2020. https://www.clickondetroit.com/news/2019/12/05/man-arraigned-on-16-charges-in-connection-with-fatal-shooting-of-detroit-police-officer-rasheen-mcclain/

810 Brand-Williams, Oralandar. 2020. "Judge grants request for competency exam for accused police killer." *The Detroit News*, March 5. Accessed October 15, 2020. https://www.detroitnews.com/story/news/local/detroit-city/2019/12/18/court-prison-records-paint-troubling-picture-accused-police-killer/2639897001/

811 Associated Press. 2019. "Suspect appears in court after Alabama sheriff is killed in the line of duty." *FOX4 Beaumont*, November 25. Accessed October 15, 2020. https://fox4beaumont.com/news/nation-world/suspect-in-sheriffs-death-appears-in-court

812 Express Digest. 2019. "Man arrested for shooting dead an Alabama sheriff is son of neighboring county's deputy sheriff." *Express Digest*. Accessed October 15, 2020. https://expressdigest.com/man-arrested-for-shooting-dead-an-alabama-sheriff-is-son-of-neighboring-countys-deputy-sheriff/

813 Roney, Marty, and Kirsten Fiscus. 2019. "Lowndes County Sheriff John Williams shot, killed. Suspect caught, charged with murder." *Montgomery Advisor*, November 24. Accessed October 15, 2020. https://www.montgomeryadvertiser.com/story/news/crime/2019/11/23/lowndes-county-sheriff-john-williams-shot-killed-alabama-sheriff/4288490002/

814 Harper, Jane. 2019. "Driver charged with killing sailor at Fort Story was going 3 times the speed limit, court record says." *The Virginian-Pilot*, December 10. Accessed October 15, 2020. https://www.pilotonline.com/news/crime/vp-nw-fort-story-driver-20191210-g445lhi66vaqtatkqt2bcdq6wu-story.html

815 Mabeus, Courtney. 2019. "Here's the man charged in the fatal Fort Story crash." *Navy Times*, December 5. Accessed October 15, 2020. https://www.navytimes.com/news/your-navy/2019/12/05/driver-charged-in-fatal-fort-story-crash/

816 Mabeus, Courtney. 2019. "Fatal Fort Story crash suspect arraigned in Virginia Beach." *Navy Times*, December 6. Accessed October 15, 2020. https://www.navytimes.com/news/your-navy/2019/12/06/fatal-fort-story-crash-suspect-arraigned-in-virginia-beach/

817 Heron, Michelle. 2019. "Why one of the 'worst of the worst suspect' was out of jail at time of deadly AL officer shooting." *WRBC TV*, December 10. Accessed October 16, 2020. https://www.wrcbtv.com/story/41427674/why-one-of-the-worst-of-the-worst-suspect-was-out-of-jail-at-time-of-deadly-al-officer-shooting

818 Bedrosian, Shosh. 2021. "WAAY 31 I-TEAM: COURT RECORDS SHOW LAJEROMENY BROWN VIOLATED FEDERAL SUPERVISED RELEASE MANY TIMES." *WAAY 31*, May4. Accessed October 16, 2020. https://www.waaytv.com/content/news/WAAY-31-I-Team-Court-records-show-LaJeromeny-Brown-violated-his-federal-supervised-release-566154641.html

819 Albritton, Casey. 2020. "INVESTIGATOR: SUSPECT IN HUNTSVILLE POLICE OFFICER BILLY CLARDY III MURDER SHOT AT HIM 8 TIMES." *WAAY TV*, January 27. Accessed October 16,

2020. https://www.waaytv.com/content/news/Investigator-Suspect-in-Huntsville-Police-Officer-Billy-Clardy-III-murder-shot-at-him-8-times-567337071.html

820 Roop, Lee. 2020. "State will seek death penalty in Huntsville police officer's killing." *Al.com*, January 27. Accessed October 16, 2020. https://www.al.com/news/2020/01/state-will-seek-death-penalty-in-huntsville-police-shooting.html

821 Remkus, Ashley. 2019. "Alabama Police Officer Fatally Shot." *Officer.com*, December 8. Accessed October 16, 2020. https://www.officer.com/command-hq/news/21117325/alabama-police-officer-fatally-shot

822 WTVC Staff. 2019. "Tennessee man charged in the murder of Huntsville police officer." *News Channel 9*, December 7. Accessed October 16, 2020. https://newschannel9.com/news/local/report-tennessee-man-charged-in-the-murder-of-huntsville-police-officer-billy-clardy-iii

823 Lee, Yuna. 2019. "First look at suspected Fayetteville officer shooter London T. Phillips." *4029 News*, December 9. Accessed October 16, 2020. https://www.4029tv.com/article/london-t-philips-fayetteville-shooting-stephen-carr/30168367

824 McKinley, Mitch. 2019. "Footage released showing that Officer Carr's killer shot him 10 times in the head during the ambush." *Law Enforcement Today*, December 14. Accessed October 16, 2020. https://www.lawenforcementtoday.com/footage-released-showing-that-officer-carrs-killer-shot-him-10-times-in-the-head-during-the-ambush/

825 Andone, Dakin. 2019. "Officials release video that shows ambush killing of Arkansas police officer who was shot 10 times." *CNN*, December 16. Accessed October 16, 2020. https://www.cnn.com/2019/12/15/us/arkansas-police-officer-surveillance-video/index.html

826 Reese, Brittany. 2020. "Fayetteville Police Department clears officers in killing man in cop slaying case." *KATV*, January 13. Accessed October 16, 2020. https://katv.com/news/local/fayetteville-police-department-clears-officers-in-killing-man-in-cop-slaying

827 Friend, Daniel. 2019. "Houston Police Chief Politicizes Officer's Death to Criticize Cornyn, Cruz." *The Texan*, December 10. Accessed October 16, 2020. https://thetexan.news/houston-police-chief-politicizes-officers-death-to-criticize-cornyn-cruz/

828 Associated Press. 2019. "Houston Mayor Sylvester Turner announced Sgt. Christopher Brewster's death at a news conference late Saturday." *WAAY 31 ABC*, December 8. Accessed October 16, 2020. https://www.waaytv.com/content/news/Houston-police-sergeant-shot-and-killed-suspect-in-custody-565950961.html

829 The Count. 2019. "TX 'Repeat Offender' Arturo Solis Lengthy Rap Sheet Admits Fatally Shot Houston Police Officer To 'Avoid Arrest'." *The Count.com*, December 8. Accessed October 16, 2020. https://thecount.com/2019/12/08/arturo-solis-houston-officer-christopher-brewster-killer-lengthy-rap-sheet/

830 Lenthang, Marlene. 2019. "Houston cop, 32, is fatally shot responding to call from a woman being assaulted by her armed boyfriend - as police say killing was captured on bodycam and suspect, 25, is in custody." *Daily Mail*, December 8. Accessed October 16, 2020. https://www.dailymail.co.uk/news/article-7769033/Houston-sergeant-32-fatally-shot-responding-domestic-dispute.html

831 McCarthy, Craig, Alex Taylor, Ruth Weissmann and Gabrielle Fonrouge. 2019. "Jersey City shooters were lovers who lived in a van." *New York Post*, December 11. Accessed October 16, 2020. https://nypost.com/2019/12/11/jersey-city-shooting-suspects-were-lovers-who-lived-in-a-van/

832 Racioppi, Dustin, and Abbott Koloff. 2019. "Jersey City shooter was Army veteran with a lengthy criminal history." *NorthJersey.com*, December 12. Accessed October 16, 2020. https://www.northjersey.com/story/news/hudson/2019/12/12/jersey-city-shooting-suspect-was-army-veteran-with-history-of-weapons-violence-offenses/4411802002/

833 Baldwin, Carly. 2019. "Slain Jersey City Police Officer 'An American Hero,' His Son Says." *Patch*, December 17. Accessed October 16, 2020. https://patch.com/new-jersey/jersey-city/slain-jersey-city-police-officer-american-hero-his-son-says

834 Porter, David. 2020. "Officials: NJ kosher deli shooters planned attack for months." *FOX 29*, January 13. Accessed October 16, 2020. https://www.fox29.com/news/officials-nj-kosher-deli-shooters-planned-attack-for-months

835 Dienst, Jonathan, and Brian Thompson. 2019. "Jersey City Shooters Identified, Were Prime Suspects in Other Homicide." *NBC New York*, December 12. Accessed October 16, 2020. https://www.nbcnewyork.com/news/local/jersey-city-shootout-developing-details-3-2/2239660/

836 Kamath, Tulsi and Joel Eisenbaum. "What we know about the suspect wanted in Nassau Bay police sergeant's death." *Click2Houston*, December 11. Accessed October 27, 2020. https://www.click2houston.com/news/local/2019/12/11/what-we-know-about-the-suspect-wanted-in-nassau-bay-police-sergeants-death/

837 ABC 13. 2019. "Police sergeant dies after being hit by suspect in traffic stop." *ABC 13*, December 11. Accessed October 16, 2020. https://abc13.com/police-sergeant-dies-after-being-hit-by-suspect-in-traffic-stop/5745647/

838 DFW-CBS. 2019. "Authorities Arrest Man Suspected Of Murdering Texas Officer Kaila Sullivan With Vehicle." *CBS DFW*, December 12. Accessed October 16, 2020. https://dfw.cbslocal.com/2019/12/12/authorities-arrest-tavores-henderson-suspected-murder-texas-officer-kaila-sullivan/

839 Carlisle, Zac. 2019. "Report: 2 teens charged with murder in death of Panola County constable." *WTVA*, December 13. Accessed October 18, 2020. https://www.wtva.com/content/news/Report-2-teens-charged-with-murder-in-death-of-Panola-County-constable--566175091.html

840 Fowler, Sarah. 2019. "Teens charged with murder after constable killed during police chase." *Mississippi Clarion Ledger*, December 13. Accessed October 18, 2020. https://www.clarionledger.com/story/news/local/2019/12/13/constable-raye-hawkins-killed-police-chase-teen-charged-murder-panola-county-batesville-car-accident/2636175001/

841 FOX 13. 2019. "Teens face murder charges after Mississippi constable killed during police chase." *FOX 13 Memphis*, December 12. Accessed October 18, 2020. https://www.fox13memphis.com/news/local/officer-killed-during-police-chase-north-mississippi/DLNOZ53TJVBYFJDGLDKCJRNDFM/

842 Malik, Alia. 2020. "Officers turn out for slain San Antonio ISD detective's funeral." *My San Antonio*, January 7. Accessed October 18, 2020. https://www.mysanantonio.com/news/education/article/Funeral-service-underway-for-slain-San-Antonio-14956007.php

843 Zavala, Elizabeth. 2020. "2 men accused of running over, killing SAISD officer indicted on capital murder charge." *San Antonio Express-News*, March 20. Accessed October 18, 2020. https://www.expressnews.com/news/local/article/2-men-accused-of-running-over-killing-SAISD-15146734.php#photo-18793540

844 Oliveira, Nelson. 2019. "Off-duty, veteran cop killed after trying to break up fight, getting run over outside IHOP." *New York Daily News*, December 21. Accessed October 18, 2020. https://www.nydailynews.com/news/crime/ny-offduty-cop-killed-at-san-antonio-ihop-while-breaking-up-fight-20191221-4g4mrheg4fha7il3xcbv2hdvly-story.html

845 McBride, Ashley. 2019. "Police arrest second man in San Antonio ISD officer's killing." *San Antonio Express-News*, December 22. Accessed October 18, 2020. https://www.expressnews.com/news/local/article/Police-arrest-second-man-in-San-Antonio-ISD-14926229.php

846 KSAT. 2019. "Off-duty officer intentionally run over, killed in San Antonio." *KBTX.com*, December 21. Accessed October 27, 2020. https://www.kbtx.com/content/news/Off-duty-officer-killed-in-San-Antonio-566411661.html

847 Ball, Megan. 2019. "UPDATE: Second suspect arrested in SAISD officer's death." *KENS 5*, December 23. Accessed October 18, 2020. https://www.kens5.com/article/news/local/update-police-arrest-murder-suspect-in-death-of-off-duty-saisd-officer-killed-outside-of-ihop/273-2ed691ff-06b2-4cbc-90f8-d084c6f67180

848 Salinas, Rebecca. 2020. "2 suspects indicted on capital murder charge in death of off-duty SAISD officer." *KSAT*, March 20. Accessed October 27, 2020. https://www.ksat.com/news/local/2020/03/20/2-suspects-indicted-on-capital-murder-charge-in-death-of-off-duty-saisd-officer/

849 Associated Press. 1998. "METRO NEWS BRIEFS: NEW JERSEY; Suspect Is Killed in Arrest And Officer Is Wounded." *The New York Times*, February 15. Accessed April 20, 2021. https://www.nytimes.com/1998/02/15/nyregion/metro-news-briefs-new-jersey-suspect-is-killed-in-arrest-and-officer-is-wounded.html

850 ODMP. 2019. "Lieutenant Leroy G. Palmer." *ODMP.org*, December 24. Accessed April 21, 2021. https://www.odmp.org/officer/25146-lieutenant-leroy-g-palmer

851 Weidman, Payton. 2020. "Who is Gregory Newson? | Looking into the criminal history of Deputy Chris Dickerson's alleged killer." *CBS 19*, January 3. Accessed October 16, 2020. https://www.cbs19.tv/article/news/local/who-is-gregory-newson-looking-into-the-criminal-history-of-deputy-chris-dickersons-alleged-killer/501-2274dfd8-869e-452c-a644-ffda80ca1e35

852 Cunningham, Patrick. 2020. "Man officially charged with capital murder in slaying of East Texas deputy after extradition from Shreveport." *KETK*, July 30. Accessed October 16, 2020. https://www.easttexasmatters.com/news/crime/man-officially-charged-with-capital-murder-in-slaying-of-east-texas-deputy-after-extradition-from-shreveport/

853 Frazier, Stephanie. 2020. "Man accused of killing Panola County deputy extradited back to Texas." *KLTV*, February 27. Accessed October 16, 2020. https://www.kltv.com/2020/02/28/man-acused-killing-panola-county-deputy-extradited-back-texas/

854 Shamburger, Meredith. 2020. "Shreveport man extradited to face capital murder charge in Panola County deputy's death." *Longview News-Journal*, April 16. Accessed October 16, 2020. https://www.news-journal.com/news/police/shreveport-man-extradited-to-face-capital-murder-charge-in-panola/article_fc05995f-b121-561c-b611-2e00e5a45db7.html

855 Seiger, Theresa. 2019. "Texas sheriff's deputy shot, killed during traffic stop; suspected gunman arrested." *Cox Media Group National Content Desk*, December 31. Accessed October 16, 2020. https://www.kiro7.com/news/trending/texas-sheriffs-deputy-shot-killed-during-traffic-stop-suspected-gunman-arrested/Y3TVSU6UPRCQ7FINVF52HBVSUI/

856 Brown, Tonya. 2020. "Suspect in officer's killing charged in armed robbery." *ABC 15 News*, January 7. Accessed October 30, 2020. https://wpde.com/news/local/suspect-in-officers-killing-suspected-in-armed-robbery

857 Christian, Matthew. 2020. "James Edward Bell has long history with police." *SC Now*, January 8. Accessed October 30, 2020. https://scnow.com/news/local/james-edward-bell-has-long-history-with-police/article_37f7acc0-5b57-5424-a2b7-c21545a959b1.html

858 Robertson, Matthew. 2020. "Florence Regional Airport Public Safety officer shot, killed in traffic stop." *SC Now*, January 5. Accessed October 5, 2020. https://scnow.com/news/local/florence-regional-airport-public-safety-officer-shot-killed-in-traffic/article_0a1b5739-ef26-59a0-b70b-b3aeac2383d6.html

859 Brown, Tonya. 2020. "Man charged in murder of Florence airport police officer requested preliminary hearing." *ABC 15 News*, February 24. Accessed October 30, 2020. https://wpde.com/news/local/man-charged-in-murder-of-florence-airport-police-officer-requested-preliminary

860 WLTX Staff. 2020. "Suspect charged with murder in killing of SC airport officer." *WLTX*, January 6. Accessed October 30, 2020. https://www.wltx.com/article/news/crime/jackson-winkeler-south-carolina-officer-killed/101-b50b54ac-5cf5-4b29-9939-f3a9bc37f369

861 Ako, Diane. 2020. "Suspect Jerry Hanel: what we know." *KITV*, January 20. Accessed October 30, 2020. https://www.kitv.com/story/41583676/suspect-jerry-hanel-what-we-know

862 POL Staff. 2020. "2 Honolulu PD Officers Killed Responding to Stabbing Call Identified." *Police Magazine*, January 20. Accessed October 30, 2020. https://www.policemag.com/539284/2-honolulu-pd-officers-killed-responding-to-stabbing-call-identified

863 Lyte, Brittany. 2020. "Plenty Of Warning Signs But Few Treatment Options In Police Killer Case." *Honolulu Civil Beat*, January 23. Accessed October 30, 2020. https://www.civilbeat.org/2020/01/plenty-of-warning-signs-but-few-treatment-options-in-police-killer-case/

864 Ibid 861.

865 Ibid 862.

866 Schaefers, Allison. 2020. "Honolulu LEO killed in ambush remembered as 'rock' of community." *The Honolulu Star-Advertiser*, March 9. Accessed October 30. https://www.police1.com/police-heroes/articles/honolulu-leo-killed-in-ambush-remembered-as-rock-of-community-fNO3LHrrhrOKzcKM/

867 Waitt, Tammy. 2020. "Heroes Down: Two Honolulu Police Officers Shot and Killed ILOD." *American Security Today*, January 20. Accessed October 30, 2020. https://americansecuritytoday.com/heroes-down-two-honolulu-police-officers-shot-and-killed-ilod/

868 Ibid 863.

869 Dujardin, Peter. 2020. "Feds turned down robbery prosecution for man later accused of killing Newport News police officer." *Daily Press*, February 1. Accessed October 30, 2020. https://www.dailypress.com/news/crime/dp-nw-officer-killing-case-20200131-sj2jeezjffesdeeffuym3sojba-story.html

870 Jones, Matt. 2020. "Man charged in Newport News officer's death indicted on federal gun, drug charges." *Daily Press*, July 6. Accessed October 30, 2020. https://www.dailypress.com/news/crime/dp-nw-thyne-green-federal-indictment-20200706-3xluovgulzdefmjcgw7rvht4py-story.html

871 Dugan, Kelli. 2020. "Virginia police officer dragged to her death after suspect attempts to elude traffic stop." *WSB TV*, January 25. Accessed October 30, 2020. https://www.wsbtv.com/news/trending/virginia-police-officer-dragged-her-death-after-suspect-attempts-elude-traffic-stop/BIRS7AIFEND4NI6ISUTMA227J4/

872 Ibid 869.

873 KTRK-TV. 2019. "Pavol Vido: What we know about suspect in deputy involved shooting." *ABC13.com*, May 29. Accessed October 30, 2020. https://abc13.com/man-on-the-run-after-multiple-shot-1-found-dead-deputy-injured/5321463/

874 Campion, Steve. 2019. "Two victims have died, deputy injured following Liberty Co. shooting." *ABC 7 Chicago*, June 1. Accessed October 30, 2020. https://abc7chicago.com/richard-whitten-pavol-vido-liberty-county-deputy-shot-in-cleveland-texas-shooting-at-business/5321381/

875 Taylor, Brittany and Jacob Rascon. 2020. "Liberty County deputy recovering from being shot in neck in May, dies from apparent heart attack, officials say." *Click2Houston*, February 4. Accessed October 30, 2020. https://www.click2houston.com/news/local/2020/02/04/liberty-county-deputy-recovering-from-being-shot-in-neck-in-may-dies-from-apparent-heart-attack-officials-say/

876 Anaya, Leah. 2020. "Deputy fighting back after being shot in the neck loses his battle, leaves behind wife and kids." *Law Enforcement Today*, February 5. Accessed October 30, 2020. https://www.lawenforcementtoday.com/deputy-fighting-back-after-being-shot-in-the-neck-loses-his-battle/

877 Robinson, Carol. 2020. "Slain Kimberly officer identified as Nick O'Rear; capital murder suspect has lengthy criminal history." *AL.com*, February 5. Accessed November 2, 2020. https://www.al.com/news/2020/02/kimberly-police-officer-shot-during-chase-on-i-65.html

878 Quinn, Stephen. 2020. "New details of interstate pursuit which killed Kimberly police officer revealed in court." *ABC 3340*, March 5. Accessed November 2, 2020. https://abc3340.com/news/local/new-details-of-interstate-pursuit-which-killed-kimberly-police-officer-revealed-in-court

879 Greenlee, Will. 2020. "New details in FHP trooper homicide: First accounts from tow driver, Riviera Beach police detective." *TC Palm*, February 24. Accessed November 2, 2020. https://www.tcpalm.com/story/news/crime/martin-county/2020/02/24/franklin-reed-appeared-normal-before-shooting-new-details-fhp-trooper-death/4860670002/

880 ABC 7 Staff. 2020. "Investigators say man who shot, killed Trooper Joseph Bullock was angry over tow company bill." *ABC 7 WWSB*, February 21. Accessed November 2, 2020. https://www.mysuncoast.com/2020/02/21/investigators-say-man-who-shot-killed-trooper-joseph-bullock-was-angry-over-tow-company-bill/

881 Greenlee, Will and Sara Marino. 2020. "Martin County Sheriff's Office reveals videos, timeline leading to death of FHP Trooper Joseph Bullock." *TC Palm*, February 21. Accessed November 2, 2020. https://www.tcpalm.com/story/news/crime/martin-county/2020/02/21/fhp-trooper-joseph-bullock-tapes-provide-some-clarity-into-moments-before-fatal-shooting/4820060002/

882 Maricopa Public Records. 2020. "Jeremy Cruz Dewey." Accessed November 3, 2020. https://www.maricopapublicrecords.com/full-record-display.php?id=147288

883 White Mountain Independent. 2020. "Pinetop-Lakeside Police." *WMICentral.com*, February 18. Accessed November 3, 2020. https://www.wmicentral.com/news/pinetop_lakeside/pinetop-lakeside-police/article_8cec24ef-a162-5434-b578-6d22798f1cf8.html

884 ABC15.com Staff. 2020. "White Mountain Apache Tribe police officer shot, killed during confrontation near casino." *ABC15.com*, February 15. Accessed November 2, 2020. https://www.abc15.com/news/region-northern-az/white-mountain-apache-tribe-police-officer-killed-in-line-of-duty

885 AZ Family. 2020. "White Mountain Apache Police Officer David Kellywood killed in shooting." *KOLD News 13*, February 17. Accessed November 2, 2020. https://www.kold.com/2020/02/17/white-mountain-apache-police-officer-david-kellywood-killed-monday-morning/

886 KOLD News 13 Staff. 2020. "Autopsy for fallen White Mountain Apache police officer David Kellywood to be done in Tucson." *KOLD News 13*, February 18. Accessed November 2, 2020. https://www.kold.com/2020/02/18/autopsy-fallen-white-mountain-apache-police-officer-david-kellywood-be-done-tucson/

887 Planalp, Carissa. 2020. "Arizona woman says son was involved in deadly shooting of Officer David Kellywood." *AZFamily*, February 18. Accessed November 2, 2020. https://www.azfamily.com/news/arizona-woman-says-son-was-involved-in-deadly-shooting-of-officer-david-kellywood/article_59b6ce00-52c4-11ea-adfb-9b8fb3be6d84.html

888 Collins, Jeffrey. 2020. "Prosecutor: Slain deputy a 'hero' for firing back." *Associated Press*, July 23. Accessed November 2, 2020. https://www.sandiegouniontribune.com/news/nation-world/story/2020-07-23/prosecutor-slain-deputy-a-hero-for-firing-back

889 Hagwood, Kayland. 2020. "Body cam footage released in shooting death of Sumter deputy, suspect." *NEWS 19*, July 23. Accessed November 2, 2020. https://www.wltx.com/article/news/crime/body-cam-footage-released-in-shooting-death-of-sumter-deputy-suspect/101-d65ef007-11b4-47ae-8df2-b2007e557be0

890 Cannon, Celeste and Sooji Nam. 2020. "Body cam footage released in February fatal shooting of Sumter Co. deputy." *WACH FOX 57*, July 23. Accessed November 2, 2020. https://wach.com/news/local/body-cam-footage-released-in-february-fatal-shooting-of-sumter-co-deputy

891 Ibid 888.

892 Mross, Steven. 2020. "Man enters plea in officer's death." *Northwest Arkansas Democrat Gazette*, March 19. Accessed November 7, 2020. https://www.nwaonline.com/news/2020/mar/19/man-enters-plea-in-officer-s-death-2020/

893 Mross, Steven. 2020. "Man, woman charged in fatal shooting of officer." *The Sentinel-Record*, March 12. Accessed November 7, 2020. https://www.hotsr.com/news/2020/mar/12/man-woman-charged-in-fatal-shooting-of-/

894 Cipriano, Ralph. 2020. "'I Will Try To Make Our District Attorney's Life Miserable'." *Big Trial*, July 12. Accessed November 7, 2020. https://www.bigtrial.net/2020/07/police-widow-i-will-try-to-make-our.html

895 Argos, Greg. 2020. "Two More Men Charged With Murder In Shooting Death Of Philadelphia Police Sgt. James O'Connor." *CBS Philly*, April 17. Accessed November 7, 2020. https://philadelphia.cbslocal.com/2020/04/17/three-men-charged-in-connection-to-shooting-death-of-philadelphia-police-sgt-james-oconnor/

896 Palmer, Chris, and Julie Shaw. 2020. "Philadelphia Police Cpl. James O'Connor IV was finally laid to rest Friday. His funeral had been delayed by the coronavirus." *The Philadelphia Inquirer*, May 8. Accessed November 7, 2020. https://fusion.inquirer.com/news/philadephia-police-sgt-james-oconnor-iv-funeral-private-coronavirus-20200508.html

897 Palmer, Chris. 2020. "Philly DA's Office to charge Hassan Elliott, 21, with murder in killing of Cpl. James O'Connor IV." *The Philadelphia Inquirer*, March 17. Accessed November 7, 2020. https://fusion.inquirer.com/news/hassan-elliot-charged-murder-philadelphia-swat-police-james-oconnor-iv-20200317.html

898 Ibid 897.

899 McBride, Jessica. 2020. "Christopher Walsh: Tribute to the Springfield, Missouri Officer." *Heavy*, March 16. Accessed November 7, 2020. https://heavy.com/news/2020/03/officer-christopher-walsh/

900 Bonvillian, Crystal. 2020. "'I've been shot': Audio paints frantic picture of shooting that killed Missouri officer, 3 others." *WSBTV*, March 19. Accessed November 7, 2020. https://www.wsbtv.com/news/trending/ive-been-shot-audio-paints-frantic-picture-shooting-that-killed-missouri-officer-3-others/THC32OGO75BR7FLTMXL4VUFYFE/

901 Ibid 900.

902 Baker, Jennifer Edwards. 2020. "Police: Suspect in officer's death broke into wife's home, pistol-whipped man, threatened 'suicide by cop'." *FOX 19 Now*, March 24. Accessed November 7, 2020. https://www.fox19.com/2020/03/23/police-suspect-officers-death-broke-into-estranged-wifes-home-pistol-whipped-her-boyfriend/

903 WCPO Staff. 2020. "Driver accused of killing Officer Kaia Grant shot himself in the head, prosecutor's office says." *WCPO*, April 8. Accessed November 7, 2020. https://www.wcpo.com/news/crime/officials-announce-aggravated-murder-charge-for-man-accused-of-killing-springdale-officer-kaia-grant

904 WXIX Staff. 2020. "Hamilton Co. prosecutor announces death penalty indictment for accused cop killer." *FOX 19.com*, May 27. Accessed October 28, 2020. https://www.fox19.com/2020/05/27/proseuctor-deters-discuss-case-against-driver-charged-killing-springdale-officer/

905 Gardner, Jackson. 2020. "Man Accused of Killing Washington State Patrol Trooper Found Not Competent to Stand Trial." *Nisqually Valley News*, April 22. Accessed November 8, 2020. http://www.yelmonline.com/article_3fd04336-0299-5bf4-be08-5adafeb10305.html

906 Miller, Shelby. 2020. "Suspect who killed WSP trooper faces charges." *KIRO 7*, March 28. Accessed November 8, 2020. https://www.kiro7.com/news/local/suspect-who-killed-wsp-trooper-appears-court/JOFY4WWELFFXXIWPJ3DLFPGPWM/

907 Takahama, Elise. 2020. "State Patrol trooper, 28, struck and killed by driver during pursuit on I-5 in Chehalis." *Seattle Times*, March 25. Accessed October 28, 2020. https://www.seattletimes.com/seattle-news/crime/state-patrol-trooper-struck-killed-by-driver-during-pursuit-on-i-5-in-chehalis/

908 Ibid 906.

909 Gephardt Daily Staff. 2020. "New details released after fatal shooting of Nevada trooper, arrest of suspect." *Gephardt Daily*, March 28. Accessed November 8, 2020. https://gephardtdaily.com/top-stories/new-details-released-after-fatal-shooting-of-nevada-trooper-arrest-of-suspect/

910 Lacanlale, Rio. 2020. "Suspect in Nevada Highway Patrol sergeant's killing found competent." *Las Vegas Review-Journal*, October 6. Accessed November 8, 2020. https://www.reviewjournal.com/crime/courts/suspect-in-nevada-highway-patrol-sergeants-killing-found-competent-2141003/

911 Ibid 909.

912 Associated Press. 2020. "Sergeant shot, killed while stopping to assist motorist in Nevada; Suspect caught with possible explosives." *St. George News*, March 27. Accessed November 8, 2020. https://www.stgeorgeutah.com/news/archive/2020/03/27/apc-prc-sergeant-shot-killed-while-stopping-to-assist-motorist-in-nevada-suspect-caught-with-possible-explosives/

913 Roberts, Harrison. 2020. "Nevada Highway Patrol officer fatally shot while assisting motorist." *KCBD 11*, March 27. Accessed November 8, 2020. https://www.kcbd.com/2020/03/27/nevada-highway-patrol-officer-fatally-shot-while-assisting-motorist/

914 KVVU. 2020. "Man accused of killing Nev. trooper was paranoid over coronavirus, court documents say." *Hawaii News Now*, April 2. Accessed November 8, 2020. https://www.hawaiinewsnow.com/2020/04/02/man-accused-killing-nev-trooper-was-paranoid-over-coronavirus-court-documents-say/

915 Longa, Lyda. 2020. "Accused cop killer formerly lived in Sierra Vista, sheriff's office says." *My Herald Review*, March 30. Accessed November 8, 2020. https://www.myheraldreview.com/news/cochise_county/accused-cop-killer-formerly-lived-in-sierra-vista-sheriffs-office-says/article_baf93132-7379-11ea-abc9-6bf0ae5b7a03.html

916 NBC 29 Staff. 2020. "Phoenix officer killed, 2 others wounded; gunman killed." *NBC 29*, March 30. Accessed November 8, 2020. https://www.nbc29.com/2020/03/30/phoenix-police-officer-killed-others-injured-shooting/

917 FOX 10 Staff. 2020. "Phoenix police released bodycam video of the night Commander Carnicle was killed." *FOX 10 Phoenix*, July 2. Accessed November 8, 2020. https://www.fox10phoenix.com/news/phoenix-police-released-bodycam-video-of-the-night-commander-carnicle-was-killed

918 Hill, Crystal. 2020. "What we know about the fatal shooting of Indianapolis police officer Breann Leath." *IndyStar*, April 15. Accessed November 8, 2020. https://www.indystar.com/story/news/crime/2020/04/09/what-we-know-shooting-indianapolis-police-officer-breann-leath/5126229002/

919 Martin, Ryan. 2020. "What we know about the suspect in the fatal shooting of IMPD officer Breann Leath." *IndyStar*, April 14. Accessed November 8, 2020. https://www.indystar.com/story/news/crime/2020/04/14/impd-officer-shot-what-we-know-suspect-fatal-shooting-indianapolis/2991705001/

920 Burke, Caroline. 2020. "Who is Elliahs Dorsey (accused of Murder of IMPD agent Breann Leath)? Elliahs Dorsey Biography, Wikipedia, Age, Charge, Twitter, Facebook, Instagram, Net Wealth and More Interesting Facts Need to Know." *Wiki Fox News*, April 11. Accessed November 8, 2020. https://wikifoxnews.com/elliahs-dorsey-wiki-bio-arrested/

921 Ryan, Shannon and Matthew Quick. 2020. "San Marcos police officers, suspect identified in ambush shooting." *FOX 7 Austin*, April 19. Accessed November 8, 2020. https://www.fox7austin.com/news/san-marcos-police-officers-suspect-identified-in-ambush-shooting

922 Sabawi, Fares. 2020. "San Marcos police shooter was undocumented, may have operated under different names." *KSAT*, May 12. Accessed November 8, 2020. https://www.ksat.com/news/local/2020/05/13/san-marcos-police-shooter-was-undocumented-may-have-operated-under-different-names/

923 Warner, Joe. 2020. "San Marcos officer killed in ambush attack was Justin Putnam, a 'fine young man, a faithful officer and a friend'." *Community Impact Newspaper*, April 19. Accessed November 8, 2020. https://communityimpact.com/austin/san-marcos-buda-kyle/public-safety/2020/04/19/san-marcos-officer-killed-in-ambush-attack-was-justin-putnam-a-fine-young-man-a-faithful-officer-and-a-friend/

924 Tracy, Gerald. 2020. "Undocumented immigrant identified as shooter who killed officer, injured two others." *News 4 San Antonio*, May 12. Accessed November 8, 2020. https://news4sanantonio.com/news/local/undocumented-immigrant-identified-as-shooter-who-killed-officer-injured-two-others

925 Dickey, Fred. 2013. "Paralyzed cop doesn't want to be forgotten." *The Sand Diego Union-Tribune*, November 11. Accessed May 2, 2020. https://www.sandiegouniontribune.com/lifestyle/people/sdut-dickey-cop-2013nov11-story.html

926 Irvine, Chris. 2020. "Ex-San Diego Padre-turned-cop who was paralyzed during on-duty shooting 17 years ago dies." *Fox News*, April 24. Accessed November 14, 2020. https://www.foxnews.com/us/san-diego-padre-dan-walters-paralyzed-dies

927 Maffei, John. 2020. "Dan Walters, former Padre and San Diego police officer, dies at 53." *The San Diego Union-Tribune*, April 23. Accessed November 14, 2020. https://www.sandiegouniontribune.com/sports/story/2020-04-23/dan-walters-padres-catcher-san-diego-police-dies

928 Kemker, Austin. 2020. "Suspect accused of killing BRPD officer, critically wounding another previously threatened to kill officers." *WAFB*, April 27. Accessed November 14, 2020. https://www.wafb.com/2020/04/27/suspect-accused-killing-brpd-officer-critically-wounding-another-previously-threatened-kill-officers/

929 Rambaran, Vandana. 2020. "Baton Rouge police shooting suspect stood over dead officer and kept firing, investigators say." *Fox News*, April 27. Accessed November 14, 2020. https://www.foxnews.com/us/baton-rouge-police-shooting-suspect-stood-over-dead-officers-body-kept-firing-investigators

930 Bonvillian, Crystal. 2020. "Baton Rouge police officer killed, colleague wounded in ambush by murder suspect, police say." *WPXI*, April 30. Accessed November 14, 2020. https://www.wpxi.com/news/trending/baton-rouge-police-officer-killed-colleague-wounded-ambush-by-murder-suspect-police-say/4JFNLJINPBHN5P3VG5ABPNGH3I/

931 Rothfield, Ariel. 2020. "Suspect in deadly shootout with officer burglarized Lawrence business." *KSHB*, May 5. Accessed November 15, 2020. https://www.kshb.com/news/local-news/op-hit-and-run-suspect-burglarized-lawrence-business

932 Nozicka, Luke. 2020. "Man who killed OP officer had 'violent' past; prosecutor wanted his bond revoked." *The Kansas City Star*, May 6. Accessed November 15, 2020. https://www.kansascity.com/news/local/crime/article242513551.html

933 Anaya, Leah. 2020. "Kansas off-duty officer killed confronting hit and run suspect. He was a young dad." *Law Enforcement Today*, May 4. Accessed November 15, 2020. https://www.lawenforcementtoday.com/officer-down-kansas-off-duty-officer-killed-confronting-hit-and-run-suspect/

934 Tactical Life. 2020. "Overland Park Police Officer Mike Mosher Killed in Shootout with Suspect." *Tactical Life*, May 4. Accessed November 15, 2020. https://www.tactical-life.com/news/mike-mosher-killed-in-duty/

935 Beeman, Amy. 2020. "Mike Mosher: Overland Park, Kansas, Police Officer Killed in Shooting." *Heavy*, May 5. Accessed November 15, 2020. https://heavy.com/news/2020/05/mike-mosher-officer-killed-in-shooting/

936 Bernard, Katie. 2020. "Video shows fatal encounter between Overland Park officer Mike Mosher and suspect." *The Kansas City Star*, August 14. Accessed November 15, 2020. https://www.msn.com/en-us/news/us/video-shows-fatal-encounter-between-overland-park-officer-mike-mosher-and-suspect/ar-BB17W43H

937 Henson, Matt. 2020. "Family: Man accused of killing Grand Forks police officer was 'amped up' over coronavirus." *InForum*, May 29. Accessed November 18, 2020. https://www.inforum.com/news/6513813-Family-Man-accused-of-killing-Grand-Forks-police-officer-was-amped-up-over-coronavirus1

938 Shirley, Hannah. 2020. "Man accused in Grand Forks cop's death fired 41 rounds from AK-47, charges say." *Forum News Service*, May 29. Accessed November 18, 2020. https://www.twincities.com/2020/05/29/man-accused-in-grand-forks-cops-death-fired-41-rounds-from-ak-47-charges-say/

939 Kolpack, Dave. 2020. "Man accused of killing North Dakota officer has long record." *Associated Press*, May 28. Accessed November 18, 2020. https://abcnews.go.com/US/wireStory/hundreds-vigil-victims-fatal-grand-forks-shooting-70929153

940 Kolpack, Dave. 2020. "Man Charged With 2 Counts of Murder in Grand Forks Shooting." *Associated Press*, May 29. Accessed November 18, 2020. https://www.usnews.com/news/best-states/north-dakota/articles/2020-05-29/wounded-deputy-in-fatal-shootout-leaves-hospital

941 Curtis, Larry D. 2020. "Man suspected of killing Ogden police officer had past weapons charge." *KUTV*, May 29. Accessed November 18, 2020. https://kutv.com/news/local/what-we-know-about-man-suspected-of-shooting-ogden-police-officer

942 Ponce, Hector. 2020. "Weber County Attorney's Office releases details in fatal officer-involved shooting in Ogden." *FOX 13 Now*, June 3. Accessed November 18, 2020. https://www.fox13now.com/news/local-news/weber-county-attorneys-office-releases-details-in-fatal-officer-involved-shooting-in-ogden

943 Roberts, Alyssa. 2020. "County attorney: Man who killed Ogden officer appeared prepared for shootout." *KUTV*, June 3. Accessed November 18, 2020. https://kutv.com/news/local/county-attorney-man-who-shot-ogden-officer-appeared-prepared-for-shootout

944 Owusu, Mercy. 2020. "New details shed light on shooting that killed Ogden police officer." *ABC 4*, June 4. Accessed November 18, 2020. https://www.abc4.com/news/fallen-officer/new-details-shed-light-on-shooting-that-killed-ogden-police-officer-lyday/

945 Lewis, Brooke A. 2020. "Fort Bend deputy charged with homicide, fired in connection to shooting of Caleb Rule." *Houston Chronicle*, July 2. Accessed October 28, 2020. https://www.houstonchronicle.com/neighborhood/fortbend/article/Fort-Bend-deputy-charged-homicide-fired-caleb-rule-15425888.php

946 Delony, Doug. 2020. "Friendly fire killing: Fort Bend sheriff's deputy fired, indicted for shooting of deputy constable." *KHOU 11*, July 22. Accessed October 28, 2020. https://www.khou.com/article/news/local/deputy-chadwick-mcrae-indicted-in-fort-bend-shooting/285-e400647f-e7c4-4b9f-9b31-49ef73219d20

947 Cochran, Amanda. 2020. "Former Fort Bend County sheriff's deputy charged in death of deputy constable." *Click 2 Houston*, July 22. Accessed November 19, 2020. https://www.click2houston.com/news/local/2020/07/22/fort-bend-county-sheriffs-deputy-charged-in-death-of-deputy-constable/

948 Zaniewski, Ann. 2017. "Suspect identified in Detroit police shooting." *Detroit Free Press*, May 1. Accessed November 18, 2020. https://www.freep.com/story/news/local/michigan/wayne/2017/05/01/detroit-police-shooting/101173678/

949 Hutchinson, Derick. 2017. "Man suspected of shooting Detroit police officer identified as James Edward Ray." *Click on Detroit*, May 1. Accessed November 18, 2020. https://www.clickondetroit.com/news/2017/05/01/man-suspected-of-shooting-detroit-police-officer-identified-as-james-edward-ray/

950 Droney, Pat. 2020. "Detroit police officer dies after being shot in the head and fighting for his life. He was a proud dad of three. His life mattered." *Law Enforcement Today*, June 28. Accessed November 18, 2020. https://www.lawenforcementtoday.com/officer-dies-after-being-shot-in-the-head-and-desperately-fighting-for-his-life-2/

951 Ramirez, Charles E. 2020. "Detroit police officer shot in 2017 dies from injuries." *The Detroit News*, June 2. Accessed November 18, 2020. https://www.detroitnews.com/story/news/local/detroit-city/2020/06/02/detroit-police-officer-shot-2017-dies-injuries-waldis-johnson/3122254001/

952 Clark, Michael. 2020. "Grand jury to hear cases against suspects accused in Moody police officer's death." *CBS 42*, July 7. Accessed November 19, 2020. https://www.cbs42.com/news/local/grand-jury-to-hear-cases-against-suspects-accused-in-moody-police-officers-death/

953 Robinson, Carol. 2020. "2 charged in fatal shooting of Moody police Sgt. Stephen Williams." *AL.com*, June 5. Accessed November 19, 2020. https://www.al.com/news/birmingham/2020/06/2-charged-in-fatal-shooting-of-moody-police-sgt-stephen-williams.html

954 Mitchell, Taylor. 2020. "The death of Lt. Stephen Williams: DETAILS EMERGE IN PRELIMINARY HEARINGS. At least four weapons that had been fired found in room of suspects in officer's death." *St. Clair Times*, July 7. Accessed November 19, 2020. https://www.annistonstar.com/the_st_clair_times/at-least-four-weapons-that-had-been-fired-found-in-room-of-suspects-in-officers/article_c8a08f3c-c0b4-11ea-a509-b3553b866de7.html

955 Mitchell, Taylor. 2020. "Woman charged in shooting death of Moody police officer." *The Daily Home*, July 31. Accessed November 19, 2020. https://www.annistonstar.com/the_st_clair_times/woman-charged-in-shooting-death-of-moody-police-officer-denied-bond/article_b0bf7c9c-d389-11ea-aa26-f729dcd04be9.html

956 Moseley, Brandon. 2020. "Marshall says Moody officer's death was not related to unrest." *AL Reporter*, June 4. Accessed November 19, 2020. https://www.alreporter.com/2020/06/04/marshall-says-moody-officers-death-was-not-related-to-unrest/

957 Bonvillian, Crystal. 2020. "Cop who threatened to kill protesters shoots, kills colleague who knocked on door, affidavit says." *Cox Media Group National Content Desk*, July 14. Accessed April 21, 2021. https://www.kiro7.com/news/trending/cop-who-threatened-kill-protesters-shoots-kills-colleague-who-knocked-door-affidavit-says/BMAXC27P7FA7LMIAXFQUJAHZJE/

958 Ibid 957.

959 Sanders, William. 2020. "Charge filed in Alexander officer's death; ex-colleague shot through door, police inquiry finds." *Arkansas Democrat Gazette*, July 10. Accessed April 21, 2021. https://www.arkansasonline.com/news/2020/jul/10/charge-filed-in-alexander-officers-death/

960 Shapiro, Emily and Luke Barr. 2020. "Suspect in sergeant's slaying now charged in killing of federal officer in Oakland: Officials." *ABC News*, June 16. Accessed November 18, 2020. https://abcnews.go.com/US/suspect-sergeants-slaying-now-charged-killing-federal-officer/story?id=71280724

961 Noyes, Dan and Lauren Martinez. 2020. "'We lost a hero': 38-year-old deputy killed, 2 officers injured after ambush in Santa Cruz County, sheriff says." *ABC 7 News*, June 7. Accessed November 19, 2020. https://abc7news.com/deputy-killed-in-santa-cruz-shooting-damon-gutzwiller-sergeant/6235296/

962 Larson, Amy. 2020. "FBI documents describe motive of Santa Cruz deputy's accused killer and Boogaloo." *KRON 4*, June 17. Accessed November 19, 2020. https://www.kron4.com/news/bay-area/fbi-documents-describe-motive-of-santa-cruz-deputys-accused-killer-and-boogaloo/

963 Edinger, Marie. 2020. "Good Samaritan credited with capturing Santa Cruz deputy's killer." *FOX 26 News*, June 7. Accessed November 19, 2020. https://kmph.com/news/local/deputy-killed-2-other-officers-injured-in-ambush-in-santa-cruz

964 Noyes, Dan. 2020. "I-TEAM: Air Force sergeant arrested on suspicion for killing of deputy in Santa Cruz County." *ABC 7 News*, June 7. Accessed November 19, 2020. https://abc7news.com/steven-carrillo-santa-cruz-carillo-california-sheriff-deputy-killed/6236742/

965 Dolan, Maura, Richard Winton, and Anita Chabria. 2020. *Los Angeles Times*, June 16. Accessed November 19, 2020. https://www.latimes.com/california/story/2020-06-16/suspects-charged-killing-santa-cruz-cop-and-oakland-federal-officer

966 Mott, Ronnie. 2020. "Simpson County shooter captured across the street from the crime scene." *Vicksburg Daily News*, June 14. Accessed November 20, 2020. https://www.vicksburgnews.com/simpson-county-shooter-captured-across-the-street-from-the-crime-scene/

967 Honea, Sue. 2020. "Simpson County Deputy James Blair Shot & Killed." *Magee News*, June 12. Accessed November 20, 2020. https://mageenews.com/simpson-county-deputy-james-blair-shot-killed/

968 Vicory, Justin. 2020. "Family, law enforcement honor Mississippi deputy shot to death in the line of duty." *Clarion Ledger*, June 18. Accessed November 20, 2020. https://www.clarionledger.com/story/news/2020/06/17/hundreds-honor-ms-deputy-james-blair-shot-death-line-duty/3203615001/

969 Carrega, Christina. 2020. "Escaped inmate accused of killing sheriff's deputy in Mississippi captured." *ABC News*, June 13. Accessed November 20, 2020. https://abcnews.go.com/US/mississippi-law-enforcement-searching-escaped-inmate-accused-killing/story?id=71235881

970 Fowler, Sarah. 2020. "Suspect in deadly shooting of Simpson County deputy apprehended." *Clarion Ledger*, June 13. Accessed November 20, 2020. https://www.clarionledger.com/story/news/2020/06/12/simpson-co-deputy-killed-suspect-considered-armed-and-dangerous/3179221001/

971 Browne, Don. 2020. "Eliceo Hernandez Arrested In Julian Keen Homicide." *Southwest Florida Online*, June 15. Accessed November 22, 2020. https://swflorida.blogspot.com/2020/06/eliceo-hernandez-arrested-in-julian.html

972 Tisch, Chris. 2020. "Arrest made in shooting death of Florida wildlife officer." *Tampa Bay Times*, June 20. Accessed November 20, 2020. https://www.tampabay.com/news/crime/2020/06/15/arrest-made-in-shooting-death-of-fwc-officer/

973 Braun, Michael. 2020. "'Our hearts are aching': Florida man charged in shooting death of wildlife conservation officer." *Ft. Myers News-Press*, June 16. Accessed November 20, 2020. https://www.usatoday.com/story/news/2020/06/15/julian-keen-jr-florida-wildlife-conservation-officer-fatally-shot/3192052001/

974 Portal, Lizandra. 2020. "Arrest made in murder of off-duty Florida Wildlife officer." *WEAR TV*, June 15. Accessed November 20, 2020. https://weartv.com/news/local/arrest-made-in-murder-of-off-duty-florida-wildlife-officer

975 WFTX Digital Team. 2020. "Suspect in local officer's death faces additional charges." *FOX 4*, July 9. Accessed November 20, 2020. https://www.fox4now.com/news/local-news/suspect-in-local-officers-death-faces-additional-charges

976 Eger, Andrea, and Samantha Vincent. 2020. "Tulsa police officer killing: Suspect's 14-year history of run-ins with local police began with assault on very same officer," *Tulsa World*, July 8. Accessed November 20, 2020. https://tulsaworld.com/news/local/crime-and-courts/tulsa-police-officer-killing-suspects-14-year-history-of-run-ins-with-local-police-began/article_ec94b83e-6914-5db5-bcf6-8208b37e61bb.html

977 KTUL Staff. 2020. "Suspect captured after 2 Tulsa police officers shot, critically wounded." *KTUL*, June 29. Accessed November 23, 2020. https://ktul.com/news/local/2-police-officers-shot-in-east-tulsa

978 Goforth, Dylan. 2020. "Videos released showing fatal shooting of Tulsa police officer, wounding of another." *The Frontier*, September 14. Accessed November 20, 2020. https://www.readfrontier.org/stories/videos-released-showing-fatal-shooting-of-tulsa-police-officer-wounding-of-another/

979 Officer.com News. 2020. "Tulsa Police Chief Asks Public Not to Watch Videos of Shooting That Left Sergeant Dead and Officer Wounded." *Officer.com*, September 15. Accessed November 20, 2020. https://www.officer.com/command-hq/news/21154371/tulsa-police-chief-asks-public-not-to-watch-videos-of-shooting-that-left-sergeant-dead-and-officer-wounded

980 Daily Telegram Staff. 2020. "Morenci man who shot officer had long criminal history." *The Monroe News*, July 7. Accessed November 23, 2020. https://www.monroenews.com/news/20200707/morenci-man-who-shot-officer-had-long-criminal-history/1

981 Choiniere, Alyssa. 2020. "Edward Henry: 5 Fast Facts You Need to Know." *Heavy*.com, July 4. Accessed November 23, 2020. https://heavy.com/news/2020/07/edward-henry/

982 Clo', Renata. 2020. "TPD mourns life of officer killed in the line of duty." *WTOL*, July 5. Accessed November 23, 2020. https://www.wtol.com/article/news/crime/toleod-police-officer-anthony-dia-shot-killed-home-depot-parking-lot/512-a4f9e7d3-9045-48bb-9f11-b73c2800a0f6

983 Norman, Greg. 2020. "Fallen Ohio police officer had final message for his family." *FOX News*, July 6. Accessed November 23, 2020. https://www.foxnews.com/us/ohio-officer-killed-in-line-of-duty

984 Associated Press. 2020. "Father-of-two Ohio cop, 26, is shot dead outside Home Depot by intoxicated man holding a beer who then took his own life." *DailyMail.com*, July 4. Accessed November 23, 2020. https://www.dailymail.co.uk/news/article-8489417/Ohio-officer-shot-killed-responding-disturbance-call.html

985 WTOL Newsroom. 2020. "'He died protecting Toledo' | Chief George Kral and Officer Anthony Dia's father discuss the young man who died a hero July 4." *WTOL*, July 7. Accessed November 23, 2020. https://www.wtol.com/article/news/local/honoring-officer-dia/tpd-press-conference-anthony-dia/512-a5f6a3c2-4607-492d-a4a2-f0ba8d1b3b65#:~:text=Kral%20outlined%20the%20events%20before,dumb%20luck.%22%20There%20was%20no

986 Phillips, Jack. 2020. "Suspect Who Killed 2 Texas Police Officers Had Criminal Past: Chief." *The Epoch Times*, July 12. Accessed November 23, 2020. https://www.theepochtimes.com/suspect-who-killed-two-texas-police-officers-had-criminal-past-chief_3421683.html

987 Curren, Jenna. 2020. "Police: Suspect who ambushed and murdered two police officers attacked own mother first." *Law Enforcement Today*, August 14. Accessed November 23, 2020. https://www.lawenforcementtoday.com/suspect-who-killed-two-mcallen-officers-attacked-mother-prior-to-incident/#more-118567

988 Romero, Dennis. 2020. "Two Texas officers shot and killed while responding to domestic disturbance call." *NBC News*, July 11. Accessed November 23, 2020. https://www.nbcnews.com/news/us-news/two-texas-police-shot-killed-while-responding-domestic-disturbance-call-n1233594

989 De Leon III, Jose. 2020. "'They were just doing their job.'." *Progress Times*, July 17. Accessed November 23, 2020. https://www.progresstimes.net/2020/07/17/they-were-just-doing-their-job/

990 Ibid 986.

991 Ibid 987.

992 Ibid 988.

993 Ibid 989.

994 Labone, Rosel. 2020. "Henry Eugene Washington: Man Accused of Killing Police Officer in Bothell, Washington." *Heavy.com*, July 15. Accessed November 26, 2020. https://heavy.com/news/2020/07/henry-eugene-washington/

995 Choe, Jonathan, and Alfred Charles. 2020. "Henry Eugene Washington: Suspect in Bothell officer's slaying facing murder charge." *KOMO News*, July 15. Accessed November 26, 2020. https://komonews.com/news/local/henry-eugene-washington-suspect-in-bothell-officers-slaying-facing-murder-charge

996 Matkin, Holly. 2020. "Hero Down: Bothell Police Officer Jonathan Shoop Killed By Friendly Fire." *The Police Tribune*, July 15. Accessed November 26, 2020. https://policetribune.com/hero-down-bothell-police-officer-jonathan-shoop-murdered-by-gunman/

997 Hutton, Caleb. 2020. "Charge: Man said, 'Come on, pig,' before killing Bothell cop." *HeraldNet.com*, July 15. Accessed November 26, 2020. https://www.heraldnet.com/news/no-bail-for-man-accused-of-killing-bothell-police-officer/

998 Cornwell, Paige. 2020. "Bothell Police Officer Killed by Friendly Fire; Prosecutors Charge Man Accused of Starting Gunfight With Murder." *The Seattle Times*, July 18. Accessed November 26, 2020. http://www.chronline.com/northwest_regional_news/bothell-police-officer-killed-by-friendly-fire-prosecutors-charge-man-accused-of-starting-gunfight-with/article_85dbe806-c904-11ea-b67d-b79e09c1c33b.html

999 Matkin, Holly. 2020. "Hero Down: Puerto Rico Police Sgt. Ricardo Perez-Ortiz Murdered By Gunman." *The Police Tribune*, September 2. Accessed November 28, 2020. https://policetribune.com/hero-down-puerto-rico-police-sgt-ricardo-perez-ortiz-murdered-by-gunman/

1000 Ibid 999.

1001 Carranza, Rafael, Uriel J. Garcia, and Debra Utacia Krol. "Tohono O'odham police Officer Bryan Brown killed in southern Arizona, FBI confirms." *Arizona Republic*, August 27. Accessed November 28, 2020. https://www.azcentral.com/story/news/local/arizona/2020/08/27/tohono-oodham-police-officer-shooting-near-why-arizona/5648995002/

1002 Wildmoon, KC. 2020. "Tribal police officer killed by suspect 'high on meth' who stole his patrol vehicle and ran him over." *Crime Online*, August 30. Accessed November 28, 2020. https://www.crimeonline.com/2020/08/30/tribal-police-officer-killed-by-suspect-high-on-meth-who-stole-his-patrol-vehicle-and-ran-him-over/

1003 Neff, Terri Jo. 2020. "Grand Jury Hands Down A Dozen Federal Charges After Death Of Tohono O'odham Officer." *Arizona Daily Independent News Network*, October 23. Accessed November 28, 2020. https://arizonadailyindependent.com/grand-jury-hands-down-a-dozen-federal-charges-after-death-of-tohono-oodham-officer/

1004 McKinley, Mitch. 2020. "Man arrested for murdering one officer, shooting second one is upset about his broken nose." *Law Enforcement Today*, October 2. Accessed November 28, 2020. https://www.lawenforcementtoday.com/man-arrested-for-murdering-officer-is-upset-about-his-broken-nose/

1005 Trager, Lauren. 2020. "Man charged in St. Louis officer's death has a lengthy criminal history." *KMOV*, September 1. Accessed November 28, 2020. https://www.kmov.com/news/man-charged-in-st-louis-officers-death-has-a-lengthy-criminal-history/article_dd7d1220-eb27-11ea-8ec1-17b2bd7e73fb.html

1006 Casiano, Louis. 2020. "Suspected St. Louis cop killer charged, has lengthy criminal history." *Fox News Channel*, September 1. Accessed November 28, 2020. https://www.foxnews.com/us/st-louis-cop-killer-criminal-thomas-kinworthy

1007 Naham, Matt. 2020. "'Very Dangerous' Man with Lengthy Criminal Record Allegedly Shot Two Black Police Officers in St. Louis, Killing One." *Law & Crime*, September 2. Accessed November 28, 2020. https://lawandcrime.com/crazy/very-dangerous-man-with-lengthy-criminal-record-allegedly-shot-two-black-police-officers-in-st-louis-killing-one/

1008 Aaro, David. 2020. "St. Louis police officer dies after being shot in head; family writes heartfelt letter." *Fox News*, August 30. Accessed November 28, 2020. https://www.foxnews.com/us/st-louis-police-officer-shot-in-head-after-responding-to-call-dies

1009 King, Chris. 2020. "Thomas Kinworthy accused of shooting two Black cops, killing one." *The St. Louis American*, September 2. Accessed November 28, 2020. http://www.stlamerican.com/news/local_news/thomas-kinworthy-accused-of-shooting-two-black-cops-killing-one/article_d7460a2c-ec91-11ea-b1dc-5b20f8de7890.html

1010 Gallek, Ed. 2020. "First clues that led to arrests in murdered Cleveland detective investigation." *FOX8*, September 8. Accessed December 7, 2020. https://fox8.com/news/i-team/i-team-video-shows-first-clues-that-led-to-arrests-in-murdered-cleveland-detective-investigation/

1011 Canaan, Michael. 2020. "Cleveland police detective and informant murdered – here's who police now say is responsible." *Law Enforcement Today*, September 9. Accessed December 7, 2020. https://www.lawenforcementtoday.com/arrests-made-in-double-homicide-of-cleveland-police-detective/

1012 Ibid 1010.

1013 Gillispie, Mark. 2020. "Undercover drug detective, informant killed; 3 are arrested." *Associated Press*, September 4. Accessed December 7, 2020. https://abcnews.go.com/US/wireStory/shooting-leaves-cleveland-officer-dead-suspects-sought-72813359

1014 Tullos, Julia. 2020. "3 teenagers charged in connection with the murder of Cleveland Police Det. James Skernivitz." *WISTV*, September 8. Accessed December 7, 2020. https://www.wistv.com/2020/09/08/additional-arrests-connection-with-murder-cleveland-police-det-james-skernivitz/

1015 Steer, Jen. 2020. "18-year-old indicted in murder of Cleveland police detective; Two more charged." *FOX8*, September 17. Accessed December 7, 2020. https://fox8.com/news/18-year-old-indicted-in-murder-of-cleveland-police-detective-two-more-charged/

1016 Halm, Laura. 2020. "Investigator Mario Herrera passes away following August shooting while serving warrant." *1011NOW*, September 7. Accessed December 7, 2020. https://www.1011now.com/2020/09/07/officer-mario-herrera-passes-away-following-august-shooting-while-serving-warrant/

1017 KOLN Staff. 2020. "Court Records: Suspect was locked in room before shooting officer with stolen gun." *1011NOW*, August 28. Accessed December 7, 2020. https://www.1011now.com/2020/08/28/court-records-suspect-was-locked-in-room-before-shooting-officer-with-stolen-gun/

1018 KOLN Staff. 2020. "Police identify officer shot serving a warrant on Wednesday." *WOWT*, August 27. Accessed December 7, 2020. https://www.wowt.com/2020/08/27/police-identify-officer-shot-serving-a-warrant-on-wednesday/

1019 10/11 NOW. 2020. "Suspect who shot LPD officer faces murder charges." *WOWT*, September 8. Accessed December 7, 2020. https://www.wowt.com/2020/09/08/suspect-who-shot-lpd-officer-faces-murder-charges/

1020 Conklin, Audrey. 2020. "Family of NC officer killed on duty has message as community mourns." *Fox News*, September 12. Accessed December 7, 2020. https://www.foxnews.com/us/nc-officer-marine-veteran-shot-face-2-kids

1021 WBTV Web Staff and WYFF. 2020. "N.C. deputy killed, suspect dead after officer-involved shooting in Henderson Co." *NBC 12*, September 11. Accessed December 7, 2020. https://www.nbc12.com/2020/09/11/nc-deputy-killed-suspect-dead-after-officer-involved-shooting-henderson-co/

1022 Rizzo, Patrizia. 2020. "'BRAIN DEAD' Who was Henderson County Deputy Ryan Hendrix and how did he die?" *The Sun*, September 11. Accessed December 7, 2020. https://www.thesun.co.uk/news/12645519/henderson-county-deputy-ryan-hendrix-killed-north-carolina/

1023 Malone, Sandy. 2020. "Hero Down: Myrtle Beach Patrolman Jacob Hancher Murdered At Domestic Call." *The Police Tribune*, October 5. Accessed December 8, 2020. https://policetribune.com/hero-down-myrtle-beach-patrolman-jacob-hancher-murdered-at-domestic-call/

1024 Boschult, Christian. 2020. "'No, it couldn't be John': Gunman's friends stunned by shootout that killed Myrtle Beach officer." *My Horry News*, October 12. Accessed December 8, 2020. https://www.myhorrynews.com/news/crime/suspected-gunman-in-fatal-shooting-was-a-fan-of-guns-and-motorcycles/article_8162da1a-074c-11eb-9cdc-6be89b37e50f.html

1025 Hutchinson, Bill. 2020. "Myrtle Beach, South Carolina, police Officer Jacob Hancher fatally shot in line of duty." *ABC News*, October 4. Accessed December 8, 2020. https://abcnews.go.com/US/myrtle-beach-south-carolina-police-officer-jacob-hancher/story?id=73414543

1026 Flaherty, Joseph. 2020. "Man, 19, jailed in officer's death in Pine Bluff," *Arkansas Democrat Gazette*, October 7. Accessed December 9, 2020. https://www.arkansasonline.com/news/2020/oct/07/man-jailed-in-officers-death-in-pb/

1027 THV11 Digital. 2020. "Man arrested in connection to death of Pine Bluff police officer." *THV11*, October 7. Accessed December 9, 2020. https://www.thv11.com/article/news/crime/2-police-officers-shot-in-pine-bluff-police-confirm/91-6b06550f-8285-463e-bf62-d1a7451f3173

1028 Wainwright, Alexis. 2020. "Man arrested in connection to death of Pine Bluff police officer." *KARK 4 News*, October 7. Accessed December 9, 2020. https://www.kark.com/news/local-news/man-arrested-in-connection-to-death-of-pine-bluff-police-officer/

1029 LMT Online Staff. 2020. "Court date changed for suspect in Pine Bluff officer's death." *LMT Online*, November 19. Accessed December 9, 2020. https://www.lmtonline.com/news/article/Court-date-changed-for-suspect-in-Pine-Bluff-15741182.php

1030 Holt, Tony. 2020. "Pine Bluff detective killed in shootout." *Arkansas Democrat Gazette*, October 6. Accessed December 9, 2020. https://www.arkansasonline.com/news/2020/oct/06/pb-detective-killed-in-shootout/?news

1031 Schladebeck, Jessica. 2020. "Arson investigator fatally shot while probing string of fires in Texas." *New York Daily News*, October 17. Accessed December 9, 2020. https://www.nydailynews.com/news/crime/ny-arson-investigator-shot-working-texas-20201017-ngswniwiang4tbbkm7akimzr3a-story.html

1032 KTRK. 2020. "Suspect who killed HFD investigator dies from self-inflicted gunshot wound." *ABC 13*, October 19. Accessed December 9, 2020. https://www.msn.com/en-us/news/crime/suspect-who-killed-hfd-investigator-dies-from-self-inflicted-gunshot-hpd-says/ar-BB1a5CYk

1033 Parker, T.J. 2020. "Grief-stricken Houston firefighters give testimonials about fallen arson investigator Lemuel 'DJ' Bruce." *ABC13*, October 23. Accessed December 9, 2020. https://abc13.com/hfd-arson-investigator-to-be-honored-at-memorial-service/7228432/

1034 WSPA Staff. 2020. "SLED releases new details into I-85 traffic stop, crash that resulted in the death of a Greenville Co. deputy." *WSPA*, October 22. Accessed December 10, 2020. https://www.wspa.com/news/sled-releases-new-details-into-i-85-traffic-stop-crash-that-resulted-in-the-death-of-a-greenville-co-deputy/

1035 Snipes, Anisa, Dal Kalsi, Jon Randall, and Matthew Ablon. 2020. SLED: One suspect charged with murder, more in death of Greenville Co. deputy." *Fox Carolina*, October 21. Accessed December 11, 2020. https://www.foxcarolina.com/news/sled-one-suspect-charged-with-murder-more-in-death-of-greenville-co-deputy/article_0681fd80-1309-11eb-8dc1-1f6f16ac4cdf.html

1036 Boyd, Tamia, and Nikie Mayo. 2020. "2 in custody after traffic stop that led to death of Greenville County sheriff's deputy." *Greenville News*, October 22. Accessed December 10, 2020. https://www.greenvilleonline.com/story/news/local/2020/10/21/2-held-after-traffic-stop-led-death-greenville-county-deputy/6004289002/

1037 Matney, Mandy. 2020. "Man And Woman From New York Charged In Incident That Killed Greenville Deputy." *FitsNews*, October 22. Accessed December 10, 2020. https://www.fitsnews.com/2020/10/22/man-and-woman-from-new-york-charged-in-incident-that-killed-greenville-deputy/

1038 Shay, Mia, T.J. Parker, and Mycah Hatfield. 2020. "1 HPD sergeant killed, 1 officer wounded in shooting at apartment complex in SW Houston." *ABC 13*, October 21. Accessed December 10, 2020. https://abc13.com/houston-police-officers-shot-hpd-sergeant-harold-preston-courtney-waller-department/7186259/

1039 Heine, Debra. 2020. "Houston Police Sgt. Killed By Repeat Offender After Soros-Funded D.A. Refused to Press Charges." *The Tennessee Star*, October 22. Accessed December 10, 2020. https://tennesseestar.com/2020/10/22/houston-police-sgt-killed-by-repeat-offender-after-soros-funded-d-a-refused-to-press-charges/

1040 McCord, Cory. 2020. "Criminal history: Who is Elmer Manzano, the man accused of shooting 2 HPD officers?" *MSN*, October 20. Accessed December 10, 2020. https://www.msn.com/en-us/news/crime/criminal-history-who-is-elmer-manzano-the-man-accused-of-shooting-2-hpd-officers/ar-BB1aehXV

1041 Diaz, Mario. 2020. "Elmer Manzano: What we know about the man accused of killing 1 HPD officer, wounding another." *Click 2 Houston*, October 21. Accessed December 10, 2020. https://www.click2houston.com/news/local/2020/10/20/elmer-manzano-what-we-know-about-suspect-after-2-houston-police-officers-shot/

1042 CBS DFW. 2020. "Man In US Illegally Charged In Houston Police Officer's Murder Could Face Death Penalty." *CBS DFW*, October 21. Accessed December 10, 2020. https://dfw.cbslocal.com/2020/10/21/man-elmer-manzano-charged-houston-police-officer-murder-death-penalty/

1043 WBRZ Staff. 2020. "Officer allegedly shot by suspect previously wanted for armed robbery while dressed as chipmunk." *WBRZ*, October 19. Accessed January 2, 2021. https://www.wbrz.com/news/part-time-officer-shot-during-traffic-stop-suspect-arrested

1044 KATC News. 2020. "Richland Parish police officer dies following October shooting." *KATC*, November 5. Accessed December 14, 2020. https://www.katc.com/news/covering-louisiana/richland-parish-police-officer-dies-following-october-shooting

1045 Matkin, Holly. 2020. "Hero Down: Mangham Police Officer Marshall Waters Murdered By Gunman." *The Police Tribune*, November 6. Accessed December 14, 2020. https://policetribune.com/hero-down-mangham-police-officer-marshall-waters-murdered-by-gunman/

1046 Mott, Ashley. 2020. "Mangham Police officer shot in the line of duty has died." *Monroe News-Star*, November 5. Accessed December 14, 2020. https://www.thenewsstar.com/story/news/2020/11/05/mangham-police-officer-shot-line-duty-has-died/6172334002/

1047 Robinson, Perry. 2020. "Community mourns fallen Mangham officer at memorial service." *KNOE*, November 12. Accessed December 14, 2020. https://www.knoe.com/2020/11/13/community-mourns-fallen-mangham-officer-at-memorial-service/

1048 Barajas, Bill, Brittany Taylor, and Amanda Cochran. 2020. "Bond set at $500,000 for man accused of killing HPD Sgt. Sean Rios." *Click2Houston*, November 12. Accessed December 14, 2020. https://www.click2houston.com/news/local/2020/11/11/man-charged-in-connection-with-hpd-sergeants-death-expected-to-appear-in-court/

1049 CBS DFW. 2020. "24-Year-Old Charged With Murder Of Houston Police Sgt. Sean Rios." *CBS DFW*, November 11. Accessed December 14, 2020. https://dfw.cbslocal.com/2020/11/11/24-year-old-robert-soliz-arrested-for-murder-houston-police-sergeant-sean-rios/

1050 Homer, Michelle. 2020. "Suspect arrested in fatal shooting of Houston police officer." *KHOU*, November 10. Accessed December 14, 2020. https://www.khou.com/article/news/crime/houston-officer-killed-shooting-i-45/285-667e770f-124c-43e7-b4a1-81284151014e

1051 Romo, Steven. 2020. "Who is Robert Soliz? Man accused of killing HPD Sgt. Rios." *KTRK*, November 11. Accessed December 14, 2020. https://www.msn.com/en-us/news/crime/who-is-robert-soliz-man-accused-of-killing-hpd-sgt-rios/ar-BB1aTAjE

1052 Malone, Sandy. 2020. "BREAKING: Suspected Cop Killer, Accomplice Captured In Mississippi." *The Police Tribune*, November 13. Accessed December 15, 2020. https://policetribune.com/breaking-suspect-cop-killer-accomplice-captured-in-mississippi/

1053 Farrar, Lara. 2020. "Pair arrested in death of lawman in Helena." *Arkansas Online*, November 14. Accessed December 15, 2020. https://www.arkansasonline.com/news/2020/nov/14/pair-arrested-in-death-of-lawman-in-helena/?news-arkansas

1054 O'Leary, Fionnuala. 2020. "'COP KILLER' CAUGHT Cops capture '29-year-old gunman who fled after shooting police officer dead at motel'." *The U.S. Sun*, November 14. Accessed December 15, 2020. https://www.the-sun.com/news/1794693/cops-hunt-gunman-shot-police-dead-motel-arkansas/

1055 Brantley, Max. 2020. "Helena-West Helena police officer killed, suspect arrested in Mississippi." *Arkansas Times*, November 13. Accessed December 15, 2020. https://arktimes.com/arkansas-blog/2020/11/13/helena-west-helena-police-officer-killed-suspect-arrested-in-mississippi

1056 WMCAAction5News.com Staff. 2020. "2 suspects wanted in connection with Arkansas officer's killing captured by U.S. Marshals; officer identified." *WMCA Action News 5*, November 13. Accessed December 15, 2020. https://www.wmcactionnews5.com/2020/11/13/suspect-wanted-killing-arkansas-officer-captured-by-police/

1057 Ibid 1052.

1058 Niland, Susan. 2020. "TBI Agents Investigating Officer-Involved Shooting in La Vergne." *TBI Newsroom*, November 18. Accessed January 3, 2021. https://tbinewsroom.com/2020/11/17/tbi-agents-investigating-officer-involved-shooting-in-la-vergne/

1059 Hoyt, Gregory. 2020. "Police K9 murdered during ambush attack while officer sitting inside of his patrol vehicle." *Law Enforcement Today*, November 20. Accessed January 3, 2021. https://www.lawenforcementtoday.com/police-k9-murdered-during-ambush-attack-while-officer-sitting-inside-vehicle/

1060 Noon, Erin. 2020. "What do we know about the shooter of Officer Cassie Johnson." *WOWK 13,* December 2. Accessed January 6, 2021. https://www.wowktv.com/news/local/what-do-we-know-about-the-shooter-of-officer-cassie-johnson/

1061 Matkin, Holly. 2020. "Hero Down: Charleston PD Officer Cassie Johnson Murdered During Parking Complaint." *The Police Tribune*, December 3. Accessed January 6, 2021. https://policetribune.com/hero-down-charleston-pd-officer-cassie-johnson-murdered-during-parking-complaint/

1062 Hedrick, Chad. 2020. "Man accused of killing Charleston officer to be arraigned on charges." *WSAZ*, December 12. Accessed January 6, 2021. https://www.wtap.com/2020/12/12/man-accused-of-killing-charleston-officer-to-be-arraigned-on-charges/

1063 Severino, Joe. 2020. "Charleston police officer Johnson dead at 28; sheriff's office provides some details on shooting." *The Herald-Dispatch*, December 3. Accessed January 6, 2021. https://www.herald-dispatch.com/news/charleston-police-officer-johnson-dead-at-28-sheriff-s-office-provides-some-details-on-shooting/article_c8a26f24-bf75-5b0c-b901-3246a45901e8.html

1064 Wood, Cassidy. 2020. "Charleston mourns CPD Patrolman Cassie Johnson." *WOWK 13*, December 4. Accessed January 6, 2021. https://www.wowktv.com/news/local/charleston-mourns-cpd-patrolman-cassie-johnson/

1065 Stewart, Gavin. 2020. "Mount Holly Police officer killed in shootout; man charged with murder." *The Gaston Gazette*, December 11. Accessed January 6, 2021. https://www.gastongazette.com/story/news/2020/12/11/3-hurt-gaston-shooting-involving-police/3893099001/

1066 WCNC Staff, Meilin Tompkins, Brandon Goldner. 2020. "'We lost a hero today' | Mount Holly officer killed in the line of duty, two days shy of 26th birthday." *WCNC*, December 11. Accessed January 6, 2021. https://www.wcnc.com/article/news/crime/officer-involved-shooting-gastonia/275-6d585953-b8d0-456a-b4eb-2f4d1960be44

1067 Zhou, Amanda. 2020. "Grand jury indicts suspect in the killing of a police officer in a small NC town." *The Charlotte Observer*, December 15. Accessed January 6, 2021. https://www.charlotteobserver.com/news/local/crime/article247843055.html

1068 Boraks, David. 2020. "Officer And Suspect Killed In Shootout Near Concord Mills." *WFAE 90.7*, December 17. Accessed January 6, 2021. https://www.wfae.org/crime-justice/2020-12-17/officer-and-suspect-killed-in-shootout-near-concord-mills

1069 Ibid 1068.

1070 Price, Mark, & Amanda Zhou. 2020. "Concord police officer dead, another wounded after confronting suspect, NC officials say." *The Charlotte Observer*, December 18. Accessed January 6, 2021. https://www.charlotteobserver.com/news/article247912240.html

1071 Korynta, Emma, Natalie Ridley (WCNC), Billie Jean Shaw, Lana Harris, & James Brierton (WCNC). 2020. "Concord police officer shot, killed by carjacking suspect." *WCNC*, December 18. Accessed January 6. 2021. https://www.wcnc.com/article/news/crime/concord-police-officer-killed-shooting-north-carolina-line-of-duty/275-536ad955-1d26-46b2-ba2b-2e2a931764a1

1072 Robinson, Carol. 2021. "Former Birmingham police Officer Randy Smith dies 25 years after on-duty shooting." *Al.com*, January 1. Accessed April 21, 2021. https://www.al.com/news/birmingham/2020/12/former-birmingham-police-officer-randy-smith-dies-25-years-after-on-duty-shooting.html

1073 CBS 42 Digital Team. 2020. "Former Birmingham police officer Randy Smith dies 25 years after line-of-duty shooting." *CBS 42*, December 30. Accessed April 21, 2021. https://www.cbs42.com/news/former-birmingham-police-officer-randy-smith-dies-25-years-after-line-of-duty-shooting/

1074 United States Census Bureau. 2019. "Quick Facts: United States." *Census.gov*. Accessed May 1, 2021. https://www.census.gov/quickfacts/fact/table/US/RHI225219

1075 Ibid 724.

1076 Ibid 930.

1077 Ibid 995.

1078 Concha, Joe. 2015. "Network Media, Black Leaders Sit Idly By as #BlackLivesMatter Rhetoric Grows Dangerous." *Mediaite*, August 31. Accessed June 13, 2021. https://www.mediaite.com/online/network-media-black-leaders-sit-idly-by-as-blacklivesmatter-rhetoric-grows-dangerous/

1079 Hemmer, Nicole. 2021. "What Jim Crow looks like in 2021." *CNN*, March 25. Accessed April 8, 2021. https://www.cnn.com/2021/03/25/opinions/voting-rights-suppression-is-jim-crow-suit-and-tie-hemmer/index.html

1080 Luckerson, Victor. 2015. "New Report Documents 4,000 Lynchings in Jim Crow South." *Time*, February 10. Accessed April 8, 2021. https://time.com/3703386/jim-crow-lynchings/

1081 Mack, Eric. 2018. "Texas Dem O'Rourke Rips Modern Policing as 'the New Jim Crow'." *Newsmax*, September 20. Accessed April 8, 2021. https://www.newsmax.com/politics/beto-orourke-modern-law-enforcement-jim-crow/2018/09/20/id/882685/

1082 Kaplan, Talia. 2021. "Alveda King slams Biden's 'Jim Crow' rhetoric over Georgia's law: 'He is not telling the truth'." *Fox Business*, April 7. Accessed April 8, 2021. https://www.foxbusiness.com/politics/alveda-king-slams-bidens-jim-crow-rhetoric-over-georgias-law-he-is-not-telling-the-truth

1083 Wallace, Danielle. 2021. "Minneapolis 'autonomous zone' jeopardizes residents amid Derek Chauvin trial, police association says." *Fox News*, March 11. Accessed April 11, 2021. https://www.foxnews.

com/us/george-floyd-square-minneapolis-autonomous-zone-derek-chauvin-trial-rioting-defund-police

1084 Pagones, Stephanie. 2021. "Police defunded: Major cities feeling the loss of police funding as murders, other crimes soar." *Fox News*, April 1. Accessed April 9, 2021. https://www.foxnews.com/us/police-defunded-cities-murders-crime-budget

1085 Cuomo, Andrew M. 2020. "No. 203: New York State Police Reform and Reinvention Collaborative." *New York State Governor*, June 12. Accessed April 12, 2021. https://www.governor.ny.gov/news/no-203-new-york-state-police-reform-and-reinvention-collaborative

1086 Associated Press. 2021. "Plan to revamp police force proceeds in Ithaca, New York." *ABC News*, April 1. Accessed April 11, 2021. https://abcnews.go.com/US/wireStory/plan-revamp-police-force-proceeds-ithaca-york-76810978

1087 Moore, Tina. 2021. "NYPD cop-killer is now helping reform the police in New York." *New York Post*, March 29. Accessed April 11, 2021. https://nypost.com/2021/03/29/nyc-cop-killer-now-helping-to-reform-the-police/

1088 Suffolk County Police Reform & Reinvention Task Force. 2021. "Police Reform / Forum and Public Comments." *Suffolk County NY*. Accessed June 13, 2021. https://suffolkcountyny.gov/Police-Reform/Forum-and-Public-Comments

1089 DeSantis, Michael. 2020. "2 Police Officers Assaulted In Brentwood; 4 People Arrested: SCPD." *Patch*, August 31. Accessed June 13, 2021. https://patch.com/new-york/brentwood-central-islip/2-police-officers-assaulted-brentwood-4-people-arrested-scpd

1090 POL Staff. 2020. "Majority of Seattle Council Wants to Cut Police Funding by 50%." *Police Magazine*, July 10. Accessed April 11, 2021. https://www.policemag.com/563608/majority-of-seattle-council-wants-to-cut-police-funding-by-50

1091 Ibid 1084.

1092 Stole, Bryn and Pamela Wood. 2021. "Maryland legislators pass landmark police reform package into law, overriding Gov. Hogan's vetoes." *Baltimore Sun*, April 10. Accessed April 11, 2021. https://www.baltimoresun.com/politics/bs-md-pol-saturday-session-20210410-eyfrbxrlevhrvohrm43lbntvyq-story.html

1093 Ali, Safia Samee. 2021. "Illinois becomes first state to end cash bail as part of criminal justice reform law." NBC News, February 24. Accessed April 29, 2021. https://www.nbcnews.com/news/us-news/illinois-becomes-first-state-end-money-bail-part-massive-criminal-n1258679

1094 Chamberas, Nicholas. 2021. "'War On Police' Gives Rise To Violent Crime." *Newsmax*, April 5. Accessed April 9, 2021. https://www.newsmax.com/nicholaschamberas/war-on-police-crime-justice-reform/2021/04/05/id/1016418/

1095 Davis, Scott A. 2021 "New York City removes qualified immunity from police in first major shot in the battle over police protections." *Law Enforcement Today*, March 26. Accessed April 14, 2021. https://www.lawenforcementtoday.com/new-york-city-removes-qualified-immunity-from-police-in-first-major-shot-in-the-battle-over-police-protections/

1096 Richard, Lawrence. 2021. "NYPD experiences mass exodus of police officers with 75% spike in departures and retirements." *The Denver Gazette*, April 24. Accessed April 27, 2021. https://denvergazette.com/wex/nypd-experiences-mass-exodus-of-police-officers-with-75-spike-in-departures-and-retirements/article_322aa218-397d-58fb-9e88-8fefa9bffebe.html#:~:text=In%202020%2C%20more%20than%205%2C300,to%20the%20New%20York%20Post

1097 Bykofsky, Stu. 2021. "PHILLY COPS ARE DEFUNDING THEMSELVES." Philadelphia Weekly, February 4. Accessed April 29, 2021. https://philadelphiaweekly.com/philly-cops-are-defunding-themselves

1098 Bernstein, Maxine. 2020. "August's 62 Portland police, firefighter retirements mark record month -- more than most years." *The Oregonian*, September 23. Accessed April 29, 2021. https://www.oregonlive.com/crime/2020/09/augusts-62-portland-police-firefighter-retirements-mark-record-month-more-than-most-years.html

1099 Bernstein, Maxine. 2021. "'Overworked, overwhelmed and burned out'. Why Portland cops say they're leaving in droves." The Oregonian, April 5. Accessed April 29, 2021. https://www.oregonlive.com/crime/2021/04/overworked-overwhelmed-and-burned-out-why-portland-cops-say-theyre-leaving-in-droves.html

1100 Rantz, Jason. 2020. "Rantz: Seattle Police on pace to lose nearly 200 officers in mass exodus this year." Mynorthwest.com, December 28. Accessed April 28, 2021. https://mynorthwest.com/2392075/rantz-seattle-police-lose-nearly-200-officers-mass-exodus-2020/

1101 Ibid 1094.

1102 Wojcicki, Ed. 2021. "LE coalition opposes Illinois 'anti-police' bill and here's why." *Police1.com*, March 5. Accessed April 9, 2021. https://www.police1.com/chiefs-sheriffs/articles/le-coalition-opposes-illinois-anti-police-bill-and-heres-why-c8WxqxsudxWwk0j2/

1103 Ibid 1102.

1104 Ibid 1102.

1105 Axelrod, Tal. 2020. "New York AG suggests NYPD get rid of traffic stops to prevent deadly force incidents." *The Hill*, September 25. Accessed April 3, 2021. https://thehill.com/homenews/state-watch/518395-new-york-ag-suggests-nypd-get-rid-of-traffic-stops-to-prevent-deadly

1106 Ibid 1105.

1107 Hope, Patrick A. 2020. "HB 5058 Marijuana and certain traffic offenses; issuing citations, etc." *Virginia's Legislative Information System*, November 9. Accessed April 11, 2021. https://lis.virginia.gov/cgi-bin/legp604.exe?ses=202&typ=bil&val=hb5058

1108 Moore, Tina. 2021. "NYC shootings and homicides soared in 2020, crime data shows." *New York Post*, January 6. Accessed April 9, 2021. https://nypost.com/2021/01/06/nyc-shootings-and-homicides-soared-in-2020-crime-data-shows/

1109 Ibid 1084.

1110 Abusaid, Shaddi, & Christian Boone. 2021. "Atlanta's deadliest year in decades has city on edge and demanding change." *The Atlanta Journal-Constitution*, January 15. Accessed April 16, 2021. https://www.ajc.com/news/atlantas-deadliest-year-in-decades-has-city-on-edge-and-demanding-change/WAF3MV7AVBD2BO2RZVANXDI6E4/

1111 Chicago Tribune. 2021. "Tracking Chicago homicide victims." *Chicago Tribune*, April 14. Accessed April 16, 2021. https://www.chicagotribune.com/news/breaking/ct-chicago-homicides-data-tracker-htmlstory.html

1112 D'Onofrio, Jessica & Craig Wall. 2021. "2020 Cook County deaths break records due to gun violence, opioid overdoses, COVID-19, ME says." *ABC 7 Chicago*, January 1. Accessed April 16, 2021. https://abc7chicago.com/chicago-shootings-2020-shooting-crime-stats-statistics/9250374/#:~:text=Chicago%20police%20also%20released%20the%20final%20crime%20number,a%20big%20jump%20from%202%2C140%20shootings%20in%202019

1113 Ibid 1084.

1114 Bernstein, Maxine. 2021. "55 homicides in Portland in 2020 -- the most in 26 years -- involved victims from 8 months old to 71." *The Oregonian*, January 15. Accessed April 16, 2021. https://www.oregonlive.com/crime/2021/01/55-homicides-in-portland-in-2020-the-most-in-26-years-involved-victims-from-8-months-old-to-71.html

1115 Stepman, Jarrett. 2021. "Violence Is Out of Control in Portland. Maybe Defunding Police Wasn't Such a Great Idea." *The Daily Signal*, March 17. https://www.dailysignal.com/2021/03/17/violence-is-out-of-control-in-portland-maybe-defunding-police-wasnt-such-a-great-idea/

1116 Associated Press. 2020. "Shootings in Portland More Than Double in 2020." *US News & World Report*, December 28. Accessed April 17, 2021. https://www.usnews.com/news/best-states/oregon/articles/2020-12-28/shootings-in-portland-more-than-double-in-2020

1117 Craighead, Callie. 2021. "2020 crime report: Seattle saw highest homicide number in 26 years; overall violent crimes lower." *Seattle PI*, January 12. Accessed April 17, 2021. https://www.seattlepi.com/local/seattlenews/article/2020-crime-Seattle-highest-homicide-rate-15864266.php

1118 Gockowski, Anthony. 2021. "105% increase in shootings, 70% increase in homicides in Minneapolis last year." *Alpha News MN*, January 26. Accessed April 18, 2021. https://alphanewsmn.com/105-increase-in-shootings-70-increase-in-homicides-in-minneapolis-last-year/

1119 Goyette, Jared. 2021. "Amid complaints of violence, Minneapolis moves to reopen intersection where George Floyd was killed." *The Washington Post*, March 18. Accessed April 11, 2021. https://www.washingtonpost.com/nation/2021/03/18/george-floyd-autonomous-zone-open/

1120 Ibid 1083.

1121 Sexton, John. 2021. "A man was killed Saturday inside the police no-go zone known as George Floyd Square." *Hot Air*, March 9. Accessed April 11, 2021. https://hotair.com/john-s-2/2021/03/09/man-killed-saturday-inside-police-no-go-zone-known-george-floyd-square-n380531

1122 O'Neil, Tyler. 2020. "Seattle Mayor Finally Sends Police to Restore Law and Order to CHOP Antifastan." *PJ Media*, June 23. Accessed April 18, 2021. https://pjmedia.com/news-and-politics/tyler-o-neil/2020/06/23/seattle-mayor-finally-admits-chop-antifastan-hurt-businesses-and-residents-after-shootings-n567320

1123 Eustachewich, Lia. 2020. "How the Seattle CHOP zone went from socialist summer camp to deadly disaster." *New York Post*, July 1. Accessed April 11, 2021. https://nypost.com/2020/07/01/how-seattle-chop-went-from-socialist-summer-camp-to-deadly-disaster/

1124 Ibid 1123.

1125 Yancey-Bragg, N'dea. 2020. "Portland mayor bans cops from using tear gas after months of protests and criticism." *USA Today*, September 11. Accessed April 11, 2021. https://www.usatoday.com/story/news/nation/2020/09/11/portland-mayor-bans-use-tear-gas-police-during-protests/3466804001/

1126 Garger, Kenneth. 2021. "Portland Mayor Ted Wheeler pepper-sprays man who accosted him outside pub." *New York Post*, January 25. Accessed April 11, 2021. https://nypost.com/2021/01/25/portland-mayor-pepper-sprays-man-who-accosted-him-outside-pub/

1127 Boroff, David. 2020. "TROUBLED PAST Did Walter Wallace Jr have a criminal record?" *The Sun*, October 28. Accessed April 19, 2021. https://www.thesun.co.uk/news/13045351/walter-wallace-criminal-record-philadelphia-police-shooting/

1128 Burkholder, Lori. 2020. "Lancaster police video: Man fatally shot ran at officer while holding knife." *WGAL 8 News*, September 14. Accessed April 19, 2021. https://www.wgal.com/article/lancaster-police-body-cam-video-shooting-man-armed-with-knife-ricardo-munoz/34009627

1129 Deliso, Meredith. 2020. "Body camera footage shows 'graphic' police shooting of Walter Wallace Jr. in Philadelphia." *ABC News*, November 10. Accessed April 19, 2021. https://abcnews.go.com/US/body-camera-footage-shows-graphic-police-shooting-walter/story?id=74018244

1130 Sorace, Stephen. 2020. "Atlanta police release bodycam video leading up to death of Rayshard Brooks." *Fox News*, June 14. Accessed April 20, 2021. https://www.foxnews.com/us/atlanta-police-release-bodycam-video-leading-up-to-death-of-rayshard-brooks

1131 Stocking, Bronson. 2020. "WATCH: DA in Brooks Shooting Called Tasers Deadly Weapons Two Weeks Ago." *Townhall*, June 17. Accessed April 19, 2021. https://townhall.com/tipsheet/bronsonstocking/2020/06/17/da-in-brooks-shooting-used-to-think-tasers-were-deadly-weapons-n2570858

1132 Chasmar, Jessica. 2020. "Secoriea Turner's parents: 'They say Black lives matter. You killed your own.'" *The Washington Times*, July 6. Accessed April 11, 2021. https://www.washingtontimes.com/news/2020/jul/6/secoriea-turners-parents-they-say-black-lives-matt/

1133 Bonvillian, Crystal. 2021. "Video shows Nashville police officer, female driver shoot one another outside Dollar General store." *WFTV*, March 16. Accessed April 20, 2021. https://www.wftv.com/news/trending/video-shows-nashville-police-officer-female-driver-shoot-one-another-outside-dollar-general-store/HJYRTF3MTVDMZCHCCWP7OGWLOU/

1134 Ferenchik, Mark, Christine Fernando, & Bethany Bruner. 2021. "Columbus police release bodycam footage, identify officer in fatal shooting of Ma'Khia Bryant: What we know." *Detroit Free Press*, April 21. Accessed April 25, 2021. https://www.freep.com/story/news/nation/2021/04/21/columbus-police-shot-killed-teen-girl-what-we-know/7316707002/

1135 O'Brien, Cortney. 2021. "Left-leaning outlets publish 'deliberately misleading' videos about Columbus shooting." *Fox News*, April 22. Accessed April 24, 2021. https://www.foxnews.com/media/daily-beast-ripped-publishing-misinformation-columbus-police-shooting

1136 Wulfsohn, Joseph A. 2021. "'NBC Nightly News' under fire for editing out key part of 911 call before Ma'Khia Bryant shooting." *Fox News*, April 22, Accessed April 25, 2021. https://www.foxnews.com/media/nbc-nightly-news-makhia-bryant-shooting-911-call-edit-out

1137 Flood, Brian. 2021. "MSNBC's Joy Reid says it's 'very difficult' to trust cops, claims even unarmed teachers break up knife fights." *Fox News*, April 22. Accessed April 25, 2021. https://www.foxnews.com/media/msnbcs-joy-reid-makhia-bryant

1138 Rutz, David. 2021. "CNN's Keilar refers to girl attacked by Ma'Khia Bryant as being 'so close to Ma'Khia when she was shot'." *Fox News*, April 23. Accessed April 25, 2021. https://www.foxnews.com/media/brianna-keilar-makhia-bryant-shooting-girl-attacked-cnn

1139 Canova, Daniel. 2021. "LeBron James now-deleted tweet targets officer in Ohio police shooting: 'YOU'RE NEXT'." *Fox News Channel*, April 21. Accessed April 24, 2021. https://www.foxnews.com/sports/lebron-james-ohio-police-shooting-tweeting-photo-officer-youre-next

1140 Salo, Jackie. 2021. "Over 100 protesters demonstrate against police shooting of Ma'Khia Bryant." *New York Post*, April 22. Accessed April 25, 2021. https://nypost.com/2021/04/22/over-100-protest-against-police-shooting-of-makhia-bryant/

1141 Casiano, Louis. 2021. "Ohio State students demand university cuts ties with Columbus police after Ma'Khia Bryant shooting." *Fox News Channel*, April 21. Accessed April 25, 2021. https://www.foxnews.com/us/ohio-state-columbus-makhia-bryant-shooting

1142 Fordham, Evie. 2021. "Democrats condemn Ma'Khia Bryant shooting despite bodycam footage showing 15-year-old wielding knife." *Fox News*, April 21. Accessed April 25, 2021. https://www.foxnews.com/politics/democrats-makhia-bryant-shooting-bodycam-footage-knife

1143 Canzano, Julia. 2021. "'Life Was Taken By Columbus Police': Ilhan Omar Criticizes Officer Who Shot Ma'Khia Bryant During Knife Attack." *Daily Caller*, April 23. Accessed April 25, 2021. https://dailycaller.com/2021/04/23/ilhan-omar-makhia-bryant-daunte-wright-funeral/

1144 Phillips, Morgan. 2021. "Psaki calls Ohio fatal police shooting of teen who appeared to attack others 'tragic'." *Fox News*, April 21. Accessed April 25, 2021. https://www.foxnews.com/politics/psaki-ohio-fatal-police-shooting-teen-tragic

1145 Varian, Ethan. 2021. "Santa Rosa Police Department draws criticism for thin blue line flag in Facebook post." *The Press Democrat*, January 21. Accessed January 24, 2021. Santa Rosa Police Department draws criticism for 'thin blue line' flag in Facebook post (pressdemocrat.com)

1146 Ibid 1145.

1147 DeSantis, Michael. 2021. "Smithtown FD Removes 'Thin Blue Line' Flag Following Complaint." *MSN*, February 21. Accessed April 21, 2021. https://www.msn.com/en-us/news/us/smithtown-fd-removes-thin-blue-line-flag-following-complaint/ar-BB1e1iPL

1148 Davis, Scott A. 2021. "Fire Department reverses decision to remove Thin Blue Line flag following 'overwhelming' community outcry." *Law Enforcement Today*, March 3. Accessed April 21, 2021. https://www.lawenforcementtoday.com/fire-company-returns-thin-blue-line-flag-to-truck-following-public-outcry/

1149 Feris, Sachi. 2016. "TELLING MY WHITE FOUR-YEAR-OLD ABOUT ALTON STERLING AND PHILANDO CASTILE." *Raising Race Conscious Children*, July 8. Accessed June 15, 2020. http://www.raceconscious.org/2016/07/telling-four-year-old-alton-sterling-philando-castile/

1150 Tastrom, Katie. 2016. "7 Tips for White Parents Talking to Kids About Police Murders of Black People." *Everyday feminism*, November 29. Accessed June 15, 2020. https://everydayfeminism.com/2016/11/talking-kids-police-brutality/

1151 CBS/Associated Press. 2016. "Dallas suspect said he wanted to kill whites." *CBS News*, July 8. Accessed March 17, 2021. https://www.cbsnews.com/news/dallas-shooting-suspect-kill-whites/

1152 Southern Poverty Law Center. "NEW BLACK PANTHER PARTY." *SPLCenter.org*. Accessed March 17, 2021. https://www.splcenter.org/fighting-hate/extremist-files/group/new-black-panther-party

1153 Romain, Alana. 2016. "How to talk to your kids about the Dallas shooting, because it shouldn't be ignored." *The Child Mind Institute*, July 8. Accessed August 10, 2020. https://www.romper.com/p/how-to-talk-to-your-kids-about-the-dallas-shooting-because-it-shouldnt-be-ignored-13931

1154 TVVideoClips.com. 2021. "Michael Simonelli – Police Bias." *Fox News Channel*, May 15. Accessed July 1, 2021. https://app.box.com/s/a7msu0x38ahm4gi7lerdieia9522mt9x

1155 McCaughey, Betsy. 2021. "Parents CAN beat critical race theory — by running for school boards." *DailyNewsWeek*, June 2. Accessed July 10, 2021. https://dailynewsweek.com/parents-can-beat-critical-race-theory-by-running-for-school-boards/

MIKE SIMONELLI HAS OVER 50 COMBINED YEARS OF DECORATED and honorable service to the nation and New York. From 1989-2019 he served in the U.S. military. Graduating from the Air Force Academy with a B.S., Mike was an active-duty Air Force officer for five years before transferring to the U.S. Army National Guard and then Reserves. As a Civil Affairs Special Operations Army officer, Mike deployed to Iraq from 2003-2004 and then Afghanistan for the surge of 2010. Retiring as a lieutenant colonel, his awards include the Bronze Star Medal with one oak leaf cluster, Army Combat Action Badge, and Air Force Combat Action Medal. From 2000-2021 Mike was an active law enforcement officer assigned to patrol, highway patrol, community-oriented police enforcement and the Police Benevolent Association (PBA). He received numerous commendations and three times was overwhelmingly voted by his fellow officers to be on their PBA Executive Board. Most recently, Mike earned his M.S. in National Security Studies from American Military University in 2020.

CPSIA information can be obtained
at www.ICGtesting.com
Printed in the USA
JSHW022154041121
20146JS00005B/18

9 781685 150105